EIGHTH EDITION

Check In

Check Out

Managing Hotel Operations

Gary K. Vallen

Northern Arizona University

Jerome J. Vallen

University of Nevada, Las Vegas, Emeritus

PEARSON

Prentice
Hall

Pearson Education International

Vice President and Executive Publisher: Vernon R. Anthony
Acquisitions Editor: William Lawrensen
Editorial Assistant: Lara Dimmick
Project Manager: Maren L. Miller
Production Coordination: Pine Tree Composition
Design Coordinator: Diane Y. Ernsberger
Cover Designer: Mike Fruhbeis
Cover Image: Superstock
Operations Specialist: Deidra Schwartz
Director of Marketing: David Gesell
Marketing Manager: Leigh Ann Sims
Marketing Coordinator: Les Roberts

This book was set in 10 point Sabon by Laserwords. It was printed and bound by Edwards Brothers. The cover was printed by Phoenix Color Book Group.

If you purchased this book within the United States or Canada you should be aware that it has been wrongfully imported without the approval of the Publisher or the Author.

Pearson Education Ltd., London
Pearson Education Singapore, Pte. Ltd.
Pearson Education Canada, Inc.
Pearson Education—Japan
Pearson Education Australia PTY, Limited

Pearson Education North Asia, Ltd., Hong Kong
Pearson Educación de Mexico, S.A. de C.V.
Pearson Education Malaysia, Pte. Ltd.
Pearson Education Upper Saddle River,
   New Jersey

10   9   8   7   6   5   4   3   2   1
ISBN-13: 978-0-13-503630-3
ISBN-10:   0-13-503630-5

• • •

To fathers and sons who work together

Brief Contents

• • •

Contents

• • •

Preface

• • •

The lodging industry's most senior and comprehensive text has been updated once again. Welcome to the eighth edition of *Check-In Check-Out: Managing Hotel Operations*. Eight editions in some 30 years makes this the most current and complete work in the field of Hotel Management. Excellence—excellence in presentation, content, and exhibits—enhances an exceptional depth of knowledge to make the book readable and practical. Hospitality faculty and students who know the book are not surprised to see it on the shelves of professional hoteliers. It has become a reference text for operators as well as a course text for students. A complete, cross-referenced index allows for both quick inquiries and thorough investigations.

Sales of guest rooms is the lodging industry's largest income producer and its most profitable operating department. The success of this critical division determines the success of the entire enterprise. That's why the content extends beyond the front desk. It looks broadly to supporting departments, markets and agencies, many outside of the hotel building itself. The reader gains insight into the many aspects of *Managing Hotel Operations*.

Previous users will find new resources; international users have already had editions in Chinese and Portuguese as well as a special Canadian Edition. A completely revised technologies chapter (Chapter 14) updates the rapid changes in electronics, both for guest use and operational efficiency. New exhibits reinforce new content; previous exhibits strengthen basic concepts and improve understanding. *Check-In Check-Out* is complete, as it has always been.

ONLINE INSTRUCTOR'S RESOURCES

Instructor
Resource
Center

Register today at www.prenhall.com
to access instructor resources digitally.

To access supplementary materials online, instructors need to request an instructor access code. Go to **www.pearsonhighered.com/irc**, where you can register for an instructor access code. Within 48 hours after registering, you will receive a confirming e-mail, including an instructor access code. Once you have received your code, go to the site and log on for full instructions on downloading the materials you wish to use.

Welcome to the latest edition of an industry tradition!

Acknowledgments

• • •

It takes many individuals to prepare this text for publication. Even the authors don't know everyone. There are artists and printers; reviewers and editors; photographers and lawyers. With thanks, we acknowledge them and the industry professionals who have provided many of the exhibits. Company names are registered trademarks. As reminders, we have marked these periodically.

We have had a more immediate relationship with three direct contributors. So we extend a more personal note of appreciation to them:

Phil Arce, Hotel Manager at the Colorado Belle Hotel and Casino, Laughlin, Nevada, for providing resource documents;

Cihan Cobanoglu, Ph.D., CHIP, Associate Professor of Hospitality Information Technology at the University of Delaware for updating Chapter 14;

John Peiser, Instructor in the Department of Resort & Gaming at the College of Southern Nevada and President of Peiser Hospitality, for suggesting and providing incidents* for each chapter.

Direction and guidance from colleagues who reviewed the manuscript helped point us toward new and relevant issues. We appreciate the input from: Christian Celis-Schemidt, Indiana University–Purdue University; Julie A. Doyle, Ferris State University; Myron S. Levy, Roosevelt University; Chris Brandmeir, Highline Community College; Elizabeth Bender, University of South Carolina; Sheryl Kline, Purdue University; Bharath M. Josiam, University of North Texas; and Terry Jones, College of Southern Nevada.

And a special thanks to you, the readers. Your suggestions and feedback have helped keep the revisions current and accurate. We appreciate hearing from friends in education and industry.

---

*Incidents follows the terminology of the outline.

About the Authors

• • •

Coauthored texts are not unusual unless the authors are father and son. Jerry Vallen, the father, launched the book in 1974. Gary Vallen, the son, pursued several degrees and a professional career before becoming a joint author of the fourth edition.

Dr. Gary K. Vallen is Professor in the School of Hotel and Restaurant Management at Northern Arizona University. He joined that program in 1988 as one of its founding faculty, bringing 16 years of industry experience to the classroom. Part of that resumé included vice president and assistant general manager of a casino, hotel sales manager, financial and operational analyst, and associate manager for private clubs.

Dr. Vallen received his undergraduate degree in hotel administration at the University of Nevada, Las Vegas. Despite the long hours of industry, he simultaneously worked and earned an MBA at the University of Nevada, Reno. His Ed.D. degree with an emphasis in hospitality education (Northern Arizona University) was earned after he began teaching. In addition to *Check-In, Check-Out*, Dr. Vallen coauthored *An Introduction to Hospitality Management* and has published over three dozen refereed articles and conference proceedings. He is on the editorial boards of six professional journals.

Professor Vallen operates *Gary Vallen Hospitality Consultants*, which specializes in hosted casino nights for clients of destination management companies, and in visitor analyses for festivals, fairs, rodeos, and ski slopes. He has developed and carried out numerous secret-shopper evaluations for both hotels and restaurants. The Southwest location has enabled him to assist many Native American groups, including the Hopi and Navajo, but he is also well known for his rural tourism expertise.

Dr. Jerome J. Vallen was the founding Dean of the College of Hotel Administration, University of Nevada, Las Vegas, and served in that capacity for 22 years. He is now Professor Emeritus/Dean Emeritus. Jerry Vallen returned to the classroom for a short period before taking an assignment as founding dean of the Australian International Hotel School, Canberra.

After earning a baccalaureate degree at Cornell, he entered the hotel industry, carrying with him the food experience gained from the family's small chain of four restaurants. For several years, he taught and worked in industry. Dr. Vallen earned a master's degree in educational administration (St. Lawrence University) and a doctoral degree from Cornell's School of Hotel Administration.

He has coauthored a book on hotel management and edited a work on the legal basis for obtaining a gaming license in Nevada. Professor Vallen has served as a consulting editor for textbook publishers; a traveling consultant to the U.S. Department of

Commerce that has carried him to over three dozen countries; an outside examiner for the University of the West Indies; president of a consulting company; member of the board of several private companies and public entities; and president and chairman of the Council on Hotel, Restaurant and Institutional Education (CHRIE).

Such diverse groups as the University Alumni Association, the Educational Foundation of the National Restaurant Association, and the Educational Institute of the American Hotel & Lodging Association have honored him. So has CHRIE, with its prestigious H.B. Meek Award. Jerome Vallen has been cited in the *Congressional Record* and named among the 100 most important Las Vegans of the 20th century.

PART I
The Hotel Industry

The Traditional Hotel Industry

Outline

Hotels have their origins in the cultures of ancient societies. But the word "hotel" didn't appear until the 18th century. It came from the French *hôtel*, large house, and originated in the Latin roots *hospitium* or *hospes*. *Hospitality*, *hostile* and *hotels* are all related words. The difficulty of identifying early travelers as friends or foes probably accounts for the conflict in meanings. Friendly travelers found security and accommodations through the hospitality of their hosts. As the number of travelers increased, personal courtesy gave way to commercial enterprise. The hotel was born carrying with it a culture of hospitality.

UNDERSTANDING THE HOTEL BUSINESS

The Service Culture

The hotel industry grew and flourished through the centuries by adapting to the changing social, business and economic environment that marked human progress. During modern times, these stages have been labeled for easy reference. The 18th century was the agricultural age; the 19th, the industrial age. The 20th century has been the age of service. The sale of services, such as medicine, banking, education and hotelkeeping, has outpaced the manufacture and distribution of goods. The 21st century has opened with that same service culture even as it launches what is likely to be the age of technology.

A Cyclical Industry

Hotelkeeping is a cyclical industry that closely follows the nation's economic phases. Wide swings carry the hotel business between peaks of exceptional profits and troughs of outright distress. Unfortunately, the industry both lags the general recovery and precedes the start of the decline.

This rollercoaster has been very evident over the past half century. The entire travel industry, including innkeeping, was brought to its knees by the oil embargo of 1973. Hundreds of hotels[1] went through bankruptcy. Then came recovery. A decade later, the early 1980s, saw a second collapse when the federal government changed the income tax laws on real estate. That debacle took down many banks as well. (Remember: Hotels are pieces of real estate above all else, and real estate is the basis of bank loans.) Recovery followed once again. A dozen years later, late 1990s, hotel profits began to appear. Just as the recovery was consolidating came the tragedy of the World Trade Center (2001). Travel and tourism bottomed out again. Recovery was faster this time. About 100,000 new rooms were announced in 2005 alone. The 2004–2008 period has been one of great prosperity. Rising oil costs beginning in 2005 laid the groundwork for another scenario reminiscent of 1973. Equally devastating has been the industry's rush to build.

Hoteliers stop building during the downturns. Three years is the typical span between planning and opening a hotel, even longer if there are special financing, zoning, or environmental issues. Over half of the projects are never built and those that are often have fewer rooms than announced. Hotel occupancy and profits boom before the competition revs up new properties. So new rooms usually come on as the cycle peaks. That increased inventory accelerates the next downward dip. Supply and demand play their traditional roles in hotel economics, as they do for general business. Overbuilding, excess supply, exaggerates the downturns far, far more often than does insufficient demand, fewer customers.

---

[1]In Australia, hotel means a bar or pub; on the subcontinent, it means a restaurant.

How Hotels Count and Measure

New hotels and hotel rooms are built at the cyclical peaks. Old hotels and old rooms are removed in the troughs. One can never say for certain, therefore, how many hotel buildings or hotel rooms are available for sale at a given time. Governmental agencies (Bureau of the Census[2]), trade associations (American Hotel & Lodging Association, AH&LA) and private firms (Smith Travel Research) count, track, and report the statistics. Other interested parties include the World Tourism Organization (WTO) of the United Nations, the International Hotel and Restaurant Association (IH&RA), and several accounting/consulting firms (such as PricewaterhouseCoopers and PKF Consulting). As one would expect from such a dynamic industry and so diverse a group of reporters, none of the figures agree exactly.

The Bureau of the Census counts once every decade and then takes several years to report. By then, the dynamic industry has produced many more offspring. Estimates today suggest that there are approximately 65,000 hotels in the United States with some 5,500,000 hotel rooms. Averaging, the typical hotel has some 85 rooms. Industry professionals value hotels on a per-room cost, either the cost per room to build or the resale price per room—sometimes expressed as a *per-key cost*. Valuing each room at, say, $250,000,[3] the worth of U.S. hotel properties is about $1 trillion. In "good times," that investment produces industry profits in the range of $20–25 billion on total revenues of $120 billion.

Exhibit 1–1 illustrates what is apparent. Despite the swings, the industry continues to grow in size and importance.

Worldwide, there are an estimated 12,000,000 hotel rooms. Traditionally, Europe's 3,000,000 rooms—Italy leads, with nearly half—and the United State's ±5,000,000 rooms have accounted for some two-thirds of the total count. Rapid growth in developing Asia and the subcontinent as well as the rebirth of the Japanese economy are certain to change those percentages over the next decade.

The Hotel Industry: A Quarter Century of Growth			
Cico Edition	**Date[a] Published**	**Estimated Number of Hotels**	**Estimated[c] Number of Rooms**
8th	Current	58,000	4.8 million
7th	2005	56,200	3.5 million
6th	2000	48,000	3.1 million
5th	1995	40,424	2.9 million
4th	1988[b]	27,000	2.8 million
3rd	1985[b]	N/A	2.7 million

[a] Figures lag because the publication date may be 1–2 years after the authors researched and prepared the text.

[b] Source is Smith Travel Research, because this data was not included in the 3rd and 4th editions.

[c] Despite the huge growth in both hotels and rooms, the typical hotel still averages about 100 rooms.

Exhibit 1–1　The lodging industry continues to grow in size and economic impact. It gains momentum at the top of economic cycles such as that of 2005–2008. Smith Travel Research reported total industry revenues for 2005 of $123 billion with profits of $23 billion. (*Wall Street Journal*, June 5, 2006, p. B7.)

---

[2]Facts about the lodging industry are reported in the *SC Series*.

[3]All-suite properties of 125 rooms or so cost about $120,000 per key.

Occupancy.   Occupancy measures the economic health of the hotel industry. It reflects both supply and demand. An improving business environment encourages new construction. Falling demand seals the fate of old hotels. Worn-out rooms are kept in place only during boom periods, when there is a room shortage. They fall to the wrecker's ball or are converted when they are competitive no longer. Historically, many were renovated into dormitory rooms. Today, condo conversion is the hot move because residential rental values have overheated. There is more value in luxury residential units than in luxury hotel units. The conversion of New York's world-famous Plaza Hotel pays witness to the contrast.

At any given time, the number of rooms available for sale reflects the mathematics of the old and the new (see Exhibit 1–2).

During the upward cycle, more guests are buying, but fewer rooms are available. It's just the opposite in a downward cycle: fewer buyers and more rooms. Customer demand is measured by the *number of rooms occupied*, also called the *number of rooms sold*. This information is counted every night by every hotel.

Although the number of rooms in the world is an estimate at best, hotel managers know accurately the number in their own hotels. Whether for the world, the nation, the region or the individual hotel, that number is called *the number of rooms available for sale*.

The relationship (or ratio) between the number of rooms sold (demand) and the number of rooms available (supply) is a barometer of the property's health. It is a closely watched value that asks, "What is our share of the market? How well did we

How the Number of Rooms Available for Sale Is Estimated[a]					
Year	2005[b]	2006[b]	2007[b]	2008[b]	2009[b]
Rooms available at start of year (last year's close)	4,355	4,400	4,500	4,600	4,725
Plus rooms completed	70	110	130	150	95
Total	4,425	4,510	4,630	4,750	4,820
Less rooms removed	25[c]	10[d]	30[d]	25[d]	20[d]
Rooms available (Next year's start)	4,400	4,500	4,600	4,725	4,800

[a] In thousands, add 000 to each figure.

[b] Figures are hypothetical based on historical averages, but represent the largest numbers ever recorded for the hotel industry.

[c] Some 42,000 rooms were lost to Hurricane Katrina along the Gulf Coast during the summer of 2005; some reopened before the year was out. In 2001, New York City lost rooms following the attack on the World Trade Center.

[d] Usually, fewer rooms are removed during "good times"; these estimates include conversions from guest rooms to condos.

Exhibit 1–2   The number of rooms available for sale is the net of available rooms at the start of the year (last year's closing number) plus and minus rooms added and lost this year. The figure obtained (number of rooms available for sale) is the denominator of the fraction used to compute the national percentage of occupancy (number of rooms sold nationwide ÷ number of rooms available for sale nationwide).

sell rooms relative to the number of rooms that could have been sold?" That big mouthful has a shortcut called the *percentage of occupancy,* or *occupancy percentage* or, simply, *occupancy.*

The occupancy calculation is a simple division. The number of rooms available for sale is divided into the number of rooms sold (see Exhibit 1–3):

$$\frac{\text{number of rooms sold}}{\text{number of rooms available for sale}}$$

Occupancy can be computed by one hotel for one night, one month or one year. Citywide occupancy, regional occupancy (the Northeast, for example), or national

---

Given   Number of rooms in the hotel available for sale   800
Number of rooms in the hotel   820
Number of rooms sold to guests   600
Number of dollars received from guests for rooms $48,000
Number of employees on staff   500
Number of guests   700

Computations

Percentage of occupancy is 75%.

$$\frac{\text{number of rooms sold (to guests)}}{\text{number of rooms (in the hotel) available for sale}} = \frac{600}{800} = \frac{3}{4} = 75\%$$

Sales per occupied room (average daily rate, ADR) is $80.00.

$$\frac{\text{room sales (as measured in dollars)}}{\text{number of rooms sold (to guests)}} = \frac{\$48,000}{600} = \$80.00$$

Sales per available room (RevPar) is $60.00.

$$\frac{\text{room sales (as measured in dollars)}}{\text{number of rooms (in the hotel) available for sale}} = \frac{\$48,000}{800} = \$60.00$$

Mathematical check:

$$\text{ADR} \times \text{occupancy} = \text{RevPar} \qquad \$80 \times 0.75 = \$60.00$$

Number of employees per guest room is 0.625.

$$\frac{\text{number of employees (on staff)}}{\text{number of rooms (in the hotel) available for sale}} = \frac{500}{800} = 0.625$$

Percentage of double occupancy is 16.6%

$$\frac{\text{number of guests} - \text{number of rooms sold}}{\text{number of rooms sold}} = \frac{700 - 600}{600} = 16.6\%$$

Exhibit 1-3 Hoteliers track the health of the industry through the measures and ratios shown. Outside of the United States, bed occupancy percentage (number of beds sold ÷ number of beds available) is often substituted for the percentage of room occupancy. Bed (or guest or sleeper) occupancy of 50% approximates room occupancy of 70%.

occupancy are tracked by many agencies. Among them are the hotel chains, convention bureaus, and state tourism offices.

Values become less accurate as the breadth of the count moves away from the individual property to a worldwide number. Nevertheless, everyone is engrossed in occupancy figures. More so when executives of major companies announce that a mere 1% rise in chain occupancy represents millions of dollars of improved profits. The mayor of Atlanta offered a different perspective. He said that each 1% rise in hotel occupancy represented 400 new jobs for his city.[4]

Sales Per Occupied Room.   Occupancy measures the hotel's "share of the market," so it measures *quantity*. The *quality* of the business being done is measured by the amount received for each room sold, *sales per occupied room*. Sales per occupied room goes by another, more commonly used name, *average daily rate* (ADR). ADR is the second of several ways that hotels count and measure. It too is computed with a ratio or fraction:

$$\frac{\text{room sales (measured in dollars)}}{\text{number of rooms sold}}$$

Note that the number of rooms sold (or occupied) appears in both formulas (see Exhibit 1–3).

The health of the hotel business depends on a combination of occupancy and price. Normally, price (ADR) increases as occupancy percentage increases. That is, the more customers want rooms, the more they'll pay. As the industry goes through a declining cycle, it is sometimes possible to keep the ADR climbing for a short time, sometimes even faster than the consumer price index, even as occupancy is falling. That's true for both an individual property and the industry as a whole. As more vacancies occur, prices (ADR) begin to level off because front-office managers reduce rates to maintain higher occupancies. How well they do their job of filling rooms without cutting prices is what the next measure gauges.

RevPar (Revenue Per Available Room).   RevPar is an old industry standby that has reemerged recently as a far more important value than it was 25 years ago when it had a different name, *average rate per available room*.[5] Yield management has come onto the scene during that time. Yield management balances demand and price. Normally, as guest demand (occupancy) falls, price (room rate) declines. One hears that old standby, "hotels fill from the bottom up," meaning that guests elect lower rates when an empty house allows it. The superior manager strives to stabilize or even increase both price and occupancy, especially during dips in the cycle. RevPar (sometimes written as REVPAR) measures that performance. It measures revenue (or sales) per room relative to the total room inventory available. In contrast, ADR measures revenue per room relative to the number of rooms actually sold.

Exhibit 1–3 illustrates the computation. Keep in mind that room revenue and room sales are two different terms for the same value! So the fraction is:

$$\frac{\text{room revenue}}{\text{number of rooms available for sale}}$$

---

[4]*Hotels & Restaurants International,* June, 1989, p. 40, quoting John Kapioltas, Sheraton's CEO; and Andrew Young's keynote speech to CHRIE, Washington, D.C., August 12, 1996.

[5]*Average rate per available room* was the terminology used in the first four editions of this book. The concept and the name fell into disuse only to reemerge as *RevPar.* Similarly, the *average daily rate* was originally called the *average room rate*. It, too, fell into disuse when some misinterpreted it to mean the rate the hotel was charging.

Both values, room revenue and the number of rooms available, are easily misstated. Room revenue must exclude room taxes, costs associated with free parking, and be net of any breakfasts included in the rate. Similarly, the number of rooms available should include vacant rooms, but exclude rooms that have been permanently removed from sale, converted to offices for example. Out-of-inventory rooms, permanent rentals, and the like are also excluded from rooms available. Some argue the contrary; they say measuring management's ability requires the denominator to be all the rooms in the house, not just those available for sale at the moment.

RevPar has become a key indicator of industry health. It's a top-line indicator, meaning it measures demand above all else. RevPar showed double-digit growth in major U.S. cities during the fabulous recovery of 2005–2008. It was especially good for managers whose salaries and bonuses were based on RevPar.

RevPar is easy to compute, and that's its strength. It measures room income only, and that's its weakness. It does not reflect management's ability to control costs and produce sales and profits in other departments. For smaller, rooms-only hotels that lack other revenue departments, RevPar is an ideal measure.

Although not widely used (the computation is too lengthy), gross operating profit (GOP) per available room would better reflect management's overall strengths.

Double Occupancy.   This term refers to any room in which there is more than one guest. So *multiple occupancy* is sometimes used. Therefore, the formula isn't exactly true:

$$\frac{\text{number or guests} - \text{number of rooms occupied}}{\text{number of rooms occupied.}}$$

Assume two rooms occupied with 3 persons in one room and 1 person in the other. The formula would be $4 - 2 = 2 \div 2$ or 100% double occupancy, which isn't the case. Double occupancy's impact on room revenue is much clearer. Additional charges may be levied for second and third occupants. Families, skiers, and tour groups are typical double-ups. Even business travelers share rooms as corporate management focuses on cost-cutting. Two execs to a room is standard procedure at company meetings and conventions because it promotes professional friendships. Casino/hotels want bodies on the casino floor, so they don't charge for dual occupancy. High double occupancy is a characteristic of resort properties. It skews upward both room revenue and ADR.

Another statistical fudge occurs when *comp* (complimentary—free) rooms are counted as occupied. There is no charge, so occupancy increases as ADR decreases. RevPar would not be affected since the denominator of the fraction, number of rooms available for sale, would be unchanged.

Just as the averages of individual hotels can be skewed, so too can the averages of the entire industry. Any computation of *average* is impacted by extreme numbers. National or regional occupancy, ADR, and RevPar figures are influenced by the large hotels, which tend to provide more information and more extreme data than do hotels of 50 rooms or less.

Break-Even Point.   To break even is to have neither profit nor loss. At the break-even point, inflows from revenues exactly match outflows for costs. A large portion of a hotel's costs are fixed expenses: debt payment on funds borrowed to erect the building, for example. Reducing fixed costs such as interest rates drops the amount of occupancy needed to break even. Similarly, raising the ADR, or doing more food and beverage sales, increases the flow of income. More income per room sold, a higher RevPar, means that a smaller percentage of occupancy is needed to pay off the costs, to break even.

Break-even points are important because there are no profits until that point is reached. Until the business pays its fixed expenses (interest, for example), its semifixed expenses (power, for example), and its variable expenses (wages, for example), there are no profits. But once that point is reached, profits accumulate quickly. Each dollar before the break-even point has a mission: Pay off the debt, pay the electricity, pay the employee. Each dollar after the break-even point has a lesser mission because fixed expenses no longer need to be paid! Even some of the semifixed expenses have been met. Therefore, each dollar beyond the break-even point makes a huge contribution to profits.

Break-even points are expressed in percentage of occupancy. That value has been declining over the past decades. Better hotel design and better financing have held down costs, both variable and fixed. Changes in market mix and higher room rates have improved revenues, the other component of the computation. Break-even points have fallen throughout the past quarter-century. Whereas the break-even point was once in the 70% range of occupancy and later in the 60% range, it is now in the high 50% range: Great news for the industry's economic health. The values of Exhibit 1–4 are the best the industry has seen!

Special Characteristics of the Hotel Business

Executives in the lodging industry have to work around several industry characteristics that limit management's flexibility. Some are lodging-only issues and some are also found in other industries, especially the airlines.

Perishability.   Vacant rooms are perishable. The industry's mantra is an unsold room tonight can never be sold again. Unlike a can of fruit which inventories on the grocer's shelf, hotel rooms are time restricted. No way to take last night's empty room to meet an overflow situation tonight. Like empty airline, theater, or sport-arena seats, hotel rooms cannot be stored, cannot be saved, and cannot be used a new.

How's Business? Let The Good Times Roll!				
Year	Percentage of Occupancy[a] %	×	Average Daily Rate (ADR)[a] $	= Revenue Per Available Room (RevPar)[a] $
2005	68.7		94.57	64.97
2006	70.1		95.65	67.05
2007	69.6		95.92	66.76
2008	68.9		97.31	67.05
2009	68.1		97.75	66.57
2010	66.8		98.15	65.56
Approximate Mean	68.8%		$95.60	$65.77

[a] Author estimates. Values vary widely among reporting agencies because there are many variables; ADR is one example. Luxury brands have ADRs 4–6 times greater than those of economy brands.

Exhibit 1–4   Industrywide statistics are estimates at best because the lodging industry is highly segmented (see Exhibit 2–2) and different reporting agencies use different data. However, several trends have been constant: ADR increases even as occupancy falls; and occupancy falls, in part, because new hotel construction (more rooms) is powered by good economic times.

Location.   Ellsworth Statler, who sold his Statler chain to Hilton, has been credited with a frequently quoted expression. He cited "Location, location, location" as the three most important aspects of [hotel] real estate. Good locations are not easy to acquire. Changing neighborhoods and shifting demographics sometimes doom a hotel whose original location was good. Unlike an airline seat, there is no way to move the hotel room. A fixed location in an uneven neighborhood means management must depend more on good marketing and sales and less on location; more on a good reservation systems and less on drive-by and walk-in traffic.

Fixed Supply.   Just as the hotel's location is fixed, so is its supply of rooms. Airlines adjust to demand by temporarily adding or removing flights. Not so with hotels. What you see is what you have.

High Operating Costs.   Unlike manufacturing industries, which offset labor with large capital investments, hotels are both capital- and labor-intensive. The result is high fixed costs (a *large nut* in the jargon of the industry), which continue whether or not the hotel has business. Thus, a high percentage of occupancy is needed just to break even.

Seasonality.   Throwing away the key is a traditional practice when a new hotel is opened. The act signifies that the hotel never closes. Yet hotelkeeping, even for commercial hotels, is a very seasonal business. The cyclical dip strikes the commercial hotel every seven days as it struggles to offset poor weekend business. The federal holiday law, which assigned Mondays to national holidays, reinforces the negative pattern of the commercial hotel.

Occupancy computations must account for this weekend phenomenon. Especially so since the business traveler—the one who is not in the hotel during the weekends—still accounts for the majority of the lodging industry's business. Given the usual profile of the commercial, urban hotel (see Exhibit 1–5), national occupancy percentages in the high 70s and 80s remain an elusive goal.

Annual cycles compound the problem. Commercial business is down even in midweek between Thanksgiving and New Year's Day and from May through Labor Day. But Christmas Day has been rising.

The resort pattern is the opposite of the commercial pattern. Weekends are busy and midweek less so. The slack period of the commercial hotel is the very season of the resort. At one time, resorts opened Memorial Day and closed Labor Day. This 100-day

Monday	100%
Tuesday	100
Wednesday	90
Thursday	90
Friday	40
Saturday	20
Sunday	20
Total	460%
Average per 7 days	66%

Exhibit 1–5   The difficulty of achieving a national occupancy in the mid-70% range is highlighted by the typical cycle of weekly occupancy for commercial hotels. The challenge is convincing groups, whose members work all week, to hold conventions on the weekends. (*Smith Travel Research* now tracks U.S. occupancy daily and weekly as well as annually.)

pattern made the hotel's success dependent on the weather. Two weeks of rain are devastating when the break-even point is 80 days of near-full occupancy.

Although the dates of the winter season differ, there are still only 100 days between December 17 and March 15.

Both winter and summer resorts have extended their seasons with groups, conferences, and special activities. Hotels that operate on the four-day season may be worse off now than those on the four-season year. At least the latter have a higher double occupancy.

TRADITIONAL CLASSIFICATIONS

Lodging is an industry of rapid transformation. The inns of old evolved from private homes located along the traveler's route. Today's hotel is often a point of destination even as it serves its traditional role of accommodating those in transit. Yesterday's tavern offered meals with the family. Dining today is a created experience in design, décor and menu. Early inns were indistinguishable from their neighbor's homes. Today's edifice is a sharp contrast in style and packaging.

The industry still delivers the basic accommodations of shelter, food and hospitality. It's the means of delivery that has changed. These variations have been marked by shifting terminology: hostel, tavern, public house, inn, guest house, hotel, resort, motel, motor lodge, motor inn, bed and breakfast, airtel, boatel, hometel, skytel, condotel.

In keeping with the pace of change, the industry's trade association has undergone similar shifts in identity. What started as the American Hotel Association became the American Hotel & Motel Association, and more recently the American Hotel & Lodging Association. "Motel" has been replaced in the professional vocabulary with new hotel types, as we shall see throughout this chapter and the next.

Notwithstanding the changes, several traditional classifications have withstood the test of time. They are size, class, type and plan. These are not definitive, objective measures. Nor are they exclusive. Hotels fall into all categories or just some, and there are even degrees of belonging. Each category impacts differently on the text's subtitle, "Managing Hotel Operations."

Size

The number of rooms available for sale, the very same figure used in occupancy computations (see Exhibit 1–3) is the standard measure of size. Other possible measures such as the number of employees or gross dollar sales are simply not used. Of course, there is a relationship between them and the number of rooms available.

Counting available rooms is not as certain a gauge as one would first believe. More rooms may be advertised than are actually available. Older hotels have rooms that are no longer saleable. Newer properties lose guest rooms to unplanned offices and storage. As a rule, the older the hotel, the fewer rooms available relative to total room count:

$$\frac{\text{number of guest rooms available for sale}}{\text{number of guest rooms originally constructed}}$$

Hotels are grouped by size for financial reporting, for the U.S. Census and for trade association dues. Traditionally, large hotels are 300 rooms, or more. Medium hotels are 100 to 300 rooms, and small hotels are less than 100 rooms. Recognizing that these definitions are getting dated, the AH&LA boosted its definition of small to 150 rooms. About 25% of the AH&LA's membership falls into the small category.

For hotels seeking government loans, the Small Business Association's (SBA) definition of "small" is based on annual sales. They change that value periodically. At $3 million, an 80-room hotel with 70% occupancy and an ADR of $90 would qualify. It would only generate $1,839,600 annually (80 rooms × 70% occupancy × $90 ADR × 365 days per year).

Visualizing small and medium-sized hotels as *the* lodging industry is difficult when one thinks of famous hotels such as the Waldorf-Astoria in New York City with 1,852 rooms, or the New Otani in Tokyo, 2,057 rooms (see Exhibit 1–6). Small hotels are more common in Europe where traditionally they have been family owned and operated. The shift to chains and franchised hotel names has accelerated recently in both Europe and Asia and is changing the structure of the business there. Still, only 30% of Europe's hotels are branded versus 70% in the United States.

Mom-and-Pop Motels.   The term "motel" (motor + hotel) was coined after World War II when Americans took to the highways. The concept was refined by Kemmon's Wilson, who created the Holiday Inn chain. Motels replaced the very limited facilities known as motor courts (see Exhibit 1–7). Many motels—the term has now fallen from favor—were family owned and operated. Whence comes the term "mom-and-pop". There were some 60,000 mom-and-pop motels along the 1960s' highways. Rising construction, financing, and labor costs headed a list of hurdles that such small entrepreneurs could not overcome. They did not purchase in quantity; they were unable to advertise widely; and they competed against the better management talent that worked for their chain/franchise competitors.

Class

The class of hotel is sensed as often as it is measured, although two objective measures are available. One is price (ADR); the other is rating systems.

Average Daily Rate.   Delivering class, elegance, and service costs money. Larger rooms, costly construction, upgraded furnishings and extra employees incur larger financing costs, depreciation, energy, salaries, wages and more. All are recovered by higher rates. So too are better levels of maintenance, 24-hour room service, saunas, and similar extras. The better the class of hotel, the higher the rate.

Driven by inflation, ADR has been increasing industrywide for decades. So a higher room rate over time is not the measure. A higher room rate relative to competition is the critical number. Location, location, location also plays a role. Hotels in small towns are different from their big-city counterparts. A $55 rate in Los Angeles conjures up a totally different class of lodging than does that same rate in a small rural town, However, at a given time and with a judicious concern for size, type, and location, ADR is a fair measure of class.

Published rates help classify the nation's hotels (see Exhibit 1–8).

Full-Service to Limited-Service.   Hotels are as diverse as the traveling public that fills them. Responding to many varied needs, the industry has created a range of accommodations from the full-service high-rise to the squat motor inn. One group of hotel investors offers nothing more than a clean room and a good mattress. Guests do not need swimming pools, closets, or lobbies, goes the argument. This hotelier offers limited service at minimum prices (see Exhibit 1–8).

One hundred eight degrees away is the full-service, upscale property. This hotel has superior facilities and a full complement of services. Limited services means lobby vending machines or a nearby restaurant servicing several properties in the area. Full-service has a menu of dining options and a range of extras such as lounges, room service, newspapers to the room, exercise facilities and a wide range of electronic options. Expense-account travelers patronize the full-service property, although something less costly may do when the family travels.

Hotel	Number of Rooms[a]	Location
Asia-Asia	6,500[d]	Dubai, United Arab Emirates
MGM Grand[b]	5,000	Las Vegas
Ambassador City	4,700	Jomtlen, Thailand
Luxor[b]	4,400	Las Vegas
Excalibur[b]	4,050	Las Vegas
Circus Circus[b]	3,700	Las Vegas
Flamingo[c]	3,650	Las Vegas
Mandalay Bay[b]	3,225	Las Vegas
Las Vegas Hilton	3,200	Las Vegas
Opryland Hotel	3,100	Nashville
Mirage[b]	3,050	Las Vegas
Venetian[e]	3,050[e]	Las Vegas
Monte Carlo[b]	3,000	Las Vegas
Bellagio[b]	3,000	Las Vegas
Paris[c]	2,925	Las Vegas
TI (Treasure Island)[b]	2,900	Las Vegas
Bally's[c]	2,825	Las Vegas
Wynn[e]	2,700[e]	Las Vegas
Imperial Palace[c]	2,600	Las Vegas
Aladdin	2,575	Las Vegas
Hilton Hawaiian Village	2,850	Honolulu
Atlantis	2,450	Paradise Island, Bahamas
Caesars Palace[c]	2,425	Las Vegas
New York Hilton	2,000	New York City
Caribbean Beach	2,100	Orlando
Riviera	2,075	Las Vegas
New York, New York[b]	2,000	Las Vegas
San Francisco Hilton	1,900	San Francisco
Adam's Mark	1,850	Dallas
Chicago Hilton	1,550	Chicago
Gaylord Texan Resort	1,500	Grapevine

[a] Room numbers have been rounded.
[b] Identifies hotels owned by MGM Grand Hotels.
[c] Identifies hotels owned by Harrah's.
[d] Under construction.
[e] Additional rooms under construction.

Exhibit 1-6 Megahotels, once exclusive to Las Vegas, are appearing worldwide. The Opryland Hotel, Nashville, TN, bills itself as the largest U.S. hotel outside of Las Vegas. With its Texan Resort (final entry) Gaylord Entertainment now has two entries, although it dropped the Opryland designation from all of its non-Nashville properties.

Exhibit 1-7   Tourist courts predated the highway motel, which gained momentum from the federal, interstate road construction boom following World War II. Kemmons Wilson's Holiday Inn chain (1952) set the initial standard for motels. Then came amenity creep (see Chapter 2).

Between the two lies the bulk of facilities. Services are added as competition demands and costs allow. Services are pared as markets shift and as acceptable self-service equipment appears. Chapters 2 and 3 introduce some newer in-between hotels.

Number of Employees.   Class as measured by full service or limited service refers as much to the size of the staff as to the physical amenities. Thus, the number of employees per guest room

$$\frac{\text{number of employees on staff}}{\text{number of rooms available for sale}}$$

is another measure of class (see Exhibit 1–3).

Budget properties, those without restaurants or other amenities such as bars or room service, operate with as few as 0.25 (one-fourth) employee per guest room. An 80-room house might have as few as 20 employees. There's a limit to how small the staff can shrink. If the property wants the legal benefits of being a hotel, common law requires it to provide around-the-clock coverage. Add in staff days off plus a minimum housekeeping crew, night security, someone for repairs and maintenance, and the total grows.

Because a minimum staff is needed, a hotel of 60 rooms might have almost the same number of employees as one of, say, 100 rooms. Each property needs a minimum number at the desk, a manager, a head housekeeper, an accountant, and someone in maintenance. Housekeeping would be the major difference. If a housekeeper cleans 15 rooms per shift, every additional 15 rooms requires an extra employee and eventually a supervisor. Hotels minimize that number by using and paying for call-in housekeepers only when volume dictates.

The in-between class of hotel uses an in-between number of employees. That ratio ranges from 0.5 (one-half) an employee per room to as much as a 1:1 ratio. Depending on the services offered, a 300-room hotel could have as few as 150 employees or as many

Classification of Hotels by Average Daily Room Rate
Deluxe Hotels (typical room rate: $600 plus/night)
Fairmont Hotels
Four Seasons Hotels
Ritz-Carlton Hotels
Upper Upscale Hotels (typical room rate: $400/night)
Le Meridien Hotels
Sofitel Hotels
W Hotels
Upscale Hotels (typical room rate: $300/night)
Hyatt Hotels
Marriott Hotels
Omni Hotels
Midprice Hotels with Food (typical room rate: $150/night)
Four Points (Sheraton)
Garden Inns (Hilton)
Best Western
Midprice Hotels without Food (typical room rate: $90/night)
Amerisuites
Hampton Inns
La Quinta
Economy Hotels (typical room rate: $65/night)
Baymont Inns and Suites
Red Roof Inns
Super 8
Budget Inns (typical room rate: $60/night)
EconoLodge
Microtel
Motel 6

Exhibit 1-8   ADR, average daily rate, identifies the class of hotel, offering consumers a range of accommodations from the bare-minimum budget facility to the full-service, super-deluxe property.

as 250 or so. The number is most likely to be about 200 to 225 if there's food service and a bar that needs staffing.

Full-service hotels staff a full complement of departments, including bell service, restaurants, turn-down bed service, and telecommunications persons, among others. Hotels with theater shows, acres of grounds to be maintained, casinos, and 24-hour services require extra personnel and have still higher ratios, perhaps 1.5 employees per guest room. A 1,000-room hotel/casino operating fully over 24 hours could easily have 1,250 to 1,500 employees.

Hotels employ many low-wage workers. That point has been used to argue in favor of casino/hotels when there are moral objections.

Asian properties offer the best in service. Labor is less costly, so the number of employees per room is the world's highest. At the Bangkok Shangri-La, for example, 1,073 staff members handle 697 rooms, a ratio of 1.5:1. Hong Kong's Peninsula Hotel ranks better still, with a staff of 655 for its 300 rooms, better than 2:1.

Worldwide, the workforce is huge. The United States alone has some 2 million hotel workers. The privately funded World Tourism and Travel Council (WTTC) estimates 225 million employees in the world's tourism industry. That includes about 13% of Europe's total labor force.

Rating Systems.　　Room rates provide good guidance to the class of hotel even when rating systems are in place. Some rating systems have been formalized; some have not. Some are government run; some are not. Most are standardized within the single country, but not so across its borders. Members of the World Tourism Organization have done much to standardize their systems by adopting the WTO's five recommended classes. Deluxe or luxury class is at the top. First-class, which is not top-of-the-line despite its name, comes next. Tourist class, sometimes called economy or second class, is actually third in line. Third and fourth class (really the fourth and fifth ranks) usually have no private baths, no centralized heat, not even carpeting.

International travelers avoid third-and fourth-class facilities. They also know to discount the deluxe category of many Caribbean properties. Similarly, experienced travelers limit stays in Africa and the Middle East to deluxe properties.

Worldwide.　　There are some 100 rating systems. Almost all of them use stars for ranking, but coffee pots, alphabets, and even feathers have been used. Britain uses ticks for its holiday parks, which are upscale caravan parks.

Europe's system is the most developed. Its four-and five-star hotels have restaurants and bars. *Hotel garni* means no restaurant but a continental breakfast is usually served. That's the usage in England as well as on the Continent and both correspond to the U.S. phrase, "breakfast included."

The Swiss Hotel Association is unique because it is a private organization rating itself. Mexican hotels are also trade-associated rated. They use the WTO's five classifications plus a luxury class termed Gran Tourism or Gran Especial. The Irish Tourist Board takes a different tack, listing the facilities available (elevator; air conditioning; laundry) rather than grading them. Directories of the European Community do the same and also classify by location: seaside/countryside; small town/large city. European auto clubs go further by distinguishing privately owned from government-run accommodations.

Spain has standardized the rating system of its *paradors* ("stopping places") despite the great differences in physical facilities and furnishings. The government-operated chain of nearly 100 inns maintains approximately one-third at the four-star level. All but a few of the remaining group are two- or three-star properties.

Japanese *ryokans*, which are traditional inns, are rated according to the excellence of their guest rooms, kitchens, baths, and—of all things to Western values—gardens. These very traditional hotels serve two meals, which are often taken in the uncluttered guest room that opens onto those gardens. About 1,000 *ryokans*, have been registered by the Japanese Travel Bureau as appropriate for international guests.[6]

Like Japan, Korea has fine, Western-style hotels at top international standards. It also has budget-priced lodgings called *yogwans* (or inns). Unlike the *ryokans*, most *yogwans* have Western-style accommodations, including private baths. Upscale *yogwans* can be identified because their names end in *jang* or *chang*.

The United Kingdom probably has the largest number of rating systems by the greatest range of organizations. Among them are the National Tourist Board (NTB), the Automobile Association (AA), the Royal Automobile Club (RAC), and commercial enterprises such as Egon Ronay and the better known Michelin. The ratings are by crowns (NTB) and stars (both the AA and the RAC) and pavilions or small buildings (Michelin). Each classification is then subdivided by grades or percentage marks. Thus the AA might rate a property as Four Star, 65%.

---

[6]International guests have been the savior of the ryokans, whose revenues have declined by half as resident Japanese forsake their complexity for Western-style hotels.

The U.S. System.   The U.K. has both private and governmental rating systems. U.S. ratings rely solely on private enterprise. The American Automobile Association (AAA) has been one of two major participants. Mobil, the other, was started in the motor-lodge era of the late 1950s as a subsidiary of Mobil Oil. Both face a wide range of competitors that has Mobil urgently restructuring. Michelin, which is very popular in Europe, now has U.S. guidebooks. Zagat started with restaurant guides and only recently with hotel ratings. J. D. Powers, famous for ratings consumer goods, has also entered the market. Many Web sites (Expedia, for one) carry evaluations, as do a wide range of publications. There are bed-and-breakfast guides, magazine guides, regional guides, even one by the NAACP. None are government affiliated. All are crowding out the traditional star system of Mobil and the diamond ratings of AAA (see Exhibit 1–9).

Historically, a good Mobil listing boosted occupancy by 20% or so. Similarly, as much as 40% of volume in small hotels has been attributed to an AAA listing. Both agencies rely on on-site, anonymous inspections, each covering about 25,000 properties. AAA personnel identify themselves after their annual visit. Mobil inspectors come every 18 months but remain anonymous. Online reservation (res) systems such as *Priceline* also send inspectors, but they solicit business at the same time. AAA includes information for handicapped travelers; the Scottish Tourist Bureau does the same using three levels of accessibility. All travel guides accept input from their users.

By building different facilities for different markets, hotel chains have unintentionally created internal rating systems, but few consumers recognize them. Exhibit 2–1 illustrates the point.

Membership in Preferred Hotels, a loosely knit affiliation of independent hotels, requires ratings of superior or above from one of the recognized services. So just belonging to Preferred gives the property a superior-plus rating.

Not all guides are consumer oriented. Several list conference and meeting facilities, an American specialty. Others are important to travel agents and meeting planners. Among the publications that focus on the trade are the *Official Meeting Facilities Guide* and the *Hotel & Travel Index*. The *Official Hotel Guide (OHG)*, whose ratings are favored by the cruise lines, uses subjective assessments of service as well as objective listings of actual accommodations.

We may eventually see a new environmental rating. Research from the United States Travel Data Center indicates a willingness of guests to pay more for environmentally friendly lodgings (EFLs). EFL could be another criterion for, or a completely separate rating from, the usual standards.

Type

Size and class, two of lodging's four traditional classifications, have already been discussed. Now we exam number three, types of hotels. Type has three traditional subdivisions of its own: commercial hotels, resort hotels, and residential hotels. As with so many other definitions in a dynamic industry, there are sharp distinctions no longer. Chapter 2 goes further by describing emerging hotel patterns. Some are new concepts and some build on the traditional types.

Commercial Hotels.   Commercial hotels, or transient hotels, make up the largest category of American hotels (see Exhibit 1–10). They service short-term, transient (not permanent) visitors. Businesspersons are the chief market of commercial houses. Conventioneers, engineers, salespersons, consultants and small businesspersons form the

The key criteria for every rating are cleanliness, maintenance, quality of furnishings and physical appointments, service, and the degree of luxury offered. There are some regional differences, as customers have different expectations for a historic inn in northern New England, a dude ranch in the Southwest, and a hotel in the center of a major city.

★

One-star establishments should be clean and comfortable and worth the prices charged when compared to other accommodations in the area. If they are below average in price, they may receive a checkmark for good value in addition to the one star. They offer a minimum of services. There may not be 24-hour front desk or phone service; there may be no restaurant; the furniture will not be luxurious. Housekeeping and maintenance should be good; service should be courteous; but luxury will not be part of the package.

★★

Two-star accommodations have more to offer than one-star and will include some, but not necessarily all, of the following: better-quality furniture, larger bedrooms, restaurant on the premises, color TV in all rooms, direct-dial phones, room service, swimming pool. Luxury will usually be lacking, but cleanliness and comfort are essential.

★★★

Three-star motels and hotels include all of the facilities and services mentioned in the preceding paragraph. If some are lacking, and the place receives three stars, it means that some other amenities are truly outstanding. A three-star establishment should offer a very pleasant travel experience to every customer.

★★★★

Four-star and five-star hotels and motels make up a very small percentage (less than 2%) of the total number of places listed; therefore they all deserve the description of "outstanding." Bedrooms should be larger than average; furniture should be of high quality; all of the essential extra services should be offered; personnel should be well trained, courteous, and anxious to please. Because the standards of quality are high, prices will often be higher than average. A stay in a four-star hotel or motel should be memorable. No place will be awarded four or five stars if there is a pattern of complaints from customers, regardless of the luxury offered.

★★★★★

The few five-star awards go to those places which go beyond comfort and service to deserve the description "one of the best in the country." A superior restaurant is required, although it may not be rated as highly as the accommodations. Twice-daily maid service is standard in these establishments. Lobbies will be places of beauty, often furnished in antiques. If there are grounds surrounding the building, they will be meticulously groomed and landscaped. Each guest will be made to feel that he or she is a Very Important Person to the employees.

Exhibit 1-9   The authors have created criteria for rating U.S. hotels, which are expressed traditionally with stars and diamonds. Other symbols are used worldwide where rating systems are usually government controlled. Private organizations, such as *Mobil's Travel Guide*, do the job in the United States.

Exhibit 1-10   Location, location, location is the mantra of commercial hotels, which serve several markets but chiefly business clientele. Thus, their usual locations are business parks, research centers, ring roads or urban downtowns. *Courtesy of New York Marriott Marquis, 45th and Broadway, New York, New York.*

core of the customer base. Indeed, commercial guests are the backbone of the entire lodging industry. They are equally important to the urban property and the roadside motor hotel. Still, there are plenty of rooms to accommodate leisure guests, and commercial hotels do so with pleasure.

Commercial hotels locate close to their market—the business community, usually an urban area. As business centers have left downtown cities, so has the commercial hotel. Arterial highways, research parks, airports, and even suburban shopping centers have become the new locations for commercial properties.

Many businesspersons relax on weekends, which explains the poor weekend occupancy of the commercial hotel (see Exhibit 1–5). Attempts to offset this decline with tourists, groups, and special local promotions have been only moderately successful.

Large, commercial hotels are almost always full-service properties. Businesspersons are usually expense-account travelers who can afford four-star and even five-star accommodations. Travel offices of many businesses began to closely monitor employee travel costs following the dip in business after the World Trade Center disaster. Furthermore, Congress had enacted restrictions on the amount of tax-deductible business expenses.

Strong economic recovery beginning in late 2004 eased concerns about the demise of expense-account travelers. They've come on strong!

Residential Hotels.

Unlike the transient nature of the commercial hotel guest, residential guests take permanent residency. This creates a landlord–tenant relationship that differs in legal rights and responsibilities from the traditional guest–innkeeper relationship. In some locales the room occupancy tax is not payable for residential (sometimes called *permanent*) guests in a transient hotel.

The last census reported two-thirds of all commercial hotels had permanent guests. New York City's Waldorf-Astoria is a good example. Its Towers (a section of the hotel) houses residential, often famous, guests. Less common is the residential hotel that caters to transient travelers.

Extended-Stay Hotels. Extended-stay hotels are different from either commercial or residential properties. Rooms are designed differently because guests are there for long-term stays. But that timing is loosely defined. Guests are not in permanent residency as they are in residential hotels. Neither are they the transient, 2–4 day commercial guests.

Extensive travel and suitcase living quickly lose their glamour. Something different is needed for those persons moving locations or having extended business assignments away from homes and home offices. Keeping workers comfortable and productive takes more than a traditional hotel room. Extended-stay hotels provide kitchens, grocery outlets, office space, office equipment, fireplaces, exercise rooms, laundry facilities, and more—even secretarial support—but all with maid service.

Accommodations at an extended-stay hotel are similar to those at the all-suite hotel. In fact, the all-suite emerged from the extended-stay as management sought to broaden an otherwise narrow market. So the distinctions have blurred. The same building caters to both long-term business travelers and all-suite users (families, interviews, small in-room meetings, and the like).

Resort Hotels.

Transient hotels cater to commercial guests, residential hotels to permanent guests and resort hotels (see Exhibit 1–11) to social guests—at least traditionally they do.

Economics has forced resorts to lengthen their operating period from the traditional summer or winter season to year-round operations. Resorts have marketed to the group and convention delegate at the expense of their social guest. As this began happening, the commercial hotel shifted its design and markets toward the resort concept, dulling once again the distinctions between types. What emerged is a mixed-use resort. Sometimes these resorts are found in residential areas as part of a master-planned community.

Many believe that the modified resort is the hotel of the future. It is in keeping with the nation's move toward increased recreation and is compatible with the casual air that characterizes the vacationer. Unlike the formality of the vacationer of an earlier time, today's guest is a participant. Skiing, golfing, boating, and a host of other activities are at the core of the successful resort.

The Megaresort. Megaresorts are large, self-contained resorts. Entertainment and recreational facilities are so numerous and so varied that guests need not leave the property during their entire stay. There are other self-contained resorts. The Sandals chain in the Caribbean is one example. Size distinguishes the megaresort from these other all-inclusive accommodations.

Exhibit 1-11   Resorts have broadened their appeal beyond the "social guests" that persisted through the middle of the 20th century. Amenities, including executive conference centers, spas, tennis clubs, water sports and more, appeal to groups as well as leisure guests. *Courtesy of the Sagamore, Bolton Landing, New York.*

Although megaresorts are a feature of Las Vegas (see Exhibit 1–6), they are not limited to that location. The 900-room Marriott Desert Springs and Spa near Palm Springs, California, and Hilton's Hawaiian Village on Oahu (over 2,500 rooms) also represent this genre.

Single-feature, specialty resorts have also proven quite successful. They appeared even earlier than the hotel industry's general move toward segmentation. Tennis clubs (all types of sports clubs), spas, and health resorts ("diet farms") have opened and flourished (see Exhibit 1–12). Club Meditérrannée became the prototype of a new style of resort: one that features an all-inclusive price, with tips included.

America's changing demographics (age distribution) is certain to impact the type and variety of resort hotels. The wealthy baby-boom generation is moving toward retirement, and its children, generation X (or echo boomers), are reaching economic maturity. Condominium resorts are a favorite of the parents; all-inclusive resorts are a favorite of the offspring. In every case, weather and location play key roles. Geography is to the resort as commerce is to the transient hotel and population is to the residential property.

Plan

Plan identifies which meals, if any, are included in the quoted room rate. Rates are higher, obviously, if meals are provided. Classification by plan is more objective than classification by any of the other three categories: size, class, or type. Either meals are included or they are not. With few exceptions, hotels in the United States operate on the European Plan: no meals.

European Plan. Rates quoted as European plan (EP) include room accommodations only. Meals taken in the dining room are charged at menu prices. Evidence of the widespread use of the European plan is its lack of designation. Guests are not told, "This is the European plan"; it is assumed unless otherwise stated.

Continental Plan (Continental Breakfast). More than any other meal, travelers eat breakfast in the hotel. European hotels often include a limited breakfast with the European plan. This continental breakfast (mainland Europe being the continent) consists of coffee or hot chocolate, a roll, and a bit of cheese (cold meat or fish in Holland and Norway). Breakfast is on the wane in Europe even as it gets a boost in North America. All-suite hotels have gained popularity by including free breakfasts as part of their marketing approach. It is a revival of America's view of the continental plan, which took form in the no-restaurant format of the 1950s motel. In-room coffee makers, coffee in the lobby, or coffee and sweet rolls in the small proprietor's kitchen were all touted as continental breakfast.

Continental breakfast has still other meanings. A coffee urn with sweet rolls and juice left in the lobby when the dining room closes is often called a continental breakfast. A similar setup at a group registration desk or at the rear of a meeting room during a speaker's talk appears on the program as continental breakfast. Juice is included in the United States or when the delegates are Americans, but it is not usually served elsewhere.

In some parts of the world, this abbreviated breakfast is called a bed-breakfast. That should not be confused with the Bermuda plan, which includes a full breakfast in the rate. A very hearty breakfast called an English breakfast is served in Ireland and the United Kingdom. It includes cereal, eggs with a choice of meat, toast with butter and jam, tea, and coffee, but no juice. However, unlike the Bermuda plan, it is rarely included in the room rate quote.

Café complet, a midmorning or afternoon coffee snack, is mistakenly called a continental breakfast. The distinction is neither the time of day nor the menu items, but the manner of payment. *Café complet* is not included in the room rate.

The appearance of late afternoon tea as a pleasant supplement to the overworked happy hour is certain to bring further confusion in terminology. Many top U.S. hotels and cruise lines have latched onto that quintessential British ritual, afternoon tea. Delicate sandwiches and small sweets served with tea, or even sherry, comprise this light snack. It is not to be confused with high tea, which is a supper, a substantial meal almost always served with meat. High tea is a rarity today, even in British hotels.

American Plan. Rates quoted under the American plan (AP) include room and all three meals: breakfast, luncheon, and dinner. The American plan, which is occasionally called *bed and board,* had its origin in colonial America, when all guests ate at a common table with the host's family. The plan was still in use when the affluent resorts of the Northeast began operating in the late 1800s. They adopted and held onto the plan until World War II.

New England's resorts retained the American plan for the same reason that the colonial innkeeper offered it in the first place. Both were isolated, so there was no place else to eat. Better roads and better cars gave guests the mobility that spelled the end of the plan.

Europe's full *pension* (pen'-si-own) is almost equivalent to the American plan. Breakfast is the big difference. Full *pension* includes an abbreviated continental breakfast, not the complete breakfast of the American plan. To market the American plan to international guests, European hotels rely on the more descriptive "inclusive terms." The *pension* of Europe is the guest house or boardinghouse of Britain and the United States, with residential hotels in Europe using the term *en pension*. *Pensiones* are usually longer-stay facilities with limited services, so guests become members of an extended family.

Adaptations of the American Plan.   Many guests view the American plan negatively. It requires them to adhere to the hotel's meal schedule and to pay a fixed price for the meal no matter what they eat. Although not as popular as it once was, the American plan is still alive but under different names.

Cruise ships provide American-plan dining, but they don't use that terminology. Neither do the all-inclusive resorts of the Caribbean which add drinks, tips, and activities for one price.

A *dine-around* plan is another variation. AP hotels allow guests to dine at other hotels in the vicinity. The cooperating hotels might be members of the same chain or a local consortium of competitors that understands the marketing value of the option.

Conference centers, which cater to groups, call their variation CMP, *complete meeting package*. The quoted room rate includes room, meals, coffee breaks, meeting setups, and gratuities. Of the rate quoted, 50% might be attributed to rooms, 33% to food and beverage, 10% to gratuities and the remaining 7% to meeting space and audio-visual/electronic support. This accounting is for internal use and would not be communicated to the guest.

Modified American Plan.   The modified American plan (MAP) is an astute compromise offered by some hotels, including those running a full American plan. The hotel retains some of the AP advantages, and the guest feels less restricted. Guests get breakfast and dinner as part of the room rate quote, but not luncheon. This opens the middle of the day for a flexible schedule of activities. Guests need not return for an inconveniently scheduled luncheon nor suffer the cost of a missed meal. The hotel retains the obvious benefits of a captive market for the dinner hour. In an effort to make the difference clear, some APs are now called FAP—full American plan.

Half-pension or *demi-pension* (DP) is the European equivalent of the MAP. It includes breakfast and one other meal along with the lodgings. Granting either luncheon or dinner gives the foreign guest the same flexibility of scheduling offered with the modified American plan.

Variations on the Themes

The hotel business is a dynamic one because it is run by clever hoteliers. They innovate by modifying the standard into something different even as the basic industry remains the same (see Exhibit 1–12). Bed and breakfasts and boutique hotels are two great examples.

Bed and Breakfast (B&B).   Bed and breakfast surged onto the American scene so strongly that one might think it a whole new concept in hotelkeeping. It's hardly that. Bed and breakfast in the United States takes its cue from the British B&B, the Italian *pensiones*, and the German *zimmer frei* (room available)—lodging and breakfast offered by families in their own homes. The Japanese B&B is *minshuku*.

Specialty Hotels That Fit No General Category	
Backpackers	And camping
Club Med	Vacation villages
Couples only	Honeymoon resorts and gay groups
Dude ranches	For the horsey set
Eco lodges	Safari lodges; wilderness accommodations
Exclusive-use	Resorts that limit use to one group of guests at one time
Floating	House boats; as hotel rooms in India
Grand dames	Ladies with aristocratic bearings; hence grand, elegant hotels
Historical	Buildings (not only hotels) listed with the National Trust
Ice hotels	Made of ice, popular in Iceland and Canada
Kosher	For Jewish and Muslim diets
Landmarks	Former jails and prisons; famous homes; lighthouses[a]
Luxury camping	With creature comforts
Mi Casa Es Su Casa	Joining families in private homes
Military hotels	The army alone has some 22,000 commercial hotel rooms
National parks	Operations, including rates, set by the government
Native American	American Indian operations
Nudists	Camps, colonies, beaches
Resident clubs	Private facilities, often with golf clubs
Retreats	Centers for rehabilitation from drug and alcohol addiction
Singles	May be religious affiliated
Sleep clinics	For giving polysomnograms, sleep tests
Tree houses	Popular in Turkey
Yurts	Round, cloth-covered tents

[a]After World War II, Europe's old bomb shelters served as hotels for a brief period.

Exhibit 1–12   Innovative operators and marketeers have created many new hotel niches that do not fall within lodging's traditional classifications of size, class, type and plan.

American B&Bs are modern versions of the 1930s rooming houses, once called tourist homes. Running a B&B is an adventure for some owners; for others a hobby; for many a livelihood. Guests take rooms with private families, who furnish camaraderie along with the mandatory second B, breakfast. The lack of privacy—conversation at breakfast and sometimes even a shared bath—forces the host and guest into a level of intimacy that brings new friendships along with new business.

Like the rest of the industry, change is part of the B&B's vocabulary, and no one definition fits all the parts. There are many subcategories because the business is very individualized and localized. The B&B changes identity as it moves across the country. The B&B Inn, for example, is a product of California. It is a large version (over half the B&Bs in the United States are 8 rooms or less) and is usually the owner's primary occupation. Another subcategory, the Country B&B, is an upscale boardinghouse because it serves all meals, not just breakfast. Country B&Bs have their origin in New England. Between the coasts are a variety of facilities serving their local markets (see Exhibit 1–13). Like other small businesses, B&Bs often lack staying power. Results can be ruinous where zoning laws prohibit even a "rooms-for-let" notice in the window. One positive sign is

(a)   (b)

Exhibit 1–13   Bed and breakfasts operate under a variety of names. *B&B inns* are popular on the west coast; *country B&Bs* in New England. In between are many wonderful stopping places with award-winning breakfasts and distinctive guest accommodations. *Courtesy of The Inn at 410, Flagstaff, Arizona.*

the new Yellow Pages listing of B&B referral organizations under "B&B" rather than under their previous category of "hotels, motels, and tourist homes."

In one way, B&Bs are no different from other American hotels. They fight for business and rely on themselves for referrals. In Europe and Japan, government tourist agencies make B&B referrals and even rate them by price and accommodations. The French call them *café-couette* (coffee and quilt), and their rating system uses three to six coffee pots instead of stars. Since the U.S. government has never entered the tourist-rating business, several private rating and referral systems have emerged. Like the B&Bs themselves, these rating/referral systems come and go quickly, for they too lack staying power.

Boutique Hotels.   Boutique hotels are the rage among the hip, the chic, and the cool. So sometimes the pool-party buzz that they create hides their true identity. They're just hotels; hotels with special issues. Balancing paying customers and trendy clubgoers is one of those challenges. Using word-of-mouth rather than traditional advertising and restricting house guests from some of the parties contribute to the problem. Defining a boutique is even more difficult.

Boutique hotels have small inns as their prototypes, but they provide the amenities of fine hotels. Although many now number in hundreds of rooms, boutiques remain fashionable because of their good urban locations. They are proof positive of "location, location, location." Two reasons account for their popularity in London, San Francisco, and New York. Relatively small, they can find affordable land in crowded urban areas. Indeed, once they were called *urban inns. European-style hotels* or, in Britain particularly, *baby grand hotels* were also once widely used. Secondly, the boutique's guest is an urbancentric customer: One who willingly pays a 10–15% room premium for the design and excitement of the urban inn.

The very nature of boutique hotels—something different—precludes a single definition. The term has been attributed to Steve Rubell, one of the founders of New York City's *Studio 54,* but the concept predates him. Asked to describe his hotel, The Morgans, Rubell said that other hotels are large department stores, but Morgans is a small boutique.[7] Boutique suggests something different, very eclectic, always with

---

[7]Derived from the Greek for *storehouse.* "Perhaps that's where the notion that boutique hotels need to be small began." Jeff Higley, Editor-in-Chief, *Hotel Design*, October/November, 2005, p. 4.

flair, funky, and artsy (see Exhibit 1–14). The modern boutique aims to mirror its guests: Wannabes who often see themselves experiencing the lifestyle of celebrities. Nevertheless, boutique executives still talk about service, the guest's experience, and the quality of the operating team, issues for any hotelier.

Ian Schrager, Rubell's partner, helped develop the boutique concept, but left after the idea was widely adopted by the hotel chains. Starwood Hotels introduced the W Hotel (for warm, welcoming, and witty). Marriott redeveloped its Renaissance chain with a facelift into the unexpected. The brand chains have entered the fray because boutiques have higher RevPar and occupancy figures (lower break-even points) than traditional establishments.

The question remains whether a branded chain can deliver the unexpected and the quirky, which are the hallmarks of a boutique. Can a hotel be both mainstream and boutique? Can hotels larger than 100 to 150 rooms with banquet and meeting space maintain the connection that boutiques develop between guests and staff? (W Hotel's flagship is the New York W, with 722 rooms.) Perhaps there is a second-generation boutique hotel coming, one with both style and substance. Meridian Hotels use the term *Art and Tech:* hotels that can be provocative and still provide the basics.

Exhibit 1-14   Boutique hotels have become a distinct segment of the lodging industry. Like the B&B, there is no one standard. Indeed, breaking the stereotype of the hotel is the very appeal of the genre. *Courtesy of the Georgian Hotel, Santa Monica, California.*

Trophy Hotels.   Trophy hotels are those that add to the owner's reputation, similar to a trophy on the shelf. Many *grande dames* of the hotel business have such wonderful reputations and historical lineage that hoteliers acquire them just to claim ownership. Some are profitable, ongoing properties, such as Denver's Brown Palace. But many trophy hotels struggle during economic dips, although they may be profitable during up-cycles. Listing these unique buildings in the National Register of Historic Places provides some helpful tax relief if the hotel is a historical site or if the boutique hotel results from a historical conversion, as it sometimes does.

SUMMARY

The lodging industry continues to play an important role in the development of commerce and culture even as it undergoes rapid changes. Despite the introduction of many new lodging types, the industry retains its traditional measures of success: occupancy (%), average daily rate (ADR), and revenue per available room (RevPar).

To maximize the values of these measures, management must overcome several limitations that are inherent in the hotel business. These include a highly perishable product, an unmovable location, a fixed supply of inventory, a high break-even point, and seasonal operating periods. In addition, hotelkeeping is a cyclical industry, with long up and down waves that sometimes last a decade: tough hurdles all.

Understanding the industry's traditional identifications (size, class, type, and plan) helps in identifying the new permutations (all-suite, B&B, boutique) that keep the industry economically sound and exciting as a career. Competition sharpens the new direction, and rating systems keep the individual hotel attuned. As the changes continue, new classifications and new categories are needed. Those identities are provided in Chapter 2.

RESOURCES AND CHALLENGES
Resources

WEB SITES

http://www.ahla.com (American Hotel & Lodging Association [AH&LA]—New York. The lodging industry's chief trade association.)

http://www.lodging-econometrics.com (Lodging Econometrics—Portsmouth, NH. Hotel statistics from the research division of National Hotel Realty, dealing with the value of hotel real estate.)

http://www.rkmillerinc.com (Richard K. Miller & Associates—Loganville, GA. Lodging industry research.)

http://www.smithtravelresearch.com (Smith Travel Research—Hendersonville, TN. Statistical analysis of the lodging industry in conjunction with the AH&LA.)

http://www.census.gov (United States Census—Washington, DC. Counts the nation's lodging establishments.)

Web Assignment

Use references from the Web site (or elsewhere) to update the chapter's statistics. Provide national or local values as assigned by the instructor. Cite sources for the number of hotels, the number of rooms, the percentage of occupancy, ADR, and RevPar.

INTERESTING TIDBITS

➤ Mr. Chase Burritt, Ernst & Young LLP's hospitality group, says that half of the nation's 4,000,000 hotel rooms are owned by small, independent (non–chain affiliated) operators. *The Wall Street Journal*, December 11, 2001, p. B1.

➤ *Eloise*, a 1955 book about a 6-year-old girl who lived in New York's Plaza Hotel, helped the hotel receive a 1998 declaration as a "literary landmark." Eloise books, paintings, even a special room set aside for tourists were highlighted for the book's 50th year. The conversion of the Plaza into condos leaves Eloise's fate unclear. A recent novel, *Snowing on Palm Trees*, by Hubert de Maximy, has created a new hotel heroine, an adult businesswoman. The setting is Hilton's Paris Hotel, Arc de Triomphe.

➤ The Las Vegas Sands Corporation's integrated megaresort/casino in Singapore has 2,500 rooms and 20,000 employees. That's 8 employees per guest room! *Las Vegas Review Journal*, May 27, 2006, p. D1.

Challenges

TRUE/FALSE

Questions that are partially false should be marked false (F).

___ 1. A budget hotel would have a 1:1 employee to guest ratio, while a casino/hotel would provide better service, say, 0.5 employees to each room (0.5:1).

___ 2. Simply put: Occupancy (%) measures quantity and ADR ($) measures quality.

___ 3. Since there are about 100,000 hotels in the US and about 25,000,000 hotel rooms, the average hotel is about 250 rooms in size. That sounds about right.

___ 4. The hotel industry is counter-cyclical: That is, it improves when the general economy falls and declines when the general economy booms.

___ 5. As a member of the United Nations, the United States adheres to the hotel rating system adopted by the World Tourism Organization.

PROBLEMS

1. A natural disaster such as an earthquake or man-made disaster like the attack on the World Trade Center has an immediate effect on hotel occupancy. Explain step by step how you would estimate the loss in room income to New York City's hotels when approached by the news media. (*Hint:* New York City has an estimated 63,000 rooms. Use figures and values from Chapter 1 and/or make assumptions; assumptions should be identified.)

2. Create a checklist with two dozen objective listings that could be used by an evaluator inspecting guest rooms for a national rating system.

3. Explain where the hotel industry is in its economic cycle. Be specific. Is it at the bottom of the trough? The highest point of its rise? Somewhere in between? If so, moving in what direction? Submit evidence to support your position.

4. Give three to five examples of each type of expense that is used to determine the cost portion of a hotel's break-even point: fixed expenses; semifixed expenses; variable expenses.

5. How many rooms does the MGM Grand Hotel need to sell annually if it budgets operations on an annual occupancy of 82%? (*Hint*: See Exhibit 1–6.)

6. Using information contained in Chapter 1, justify or challenge the statement of Andrew Young, the former mayor of Atlanta, who said that a 1% rise in room occupancy creates 400 new jobs for that city. (*Hint*: You will need to know the approximate number of rooms in the city and an estimate of the staff-to-room ratio.)

AN INCIDENT IN HOTEL MANAGEMENT

Hit with a Stinging Towel

The resort was living up to everything the family had heard about it. The view was magnificent; the rooms were large, and the food was great. There were three swimming pools in addition to the beach by the ocean. Getting a towel was the big problem. An in-room sign read,

PLEASE DO NOT TAKE BATH TOWELS TO THE POOL OR BEACH; TOWELS ARE AVAILABLE THERE.

Except there were no towels for two days straight. The attendant said that the laundry couldn't keep up with the demand because the house was full. It was true that the beach and the pools were packed with crowds. So the children took towels from their bath on their final day. Kids! Both left their towels on the beach.

The family's upbeat vacation and positive image of the resort took a wide U-turn when they found a $22 charge on the bill for 2 towels missing from Room 319. And the dad said so aloud.

Questions: Was there a management failure here; if so, what?

What is the hotel's immediate response (or action) to the incident?

What further, long-run action should management take, if any?

ANSWERS TO TRUE/FALSE QUIZ

1. False. Values are reversed. A budget property would have an employee ratio of, say, one-half employee per room (0.5:1), and a full-service property would have a 1:1 ratio or even higher—1.5:1, or superior luxury properties even 2:1.

2. True. Occupancy measures the number of guests in the house relative to the number that could be accommodated (quantity). ADR measures what those guests pay. The higher the rate (the quality of the purchase), the higher the ADR.

3. False. The hotel industry is not that large; see Exhibit 1–1. Moreover, the answer is doubly false, because the typical hotel is closer to 100 rooms rather than 250 rooms.

4. False. The hotel industry follows the national economic cycle. Unfortunately it often precedes the national decline and lags the national recovery.

5. False. The United States government does not rate hotels. That job is left to private enterprise, typically AAA and Mobil Guides.

The Modern Hotel Industry

Hotels originally served as the storage arm of transportation. They were located along the travelers' route, waiting there for potential guests to tire and seek shelter. Today's guests use a wide range of transport to find an array of routes, a variety of destinations, and a host of reasons to travel. Only by recreating itself over and over again has the lodging industry been able to meet these changing challenges. New patterns have resulted and this chapter examines four of them: product, market, ownership, and management.

NEW PRODUCT PATTERNS

The four patterns are actually interlaced. Change in one invariably impacts another. New methods of financing may create new management patterns, for example. Or new products emerge when driven by new markets. One size no longer fits all. Recognizing this, lodging executives began *brand stretching*, later called *brand segmentation*,[1] as one means of offsetting a dip in the demand curve.

Segmentation, Brand and Image

Segmentation. To counter falling occupancies during the 1990s, upscale hotels moved vertically downward (stretched their brands) into midscale operations. Marriott introduced Fairfield Inns, for example. Midscale chains countered, moving both upward and downward. Choice Hotels, for example, stepped up with its Clarion brand and down with its Sleep Inn (see Exhibit 2-1). Now, Choice has begun re-inventing itself again. It is enhancing its Quality brand with property improvements and an inclusive breakfast. It is differentiating its Sleep Inn from its Comfort Inn. And it is increasing the rates and services of its Comfort Suites. Adding to the richness—some think confusion— Choice has added Cambria Suites, to its group, designating it as a "lifestyle chain."

Other chains made different moves. Holiday Inn Hotels launched a new brand, Crown Plaza. That altered its identity. No longer just a roadside, motor-inn company, it now competes with the urban likes of Starwood's Sheraton and Hilton's Doubletree brands. Hyatt, an urban chain strong on conventions and group business, recently acquired AmeriSuites, a leisure-oriented chain. Other shifts brought resort companies into commercial businesses, and vice versa. Segmentation spilled over from product differentiation into other aspects of the industry (see Exhibit 2–2).

---

[1]The lodging industry uses *segmentation* to mean different products, hotel types. The word has an opposite meaning in general marketing terminology. There it means developing a product for just one market segment.

Company Name	Brand Names			
	Low End	Midscale	Upscale	Suites
Choice Hotels International	Comfort Inn Econo Lodge Rodeway Inn Sleep Inn	Quality	Clarion	Cambria Suites Comfort Suites MainStay Suites Suburban[b]
Marriott International[a]	Fairfield Inn	Courtyard Residence Inn	JW Marriott Marriott Hotels Ramada International Renaissance Ritz-Carlton	ExecuStay Marriott Suites Renaissance Suites SpringHill Suites TownePlace Suites
InterContinenal[c]	Holiday Inn Express	Holiday Inn Indigo	Crowne Plaza InterContinental	Candlewood Suites Staybridge Suites

[a] Marriott's list is not complete.
[b] Suburban is advertised as an extended-stay hotel; its complete name is Suburban Extended-Stay Hotels.
[c] InterContinental has gone through several name changes: From Holiday Inn to InterContinental to Bass Hotels to Six Continents and back to InterContinental.
Note: Read horizontally, not vertically. Brand comparisons are valid only within the same chain. They are not valid between companies. Choice's mid-scale brand, for example, is not equated to Marriott's mid-scale brand.

Exhibit 2-1   Hotel companies stretch up and away trying to establish new brands. The result is more names, more buzz, and more confusion. Adding to the muddle, chains use different, unrelated names for their frequent guest programs. Exhibits 2–14 and 2–15 pile on still more names. (Five brands have been added and two have been deleted from this exhibit in three years.)

Brand.   Segmentation has created issues as well as solutions. Identification of new products can be muddled by too many new designs, new logos, and new promotions. It took time for hoteliers to realize that collecting a group of like hotels—or even worse, unlike hotels—under one name did not automatically create a brand.

Customer recognition is what defines a brand: recognition of the name and the logo. To that end, hotel chains have poured advertising dollars into the creation of new brands. But how many guests know that Renaissance Hotels are actually Marriotts (see Exhibit 2–1), or that Le Méridien and Westin are both children of Starwood? Like Marriott and Starwood, most large chains have several brands. Some of them have been created, others purchased. There are advantages to multiple brands if the parent company can sell the differences and values of each (Sheraton's Four Points versus W's boutique brands, for example) and yet retain the umbrella of the still broader brand (that's the Starwood example again).[2]

[2]Starwood recently announced that it will cross-market its brands with nonhotel brands. Neither the mechanics of the arrangement nor the results are evident at the time of publication.

A Segmented Industry

Segmented by Activity	**Segmented by Plan**
Casino hotel	American plan
Convention hotel	Continental plan
Dude ranch	European plan
Segmented by Financing	**Segmented by Price (ADR)**[a]
Public corporation	Deluxe
Private individual	Midrange
REIT	Budget
Segmented by Location	**Segmented by Ratings**
Airport	Five-star
Highway	Four-star
Seaside	Three-star
Segmented by Management	**Segmented by Service**
Chain	Full service
Management company	Moderate service
Self-managed	Self-service
Segmented by Markets	**Segmented by Structure**
Business	High rise
Groups	Low rise
Leisure	Outside corridor
Segmented Miscellaneously	**Segmented by Type**
Collar	Commercial
Hostel	Residential
Mixed-use	Resort
Segmented by Ownership	**Segmented by Use**
Chain	Bed and breakfast
Condominium	Extended stay
Mom-and-pop	Health spa

[a] See also Exhibit 1–8

Exhibit 2-2   The lodging industry can be divided and subdivided into many segments. None are self-exclusive. Both individual hotels and entire hotel chains fall under many categories simultaneously. For example, a commercial, three-star property near an airport can be REIT-owned, chain-managed, franchised-flagged operation.

Establishing a brand is more difficult when the chain is foreign based. Not only is it unfamiliar to the traveler, it may use a foreign-sounding name. Recent North American entries include Sol Meliá (Spanish) and Taj Hotels (Indian). (See Exhibit 2–13.)

Brand Equity.   Brand equity is the inherent value that the shopper's recognition gives to the brand. There is equity (value) in the brand only if that recognition carries a positive image. There is no brand equity if guests know the brand but will not stay. Travelodge is a good example of strong brand recognition with weak brand equity. At least that's so in the United States, where it is a Wyndham company. Non-Wyndham Travelodge has both recognition and equity overseas, particularly in Australia, with its mid-range rating of three stars on a five-star system.

Equity develops when hoteliers identify promising segments of the industry, promote the brand associated with that segment, and deliver a product that appeals to the buyer. Basic to developing brand equity from mere brand recognition are four criteria: instant identification (the Marriott name comes immediately to mind); broad distribution (Holiday Inn Hotels is the best example); consistent quality (Hampton Inns has achieved that reputation), and an assured level of service (Four Seasons tops the list).

Branding is about consistency far more than it is about identification with its parent. Branding is about quality far more often than it is about advertising. Branding is about the chain's personality far more often than it is about location. Branding is about individualizing the experience more than it is about cluttering the landscape.

Price—in the lodging industry that's room rate—is the offset to brand equity. With so many choices, the guest's decision often depends on nothing more than the quoted rate. When hotel rooms are viewed as a product rather than as a service, they are characterized as a commodity, much like wheat or oil. In the extreme, guests see every hotel room like every other, and brand managers fight an uphill battle for identity. Web sites such as *Priceline.com* focus the buyer's attention on price, not brand.

New Product Segments

Some efforts at segmentation merely add new faces to tired properties whose logos no longer have equity. More dramatic efforts put entirely new products onto the market. These materialize when hoteliers recognize the need and match their innovations to contemporary demands. Among them are economy hotels, all-suite hotels, casino/hotels, spas, and conference centers. None of which quite meet the traditional hotel definitions of Chapter 1. Let's check in to each.

Economy (Budget, or Limited-Service) Hotels. Budget hotels evolved from the roadside motor courts of the 1930s (see Exhibit 1–7). Then came Holiday Inn Hotels, Kemmon Wilson's chain of clean, no-frills accommodations. Except, existing motor-court operators saw the chain very differently. They saw it as *amenity creep*! Every hotel class fights the battle of amenity creep, but it seems to impact most on the economy segment.

Amenities and Amenity Creep. The history of the industry's ever-improving levels of service is the story of amenity creep. An amenity is a special extra used to distinguish the property from its competitors. It's used in part to establish the brand and to give it equity. After a time, guests expect the amenity. No longer do they view the product or service as an "extra." It is now offered throughout the industry because competitors have first met the challenge and then launched their own, new amenity. Rather than a competitive advantage, the amenity is now a fixed cost.

So little by little, small hotel rooms grew larger. Direct-dial telephones replaced the lobby booth to be replaced in turn by free, wireless connectivity. Free television replaced coin-operated sets, to be replaced in turn by multiple, flat screens. Expensive, but rarely used swimming pools became the norm. Air-conditioners replaced electric fans. Inclusive breakfasts replaced in-room coffee makers. Two wash basins holding a variety of soaps, combs and lotions replaced the disposable shower cap and the free shoeshine cloth. At one point, the cost of toiletry amenities exceeded $10 per room per night! Exhibit 2–3 contrasts the special amenities of yesteryear to the new ones now in place.

Signs of Amenity Creep	
One-Time Amenities	**Today's Amenities[a]**
Bathrobe	Sleep CD
Bottle opener	Flat, plasma screen TV
Chocolate mint on the pillow	Luxury bedding [b]
Direct-dial telephone	Wireless Internet
Double sink in the bathroom	Global positioning unit
In-room coffee maker	All-inclusive breakfast
Iron and ironing board	Ergonomic furniture
Plastic shower cap	Check-in kiosk
Radio alarm clock	Satellite radio
Shoeshine cloth	Perfumed guest room spray
Soap and shampoo	Overnight pets (cats, dogs, fish)
Swimming Pool	Spa

[a] Estimates suggest that the industry spent a total of $10 billion on upgrades and renovations in the two-year period 2006–2007.

[b] See also Chapter 7.

Exhibit 2-3   Amenities are limited only by the hotelier's imagination. Guests at San Francisco–based Kimpton Hotels—not quite a boutique chain but not a mass-marketed chain either—are offered chocolate drinks, Yoo-Hoos, and Twinkies. The company's Topaz Hotel in Washington, D.C., gives horoscopes.

Each upgrade pushed room rates higher. Hotel companies that started in the economy segment (Holiday Inn, Ramada) found themselves in the midrange. Undoubtedly, personal egos played a role in upgrading the chains. So did the introduction of franchising. Franchise fees are based on room revenues. As amenity creep pushes up room revenues, franchise fees to the parent company also increase.

How Budgets Compete.   As room rates inch upward, new chains fill the void at the lower end. Some date the start of this rotation from 1964, when Motel 6 entered the market. By 1999, Motel 6—now owned by Accor—had interior corridors, improved heating and air-conditioning, and upgraded baths. Amenity creep had set in. New budget entries forego some amenities, but many, such as remote television, acceptance of credit cards—even breakfasts and frequent-stay programs are now seen as basic services. Today's budgets are competing with fewer bathroom amenities, better values in construction and attention to operations and management.

Newer economy chains employ newer techniques. Rooms smaller than the standard 300 to 325 square feet are being offered. (Microtel rooms are 178 square feet.) Chains are selecting less costly land, and they are building on smaller sites, 1.5 acres or less for 100 rooms. Nonbasic amenities such as pools, lobbies, meeting space, and restaurants have been eliminated once again. Providing free continental breakfasts is actually less costly than operating a restaurant that loses money. Besides, budget hotels/motels are almost always located near outlets of national restaurant chains, with one restaurant often serving several competitors.

The latest round of budgets has focused on design and construction. Economy is coming from standardized architectural plans and from using just a few builders. New structures have low ceilings and improved insulation. Better construction has reduced subsequent operating costs; the offset has been amenity creep. Interior corridors, now required for better guest security, have replaced the exterior access of the traditional roadside property and added substantially to construction costs.

Some budgets employ fewer than 20 employees per 100 rooms, almost 60% less than the traditional figures suggested in Chapter 1. Eliminating the dining room is just one technique for reducing labor. Hanging guest room furniture and providing a shower but not a tub increase the productivity of the housekeeping department. Automating telephone calls and assigning extra duties (including laundry operations) to the night clerk improve productivity on that side of the house.

It takes about 250 properties to ensure brand identification. To achieve market identity quickly, some chains acquired and then franchised old mom-and-pop operations at fire-sale prices. Days Inns was chief among them (see Exhibit 2–4).

Hard Budgets.   The economy group of hotels has performed very well during both the upswings and the down cycles. As amenity creep has forced some budgets into higher-rate classes, a still more limited service hotel has emerged. Among the euphemisms for these inexpensive accommodations are: economy, budget, limited-service and low-end. Adding confusion to the terminology are upscale budgets—what an oxymoronic term— (La Quinta, for example), intermediate budgets (Red Roof Inns) and low-end budgets (Super 8).

Hard budgets are found worldwide. They are favored at airports and at the hundreds of truck stops that dot the interstate roads. The airports at both Los Angeles and Honolulu offer budget rooms for rest and showers between connections. They measure 75 square feet, less than 1/3 a normal sized hotel room. Tokyo's airport offering is smaller still. Its "capsule rooms," something like railroad sleeping berths, measure

Among the Budget Chains Are ...		
Name	**Parent Company**	**Approximate Number of Rooms**
Comfort Inn	Choice	120,000
Days Inn	Wyndham	150,000
Econo Lodge	Choice	50,000
Howard Johnson	Wyndham	15,000
Knights Inn	Wyndham	15,000
Motel 6	Accor[a]	100,000
Red Roof Inn	Accor	40,000
Sleep Inn	Choice	25,000
Super 8	Wyndham	125,000
Travelodge	Wyndham	40,000

[a] Accor, a French company, has some 18 different brands, but has recently divested its Club Med.

Exhibit 2–4   Budget hotels are controlled by a few large chains. These ten account for nearly 700,000 rooms. The typical budget hotel is less than 100 rooms in size, located on the highway, and flying the franchise flag of one of these companies.

$5' \times 5'$. London is working on the "Yotel," about the size of an airplane's first-class cabin. It will be some 100 square feet ($9' \times 12'$). Clean bathhouses have served as the hard-budget accommodations of China's growing middle class. In preparation for the 2008 Olympics, Beijing opened the field to Wyndham, formerly Cendant, and other hard-budget operators. Hard budgets are growing quickly in Europe. France has the largest number because its costly social services are paid for by high payroll taxes. There is a real need to minimize labor, something that hard budgets do well.

Hostels are a special case of hard budgets. They have been favored by the young, the single, and the not-too-discriminating traveler. Dorm sleeping and a complete lack of privacy has discouraged a broader audience. But amenity creep is noticeable here too. Smaller rooms are now available for families and traveling friends. Security of personal items, better beds, and even *en suite* baths are attracting new clientele. Hostelling International, which represents some 4,000 hostels, has been working to upgrade facilities and assure stricter standards, even sending out inspectors.

All-Suite Hotels.

Each segment of the industry offers something unique. Boutique hotels emphasize soft attributes (fashion and spas) over hard values (room size and meeting space). Budget hotels offer rooms at reduced prices. The all-suite appeal is two rooms for the price of one, which is a shift from the original appeal to extended-stay guests. All-suite investors have their own draw: higher weekend occupancy and sustaining profits.

The extended-stay concept, Hometel, was conceived in Phoenix in 1969. It matured during the Texas oil boom, where temporary but long-term housing was needed. The idea was innovative—some say the best in a generation—but it borrowed from the traditional, the residential hotel.

The all-suite idea flourished after Holiday Inn acquired Hometel. With Residence Inns and Embassy Suites (Hometel renamed), Holiday Inn Hotels became the largest all-suite chain. Embassy was spun off to Promus when the Holiday Corporation was broken up (1990). In turn, Hilton bought Promus and with it Embassy Suites (1999). Hilton now has Embassy Suites, Homewood Suites, and Hampton Suites.

Holiday Inn's other chain, Residence Inns, was sold to Marriott in 1987. Now Marriott has five, including ExecuStay, SpringHill Suites, and TownePlace Suites (see Exhibit 2–1).

Separate living–sleeping accommodations (see Chapter 3, Exhibit 3–17) are attractive to personnel conducting interviews, to women executives, and to others who require private space outside the intimacy of a bedroom. That's why the market shifted away from just extended-stay use. The living space contains a sofa bed and sometimes a second bath. That opened still another market: traveling families seeking economical accommodations.

Despite all-suites' tilt toward transient accommodations, two subdivisions, extended stay and corporate housing, continue to market the segment's original appeal.

Extended Stay.

Extended stay (5 nights or more—18 nights is the average stay) was the original concept of the all-suite hotel, and corporate users were the target market. The annual expenditure of extended-stay guests is four to five times that of transient guests, who stay but a night or two. Better to sell four weeks to one guest than 28 room nights to, say, 20 guests. Consequently, extended-stay hotels have higher occupancies than the norm and lower ADRs. Higher occupancy requires a good revenue management system (see Chapter 5), but problems are minimized by reduced room turnover and by the ability to supplement with transient guests.

Long-term business travelers are not the only market: Families that are relocating and military personnel awaiting new assignments are two other sources. So too are company training sessions and employees on long-term, but temporary, assignments. Among them are movie crews, federal agents, FEMA employees, and utility workers. Leisure travelers fill in the vacancies and broaden the market still further.

The kitchenette is to the all-suite what the swimming pool is to the motor hotel. Everyone looks for the amenity, but few use it. Having restaurants nearby is therefore a plus. Some extended-stay chains jump from minimum service to closing the desk and locking the door overnight. That will prove troublesome in law suits. Hotels must be staffed around the clock to have the legal benefits of innkeeping.

Corporate Housing.   A large business sends a variety of staffers from many departments to one city. It makes sense for the company to take a long-term lease on housing accommodations, provided hotel services are included. A new type of facility, corporate housing, is being explored. Such buildings are exempt from local room taxes and are permitted in areas not zoned for hotels. Using one dedicated site makes more sense than scattering managers around a large city. Marriott's Executive Apartments, a division of its all-suite Execustay chain, is the most apparent participant in this business segment.

Mixed-Use Projects and Other Hotel Segments

The dynamic nature of the hotel business—out with the old; in with the new—brings innovation and excitement to the industry. One curious example: Elderhostel programs have married hotels with universities. At the other end of the age spectrum are children's camps within hotels. (They even give frequent-stay points to the kids.) Mixed-use, the current buzz word in real estate, takes innovation to the next step.

Mixed-Use Projects.   Every developer is talking and investing in mixed-use ventures. Apartments, hotels, resorts, condominiums, shopping marts, and business towers are being merged into one development, the mixed-use concept. Resort communities embrace the idea, bringing tennis, golf, skiing, and swimming to the mix. Combining residential and business with retailing, recreation, and entertainment, usually by means of high-rise buildings, is a modern version of the small city that everyone aspires to.

Mixed-use communities are feasible because of demographic shifts in society. Retirees find them to be ideal. Urban centers accommodate the working-from-home employee. Marrying vacation environments and residential facilities seems the best of all worlds. It certainly fits for space-challenged cities. Hotels, in the broadest definition of the word, are at the core of the development.

Mixed-use in the urban landscape is illustrated by Marriott's plan to "stack" two hotels into one building as part of Los Angeles' mixed-use broadcast center that includes theaters, studios, and retail outlets. Across the nation, the Rockefeller Center Hotel occupies one part of a larger building within the business center of Rockefeller Plaza.

Mixed use in the resort corridor is best illustrated by MGM Grand's $7 billion (!) City-Center development of hotels, retailing, and casinos in the center of the Las Vegas Strip.

Casino/Hotels.   Not every mixed-use project has a hotel casino, but the possibility has increased many fold. Casinos, which once were limited to Nevada and then to Atlantic City, have spread across the nation and the world.[3] Tax-starved states have licensed them and Indian tribes have built them. The jobs and the dollars they create have all but silenced critics.

---

[3] France and England are Europe's biggest gaming countries. Construction of mixed-use projects in Macau and interest from Singapore and mainland China signal Asia's intent to become a major casino destination. (Many countries, Korea and the Caribbean Islands among them, deny access to local citizens, reserving the casinos for tourist dollars.)

Casinos are almost never free standing. They are hotel/casinos; more accurately resort casinos, best typified by the Atlantis Casino & Resort in the Bahamas. Casino/resorts show every sign of becoming lodging's dominant segment. They're certainly the largest hotels around (see Exhibit 1–6), and their cash flow is immense. It needs to be, when the break-even point that Chapter 1 discussed can exceed $1 million per day!

Casino/hotels have a different focus from traditional hotels. Gaming revenue (called win), not room sales, is the major income producer. Therefore, having rooms occupied (having potential gamblers in the house) is more important than ADR or even RevPar. Similarly, two guests in the same room double the casino "action." Obviously then, single and double rates are kept the same. Some of the truisms that one quotes for casinos are changing. Pushed by very heavy demand casino occupancy has risen dramatically. So some casino/hotels have reported higher revenues from traditional hotel sales and other mixed-use income than from casino win. And that's a first.

Conference Centers.   As a separate category, conference centers (CCs) first appeared in the 1960s. What began in renovated mansions morphed into highly specialized facilities designed for meetings and conferences. CCs provide specialized space, audiovisual equipment, interactive seminar rooms, theaters, closed-circuit television, and simultaneous translation capabilities. They supply whatever is needed to make the meeting/conference successful (see Exhibit 2–5).

Unlike convention hotels, conference centers take no transient guests. Similarly, food service is not open to the public. The centers serve a special niche in the meeting market, so they number in the hundreds; as Chapter 1 points out, hotels number in the tens of thousands. Conference centers need not be separate and distinct from hotels, but they must have separate and permanent space. To secure membership in the International Association of Conference Centers, no less than 60% of the facility must be dedicated. Hotel space is not dedicated. Its function changes to accommodate meetings, banquets, trade shows, weddings, dances and more (see Exhibit 2–6).

Double occupancy is high in CCs. Even senior managers are doubled up. Two to a room encourages familiarity, one goal of conference planners. Upper and lower managers get to know one another.

Rates at conference centers are bundled. Everything—guest rooms, meeting rooms, food, drinks, and equipment—is included in the rate quote, called a *corporate meeting package (CMP)*. The CMP is a modern version of the American, all-inclusive plan. But then the conference center itself is a modern marriage of the convention hotel and the traditional resort. The combination houses a five-day workweek in the center (the convention hotel), followed by a two-day weekend in the resort portion. Much like convention hotels, weekend occupancy is low. The business model is static; it certainly isn't an expanding market. Nothing like the growth in spas.

Spas.   Spas offer curative waters. The term originated in the city of Spa, Belgium, where the ancient Romans "took the waters." The resorts of 19th century New England developed around mineral springs, so the resorts themselves became known as spas. Today's spas are far different from their famous namesakes at Saratoga Springs in New York, White Sulphur Springs in West Virginia, and the Broadmoor in Colorado Springs. Originally sought for their restorative properties, these resorts became the playgrounds of the rich and socially well placed. Horse racing, casinos, and other entertainment replaced the waters as the main attraction.[4]

---

[4]The curved top of the Saratoga trunk, named for its appearance at Saratoga Springs, was designed around the elaborate wardrobe of ruffles, bustles, parasols and petticoats that fashionable ladies brought to the resort.

Exhibit 2–5   Conference centers blend business and high-tech facilities in dedicated meeting space with pleasant, resort-like surroundings. Hotels that compete for this market segment do so with multiple-use space (see Exhibit 2–6). *Courtesy of Barton Creek Resort, Austin, Texas.*

Exhibit 2–6   The versatile space of convention hotels accommodates meetings and banquets, trade shows and weddings, proms, seminars, and more. Contrast this to the dedicated space of Exhibit 2–5. *Courtesy of Radisson Hotel Orlando, Orlando, Florida.*

Early spa-goers sought better health in the healing qualities of the waters. That pretty well determined the spa's location. Modern spas are everywhere because water is not the attraction; health is. Health remains the essence of the spa experience. Attendance evokes an almost religious fervor of health, exercise, massage, and diet.

Spa installations continue to grow because they are profitable. Unlike unused swimming pools and kitchenettes, guests take to the spas and pay handsomely to do so! Travelers and tourists expect to find them even in modest properties under one of three identities. There are spa destinations, "stay spas," which are spas with a resort component. There are "day spas," which may or may not have a lodging component. And in between are resorts with all amenities, spas among them (see Exhibit 2–7).

Stress reduction—there should be no competition—is a mantra of the spa-goer and the spa-provider. As such it fits perfectly with the industry's latest catchphrase, "lifestyle hotels." Choice Hotel's Cambria Suites, mentioned earlier in the chapter, latched on to that lifestyle terminology. So, too, has aloft hotels, a brand recently spun off from Starwood's boutique division, W Hotels. It's no coincidence that Bliss, which operates spas for W Hotels, designed aloft's baths and showers. So once again, the spa has changed course. Now it's lifestyle. Beauty care (see Exhibit 2–8) for men as well as women is part of that current theme.

Fitness Centers.   Rarely do spa managers bring the noisy energy of the fitness center into the operation. Fitness centers, euphemistically called health clubs, appeal to the work-out patron. Such facilities preceded the introduction of the spa because they are less costly to launch and to manage. Indeed, when there are a few pieces of equipment in an old storeroom, they are not being managed at all. The other extreme is a cadre of accredited trainers and expensive equipment. Since the users are usually businesspersons on the road, staff must be scheduled at the user's convenience: mornings and evening, before and after work. These are also the times when guests are most frustrated, waiting for a turn on the busy equipment. It is more exasperating when nonguest/outsiders (local resident-memberships which increase the center's revenues) compete for their turn. Portable equipment brought to the room is an expensive alternative, an amenity offered by some upscale properties.

Minimum equipment includes stationary bikes, treadmills, and stair-climbing machines. Users like to see familiar brands that operate without a learning curve. Management must be diligent about maintainance. It must assign periodic inspections and repairs to the gym

Exhibit 2–7   Spas, which are rated by the *Mobil Travel Guide*, are profitable amenities. The International Spa Association lists seven spa types: club; cruise-ship; day; destination; medical; mineral springs; and the resort/hotel type illustrated here. This spa at the Hotel Hershey features a Whipped Cocoa Bath. *Courtesy of Hotel Hershey, Hershey, Pennsylvania.*

equipment as it does for other major machinery such as ice machines and elevators. Broken and dirty equipment undermine the image. They might even undermine insurance coverage, an absolute necessity for both spas and fitness centers.

NEW MARKET PATTERNS

Today's consumers have a rich selection of choice from bottled water, to investment options, to lodging accommodations. The old conundrum Which came first, the chicken or the egg? has application here. Have all the new products just discussed been a response to market demand? Or have these product changes caused the demand? Conjecture aside, the challenge lies in enticing the customer in.

Marketing to the Individual Guest

By law, hotels must accept all who come in good condition. In practice, hotels cater to particular market segments (niches). What appeals to one type of guest may be of indifference to another. So the guest's very presence tells us as much about the hotel as about the guest.

SPA Services	
Acupresssure	Aromatherapy
Ayurveda[a]	Bikini wax
Body treatment	Body wax
Brow wax	Exfoliation
Facial	Fango[b]
Gommage[c]	Herbal Treatment
Hydrotherapy	Lip wax
Loofa scrub	Massage
Mud bath	Nail care
Oxygen treatment	Pedicare
Shiatsu[d]	Wraps

[a] Folk medicine from India.
[b] Upgraded mud bath.
[c] Rehydration massage.
[d] Japanese acupuncture.

Exhibit 2-8   Spa services are highly specialized so hotels often lease the space rather than operate it. Services are very personal, individualized, and costly. Many products are similar despite their different names. One leisurely afternoon at the spa might produce $200–$500 on the folio.

Guest Profiles.   Guests have several profiles; they wear different hats under various circumstances. Personas change depending on the reasons for the visits. Sometimes they're business persons, sometimes family members. They may be transient travelers, convention goers, tour group members, or excited tourists. They may be urbane or unsophisticated; they be nationals or foreign visitors.

Knowing guests in various circumstances, developing profiles, enables hoteliers to manage a variety of market segments. Profiles are gathered by many agencies, not just the hotel. Among them are trade associations, and convention and tourist bureaus. The typical study focuses on demographics. Age, income, job, gender, residence, education, and the number of persons in the party can be determined with a good deal of accuracy. Knowing one's guests is the staring point for servicing them.[5]

Some patterns are less measurable than demographics. Developers differentiate between upstairs and downstairs buyers. *Upstairs buyers* want larger sleeping rooms and comfortable work spaces. For this, they sacrifice theme restaurants, intimate bars, and other lifestyle accoutrements. Not so *downstairs buyers*, who use the concierge, want public space above all else, and are more extroverted. Generalizing, women are upstairs buyers and men downstairs buyers.

Profiles of extended-stay guests show something else entirely. They try to recreate a little bit of home by bringing personal items such as pillows, photos, and stuffed animals. Very long-term guests actually rearrange furniture. Both groups use the kitchenette sparingly. Both groups, along with almost every other class of guest, want good lighting and work space.

---

[5]A business guest's profile might read: "Male, 28–45 years old, married, holding a middle-manager's job, salaried between $75,000 and $120,000. He is a solitary traveler, dependent on lap-top connectivity. A heavy cell-phone user, who comes by air, arrives early evening, holds a reservation, and looks for accommodations in the $135 range."

Business/Leisure Travelers.   Businesspersons need to be at a given place at a given time. Therefore, price is less important—not unimportant, but less important—to the business guest than to the leisure traveler. Businessmen and women are not apt to cancel a trip because of high rates, and they are not apt to make a trip because of low rates. Theirs is an *inelastic* market—there is very little change in demand from a change in price. The response from leisure guests is more dramatic: High rates repel them and low rates attract them. By responding to price changes, leisure guests represent a more *elastic* market.

All guests demonstrate some degree of elasticity. Even leisure guests may be inelastic; they just have to be there—a wedding, a funeral, and so on. Business guests may be elastic, rescheduling or postponing their meetings. Companies with travel desks, which schedule and buy travel (air, hotels, and car rentals) for their personnel, are more price sensitive. With someone other than the traveler doing the planning, businesses have shifted toward the elastic side. This shift helps explain the buyer's focus on the value of all-suite hotels.

Business guests are mostly men; tourists are mostly couples. Almost everyone watches television from the bed. Business travelers use the telephone, the shower, and the TV movie channel more than leisure travelers do. Tourists hold the edge on the pool and other recreational facilities. Leisure tourists tend to be 5 to 10 years older than businesspersons. They make reservations less often and pay less for their rooms than business travelers do.

Women are about one-third of all business travelers. That's a demographic measure. How best to please that market is a psychographic issue. Psychographic profiles detail traits, personalities, desires, and inner motivations. Every profile, whether demographic or psychographic, is flawed because no guest is ever 100% of the composite study. Besides, as the next few pages explain, the guest staying at the hotel, the one we profile, is probably not the person who actually selected the hotel. Demographic profiles tell us that male business travelers usually make their own arrangement more often than do female business travelers.

Both male and female business travelers use their rooms as offices. They give high priority to comfortable furniture and convenient work areas. Women executives (upstairs buyers) rank in-room coffee makers almost as important as the work area. Men rank coffeemakers at the bottom of their priority list.

Leisure guests still seek the sun and surf. But many have moved beyond that to nontraditional vacations. Niche resorts are offering out-of-the-ordinary experiences such as mountain climbing, rafting and archeological digs. Guests are coming, buying, often paying handsomely for such adventures.

The economy market is just the opposite. Price-sensitive guests form the core of the budget customers. Who are they? Government employees on a fixed per diem (per day) allowance make up one segment. Retirees, whose time is more flexible than their budgets, go to the less convenient and less costly locations that economy properties require. Family vacationers and small-business persons sensitive to travel costs help round out this segment. International guests, who have different expectations from domestic travelers, are also part of the budget market, especially when the U.S. dollar is strong.

The International Guest.   Globalization requires special attention to the profile of the international guest. Foreign visitors are big business. The World Tourism Organization (WTO) forecasts 102 million visitors to the United States by 2020. Since they spend more time and more money reaching their destinations, international guests stay longer than do domestic guests. Typically, theirs is a six-day visit, nearly twice the usual domestic stay. International visitors to the United States help the nation's balance of trade, representing some $50 billion in export equivalence.

Japanese visitors to Hawaii spend three times that of the U.S. tourist to Hawaii. Japanese visitors frequently tour in groups, even when they are honeymooning. Office groups (women), ski groups (men), business groups (rarely women), and silver groups (retired couples) are the profiles of the Japanese traveler. Hotels seeking foreign guests need to provide accommodations (Japanese, for example, want bedroom slippers provided), and meals, especially breakfasts, that cater to the tastes of their international patrons.

Preferred Guest Programs.   Guest profiles have been sharpened by the introduction of preferred guest programs (PGP). Electronic recordkeeping and intrachain networks enable hotel companies to track their clientele. Just as frequent fliers earn points with airlines, guests earn points with hotel chains. Points are turned into gifts and free stays. To qualify, guests must provide information about their travel and personal habits. Hotel companies maintain demographic and psychographic information on millions of names. Marriott's list numbers some 20 million. The cost of maintaining these systems is borne largely by franchisees and hotel owners, not the chains. (Chains don't own many hotels, as the next segment of this chapter explains.)

Rewards range from the simple to the expensive. Among the less costly one are check-cashing privileges, room upgrades, daily newspapers, late check-outs, express check-ins, special telephone access for reservations and guaranteed rates. Up a stage and the reward becomes a fruit basket, a bottle of special water, or free in-room films. Under certain circumstances, even nonmembers can access some of these services.

Elite club memberships, achieved by earning many, many points, carry elite awards. Among them are rate discounts, health club memberships, accommodations in the chain's exotic destinations and U.S. savings bonds or even cash. Ethical issues are raised when cash and cash equivalents are the rewards. Hard-core PGP participants are almost always traveling on expense accounts paid by someone else. Cash rewards paid to the traveler are not well received. They might encourage employees to book at higher rates than could be obtained elsewhere.

PGPs cycle in tandem with economic conditions. Tough times bring additional perks such as double or triple points. During the downturn that followed 9-11, dramatic upgrades were offered throughout the industry. Like other amenities, preferred guest programs follow the competitors. One adds lower brands to the coverage; others follow. Some partner with competing chains; others follow. Expensive gift vouchers of the likes of Saks Fifth Avenue are distributed through gift catalogs; others follow. Tie-ins allowing hotel points to be used for airline travel are introduced; others follow.

During the last downturn, blackout dates were dropped, elite travel status was eased, more brands were placed under the one umbrella, stockholders were automatically included. And amenity creep crept in. Once in place, upgrades are difficult to withdraw when the good times roll. Moreover, there is little distinction anymore among the offerings. Frequent guests have suggested that the companies improve the telephone service and procedure used to redeem the amenity rather than broadening coverage that was already stifling.

No one really knows how much business PGPs actually represent. It is known that they add more name confusion to branding. Wyndham adds *Trip Rewards* to the 19 chain names under its umbrella. Hilton has *HHonors Club* and 12 other brand names. There are two golds, *Gold Crown Club* (Best Western), and *Gold Passport* (Hyatt). Marriott, with 19 brands has finally changed its PGP name from *Honored Guest Awards* to *Marriott Awards*.[6]

Despite the cost, the real lack of competitive difference, and the uncertainty of their effectiveness, no company dares close its program. Airlines have the same dilemma. It

---

[6]These and other brand names used throughout the text are registered trademarks.

was the chairman of American Airlines, Robert Crandall, who invented frequent fliers. Hotels will likely do what airlines have done: gradually tighten access, increase points, and reduce awards. At least they'll do that until the next downturn in business.

Nonguest Buyers.   Nonguest buyers are intermediaries who buy guest rooms. They are not guests and have no intention of becoming guests. These third parties may be actual persons, but just as often they are legal persons (companies, associations, and organizations). Later chapters on reservations and room rates deal more thoroughly with the mechanics of this type of buyer. Nonguest buyers add costs to, and organizational levels between, the hotel and the eventual room occupant. It's obviously not to the industry's advantage. The idea came from outside, not from within, lodging. With nonguest intermediaries, hotels are not selling rooms to guests. They are buying guests through new marketing channels.

Nonguest buyers negotiate from strength. The American Automobile Association (AAA) and the American Association of Retired Persons (AARP), for example, haggle with hotel chains over room rates. They obtain special rates for their members, although neither the associations nor the hotels know who those guests will be. So widespread is this practice that almost every hotel grants the guest's request for a special AAA rate. Hotels often do so without verifying that the guest is an AAA member. Travel clubs such as Amoco Traveler and Encore Travel negotiate a different commitment: second nights free.

A second type of nonguest buyer actually buys the rooms, rather than just negotiating rates. More and more business travel is arranged by "travel desks." Either the business operates its own desk or employs an outside agency. Whichever, the buyer is not the arriving guest.

Franchisees rely on the franchisor's reservation system, another type of nonguest buyer, to generate room occupancy. The room commitment is made by the system, a third party. Quite possibly, the system isn't even owned by the franchisor, rather by still another party.

The broad range of third-party buyers is detailed next. Group tours, incentive firms, and wholesalers make huge room commitments, but someone else occupies the room. The same is true with travel agents: They buy rooms, but it's their clients who come. Airlines, Web sites, and auto-rental companies round out a growing list of nonguest buyers.

Marketing to the Group

Group business is a post–World War II (1950s) innovation that changed the very concept of hotelkeeping. Modern hotels became destination sites without giving up their historic role of transient accommodations. Now, instead of selling one buyer one room, hoteliers sell dozens, hundreds, or even thousands of room nights at one time. One constant remains, the guest's profile. Buyers are either tourist/leisure visitors or business/commercial groups.

Tourist/Leisure Visitors.   Rising disposable income and broader travel horizons have made travel appealing to every level of society. Packaging travel and accommodations has brought costs low enough to attract huge numbers of the world's citizens. The travel and hotel industries have embarked on the same kind of mass production techniques that have increased efficiency in manufacturing. The move was delayed until the transport carriers and the destination hotels were large enough to move and house these large numbers.

The Tour Package.   Groups of tourists, especially first-timers, travel together in tours. A new entrepreneur, the wholesaler, another nonguest buyer, has emerged to handle the mass movement of leisure guests. Wholesalers buy at wholesale (reduced) prices because they buy in quantity. They buy blocks of rooms (commitments to buy so many rooms for many nights), blocks of airline seats, and blocks of bus seats. Then the wholesaler tries selling the "package." By this time, the offer includes ground handling and baggage along with other goodies that the wholesaler either buys inexpensively or gets without cost from the hotel (see Exhibit 2–9).

Wholesalers promise year-round, back-to-back charters (each departing group is matched by an new, arriving group). Hotel sales executives and accountants sharpen their pencils to accommodate the price. One sale books hundreds of rooms. One correspondence confirms all the reservations. One billing closes the account. Bad debts are minimized and credit-card costs are eliminated. It is a bargain buy for the traveler, a profitable venture for the wholesaler, and free advertising for the hotel. More importantly,

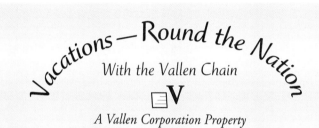

Vacations—Round the Nation
With the Vallen Chain
▤V
A Vallen Corporation Property

$697.20	**$767.50**	**$933.33**
In Las Vegas	*In Orlando*	*In Maui*
Round Trip Air	Round Trip Air	Round Trip Air from LA
4 Days/3 Nights	4 Days/3 Nights	5 Nights/4 Days
HOTEL PARADISE	HOTEL CARTOON	THE VALLEN MAUI
Taxes Included	Room Upgrade If Available	6th Night Free
Airport Transfers	$40 Daily Car Rental	Includes Full Breakfast
Free Gaming Lesson	Nonstop Flights from Major Cities	Guaranteed Ocean View or Suite

$715.00	**$617.76**
In New York City	*In Boston*
4 Days/3 Nights	4 Days/3 Nights
2 Broadway Shows	Bottle Champagne Nightly
THE BIGGEST APPLE	FREEDOM TRAIL HOTEL
Apple Before Bed	Guided Walking Tour of Historic Boston
One Breakfast-in-Bed	$25/Day Food or Beverage Credit
City Bus Tour	Surprise Amenity

CALL: 1-888-555-5555 OR YOUR TRAVEL PROFESSIONAL

Rates are quoted per person, double occupancy and are available until September 30. Unless otherwise stated, taxes and service charges are not included. Las Vegas offering is good Mondays to Thursdays only. All vacations earn Club Vallen points. Air trips, where included, require specific flights on carriers of the company's choosing. Other restrictions may apply. The company strives for accuracy but will not be held responsible for errors or omissions in this advertisement.

Exhibit 2–9   Sample of print advertising used by this hypothetical tour operator, *Vacations— Round the Nation*, to sell packaged vacations. Buying in quantity puts this wholesaler at risk of not reselling all of the spaces. But quantity purchasing reduces costs from hotels and airlines making possible huge savings. (See also travel pages of local newspapers.)

the hotel now has a basic occupancy on which to build its room rates (see the discussion on yield management).

Group tours are packaged in a variety of wrappings, some reminiscent of the old American plan. Transportation, room, food, beverage, entertainment, tips, and baggage are offered for one fixed price. (Unlike the all-inclusive plan, not all items—not every meal or every drink—are included, so the hotel stands to gain from additional business outside the package.) Often, the wholesaler can sell the entire package for less than the cost of the airfare alone, having earned sharp discounts from the hotel and the airline.

The wholesaler also benefits from *breakage*. Every guest does not use every part of the package. Some may not play golf. Others may not use the drink coupon. Others may skip the buffet for a specialty meal that they pay for separately. If the guest does not use the service, the hotel is not paid. Still, the item was computed in setting the package price. That small gain per guest, multiplied by many guests, accrues to the wholesaler as breakage.

The guest gains too, buying services at a fraction of their separate costs. The travel industry, hotels included, gain as well because mass marketing introduced new customers to travel. Inexperienced guests find comfort in the safety of the group; experienced travelers find irrefutable savings. The downside is a loss of guest identity. Even the hotel staff senses a reduced responsibility when guests buy and pay through a third party.

Almost any hotel can host a tourist group if it can attract the group to the site. It must meet the price of a very competitive market to appeal to the wholesaler, and it must be large enough to accommodate the group and still handle its other guests. Hotels in out-of-the-way places cater to bus groups. They're a broader market because the number of guests is smaller and almost any hotel can handle them. With bus tours, hotels provide a mix of destination and transient service because after touring the area, the bus moves on, usually after one night.

The Inclusive Tour (IT) Package.   The IT package is marketed to individual guests. Logically, it should have been discussed under the heading, "Marketing for the Individual Guest." It's here as part of "Marketing to the Group" because the IT package so closely resembles the just-discussed wholesaler's tour package. The tour package requires numerous buyers to make it profitable. Couples or small groups of friends are the target of the IT package.

Group tours involve financial risks (air and land transportation) outside the hotel's control. The hotel's IT package is the same as the wholesaler's tour package without the risks. Guests get to the hotel on their own. Once there, the package is the same; often it is better. The basics remain: room, food and beverage, hotels add "freebies." One or more extras are included, such as free tennis or putting green, shuffle board, etc. Free admissions sweeten the deal. So tickets may be included to theaters, formal gardens tours, spas, or tournaments. The deal looks better if these extras normally require a fee. Casino ITs include one free play at a table. Breakage now accrues to the hotel; the wholesaler is no longer in the picture.

Both the wholesaler and the hotel market directly to the public. Exhibit 2–9 would be a newspaper advertisement. Exhibit 2–10 could also be used similarly or distributed individually across the desk, through the mail, or to convention attendees. Travel agents are traditional advertising outlets. Travel agents normally receive a 10% commission on rooms booked for their clients. Because ITs do not break out room costs from other services, the hotel pays 10% on the entire package price.

One hotel may offer several IT packages. Each (a golf package, a spa package, a valentine package) is aimed toward a different market. Commercial hotels use them extensively to offset weekend doldrums—the Run Away with your Wife package. The

Exhibit 2–10   Inclusive tour (IT) packages are the hotel's method of competing with the tour wholesaler (see Exhibit 2–9) except transportation is not included. The package is complete within the hotel. IT packages compete with individual room rates, so they are offered and withdrawn by the hotel as occupancy dictates under a yield management system (see Chapter 5).

contents and price of each varies. Care must be exercised because the hotel competes with itself. Inclusive tour packages are discounted rooms with extra services that sell for less than the normal room rate. So ITs are discontinued during high occupancy periods. Later chapters deal with discounted rooms, under the topic of yield management.

Business/Commercial Groups.   Our fondness for forming into groups has produced an astonishing number of organizations. People come together under many umbrellas: business, union, fraternal, social, historical, veteran, health and medical, educational, religious, scientific, political, service, athletic, and on without end. For short, the industry uses the acronym SMURF: societies, medical, university, religious, fraternal, or sometimes SMERF: social, military, educational, religious, fraternal.[7] Each classification translates into numerous organizations, societies, clubs, and associations. Each of them meets, holds shows, and stages conventions. Functioning at local, state, regional, national, and international levels, these groups offer business to a variety of destination facilities.

Conventions.   Conventioneers assemble to promote their common purposes. These aims are as diverse as the list of associations that hold conventions (see Exhibit 6–14). Meetings, speeches, papers, and talks are given on a range of topics during the gathering of two, three, or four days. Some are professional and some merely entertaining. The members also interact individually, discussing common goals and problems. Professional conventions may serve as formal or informal job-placement forums.

Both urban and resort properties vie for convention business as the growth of mixed-use facilities spreads. To be competitive, the convention hotel must provide a range of self-contained facilities. Meeting space with appropriate furnishings and equipment and food facilities large enough to accommodate the groups at banquets are the minimum facilities needed (see Exhibit 2–6). Conventioneers are a captive audience for the program and the planned activities. The more complete the property, the more appealing the site.

Sports activities, a change of scenery, and isolation from the hubbub of busy cities are touted by a resort's sales department. Urban properties compete with theaters, museums, and historical locations. Urban areas may have the advantage of publicly financed convention halls (see Exhibit 2–11).

Hotels sometimes combine facilities with those of nearby competitors when the convention size is too large for one property. Although not the rule, conventions of 50,000 to 100,000 delegates have been recorded, usually when combined with trade shows.

Trade Shows.   Trade shows are exhibits of product lines shown by purveyors to potential buyers. Conventions and trade shows are often held together. Shows require a great deal of space, particularly if the displays are large pieces of machinery or equipment (see Exhibit 2–11). Space requirements and the difficulty of handling such products limit shows to a small number of hotels. The city convention bureau has a role here. It builds halls to accommodate the exhibits, leaving the housing and guest service to the local hotels.

Exhibits of small goods such as jewelry or perfume can be housed almost anywhere. They do not need convention halls of 1,000,000 square feet. Any hotel can pursue small trade shows. Although not commonly done, several sleeping floors can be assigned to small-product exhibits. Guest rooms are converted into a combination of exhibit space and sleeping accommodations. Shoppers visit the room to do business. At day's end, the exhibitor occupies the room as a registered guest.

Competition for conventions and trade shows is coming from a new source, corporate training centers. Not hotels and not conference centers, training centers were built by and run for specific companies. They are in-house training sites that, like hotels and conference centers, abhor vacancies. So the likes of U.S. Postal Service (Norman, OK) and Aetna Insurance (Hartford, CT) will happily book transient guests or group business and trade shows into facilities built for their own training purposes.

---

[7] Asian hoteliers use MICE as the acronym: meetings, incentives, conventions, and exhibits.

Exhibit 2–11   Publicly supported convention centers solicit and house trade shows whose delegates may number in the tens of thousands. What is good for the local hotel business is good for the community's economic health. That value approximates $266 per day per delegate (see Exhibit 6–10) during a three- or four-day convention. *Courtesy of Las Vegas Convention and Visitors Authority, Las Vegas, Nevada.*

The Single Entity.   The single entity is neither a tour package nor a convention/trade show. As its name implies, *single entity* has an adhesive that binds its members together. Attendees already belong to "the" group (a company, an orchestra, a college football team) before they come to the hotel. The unit (the company, the orchestra, the college football team) makes the reservation, and the unit pays the bill. The single entity stays together during the engagement: They hold meetings; they perform; they play ball.

Although the visiting athletic team is the best example of a single entity, hotels cater to a wide range of other groups. There are company sales and technical meetings, new product–line showings, traveling concert groups, annual high-school graduation trips, and others. Hotel/casinos have their own form of the single entity, the gambling junket. High rollers are brought in to the hotel for several days of entertainment and play.

The tour group offers a contrast. Tour group members have no previous relationships. They come together only for the trip. Each member pays the wholesaler a share of the cost plus profit. With a single entity, the entity pays the hotel bill, not the individual members. There are no profits. Tour groups dissolve after the trip; single entities retain their original relationships.

Certain single entities (say, a church group) may contribute prorated costs. Business entities (say, a company training program) would pay the entire cost. Single entities are arranged and paid for by the entity's leader, who is a member of the entity. The tour group negotiator is a for-profit businessperson. There are similarities: Both commit to a block of rooms and both pay a single bill (called a folio) for the rooms (see Chapter 10).

Attendees at conventions and trade shows are unlike either the tour group or the single entity. The room block is most likely made by a nonguest buyer, a professional trade-show executive. Convention delegates make individual room reservations within that room block. Delegates, who represent a wide range of companies and geographies, pay their own bills. Each conventioneer comes and goes without concern for the schedule of other delegates. The subject matter of the convention may be their one common interest. Convention-goers may not know other attendees, or they may have come with others from the same company. If there are many representatives from the same organization, they may be billed as a single entity within the convention.

Incentive Tours.   Incentive tours are special, highly prized single entities. Businesses run incentive programs to motivate employees. Cash bonuses, prizes, and incentive trips—a free vacation for two—are rewarded to those who meet announced goals. Many winners from one company make up an incentive tour, a single entity.

Resorts covet incentive tours. The winners are the company's top people. Only the best accommodations will do. Unfortunately for the resorts, incentive tours have grown so important that most companies hire incentive-company specialists. Hotels know them as nonguest buyers!

Incentive companies run incentive programs for many businesses. This gives the incentive company leverage against the hotel. The two sides bargain tough when bookings for several incentive groups are possible. The incentive company exerts the same pressure on the hotel/seller as does the tour operator. More than one sale is at stake. Price and quality are the difference. Cost is critical for the wholesaler, quality for the incentive buyer.

NEW OWNERSHIP PATTERNS

The State of the Industry

Historically, the inn was a family affair with the host–guest relationship paramount. That began to change after World War II (early 1950s) when ownership and management became separate activities. Those who owned the hotel did not operate it. Those who operated the hotel did not own it! As the separation widened, hotel chains concentrated on managing both their own hotels and those belonging to others. Those who owned the buildings and the lands on which the hotels stood were concerned more with the hotels as properties, pieces of real estate. Income taxes, depreciation, rent, and financing are more important to owners than are day-to-day operational problems. That difference brought huge changes in the lodging industry.

Turmoil and Churning.   Chapter 1 explained the cyclical nature of hotelkeeping. Good and bad times roll in on the waves of change. The cycle is dramatic because unforeseen events come quickly and from a variety of causes. For example:

Income tax laws were changed in the 1970s. Before that, speculators bought and sold hotels at ever-increasing values. The gains came from turning the real estate, not from operational profits. Then Congress repealed the tax advantages. Suddenly, there was no point in trading hotel equity. Earnings from operations were insufficient to pay the mortgage debt on the high values of the real estate. Estimates placed about two-thirds of nation's hotels in financial distress. Prices plummeted and the industry went into shock. For those who had waited, there was a silver lining. Bankrupt hotels resold at distressed prices. Now earnings were adequate to meet the lower mortgage obligations.

Recovery brought optimism, the first good signs in more than a decade. Business travel was increasing, occupancy improving. Distressed hotels had closed, so room supply had fallen. Increased demand and reduced supply meant a healthy industry once again.

The turnaround gained momentum beginning in the early 1990s. Sales climbed; operating costs were held in check by low inflation. By 2000 new construction (increased room supply) was hinting at another cycle of overbuilding and another downward spin. Before the trend was clear, the nation was hit by the horrific events of September 11, 2001 in New York City. The entire nation, but especially travel and tourism, experienced sudden churning and unforeseen turmoil. Occupancy and RevPar plunged. Searching desperately for business, hotels, and airlines, too, allowed another market source to gain hold, another nonguest buyer, Web sites.

Churning.   Churning is rapid buying and selling, buying and selling anything—including hotels. Oddly, one of the major hotel churners is not even a hotel company. The Blackstone Group is a private-equity firm that invests in real estate. It became interested in hotel real estate when the values plummeted after 9-11.

A small extended-stay chain, Homestead Village, was its first acquisition. Blackstone subsequently bought Extended Stay America, Boca Resorts, Prime Hospitality, and Wyndham Hotels. Each had additional brands. It diversified next by paying some $3.5 billion for La Quinta and La Quinta's seven brands, including Baymont Inns. In rapid succession, Blackstone then sold Amerisuites and the management and franchising rights for Wyndham Hotels. In keeping with its own mission, Blackstone did not sell Wyndham real estate. Next it sold the Baymont brand. These sales/deals were negotiated with Cendant Hotels, a churner in its own right.

Cendant owned 19 different hotel chains, among them Days Inn, Howard Johnson, and Wyndham. It also owned travel, auto-rental, tax, and real estate companies. Cendant no longer exists: It broke itself into four separate companies. The hotel division was renamed Wyndham Worldwide, the very brand that it acquired from Blackstone shortly before its breakup.

There are many real estate churners in the lodging industry. Large hotel companies have no desire to own hotel real estate; we will see why in detail shortly. So companies such as Starwood sold several dozen hotels to a REIT named Host Marriott, later renamed Host. Colony Capital, another equity firm, bought the Raffles Hotel Chain (Singapore), the Bahamas-based Kerzner casino company, and the Fairmont Hotel Chain, San Francisco.

Hotel real estate transactions during the height of the industry's 2006–2009 peak are estimated to be as high as $60 billion annually.

A Consolidating Industry.
Consolidation—bigger hotel companies and fewer of them— has contributed immensely to the industry's churning and turmoil. Whether the cycle is up or down, the big guys have grown bigger (see Exhibit 2–12). Growth comes from acquisitions, from adding new properties to existing brands, and from inventing new products. Growth is facilitated when the stock market booms. Shares of hotel companies increase in value. These shares, rather than cash (money), are used as currency to buy competitors or smaller companies.

Acquiring other companies is more than a stock market game. Consolidation promises economies of scale and larger marketing and distribution networks for the chains. Growth comes faster and flashier from acquisitions than from internal growth. Buying instead of building produces immediate increases in revenues. It also makes good business sense. Acquiring hotels from an existing company costs less than building new ones. During the past several years, hundreds of acquisitions with multiple brands have consolidated into just a few large holding companies.

One of many ongoing examples follows. The explanation is neither complete nor current because the lodging industry is in continuous movement. Quite likely, Hilton's company structure will have changed even before this text's publication.

The Big Guys of the U.S. Hospitality Industry		
Company Name[a]	Estimated[b] Number of Hotels	Estimated[b] Number of Rooms
Best Western	4,250	325,000
Carlson	1,000	150,000
Choice	5,000	425,000
Hilton	2,500	375,000
Marriott	2,750	500,000
Starwood	1,000	250,000
Wyndham	7,000	550,000

[a] Generally used name, not official, legal name.
[b] Figures are estimated and rounded.

Exhibit 2-12   Growth, consolidation and churning within the lodging industry have created large companies. They're big, tough competitors. These seven chains control an estimated 2.5 million rooms.

Hilton Hotels Corporation.   Hilton grew during the late 1990s by acquiring DoubleTree Hotels. DoubleTree already owned Homewood, Hampton, and Embassy Suites. These were acquired when DoubleTree bought Promus, which was spun off from Holiday Inn.

DoubleTree also owned Guest Quarters, Red Lion Inns, Candlewood Hotels, Patriot America, and Harrison Conference Centers. Hilton was after the brands, not the real estate. Hilton is a management company, not a landlord. Not long afterward, Hilton sold many of these brands and all of its gaming properties, including those in Las Vegas. It kept its Vegas timeshare property, branded as Grand Vacations.

Hilton's biggest coup was still to come. In 2006, Hilton bought Hilton International from its British owners for about $6 billion. The seller's official name is The Hilton Group, PLC. Pressed for cash in 1964, Hilton had sold the international rights to its name. Later, it created the Conrad brand—Hilton's founder was Conrad Hilton—to compete overseas. In reacquiring its offspring, and with it the Scandic brand, The Hilton Corporation reemerged as an international player. Hilton used cash, not stock to make the deal. In 2007, Hilton sold itself to the Blackstone Group for $20 billion.

As an aside, Hilton enlarged its real property ownership. As mentioned earlier, modern hotel companies do not own hotels. In fact, Hilton had sold two dozen properties, including the Palmer House, a Chicago landmark, right before its new acquisition. Whereas the Hilton Group owned about 10% (40 hotels) in its group, The Hilton Corporation owned only 8 hotels before the purchase. Eight hotels is less than one-third of 1% of Hilton's 3,000 properties. As expected, Hilton sold off most of the newly acquired real estate within the first year, retaining the management contracts.

The Corporation also launched a new brand as part of its invigorated realignment. The Waldorf=Astoria Collection builds on the reputation of New York City's famed Waldorf=Astoria Hotel, one of the eight properties that Hilton owns.

The Global Village.   The global village, shorthand for shrinking political differences and interlocking economies worldwide, has enabled businesses to cross borders and jump oceans. Hotel companies have been among the leaders. Consolidation has been possible, in part, because of the global village. The Hilton experience with a British acquisition highlights the point. So do the sales reported in the "churning" segment above. Among them is Starwood's takeover of Le Méridien, which operates in 21 different countries. It's the same story with Colony Capital's purchase of Raffles (see Churning). Raffles owns Swissotels, which has some three dozen locations.

Who pursues whom often depends upon the value of international currencies. If foreign investors want to buy a U.S. hotel, they need U.S. dollars. When the dollar is weak, fewer units of the foreign currency are needed to buy the necessary dollars (see Exhibit 12–12). The international buyer with the strong currency gets a bargain. China is in that position now. Japan was similarly situated 30 years ago. All currencies, including dollars, go up and down in value. The United States started the overseas movement in the 1950s when the dollar was very strong.

Many international chains have moved globally (see Exhibit 2–13), and many U.S. chains have made subtle name changes. Best Western, for example, became Best Western International; Quality Inns became Choice Hotels International.

There is more to global participation than currencies. Companies go international to acquire a foothold on another continent, to acquire assets (management talent or reservation systems) and to open new markets for their brands. Consumers prefer branded products, seeking the security and certainty of a brand they know. That works for U.S. travelers going abroad and for international travelers coming to the United States.

Political stability is another factor. Foreign investors may face serious financial loss from political uncertainty. Better to invest elsewhere even if the price is higher than risk loss from confiscation of the hotel. The United States is attractive to foreign investors because the loss from political uncertainty is unlikely. That's especially important to non-American developers. They have longer business horizons and are more focused on the real estate property than are their U.S. counterparts.

Half-Dozen International Hotel Chains that Also Operate in the United States		
Company Name and Identity	**Estimated[a] Number of Rooms**	**Countries of Operation[b]**
Accor (France)	500,000	China, France, India, Sweden
InterContinental (U.K.)	550,000	Andorra, Gabon, Kazakhstan, Rwanda
JAL Hotels (Japan)	20,000	China, Germany, Myanmar, Taiwan
Rezidor[c] (Denmark)	45,000	Croatia, Ireland, Senegal, U.K.
Sol Meliá (Spain)	85,000	Costa Rica, Mexico, Spain, Venezuela, Viet Nam
Taj Group (India)	9,000	Malaysia, Maldives, India, Seychelles

[a] Values are rounded.
[b] Representative; lists are not complete.
[c] Strategic partnership with Radisson SAS (Carlson).

Exhibit 2–13   Maturing markets abroad and the relative strengths of world currencies encourage both American and foreign chains to operate domestically and internationally.

Ownership and Financing Alternatives

Early inns were family homesteads under the direct control of the innkeepers. Owners and managers were the same persons. The arrangements grew more difficult as the size of hotels increased. Large hotels require large amounts of money, sums beyond the means of most families. Gradually, the financing/ownership of the building separated from the operation/management of the hotel. The separation gained momentum from two developments. Corporations became another legal means of ownership and larger hotels were built using new construction techniques.

Individual Ownership.   There are still large numbers of individually owned hotels. Many are held by members of the Asian American Hotel Owners Association (AAHOA). They are usually small, fall within the economy class of roadside motels, and carry a franchise flag. Best Western International is another affiliation of individual owners, but it is not a franchise group.

Owning a single hotel or even several is not the same as maintaining a family homestead. The issue is not where the family dwells, but where the financing originates. There are still instances when the cash to buy or build come from the extended family. Uncles and aunts, cousins, and in-laws are tapped for the equity (the ownership portion). A localized hotel may get equity from community professionals and businesspersons who invest because of public pride.

Borrowed funds supplement equity monies. Lenders are local banks and investment groups or even the franchise company bidding for the flag. The money needed to complete the deal can be borrowed with government support. Small business loans are financed by local and regional banks. Portions of the loan can be guaranteed by two agencies of the federal government. One is the Small Business Administration (SBA), another the Business and Industry Loan Guarantee Program of the Department of Agriculture. Small entrepreneurs borrow more easily and less expensively when lenders are guaranteed 80% of their loans by these agencies.

More equity money is needed as the project grows. Then the effort shifts from Main Street to Wall Street and the sale of shares (stock). En route, borrowed money comes from regional and national banks, from insurance companies and pension funds. At one time, labor unions were a source. Investment bankers and mortgage brokers and private equity firms join the flow that supports hotel development. During the downturn of the 1980s, when prices fell so low, some franchise companies, Choice Hotels particularly, began buying. About the same time, a new financing vehicle emerged to energize the market once again, the REIT.

Real Estate Investment Trusts (REITS).   REITS can own hotel properties just as individual owners or corporations do. Although the concept has been around for some time, it was rediscovered during the 1990s and provided the funds for that upturn.

REITs are public companies that raise capital through the sale of stock. Individual investors easily buy or sell small pieces of the REIT through the stock market. The REIT uses these funds along with borrowed funds to acquire hotels. Risk is spread among many hotels and many investors. There are also nontraded REITs.

Prior to 2001, there were legislative limitations placed on REITs. They were not permitted to be in any business other than real estate ownership. A REIT could own a hotel, but not operate it. A REIT could not provide services to its tenants. REITs could not have earnings from rooms, food, or beverage sales. One big advantage offset these disadvantages: REITs pay no income taxes so long as 95% of their taxable income (90%, under the new law) is returned to shareholders. That increases the REIT's appeal to the typical stock market investor, who may know nothing about hotel ownership or operations.

Some restrictions, but not the tax advantages, were lifted by Congress in the REIT Modernization Act of 2001. Entrepreneurship was the essence of the 2001 change. Old REITS were merely rent collectors. New REITs were able to sell services through wholly owned subsidiary companies that do pay income taxes. To aid the distinction, the REITs' tax-paying subsidiaries are called C Corporations. REITS are not limited to lodging. There are REITS specializing in apartments, hospitals, retail malls, and other types of real estate.

The story of hotel REITS is put into perspective by following what happened at Marriott. In 1993, Marriott formalized the distinction between management and ownership. The company split into two parts, Marriott International (management) and Host Marriott (equity). Just three years later, Host Marriott broke itself into two pieces, converting one into a specialized hotel company, a real estate investment trust. That REIT took advantage of the new 2001 law to buy Crestline Capital. Crestline separately owned the operating subsidiaries required under the old law. The REIT Modernization Act now allowed REITs not only to own the hotel real estate, but to own as subsidiaries the companies that operated the hotels. Host Marriott (the original 1996 REIT) bought and sold innumerable hotels in 2006. It bought 38 from Starwood in one transaction. (Talk about churning!) Host Marriott then dropped the old Marriott name to become Host Hotels, the world's largest hotel REIT.

Condominiums and Timeshares.   Condominiums (condos) and timeshares (interval or vacation ownerships) are two other ownership patterns. They differ from individual ownerships, from partnerships, from corporations, and from REITS.

Both have their origins in destination resorts. Condos are an American innovation that first appeared in ski resorts, such as Aspen and Stowe. Timeshares, a later development, are a European idea that took hold in North America's sunshine coasts, Florida and Hawaii. Florida ownership has been fueled by the weakness of the dollar. Foreign buyers have come because of the currency imbalance and the security of domestic real estate. The United States is now the world's largest market, but condominiums are gaining worldwide. Europe, especially, is experiencing growth in condo hotels.

Condominium Ownership.   Condos and timeshares are often confused because the physical buildings look alike. The ownership of the units is the distinction, not the blueprint of the building. Condos are real-estate purchases; timeshares are not. The craze for condo ownership was nurtured in a favorable income-tax environment. Measured growth continues even though tax incentives have been removed.

Today's condominium may be the owner's home, a second home, or a speculative buy. Guests finance the unit as they would any home purchase, but real-estate gains are still part of the play. Owner/guests own their own units and furnish them to personal preferences. As members of the condo association, they also own the common space and grounds.

The concept of mixed-use facilities grew from these new ownership patterns. Because owners are not always in residence, there's an opportunity to rent the unit. On-site management is needed to service the transient guest: to provide linens, maintenance, and more. A hotel company is the perfect answer, and adding an adjacent hotel a logical extension. Then both owners and guests can access all the services and amenities. Next came retail outlets, health clubs, entertainment venues, timeshares, and white-collar businesses. The mixed-use development, which is so popular today, was born.

There are endless permutations to the basic plan. In its simplest form, the guest reserves so many days per year for personal use, and puts the unoccupied times into the rental pool or not, as preferred. Profits, if any, from the participating unit are paid to the homeowner under some rotating, pro-rata plan. Homeowners may elect to have their own management company handle rentals. If so, the owners, who have helped the developer finance the construction, now occupy the units as guests and hire the management to rent to themselves.

A new variation on condo ownership is taking place by the swimming pool. Cabañas, poolside huts, at upscale resorts (some with baths and even kitchens) are being sold as timeshare and condominiums. Costs can run into the tens of thousands of dollars.

Condo Hotels.   No surprise that a *condo hotel* would be part of a resort project. Locating condos within commercial hotels is a more recent development. Residential guests are buying condominiums as parts of urban hotels rather than as adjacent supplements to free-standing hotels. The idea is part of a broader social movement that is bringing residents back to city centers. The Ritz-Carlton in downtown Boston is a good example. Internal condos help the developer in financing. They also upgrade the type of accommodations available to long-term, residential guests. (See also residential hotels in Chapter 1.)

Unlike resort condominiums, the space of the permanent occupant is not available to transient guests. What if circumstances change and permanent occupants decide to make their condos available? Is such space computed in occupancy and RevPar? Are rooms not owned by the hotel available for occupancy if not occupied by the owner? If so, or even if not, how is the occupancy percentage calculated? If left vacant, are these room computed in the revenue per available room? A more pressing current issue is the conversion of older hotels to condo hotels.

The switch, which is accelerating nationwide, has alarmed many city fathers because conversions reduce the number of rooms available. Fewer transient rooms threaten to impact local tourism and convention solicitation. Moreover, there is a loss of municipal income from fewer transient rooms subjected to room taxes. New York City lost some 10,000 rooms including the Plaza Hotel's renovation, the most publicized nationwide. Government officials both there and elsewhere are threatening regulations to stem the movement. Pressure from New York officials forced the Plaza to retain more transient rooms than first planned.

Timeshares.   Unlike condominium sales, the first timeshares were not real-estate purchases. Buyers did not buy a unit; they bought only the right to use the unit for so many days each year over a fixed time period. There was no property deed. At the end of the period, 20–40 years, the developer—not the guest who had paid upfront money as well as fees for many years—owned the unit. In contrast, condominium owners took title immediately.

Timeshares started out with very sleazy reputations. Sales without titles were not real-estate sales, so none of the 50 states regulated the industry. Numerous consumer complaints about pushy, unethical sales techniques forced state regulation of the industry. Cooling-off periods of 10 to 30 days, when buyers are out from under the high-pressure tactics of the timeshare seller, was one critical regulation. Once credibility to timeshare ownership was established, large hotel companies entered the business. Disney, Hilton, Hyatt, and Marriott among others reassured buyers. Timeshare sales entered a new phase.

Marketing executives of the chains contributed to the turnaround simply by changing the name. Timeshares became *interval ownerships, vacation clubs, vacation ownerships,* or *fractionals. Private residence clubs* are expensive timeshares with longer commitments than the standard one or two weeks.

Names aside, timeshares remain a very poor investment. Getting out from the contract's annual cost is almost impossible; resale is practically unknown. Buyers who give them back may still be responsible for annual fees. eBay often lists units for sale at 10%

of their original cost. The other major negative, coming to the same place at the same time for 30 years, has been alleviated by two types of exchange arrangements, but not without cost.

Exchanges.   Exchange clubs developed almost at the start of the timeshare idea. Like the industry itself, exchange clubs have matured to provide a legitimate service to a booming industry. Resort Condominiums International (RCI) and Interval International (II) are two of the better known names. For a fee, plus the deposit of the unit into the exchange pool, accommodations can be traded. Resorts at both ends of the trade must be affiliated members. RCI advertises over 3,500 resorts worldwide, II about 2,000 properties.

The importance of swapping was not lost to hoteliers. Two types of exchanges have developed. One builds on the hotel companies' preferred guest programs (PGPs). Timeshare guests can trade vacation units for other PGP values, including airline tickets. Disney goes one better, allowing exchanges for cruises.

The second type of exchange integrates resorts with timeshare facilities. It is so natural an affiliation that the two facilities are very often built side by side. Prospects are offered free or discounted minivacations at the resort, provided they listen to a timeshare sales pitch. These are long, pressurized sessions. The gift(s) is/are rescinded if the guests leave early. The synergy is reinforced by housing the guest-client in one of the units. As with condominiums, the marriage of timeshare units and hotels is logical. The hotel offers the infrastructure (spas, golf courses, restaurants) that the fractional lacks. The large size of the party in the timeshare and the continuous occupancy of the unit offsets the less consistent base of the hotel's clientele.

Role of the Timeshare.   Timeshares and condos are financing alternatives, additional capital for the developer. Converting existing resorts, or parts of them, was the first step in timeshare development. The funds were used to pay debts, upgrade and refurbish facilities, or line the pockets of the owner. This conversion phase failed because buyers wanted more than renovated hotel rooms. Converting larger, extended-stay facilities with kitchenettes was equally unsuccessful.

Developing new buildings with upscale accommodations and space takes capital. So the developer sets out to sell each unit 50 times, once each week. The more desirable the time purchased, in-season versus off-season or shoulder season, the more the unit costs. An 80-unit property may have as many as 4,000 participants annually (50 weeks × 80 units). The figure swells when the actual number of persons in each unit (2–6) is added in. For this illustration, a lucky developer could gross $100,000,000 upfront to finance the projects. All the units would need to sell at an average of, say, $25,000 each ($25,000 × 80 units × 50 weeks). This substantial sum is reduced by very high sales and marketing costs, including commissions to salespersons.

The up-front calculations must be tempered by several realities. Only a percentage of the units are actually presold and two weeks of the year are held back for maintenance. California law actually limits sales to 50 weeks. Unlike condominiums, where upkeep is the owner's responsibility, timeshare repairs, services, and furnishings are the developer's costs. Some expenses are offset by weekly maintenance and housekeeping fees levied on the occupants for T&T—trash and towels—but may also cover insurance costs.

Innovations have followed the legitimizing of the industry. The first was the *deeded timeshare*, where buyers actually take title, just as they do with condominiums. Deeded timeshares can be resold (but not easily), gifted, exchanged, willed, or rented. They may even appreciate in value. But that is so unlikely that suggesting it to new buyers is forbidden by the American Resort Development Association, the timeshare industry's trade group.

Limiting the number of participants is another idea being tested. Rather than 50 buyers per unit, the property is sold in, say, eight-week blocks to, say, six buyers. Rotating weeks is yet another innovation. It takes advantage of the two- to four-week break in the schedule. Buyers rotate throughout the years, so no one buys the best times and no one the worst. Of course, it might take a decade to get a one-time chance at Christmas or the Fourth of July weekend.

Joint Ventures and Strategic Alliances.   Joint ventures are similar to partnerships created by two or more individuals. With joint ventures, the individuals are not persons. They are one of several entities. Joint ventures are partnerships of corporations, of existing partnerships, or even of governments. For example, privately owned Radisson Hotels formed a three-way venture with the Russian Ministry for Foreign Tourism and a publicly owned business-center company, Americon. The new entity opened the 430-room Radisson Slavjanskaya in Moscow.

Similar developments in China almost always involve governmental agencies; they own the land. Free enterprises make up North America's joint ventures. Canadian Pacific Hotels formed such an alliance with Fairmont Hotels and Kingdom Hotels.[8] Of the four members, three were hotel companies and one was an already existing joint partnership. Even players as big as Marriott and Wyndham have united in joint ventures. Marriott's partner, Mitsui Fudosan, built the Tokyo skyscraper for Marriott's Ritz-Carlton chain to manage.

Joint ventures are usually financial marriages warranted by rising land and construction costs and ever-larger megadeals. The alliance spreads the risk, but it also taps the capabilities of different organizations. Financial, managerial, operational, and government expertise may not be found in a single company. Gaming management is one such skill. New gaming ventures in Singapore and Macau have recently turned to Nevada expertise to make certain of their success.

NEW MANAGEMENT PATTERNS

The era of the small innkeeper and the individual entrepreneur is waning. Costly and risky enterprises facing intense competition require the management talent and capital funding that only large, public companies—hotel chains—can provide.

Hotel Chains

Travel evokes the unknown and the unfamiliar. Within that environment, travelers seek a rather personal service—a bed for the night. Since it isn't possible to test the facilities beforehand, the decision rests on the reputation of the hotel or, more likely, on its chain membership.

Chain-controlled hotels now dominate the U.S. hotel industry (see Exhibit 2–14). Some 75% of all hotels are under the flag of one chain or another. That's up from 40 years ago, when the figure was about 33%. The momentum is evident overseas as well where chains are replacing the traditional hotelkeepers, individuals and families.

The reasons are simple. Chains bring strengths in site selection, access to capital, and economies of scale in purchasing, advertising, and reservations. Chains attract the best management talent and provide the consumer with brand recognition.

---

[8]The Kingdom Hotels Investment Company of Dubai, which is heavily invested in hotels worldwide, is owned by Saudi Prince Alwaleed bin Talal, one of the world's wealthiest persons.

20 Hotel Chains: Some Old and Well Known; Some New and Unproven	
Name	**Parent Company**
aloft Hotels[a]	Starwood
Crillion[a]	Starwood Capital[b]
Disney	Its Own Brand[c]
Element[a]	Starwood
Fairmont	Canadian Pacific Hotels
Four Seasons[d]	Its Own Brand
Harrah's	Its Own Brand
Historic Hotels of America	Referral Group
Host Hotels	Its Own Brand
Hyatt	Global Hyatt
Indigo[a]	InterContinental
Loews	Its Own Brand
MGM Mirage	Its Own Brand
Morgans	Its Own Brand
NYLO (New York Loft)[a]	Its Own Brand
Omni	Its Own Brand
Onyx[a]	Kimpton Hotel Group
Renaissance	Marriott
Ritz Carlton	Marriott
Sheraton	Starwood
Westin	Starwood

[a] New brand, recently introduced.
[b] Not to be confused with the Starwood Hotels and Resorts Worldwide.
[c] Companies with their own brands have different names for their individual hotels.
[d] No longer a publicly traded company.

Exhibit 2-14   An alphabetical register of hotel chains, some old and some new, that have not been identified in previous exhibits. New brands such as aloft Hotels, Hotel Victor, Hyatt Place, Indigo, and NYLO are featuring "lifestyle alternatives" for Generation Xers. They're either a really new option, or just a new brand name. (See also Exhibits 2–1, 2–4, 2–12, 2–13, and 2–15 for a full view of hotel options.)

As this chapter has stressed, hotel chains are no longer hotel builders. In fact, the builders may not be the owners. For certain, hotel owners are not hoteliers. So builders, money lenders, and owners turn to the chain.

Parties to the Deal.   Five different parties are involved in the development and operation of a hotel. That need not be five separate entities. One of the participants could assume several roles. The *developer* (party 1) sees an opportunity, acquires the site, and puts the plan together. The hotel might be a project of the community. It might be part of one element in a business park or a timeshare in a resort complex. The developer could be the owner (party 3), which would fold the five parties into four identities.

Financing loans are arranged from banks, insurance companies, government agencies, pension funds, REITS, or elsewhere. The *financier* is party 2. Some of the financing might come from one or more of the other parties. *Mezzanine financing* is a secondary source of borrowed money so it carries higher interest rates. Mezzanine financing is sometimes used as a construction loan. Sometimes it is treated as if it were equity money. If Marriott, for example, were to be the management company (party 4), it might lend short-term funds, mezzanine financing, to the developer (party 1) or to the owner (party 3).

Party 3 is the equity, that is, the *ownership*. This party could be any of the others or an individual, a joint venture, a REIT, a public corporation, or a separate entity making a passive investment.

If none of the others are capable of running a hotel, a *management company* (party 4) will be needed. It is desirable that the management company have a recognizable logo. If the management company (see Exhibit 2–15) is not known to the public, *a franchise* license is obtained from another company (party 5) that does have brand recognition (see Exhibit 2–16).

Hotel chains (see Exhibits 2–12, 2–13, and 2–14) are likely to be some combination of all five parties. They help with development and financing, hold a piece of the ownership equity, and supply management talent. Chains provide brand recognition and the essential reservation systems.

Consortia and Membership Organizations. Independent operators are at a disadvantage, struggling against the logos and reservation systems of their chain-linked competitors. Fighting back shifts the issue from "if and when to join" to "how to choose the right organization." So they, too, have affiliated. Their associations are looser, focusing chiefly on logos and reservations systems. There is some training and advice, but restrictions are fewer and autonomy is greater.

Reservation referrals are cooperative organizations designed to provide only one service: marketing. Centralized reservations, standardized quality, joint advertising, and a recognizable brand with a logo are the limited objectives of most referral groups. This enables the individual property to compete but still maintain its independence.

Hotel Management Companies		
Name of the Management Company	**Approximate Number of**[a]	
	Properties	**Guest Rooms**
Boykin Management Company	25	6,700
John Q. Hammons Hotels	65	15,000
Interstate Hotels Corporation	280	64,000
Janus Hotels & Resorts	45	10,000
Lane Hospitality	20	3,500
Lodging	20	2,000
MeriStar Hotels & Resorts	225	45,000
Richfield Hospitality Services	40	11,000
Sage Hospitality Resources	45	8,000
Westmount Hospitality Group	400	40,000
Winegardner & Hammons	30	7,500

[a]Rapid consolidation means values are best estimates. Some companies give different values even within their own Web sites.

Exhibit 2–15　Hotel management companies are not as distinct a class as once they were. Other than size and name recognition, the companies of Exhibit 2–15 and 2–12 are much the same. Although this group is chiefly into hotel management, they also develop, lease, and even own properties outright.

Representative Franchise Fees[a]		
Fee	**Representative Terms**	**Alternative Terms**
Application[b]	The greater of $45,000 *or* $400 times the number of rooms	A lesser fixed amount plus a per-room fee over, say, the first 75 rooms.
Royalty	4%–6% of room revenue	3% of gross revenue; *or* a minimum per night, say, $8
Advertising/ Marketing	1.5%–3.5% of room revenue	2% of gross revenue, *or* a minimum per night, say, 1.50 per room
Training	0.5% of gross revenue plus cost of attending school	None; franchisee bears all schooling costs for employees sent away.
Reservation	3% of room revenue plus $5 per reservation	$10 per reservation, *or* a minimum per night, say, $10 per room

[a] Other possibilities include email costs, global reservation costs, termination costs, accounting charges, and participation in frequent guest promotions.

[b] All or some (90%–95%) of the application fee is returned if the application is not approved.

Exhibit 2–16   Hotel franchisors (those who sell franchise rights) charge franchisees (buyers) a variety of fees that total as much as 8–10% of gross sales. *Reminder*: As room rates rise, so does the innkeeper's dollar cost as a fixed percentage of the higher rate. Franchisees gain access to national reservation systems, which may account for a large percentage of their occupancy.

There is no interlocking management, no group buying, no common financing—nothing but a unified sales effort. Unlike the franchise contract, which is discussed soon, individual identity is encouraged. There is no prescribed limitation on the location or configuration of the building so long as the guest rooms meet standards. That said, Best Western International, the largest of the referral groups, has introduced several prototype rooms.

Best Western International is the best known membership/referral group (see Exhibit 2–12). Each of its 4,250 properties in some 80 countries is individually owned. Members have voting status for the board of directors that operates the association. By maintaining standards, quality accommodations, and fair pricing, Best Western provides the traveling public with consistency among the properties, whose uniqueness reflects the individual ownership that is still maintained.

Preferred Hotels and Resorts Worldwide is a different type of membership group. Its rates are at the other end of the price scale from Best Western. Although both are international in scope, Preferred's membership has been less than 150 hotels. Recently, it created a new holding company, IndeCorp Corporation, with several wholly owned brands. Preferred is now one of those brands. Under IndeCorp's umbrella are other independent brands such as Summit Hotels and Resorts, and Sterling Hotels and Resorts. By developing brands, IndeCorp emphasizes its consortium strategy with now nearly 1,000 hotels. The Sagamore Resort (see Exhibit 1–11) is a member of Preferred Hotels & Resorts Worldwide.

Consolidation of the consortia follows the general consolidation movement of the whole industry. Leading Hotels of the World, which had been the largest consortium of the luxury independents, less than 500 members, also began consolidating. They have added the Leading Small Hotels group of 70 hotels and Leading Spas of the World. It is likely that competition may force the consortia to move beyond mere branding to begin managing, even owning, hotels.

Management Contracts and Management Companies

Management Contracts.   A management contract is an agreement between the hotel owner (party 3) and a management company (party 4). The contract is a complex legal instrument by which the management company (see Exhibit 2–15) operates the hotel within the conditions set down by the contract. For this, the owner pays the management company a fee of between 2% and 4% of revenues plus incentive fees based on other values as well: net profits, for example.

Fees are paid whether there are profits or not. Profits, if any, belong to the owners, as do losses. Since management fees are paid whether there are profits or not, big management companies such as Marriott and Starwood have grown rapidly. They have little invested capital and almost no risk. Risk lies with parties 1, 2 and 3. Besides, most contacts provide large incentive fees if the management company hits preestablished goals.

The relationship between owner and management company is not always smooth. Lawsuits arise over the many issues that contracts invariably overlook. One, for example, deals with the revenue the management company earns from selling guests' names and addresses. Another deals with their rebates from purveyors. As expected, lawsuits are fewer during the up-cycles and greater during the downturns when owners suffer losses. Contract terms favorable to one party or the other reflect the time in the cycle that the agreement was made.

If early in the project's development, the management company may provide advice on construction, on systems, on financing, and so on. When times were bad, owners accepted many restrictive terms in the contract in order to secure the management company's services. An improving economy shifts the advantage. Lenders have disposed of their excess hotel inventory, and hotels have turned profitable. Simultaneously, the number of management companies has increased. This tight competition forces concessions from the management companies as they bid for contracts. Owning companies are able to negotiate shorter contracts, less costly fees, and more capital investments from management companies.

Management Companies.   Management companies are of recent origin in the long history of innkeeping. These professional managers, as distinct from owner managers, emerged and grew important because of three different events. Although the causes varied, the positive impact on the management companies was the same.

Lenders (party 2), usually banks, take control of hotels when owners (party 3) are unable to repay their mortgage loans. Bankers dislike holding physical assets (buildings) so they try to sell them as quickly as possible. Knowing that the resale value of the hotel is greater if the hotel is up and running, banks hire management companies to operate defunct hotels.

Event 1 was the Great Depression (1930s), when most of the nation's hotels went into bankruptcy. Event 2 was the oil embargo of 1973. Without oil, travel shut down and many of America's hotels fell to the auctioneer's hammer again. In the 1980s, the whole banking system collapsed partly because the hotel industry collapsed. This time, the remedy required the intervention of the federal government. Poor times for hotel owners proved to be good times for hotel management companies.

A pure management company is almost unknown today. Companies like those in Exhibit 2–15 are not pure plays. They have the same mixed characteristics as their competitors, Exhibits 2–12, 2–13, and 2–14. Consolidation and brand identification have enabled the better known chains to dominate the management field. The number of independent properties that look to smaller management companies is declining. At the same time, there is greater competition from and among the big guys. REITS are another of those big guys.

REITS add another issue. Earlier, the chapter pointed out that REITS were not legally able to manage the hotels they own. However, under the REIT Modernization Act, REITS may now own the leasing company. And it's the leasing company that hires the management company! So a REIT named Host Marriott, now renamed Hosts Hotels, had Marriott International operating many, not all, of the hotels that Host Marriott owned.

Leasing (Renting).   Management contracts and lease contracts are almost opposite views of the industry's health. One or the other becomes popular depending on the position of the economic cycle. Leases are popular when times are good.

Hotels once owned the real estate and managed the operation. Owning real estate takes large sums of invested equity and significant risks from borrowing. As hoteliers became more sophisticated about finance (1960s), sale-and-leaseback became popular. The hotel company would sell the building to outside investors. The new investors would then lease (rent) the operation of the hotel back to the very hotel company that had sold the the real estate. Since the operation was profitable, both parties won. The operating companies of Exhibit 2–12 had profits after they paid the lease rent. The owning company had a fixed flow of rental income with which it could secure the borrowing. The lease's long and successful history gives precedent to current REIT arrangements.

Management contracts gain popularity when the industry goes into a slump. The operating company cannot visualize any operating profits, so it steps back from lease arrangements. The owning company still has a hotel that needs management skills. It hires the management company, paying the company a management fee as prescribed by the management contract. Incentives are paid to the management company if it produces profits through increased sales or reduced costs.

The dynamics of hotelkeeping allow for a variety of possibilities. Some hotel companies own and operate hotels. Sometimes, it is as a joint venture. Some hotel companies manage for a fee but contribute some of the equity (ownership). Some hotel companies just manage. Franchising is another option.

Franchising.   Franchising is not a new idea, nor is it unique to the hotel industry. Tires, speedy printers, diet clinics, and many other industries (hamburgers) have franchises. A franchise buyer (called a *franchisee*) acquires rights from a seller (called a *franchisor*). Those rights give the franchisee exclusive use (a franchise) of the name, the product, and the system of the franchisor within a given geographic area. Buying a franchise enables the small businessperson to operate as an independent but still have the benefits of membership in the chain. The membership comes with costs.

The franchisee pays a variety of fees to adopt the name and trademark of the franchisor (see Exhibit 2–16). In addition to an initial signing fee, the franchisee pays so much per room per night throughout the life of the contract. But that's not all. The franchisee also pays a rental for the company sign, a fee to access the reservation system, and a per reservation fee for each room booked. In addition, the franchisee buys amenities from the parent company in order to get the franchise logo. Extra fees are charged for required training and for participating in the frequent guest program. Competition has encouraged some management companies to pay all or part of the owner's up-front franchising costs in order to win the management contract.

Franchise fees have almost doubled during the past 20 years. They now represent 9% to 10% of room sales—some 8% of sales from all sources. The impact is significant because net earnings from all departments is only in the 20% range. (Franchise expense fees are already included in that calculation.) If net earnings are only 20% of sales, franchise fees represent a good chunk of operating costs. On the other hand, brand affiliation may add 10 percentage points to occupancy and $20 or more to ADR. That, too, is a significant amount.

With those fees come a variety of services. How many and which services depend on which franchise is purchased. The most extensive franchise might include feasibility studies, site selection advice, financing support, design and planning, mass purchasing, management consultations, advertising, and systems design. The central reservation system, discussed in Chapter 5, is the major reason by far that franchisees sign up. Estimates place the number of reservations coming through the system as high as 30% of the chain's total reservations and upward of 50% of all reservations for individual properties.

Fees versus services have split the direction of franchise development. Franchising is growing in Europe and Asia, especially in China as it prepares for the Olympics. Contrariwise, some American hotel owners are dropping their franchises in favor of membership groups. Membership affiliation (sometimes called *brand affiliation*) has lower fees, shorter contracts, and fewer restrictions. Franchise fees typically cost 4–5 times more than memberships. Moreover, franchisors are among the first with the costly amenity creep that owners must pay for. Still, many owners weigh the costs and buy in.

Best Western International is the oldest, largest, and best known of the brand-affiliated groups. Others—Best Value Inns, Superior Small Lodging and Payless Lodging—are emerging. They now coexist with more senior alliances such as Historic Hotels of America, Budget Host, and Utell.

The Franchise and the Flag.   Hotel franchising probably began during the late 19th century. Cesar Ritz—*ritzy* now means the finest accommodations—gave his name to a small number of hotels whose management he supervised. Kemmons Wilson made the next advance in hotel franchising with the development of the Holiday Inn chain.

Franchising is all about brand recognition. The franchisor delivers immediate brand identity by selling its "flag" to the franchisee. Franchisee and parent company are so alike that guests do not distinguish between them. The physical hotels look identical. It's the ownership and management structures that differ. The chain (the franchisor) does not own the franchise property, the operator (the franchisee) does. The franchisor does not manage the property, the franchisee does. If the franchisee elects not to manage, it could hire the franchisor as its management company under a separate management contract. Or instead, it could hire an entirely different management company. So now another party, the franchisor, has been added to the interaction of the developer, the owner, the lender, and the management company.

Each flag denotes a certain type of facility in the buyer's mind. A franchisee intent on developing long-stay facilities wouldn't shop for a franchise flag of a budget property such as Holiday Inn Express.

Canceling a franchise contract is difficult and expensive. Franchisees are usually small businesspersons. The franchisor is a multifaceted company whose attorneys wrote the franchise contract. Competition and court decisions have helped balance the scales. Still, tension often exists between franchisees and franchisors. When issues become widespread, franchisees have formed organizations to counter the strength of their franchise parent. That was the source of the Owners Association of Intercontinental Hotels (IAHI), a franchise owners' group within one brand, Holiday Inn initially. The Asian American Hotel Owners Association (AAHOA) is an owners' group across many brands. Franchisees often franchise multiple properties with multiple flags.

Among the defining issues are:

1. Defense from competing franchises within the supposedly protected area, especially as consolidation among franchisors puts many heretofore competing brands under one umbrella and on the same reservation platform;
2. Unexpected upgrade demands by the franchisor, particularly when the franchisee sells the hotel;
3. High liquidation damages when the franchisee tries to change flags.

Despite the negatives, buying a franchise flag is equally popular with both large absentee owners and small owner/operators. Branding is essential for attracting the transient traveler who may never come that way again.

SUMMARY

Partly because of the industry's willingness to try new things—its dynamic approach to competition—hotelkeeping opens the 21st century at the peak of its cycle. New products using new marketing techniques are being tested. New ownership patterns are calling for new management structures. Strategic changes such as these require rapid responses and decisive moves to meet worldwide competition head on. Many new flags (brands) are flying even as consolidation shrinks the number of, and grows the size of, surviving hotel companies.

Shifts in the lodging industry take place within the global village, where ideas and innovations move swiftly between continents. Their speed and direction depend, in large measure, on the relative strengths of currencies. Hoteliers worldwide know that name recognition attracts the transient traveler. High fees notwithstanding, franchising is one concept that has jumped the oceans to further consolidate lodging and make it a true global industry.

For now, the inelastic business market continues to underpin the basic business of hotelkeeping. Many predict that the rapidly growing elastic market of tourism and leisure will soon replace the business traveler as lodging's major guest profile.

The 21st century will build on the dynamic changes in products, markets, financing, and operations that continue to reshape this ancient industry.

RESOURCES AND CHALLENGES
Resources

WEB SITES

http://www.hotelinteractive.com (E-mail newsletter—Smithtown, NY. One source for tracking the dynamics of modern innkeeping.)

http://www.hotelmotel.com (*Hotel & Motel Management*, trade periodical—Duluth, MN. One source for tracking the dynamics of modern innkeeping.)

http://www.hotelsmag.com (*Hotels,* international trade periodical—New York; London. One source for tracking the dynamics of modern innkeeping.)

http://www.meetings-conventions.com (*M&C, Meetings and Conventions*, trade periodical—Northstar Travel Media, Secaucus, NJ. One source for tracking the dynamics of modern innkeeping.)

http://www.hotelreports.com (Smith Travel Research—Hendersonville, TN. One source for tracking the dynamics of modern innkeeping.)

Web Assignment

Hotel & Motel Management has "The Hotel Franchise Fee Calculator" by HVS International on its Web site.

Select a franchise for your 110-room hotel which has an ADR of $68 and an occupancy of 60%. Make your selection by contrasting two choices from the franchise calculation using two years of comparison and assuming: (1) Every value increases by 2% annually; (2) frequent travelers account for 10% of the occupancy; (3) third-party reservations account for 1/8 of total reservations; and (4) the Internet accounts for 5% of reservations.

Explain the reasons for your choice over the second brand by showing your calculations for both and listing any assumptions that you make.

INTERESTING TIDBITS

➤ Motels are said to be autocentric, which is a play (pun) on the prefix "auto." Auto means both (1) the inward self and (2) automobile. So motels emphasize both privacy and anonymity (exterior entrance to the rooms, for example) as part of the guests' arrival by auto.

➤ The Sheraton Corporation, which is now the largest brand of Starwood Hotels & Resorts, was the first hotel company to be listed on the New York Stock Exchange (1945).

➤ A rule of thumb is a general principle based on experience rather than on scientific testing. The "36/12 rule" emphasizes the importance of long-stay/repeat guests. The rule says that 36% of the industry's room nights come from 12% of guest stays. The growth of extended-stay facilities seems to support this rule.

Challenges

TRUE/FALSE

Questions that are partially false should be marked false (F).

___ 1. Segmentation (breaking lodging into separate segments) is the federal government's effort to increase competition in the lodging industry.

___ 2. Timeshares are also called by other names, including interval ownerships, vacation clubs, and fractionals.

___ 3. The hotel's inclusive tour package (IT) is the same concept as the wholesaler's tour package, but without the cost and risk associated with transportation.

___ 4. Management companies favor management contracts when the business cycle is up and profits are certain; they favor management leases when the cycle is low and profits uncertain.

___ 5. Lodging depends on two major classes of buyers (guests): the businessperson (an inelastic consumer) and the leisure buyer (an elastic consumer).

PROBLEMS

1. Using the trade press, your own management skills, or Web sites, prepare a list of six amenities, other than those cited in the text, that hoteliers use to attract business. *Hint*: Start the list with "free parking."

2. Identify the advantages and disadvantages to the personal career of a student who takes a job after graduation with a Hilton Inns franchise and passes up an offer from Hilton Hotels, the parent company.

3. Why is Best Western International not listed among the large management companies of Exhibit 2–15 After all, Best Western has some 300,000 rooms in its brand! Explain in detail.

4. Someone once said, "If you try to be all things to every guest, you'll likely end up as every guest's second choice." Is that an accurate statement? Why or why not? Answer with special attention to the segmentation of the industry's product line.

5. A traveler driving along Interstate 36 stops at two different hotels on successive evenings. Explain, and differentiate between, the signs posted by the front desk in terms of the text discussion about ownership, management, franchising, and joint ventures.

   Hotel A: This Hampton Inn is owned by Jerome J. Vallen and Sons, Inc., under license from Promus. Richfield Hotel Management.

   Hotel B: This Hampton Inn is owned by Promus. Jerome J. Vallen, General Manager.

6. Obtain a copy of a management contract from a local hotel, or review a book in the library on hotel management contracts. Discuss three terms (for example, life of the contract, payment, maintenance of the property, or investment by the management company) that intrigue you.

AN INCIDENT IN HOTEL MANAGEMENT

Taken for a Ride

The hotel advertised the availability of free shuttle service. A business guest relied on that information when she booked for a meeting at company headquarters about one mile away. She tried to arrange the trip, only to be told that first priority went to airline employees. (The hotel has a rooms contract with the airline). As a result, she was late for appointments the first day.

The guest complained and was told that the shuttle would be available if she called with a 30–45-minute lead time. On the second day, she did that from the office, but the pickup was never made; she took a cab back. Arrangements worked both ways the other days. On the last morning, she was stunned to learn that the shuttle was leaving in 5 minutes, not between 30 and 45-minutes after her call. She had not finished dressing and had had no breakfast.

Questions   Was there a management failure here; if so, what?
What is the hotel's immediate response (or action) to the incident?
What further, long-run action should management take; if any?

ANSWERS TO TRUE/FALSE QUIZ

1. False. First of all, lodging is highly competitive and the federal government is not a party to any action against the industry. Segmentation is the industry's own action to be more competitive whereby individual companies enter new markets with new products to compete against other brands.

2. True. Renaming timeshares, which had a very poor reputation, was one of the techniques used by the reputable hotel companies, which were entering the timeshare market, to change buyer attitudes.

3. True. The hotel IT package is 100% controlled by the hotel. It is added or removed from availability depending on occupancy projections without the fear of losses from prepurchased travel commitments.

4. False. Just the opposite. Management companies prefer *paying the hotel owner* a lease rental when profits are expected to be high. They prefer *receiving* the fixed payment *from a management contract* when profits are low or uncertain.

5. True. Lodging has two major guest classes, business travelers and leisure travelers. Businesspersons are inelastic buyers. Changes in rates or other circumstances will neither encourage nor deter their visits. Leisure guests are the opposite. They will be attracted by concessions (they are elastic) and turned away by restrictions.

The Structures
of the Hotel Industry

Two distinct structures frame the operation and form of the modern hotel. Every hotel, no matter its size and complexity, has an organizational structure that enables it to carry out its daily operations. That business takes place within a building that also has structure. Both forms differ substantially depending on the size and market of the individual property.

Physical differences are the most visible. The ski lodge has individual units hidden in the woods. Resorts offer low-rise buildings hugging the swimming pool (see Exhibit 1–11). How different these hotels are from the urban, commercial giant squeezed by higher land costs into a narrow high-rise configuration (see Exhibit 1–10).

Organizational structures can be as unique, although not nearly as visible, as the physical structures. Each organization takes form from a basic pattern common to the industry. Commonality aside, the 1,000-room commercial hotel is going to differ substantially from the mom-and-pop highway property. The all-suite, long-stay property will not be at all be like the Native American casino operation.

Differences notwithstanding, both the organizational structure and the building structure adhere to basic blueprints. Organizations are built around guest services, sleeping rooms around guest sensibilities. This chapter explores both.

THE ORGANIZATIONAL STRUCTURE

Hotels employ a vast number of people with a variety of skills. Among them are plumbers and accountants, bartenders and cooks, groundskeepers and water purification experts, computer troubleshooters and telecommunication specialists. The larger the hotel, the more specialized are the tasks. Some hotels have larger resident populations than do many small towns.

Each hotel organizes this diversified workforce in different ways. Human and physical resources are combined to achieve company goals in the most efficient manner. Although each organization takes a unique form, the patterns that emerge are based on the industry's best practices.

Hotel organizations follow the pattern of other businesses or social institutions. The workforce is separated into specialized departments. Each is entrusted with a share of duties and services. Good management works to minimize the differences that invariably arise among the various departments. Poor performance in one department undermines the best efforts of all. Coordinating the whole, unifying the specialties, and directing joint efforts is the job of the general manager. General managers get the authority they need from the ownership interests of the management company.

Ownership

From atop the organizational pyramid, ownership oversees the unfolding organization (see Exhibit 3–1). Ownership can rest within an individual, a partnership, a joint venture, a REIT or a public corporation. This discussion on organization references ownership of the managing company. Previous chapters made clear that the management company is, most likely, not the owner of the physical structure, the building. The management company could be relatively small (see Exhibit 2–15) or extremely large (see Exhibit 2–12). Control could be in the hands of one person or vested in as many as the 800 million shares authorized for the Marriott Corporation.[1]

Companies that both manage and own hotels can also own and manage other companies, subsidiaries of the parent. That's Marriott's relationship with its several subsidiaries, among them its Ritz-Carlton and Renaissance chains.

Public corporations are legal persons with all the rights and responsibilities of legal individuals. Corporations are favored because investors have limited liability. Individuals who own shares are not liable for company obligations. If a hotel company fails, shareholders may lose their investment, but they are not responsible for the company's debts to the bank, to the purveyors, or to the employees. The corporate "person" is the one responsible. The corporate person buys and sells hotels, it borrows, pays taxes, and hires the general managers who make the organization work.

The General Manager

Management titles vary from hotel to hotel just as their organizations do. Large hotel chains use titles at the corporate level similar to other American businesses: CEO (chief executive officer); CFO (chief financial officer); COO (chief operating officer).

General manager (GM or *The* GM) is the favored title at the unit level—the operating hotel. If the GM is an executive of the corporation that owns or operates the hotel, his or her title might reflect that: *president* (of the corporation) *and general manager* (of the hotel). Owner-manager is used for a GM who actually owns the hotel. Standing alone, the title of general manager indicates no ownership interests. The GM is simply the employee most responsible to ownership, corporate or otherwise, and the one person accountable for the full scope of the operation. Total responsibility for all that happens in every department rests with the GM.

---

[1]The Marriott family owns about 20% of the 400 million shares that are issued and outstanding. The company and the family now face a succession issue: Who will follow the current Chief Executive, J.W. (Bill) Marriott? Bill is the second Marriott generation; his father, J. Willard Marriott, was the founder. With a publicly held corporation there is no assurance that Bill Marriott's son, John, will succeed his father.

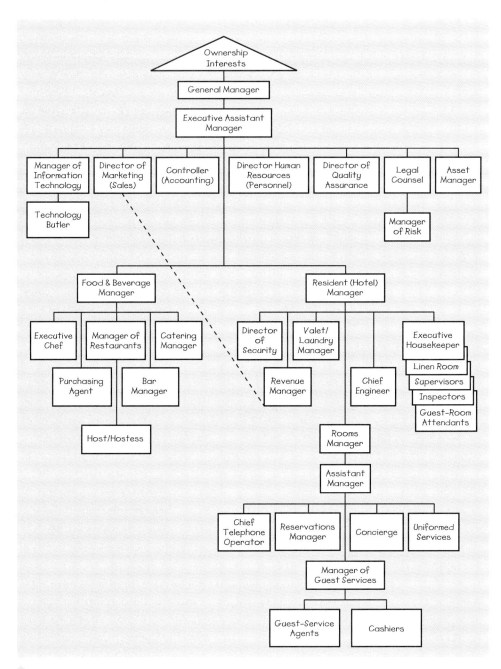

Exhibit 3-1 Hotel organizations are changing to keep pace with social and economic shifts. Flatter organizations (fewer supervisory levels) notwithstanding, new positions are being added even as older ones are being retrenched. The chart is incomplete except for the Resident Manager's line, which is the thrust of the chapter and the text. Even here, flatter organizations are the trend, so many hotels lack all of the intermediate managers discussed in the chapter.

The GM deals either directly with ownership or indirectly through layers of corporate levels and titles: area vice president for operations; regional director of marketing; food and beverage manager, eastern division.

GMs of large organizations have an assistant, the *executive assistant manager*. Like the boss, the executive assistant has jurisdiction over the entire organization. That distinguishes the job from the post of *assistant manager,* a rooms department position (see Exhibit 3–1). Small hotels lack both executive assistants and assistant managers, whereas large hotels may use several assistant managers to cover the desk around the clock.

"Around the clock" because hotels never close: 7/24/365 places great demands on the time and energy of hotel executives. The work week, which is limited for operative employees by federal and state labor laws or labor contracts, is open ended for management. The burden is heavy on every department head as well as on the GM. An *executive-on-duty* program offers relief for all executives and their assistants. Slow periods (such as nights, weekends, and holidays at commercial hotels) are covered by rotating the entire management staff. Every department head of Exhibit 3–1 takes a turn as GM with responsibility for every department. The reservoir of management talent is deepened; the experience of the individual manager is broadened; and family time is strengthened.

From Host to Executive.   The role and responsibility of the GM has changed as expectations of the job to be performed have changed. During the period of one-person ownership, general managers personified their hotels. The GM of the era was either the actual owner or a representative who stood in the owner's place. He (and in those days, the position was invariably held by a man) was known as "Mine Host." His name was part of the advertising, his personality part of the aura, his presence part of the hotel's very identity. Hotels were smaller, and the manager often visited with arriving and departing guests. The property reflected the host's qualities, the personality, the leadership, the essence of this very special person (see Exhibit 3–2).

How different from today, when…

> …the amount of time spent with customers versus budgets is totally reversed. In fact, one room clerk working at a hotel for more than six months…[said] she had never seen the general manager [at] the front desk.[2]

A statement like this reflects the reduced importance of being a "greeter" in the manager's overall responsibility.

> …the term "Hotel Greeter" appears to have been rather loosely defined. In the 1930s and 40s…the Association of Hotel Greeters was open to any hotel employee whose work involved meeting the public—most were in management.…[3]

The issues are different 75 years later. Labor and law, community relations and advertising, energy and communications, and more—all cited in Exhibit 3–2—preempt executive time. These are some of the reasons behind the continued demise of the small, privately owned establishment. Chain operations, not family finances, are needed to fund the expensive expertise that supports the individual GMs in these critical areas of operation.

Mobility is another explanation for the decline of Mine Host. GMs of an earlier period put their marks on properties because they were in one location for a long time. Not so today when the company's need for the special talents of a particular manager often means frequent transfers. Guests have also changed: Mass marketing and one-time arrivals make Mine Host less relevant. Executive talents now focus on a growing list of nonguest issues. Hence, many observers worry that "the business of hotels is no longer the hotel business."

---

[2]Jeff Weinstein. "Old-Fashioned Hotelkeeping." *Hotels*, February 2001, p. 5.
[3]Joy Kingsolver. Web site for Archives and Archivists, March 3, 2000.

Exhibit 3-2 The shift from hotel host/greeter to hotel manager/executive is described lightly in this well-known ditty that the authors have changed to modernize the phrasing. Time has not changed the numerous disciplines required of the general manager even as qualifications shift from specialist to generalist and back again.

What Has Become of Our Genial Hosts?

What was it in bygone days
That served the famous hoteliers?
Smiles and friendships, *bon mots* and more.
To know them, guests flocked through the door.

Schooled in the fine art of conversation
Made hotelkeeping an endless vacation,
Chatting and supping and drinking one's fill
While the cream of society fattened the till.

What has become of our Genial Hosts?
Alas, conditions have altered their posts.
They rarely see their fashionable clients.
Their careers have become mathematical science.

Occupancies, percentages, rooms income,
Wages, break-even, taxes, and then some!
Their carefree pasts have become archaic.
The innkeepers' life is today algebraic.

Each acts like an Einstein, a judge, and a foreman,
A housekeeper, a chef, an art critic, a doorman.
And there on the desk, a great volume about:
Hotel management; titled, *Check-In Check-Out*.

Consultants and salespersons vie for a visit
Then the new decorator with the latest what-is-it.
They're umpires and referees; they pacify all
From the board of directors to the charity ball.

And leaving the office, they find in the corridors
Anxious sales staffers and tired night auditors.
And if that's not enough, alack and egad
There's always the competitor's TV ad!

What's to be done about REITS and franchisees,
And what about the competition overseas?
Consolidation? Segmentation?
Rising prices of electrification?

Hearing the reverberations about minimum wage
Helped bring the change from host to sage.
Entertainment centers, computerization, what more?
Environmental concerns and a concierge floor.

What has become of our Genial Hosts?
What else: they're figments, relics, ghosts.
And when will they rest from their toil so hard?
When they hang o'er their tombs a "Do Not Disturb" card.

Strength and Salaries.   Outsiders still believe that the GM's job is all about meeting celebrities and enjoying free dining and drinks. But another night out for cocktails and dinner is not a hotelier's idea of a nice evening. Studies of general managers—and GMs are heavily studied—indicate work weeks of up to 65 hours. Long hours wreak havoc on marriage and family time; with chronic fatigue and reduced productivity.

Similar studies point out the importance of a manager's people skills. That means, in part, developing the social and communicative abilities required of an important community person. Having such skills is even more critical to managing the hotel's human resources. Many staff members are minimum-wage workers dependent on tips and gratuities. Low wages account, in part, for the high rate of employee turnover and the difficulty of communicating company values.

Incentive bonuses and rewards are one technique for supplementing employee wages and retaining good people. The same is true for general managers. Executive incentives and bonuses range between 20 and 40% of annual salaries. GM salaries are dependent on several criteria: the size of the hotel (number of rooms); the ADR the manager is able to deliver; and the revenue (both gross and net revenue) generated by the property. Chapters 1 and 2 treated the wide range of hotels, which accounts for manager's salaries ranging between $50,000 and $2,000,000 per year. The median salary for general managers is over $125,000 plus incentives.

GM salary packages are negotiated. Housing (no rent, telephone, or utility bills) for the manager and family might be added to the cash salary and bonus/incentive. Family meals in the dining room may be included. Free laundry and dry cleaning are common benefits. Membership fees for local clubs and associations are appropriate if the manager is expected to be a very visible community leader. Stock options (shares of stock sold to the executive at reduced prices) is another fringe benefit, an advantage of the corporate structure.

"Professional courtesy," by which one hotelier extends comp (free) accommodations to traveling executives of other hotels, is an extra benefit, but certainly not a negotiated one.

Support Departments.   GMs contend with an ever-growing list of issues that require special knowledge and expertise. Exhibit 3–2 treats these lightly but hotel companies support their managers with experts in specialized areas of law, employment, environment, taxes and technology. Some of these specialists are available only at organizational levels higher than the operating hotel. Others are part of the property's organizational chart (see Exhibit 3–1). If the general manager carries a corporate title, so may the support staff. A GM entitled president and general manager may have a vice president of marketing, a vice president for human resources, etc., rather than a director of marketing or manager of human resources. Whatever the titles, the probability that the organization is a corporation is about 100%.

Staff positions support the operating departments as well as the general manager. The hotel (or resident) manager, discussed soon, looks to human resources for help in filling job openings. The marketing department makes room sales, and accounting is responsible for billing and collection. Staff is not isolated; it, too, has guest contact. Legal counsel may be involved with accidents; accounting with unpaid bills; technology with guest support.

The Food and Beverage (F&B) Department.   Unlike the advisory nature of the support staff, the *food and beverage manager* has direct operating (line) responsibilities. Where present, F&B is one of the hotel's two operating departments (see Exhibit 3–1). The rooms department, the thrust of this text, is the other.

The importance of F&B continues to erode. Many hotels have no F&B department. At one time, food and beverage accounted for nearly half of hotel revenues industry wide. That value has declined by over 50% (see Exhibit 3–3), reflecting the large number of hotels

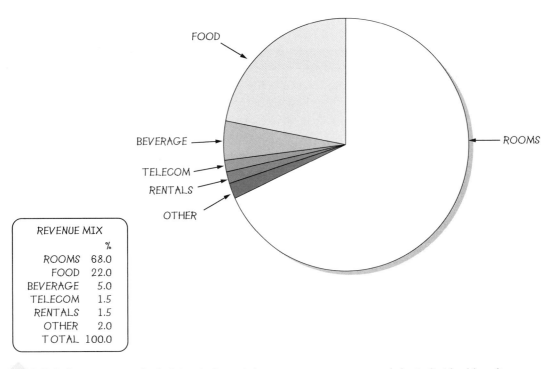

Exhibit 3-3   Rooms is the lodging industry's largest revenue earner and the individual hotel's most profitable department, approximately $0.70 of each dollar sale. The percentage of nonroom revenue is higher in full-service properties and resorts because they offer many additional services. Food and beverage sales have fallen as a percentage of industry revenues because many hotels have done away with restaurants. Similar declines have occurred in telephone revenues since their peak in 2000 because guests have increased their use of wireless communication devices.

that either offer no meals or include breakfast within the room rate. Food revenues have fallen even in full-service hotels. F&B's declining importance has impacted many middle-management positions in that department. Fewer managers mean that decisions have been pushed onto the operating employees. Chapter 7 examines the implications of this issue.

The Hotel (or Resident) Manager

The hotel manager, also called the *house manager* or *resident manager*, is the front-of-the-house counterpart to the food and beverage manager, if one exists. All operating departments, other than food and beverage, report to this position. Exhibit 3–1 illustrates the scope of the resident manager's responsibilities. Every department that services guests falls within the purview of this manager, who, in turn, reports to the GM.

Like other industries, lodging has been moving toward flatter organizations. Fewer management levels between the top and the bottom of the chart speed communications and decision making and hold down costs. So not many hotels have all the management positions shown in the illustration. The offset is greater fatigue among the remaining staff. Fewer managers mean a broader span of control, which translates to less supervision. Without a resident manager, the department heads shown in Exhibit 3–1 report directly to the GM. A still smaller hotel would even do away with some department heads. Either a senior employee would be the responsible person or operative employees would turn to the general manager.

All positions are retained here to facilitate the discussion. Besides, large hotels do have resident managers and all the support positions. Included are housekeeping; security; rooms; engineering (repairs and maintenance); laundry and valet; revenue control; shops, rentals and business centers; concierges; pools and spas.

Housekeeping. Responsibility for the delivery of the hotel's basic product, a clean room, rests unconditionally with this department. Yet it has never enjoyed the status afforded other units within the orbit of the resident manager. The explanation lies in part with the productive nature of the physical job: servicing guests rooms and cleaning public space. Besides, floor housekeepers usually work in isolation, while other front-of-the-house positions enjoy a rich social environment.

Floor housekeepers or *guest-room attendants* are among the hotel's poorest paid employees. Tips, which supplement the minimum salary of other low-wage jobs, are less available to the housekeeping crew. Therefore, the job attracts the least educated, particularly those with a limited knowledge of English—often recent immigrants. It is no surprise, then, that simple clerical duties—completing request forms for minor in-room maintenance—add to job stress. Without salable skills, housekeepers face another large negative: a great deal of part-time/call-in work. As occupancy falls, housekeeping jobs disappear. So uncertainty about the weekly pay check is piled atop physical labor and low status.

Nothing in this list of issues takes away from the amazing job that's done each day in hotels around the world. Cleanliness is the very essence of what the hotel sells and is a prime factor in winning high ratings from agencies such as AAA. A superb level of delivery is achieved because the housekeeping crew is hardworking and carefully supervised. A lack of language skills does not lessen one's motivation; minimum salary does not mean minimum commitment. But these factors, when combined with a high rate of employee turnover, do make the management job more difficult.

Organization of the Department.   Not surprisingly, the manager of the housekeeping department is called, the *housekeeper*. Small hotels need this person to clean rooms as well as to supervise. *Working housekeeper* may then be the job title. Large hotels favor *executive housekeeper*. (Similar titles are found in the kitchen: *working chef* and *executive chef*.)

The housekeeper's location in the organizational chart is in flux more than other department heads. Responsibilities are added or deleted depending on the inclination of the general manager and the capabilities of the current housekeeper. Traditionally, housekeepers have been women who have risen in the ranks from guest-room attendants. That still holds true in small hotels that rely chiefly on menial skills. Elsewhere, the management skills of the housekeeper have become the measure of success. After all, housekeeping is the largest department in the hotel.[4] This recognition has opened the competition to professional managers, men as well as women, who have never worked the floor.

The size of the hotel, the ability of the housekeeper, and the biases of the general manager dictate the span of responsibility assigned to the position. The housekeeper may or may not have responsibility for laundry and valet. Housekeeping may or may not be responsible for the pools, outdoor ponds or other water attractions. Housekeeping may or may not be responsible for advice on guest-room design and décor. Housekeeping may or may not be responsible for some areas that might otherwise be assigned to engineering. To emphasize the importance of housekeeping (Chapter 7 treats this in detail), some GMs have the position report directly to them. Others hold to the more traditional resident-manager reporting line of Exhibit 3–1.

Duties of the Department.   Housekeeping is charged with the general cleanliness of guest rooms, corridors, and public spaces such as lobbies and restrooms. Special attendants may be assigned to employee locker rooms, guest bathhouses and spas, or other amenities special to the particular hotel. Housekeeping in the food and beverage department, including the banquet floor, is not normally the responsibility of the housekeeping department, but it may be. If not, the job is assigned to the stewar*d* (not stewar*t*), a food and beverage supervisor not shown in Exhibit 3–1.

---

[4]The Excalibur, a 4,000-room Las Vegas Hotel, has 750 persons in housekeeping. Housekeeping in Caesars Palace, another Las Vegas property, needs a computer program to track the clothing of nearly 7,000 uniformed employees.

Guest-room attendants service 12 to 18 rooms per day, taking about 30 minutes per room (see Exhibit 3–18). Check-out rooms being readied for new occupants require more time to prepare than do stay-over rooms. Some hotels use two-person teams, hoping to offset job isolation and improve productivity. Housemen are available to help with heavier work, including wall- and window-washing, carpet vacuuming and shampooing, and moving furniture. Several of these jobs, window-washing in particular, may be outsourced to specialty firms. Housemen (or special "runners") move clean and soiled linens between the maids' closets on the guest floors (see Exhibit 3–14 adjacent to room 11) and the laundry.

A wide variety of guest supplies (shampoos and other amenities), cleaning supplies (rags and cleansers), and small equipment (buckets and vacuums) necessitates careful control of inventory. Help is available from the accounting department, which usually assigns a number for each item based on occupancy patterns. Thus, so many bars of soap are ordered if occupancy for the quarter (of a year) is running at, say, 68%. Replacements, which may be purchased directly by the housekeeper or through the hotel's purchasing department (not shown in Exhibit 3–1) are charged against the housekeeper's budget.

Other departmental duties include monitoring sick guests, lost-and-found property,[5] and linen control. Counting and weighing linens (about 9 pounds per midrange room) are important if the hotel has no laundry. Outside laundries base charges on linen count and weight. Moreover, many hotels rent their linen from the laundry company. Other chores include dry cleaning drapes and bedspreads, disinfecting after animal occupancy, pest control, and the difficult cleanups that follow fire and death. Linen repair is handled by a seamstress who works in the *linen room,* the central office–complex of the housekeeper. This person also fits and maintains uniforms for staff across the entire hotel. All uniformed personnel visit the linen room to trade soiled uniforms for fresh ones.[4]

Coordination between the front desk and the housekeeping department is essential. Hundreds of persons arrive and depart daily. Rooms must be serviced quickly to placate waiting guests and maximize room revenue. A *floor supervisor* or *floor housekeeper* inspects (hence also *inspectress*) and approves rooms recently vacated and cleaned by the guest-room attendant. The room is held *on-change* by the front desk until approved by the inspection. Rooms must be reclassified from on-change to *ready* before guest occupancy. Waiting guests may be assigned to, but not housed in, on-change rooms.

Continuous training and supervision are important elements of housekeeping management. Security awareness should be high on the list of topics, because most property losses (both the hotels' and the guests') originate in guest rooms. This makes guest-room attendants and floor supervisors the first line of security defense. Unfortunately, it also places them in the first line of suspicion; they have the master keys. It's a matter of self-interest for everyone on the floor to abide by basic security principles: to watch for suspicious persons; to keep floor closets locked; to secure master keys, which access the rooms (see Chapter 14), by attaching them to their persons with retractable cords. Properly trained guest-room attendants will never, ever open doors for guests without keys or allow guests to enter open rooms. That's why security training teaches housekeepers who are working a room to block open doors with their carts. Equally important, room attendants must report suspicious activity in the corridors or unusual items (burglary tools, printing paraphernalia, etc.) in the rooms.

As we shall see in the following sections, housekeeping is but one arm of hotel security.

---

[5]The lost-and-found department of Chicago's Hyatt Regency (2,000 rooms) catalogs 113 pieces of underclothing, 31 pairs of eyeglasses, 30 cell phones and 2 sets of dentures each month. *H&MM,* November 6, 2000, p. 142.

Security.   Automation and social change are restructuring the industry's organizational charts. Reductions in the uniformed services and telephone operators have been offset by the creation of security departments.

At best, security previously had an informal structure.[6] The new focus arose, in part, because of liability claims and rising insurance costs. Street crimes have entered the lobbies and corridors of even the most fashionable hotels. More telling, security awareness has grown exponentially after the tragedies at the World Trade Center (2001), which included the loss of a Marriott hotel, and the "war on terror."

Knee-jerk decisions were part of the industry's earliest response. Some hotels refused to hold guests' baggage at the bell desk. Packages and loading-dock deliveries were subjected to inspection and X-rays. Auto trunks were examined before cars were garage parked. Baggage had to be removed directly from the guest rooms, and corridor pickups were no longer allowed, even for large tour groups.

More measured changes had been initiated long before these seminal events. The single house detective or night watchman walking a fire patrol already had been upgraded to a full-time security staff. Several widely publicized events had forced the changes. Topping the list was the 1971 in-room rape of a well-known Hollywood actress. That occurred just as the industry was promoting travel for unaccompanied women. Then came exposés by the press attacking the quality of hotel security even though crime rates in hotels are much lower than in the surrounding cities. Disastrous fires in Las Vegas focused attention on hotel fire safety, sprinkler systems, and evacuation plans. British tourists were targeted in southern Florida in a series of ugly incidents that required government intervention.

The lodging industry first responded with basic security measures and then moved toward professionalizing its security forces. Better, not merely more, security measures were implemented (see Exhibit 3–4). First came the widespread installation of electronic locks (see Chapter 14), observation ports (peepholes in corridor doors), and better fire protection, including public address outlets in guest rooms. Perimeter lighting was improved. Smoke alarms and sprinkler systems were mandated. Properties that failed to comply suffered downgrades by rating agencies such as AAA and lost their franchise affiliations.

A second phase of equipment upgrades is currently underway. It reflects improvements in security equipment of all types. CCTV (closed-circuit television) with improved video cameras enables one security person to monitor a vast array of corridors, parking areas, and public space. Special in-room alarms for the hearing and visually handicapped are being installed. Upgraded telephone and radio communications add to efficiency. Remote card readers control access to hotel facilities such as pools and garage gates. Perhaps biometric

---

[6]The house detective plays an important role in Arthur Hailey's fictional book (and later film), *Hotel.*

SECURITY CHECKLIST

Item	Advantage, Concern or Solution
Above-street elevators	Use room key to limit access to guest sleeping floors
Above-street lobbies	Allows for prelobby screening at entry level
Alarms	Loud enough to be heard over ambient noise
Atrium design	Guest-room doors and glass elevators improve visibility
Babysitters	Licensed child care
Badges	No one on convention floor without identity
Cameras	Must be monitored 24/7, including elevator-mounted cameras
Communications	Alert community members to scams, employees to issues
Counterfeit litigation	Train to identify "professional" litigants
Conventions	Identify and monitor everyone on the floor
Cribs	Require high maintenance and properly sized bedding
Crowd control	For visiting VIPs, protestors; emergencies
Data security	Frequent guest; registration; credit cards
Defibrillators	Quick response to heart attacks
Employees	All vetted; training to include security awareness and detection
Equipment	Secure sliding glass doors; inspect sprinkler and alarm systems
Exit signs	Fire exit signs at floor level for those crawling below the smoke
Fire	Directions and exits posted on inside of guest-room door
Force majeure	Convention contracting and planning for acts of God
Gambling	Organized by guest in their rooms or by employees
Garage	Electric gates; install emergency telephones
Grief counseling	For employees and guests following incidents
Guest awareness	Guest receives a security message when turning on the television
Guest-room attendants	Allow no one into the room without proper identification
Guest-room safety	Peepholes; fire and smoke alarms; inside locks that retain keys
Handicapped	Provide for needs of handicapped during emergencies
High-tech	Coded passes, parking passes, panic buttons; secure with password
Homicides	Rank third against desk clerks, after cabbies and cops
Identity theft	Rampant, so it's not a lodging-industry issue alone
In-house losses	Many attributed to employees
Inspection	Investigate any occupied guest room not cleaned for 24 hours
Keys	Unnumbered plastic types have replaced numbered metal types
Lighting	Adequate-plus everywhere, especially exterior
Locks	Automatic, large spring-activated deadbolts

Exhibit 3–4   Common law holds innkeepers to a high standard of security, requiring them to provide safe premises. This duty cannot be delegated away. Heightened security concerns among the traveling public necessitate more than just a minimum response to this security checklist.

SECURITY CHECKLIST

Item	Advantage, Concern or Solution
Master keys	Secured and accounted for, including guest room attendants
Messages	Wait until writer leaves before placing message in cubbyhole
Mutual aid	Cooperation among competitors and law enforcement agencies
Notices to guests	By means of rooming slips, in-room tents, guest-service manuals
Patrols	Random schedules; escort guests to parked cars
Pickpockets and prostitutes	Keep photo lineups available with desk and security personnel
Planning	For the unexpected emergency: cyclones, flood, hurricane, tsunami
Safety	Inspections: wet, slippery floors, bathroom fixtures, etc.
Spot checks	Identifications, baggage, packages, purveyors
Staffing	Security needed regardless of hotel size
Swindlers	Make false claims; pass bad checks and currencies; rob and steal
Teens	Balancing legal right to occupy with destructive behavior
Thefts by guests	Taking home more than memories; pranks; falsified value of loss
Training	All employees get security-awareness training
Unexpected	Foreign visitors, foreign languages; health alerts
Valuables	In-room safes
Video	Cameras strategically placed; incidents accurately recorded
Visibility	Uniformed personnel as well as security in mufti

Exhibit 3–4   *(Continued)*

room systems, which are now in the pipeline, will serve as the room keys of the future. In the meantime, simple decisions such as sharing perimeter patrols with nearby competitors produce results.

An open, candid approach to the problem has been another shift in policy. Heretofore, lodging executives rarely spoke of security. Plain-clothes personnel were favored over uniforms. Today, hotels go for visibility: uniforms or distinctive blazers in the lobbies, by the elevators—where a room key is required for access—and on patrol. Not all personnel switched to uniforms. Some dress in keeping with their prior backgrounds as federal agents, military officers and police investigators. More than ever before, hotel security people hold degrees in criminology.

Security's Charge.   Security is charged with the protection of persons, both guests and staff, and of property, both guests' and hotel's. Good security has strong market appeal; everyone wants to feel safe. The hotel's reputation suffers from security lapses, but even more so from the bungling of poorly trained personnel trying to handle a security incident. Many lawsuits originate in security's (or the desk's) failure to respond compassionately and professionally to guest injuries or losses.

Protecting persons has a higher priority than protecting property. Still, property losses far outweigh personal injuries. Employees are the greatest source of larceny, but many guests take home more than memories. Pilferage is so costly that some hotels tag property with logos containing minute circuits for tracking. Both employees and guest are petty thieves of towels and even of furnishings that are not secured. Although the term usually refers to larger, more valuable assets, "asset management" is a buzz term among hotel executives. An industry that loses $100 million a year from theft (an AH&LA estimate) must certainly focus on asset management.

Theft against guests is not all employee theft. A class of professional thieves specialize in hotels. They know how easy it is to obtain room keys from the desk or from guests' belongings by the pool. Guests are not all innocent. Some lose their valuables and accuse the hotel; other pretend a loss for insurance purposes.

Risk preparedness and crisis management have shifted the focus and structure of hotel security. Large chains have added a manager (even a vice president) of loss prevention. Petty thieves, pickpockets, and prostitutes still demand attention, but many new flash points have been added to the basic assignment of loss prevention. Security now umbrellas and trains for a whole range of emergencies, including hazardous materials; bomb threats; fire; gas leaks; terrorism; riots and crowd control; elevator failures; CPR and medical emergencies, including food poisoning; and guest lawsuits. Security has focused more attention than ever before on risk management, on workman's compensation injuries, and on compliance with ADA, Americans with Disabilities Act (see Chapter 7). In certain locales, Hong Kong for one, hotel security prepares for cyclones, tornados, and floods. Loss of electric power is a closer-to-home contingency.

Security handles plenty of other tasks as well. It helps the credit manager with lockouts and luggage liens. It handles drunks and prostitutes (*night birds*). It maintains records and logs that are vital if a case goes to court. Security interfaces with insurance companies about accidents and claims. It works with police in robbery, murder, and suicide cases. (Many local jurisdictions allow police to examine registration cards without obtaining a court warrant.)

A greater openness about security has enlisted guests in the campaign. In-room notices alert guests to first-level security: Look through the peephole; lock corridor doors, sliding doors, and adjoining-room doors. Guests are urged to use front-office or in-room safes (see Chapter 14) for valuables, since temptation and opportunity are the most recognized reasons for guest theft.

Evacuation routes are now standard postings on the inside of corridor doors. Lobby signs warn against elevator use during fires. Following examples set in the Far East, fire-exit signs have been relocated near the floor, where they are visible to guests crawling under the smoke.

Competitors have also been enlisted. Governmental agencies, which might see cooperation between competing marketing departments as restraint of trade, endorse industry-wide cooperation in security. When one hotel is hit, the entire community is alerted. The likelihood of apprehending the felon increases because thieves generally work one area before moving on. Convention and visitor bureaus are part of the network. Convention crowds of tens of thousands have always created medical emergencies and petty theft. But their very size may now make them targets for coercion. Smaller, second- or third-tier convention cities are less visible and may benefit from World-Trade-Center anxiety.

Public safety, which had never been a priority in the selection of convention sites, has become a major consideration. There is increased sensitivity to booth security. Convention halls use explosive-sniffing dogs, metal detectors, package searches, and ramp control to bolster security. Off-duty police are being recruited to act as convention security. New paragraphs are hurriedly being added to standardized convention contracts to reflect the growing concern with public safety (and with ADA). New provisions for unexpected and disruptive events, force majeure (*forz ma-zhoer*), are redefining what had been previously understood to be acts of God. Tour companies and associations are adding additional reasons for canceling group bookings or reducing room commitments without penalty.

Hotel security has moved up the organizational ladder in importance, even as other departments (bells and telephone) have been downsized. However, it functions as it always has. It acts first as a deterrent, then as a restraint, and only rarely as a police force. Hotel security must remain an iron hand in a velvet glove.

Other Departments.   The organizational chart of Exhibit 3–1 reflects the hotel manager's oversight of all the operating departments except F&B. An additional duty, acting as landlord, is not shown on 3–1. Recall from earlier chapters that hotels are real estate investments above all else. They rent space. There are numerous tenants in hotels, especially in large hotels and casino/hotels. Some tenants such as florists, beauticians, and clothing shops need retail space. Commercial firms lease office space. Airlines, auto, and tour desks require lobby space. If the business center is not a hotel unit, it, too, may be a tenant. Renters turn to the hotel manager with their issues because hotel managers are the designated landlords. Supported by hotel staff in accounting and law, they negotiate leases and rental contracts.

Thousands of people pass through the hotel each week. Medical emergencies must be anticipated and preparations put in place. That's another responsibility for the hotel manager, although the assignment may be delegated, perhaps to the concierge. Many large cities have some form of *HotelDocs*, a private medical service. The physicians come without charge to the hotel; ill travelers pay for the care as they would at home.

The *facilities manager,* if the hotel has one, is likely located within the hotel manager's control. The post reports either directly to the house manager or indirectly as a member of the engineering or housekeeping departments. A facilities manager is responsible for all of the physical plant, from the engine room to the gardens. The job oversees maintenance and repair, and new construction.

The Rooms Manager

Full-service operations require some of the hotel manager's responsibilities to be moved down the organizational line. Rooms, which might include housekeeping, is then assigned to the next management level, the *rooms manager.* Reservations, telephone, concierge, and uniformed services are among the departments reporting to the rooms manager, as is the front desk. If the management load is still too heavy, the rooms manager may delegate oversight of the desk to another line officer, the *manager of guest services*, previously called the *front-office manager.* This manager assumes control over the front desk proper, including guest-service agents (front-office clerks), credit, cashiers, mail, messages, and information. The position of guest-service manager is discussed shortly.

Few hotels need so many executives for the front of the house. This chapter recognizes that by including duties of all three positions in the job description of Exhibit 3–5. Whatever the management titles, Exhibit 3–5 illustrates the need for skill in dealing with people (both staff and guests) and signals the importance of attention to detail that is expected in the rooms division.

Room Reservations. Reservations are requests for rooms from prospective guests. The inquiries are received, processed, and confirmed by the reservations department, which is supervised by a *reservations manager.*

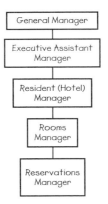

Reservations arrive by letter, fax and email and occasionally in person, across the front desk. Usually they are made by telephone. Guests may call the hotel directly, but more likely the call is made to a central reservation office (CRO) by way of a toll-free number. CROs started with chains and franchises but now include many independent agencies. (Chapter 5 explains the relationships.) With so many external reservation systems, the hotel's on-site department has been shrinking. Small hotels never had res departments, assigning the job to guest-service agents. Large hotels do the same during off-peak hours.

The importance of the guest's initial contact with the hotel dared not be overlooked. Reservationists need strong telephone personalities. They must be good salespersons, and they must have full knowledge of the hotel and the community. The quality of the reservationists' disembodied voices must close the sale, convincing the caller to commit to the room. Weak English language skills won't do it!

Reservation departments track anticipated arrivals by dates and length of stay. That information and the type of accommodations needed is sent to the front desk the day of the guest's anticipated arrival. Estimating the number of rooms sold and the number still available for sale is a major responsibility of the department. Groups and individuals must be balanced to achieve maximum occupancy. Sales, reservations, and the front desk work together to bring about a full house (100% occupancy) without overbooking (committing more rooms than are available).

Detailed reservations are maintained on a day-to-day basis for a year and in less detail for as much as three to five years. Computerization has made the job easier and decisions more accurate, as Chapter 5 explains.

The Uniformed Services. The ranks of the service department (or uniformed services, or the *bell department*) have been contracting. At one time, there were baggage

A Vallen Corporation Property

DEPARTMENT OF HUMAN RESOURCES

COMBINED JOB DESCRIPTION: Hotel Manager and Manager of Guest Services

RESPONSIBILITY: Both the Hotel Manager and the Manager of Guest Services have broad responsibility for the operation of the Rooms Division and of the Front Office.

QUALIFICATIONS

REQUIRED:
- ➤ No less than 5 years of industry experience, or 2 years with a college degree
- ➤ Previous supervisory or middle-management experience

DESIRABLE:
- ➤ Able to stand and work for long hours
- ➤ Approach problems with innovative solutions
- ➤ Demonstrate open-mindedness; willing to test ideas regardless of source
- ➤ Earned reputation for honesty; good credit rating
- ➤ Evidence good communication skills, especially verbal
- ➤ Exhibit self-confidence, poise, and an ability to retain composure under stress
- ➤ Have knowledge of computer equipment and can make minor repairs
- ➤ Is an effective listener
- ➤ Meet deadlines of all types
- ➤ Possess some level of foreign language capability
- ➤ Read professional journals and the business press
- ➤ Think quantitatively, good math skills; some understanding of accounting
- ➤ Warm guests, employees, and visitors with outgoing personality

DUTIES:
- ➤ Acknowledge and resolve complaints quickly and professionally
- ➤ Add and remove special hotel packages as demand warrants
- ➤ Approve and monitor budgets of departmental managers
- ➤ Arrange outside medical support as needed
- ➤ Assume full management responsibility during manager-on-duty assignments
- ➤ Attend and contribute to interdepartmental meetings
- ➤ Call the hotel from outside to uncover areas that warrant training
- ➤ Coordinate the duties of all staffers within the span of control
- ➤ Conduct employee appraisals, evaluations, and counseling sessions
- ➤ Develop and work within standards of industry's best practices
- ➤ Ensure that all operations fall within the guidelines of the company manual

Exhibit 3–5   The guest-service manager by whatever title (front-desk manager, rooms manager, etc.) has a broad range of responsibilities. They are described here at length because flatter organizations incorporate additional duties from positions that may no longer exist.

➤ Hire, train, supervise, and discharge, where necessary
➤ Hold security drills with the cooperation of the city's safety department
➤ Implement and manage recycling and conservation programs
➤ Increase ADR and RevPar by astute use of yield management
➤ Inspect employee dress and uniform standards
➤ Interface positively with other department heads
➤ Maintain a constructive interaction with the union and its membership
➤ Monitor the bell department's call sheets
➤ Oversee preparation of reports and recordkeeping
➤ Negotiate rentals and other leases, including charges that clear the desk
➤ Participate in and train for emergencies
➤ Post job openings and develop staff from within
➤ Prepare both oral and written reports
➤ Receive and attend to VIP guests
➤ Review and submit payroll records
➤ Safeguard arriving packages and mail
➤ Stem scams by cooperating with credit-card companies and police agencies
➤ Support the company's preferred guest program
➤ Train staff in their duties and the operation of their equipment
➤ Uncover fraud and dishonesty among employees and guests
➤ Unify the work of reservations with rooms and sales and marketing
➤ Uphold all company standards of dress, courtesy and operations
➤ Visit rest rooms to check cleanliness, supplies and appeal
➤ Walk property and note needs of repairs and maintenance

Exhibit 3–5   *(Continued)*

porters, pages, transportation clerks, and operators for both guest and service elevators. What remains is organized around a few bellpersons and the occasional door attendant.

Changes in travel habits and licensing requirements have eliminated the service department's role in arranging travel. Wheeled suitcases and lighter luggage allow guests to handle their own baggage. Self-service is part of the American culture. Guests who have handled their own luggage throughout their travels expect to do so up a few floors on an elevator. Less demand for service translates into fewer tips, less job appeal, and a smaller workforce.

Bringing ice to a room, a time-honored assignment for generating tips, is no longer a "front" (tip-earning) call. In-room refrigerators and floor ice machines reinforce the idea of self-service. Group arrivals and departures are among the department's best moneymakers. Sales departments add a contractual charge to group bookings for each bag in and each bag out. Funds are collected and distributed to the bells whether tour guests use the service or not.

Management cost-cutting has also contributed to smaller departments. Today, every employee is paid a minimum wage, whereas tips alone constituted the salary of an earlier era. Reducing staff cuts labor costs and fringe benefits, which add as much as one-third more to labor costs. So the hotel that services the entrance door around the clock is rare, and the motor hotel without any of the uniformed services is the norm. In urban properties with separate parking, someone needs to be at the door to handle garaging and other auto services. Few urban hotels own their own parking spaces. They lease the space or have an outside contractor take a parking concession. (This outsourcing is still another explanation for today's smaller uniformed staff.)

If bell services are available, they will be the guest's first contact with the hotel. Whether it's a door attendant, a bellperson, or the airport van driver (also a member of the department), the first impression will stick. The condition of the uniform, the personality of the individual, and the quality of the greeting tells the new arrival about the condition of the hotel and the level of its service (see Exhibit 8–16). In this respect, the industry's human resources departments usually do a better job hiring staff for the door and the bells than for the van.

With guest arrivals and departures as their main function, bellpersons can be scheduled at a ratio of 1 bellhop per 65 anticipated hourly arrivals/departures. If they exist at all in small hotels, the bellstaff may also handle room service, lobby cleaning, and pool maintenance along with their other duties.

The title of the modern service department head is *manager of services,* or *superintendent of services,* not nearly as romantic as the more traditional terms, *bell captain,* or its shortened version, *captain.*

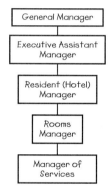

Some services that were previously handled by the captain have migrated to the desk of the concierge. With them has gone a flow of money, since tour bookings and auto rentals represent a commission to the desk that books them.

Concierge.   Not many U.S. hotels have a concierge. The position is limited to larger, upscale properties. It is more popular in small hotels overseas, especially in France.[7] Great Britain calls the front desk the front hall, so there the concierge becomes the head hall porter. Like a French idiom, translating the nuances of the job into Americanese leaves something to be desired. Many guests are uncertain what the position does, let alone how to pronounce it (*kon syerzh*).

The word comes from the Latin *con servus,* meaning "with service." Other translations offered are "fellow slave" or, more to the point, "building guard." According to the French, the *Comte de Cierges* (Count of Cierge) was in charge of the prisons, making him the keeper of the keys under the French monarchs.[8] Thus, the European concierge appeared as a door attendant (building guard) and from that to the keeper of the keys, porter, and provider of various services.

---

[7]The International Union of Concierges was founded in Paris in 1952, the U.S. chapter in 1978. Members wear the Golden Keys (Les Clefs d'Or), their professional symbol.

[8]The prison in Paris that housed Marie Antoinette during the French Revolution, the Palais de Justice, is called the Conciergerie prison.

The U.S. keeper of the door, the lobby concierge (see Exhibit 3–6), provides a variety of information and personal services, none of which involves keys. Travel assistance, messages, tickets, and reservations to a range of events outside the property, babysitters, language translation, secretarial sources, and more fall within the concierge's duties. Guests ask the concierge to arrange pet care; to find extra chairs; to search for lost items; to recommend a hair stylist; to arrange for flower delivery, or an attending physician (see Exhibit 3–7).

Exhibit 3–6   Pleasant working conditions and an aura of capable service highlight this lobby photo of a concierge at work. Some hotels limit concierge service to a specially designated concierge floor, which offers extra services at higher rates. *Courtesy of the Wynfrey Hotel, Birmingham, Alabama.*

A...	as in	Art supplies and restoration
B...	as in	Babysitting services for vacationing parents
C...	as in	Churches for all denominations
D...	as in	Dinner reservations at sold-out restaurants
E...	as in	Errand and courier services for speedy delivery
F...	as in	Flowers for that special occasion
G...	as in	Galleries for antiques and arts
H...	as in	Helicopter services
I...	as in	Interpreters for an international symposium
J...	as in	Jewelers from whom one can buy with confidence
K...	as in	Kennels for a cherished pet
L...	as in	Libraries for source materials
M...	as in	Maps to navigate the city or the subway
N...	as in	Newspapers from distant cities and foreign countries
O...	as in	Orchestra tickets at the last minute
P...	as in	Photographers for that special occasion
Q...	as in	Queries that no one else can answer
R...	as in	Restaurants of every specialty
S...	as in	Scuba diving sites and services
T...	as in	Transportation: air; auto; bus; limo; taxi; train
U...	as in	Umbrellas on a rainy day
V...	as in	Virtual reality equipment
W...	as in	Wedding chapels
X...	as in	Xeroxing a last-minute report
Y...	as in	Yoga demonstrations and instructions
Z...	as in	Zoo directions for an outing with the children

Exhibit 3–7   Concierge service runs the gamut from A to Z.

As hotels retrench some services and automate others, the post of concierge becomes increasingly important. Guests can no longer turn to transportation desks, floor clerks, and elevator operators for questions and services. Those jobs no longer exist. Many of the gratuities that previously went to the uniformed staff have been redirected to the concierge desk. For services rendered, a concierge may be tipped by the guest and commissioned by the service company (theater, rentals, etc.).

A play on words has created the new job of *compcierge*, in which *comp* stands for computer. A compcierge comes in two forms. The first is a *technology butler:* a technician or information technology (IT) expert who provides technology assistance to guests and conventioneers (see Exhibit 3–1). The second form of compcierge is a computerized console that provides information about the local scene. Guests turn to the computer for directional information, theaters, restaurants, and similar listings. A computerized compcierge can stand alone or support a concierge's desk by freeing the live concierge for more complicated services.

The Concierge Floor.   The concierge floor is one amenity not discussed in Chapter 2. It is a special accommodation available at a premium room rate or made available without charge to frequent guest members. Included among the extras are free continental breakfasts and evening cocktails. Terrycloth bathrobes, shoeshines, larger guest rooms and expedited arrival and departure procedures are other add-ons.

Access to the floor is limited and requires a special elevator key. The concierge is usually seated by the elevators adding security, as *floor clerks* (see Exhibit 3–14) did before World War II siphoned off all the labor. In this respect, the concierge floor is a throwback to the original intent of the concierge: keeper of the keys. The entry of Asian hotel companies into the U.S. market added another variation, the floor butler or floor steward. Providing around-the-clock coverage, the floor butler helps with more personal services, such as unpacking. Guests summon the butler with room bells or switches on the bed console.

All upscale chains offer a concierge floor. Hilton calls its floor "The Towers," after the famed Waldorf=Astoria Towers, one of Hilton's trademarks. Hyatt uses "Regency"; Radisson uses "Plaza Club." Add these names to those of the frequent guest programs and mix in some chain brands. The result is confusion; no one even tries to remember which name is which.

The Telephone Department.   Hotels have telephones, lots of telephones. Guest rooms may have two and another in the bath. Even as the number of instruments has grown, the size of the telephone department has shrunk. Computerization and social change (everyone carries a personal telephone) have downsized the department. The changes are similar to those taking place in the bells department.

There are fewer telephone operators because local and long-distance calls are handled by direct-dial, automatic equipment. Similarly, calls between guest rooms or from guest rooms to hotel departments, room service for example, no longer require an operator. Electronic billing automatically records the telephone company's charges on the guest's electronic bill, eliminating the old position of *charge operator*.

In no other department of the hotel has the introduction of costly and complex equipment been so rapid and so complete, and worked so well. Supervising the few employees

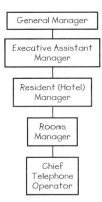

left in the department is the head telephone operator, called the *chief operator* or *telephone supervisor.* Depending on size, there might be an assistant or shift supervisor.

Operators may still answer incoming calls and direct them to their proper destinations. The caller's sole contact with the property is the voice of the telephone operator, so incoming calls must be handled professionally and pleasantly. Some hotels still have incoming messages taken by the operator. More and more, the operator doesn't answer incoming calls and doesn't take messages. Incoming calls are handled by an electronic menu from which the caller chooses a service.

If the service chosen involves a guest or guest room, the electronic voice says, "Press 1." The operator intercedes to protect guest security. Hotels never give out the room or telephone numbers of registered guests. Automation takes over again once the operator connects the incoming call to the guest's room. The system allows the caller to leave a message on the guest's telephone mailbox. Direct access assures both privacy and accuracy. Telephone operators no longer transcribe messages by trying to interpret the many accents that make up the calling public. Guests no longer look quizzically at an operator's scribbled handwriting. Automated telephone systems provide better service despite the annoyance of listening to the electronic operator.

Even morning wake-up calls have been automated, although the number of wake-up calls has been reduced by furnishing an alarm clock in each guest room. Some guests still prefer the assurance of human intervention. The telephone operator provides it with a morning wake-up call, but even that is automated.

Manager of Guest Services

One final level of management is needed for our full-service-hotel illustration, the *manager of guest services.* That title has replaced the older, more stodgy one, *front-office manager.* Large hotels have *assistant managers* supporting this position during each shift (see Exhibit 3–1). Or a senior *guest-service agent* (formerly a senior *room clerk*) might cover. With so complete an organizational structure, job responsibilities grow narrower and narrower. Guest-service managers control the immediate front-office staff, who are pivotal to the rooms department's assignment.

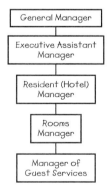

Structure of the Front Office.   Physically, the front office is an easily identifiable area of the lobby. Functionally, it is much less so despite constant reference to it as the "hub" and "heart" of the hotel. The overuse of such terms should not detract from the real importance of the front office. It is, in fact, the nerve center of guest activity: the very face of the hotel. Through it flow communications with every other department; from it emanate instructions for the service of the guest; to it come charges for final billing and settlement.

The front office is important because room sales earn about two-thirds of the hotel's total revenue (see Exhibit 3–3). Room sales total more than food, beverage, and telephone sales combined. Almost 100% of revenue comes from room sales at budget hotels. For others, much of the food and beverage sales originate in meetings and conventions, whose search for site selections begins with rooms. Furthermore, rooms is a more profitable department than are the other operating units. Each room-sale dollar produces about $0.73 in departmental profit. Profit for food and beverage combined averages to about $0.21.

Guests relate to the front office, and this adds to its importance. Guests who rarely see their housekeepers, who never see the cook, who deal with sales only on occasion, know the hotel by its desk. They are received at the desk and they depart from the desk. It is toward the desk that guests direct complaints and from the desk that they expect remedies. Guest identification, as much as profit or interdepartmental dependence, accounts for management's overriding concern with the front office.

Better to define the front office as a bundle of duties and guest services rather than as a fixed area located behind the lobby desk. Some divisions of the front office—reservations, for example—can be located elsewhere without affecting their membership in the front-office structure. Computerization's instant communication has reduced the need for all front-office segments to be within physical hailing distance of one another.

Someone once said that the front office was so named because it was close to the front door. Simple enough, except new terminology, *guest-service area*, has been adopted to emphasize the real role of the desk. By extension, the front-office manager has become the manager of guest services (see Exhibit 3–5) and room clerks are now known as guest-service agents.

Working Hours. Hotels never close. The legal definition of a hotel requires that they do not. Work schedules at the desk must accommodate that requirement, but only a few of the other departments schedule around the clock. Desk schedules must also provide for the peaks and valleys that bring daily, sometimes hourly, fluctuations to the volume at the desk.

The Shift (or Watch). Most desk employees work an eight-hour shift, which creates a good mathematical balance of three shifts per 24-hour day. The workweek is five days, with two successive days off. Sickness, vacations, and days off are covered by others, some of whom work part time. Although there are variations, especially in resort areas that have special wage-and-hour laws, the model follows that of other industries:

Day shift	7:30 AM–3:30 PM
Swing shift	3:30 PM–11:30 PM
Graveyard shift	11:30 PM–7:30 AM

The day shift is preferred by most employees because it follows the usual workday. Bellpersons opt for the swing shift, when arrivals and tips are the heaviest. Even senior front-office clerks choose the swing shift if tips are customary, as they especially are at resorts.

The graveyard shift has the least guest activity, but it is during this shift that the night audit is completed. The night audit is more specialized than the other front-office duties. Thus, night auditors cannot take advantage of the general policy that allows senior employees to select their shifts. Few workers prefer graveyard, which is one explanation for the shortage of night auditors.

A special effort is needed to maintain morale during the graveyard watch. Graveyard work should be covered by formal policies. Employees must know that they are not locked into a career of night work. They are rotated when openings appear in the more desirable shifts. In the meantime, salary supplements are paid for night work, and careful attention is paid to night meals in those hotels where the kitchen staff tends to short-change the night crew's menu.

Rotating personnel and shifts, wherever possible and where union contracts allow, builds camaraderie and morale. It also reduces the chance of collusion, which increases when the same staff always works together. Sometimes day and swing shifts are switched en masse. If so, the switch is made once each month as employees' days off allow. Shifts are not changed on two successive work days because rest time is inadequate. A guest-service agent who closed the swing shift at 11:30 at night would need to be back for the day shift at 7:30 the following morning. Large city commutes makes this impractical; state labor laws make it illegal. Shift rotations should follow the clock: day, swing, graveyard; day, swing and so on.

Cashiers, clerks, and supervisors usually change shifts in concert. Overlapping arrivals and departures by, say, 15 minutes increases continuity. A seamless transition is lost if everyone leaves and arrives simultaneously. If there are several persons in each job, individual shifts should be staggered by 15 minutes. If there is only one staff member, complimentary jobs could be overlapped. The cashier might change at 3:15 PM and the guest-service agent at 3:30 PM, for example.

THE SPLIT SHIFT.   Employees working a split shift report for work, get off, and return for a second shift the same day (see below, Employee A). Wage-and-hour laws, unionization, distance, and the difficulty of finding staff have eliminated the split shift. Isolated, seasonal resorts may still use this schedule if labor laws exempt seasonal workers and commuting distance is not an issue. It isn't where seasonal staff lives at the resort. Split shifts are not just for the desk. Where used, kitchen, dining room and housekeeping also schedule that way.

Employee A	7:00 AM–12:30 PM
Employee B	12:30 PM–6:30 PM
Employee A	6:30 PM–11:00 PM
Night auditor	11:00 PM–7:00 AM

The split shift offers a real advantage for a small property that has but one person covering the desk. That employee need not be relieved for meals. He or she eats either before or after the shift. Where the split schedule is in place, staff members rotate daily between the A and B positions (see schedule above).

FORECAST SCHEDULING.   Building work schedules for a large staff is part science and part art. Both improve with experience. The starting point is a forecast of room occupancy. The schedule builder gets this from the reservations department (see Chapter 4). Personnel needs can be envisioned once the daily number of rooms occupied has been forecasted. New computer programs help match room demand to staff numbers, even accommodating individual employees preferences for days off.

Each hotel has its own schedule design and logistics. Does cross training prepare individuals to fill several positions? Are bells supported with a concierge's desk? Do most rooms fill from walk-ins or from reservation business? Does housekeeping change linen daily even for stay-overs? Answering such questions enables management to set numerical standards for each department. The ratios vary with the size of the house and the level of luxury (ADR). If, as suggested earlier, one bellhop is needed per 65 anticipated hourly arrivals (or one guest-room attendant is needed per 13 rooms, or one guest-service agent is needed per 60 rooms occupied), the total labor force is quickly calculated. Experience for each house then dictates what hours or overlapping times to schedule the crews, taking into account the mix of full-time and part-time staff.

With forecasting and advance scheduling, employees are given their days off during the slowest part of the week. Several may be off on one day, and none on a busy day. Part-time personnel can cover peak periods, or hours of the workday may be staggered. Each technique is designed to minimize payroll costs and maximize desk coverage when required.

The amount of help needed varies during the day and even within the same shift. Cashiers are busy in the morning handling check-outs and are less busy in the afternoon when the guest-service agents are busy with arrivals. Cashiers at a commercial hotel are slower on Mondays, when agents are busier, and busier on Thursdays, when agents are slower. An employee can be hired as a cashier for some days and as a clerk for others. Computer terminals are interchangeable, so agents can respond to traffic patterns, acting as either receptionist or cashier. Two job descriptions are then reduced to one.

Design of the Lobby.   Lobby use and lobby design have gone through several roller-coaster phases. Today, even economy and midscale properties are rethinking their lobby environment. Computerization of the front desk, which is within the lobby, accounts for part of the change. Information technology reduced the mountain of paper and much of the clutter that typified the old. It also shrunk the amount of floor space that the desk required and with it the old-fashioned, bank-teller look. Today's desk is compact and efficient (see Exhibit 3–8).

Exhibit 3–8   The typical front desk of a medium-sized hotel is open to encourage a sense of welcome and enhanced security. The work level is lower than the desk level to reduce worker fatigue and encourage guest–staff eye contact.

Exhibit 3–9   Atria have revitalized stodgy lobbies into dining spots and social centers without destroying their basic services: registration; baggage; telephones; restrooms; and seating. Design elements, including lighting, differentiate the zones. Hyatt Hotels pioneered atrium architecture. *Courtesy of Hyatt Regency Atlanta, Atlanta, Georgia.*

New designs brought renewed activity to once sterile lobbies; many had no chairs! Action and eye appeal have recreated the lobby (see Exhibits 3–9 and 3–10) into the important gathering place that it was a century ago.[9]

A well-designed lobby appears as a town center. Modern lobbies are great for networking. Small furniture groupings assure privacy for cell-phone use and intimacy for cocktail gatherings. Big tables, large sofas, and heavy, overstuffed chairs have been replaced with smaller, more comfortable and eye-appealing settings. Women travelers prefer a lobby bar over a lounge bar, so hotels have enlarged their offerings with food and beverage service, afternoon tea, and continental breakfast. Adding an unusual feature or exciting landmark creates a popular meeting place for appointments. All this and jazz bands too fit within lobbies that are structured around the basics: baggage, desk, food and beverage, restrooms, seating and telephones.

---

[9]President Ulysses Grant (1869–1877) freqently walked from the White House to the Hotel Willard, now an InterContinental Hotel, to have a cigar and a drink. Petitioners, waiting to argue for their constituents, hovered in the lobby to catch the president—hence the term *lobbyists*.

Exhibit 3–10   The familiar front desk of Exhibit 3–8 gives way to the open lobby where registration pods increase staff accessibility, making the lobby more hospitable. *Courtesy of Delta Hotels, Toronto, Ontario, Canada.*

New or old, the lobby must provide easy access to the front office. Although the front office's architectural footprint has shrunk, new designs and images have made the desk more user-friendly than ever before.

Design of the Desk.   The standard front-desk counter is about 45 inches high and approximately 40 to 42 inches across. The working space on the employee's side of the desk is lower by 6 inches or so (see Exhibit ⋮ ⋮ ⋮ ⋮ ⋮ the height of the workspace enables the guest-service agent to carry out ⋮ equipment below the guest's eye level, impro⋮ ties. The desk's running length is determine⋮ or so to as much as 100 feet or more in so⋮

Informal registration pods, illustrated⋮ front desks represented by Exhibit 3–8. Po⋮ tion because conversion costs are high. Staf⋮ new ones, have not adopted the pod desig⋮ across from one another. In contrast, the a⋮ appears almost adversarial.

Pods enable agents to walk into the⋮ ify directions. Registration pods have imp⋮ the industry's response to the Americar⋮ the new design develops desk personn⋮ doing, it changes the ambience of the d⋮

Some front desks are nudged into lobby corners; others become the lobby's focal point. Whichever it is, the security of both employees and guests must be balanced with the desk's design and location. Employees, especially cashiers, must be secured (see Exhibit 3–11). Guest security is enhanced when front-office personnel have an unobstructed view of the lobby and elevator doors. Atrium hotels add a small bit of extra security because all entry doors are in full view (see Exhibit 3–9).

Internal communication is another consideration in the design. Despite the many new marvels in telecommunications, face-to-face interaction at the desk remains an important means of handling the day's business. Most designs center the guest-service agent at the hub of activity (see Exhibits 3–11 and 3–12). From this advantageous position, agents coordinate the flow of business from reservations to departures. Groups are an exception. Hotels with large tour groups (sometimes called "tour houses") often build satellite lobbies where busloads of arrivals can be accommodated without interfering with normal front-office traffic.

The desk must meet two objectives. It must provide a practical workspace and must incorporate an aesthetic design. Using lighting, form, and materials, architects must convey the image of the hotel: comfortable, open, organized, and professional—the very traits of guest-service agents themselves.

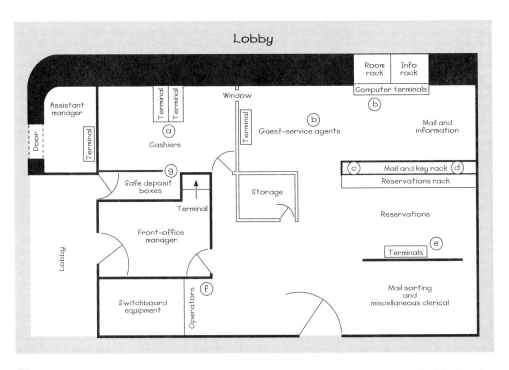

Exhibit 3–11   This schematic illustrates the design and, with Exhibit 3–12, highlights the functions of a typical front desk. Match the job description throughout the chapter with their locations at this desk. Letter references key together the two illustrations, 3–11 and 3–12. Not to scale.

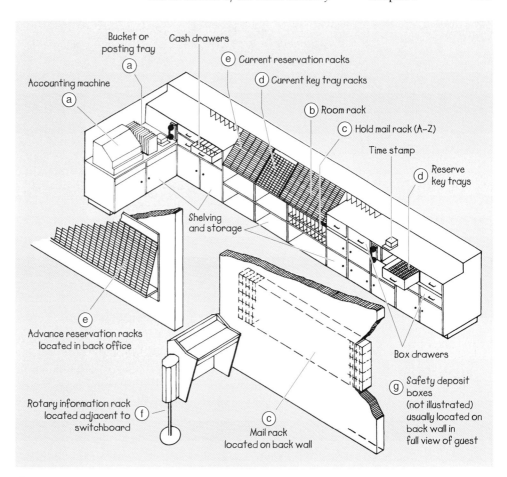

Exhibit 3–12   Similar to Exhibit 3–11, this illustration points up the tasks of the desk and identifies the relative locations of the staff. Computers have replaced the physical items identified as a, b, d, e, and f, but not their functions. Not to scale.

Guest-Service Agents.   Different titles have attempted to describe the importance of the next organizational level. *Room clerk* and *front-office clerk*, America's long-time favorites, have been replaced with *guest-service agent*. *Receptionist* is the term favored outside the United States because elsewhere the function of this position is called *reception,* not registration.

Titles aside, guest-service agents have a host of duties concentrated in four functions: room sales, guest relations, records, and coordination (see Exhibit 3–13). Agents bring together the commitments made by reservations, the availability delivered by housekeeping, the minor repairs that so annoy guests, and the billing and collection required by accounting. Room clerks adjust minor problems and buffer management from the first blasts of major complaints. They are expected to achieve the company's ADR goals by selling up (see Chapter 8). Thus, the guest-service agent is part salesperson, part psychologist, part accountant, and part manager.

As the hotel's first-line employees, agents must carry out policies that have been established—too often without input from the desk—at higher levels.

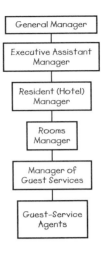

General Manager

Executive Assistant Manager

Resident (Hotel) Manager

Rooms Manager

Manager of Guest Services

Guest-Service Agents

Exhibit 3–13   The U.S. Department of Labor holds to the older *Desk Clerk* nomenclature rather than the more modern *Guest-Service Agent* terminology in this excerpt from the Bureau of Labor Statistics, *Occupational Outlook Handbook, 2006–07 Edition.* (Other job descriptions can be found in the *Dictionary of Occupational Titles.*) *Source: http://www.bls .gov/oco/ocos132 .htm.*

JOB TITLE: Hotel, Motel, and Resort Desk Clerks

NATURE OF THE WORK

Hotel, motel, and resort desk clerks perform a variety of services for guests of hotels, motels, and other lodging establishments. Regardless of the type of accommodation, most desk clerks have similar responsibilities. They register arriving guests, assign rooms, and check out guests at the end of their stay. They also keep records of room assignments and other registration-related information on computers. When guests check out, desk clerks prepare and explain the charges, as well as process payments.

Front-desk clerks always are in the public eye and typically are the first line of customer service for a lodging property. Their attitude and behavior greatly influence the public's impressions of the establishment. And as such, they always must be courteous and helpful. Desk clerks answer questions about services, checkout times, the local community, or other matters of public interest. Clerks also report problems with guest rooms or public facilities to members of the housekeeping or maintenance staff for them to correct the problems. In larger hotels or in larger cities, desk clerks may refer queries about area attractions to a concierge and may direct more complicated questions to the appropriate manager.

In some smaller hotels and motels, where smaller staffs are employed, clerks may take on a variety of additional responsibilities, such as bringing fresh linens to rooms, which usually are performed by employees in other departments of larger lodging establishments. In the smaller places, desk clerks often are responsible for all front-office operations, information, and services. For example, they may perform the work of a bookkeeper, advance reservation agent, cashier, laundry attendant, and telephone switchboard operator.

WORKING CONDITIONS

Hotels are open around the clock creating the need for night and weekend work. Extended hours of operation also afford the many part-time job seekers an opportunity to find work in these establishments, especially on evenings and late-night shifts or on weekends and holidays. About half of all desk clerks work a 35 to 40 hour week—most of the rest work fewer hours—so the jobs are attractive to persons seeking part-time work or jobs with flexible schedules. Most clerks work in areas that are clean, well lit, and relatively quiet, although lobbies can become crowded and noisy when busy. Many hotels have stringent dress guidelines for desk clerks.

Desk clerks may experience particularly hectic times during check-in and check-out times or incur the pressures encountered when dealing with convention guests or large groups of tourists at one time. Moreover, dealing with irate guests can be stressful. Computer failures can further complicate an already busy time and add to stress levels. Hotel desk clerks may be on their feet most of the time and may occasionally be asked to lift heavy guest luggage.

TRAINING, OTHER QUALIFICATIONS, AND ADVANCEMENT

Hotel, motel, and resort desk clerks deal directly with the public, so a professional appearance and a pleasant personality are important. A clear speaking voice and fluency in English also are essential, because these employees talk directly with hotel guests and the public and frequently use the telephone or public-address systems. Good spelling and computer literacy are needed, because most of the work involves use of a computer. In addition, speaking a foreign language fluently is increasingly helpful, because of the growing international clientele of many properties.

Most hotel, motel, and resort desk clerks receive orientation and training on the job. Orientation may include an explanation of the job duties and information about the establishment, such as the arrangement of sleeping rooms, availability of additional services, such as a business or fitness center, and location of guest facilities, such as ice and vending machines, restaurants and other nearby retail stores. New employees learn job tasks through on-the-job training under the guidance of a supervisor or an experienced desk clerk. They often receive additional training on interpersonal or customer service skills and on how to use the computerized reservation, room assignment, and billing systems and equipment. Desk clerks typically continue to receive instruction on new procedures and on company policies after their initial training ends.

Formal academic training generally is not required so many students take jobs as desk clerks on evening or weekend shifts or during school vacation periods. Most employers look for people who are friendly and customer-service oriented, well groomed, and display the maturity and self confidence to demonstrate good judgment. Desk clerks, especially in high-volume and higher-end properties should be quick-thinking, show initiative, and be able to work as a member of a team. Hotel managers typically look for these personal characteristics when hiring first-time desk clerks, because it is easier to teach company policy and computer skills than personality traits.

Large hotel and motel chains may offer better opportunities for advancement than small, independently owned establishments. The large chains have more extensive career ladder programs and may offer desk clerks an opportunity to participate in a management training program. Also, the Educational Institute of the American Hotel and Motel Association offers home-study or group-study courses in lodging management, which may help some obtain promotions more rapidly.

Exhibit 3–13   *(Continued)*

Guest-service agents face a wide range of difficult person-to-person encounters. Most of the issues originate in other departments. The agent is usually unaware of the problem and is not prepared to solve it. Guest complain that: "The laundry lost my shirt." Or: "My important papers are missing from the dining room." Or: "Housekeeping never made the room last night."

Unhappy guests focus on the guest-service agent. Where else would they go but to a "guest-service" agent! The situation is frustrating and stressful because the solution is more often than not out of the agent's control. Rigid policy curbs the clerk's discretion. (Chapter 7 discusses employee empowerment, which cushions this limitation.) For many issues agents must communicate with housekeeping, plead with engineering, find someone in food and beverage, or implement an arrangement made by sales and marketing. Decisions do not come promptly, and waiting guests are not patient.

Flatter and flatter organizations, which eliminate intervening management positions, always leave the guest-service agent in place. Unfortunately, this implication of importance is not always accompanied by a balance of authority or by a salary that compensates for the importance of the job done. Many years ago, a well-known hotelier noted that hotels spend large sums on building design and upgrade but never improve the position of the hotel's most visible employee, the guest-service agent/cashier.

Cashiers.   Front-office cashiers work at the desk, but report to accounting, either to the *controller* or to the *general cashier*. Contrary to a basic rule of organization that everyone should have but one boss, cashiers have a second reporting line. Their location at the desk also puts them under the guest-service manager's control.

Reorganization of the industry's front offices has blended the duties of the cashier into those of the guest-service agent. Both jobs are being rolled into one position except in large hotels. For money matters, the reporting line still flows through the general cashier.

Posting charges (recording them on guest bills), presenting final statements, resolving protests by departing guests, and handling cash and credit-card transactions are the major duties of hotel cashiers. Other services once included check cashing and loans—that is, cash advances. Changes in the way hotels do business have eliminated these banking services. Not only do hotels refuse to cash checks, they are unlikely to accept them in payment of the bill. Cash loans are limited to small payments made for guests; paid-outs for employee tips are the most common. Even guest service to safe deposit boxes (see Exhibit 3–11) has diminished as in-room safes have been installed (see Chapter 14).

As the guest-service agent is usually the guest's first contact with the front office, so the cashier is usually the guest's last. At one time, the cashier's window was a major source of guest irritation. Long lines and lengthy delays were the causes. Not so any more. Computerization allows guests to use one of several forms of express check-out (see Chapter 13). As guests became accustomed to and began to prefer checking out themselves, and as hotels reined in the various financial services that the cashier had previously rendered, it became possible to eliminate separate cashier positions. Many hotels have done so.

THE BUILDING STRUCTURE

This chapter focuses on two constructions: the organizational structure and the structure of the building. Every hotel offers both guest rooms and the organization to deliver those rooms. But the similarity ends there. The differences in the physical buildings and the differences in the delivery systems distinguish one property from another. It is these differences that segment the industry into its many parts.

The Old versus the New

There is a huge variation between hotels built before the mid-century and those built since, especially hotels of very recent vintage. Today's hotels require more land—have a larger *footprint* in real estate terms—because they are more open and because guest rooms are much larger. Exhibits 3–14 and 3–15 illustrate the differences. Some very famous hotels in the old design still exist. Best known among them are New York's Waldorf=Astoria (1931), Chicago's Drake (1920), and Cleveland's Renaissance (1918).

Exhibit 3–15's photo illustrates the exterior of the modern hotel (so does Exhibit 1–10). The rectangular room shape viewed in 3–15 is another modern-day standard. Compare rooms in Exhibit 3–15 to the strange shapes and sizes of Exhibit 3–14, especially rooms 30 to 36. It took a dozen different room rates to distinguish the accommodations of the old hotel. Three to five rates do the same job today, easing the desk's task of quoting rates and assigning rooms.

Just as room shapes have been standardized, room sizes have increased over the decades. Size is measured by square footage, and square footage translates into cost of construction. Higher construction costs obviously lead to higher room rates (see Building Cost Rate, Chapter 9). Although modern rooms are larger overall than those of 50 years ago, hotels of different classes still offer different sized rooms.

The Old: Inside Rooms.   Rooms 58 to 97 in Exhibit 3–14 form a U-shape of inside rooms around a *light court*. As illustrated, inside rooms are enclosed by wings of the building. The view is downward toward the roof on the lower floor, which is often dirty and unsightly. Inside rooms are affected by the changing position of the sun, which casts shadows into these rooms even early in the day. Inside rooms are used no longer. They have been upgraded to the outside rooms of Exhibit 3–15 just as the semiprivate (shared) baths of the 1930s have been replaced by today's private, often luxurious, baths.

The New: Suites and All-Suites.   The traditional hotel suite is comprised of a living room (or sitting room) and one or more sleeping rooms. A small, modern suite is illustrated in Exhibit 3–16 and by room numbers 72 to 74 in an older hotel (Exhibit 3–14). The suite's traditional definition, more than one room, is being challenged by modern designs. Some assign suite terminology to just one room if a 600–700 square foot facility is divided into "two rooms" either by a low wall or by strategically placed furniture. Holiday Inn's Staybridge Suites accomplishes this with a right-angle building design that separates the living area and the sleeping portion.

Larger suites add second and third bedrooms and additional living space. Very luxurious accommodations include kitchens and formal dining rooms, saunas or swimming pools, and even libraries. Most basic suites contain wet bars and several bathrooms. Balconies and patios (*lanai* suites) are common amenities. In the proper climate, suites have fireplaces. For a truly opulent experience, some hotels, especially casino hotels, offer two-floor suites. So does America's heartland: The two-floor suite of the Netherland Plaza offers a panoramic view of Cincinnati.[10] Such amenities stretch the average 300-square-foot room upward to 1,500 square feet (approximately 140 square meters) and more.

---

[10]The two-floor Governor's Suite of Miami Beach's Fontainebleau is 20,000 square feet (the size of a dozen average homes) and has five bathrooms.

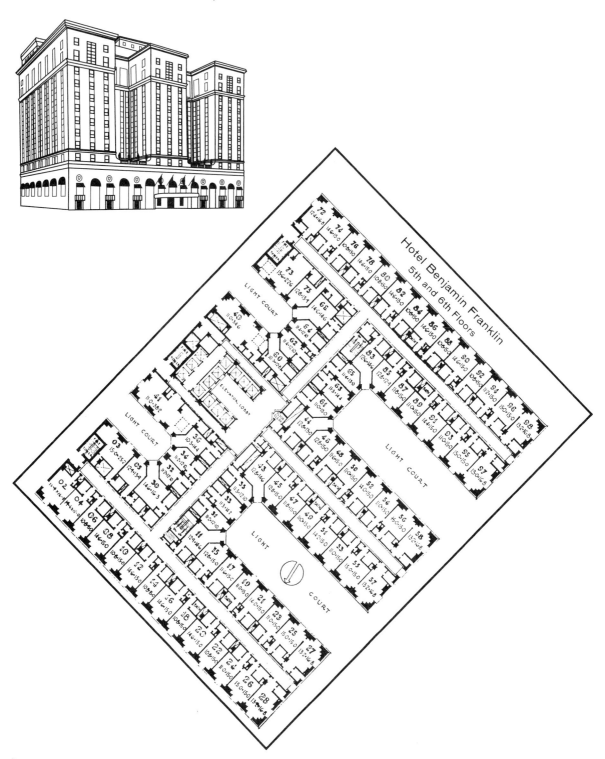

Exhibit 3–14 Typical of hotel construction between 1925 and 1945, this once upscale, commercial hotel had guest rooms smaller than today's budget inns. Light courts designed to maximize land use created oddly shaped rooms such as 44, 61, and 62. Note the floor closets (for linens and engineering supplies) on the corridor corners adjacent to rooms 11, 30, 66 and others and the floor-clerk's position opposite the elevators.

The Sofitel is a commercial hotel providing its business center and banquet/meeting facilities on the 3rd floor. Special stairwells and extra elevators service the banquet floor, but for security not the sleeping floors.

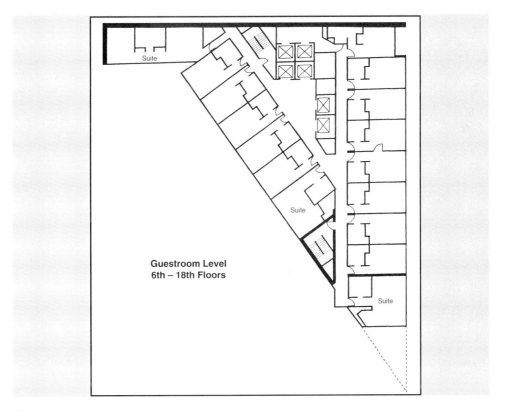

Exhibit 3-15   The open design of the 21st century urban hotel has replaced the light courts of its predecessors (Exhibit 3–14) and standardized the shape and size of guest rooms. *Courtesy of the Sofitel Chicago Water Tower Hotel, Chicago, Illinois.*

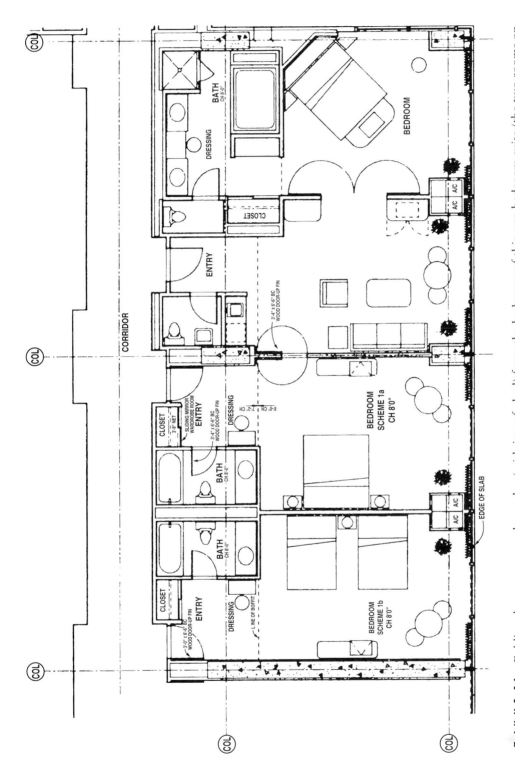

Exhibit 3–16 Folding doors separate the parlor (with its sofa bed) from the bedroom of this one-bedroom suite (the two rooms on the right side of the exhibit). On the left are two adjoining, but not connecting, rooms. The suite can be enlarged to include a second bedroom by unlocking the connecting door. Note the back-to-back plumbing and air-conditioning (A/C) shafts. *Courtesy of the Mirage Hotel, Las Vegas, Nevada.*

Speciality suites are often named instead of numbered. *Bridal suite, presidential suite,* and *penthouse suite* are popular designations. Historical figures or local references may be used to emphasize the hotel's theme: *The Kit Carson Suite,* for example.

All-suite hotels are another product altogether. They are designed for a different market and a different use (see Exhibit 3–17). All-suites compete against standard hotel rooms, not against hotel suites. To compensate for the extra square footage offered by the all-suite unit, public space is reduced. Forty percent of the typical hotel building is allocated to service areas. The all-suite hotel cuts that figure back by at least half.

All-suite and standard hotels alike employ a building technique that was invented by Ellsworth Statler in 1923. Back-to-back utility shafts reduce the amount of runs for piping, electrical, heating, and communication lines. There is economy in both the initial construction and continuing maintenance. It is not always possible, but kitchenettes, baths, and wet bars should be so constructed. Exhibits 3–14, 3–15, and 3–16 show the baths back to back.

Corner Rooms.   Corner rooms are the most desirable rooms on the floor. They provide double exposure—that is, they face two directions—and therefore command a premium price. To enhance the rate differential, corner rooms get preferential treatment from the architects. They are usually larger and are often part of a suite (see Exhibit 3–15). Corner rooms are an integral part of older hotels because the sharp angles of the floor plans create them (see Exhibit 3–14). Modern hotels have fewer building corners and thus fewer corner rooms. Of course, round buildings, and some hotels are built that way, have none at all.

Motor Inns.   The highway hotel is a child of the motel, which makes it the grandchild of the earlier tourist court (see Exhibit 1–7). Its lineage has given it a unique design. Although not applauded by architects, the simple floor plan (see Exhibit 3–18) provides easy access to outside parking, which is the market being served.

Exhibit 3-17   All-suite facilities are appealing to both transient travelers and long-stay guests, to whom the concept was originally marketed. A sofa bed or even a fold-out chair provides extra sleeping accommodations. All-suites continue to lead the growth of the lodging industry. This executive double is being remodeled as part of the company's continuing upgrade program after acquiring the chain in 2006. *Courtesy of The Gencom Group, Miami, Florida.*

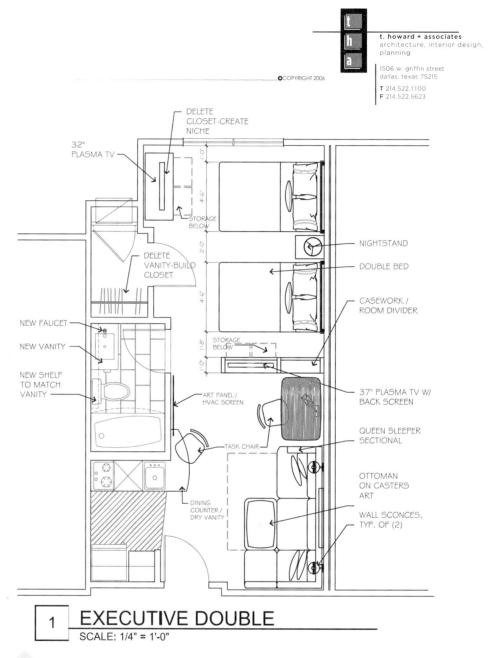

Exhibit 3–17   *(Continued)*

Room rates are at the lower end of the industry's spectrum because both land and construction costs are closely watched. Land costs are kept in check by carefully selecting locations. Construction costs are kept in check by building low-rise, one- or two-floor buildings, and designing a single strip of housing, simply a long rectangle. Building a U- or L-shape (see Exhibit 3–18) helps with exterior appeal. First impressions are important because much of the traffic is due to impulse buying rather than advanced reservations.

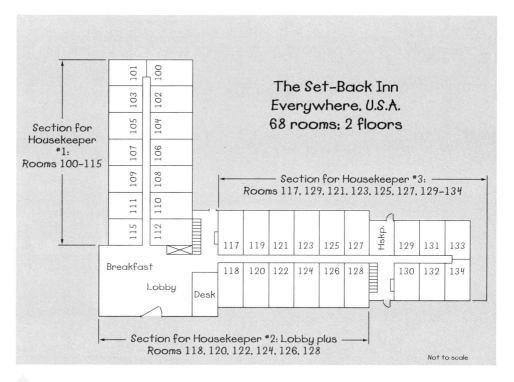

Exhibit 3-18 The typical design of a small, often two-story motor inn of 50 to 75 rooms is represented with this prototype. Ownership may still be a small company or even a mom-and-pop, but most properties such as this are franchise flagged. The design anticipates three housekeepers per floor at full occupancy.

Attractive exteriors can be achieved with landscaping, facing materials on the building, and color. First impressions are fixed by the entry, both the driveway and the port-cochère. Cleanliness and maintenance of grounds, windows, and outdoor signs set the guest's expectations.

Numbering for Identification

Everyone, guests and staff alike, uses the guest-room number for identification. Guests depend on the room number to locate their rooms. Desk personnel address guests by their names, but guests are identified by room numbers within the confines of the desk. The floor number comes first followed by the room number, 1012.

Floors are numbered sequentially in ascending order, but usually reflect the culture of their location. Most Western hotels omit the unlucky number 13 from both floors and guest rooms. The unlucky number in the Orient is 4. So 13 and 4, and in the East any number that adds to 4, may be omitted as room numbers. Better to assign guests to rooms with lucky numbers: 7 in the United States; 6 in the Far East.

Floor Numbering. Americans number the first sleeping floor as floor one regardless of the number of intervening levels between it and the ground. Mezzanine, upper-ground floor, and shopping level are interspersed without any standard order. The sequence adds an array of nonnumerical elevator buttons that confuse anyone who isn't a lifetime employee of the hotel. *M* is for mezzanine; *MM* is for the second mezzanine floor. Try to decipher *LM, SB,* and *S2* (lower mezzanine, subbasement, and subbasement 2).

The rest of the world begins numbering with the ground floor as floor number one. Even without the intermediary floors, what would be the 10th floor in the United States would be the 11th floor elsewhere.

A different numbering system is needed if the hotel has several low-rise buildings. Identically numbering each low rise unit of, say, three or four stories is one technique. Then each building is given a different name, and the keys for each are color coded. Others prefer to number the floors sequentially, moving in order from one building to the next. Guests get confused because only one unit has its ground floor numbered as floor one. Ground floors of the other units will have numbers in the teens or even 20s.

Hotels that have two or three towers have the same options. Either the towers are differentiated by name (the river tower) or direction (the east tower) with room numbers identical in each, or the floors are numbered sequentially with the bottom floor of the second tower using the next floor number in sequence.

Room Numbering.   Numbering rooms is more arbitrary than numbering floors. Each hotel is architecturally unique. Its design determines where to begin numbering and what sequence to use. Old floor plans (see Exhibit 3–14) with many right-angled corridors preclude any logical sequence of room numbers. Even a design as simple as Exhibit 3–18 offers choice.

Tradition calls for rooms to be numbered odd and even along opposite sides of the corridor. Rooms 101, 103, 105, etc. are on one side and 102, 104, and so on, are down the other side. But where to begin? The answer is obvious if the elevator is at the end of the corridor. More often, the elevator empties onto the center of the sleeping floor. Then the logic of any system breaks down. Good signage, and plenty of it, helps direct guests and visitors.

No rules govern room numbering. An atrium hotel (see Exhibit 3–9), with rooms on only one side of the corridor, is likely to be numbered sequentially. All-suite hotels are numbered in the usual manner because each room is a small suite. Numbers get confusing when a new wing or ell is added to the original structure. Rarely is the entire floor, old rooms and new, renumbered in sequence. The new wing is usually numbered without concern about interfacing with old numbers. Sometimes the old numbers are duplicated in the new wing by adding an identifying prefix, such as an N for north wing.

More and more, hoteliers opening Asian properties rely on a *feng shui* (pronounced fung shway) to position the location of everything from furniture to doors. Feng shui masters also help choose auspicious dates for opening the hotel or any of its specialty rooms.

Adjoining or Connecting Rooms.   Rooms that abut along the corridor are said to be adjoining. Using the sequence mentioned above, rooms 101, 103, and 105 would be adjoining rooms. So, too, would rooms 102, 104, and 106. If there is direct room-to-room access (a door between rooms) without using the corridor (see Exhibit 3–14, rooms 53, 55, and 57 in the center tower), the rooms connect. Obviously, every connecting room adjoins, but not every adjoining room connects.

Elevators.   The first hotel elevator, almost the first elevator anywhere, was installed in New York City's Fifth Avenue Hotel (1859). Elevators facilitated the growth of skyscrapers, so hotels became enthusiastic buyers. Early concerns dealt with lighting, ventilation, and safety. Elevators were manually operated by the bell staff until the automatic elevator was introduced in the 1950s. Then, job losses became the intermediate concern. Sixty years later, focus has shifted to the role of the elevator in a rejuvenated lobby.

How to make the elevator fun is a concern of both elevator manufacturers and elevator buyers. The atrium elevator (see Exhibit 3–9) was the first step in highlighting its contribution to guest service and its central role in the lobby. More recently, televisions with cartoons have replaced Muzak music (Le Parker Meridien Hotel in New York City).

Transparent side walls (Chambers Hotel in New York City), advertisements, and even transparent walls that present a view of the building's innards have been used to distract guests during their few claustrophobic moments in an elevator. Elevator speeds can be adjusted for smooth starts and stops or for a rapid jump from stop to full speed in just 4 seconds. Everything is open to testing so long as elevators remain an awkward ride with a dozen strangers huddled together.

Also at issue is the distance from the desk to the lobby elevator and from the elevator landings to the guest rooms. New hotel designs minimize these distances and, optimally, still maintain oversight of elevator traffic from the front desk. The 2,600-room Planet Hollywood (Las Vegas) includes a dual elevator core that puts all guest rooms within seven doors of any elevator. Often overlooked are the loud voices and other noises associated with guests exiting elevators. Room design and door insulation must anticipate this problem.

Buttonless elevators, known as *destination elevators*, are designed to speed rides and reduce waiting times. They are already in place at the Marriott Marquis in New York City (see Exhibit 1–10). It will take some time for riders to adjust. Floor number must be entered on a lobby keypad *before* getting on to the elevator. No changing one's mind once the doors close! The property management system reads the entry and directs the rider to a particular elevator car. No waiting while others enter and exit on lower floors. Lots of confusion initially, but expect to see them in new hotel buildings.

Room Shape and Size

The guest room is the hotel's product. Therefore, its shape and size are critical to customer satisfaction. Size, especially, separates the industry into its several classes. Small rooms are associated with hard budget properties, huge rooms with deluxe accommodations. As the rate discussion in Chapter 9 points out, setting the different rate classes within the hotel also depends in part on the differences in the physical rooms.

Room Shape. Little has changed in the shape of guest rooms. Interior room shapes result from the design (concave, square, round) of the hotel.[11] Research may eventually show greater guest satisfaction or reduced wear from certain shapes. Until then, the parallelogram remains the classic favorite with the room depth approximately twice its width. Increases in room size are first made by adding to the depth. Width is increased next. The 12-foot or 13-foot width is upped to 16 feet, a luxury-sized room.

Other shapes, which might look interesting from the outside, present certain internal problems. A round building of small diameter produces rooms without parallel walls. The outer wall is circular, and the inner walls are angled to accommodate the bath and the central service core within the limited cross section of the small diameter.

The presence of full or false balconies and French or sliding doors gives a sense of spaciousness to any room. Balconies are often part of a facade that adds interest to the outside of a building.

---

[11]The W Hotel in Sydney, Australia was converted from a 100-year-old wool warehouse. It required 33 different shapes in its 104 rooms.

Room Size.   Room shape is architecturally driven; room size is a financial/marketing decision. Economy class hotels have capitalized on smaller accommodations and smaller rates, resisting the general movement to larger rooms. The market, that is the rate structure, determines the room's size, furnishings and amenities. Markets vary hotel to hotel. The twin double beds of the family-oriented hotel will not appeal to upscale business travelers.

Comparing room sizes among hotels highlights the difficulty of identifying the world's hotels as one industry. Chapter 2's discussion of hard budgets identifies capsule rooms of 5 feet in width, 5 feet in height, and less than 7 feet in length. That's less than 40 square feet (not even 4 square meters).[12] London's easyHotel offers 60 square feet. Most other hard budgets are larger. The Ibis chain, Accor's European entry into the budget market, builds rooms of approximately 130 square feet (approximately 12 square meters). Econo Lodges and Super 8s have rooms of almost 200 square feet (nearly 19 square meters).

The surprise comes when comparisons are made between today's budget accommodations and the rooms of the Benjamin Franklin hotel (Exhibit 3–14), which was a first-class facility in its era. The 150- to 175-square-foot room of the prosperous 1920s was smaller than many of today's economy facilities, such as Choice Hotels International's Sleep Inn, at 210 square feet.

The Far East contributes to the other end of the scale as well. It has many of the world's opulent hotels, with large rooms and many extras. Hong Kong's Shangri-La Hotel offers a 500-square-foot facility (bath included). That size is immediately recognized as super luxury. (Guests do not get a feeling of luxury until the room size passes 400 square feet.)

The Four Seasons in New York City (370 rooms) compares favorably with luxury properties worldwide. Its rooms are 600 square feet (about 55.75 square meters), including a 120-square-foot bath. The standard American room measures between 250 and 350 square feet (approximately 23.3 to 32.5 square meters).

Total Square Footage.   The total square footage of a hotel cannot be determined by multiplying the size of the average guest room by the number of rooms. The computation must include service areas, lobbies, corridors, offices and public space. Total space is almost double that needed for guest rooms alone. Even then, allowances must be made for the size, type and class of hotel. Full-service, convention properties compute total space needed at 900 to 1,200 square feet per room. That's 2.5 to 3 times the actual room measure of 350 to 400 square feet. Economy properties with no public space are the other end of the spectrum. Total footage is calculated at about 600 square feet per room: 2 to 2.5 times the guest room size of 250 to 275 square feet.

All-suite hotels are a contrast to standard hotels and even to each other. All suites are segmented into economy, midmarket, and upscale groupings. Size is the distinction because the unit (bedroom, parlor, bath, kitchenette) is the same for the three segments. Guest Quarters pioneered the type with a 650-square-foot unit. The budget room of AmeriSuites is about 380 square feet. Fireplaces carry Homewood Suites to 550 square

---

[12]One square foot (ft^2) = 0.093 square meters (m^2). To convert square meters into square feet, divide 0.093 into the number of square feet. To convert square feet into square meters, divide 10.76 (the reciprocal) into the number of square feet. Assume, for example, a 350-square-foot guest room. It will equal 32.52 square meters: 350.00 ÷ 10.76 = 32.52 ± square meters. Conversely, 32.52 ÷ 0.093 = 350 ± square feet.

feet. Extended-stay suites that measure 400 to 650 square feet are the size of a standard apartment in many large cities of the United States!

How the Room is Used.   Hotel chains build models before proceeding with construction or renovation. They test guest acceptance, preview costs, and seek out flaws before the major project gets underway. One byproduct focuses on how the room is used.

Different kinds of guests use rooms in different ways. Within the same dimensions, a destination hotel furnishes proportionately more storage space than a transient property. A transient property allocates more space to sleeping and less to the living area than a destination facility. Such would be the case with New York City hotels, where the average daily use of the room is eight hours. Very cold or very hot climates increase usage of the room.

The use of the room dictates the type of furnishings. A destination resort wouldn't need a desk, but business travelers use their rooms as offices. Hotel rooms serve as company offices in developing countries and are furnished as such. It is no surprise that surveys of business guests give high priority to a comfortable work environment. Business guests need access to dedicated telephone lines or wireless connectivity. Hotels that provide them have been able to reduce their commitment to expensive business centers with live secretarial support. Specific requirements by business guests reduce their elasticity and make them more dependent on the hotel that meets their needs. Hotels must then decide the value of these expensive installations in attracting a single segment of the market.

Designers are good at making small rooms look larger. Eliminating nightstands is one example. Bedside lamps are then mounted on the wall. Mirrors do a good job of creating a perception of space. Wall-to-wall draperies and fewer patterned materials throughout the room add to the feeling of roominess. Designers also use mirrors and balconies to expand the sense of space. Nevertheless, it takes about 20 additional square feet (1.86 square meters) before the occupant notices the larger size. That's the point where a rate increase could be justified if spaciousness is the only basis for the increase.

Clearly, there is no standard room. The hotel industry is moving in several directions at once. Miniprices use module units and measure 12 feet from center to center. Luxury operations opt for 15-foot centers and lengths of 30 to 35 feet. (The standard carpet sizes of 12 and 15 feet dictate the dimensions unless the plan calls for a custom job.) Costs of energy, borrowed money, and labor limit expansion even as competition pushes for more space. Comparisons, therefore, begin with the marketplace.

Bed and Bath

Increases in bed sizes—Americans are getting bigger—account in part for the increased size of the guest room. Bathrooms, which have become major weapons in the competitive wars, have also contributed to total-square-footage creep.

The Bed.   Bed types, bed coverings and bed sizes vary across the world and across time. Quilted bedding appeared in Japan about 1500. It is most certain that the nomads of the Middle East were using some form of stuffing in animal skins (early futons) to ease their sleep even earlier than the 16th century. The modern American hotel room has gone through periods which favored, first, the double bed and then twin beds. Neither are popular today. The queen and king have taken over. If two beds are needed, hoteliers opt for queen-doubles rather than traditional twin beds. Of course, larger beds—kings and queens are both longer and wider—mean larger rooms. Larger rooms mean higher construction costs, and higher construction costs mean higher room rates.

Beds are being lowered as well as lengthened. Typically, mattresses and box springs measure 22 to 24 inches from the floor. Chairs stand about 17 inches. By lowering the beds to 17 inches and placing all the pieces on the same horizontal plane, designers have made rooms seem much larger. There's a negative offset, however. Guests sit on the lower beds, reducing the life of the mattresses. Good chairs—and several of them—help keep guests off the beds, but mattress management has a critical role. Mattresses can be preserved by rotating them head to foot and top to bottom. Good housekeeping departments do so as part of their quarterly deep cleaning. The position of the mattress (head versus toe and top versus bottom) is tracked by a system of arrows attached to the side of the mattress.

Although modern hotel rooms are almost the same throughout the building, there are still many variations in furnishings. Guest-service agents need to be clued in about these differences as they assign rooms in response to guest needs. The industry has developed a series of shorthand symbols to do just that for beds and bed sizes. The symbols, which were critical when hotels used room racks (see Exhibit 13–9) have carried over into computer applications.

Bed Sizes and Symbols.   The capacity of a guest room is often confused with the description of the bed. Desk personnel refer to a "single room" as one occupied by a solitary guest. It makes no difference how the room is furnished: a single bed, a double bed, a queen bed. Single and double refer with equal ambiguity to (1) the room rate, (2) the number of guests housed in the room, (3) the number of persons the room is capable of accommodating, or (4) the size and type of the beds. It is possible to have a single occupant in a double bed being charged a single rate although the room is designated as a double, meaning that it could accommodate two persons.

A single occupant in a queen double sometimes needs assurance that no additional charge is being made for the unused bed. The single-room configuration—that is, one single bed for one person—is unknown today. Thus, to the innkeeper, "single" means single occupancy or single rate.

Single Bed.   A single bed, symbol S, sleeps one person. A true single is 36 by 75 inches, but is very rarely used; it is simply too small. Instead, the rare single room (room for one person) is furnished with a single twin or, most likely, one double bed. When the room is furnished with one twin, the symbol S is used, when furnished with a double bed, the symbol is D. Single beds must measure at least 39 by 72 inches to win an AAA rating.

Twin Beds.   A twin room, symbol T, contains two beds each accommodating one person. (Two persons could also be roomed in a double, a queen, or a king bed.) Twins measure 39 by 75 inches each and use linen 72 by 108 inches. The 75-inch mattress has been replaced in all bed sizes with a longer length, called a California length. The 39-inch width remains with the twin, but the length has been stretched to between 79 and 84 inches. Additional inches are added to the linen length as well.

Because of their flexibility, twins once accounted for 60% to 70% of total available rooms. The trend shifted as twins were replaced by double–doubles, and then queens, and then by queen–doubles. Single business travelers actually prefer a two-bedded room: one for sleeping and one for spreading papers.

Because the double–double and queen–double sleep four persons, they are also called *quads* or *family rooms*. Motel owners will offer couples queen–doubles at reduced rates with the stipulation that only one bed be used. A survey done some time ago by Sheraton's franchise division showed that the second bed of a double–double or queen–double was used about 15% of the time.

Double Bed.   D is the symbol for double bed. The width ranges from 54 to 57 inches, and that's an important 3 inches. Like the twin bed, the length of the double has been stretching from 75 inches to the California 80-inch or more length. Linen sizes would be 90 to 93 inches wide and 113 inches long with a California mattress. Half a double bed is about 28 inches or so, narrower even than the single. That alone explains the double's loss of popularity among guests who are getting ever larger and heavier.

Queen and King Beds.   Queen and king beds (symbols Q and K) are extra wide (60 and 72 inches, respectively) and extra long. They made popular the California length, which has also been called a *European king.* Although designed for two, three or four persons might squeeze in when the room is taken as a family room.

Both beds require larger rooms, since the critical distance of at least 3 feet between the foot of the bed and the furniture (called *case goods*) remains a requirement. Larger sheets, 108 by 122.5 inches, are also needed. Since laundry costs are calculated by weight, larger sheets mean larger laundry bills. A larger room with extra laundry costs can only mean a higher room rate even without consideration for the extra, up-front costs of the larger bed, mattress, and linen.

Hollywood Bed.   Two beds joined by a common headboard are called a hollywood bed. Hollywoods use the symbol of the twins, T, since that's what they are. They are difficult beds to make, because the room attendant cannot get between them. To overcome this, the beds are placed on rollers and swung apart, resulting in rapid carpet wear. Because the total dimension of these beds is 78 by 75 inches (two twins), they can be converted into a king by replacing the two mattresses with one king mattress laid across both springs.

Studio Bed (Room).   A studio bed is a sofa by day and a bed by night. During the day, the bed is slipcovered and the pillows are stored in the backrest. There is neither headboard nor footboard once the sofa is pulled away from the backrest to create the bed. Today's guest room serves a dual bedroom–living room function, so studio rooms should be popular with business guests. They once were. Studios are not popular anymore because the beds are not comfortable and the all-suite hotel serves the same dual purpose.

The studio room, once called an executive room, had been used to redo small, single rooms in older hotels. *UP,* undersized parlor, is one of the symbols once used for studios. In Europe, a parlor that has no sleeping facilities is called a salon.

Sleigh Bed.   Any bed can be a sleigh bed, so named because of the sleigh-like shape of the headboard and footboard. There is no change to the integral part of the bed. The use of the sleigh shape is a designer's choice. It adds no special characteristic to the bed's sleeping qualities. (See Chapter 7 for a discussion of the bed as part of the hotel's basic service.)

Daybed.   Adding sleigh ends to a twin bed converts it to a daybed. Daybeds were once common additions to the family living room. They've made a comeback both in the home and in larger hotel rooms. Daybeds are like studio beds except they are additions to the hotel room rather than basic furnishings, as they were in the heyday of the studio room. Both daybeds and studio beds are better as beds than as sofas. At 39 inches deep, they're too wide for sitting. Removing the pillows converts a daybed into a sleeping bed, but without the struggle often associated with converting a sofa bed.

Sofa Bed.   A sofa bed is similar in function to a studio bed. It is a sofa first of all, which makes sitting more comfortable. It is usually 17 inches off the floor, whereas the studio bed may be as high as 22 inches. Unlike the studio bed, which rolls away from its frame, the sofa bed opens in accordion fashion from the seat. Since it unfolds, the sofa bed is less convenient and requires more space than the studio.

Parlors are generally equipped with sofa beds as part of a suite (see Exhibit 3–16), but a studio "bed" is usually a room unto itself. Sofa beds can be single, double, or even queen size, although the single is more like a three-quarter bed (48 by 75 inches).

Sofa beds were once called *hide-a-beds*, and thus carry an H designation. Large rooms that contain both standard beds and hide-a-beds are *junior suites*. Rooms in all-suite hotels offer a sofa bed in the parlor portion of the unit (see Exhibit 3–17).

Rollaway Bed (Cot).   A cot or rollaway is a portable utility bed that is added to the usual room furnishings on a temporary basis. A rollaway sleeps one person, and a comfortable one measures 34 by 75 inches and uses twin sheets. Cots usually come smaller—30 by 72 inches, with linen 63 by 99 inches.

Setting up cots is costly in housekeeping time, primarily because the cots are rarely located conveniently. Cot storage never seems to be high in the designer's priority, which should estimate one rollaway (mobile sleeper) per 20 guest rooms.

Crib.   Cribs for babies are rolled into the room on an as-needed basis similar to the call for rollaway beds. Deaths from unsafe cribs have made them a sensitive safety issue. Not that infants have died in hotels, but the issue was raised by a Consumer Product Safety Commission study that reported most hotel cribs were unsafe. Infants could (*could,* not *did*) catch their heads between the slats, between the mattress and the bed frame, or in cutouts in the headboards and footboards. A bigger danger is posed by the use of regular-sized sheets on a crib mattress. A call for better general maintenance (loose parts, protruding screws, broken slats) applies to rollaway beds as well as to cribs.

Water Bed.   In two decades, water beds jumped from a novelty to a hot item and then fell back again. The bed is rarely found in hotel rooms, although it offers an alternative to inner-spring and foam mattresses. Water beds have a long history, dating back to nomadic tribes, which filled goatskins with water. Their use was rediscovered by a Californian who first tried starch and gelatin as fillers. The water bed is still primarily a phenomenon of the western states.

Futon.   The Japanese futon, which is a cotton-quilted bed, is another addition to the American sleeping design. Futons come in regular mattress sizes. The thick layers of batting are easily stored and readily adapted to service as a couch or bed.

Wall Bed.   Like many other copyrighted brands that identify generic products, *Murphy bed* has come to mean any fold-up wall bed. The popularity of fold-up-into-the-wall beds waxes and wanes. They're great for dormitories, but are not now in widespread use in the commercial lodging industry. Disappearing by day and appearing at night improves on the dual use of the guest room. With the bed folded, the room is usable as a meeting place or for the commercial display of goods. Fold-up beds have an edge on studio rooms because the bed is far more comfortable. One needs to look far, indeed, to find either of the two in commercial use.

And for the future? Possibly air beds—warm air cushions that support the sleeper without bed frame, mattress, or linen. What a revolutionary thing that will be! In the meantime, there is apt to be an increasing degree of choice. One day, guests will pick from a variety of mattresses: foam, spring, hard, soft, orthopedic, adjustable, vibrating, flotation, and futons.

The Bath.   Bath is the industry's jargon for the bathroom. "Bath" does not refer to the bathtub nor to the activity that takes place in the tub. It is, rather, the industry's reference to the room containing a toilet (sometimes called a water closet), a sink (lavatory), a tub (bathtub) and a shower. The hotel bath has undergone many changes throughout this century, but its position as a sound barrier between the room and the corridor remains. That location, abutting the corridor (see Exhibits 3–14, 3–15, and 3–16), saves construction costs and leaves the desirable outside wall for windows or balconies. In more recent years, modular construction of the bath has gained some popularity. The bath is prefabricated away from the construction site and installed as one unit. Modular construction reduces the number of building trades required on the construction site and, some say, improves the quality of the work.

Stall showers, which occupy little space, gained favor as old hotels converted from rooms without baths. They fit easily into old, large closets or corners of renovated rooms. Tub and shower combinations were installed next when lifestyles changed again. Having both meets the cultural needs of all guests. The Japanese, for example, definitely favor tubs, just as they choose twin beds over all other choices. The bidet (feminine cleanliness), which is installed in many other countries, has not found acceptance in the American home and thus not in the American hotel.

The bath accounts for about 20% of the room size. Thus, the baths in hard budget inns measure about 35 square feet and in midrange properties about 70 square feet. A luxurious hotel has a bath of 120 square feet. What a contrast this is to the hotel of a century ago, when public baths served whole floors or entire wings. (Very early hotels had all their baths in the basements because the mechanics of pumping water to higher floors was not yet in place.)

Upscale properties have cut back on low-cost amenities such as soap and shampoo. Strangely, they have gone all out in building larger bathrooms with expensive appointments: in-floor scales, in-bath telephones, electric shoeshine equipment, adjustable no-fog mirrors, and plush bathrobes. The Palmer House Hilton in Chicago, which was renovated several years ago, has 300 guest rooms with his-and-her bathrooms, and one Four Seasons Hotel features bathtubs that fill in a minute!

The same "revolution" that brought untold changes to the room's beds and bedding (see Chapter 7) has impacted the bath, with the shower taking center stage. Shower rods were the beginning. Curving the rod outward keeps the sticky curtain from body contact. This minor change launched the dramatic battle of the showers. The next steps were giant leaps that have largely ignored huge increases in housekeeping costs. Glass-enclosed showers replaced the curtains. Multi-shower heads (see Exhibit 3–19), "rain showers" that direct the water onto different parts of the body, changed the very meaning of a shower. Similarly, sculptured tubs with multiple outlets were turned into quasi-spas. The most dramatic changes have taken place in boutique hotels. The walls between bedroom and bath have been eliminated or been replaced by glass panels. For those who dislike living on the edge, the glass panel may be filled with liquid crystals that turn opaque. For some avant-garde properties, the bath's frosted window panes have become clear glass overlooking gardens and fountains (and some of the neighbor's windows). By enclosing the toilets, some semblance of privacy has been retained. Questions remain whether these changes with their sexual implications can be sustained, especially for an aging population. After all, not all guests are honeymooners.

As the bath has grown larger, so has the ancillary space. Dressing areas and second lavatories outside the bath proper have added to the room's overall dimensions. Replacing closets with open hanger space has helped compensate. Consolidating furniture has also saved space. One vertical piece can incorporate several horizontal space-users. Into

Exhibit 3-19   America's hotels are undergoing a revolution in bath design and comfort. Upgraded showers are part of the amenity wars, and multiple shower heads are at the forefront of comfort. *Courtesy of Zoe Industries, Scottsdale, Arizona.*

armoires have gone television sets, bars and refrigerators, desks, and drawers for clothing. Flat-screen TVs have reversed the emphasis in upscale properties. Armoires are not needed for TV storage. Without them, the room looks larger and more chic.

Whatever the final design, it must reflect guest needs. For many travelers that is a two-night stay with hanging garment-bag luggage; but long-stay, resort guests need plenty of space to hang and store clothing. And business travelers always base their decisions on work space and electronic connectivity.

SUMMARY

Two designs structure the modern hotel. One, the building, is obvious at once. Its architecture may even be an attraction unto itself. The other structure is organization. Unlike the building, it is not visible at first. It becomes very evident, however, once the guest has stayed awhile. The first structure provides physical comfort to the guest; the second offers soothing reassurance. Both forms are changing because lodging is a dynamic industry. More space and new baths are coming from one; improved configuration of personnel and balanced service from the other.

Good building designs evolve from the diverse needs of the consumer. So not all hotels offer the same accommodations. Each structure is designed to attract portions of the traveling public, striving to cast as wide a market net as possible. The results range from hard budget hotels with rooms of 150 square feet to upscale accommodations of 600 square feet. (Square meters replace square feet outside of the United States: 0.093 square meters $[m^2]$ equal one square foot $[ft^2]$).

Good organizational designs are equally dynamic, changing as customer demand, technology, and service require. Today's guests are less inclined to pay for or wait for individualized care, opting instead for a measure of self-service. Less service has slashed the ranks of the uniformed services, even as automation has reduced the size of the telephone department. Electronics, such as self-check-in and check-out, have altered the duties of the front office.

Hotel security is one department that is growing both in size and responsibility. Recent events have focused everyone's attention on security. Although hotels are not insurers of guest safety, they must exercise reasonable care to protect guests and their property. The hotel industry has responded with better trained personnel and larger security departments. Prevention and deterrence reduce the number of security incidents and, equally important, document those that are unavoidable.

Some organizational changes have shifted assignments as much as they have altered responsibilities or department size. In this respect, reservations is probably the most dynamic of all front-office departments. The text examines reservations in the next three chapters.

RESOURCES AND CHALLENGES
Resources

WEB SITES

http://www.aahoa.com (Asian American Hotel Owners Association [AAHOA])—Atlanta, GA. An affiliation of about 8,000 Asian-American hotel owners, who control 20,000 small hotels averaging 50 rooms each.

http://www.hsmai.org (Hospitality Sales and Marketing Association International [HSMAI])—McLean, VA. An individual membership organization with a strong focus on education.

http://www.ieha.org (International Executive Housekeepers Association [IEHA])—Westerville, OH. An association of executive housekeepers and their vendor/suppliers in many professions, including hospitality.

http://www.safeplace.com (SafePlace Corporation)—Wilmington, DE. Private company providing information and accreditation about hotel security.

http://www.state.gov/travelandbusiness (United States Department of State)—Washington, D.C. Includes information about security in travel.

Web Assignment

Using these Web sites, or any other references, prepare a list of no fewer than five items detailing: (1) security measures that hotels have put into place in response to generalized heightened security concerns, and (2) security measures that hotels might put into place to prepare floor housekeepers for disasters such as earthquakes, floods, fires, or health emergencies.

INTERESTING TIDBITS

➤ Hotels have been the backdrop for several modern American tragedies. Gerald Ford was shot in front of the St. Francis Hotel (San Francisco); Robert Kennedy in the kitchen of the Ambassador Hotel (Los Angeles); Martin Luther King on the balcony of the Lorraine Hotel (Memphis); Ronald Reagan outside the Hilton Hotel (Washington).

➤ Concierges of several well-known hotels have enlarged their scope of service. They respond to guests' requests even when the guests are not registered. Nonguests telephone the concierge desk to arrange a variety of services external to the hotel. This extension of service is not free and is part of the development of a new industry, private concierge companies.

➤ *New Hotels for Global Nomads* was the first museum exhibit to feature the architecture and design of lodging facilities. The Smithsonian's Cooper-Hewitt Design

Museum held the event in New York City in 2003. Tourbus hotels, proposed for Rome, were among the showcased displays (see Exhibit 1–12). Then came a second exhibit, *In Pursuit of Pleasure*, which featured hotels of the early 20th century. The venue for this Spring 2006 show was the Wolfsonian in Miami Beach.

Challenges

TRUE/FALSE

Questions that are partially false should be marked false (F).

___ 1. Hotel organizations are getting flatter; that is, there are fewer levels of management between the top boss and the person working the floor.

___ 2. Super-luxury hotel rooms are recognized as such once the room size reaches 175 square feet (about 160 square meters).

___ 3. Cleaning a stay-over room with all the baggage, clothing, and toiletries thrown about takes a housekeeper longer than cleaning a check-out room.

___ 4. F&B has declined as a percentage of industrywide sales because so many hotels no longer offer restaurant services.

___ 5. Force majeure (a French expression) refers to unexpected events (acts of God) that relieve a hotel from delivering and a convention group from paying for obligations that were previously contracted.

PROBLEMS

1. With special attention to front-office activities, prepare a list of duties carried out by one (or more) of the fictional staff in the book *Hotel* by Arthur Hailey (Garden City, NY: Doubleday & Company, Inc., 1965; also available through Bantam Books).

2. Using information provided in this chapter or acquired elsewhere, sketch to approximate scale a typical room with furnishings that Choice Hotels might be building in Europe. (That requires dimensions to be in meters and square meters.) Above the drawing list the several assumptions as 1, 2, 3, ... n that your drawing relies upon. Cite references external to the text if used.

3. Using information provided in this book or acquired elsewhere, *estimate* the total square feet of New York City's Four Seasons Hotel. Show the several mathematical steps and label all of your figures.

4. Either as part of your travels this term or as part of a field trip, contrast the size, shape, bedding, price, and characteristics of two or more hotel rooms. Discuss.

5. Interview a hotel manager or a front-office employee. From the information obtained, construct the organizational chart of the front office, and prepare a description of any one front-office job, using Exhibits 3–5 and 3–7 as a guide.

6. Using the typical occupancy pattern of an urban hotel (see Chapter 1, Exhibit 1–5), plot the biweekly work schedule for the desk of a 300-room hotel that has separate room clerk and cashier positions. The switchboard is not at the desk. Strive for efficient coverage with minimum payroll costs. All full-time employees receive two successive days off and work an eight-hour day, five days per week.

AN INCIDENT IN HOTEL MANAGEMENT

Lost-and-Lost

The mother has called three times to inquire about a Fossil watch that her son left in the shower of room 223. He was part of a school group (three boys to a room) that checked out on the 28th. That information was taken on her first call. A promise was made then to call back, but never fulfilled. Now the mother is on the telephone with the general manager.

The housekeeper told the GM that lost-and-found had only socks, Jockey shorts, and a cap from room 223. The assistant manager, who fielded the second call, explained that he hung up when the "lady" grew belligerent and used very strong language. Among other accusations: The hotel staff was a bunch of thieves; the assistant was an ass; and worse.

Caller: "I realize people misplace things, but that happens with old people in retirement homes, not with a 17-year-old in a hotel."

Questions: Was there a management failure here; if so, what?
What is the hotel's immediate response (or action) to the incident?
What further, long-run action should management take, if any?

ANSWERS TO TRUE/FALSE QUIZ

1. True. Hotel organizations are getting flatter. Not all hotels have every job described in the chapter. Fewer levels of management put greater responsibility on line employees. So hotels must improve hiring practicing and employee training.

2. False. 175 square feet is smaller than most budget rooms. Luxury size rooms measure about 400 square feet; super luxury perhaps 600 square feet. The answer is doubly false because 1 square meter is *approximately* 10% of 1 square foot. Therefore, 175 square feet is between 15 and 17 square meters, not the 160 mentioned in the question.

3. False. A more thorough cleaning is needed when new guests are to take over a room occupied by previous guests. Housekeeping will not move personal goods about; so a thorough cleaning is not possible in a really messy room.

4. True. The introductory chapters emphasize the growing importance of all-suite hotels and the continuing existence of motor hotels. These properties add a great deal of total room revenue, but not food revenue, to the industry. Mathematically, this means a smaller percentage of industry revenue coming from F&B.

5. True. Contracts between hotels and convention groups have added this phrase to protect both parties from the uncertainties caused by both nature (storms, for example) and humankind (riots, for example).

PART II

The Reservation Process

Forecasting
Availability
and Overbooking

Outline

The next three chapters of the text cover the lodging industry's reservations process. Chapter 4, Forecasting Availability and Overbooking, examines the methods hotels use for tracking rooms sold and projecting how many remain available for sale. Chapter 5, Global Reservations Technologies, identifies many of the electronic means through which reservations are made in today's technological world. And Chapter 6, Individual and Group Reservations, addresses the type of information contained in the reservation and how that information is captured.

The processes covered in the following three chapters depend on one simple fact; there must be an available room on the receiving end of the reservation. After all, no matter how sophisticated the system that puts the guest in touch with the hotel, if no rooms are available, no reservation can be taken—or can it? Actually, there are plenty of circumstances where a fully committed hotel continues accepting reservations when no rooms remain available for sale. In such cases, overbooking the hotel is actually less risky than it sounds. It is often more conservative to overbook the hotel than just to sell the rooms available and wind up with numerous vacant rooms when cancellations and no-shows occur on the day of arrival.

The question is not "Should a hotel overbook or not?" but more accurately, how many rooms it should overbook. To answer that question, management starts by calculating the forecasted number of rooms available for sale.

FORECASTING AVAILABLE ROOMS

The concept behind rooms inventory is simple enough. There is a one-to-one match between rooms in the hotel and rooms committed either to incoming reservations or *stayover* rooms. On any given day, the hotel's available rooms inventory is equal to the physical number of rooms in the hotel less the total of today's stayovers plus today's incoming reservations.

The simplicity of the system becomes complicated as the vagaries of customer contact impact the room count. Some guests stay an extra day or two in spite of their original intention to check out. Others depart earlier than anticipated due to circumstances beyond their control. A few guests cancel their reservations hours before arrival (or worse yet, fail even to cancel their reservations and simply do not show up that day). Still others arrive a day or two early yet expect to find room. It is in the innkeeper's best interest to accommodate these *early arrivals* lest they cancel their future dates and stay elsewhere. Add to these circumstances the chance for human error—"Oh, I thought you said November 17th, not September 17th"—and the situation is further complicated.

The Simple, Unadjusted Room Count

This chapter looks at two common methods for forecasting room availability: the simple, unadjusted room count and the adjusted room count. It makes sense to start with the simple approach, where none of the more sophisticated adjustments (such as overstays, understays, cancellations, etc.) have yet been introduced. They will be introduced later in the chapter.

In this simple form, the unadjusted room count attempts to compare the rooms available in the hotel against anticipated stayovers and expected reservation arrivals. If any rooms remain uncommitted (i.e., there are more rooms available than are committed to stayovers and reservations), they are considered available for sale that day.

Automated Inventory Tracking Systems.   At a moment's notice, the reservations department must be able to determine the number (and types) of rooms available for sale for a given date. Automated property management systems offer various status reports under the reservations module. Although status reports (see Chapter 13) are determined in part by the particular property management system, most are quite similar.

➤ A 7-, 10-, or 14-day room availability report provides a window of time for which each room type is listed and the number of remaining rooms available for sale are shown by date (see Exhibit 4–6).

➤ A current or one-day inventory report details all rooms in the hotel and their particular status. An example is shown in Exhibit 4–1.

➤ A reservations forecast report projects revenues and occupancies for each of several days into the future. Such a report usually displays the room and house count (number of guests in house) as well as projects the number of stayovers for each day. As the report reads further and further into the future (three to five days from today), the forecast becomes less and less accurate because it is based on each day's assumed check-outs and stayovers.

➤ A general manager's daily report looks at the current day. Group rooms picked up, guaranteed and nonguaranteed reservations, anticipated stayovers, out-of-order and out-of-inventory rooms, walk-ins, early check-outs, and more are all displayed in such a report.

➤ An arrivals list displays information about each reservation scheduled for that day's arrival. Each anticipated guest is listed alphabetically and can also be reviewed by affiliation: group reservations, travel-agent bookings, late arrivals, and so on (see Exhibit 6–7).

More information may be included depending on the size of the hotel and the sophistication of the property management system.

Components of the Simple Room Count.   Utilizing the property management system (see Exhibit 4–1), the room count is scrutinized several days prior to the actual date of arrival. By taking a more precise look at the next several days, the reservations department prepares itself for problems that may lie ahead. The reservations department reviews the room count time and again throughout the day of arrival. Common times for careful review are before the day's arrivals begin (around 6 AM), just after the check-out hour (around 11 AM for many properties), and immediately before and after 6 PM for hotels that allow nonguaranteed (6 PM) reservations. If the hotel has rooms *available for sale* (*a plus count*), it is important to know the number and types of these rooms. Armed with this information, the reservations department and the front desk can better sell the remaining rooms in the hotel. Maximum rates are charged against the last few rooms available (a yield management approach).

The hotel also needs to know when there are no rooms remaining (an even or zero count), and it is especially important to be forewarned when the hotel finds itself in an overbooked situation (a minus or negative count)—when there are more reservations and stayovers than there are rooms available. With advance knowledge, the hotel can arrange supplementary accommodations at other hotels, alert its front-office staff to handle the sensitive situation, and encourage the reservations department to accept cancellations if and when they occur.

Business: MAY 25				1-Day Room Inventory					MAY 25 17:15:49	
				Mon MAY 25—						
Room Type	Room Cnts	Rooms Offmkt	Rooms Sold	Rooms Avail	Rates 1per	Rates 2per	Close Level	Host Status	CTA MLOS	
DDSU	15	1	5	9	85.00	85.00	4	Open		
DDSN	47	13	34	0	85.00	85.00	1	Closed		
KSU	10	0	5	5	75.00	75.00	3	Open		
KSUN	33	10	19	4	75.00	75.00	3	Open		
KHCN	3	0	1	2	75.00	75.00	2	Open		
DDHN	1	0	0	1	85.00	85.00	1	Open		
KEX	1	0	0	1	85.00	85.00	1	Open		
KEXN	5	2	1	2	85.00	85.00	2	Open		
D1HN	2	0	1	1	75.00	75.00	1	Open		
Totals:	117	26	66	25	Current occupancy 72.5%					

Key stroke action: 1 = Forward 1 Day   2 = Back 1 Day

Exhibit 4–1   An example of a one-day rooms inventory screen. This is an actual Multi-Systems, Incorporated Property Manager screen (PM Version 8.11) from a 117-room all-suite hotel. Notice that 26 rooms are offmarket (out of inventory due to an in-house renovation project), 66 rooms are sold (either to incoming reservations or stayovers), and 25 rooms are available for sale. For information on CTA (closed to arrival) and MLOS (minimum length of stay), see Chapter 5. The various room types are listed in the first column from DDSU through D1HN. DD is two double beds, K is one king bed, S or SU indicates suite, EX stands for executive room-type, N means nonsmoking (in the absence of N, the room is smoking), and H or HC means handicapped accessible. *Courtesy of AmeriSuites Incorporated, Patterson, New Jersey and Multi-Systems, Inc., Phoenix, Arizona.*

Committed Rooms.   In a computerized system, where the room count is available at a moment's notice, managers still need to understand the components included in the rooms available count. The process works on commitments. The hotel is committed to guests staying over from last night and to guests due to arrive today. If the total of these (stayovers plus reservations) is less than the total number of rooms in the hotel, there is a plus count. If the hotel has more commitments than rooms available for sale, there is a minus count (overbooked).

Overbooking is often a strategic decision made by the reservations manager in concert with the front-office manager, the sales manager, and the general manager. The idea behind overbooking hotel rooms is much the same as the reason that airlines overbook flights. Both know that some percentage of their customers will not arrive (no-show) and others will likely cancel. Therefore, the hotel reservations department plays a guessing game by projecting a series of adjustments onto the simple room count. The goal is to overbook the hotel just enough that the projected adjustments develop into a fully occupied hotel on the day of arrival. Too conservative a projection, and the hotel has unsold rooms; too aggressive a projection, and the hotel is forced to walk overbooked guests.

Refer to Exhibits 4–2 and 4–3. Exhibit 4–2 demonstrates a simple, unadjusted room count. The simple count looks at nothing more than rooms available, rooms committed to stayovers, and rooms committed to incoming reservations. These same figures are then reused in Exhibit 4–3. Exhibit 4–3, however, demonstrates an adjusted count. By including adjustments for overstays and understays, as well as for cancellations, no-shows, and early arrivals, the numbers appear substantially different.

Given:

A 1,000-room hotel had a total of 950 rooms occupied last night. Of those 950 rooms, 300 are due to check out today. In addition, there are 325 reservations for today. There are 5 rooms out of order (OOO).

Required:

Develop a simple, unadjusted room count utilizing the given information above.

Solution:

Rooms available in hotel		1,000
Occupied last night	950	
Due to check out today	300	
Equals number of stayovers		650
+ Today's reservations		325
Total rooms committed for today		975
Equals rooms available for sale		25 (with 5 OOO)

Occupancy/forecast is 975 ÷ 1,000, or 97.5%.

Exhibit 4–2   A simple, unadjusted room count. This is the first of two sample problems utilizing the same basic information (also see Exhibit 4–3).

By subtracting committed rooms (650 stayovers and 325 incoming reservations) from rooms available (1,000 rooms are available despite that 5 rooms are out of order), the reservations manager knows there are 25 rooms available for sale today (1,000 minus 650 minus 325 equals 25).

Compare these results (25 rooms) with the findings from Exhibit 4–3. Although the same basic information was used for Exhibit 4–3, the end result is a substantially different room count.

Adjusted Room Count

Mathematics carries an aura of exactness that deceives any reservations department that relies on unadjusted figures. Most of the figures must be modified on the basis of experience. The reservations department collects data over the years, and this information establishes the basis for more precise projections. But even the adjustments change from day to day depending on the day of the week and the week of the year. Percentages change with the weather, with the type of group registered and even with the news (think September 11). Gathering the data is the first step, and interpreting it is the second.

Each element in the projection can be refined over and over by using additional data or varying interpretations. Recomputing the count with these adjustments can make a substantial change in room availability (compare Exhibits 4–2 and 4–3).

Defining Rooms Available.   The actual number of rooms in the hotel (1,000 rooms for the continuing example shown in Exhibits 4–2 and 4–3) can change from day to day. Rooms available for occupancy one day may be closed to occupancy another day. When the reason is unexpected, the removal of such rooms from inventory can have a detrimental effect on the hotel's ability to accommodate reservations.

Given:

A 1,000-room hotel had a total of 950 rooms occupied last night. Of those 950 rooms, 300 are due to check out today. In addition, there are 325 reservations for today. There are 5 rooms out of order (OOO). *Note:* This is the same information given in Exhibit 4–2.

Historical Adjustments

The hotel has developed the following historical adjustment statistics: understays, 6%; overstays, 2%; cancellations, 2%; no-shows, 5%; and early arrivals, 1%.

Required

Develop an adjusted room count utilizing the given information and historical adjustments above.

Solution

Rooms available in hotel			1,000
Occupied last night		950	
Due to check out today	300		
Understays (6%; as percent of occupied last night)	+ 18		
Overstays (2%; as percent of occupied last night)	− 6		
Equals adjusted number of rooms to check out today	312 ⟶	312	
Equals adjusted number of stayovers		638 ⟶	− 638
Today's reservations	325		
Cancellations (2%)	− 7		
No-shows (5%)	− 16		
Early arrivals (1%)	+ 3		
Equals today's adjusted reservations	305	⟶	− 305
Adjusted total of rooms committed for sale			− 943
Adjusted number of rooms available for sale			+ 57 (with 5 OOO)

Anticipated occupancy percentage is 943 ÷ 1,000 or 94.3%

Exhibit 4–3 An adjusted room count. This is the second of two sample problems utilizing the same basic information (see Exhibit 4–2).

Using the same figures provided in Exhibit 4–2, this room-count calculation incorporates a series of adjustments. Stayover rooms, for example, are adjusted by understays (6% of rooms due to check out today) and overstays (2% of rooms due to check out today). Incoming reservations are adjusted by cancellations (2% of today's reservations), no-shows (5% of today's reservations), and early arrivals (1% of today's reservations).

The net result (57 rooms available for sale) is far different from the 25 rooms found in Exhibit 4–2.

Rooms removed from availability are categorized either as *out of order* or *out of inventory*. In either case, when a room is removed from availability, management needs to understand why it is unavailable and how long it will take before it is returned to availability. Short-term repairs (returned to availability within the same business day) are defined as out-of-order rooms. Longer repair horizons, or problems which affect guest safety and security, are considered out-of-inventory rooms. Minimizing out-of-inventory rooms is a critical function of rooms management, because they impact the day's occupancy statistic. Too many out-of-inventory rooms may affect management bonuses and even stock prices of publicly traded hotel companies.

Out-of-Order Rooms.　A room placed out of order is generally repairable within a short time. A minor problem such as poor TV reception, a clogged toilet, a malfunctioning minibar refrigerator, or a noisy air conditioner will usually classify a room as out of order (OOO). Out-of-order rooms pose a special problem to management because in sold-out situations they must be repaired and returned to the market quickly. In periods of low occupancy, management may wait several days before returning such rooms to inventory.

Out-of-order rooms are, by nature, minimally inoperative—the problem that placed the room out of order is slight. In some situations, out-of-order rooms may actually be sold to the public. If the hotel is facing sold-out status, management may choose to sell these rooms "as is" at a discount. A broken TV set may warrant a $10 discount; an inoperative air conditioner may warrant a $30 discount. No out-of-order room would ever be sold if it posed a hazard to the guest.

Because OOO rooms can be readily returned to market, they are included in the total rooms available for sale. In calculating room count and occupancy statistics, out-of-order rooms are treated as if there were nothing wrong with them—they are included with marketable rooms.

In the continuing example, note that five rooms are out of order. Because out-of-order rooms are counted in inventory, there are still 1,000 rooms available for sale in the hotel. The occupancy of 97.5% (see Exhibit 4–2) has not changed in the 1,000-room denominator.

Out-of-Inventory Rooms.　Out-of-inventory rooms cannot be sold "as is." Out-of-inventory rooms have significant problems that cannot be repaired quickly. Examples of major out-of-inventory (OOI) situations might include a flood that destroyed carpet and drywall in a room, a fire that blackened the walls and left a strong odor, a broken guestroom door lock or sliding glass door, and a murder investigation in which the police have ordered the room sealed until further notice. It is common practice to place blocks of rooms out of inventory during hotel remodeling projects where carpet, window and wall coverings, bathroom tile, and countertops are being repaired and replaced.

By their very nature, out-of-inventory rooms are not marketable. The problem that placed them out of inventory is significant enough to remove the room from marketability until it has been repaired. These rooms, therefore, are not included in the total figure for rooms available for sale. In calculating room count and occupancy statistics, out-of-inventory rooms are removed from the total of rooms available for sale.

Remember there are five rooms out of order in Exhibits 4–2 and 4–3. Out-of-order rooms are not removed from rooms available for sale when calculating room count and occupancy. Out-of-inventory rooms are removed from rooms available. So both the room count and occupancy statistics change. To illustrate this point, refer to Exhibit 4–4. The same ongoing example has one key difference—five out-of-order rooms have been changed to five out-of-inventory rooms.

The distinction between out-of-order and out-of-inventory rooms is an important concept. To further illustrate the point, Exhibit 4–5 provides three sample problems. Each problem is shown in two-parts (a and b). The first part of each problem shows the calculation assuming the rooms were simply out-of-order. The second part shows a different calculation assuming the rooms were out-of-inventory. Two of the problems are shown with detailed calculations and final answers. Work through the third problem on your own.

Simple, unadjusted room count

Rooms available in hotel		1,000
Less out-of-inventory rooms		5
Equals marketable rooms		995
Occupied last night	950	
Due to check out today	300	
Equals number of stayovers		650
Plus today's reservations		325
Total rooms committed for today		975
Equals rooms available for sale		20 (with 5 OOI)

Occupancy percentage is 975 ÷ 995, or 98.0%.

Adjusted room count

Rooms available in hotel			1,000
Less out-of-inventory rooms			5
Equals marketable rooms			995
Occupied last night		950	
Due to check out today	300		
Understays (6%; as percent of occupied last night)	+18		
Overstays (2%; as percent of occupied last night)	− 6		
Equals adjusted number of rooms to check out today	312	312	
Equals adjusted number of stayovers		638	638
Today's reservations	325		
Cancellations (2%)	− 7		
No-shows (5%)	− 16		
Early arrivals (1%)	+ 3		=
Equals today's adjusted reservations	305		305
Adjusted total rooms committed for today			943
Adjusted number of rooms available for sale			
Anticipated occupancy percentage is 943 ÷ 995, or 94.8%.			+ 52 (with 5 OOI)

Exhibit 4–4   The example continues with one key difference. In this exhibit out-of-order rooms have been changed to out-of-inventory rooms.

Occupancy is calculated by placing rooms available for sale in the denominator of the statistic (rooms sold ÷ rooms available for sale). Because out-of-inventory rooms reduce the number of rooms available for sale, the result is always a higher occupancy statistic. Compare the results above with Exhibits 4–2 and 4–3. The same holds true with the sample problems shown in Exhibit 4–5.

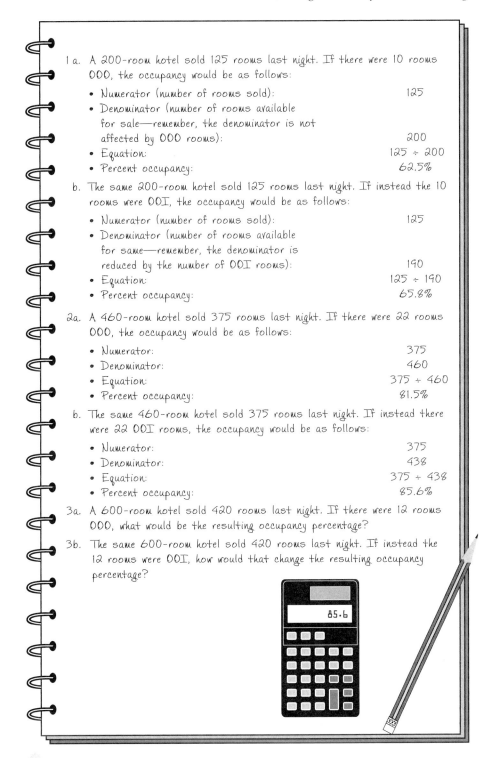

1 a. A 200-room hotel sold 125 rooms last night. If there were 10 rooms OOO, the occupancy would be as follows:
- Numerator (number of rooms sold): 125
- Denominator (number of rooms available for sale—remember, the denominator is not affected by OOO rooms): 200
- Equation: 125 ÷ 200
- Percent occupancy: 62.5%

b. The same 200-room hotel sold 125 rooms last night. If instead the 10 rooms were OOI, the occupancy would be as follows:
- Numerator (number of rooms sold): 125
- Denominator (number of rooms available for same—remember, the denominator is reduced by the number of OOI rooms): 190
- Equation: 125 ÷ 190
- Percent occupancy: 65.8%

2a. A 460-room hotel sold 375 rooms last night. If there were 22 rooms OOO, the occupancy would be as follows:
- Numerator: 375
- Denominator: 460
- Equation: 375 ÷ 460
- Percent occupancy: 81.5%

b. The same 460-room hotel sold 375 rooms last night. If instead there were 22 OOI rooms, the occupancy would be as follows:
- Numerator: 375
- Denominator: 438
- Equation: 375 ÷ 438
- Percent occupancy: 85.6%

3a. A 600-room hotel sold 420 rooms last night. If there were 12 rooms OOO, what would be the resulting occupancy percentage?

3b. The same 600-room hotel sold 420 rooms last night. If instead the 12 rooms were OOI, how would that change the resulting occupancy percentage?

Exhibit 4–5　Out-of-order rooms do not affect inventory (rooms available for sale), while out-of-inventory rooms do. These three examples illustrate the difference this distinction can have on the resulting occupancy percentage. Each example is calculated two ways: First, the occupancy is calculated assuming the rooms were OOO, then the occupancy is recalculated assuming that the rooms were OOI. Try the third example on your own . . .

Computing the Number of Stayovers.   To compute the number of stayovers, the night auditor or guest-service agent begins with the number of rooms occupied last night. Rooms occupied last night is a precise number taken during the hotel's night audit function. Rooms accounted for in front office records (whether revenue rooms or comp rooms) are counted as occupied last night. Rarely, a situation may exist where the front office records and the physical house count are off by a room or two. Examples may include a person who acquired a room key through some illegitimate means (usually a hotel employee) or a legitimate guest whose front office records were improperly recorded in the property management system. Occupied rooms for which the front office has no knowledge are often called *whos* (see Chapter 13).

The number of rooms scheduled to check out today is far less precise than the number occupied last night. Rooms due to check out are based primarily on the guests' initial plans at the time they made their reservations. Even if a well-trained guest-service agent reconfirms the departure date during the check-in process, changes still occur. Corporate guests may complete their business a day or two earlier (or a day or two later) than expected. Leisure guests may decide to sightsee in town a bit longer (or shorter) than originally planned. Emergencies also occur, where guests may need to catch the next flight home, regardless of their original plans.

Although these changes are difficult to project on an individual guest-by-guest basis, they generally form an historical trend over time. Although it is impossible to guess if Mr. Jones in room 2144 will stay an extra night, it is somewhat more certain to say that historically 2% of our scheduled check-outs do not depart (they overstay).

Each property collects historical data with which to project its understays and overstays. This data is usually expressed in terms of a percentage of the rooms due to check out that day. For example, in Exhibit 4–3, the understay percentage is 6% (0.06 times 300 rooms due out equals 18 understays). The overstay percentage is 2% (0.02 times 300 rooms due out equals 6 overstays). Although these are both fictitious percentages, a real hotel would develop similar statistical projections over time.

Understays.   Some guests leave earlier than the hotel expected; they are known as understays. They are also sometimes referred to as *earlys*. When calculating the number of rooms due to check out, any understays will be added to the projected check-outs.

Overstays.   Some guests stay past their scheduled departure date; they are referred to as overstays. They are also sometimes known as *holdovers*. When calculating the number of rooms due to check out, any overstays will be subtracted from the projected check-outs.

Occupied last night		950
Due to check out today	300	
Plus understays (6%)	+ 18	
Less overstays (2%)	− 6	
Equals adjusted number due to check out today	312	−312
Equals adjusted number of stayovers		638

By including understays and overstays in the continuing example, the number of rooms due to check out changes substantially. In the simple, unadjusted room count shown in Exhibit 4–2, the number due to check out today was 300. Once understays and overstays are included in the computation, that number changes to 312. Similarly, the number of stayovers changes from 650 (in the simple, unadjusted room count; Exhibit 4–2) to 638 (in the adjusted room count; Exhibit 4–3).

Computing Today's Reservations.   Just as some departing guests change plans and overstay or understay, some expected guests do not adhere to their original reservations. Guests often cancel reservations, arrive a day or two earlier than expected, or never arrive at all. Each of these variables must be assessed and adjusted according to historical data.

No-Shows.   Some guests with reservations never arrive at the hotel. These guests are referred to as no-shows. No-shows may be caused by a change in business or personal plans, inclement weather or closed roads, canceled or stranded flights, illness, or death. It is also possible that they simply forgot they had made a reservation.

No-shows present the hotel with a unique problem—it is difficult to know when to classify the reservation as a no-show. For nonguaranteed reservations, the industry standard is 6 PM. Nonguaranteed reservations that fail to arrive by 6 PM are considered no-shows, and those rooms are sold to walk-in guests.

Guaranteed and advance-deposit reservations are another story. The very nature of these higher-quality guaranteed or advance-deposit reservations suggests that the hotel will hold a room all night long (See Chapter 6). Therefore, it is impossible for a guest-service agent to determine when a guaranteed reservation changes from an expected arrival to a no-show. A reservation that has not arrived by 11 PM, midnight, or 1 AM is probably a no-show. But, there is always the chance that the guest has been detained and will still arrive in search of the reservation.

Asking for an estimated time of arrival at the time of reservation is one partial solution. By documenting the guest's expected arrival time, the hotel is better equipped to make difficult decisions about possible no-show guests. The earlier such decisions are made, the better the hotel's chances of selling the room to a walk-in.

Cancellations.   Cancellations are infinitely better than no-shows. Guests who cancel on the day of arrival are providing the hotel an opportunity to resell the room. The earlier the cancellation is received, the better the chance of reselling the room.

Cancellation policies may require notice at least 24 hours in advance of the reservation's arrival date. Depending on policy, cancellations made on the day of arrival may be charged one room-night. As a courtesy, most corporate hotels allow business guests to cancel, without penalty, until 6 PM the day of arrival.

Early Arrivals.   Cancellations and no-shows reduce the number of expected arrivals. Early arrivals increase the number of expected arrivals. Early arrivals are guests who arrive at the hotel one or more days prior to their scheduled reservation date.

There are a number of reasons for this. Maybe the reservations department had a different date for the reservation than the guest understood. Possibly the guest's plans changed and he or she decided to arrive one or more days early. Whatever the reason, the front office should attempt to accommodate the guest.

Even in periods of 100% occupancy, front-office personnel strive to find accommodations for the early arrival. Not only is that good guest service, but early arrivals often represent a number of room-nights to the hotel—many early arrivals stay through the end of their originally scheduled departure. An early arrival who arrives two days early for a three-night reservation may very likely stay all five nights.

Adjusting Today's Reservations.   The continuing example in Exhibit 4–2 shows an unadjusted reservations count of 325 rooms. Assuming a cancellation rate of 2%, a no-show rate of 5%, and an early arrival rate of 1%, the numbers change significantly (see the following table and Exhibit 4–3):

Today's reservations	325
Less cancellations (2%)	−7
Less no-shows (5%)	−16
Plus early arrivals (1%)	+3
Equals adjusted number of reservations	305

A certain amount of mathematical rounding is necessary to convert these equations into whole numbers (whole rooms). A 2% cancellation rate for 325 reservations results in 6.5 cancellations (rounded to 7). No shows round from 16.25 to 16 and early arrivals round from 3.25 to 3.

The Adjusted Result.   With all the adjustment components in place, the adjusted room count (Exhibit 4–3) shows a substantial change from the unadjusted room count (Exhibit 4–2). Stayover rooms have been adjusted from 650 to 638 because the number of rooms due to check out has been adjusted with understays and overstays. The number of expected reservations has been adjusted from 325 to 305 because of estimated cancellations, no-shows, and early arrivals.

The count of 57 rooms available for sale shown in Exhibit 4–3 is significantly higher than the count of 25 rooms available shown in Exhibit 4–2. With the same five rooms out of order, the hotel can now accept 57 rooms as walk-ins (assuming it quickly repairs the five OOO rooms).

Exhibit 4–3 could just as easily have projected a change in the opposite direction. Second-guessing the actions of the guest is the reservations department's burden. Projections are made from historical data gathered by the property and forecasted on the basis of experience. At best, it is a composite of many previous days and may prove disastrous on any given day. A cautious projection with too few walk-ins accepted results in low occupancy and empty rooms despite guests who were turned away earlier in the day. An optimistic projection allows the desk to accept so many walk-ins that the reserved guest who arrives late in the day finds no room.

This is the dilemma of overbooking: the need, on the one hand, to maximize occupancy and profits, and the pressure, on the other hand, to keep empty rooms for reservations who may never arrive. Selective overbooking, 5 to 15% depending on historical experience, is the hotel's major protection against no-shows, double reservations, and "guaranteed reservations" that are never paid. Conservative overbooking begins with a collection of data, structured and accurate so that the reservations office can rely on the figures. Data must be accumulated in a chronological fashion, day of the week matching day of the week. It is important for the second Tuesday in April, for instance, to match the second Tuesday in April of last year, irrespective of the calendar dates of those Tuesdays.

Dates do have importance, of course. The Fourth of July holiday is a more important date than the day on which it falls. Similarly, the days before and after such a holiday must be identified with other before and after days of previous years.

Putting the Room Count to Use.   Room forecasting starts with an annual projection and ends with an hourly report. In between are monthly, biweekly, weekly, (see Exhibit 4–6) three-day, and daily forecasts. Ten-day reports (see Exhibit 4–7) are

Royal Hotel Weekly Forecast for February 3 to February 9

	3	4	5	6	7	8	9
Rooms available for sale	1,206	1,206	1,206	1,206	1,206	1,206	1,206
Rooms occupied last night ⟶	1,121	1,190	1,193	890	480	140	611
Less anticipated departures	444	396	530	440	350	55	20
Stayovers	677	794	663	450	130	85	591
Reservations	498	386	212	25	10	501	552
Estimated out of order	3	3					
Rooms committed	1,178	1,183	875	475	140	586	1,143
Estimated walk-ins	12	10	15	5		25	63
Rooms occupied tonight ⟶	1,190	1,193	890	480	140	611	1,206
Group Arrivals							
National Water Heater Co.	80	140					
Play Tours of America			68				
Chevrolet Western Division					5	183	
PA Library Association						251	396
Chiffo-Garn wedding party							23

Exhibit 4–6   This room-availability forecast demonstrates why statistics that depend on the cumulative results of previous days' forecasts grow less reliable the further the projected horizon. Each day's values build on estimates from previous days (see arrows). If the actual number of rooms occupied in any preceding day is different than the mathematical base—and it always is—later forecasts become less and less accurate, since they begin with invalid figures.

For example, if the rooms occupied on February 3 are actually less than the 1,190 projected (less because of fewer walk-ins, more understay departures, etc.), then the rooms occupied on February 4 will also be lower than projected. The count for February 4 is based upon the number of rooms occupied the night before (1,190). If the count for February 4 is lower than projected, then the count for February 5, 6, 7, and so on may also be lower than projected.

sometimes used in place of the biweekly projections, but most reservation managers prefer to see two weekends included in a report.

Every department of a hotel uses the room count projections as a tool for labor planning. Each department makes sales and labor forecasts from the anticipated room count. Most departments depend on room occupancy for their own volume. This is certainly the situation with valet and laundry, room service, lounges, in-room minibars, and uniformed services.

Housekeeping's schedule is also a function of room sales. So, too, there is a direct relation between the number of breakfasts served and the previous night's room count. Early scheduling of shifts and days off helps build good employee relations, and the two-week forecast is generally used for that purpose. A two-week lead time may be required in hotels covered by union contracts.

The reservations department should have its closest partnership with marketing and sales. Without that alliance, the property has little opportunity to maximize yield management policies. For example, how many discounted rooms has the sales department

Occupancy Forecast Report

Santa Rae Ranch
Ann Parker

Occupancy Forecast Report
For the Period from 03-JAN- to 12-JAN-
Percentages Include Out of Order and Off Market Rooms
Percentages Exclude Tentative Group Rooms

	FRI JAN-03	SAT JAN-04	SUN JAN-05	MON JAN-06	TUE JAN-07	WED JAN-08	THUR JAN-09	FRI JAN-10	SAT JAN-11	SUN JAN-12
Total Rooms	236	236	236	236	236	236	236	236	236	236
– OOO	3	2	3	3	2	2	3	1	1	0
– OFF	0	0	0	0	0	0	0	0	0	0
Rooms Available	233	234	233	233	234	234	233	235	235	236
Rooms Occupied	94	90	83	44	33	27	21	30	42	27
– Non-Group Departures	11	18	34	14	4	5	17	2	13	4
– Group Departures	12	3	14	1	2	2	0	1	5	4
+ Non-Group Arrivals	18	13	9	4	0	1	15	14	3	0
+ Group Arrivals	1	1	0	0	0	0	12	0	0	0
Net In-House	90	83	44	33	27	21	31	41	27	19
+ Estimated Pickup	0	0	0	0	0	0	0	2	2	2
+ Excess Committed	82	60	1	0	0	0	19	9	14	0
+ Tentative Grp Rooms	5	0	0	0	0	0	2	0	0	0
Net Rooms Reserved	172	143	45	33	27	21	50	52	43	21
Net Rooms Available	61	91	188	200	207	213	183	183	192	215
Non-Group										
Projected Revenue	7113.00	6527.50	3438.50	2757.50	2446.00	1810.00	1341.88	4265.37	3415.99	2913.49
Avg. Rate	103.09	101.99	88.17	95.09	97.84	86.19	70.63	137.59	162.67	171.38
Group (Reserved)										
Projected Revenue	1064.00	965.00	221.00	175.00	47.50	0.00	1148.00	1100.50	590.00	190.00
Avg. Rate	50.67	50.79	44.20	43.75	23.75	0.00	95.67	100.05	98.33	95.00
Group (Excess Committed)										
Estimated Revenue	5340.00	3925.00	20.00	0.00	0.00	0.00	1945.00	845.00	1280.00	0.00
Avg. Rate	61.38	65.42	20.00	0.00	0.00	0.00	92.62	93.89	91.43	0.00
Group (Tentative)										
Estimated Revenue	375.00	0.00	0.00	0.00	0.00	0.00	150.00	0.00	0.00	0.00
Avg. Rate	75.00	0.00	0.00	0.00	0.00	0.00	75.00	0.00	0.00	0.00

142

Occupancy Forecast Report

	TEN/ DEF	FRI JAN-03	SAT JAN-04	SUN JAN-05	MON JAN-06	TUE JAN-07	WED JAN-08	THUR JAN-09	FRI JAN-10	SAT JAN-11
Group (Totals)										
Projected Revenue		6779.00	4890.00	241.00	175.00	47.50	0.00	3243.00	1945.50	1870.00	190.00
Avg. Rate		59.99	61.90	40.17	43.75	23.75	0.00	92.66	97.28	93.50	95.00
Totals										
Projected Revenue		13892.00	11417.50	3679.50	2932.50	2493.50	1810.00	4584.88	6210.87	5285.99	3103.49
Avg. Rate		76.33	79.84	81.77	88.86	92.35	86.19	84.91	121.78	128.93	163.34
% Occupancy Reserved		38.63	35.47	18.88	14.16	11.54	8.97	13.30	17.45	11.49	8.05
% Including Commits		73.82	61.11	19.31	14.16	11.54	8.97	21.46	21.28	17.45	8.05
American Building Consult	DEF	30/0	20/0								
Bavarian Bakeoff	*DEF	0/1									
Bob's Bablo Island Tour	*DEF	5/4	0/3								
Brady Tours	DEF								5/0		
Cardinal Group	DEF	1/0	1/0	1/0							
Cups & China	DEF	10/0									
Honda	DEF								25/11	20/11	20/6
MIPS	DEF	6/5	5/5								
Micro Data	TEN								2/0		
Presentations Now	DEF	5/0	5/0								
Sky Line Displays	TEN	5/0									
US Clowns Inc	DEF	25/2	25/2								
US Water Polo Team	DEF	12/1	12/1								

* This group's commitments must be cleaned up or all availability reports will be out of balance.

Exhibit 4–7 This computerized reservation forecast report displays a 10-day view of rooms activity. It details arrival and departure projections for individual as well as group rooms. Usually, such forecast reports also provide an estimate of each day's anticipated rooms revenues. (Note that unlike the treatment suggested by the authors, this example shows out-of-order rooms reducing rooms available.) *Courtesy of Geac Computers, Inc., Tustin, California.*

committed to wholesalers during a high-occupancy (thus, high-rate) period? The marketing department should be able to help reservations forecast no-shows, walk-ins, early arrivals, and so on, as they pertain to a particular group. Group figures differ from figures for individual guests and may vary from group to group.

Periodic Recounts.   The longer the period between the preparation of the forecast and its use, the less reliable it is. Without periodic updating, all the departments, but especially the desk, act on information that is no longer accurate. The three-day forecast permits a final push for sales and a tightening of labor schedules throughout the property to maximize occupancy and minimize costs.

By the time hourly projections are being made, responsibility has moved entirely to the front office. Overbooking problems, additional reservations, walk-ins, and stayovers are being resolved by front-office executives.

Periodic or hourly forecasts improve the system in two ways. Obviously, the information is more current (see Exhibits 4–6 and 4–7). Less obvious is the increased accuracy in percentage adjustments as the day wears on. If 80% of all the check-outs are usually gone by noon, a better guess of understays and overstays can be made at noon each day than at 7 AM. Similar refinements are possible with cancellation percentages, no-show factors, and so on. It is possible to improve the accuracy of no-show forecasts by separating the total reservations into three categories—advance deposit, guaranteed, and nonguaranteed—before applying a different no-show percentage to each.

Adjusting by Reservation Quality.   The adjusted room count can be improved even further by segregating reservations by quality. The quality of a reservation (discussed in greater detail in Chapter 6) correlates with its likelihood of no-show. Higher quality advance deposits and guaranteed reservations have lower no-show statistics than nonguaranteed reservations.

It is more accurate to maintain historical projections for each type of reservation rather than taking a 5% no-show factor across all 325 reservations. Assume that 20% of nonguaranteed reservations are no-shows, 4% of guaranteed reservations are no-shows, and 1% of advance deposits are no-shows. The total number of no-shows would now change from 16 in Exhibit 4–3 to 28. This is calculated by taking 20% of 100 nonguaranteed reservations (20), plus 4% of 175 guaranteed reservations (7), plus 1% of 50 advance-deposit reservations (0.5 rounds up to 1). See the table below.

Today's nonguaranteed reservations	100	
Today's guaranteed reservations	175	
Today's advance-deposit reservations	50	
Equals today's reservations	325	325
Less cancellations nonguaranteed reservations (0%)	−0	
Less cancellations guaranteed reservations (4%)	−7	
Less cancellations advance-deposit reservations (3%)	−2	
Equals total cancellations	−9	−9
Less no-shows nonguaranteed reservations (20%)	−20	
Less no-shows guaranteed reservations (4%)	−7	
Less no-shows advance-deposit reservations (1%)	−1	
Equals total no-shows	−28	−28
Plus early arrivals (1%)		+ 3
Equals today's adjusted reservations		291

Accuracy can also be improved by attention to the character of the market. The type of group clues the reservation department to the no-show projection. For example, teachers are very dependable. Tour groups are nearly always full because volume is as important to the tour operator as to the innkeeper. That generalization must then be balanced by knowledge about specific tour companies. Allocations versus utilization should be computed individually on wholesalers, incentive houses, associations, and other group movers.

Market research may prove that bookings from certain localities are more or less reliable. Variations would depend on transportation, weather, distance, and the kind of guest the hotel is attracting, water park goers, for example (see Exhibit 4–8). Commercial guests have a different degree of dependability than tourists, who differ again from conventioneers. A large permanent guest population needs to be recognized in any percentage computation involving stayovers and anticipated departures.

The overall goal of any room count projection is to forecast the number of rooms available for sale. This is especially critical during high-occupancy periods. When the

Exhibit 4–8   Indoor water parks are one of the latest trends hoteliers are using to boost reservations and occupancy levels. Indoor water parks attached to hotels were once confined to the upper Midwest, where they offered a warm local retreat from the cold Wisconsin and Minnesota winters (shown here is the Grand Lodge in Minneapolis). Today they are popping up everywhere, with projects underway in such sunny states as Texas, Arizona, and California—and being constructed by such hotel chains as Hilton, Holiday Inn, and even Super 8!

In 2000, there were fewer than 25 indoor water parks attached to hotels. By the end of 2006, that number had climbed to well over 100. They are expensive to build and operate, with construction costs running more than double the cost per square foot of conventional hotel swimming pools. But they work well in attracting local families to spend a night or even a weekend. Many properties claim the indoor water parks increased their hotel occupancies by 10% per year, an increase that dwarfs the overall industry growth rate. *Courtesy: Wirth Companies, Brooklyn Center, Minnesota.*

hotel is nearly full, it is important to forecast the number of rooms that may become available for sale due to understays, no-shows, and cancellations. By understanding the interrelationship of these adjustments, the front office has a better chance of filling the hotel.

Cancellations are also correlated with the quality of the reservation. Cancellations are more common with guaranteed and advance deposit reservations, because such guests have an incentive to call and cancel. (If the guest is not planning to arrive, he or she will save a no-show charge by calling and canceling). Cancellations are less common with nonguaranteed reservations. The guest has nothing to lose with the nonguaranteed reservation, because the reservation is basically a courtesy hold until 6 PM. Few guests take the time to notify the hotel that they are not arriving when they have a 6 PM hold (nonguaranteed) reservation. In our continuing example (Exhibit 4–3), assume 0% of all nonguaranteed reservations call to cancel, 4% of guaranteed reservations cancel and 3% of advance-deposit reservations cancel. The total number of cancellations changes from 7 to 9. This is calculated by taking 0% of 100 nonguaranteed reservations (0), plus 4% of 175 guaranteed reservations (7), plus 3% of 50 advance-deposit reservations (1.5 rounds up to 2).

OVERBOOKING

Even when hotel records show 100% occupancy, there are usually a few unoccupied rooms in the hotel. The hotel shows 100% occupancy because it has sold every available room, not necessarily because every available room is physically occupied. Rooms held for guaranteed reservations provide revenue in the form of no-show charges even when the guest fails to arrive. The *perfect fill* or the *perfect sell-out* occurs when every available room is physically occupied.

The Perfect Fill

Reaching the perfect fill is a challenge because guests are notoriously undependable. To compensate for this lack of dependability, hotel managers sell more reservations than the number of rooms physically available. Look back at the five adjustments covered in the first half of this chapter; overstays, understays, cancellations, no-shows, and early arrivals. These adjustments are designed to compensate for guest behavior by second-guessing the guest and selling more reservations than the number of rooms physically available. The difference between Exhibit 4–3 (plus count of 57 rooms) and Exhibit 4–2 (plus count of 25 rooms) is 32 reservations—32 more reservations than the number of rooms physically available.

Look at the strategy differently. Selling the exact number of rooms physically available in the hotel would be a mistake. Adjustments resulting in more available rooms (no-shows, cancellations, and understays) will not necessarily be balanced by adjustments requiring additional rooms (overstays and early arrivals). Adjustments resulting in more available rooms far outweigh adjustments requiring additional rooms. So managers oversell, *overbook*, their properties.

Overbooking is standard practice in the lodging industry as it is in the airline industry. Overbooking means that a hotel knowingly sells more reservations than it has rooms available. When a hotel overbooks a sold-out date, it is taking a calculated risk that more guests will understay, cancel, or no-show than the number of rooms by which the hotel has overbooked. A conservative overbooking policy rarely places the hotel in a compromising situation. More aggressive overbooking, however, can force both the hotel and the unlucky guest(s) into an unpleasant situation. (See Exhibit 4–9).

HOTEL OVERBOOKING SOLUTIONS

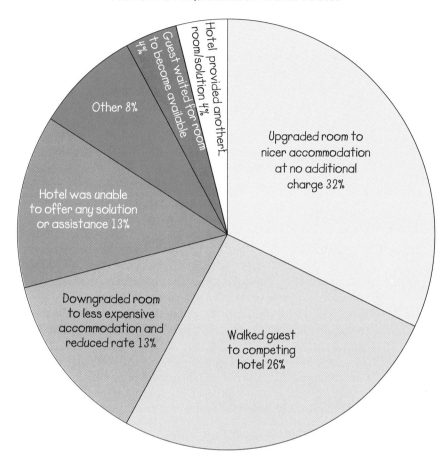

Exhibit 4–9 In a survey designed by American Express Travel Trends Monitor, an amazing 22.0% of all travelers stated they have arrived at a hotel with confirmed reservations only to find the hotel did not have a room available for them (or did not have the exact room type originally reserved). As a follow-up to that question, travelers were asked how their particular situation was handled; that information is shown in the pie-chart above.

Note that many of these overbooking problems were handled internally because other room types were available to accommodate the guest (solved by either upgrading the guest to a nicer room at no additional charge or downgrading the room type and adjusting the guest's rate accordingly). But a dismal 13% of these situations were poorly handled because the overbooked hotels were "unable to offer assistance." *Source: American Express Travel Trends Monitor.*

Reservations are Legal Contracts

Courts consider room reservations to be legal contracts. The request constitutes the offer, and the promise of accommodations represents the acceptance. Either the promise to pay or the actual transfer of a deposit is the third important element of a contract: consideration. Such promises may be verbal (as with a telephone confirmation) or written (as with a letter of confirmation (see Exhibits 6–5 and 6–6).[1] The parties are competent; the transaction is legal; and there is a mutuality of interest. All the elements of a binding contract are in place.

If one party breaches the contract, the innocent party should be compensated for the injury. However, for many years, recovery by either party has generally been limited to the natural or expected costs that the parties anticipated at the time of the agreement.

There have been few legal cases involving breach of reservation contract. There is little to be gained by bringing suit. If the guest breaches the contract by failing to show up for the room, the hotel may have an opportunity to resell the accommodation. Even if the room cannot be resold, the monetary loss to the hotel is minimal. Similarly, if the hotel breaches the reservation contract by failing to provide a room, the guest is free to seek accommodations elsewhere. Even if a room cannot be found, the actual cost to the guest is still quite small (possibly limited to taxi fares and telephone calls expended in search of alternative accommodations). And courts have not been willing to compensate the guest for inconvenience and depression.

In very few cases (usually involving group reservations or tour operators) have negligence or fraud in room reservations been alleged and then proven. The threat remains, however, especially for those hotels that overbook as a matter of operational policy. If the complaining guest can show that the hotel consistently overbooked, there might be adequate grounds to recover in a tort action.

This is also true in cases where the plaintiff can demonstrate foreseeable damage. For example, if the hotel overbooked and walked the guest during a sold-out period in the city (say, during the Olympics or the World Series, if either were being held in the city), the hotel could reasonably foresee the difficulty the guest would have in finding an alternative room. After exhausting all possibilities, if the guest decided to sleep in his or her car and was subsequently attacked and harmed, the hotel might be found liable for significant damages.

Threat of Legislation.

In the early 1980s, the Federal Trade Commission (FTC) threatened to legislate hotel overbooking, as it did airline overbooking. Having witnessed the restrictive regulations the government placed on airlines, the hotel industry took quick action. The hotel industry lobbied the FTC to allow lodging chains and individual properties the freedom to develop their own internal overbooking policies. Policies in place today look remarkably similar across the industry (see Exhibit 4–10).

State Legislation.   In response to consumer outcry, many state Attorneys General have mandated certain hotel industry overbooking practices. Florida, for example, has enacted such legislation. In addition to monetary penalties, Florida law requires the hotel to reimburse guests for prepaid reservations whether paid directly to the hotel or to a travel agency. New York and Georgia have legislated refunds for unaccommodated guests. Pennsylvania, Michigan, and Florida permit punitive damages. Hawaii, Puerto Rico, and others have enacted eviction laws permitting the physical ejection of guests who overstay their reservation. That puts the ball in the hotel's court. No longer can the excuse for overbooking be laid on other guests.

---

[1]Hotel reservations are legal contracts whether they are oral (see *Dold* v. *Outrigger Hotel and Hawaii Hotels Operating Company,* 1972) or in writing (see *Rainbow Travel Service, Inc.* v. *Hilton Hotels Corp.,* 1990). Although most cases show damaged customers or tour operators suing hotels for overbooking, hotels have also been known to sue guests for their failure to arrive (*King of Prussia Enterprises, Inc.* v. *Greyhound Lines, Inc.,* 1978).

Our Pledge to You

We will not knowingly offer for rent, space on which we already have an advance deposit or credit-card guaranteed reservation from a customer. If, for any reason beyond our control, a room should not be available for a customer who has either an advance deposit reservation or a credit-card guaranteed reservation, we shall arrange for at least comparable accommodations at another hotel or motel in this area.

The Management

Exhibit 4–10   Nonoverbooking pledge. The American Hotel & Lodging Association encourages all hotels to adopt similar policies. Reading between the lines, this pledge allows the hotel to overbook nonguaranteed (6 PM) reservations. That makes sense, in light of the extremely high no-show rate associated with nonguaranteed or "courtesy-hold" reservations. According to this pledge, however, guaranteed and advance deposit reservations are not to be oversold. *Courtesy of the American Hotel & Lodging Association, Washington, D.C.*

Whose Fault?   The fault for overbooking is not the hotel industry's alone. Tour operators, convention housing committees, and individual guests are all to blame. Each, the hotel included, attempts to maximize its own position at the risk of overbooking.

Tour operators negotiate room commitments with hotels months in advance. Yet no one knows exactly how many rooms the tour operator will fill on any given night. Convention executives tend to overstate the number of rooms their event will require as a strategy for obtaining better room rates. To forecast the group's room pick-up rate more accurately, hotels share previous years' histories with each other. The group is also encouraged to adjust its room count periodically over the weeks and days before the event, because the group will often be charged an attrition fee for each unsold room.

Guests are probably the most to blame. Guests are known to make reservations in more than one hotel and, if they do show, change their length of stay without notifying the desk. The reservation department is always second-guessing guests' moves, and this means occasional errors no matter how carefully previous statistics and experiences are projected.

Overbooking Policies.   The burden of *walking* an arriving guest—sending that person away—falls to the room/guest-service agent. (see Exhibit 4–11). Too often management leaves it at that, making no provision to train the agent. Where this is a frequent affair, the staff grows immune to the protests and even finds a bit of humor in walking one guest after the other. In doing so, the staff reflects the apparent attitude of an unconcerned management. The situation should never be treated lightly, even if a number of guests were walked that day.

No matter how well managed a hotel, no matter how well made the forecasts, overbooking will occur. Preplanning for overbooking reduces guest irritation and even offers some chance of retaining business. Arranging substitute accommodations elsewhere is what the clerk should do. Providing the training to anticipate the incident is what management should do. Preparation includes preliminary calls to neighboring properties as the situation becomes obvious. Many smaller properties depend on this type of overflow for business. Affiliated properties usually refer each other before overflowing rooms to competitors—even to the extent that a full-service chain property may walk guests to one of the same chain's budget operations and vice versa.

Managers need to be alert to unethical practices involving walked rooms. Some properties give a commission or kickback to clerks of oversold properties when they walk guests their way. Even though the oversold hotel may specify to which properties guests can be walked, $10 or $20 from a competing operation is incentive enough to disregard the rule. Some unethical clerks have been known to refer walk-in customers to the other hotel even when rooms remain available at their own property.

Overbooking and the Antiservice Syndrome.   While the majority of hotels prepare their employees to handle oversold days, poorly managed properties place the "blame" on the guest. The common antiservice approach for an overbooked situation is to act as if the reservation never existed. The guest-service agent's pretense is what guests find so frustrating. To play out the charade, the clerk consults with coworkers, types on the computer, and

Exhibit 4–11   An overbooked hotel is no laughing matter!

pretends to check racks and other resources. Finally comes a proclamation—there is no reservation! And therefore the hotel has no further responsibility.

It is this cavalier attitude that concerns the industry. A few highly publicized incidents could renew the FTC's interest in industrywide legislation. Although the great majority of hotels have established fair and consistent overbooking policies, these are voluntary guidelines. Web sites have done the same (see Exhibit 4–12).

No-Show Policies.   Hotels overbook, in part, to compensate for no-shows—guests with reservations who neither arrive nor cancel. Industrywide, no-shows run about 8%; they can reach as high as 25% in some cities on occasion.

There is a direct correlation between no-shows and the types of reservations a hotel accepts. The higher the quality of the reservation, the lower the likelihood of no-show. The highest quality, an advance deposit or prepaid Internet reservation, has the lowest incidence of no-show. Guaranteed reservations (guaranteed to a corporate account or credit card) are next in quality. The lowest quality, a nonguaranteed (often referred to as a 6 PM hold) reservation has the highest rate of no-show.

Hotels have become less willing to accept nonguaranteed reservations (see Exhibit 4–13). When nonguaranteed reservations don't show, the hotel is left with no revenue

Sample Cancellation Policies for Discount Travel Web Sites

Discount Travel Site	Change/Cancellation Policy
Expedia.com	• Changes or cancellations are charged a $25 fee. • Cancellations or changes within 72 hours of time of arrival are charged a one-night fee.
Hotels.com	• Changes or cancellations are charged a $10 fee (recently reduced from a previous $50 fee).
Hotwire.com	• Changes or cancellations are not an option—all hotel reservations are final.
Lowestravel.com	• Changes or cancellations are always charged a fee, but the exact fee depends partly on what the hotel's individual policy requires.
Orbitz.com	• Changes or cancellations are charged no fee (other than what the hotel's individual policy requires).
Quikbook.com	• Changes or cancellations are charged no fee (other than what the hotel's individual policy requires).
Travelocity.com	• Changes or cancellations are charged a $10 fee. • Cancellations or changes within 72 hours of time of arrival are charged a one-night fee.
Trip.com	• Changes or cancellations are charged no fee (other than what the hotel's individual policy requires).

Exhibit 4–12   A sampling of hotel reservation cancellation policies for some of the biggest names in travel Web sites. One of the most punitive aspects of making such reservations is the 72-hour cancellation policy shared by several discount travel sites. Customers should be very certain they know their travel plans before making such reservations.

Managing Your No-Shows

Accept only guaranteed or advance-deposit reservations. Accept few nonguaranteed reservations.

All reservations guaranteed against credit cards should be carefully documented—name, card number, expiration, and billing address. Consider charging the card during the reservation to ensure its accuracy.

The absolute safest way to accept a credit-card guarantee is with a credit-card authorization form. The hotel faxes the form to the guest for signature, and once the form has been returned, the guaranteed reservation becomes activated.

To minimize clerical errors, train reservationists always to restate reservation details: room type, dates of arrival and departure, rate, applicable discounts, and all other pertinent information before finalizing the reservation.

Be certain reservationists explain the hotel's cancellation and no-show charge policy with each and every reservation. Some hotels go so far as to have reservationists initial a computer screen field after these policies have been explained to the guest.

Provide guests a confirmation number and recommend that they keep this number in their records.

Fax, email, or mail confirmation to ensure all information has been provided to the guest.

In the event a no-show or cancellation fee is charged, the hotel should immediately send a copy of the charge to the guest via fax, email, or mail.

Guests who cancel in an appropriate timeframe should be provided a distinct cancellation number and be advised to keep the number on file.

Exhibit 4–13   Well-operated hotels take active steps toward reducing their incidence of overbooking. One of the primary catalysts for overbooking is the negative impact hotels experience from no-show rooms. Here are some steps designed to minimize no-shows while maximizing the hotel's chances of recovering rooms revenue from no-show guests.

except for reselling the room to a walk-in guest after the 6 PM hold. No-shows with guaranteed or advance deposit reservations, on the other hand, do provide the hotel with revenue.

Guests with guaranteed or advance deposit reservations are penalized for failing to cancel (or use) their reservation. Hotels usually charge the cost of one room night (one room night plus tax is the common amount requested for an advance deposit). For advance deposits, it is a simple matter for the hotel to claim the deposit. With guaranteed reservations, the process is less certain. Collecting against guaranteed reservations can be difficult when guests are unwilling to pay the charge against their credit card or corporate account. This disagreement often results in a fight between the guest and the hotel over the amount of one night's lodging. Even when the hotel wins, it loses because the guest may forever be lost as a customer. Exhibit 4–13 illustrates the steps a well-operated hotel should take to ensure no-show revenues are properly collected.

Cancellation Policies.   Cancellation policies are another source of guest irritation. After taking the time to contact the hotel and cancel the reservation, guests may be told they will still be charged one room-night. Cancellation policies differ by chain, hotel, market, and destination. The cancellation policy often reflects the quantity of walk-ins experienced by the hotel. Liberal cancellation policies allow the guest to cancel until 6 PM on the day of arrival. Such policies are generally found at corporate and chain-affiliated properties. In contrast, many resorts and isolated destination properties mandate more stringent cancellation policies. Some request notification 24 to 48 hours in advance. Others require as much as 7 to 14 days notice. More rigid cancellation policies carry a weightier penalty: Some resort properties charge the full prepaid stay.

The major credit-card companies mandate cancellation times for properties that guarantee reservations against their cards. Discover, MasterCard, and VISA all require properties to accept cancellations until 6 PM on the day of arrival (resort operations are given the option of requiring cancellations up to three hours earlier). American Express and Diners Club understand that different markets may require different cancellation policies. These two companies allow hotels to establish their own cancellation times, provided that the hotels clearly explain the policies and procedures to all guests at the time of reservation. And oral descriptions are not necessarily sufficient. VISA, for one, requires written notice of cancellation policies for reservations made at least 72 hours in advance. Exhibit 4–14 charts the policies of the several credit-card companies.

Minimizing the Overbooking Problem

There are no perfect solutions to the problem of overbooking. As long as hotels overbook to compensate for no-shows and last-minute changes in occupancy, there will be walked guests. The answer is found not in eliminating overbooking as a management tool but in minimizing the need to overbook on most occasions.

Unfortunately, guests want the best of both worlds. They want the flexibility to understay or overstay as plans change, but they also want liberal cancellation and no-show policies for the times when they don't arrive. This leaves the hotel in a difficult position. If it charges a no-show guest for the unoccupied room night, the guest might never return to the hotel. If the hotel refuses a request for an overstay or tries to charge a fee to an early-departing understay, it may also create ill will. The answer is proving to be found in more restrictive reservations policies and third-party involvement.

	Credit-Card Company				
	American Express	Diners Club	Discover Card (Novus)	MasterCard	VISA
Name of guaranteed reservations program	Assured Reservations	Confirmed Reservation Plan	Guaranteed Reservation Service	Guaranteed Reservations	VISA Reservation Service
No-show charge policy	Will support no-show charge if "assured reservation no-show" is written on signature line	Will support no-show charge if "confirmed reservation—no-show" is written on signature line	Will support no-show charge if "no-show" is written on signature line	Will support no-show charge if "guaranteed reservation/no-show" is written on signature line	Will support no-show charge if "no-show" is written on signature line
Cancellation policy	Property may determine its own cancellation times	Cancellations by 6 PM (4 PM for resorts) on day of arrival	Cancellations by 6 PM (property may select up to three hours earlier) on day of arrival	Property may determine its own cancellation times	Cancellations by 6 PM if reservation made in past 72 hours; otherwise, property may set its own policy
Overbooking policy	Property must: • Provide and pay for room in comparable hotel for one night • Pay for one 3-minute call • Forward guest contacts to new hotel	Property must: • Provide and pay for room in comparable or better hotel for one night • Pay for one 3-minute call • Provide transportation to new hotel	Property must: • Provide and pay for room in comparable hotel for one night • Pay for one 3-minute call (if requested) • Forward guest contacts to new hotel • Provide transportation to new hotel	Property must: • Provide and pay for room in another hotel for one night • Pay for one 3-minute call • Provide transportation to new hotel • Neither hotel can charge guest. Hotel 1 pays Hotel 2.	Property must: • Provide and pay for room in comparable or better hotel for one night • Pay for one 3-minute call • Forward guest contacts to new hotel • Provide transportation to new hotel

Exhibit 4-14 Third-party reservation guarantees are supported by the major domestic credit-card companies. If the room is guaranteed and the guest does not cancel within the established parameters, the hotel has the right to receive compensation for one night's stay. Of course, this means that the hotel must hold the room available for the guest until check-out time the following day. As long as hotels abide by the policies established by each credit-card company, they will be upheld by the credit-card companies in all but the most unusual customer chargeback disputes.

Increasingly Restrictive Policies.   Certainly, the airlines are strict about their flight policies. Most tickets are nonrefundable and must be paid at the time of reservation. Courtesy (nonguaranteed) holds on reservations usually expire within 24 hours of the time they were made. No-show guests (and cancellations) face $100 "change" fees when they attempt to reuse their tickets. Unused tickets are only valid a year.

The lodging industry is slowly beginning to adopt similar policies. Merely adopting such reform, however, is not enough. The airlines went through a long period of guest education. The lodging industry will have a somewhat easier time educating their customers (because the airlines already broke much of the ground). Competition between chains will surely affect the success of industrywide reservations policies reform.

Slowly, such changes are taking place. One chain puts its toe in the water, and soon another follows suit. Yield management "fences" (nonrefundable reservations, 21-day advanced purchase, and stay over Saturday night) are some of the first toes (see the yield management discussion in Chapter 5). Early departure charges are also being tested.

Early Departure Fees.   Several major lodging chains, including Starwood, Hyatt, and Hilton, have recently experimented with early departure charges. Such fees are designed to make guests think twice before departing early. Early departure fees are also expected to improve the accuracy of the reservation on the front end; once aware of an early departure penalty, guests will probably be more conservative in estimating the number of nights they plan to stay.

As with cancellation and no-show policies, early departure or understay fees must be clearly detailed at the time of reservation booking. Credit-card companies expect properties to explain the policy in detail, include a comment about the policy with mailed confirmations, and have guests sign a statement reiterating the standard during the check-in process. When these procedures are followed, credit-card companies generally support the hotel with regard to guest disputes and chargebacks (see Exhibits 4–13 and 4–14).

Third-Party Guarantees.   There is some logic in removing the hotel from direct involvement with the guest when fees or penalties are involved. It is easier for the hotel to charge a credit-card company or travel agent the no-show than to assess it directly against the guest or the guest's corporate account. Although the guest still pays the charge in the end, the hotel is one step removed from the negative connotations associated with collecting such fees.

Trip Insurance.   The increasing popularity of trip or travel insurance is predicated on this same logic. By placing a third party into the picture, some of the negative feelings associated with paying a penalty fee are assigned elsewhere and the hotel looks a little less the bad guy.

Although less common in the United States, travel insurance is quite popular in Europe. At the time of reservation, or mailed with the confirmation, is some explanation about the benefits associated with travel insurance. The benefits are simple enough: For a small fee, a third party becomes responsible for cancellation, no-show, understay, or reservation change fees assessed for a given trip. The reasons for guests changing their plans are usually described with the insurance and may include illness, death, a change in business plans, or even inclement weather. Some of the more popular companies offering travel insurance include HTH Worldwide, TravelGuard, Travel Safe, and Access America.

Credit Card Disputes.   When the hotel charges a guaranteed no-show against the guest's credit card, it may be the start of a potentially long process of guest disputes. Such disputes place the credit card company in a third-party position between the hotel and the guest. The dispute starts when the guest contacts the credit card's customer service department claiming: "I never made the reservation" or "I canceled that reservation days in advance."

Once the claim has been made, the third-party credit card company issues a temporary credit to the guest and an offsetting debit to the hotel. Temporarily, the guest does not have to pay the charge and the hotel does not receive the income.

At this point, the guest's statement is copied to the hotel and the property has an opportunity to respond. Many hotels stop at this point, believing that the case will never be settled in their favor. If the hotel chooses not to respond, the guest automatically wins the decision. Even when the hotel does respond, the case is still found in favor of the guest much of the time. Some critics believe that credit-card companies uphold the guests because they want to keep them as customers. That is really not the case; if the hotel follows the credit-card company's standard procedure, they should never lose a chargeback dispute (see Exhibit 4–14).

Best Western, for example, always provides separate confirmation and cancellation numbers (unlike some chains, which simply add an "×" to the confirmation number to signify cancellation). In this way, Best Western can insist that the credit-card company ask the guest to provide the cancellation number. No cancellation number (I lost it, I threw it away, they never gave me a number), no excuse. Similarly, Best Western does not accept the excuse "I never made the reservation." As a company, they find that excuse questionable—after all, how did the chain get the guest's name, address, phone number, and credit-card number?

Travel Agent Guarantees.   A different type of third-party guarantee utilizes the travel agent. When a guest makes the reservation through a travel agent, the hotel removes itself from dealing directly with the customer. In the event of a no-show, the hotel receives payment directly from the travel agent. Whether or not the travel agent then charges the no-show customer is the travel agent's problem.

The only weakness with this system is that the hotel must have a credit relationship with the travel agent. In today's fast-paced travel environment, there is rarely enough lead time for the travel agent to send a check and for the hotel to clear the funds.

Advance-Deposit Reservations.
Probably the best of all methods for reducing the industrywide problem of overbooking is to encourage advance deposits. Advance-deposit reservations (also known as paid-in-advance reservations) have historically maintained the lowest percentage of no-shows. Guests who pay a substantial amount in advance (usually the first-night's room charge, although some resorts charge the entire payment up front) have a strong motive to arrive as scheduled.

Advance-deposit reservations require an extra clerical step not found with other reservation trackings. If the guest responds by sending a deposit, the reservation must be changed from tentative to confirmed. If the guest doesn't respond, the reservation office must either send a reminder or cancel the reservation. Sending a reminder starts the tracking process all over again.

Handling the money, usually a check, involves bank deposits, sometimes bounced checks, and accounting records. Refunds must be made in a timely manner when cancellations are requested. Processing and writing any check represents a measurable cost of operation.

For many hotels, these operational burdens are inconsequential compared to the benefits that accrue from advance-deposit reservations. However, even those hotels using advance-deposit systems would probably switch if and when new guarantee systems become available. And that is apt to happen as new electronic systems and new innovations in money substitutes appear.

SUMMARY

Accepting a reservation is only half the battle. Tracking the reservation and forecasting house availability are also important components in the reservations' life cycle. Forecasting room availability is as much an art as it is a science. It is a simple matter to count committed rooms (those sold to stayovers and incoming reservations) as a means of forecasting the number of rooms available for walk-ins and short lead-time reservations. However, such a simple approach leaves untended a number of costly variables. When the reservations manager begins to consider the potential for such variables as no-shows, cancellations, early arrivals, understays, and overstays, the art of forecasting becomes a bit more scientific.

An error in predicting the number of cancellations and no-shows may prove disastrous to a nearly full hotel. Rooms may be overbooked, necessitating that guests be walked to a nearby property. When this is a rare occasion, the employees treat the situation with compassion and the walked guest is a satisfied one. However, when walked guests become a routine daily occurrence, the hotel is showing greed by purposely overbooking each day to compensate for the maximum potential no-shows and cancellations. In such cases, employees become jaded, guests are shown little concern, and dissatisfaction inevitably results.

The lodging industry has done a superior job reducing overbooking complaints in recent years. Partially from fear of government regulation (as with airline overbooking policies), and partially from a desire to create lasting relationships and repeat business in a highly competitive industry, few overbooking complaints have become public scandals in recent years.

RESOURCES AND CHALLENGES
Resources

WEB SITES

http://www.nolo.com/definition.cfm/Term/F4798B77-A3F6-4071-B9FBA4CC59AA5363/alpha/O/ (Legal definition of overbooking).

http://www.travellaw.com/web/articles/Getting-Walked.html (Legal answer to a guest's question about being walked).

http://www.tripinsurancestore.com (Travel insurance that pays an extra $150 if you are walked.)

http://www.tripso.com/forums/index.php?showtopic=1706 (Web posted overbooking question with responses).

http://www.law.enotes.com/everyday-law-encyclopedia/hotel-liability (A look at a hotel's liability for overbooking).

Web Assignments

These Web sites provide deeper insight into the issue of hotel overbooking. You'll find everything from a legal definition of overbooking to assorted articles on the subject, even a discussion forum. Try it yourself. Type "hotel overbooking" into Google and you'll find better than 800,000 results.

INTERESTING TIDBITS

➤ Hotels that overbook in Florida are obligated under state law to make "every effort" to find suitable accommodations for the injured party, refund the party's deposit, and potentially pay a $500 state-levied fine.

➤ In a landmark case, *Rainbow Travel Service v. Hilton Hotel Corporation* (1990), Hilton Hotels argued that their Fontainebleau Hotel was not responsible for the overbooking incident in question because it was due to factors beyond its control. Many experts believe it was the Fontainebleau Hotel's own policy manual that turned the tide of the trial against Hilton (Hilton eventually lost the trial and paid restitution to Rainbow Travel). And no doubt, that is true. The policy manual read:

Overboard

We never tell a guest we overbooked.

If an overboard situation arises, it is due to the fact that something occurred that the hotel could not prevent.

Examples:

1. Scheduled departures do not vacate their rooms.
2. Engineering problems with a room (pipe bursted, thus water leaks, air conditioning, heating out of commission, broken glass, etc.).

Always remain calm and as pleasant as possible.

➤ Finding any room available, no matter what the cost, can be the paramount issue in certain lodging markets. Cities like Las Vegas; Bangalore; and New York run sustained occupancies at or near 100% for long periods of the year. Corporate travelers are forced to negotiate room commitments with hotels as much as one year in advance in order to secure guaranteed accommodations. Some hotels won't even agree to this "bird-in-the-hand" arrangement for fear it will obligate them to a lower rate than the actual rate during these substantially overbooked periods.

➤ Plagued by bad publicity from overbooking, the Bahamas Hotel Association (BHA) formalized an areawide policy. Recognizing that being stranded on an island with no room was not going to encourage tourism, the new policy carried the paid cab ride one step further. BHA hotels must pay walked guests for air taxi transportation to another island if local accommodations are booked. A $25 cab ride is cheap compared to an air taxi in the middle of the night!

➤ An AH&LA study on customer satisfaction ranked overbooking just 19th in the frequency of guest complaints against hotels.

Challenges

TRUE/FALSE

Questions that are partially false should be marked false (F).

___ 1. The term *walking* an overbooked guest means virtually the same as the term *walk-in* guest.

___ 2. A simple, unadjusted room count does not consider understays, overstays, cancellations, no-shows, or early arrivals in the calculations.

___ 3. A *perfect fill* (a sold-out night where every hotel room is physically occupied by one or more guests) is not the same thing as 100% occupancy. Therefore, it is theoretically possible for hotel management to show 100% occupancy without actually attaining a perfect fill.

___ 4. Understays and overstays both affect the room count in the same direction. They both allow the hotel to sell a few more rooms to compensate for the projected understays and/or overstays.

___ 5. Reservations are only legal contracts if the guest mails in a deposit (or has the credit card charged at the time of reservation) and the hotel returns a receipt and/or written confirmation.

PROBLEMS

1. What is the difference between out-of-order and out-of-inventory rooms? Explain why one of these designations affects the occupancy count while the other has no bearing.

2. Prepare a simple unadjusted plus count from the following scenario: A 700-room hotel had 90% of its rooms occupied last night. Of those occupied rooms, 260 are due to check out today. In addition, there are 316 reservations scheduled for arrival today, and 10 rooms are currently out of order.

3. The rooms forecast committee is scheduled to meet later this afternoon. You have been asked to prepare remarks on group no-shows. Contrast the likelihood of no-shows for (a) business groups, (b) tour groups, and (c) convention groups. How would your remarks differ if the group reservation had been made by (a) the vice president of engineering, (b) an incentive travel company, or (c) a professional convention management company?

4. The rooms forecast is a tool for managers throughout the hotel; it is not for the front office alone. List and discuss how several other nonroom departments (housekeeping, food and beverage, etc.) would use the rooms forecast.

5. A chain's corporate office launches a national campaign advertising its policy of honoring every reservation. Each property is notified that overbooking will not be tolerated. What policies can be implemented at the hotel level to meet corporate goals and still generate the maximum occupancies on which professional careers are built?

6. Two hours before the noon check-out hour, a walk-in party requests five rooms. The following scrambled data have just been completed as part of the desk's hourly update. Should the front-office supervisor accept the walk-ins?

General no-show factor	10%
Rooms in the hotel	693
Group reservations due (rooms)	250
Rooms occupied last night	588
Total reservations expected today from all sources (including group rooms)	360
No-show factor for groups	2%
Understays minus overstays as a percentage of occupied rooms	8%
Early arrivals expected	2
Rooms that are out of inventory	7
Total forecasted departures for the day	211

AN INCIDENT IN HOTEL MANAGEMENT

Tell Me Why I Should

The accounting office received a call from a couple who said they had been at the hotel about five weeks earlier. They were calling to complain about a charge on their latest credit-card statement. The hotel has billed them as a no-show. The guests stated that they had, indeed, been there! Now they wanted a credit against the charge.

Apparently, they had two reservations. One was made directly to the hotel and one through the reservation center. The caller said that both were 4:00 PM holds and that they came on one, but did not bother to cancel the other hold since they knew it would be taken down at that time.

The person answering the telephone knows the hotel has 6:00 PM holds, not 4:00 PM holds. Furthermore, how did the Central Reservation Office get their credit-card number if they had a hold reservation, not a guaranteed one?

"No, we don't have the cancellation number, since we didn't cancel a hold."

"No, we don't have a copy of our bill during that stay; we don't keep everything!"

"No, sorry! We don't recall the room number we were in."

"Well, we were there sometime during the week of the 11th."

Questions: Was there a management failure here; if so, what?

What is the hotel's immediate response (or action) to the incident?

What further, long-run action should management take, if any?

ANSWERS TO TRUE/FALSE QUIZ

1. False. Walking a guest is what the hotel must do when no rooms are available and the guest needs to be accommodated at a different hotel elsewhere in town. A walk-in guest is a person who arrives without a reservation and yet is still accommodated because rooms are available.

2. True. Simple, unadjusted room count does not consider those adjustments listed. Understays, overstays, cancellations, no-shows, and early arrivals are only considered in the adjusted room count equation.

3. True. The question defines the perfect fill correctly. Hotels can claim 100% occupancy by showing revenues from no-show and late cancellation charges even when rooms remain physically unoccupied.

4. False. Understays do increase the number of rooms available for sale on any given day. Overstays do just the opposite and decrease the number of rooms available for sale.

5. False. Although it is good advice for consumers to use a credit card when making reservations and for hotels to send (mail, fax, even email) written confirmations with hotel cancellation policies clearly detailed, they are not required for the reservation to become a legal contract. When the offer is made and accepted (even orally, by telephone) for future remuneration, a contract has been established.

CHAPTER 5

Global Reservations Technologies

Outline

Ideal Conditions for Yield
Management
Tools for Measuring Results
Automated Yield Management
Systems
Artificial Intelligence

Rules and Triggers
Centralized Yield Management
Yield Management Controls
Resources and Challenges
Resources
Challenges

Rapid advancements in technology have changed—to the very core—the manner by which reservations are booked. Where just a few years ago a hotel's posted available rooms were manually adjusted and sold on a daily (even hourly) basis, today's rooms are sold electronically through myriad channels with little or no human interaction (see Exhibit 5–3). That represents a substantial change in methodology over a few short years. What does the future hold for hotel reservations? Imagine the following rather futuristic scenario:

> Heading to the airport for a hastily scheduled business meeting, a technologically savvy corporate businessman accesses the Internet on his handheld personal digital assistant (PDA). Through the PDA, he checks availability at his favorite New York City hotel, discovers that rooms availability is tight, but manages to reserve a Parlor Queen room for $345 that night. His credit-card guarantee is transmitted automatically, and the return confirmation number is conveniently stored in the PDA for later retrieval. As he waits for the airplane, our corporate executive downloads a podcast from the New York City hotel, complete with a virtual tour, greeting from the general manager, and highlights of dinner and drink specials he'll enjoy that evening.
>
> Several hours later, this futuristic scenario continues as our business traveler arrives at the Holiday Inn Wall Street. The moment he steps foot into the hotel's lobby, his digital cell phone alerts him that a message is waiting. The text message on his telephone asks if he would like to proceed with electronic check-in. No wonder he loves this hotel. Of course he readily agrees, and simply types "yes" into his cell phone and enters a preprogrammed personal identification number (PIN). Then, in one last attempt to up-sell to the guest, the hotel's property management system prompts him with several additional room-rate options. He decides to treat himself to an Executive King Suite for $425 and indicates as much on the cell phone.
>
> As he walks across the lobby (secretly boasting because he's avoiding the growing check-in queue), his text message provides him the room number and even directions to the room (not that he needs directions—after all, this is his favorite hotel). As he exits the elevator, the hotel's short-range radio-wave technology senses him and prompts his telephone by again requesting his PIN. As he approaches the guestroom (within, say, 15 or 20 feet), the door automatically unlocks itself.
>
> Relaxing in his room a few minutes later, his cell phone again alerts him to a text message. It is the hotel's food and beverage department prompting him through the guest history database to see if he would like the same breakfast he ordered last visit—two eggs scrambled, dry wheat toast, juice, and coffee—delivered at the same time, 6:30 AM?

What a truly seamless series of transactions our corporate guest experienced. Each transaction was fully electronic—both paperless and faceless (no printed receipts or mailed confirmations, and no one-to-one or guest-to-employee interactions). Quite futuristic, you must agree! But wait . . . that technology is already in place at many hotels across America today. Everything mentioned in the above scenario is available technology accessed regularly by today's corporate guests. The future is here!

GLOBAL DISTRIBUTION

Understanding the channels through which hotels receive reservations is challenging. There are numerous *channels of distribution* available to hotels today, with new types being introduced every year. Today, travelers can make reservations by telephoning the property directly or telephoning the chain's central reservations office, through email, via the hotel's Internet Web site, with a travel agent, or on the chain's Web site (see Exhibit 5–1).

Today's hotel reservations technologies owe their beginning to the airline reservations systems of the early 1960s. The lodging industry has historically followed the airline industry into new technologies (reservations, inventory control, revenue management, etc.), waiting for the more capital-intensive airlines to perform expensive research and development before wading in. By choosing to wait on the sidelines in the early stages of development, hotel chains saved time and money. This holds especially true for the development of the airlines' global distribution system.

Travel agents were the first step in the development of today's global distribution system. Airlines, in an attempt to improve efficiency over telephoned reservations, began installing reservation terminals in travel agencies. This allowed the travel agency access to the airlines' seats inventory and a means by which to electronically ticket clients. Larger agencies, with access to more potential bookings, received more dedicated computer terminals than did smaller agencies. More terminals meant access to more airlines, because each airline had a dedicated proprietary system.

Before long, travel agents were hooked on the increased efficiencies associated with computer access. It was a vast improvement over telephoned reservations, the method smaller travel agencies were still required to use. It wasn't long before airlines were also offering select hotel rooms and rental cars through their fledgling global distribution systems (see Exhibit 5–2).

Not all hotel chains joined the fray, because many thought it was cost prohibitive. Hoteliers were accustomed to paying a per-reservation fee for rooms booked through the chain's central reservations office. And hotels were accustomed to paying a commission to travel agents (usually 10% of the room rate for each night of the guest's stay). But this new fee, to be listed on the airline's global distribution system, seemed an expensive way to attract reservations.

Seamless Connectivity

Another early issue for the hotel was the outdated rooms inventory information listed on the airline reservations system. Because room inventory had to be updated manually on the airline global distribution system (GDS), this information was always outdated. Not only was this manual updating prone to error, it created time lags between the creation of new data and its appearance on the GDS. Even when the hotel's inventory and pricing was regularly updated, it was the source of many problems. Hotels needed to close availability when only a few rooms remained, or else they could find themselves oversold. Hotels were not able to alter rates at a moment's notice. And hotels were only allowed to sell a few categories of room types.

An important step occurred in 1989 when the airline GDSs and the central reservations systems (CRS) of the major hotel chains began exchanging real-time information. Now travel agents working through the GDS could view the same information a reservations agent working in the hotel chain's central reservations office (CRO) was able to see. Unfortunately, that wasn't much improvement.

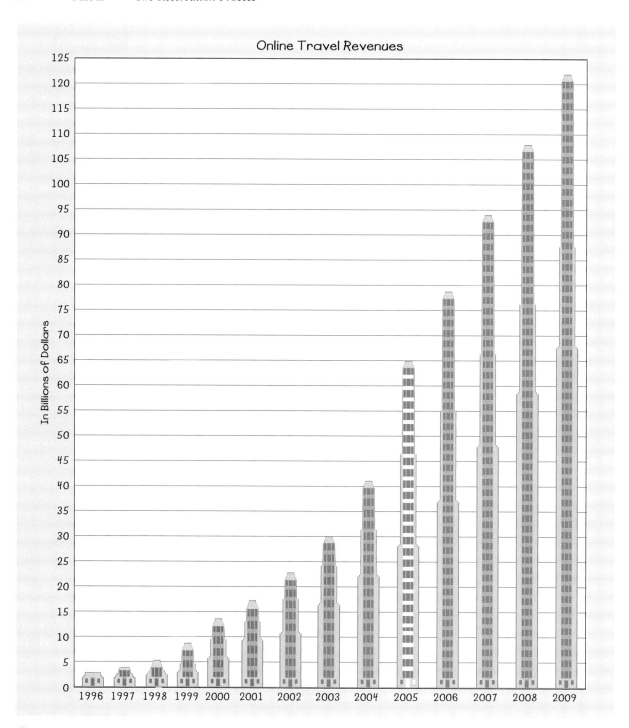

Exhibit 5-1   The United States is the global leader in online travel reservations. Online travel expenditures grew at roughly 43% per year between 1996 and 1999. The growth in 2000 was 64% (to about $13 billion) over the previous year. Between 2005 and 2009, online travel revenues are projected to double again, reaching a staggering $122 billion per year by 2009.

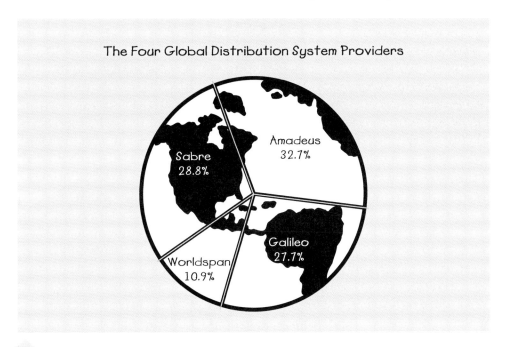

Exhibit 5–2   While many corporations and travel providers have looked at other distribution channels, the vast majority of corporate travelers continue to use travel agents and the GDS. Still, these are tumultuous times. Hotel and airline chains are constantly shopping distribution channels for the least expensive arrangement with the most promise of exposure. In fact, an arrangement in 2006 surprised the industry when rivals Sabre and Amadeus agreed to protect each other if participating suppliers drop out of either system.

What are these global distribution system providers worth? In 2001, Galileo was purchased by Cendant Corporation for a whopping $2.9 billion. In 2005, Amadeus sold a 53% share to a private investment firm (WAM Acquisitions) for an unprecedented $5.2 billion.

Hotel central reservations systems in the late 1980s were also out of date with regard to the rooms inventory information they carried. The CRS required constant manual updating by each property's inhouse reservations department. The hotel's inhouse reservations department was responsible for tracking rooms sold by the CRO and manually adding them to its first-generation property management system. Once added, a new rooms availability count (see Chapter 4) was calculated. The CRO never knew how many rooms a given hotel had available; it just knew that rooms were still open for sale. This placed an important responsibility on the property's inhouse reservations manager to notify the CRO when room availability began to tighten.

Last-Room Availability.   The result of this manual communication between each hotel of the chain and the central reservations office was anything but efficient. Inhouse reservations managers were continually monitoring rooms availability for all dates. When a date began to show signs of filling, the hotel's inhouse reservations manager closed availability with the CRO. Sometimes the decision to close availability came too soon and the hotel found itself with rooms left to sell. Sometimes the decision to close availability came too late and the hotel found itself oversold. In either case, this lack of efficiency was expensive to the chain.

Interfacing the central reservations system with each of the chain's individual properties was also expensive. That was especially true in the 1980s, because the individual hotels within the chain were often using dozens of different property management system (PMS) software vendors. Getting each of these PMSs to communicate with the CRS was viewed as a necessary investment.

It was a costly, but necessary investment. If the CRS could view each property's rooms inventory in real-time, it could sell each property's very last room (hence the name "Last-Room Availability" technology). Those last few rooms sold by the CRO represented almost pure profit to the hotel. Selling those last few rooms on nights when the hotel was close to full represented substantially increased revenues. Calculating the cost of this investment against these new found profits (number of nights each hotel filled multiplied by revenue per room multiplied by hundreds, if not thousands, of hotels in the chain) proved the investment was practical.

Lodging chains also came to realize that real-time information from each property had other advantages as well. Electronic access directly into each hotel's property management system allowed chains to perform research and corporatewide developments, including revenue management, inventory control, and guest history.

Electronic Switch Technology.   At the same time electronic interfaces were being developed with airline global distributions systems and hotel central reservations systems were being interfaced with individual hotel property management systems (last-room availability), a new inefficiency was rearing its head. Travel agencies were adding more and more proprietary computer terminals as a means for electronically booking a growing cadre of airlines, hotels, and rental cars. American Airlines' Sabre and United Airlines' Apollo were the original two global distribution systems, but others were fighting for market share.

Travel agencies were now faced with numerous systems to learn and choose from. Each of these systems was developed uniquely, and that meant a different set of rules, computer codes, and procedures for each. Not only did this growing number of terminals take up more space at the travel agency and require more training to learn how to use each system, but travel agents now found themselves spending more time moving from terminal to terminal comparing prices and availability.

It took a new innovation, switch technology, to get all the companies speaking the same language. Today, there are several major electronic switches available. One system, THISCO (known today as Pegasus Solutions; see Exhibit 5–3), was developed by 11 major lodging chains. They were Best Western, Choice, Days Inns, Hilton, Holiday, Hyatt, La Quinta, Marriott, Ramada, Sheraton, and Forte in conjunction with Rupert Murdoch's electronic publishing division. THISCO, which stands for The Hotel Industry Switching Company, was introduced in the early 1990s.

Switch technology functions like a clearinghouse. All reservations transactions are processed through the switch. The travel agent now needs access to just one terminal to communicate real-time reservations requests and confirmations to any of thousands of airlines, hotels, car rentals, and other related products. Switch technology functions as a translator as well as a real-time communicator. It translates codes from all the various hotel central reservations systems into one common switch language. Now, when the agent is interested in booking a room with, say, two queens, the agent does not need to remember the exact input code. One chain might identify two queens with a QQ code, another chain might use 2Q or DQ for double queen. The electronic switch allows the user to learn one system of codes and translates that information across each chain's particular CRS language.

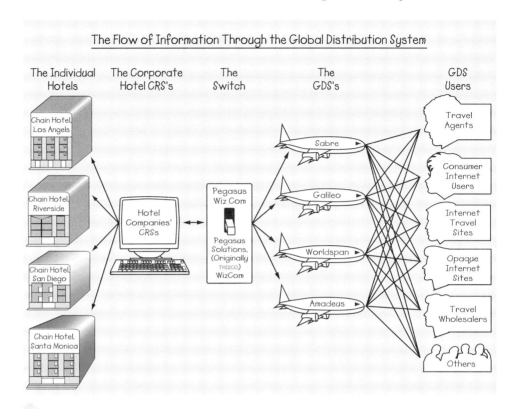

Exhibit 5–3   The Global Distribution System is enormous in scope. Each of the four airline GDS systems processes roughly 100 billion transactions per year and about 300 million requests for information per day. Galileo alone, for example, is connected to 60,000 hotel properties, 44,000 travel agencies, 500 airlines, 40 car-rental companies, 360 tour operators, and all of the world's major cruise lines.

The flow of information works like this: The supply side of the flow begins with the hotel where information (rate and availability) flows through the chain's CRS to the switches. The switches provide that information to all four airline GDSs. Travel agents, consumer Internet users, Internet travel sites, opaque Internet sites, travel wholesalers, and myriad other end users (still to be invented) access the information through the GDSs. The demand side of the flow works in the opposite direction, with the resulting room reservation finally coming to rest in the hotel's reservations system.

The introduction of the switch has allowed seamless connectivity across the spectrum of reservations. Now travel agents, airline reservationists, hotel central reservation agents, and inhouse hotel reservations clerks access the same information at the same speed. So too do Internet applications and most other channels of distribution. All reservations are made in real time and update the rooms inventory the moment the reservation is confirmed.

Application Service Providers

The historical evolution of CRSs from stand-alone call centers in the mid-1960s to today's seamlessly connected has only been possible at a substantial price. Because of the heavy investment required, not all hotel chains are in the same place today in terms of their respective levels of sophistication.

Last-room availability software requires an ability to integrate all of the chain's hundreds (if not thousands) of individual hotel property management systems. In terms of property management systems, some chains are still dealing with the mistakes they made decades ago. Allowing each hotel—franchised or corporate-owned—to select its own property management system (hardware and software) is still proving costly. Different hardware and software applications across each property in the chain require either new investment to bring like products to all properties or a myriad of programming changes to get all systems speaking the same language. It is this challenge that has lent itself to the successful introduction of application service providers (ASPs). Application service providers are software companies (Pegasus' RezView and Swan's Unirez are two such examples) that offer a suite of software applications via Internet-based access. No longer is it necessary for a hotel chain to purchase and maintain specific property management system hardware and software for each hotel. Rather, through an Internet Web site, each hotel runs off the same suite of software by simply using any Internet-ready computer—even a laptop!

Generally, ASPs offer four primary functions in their arsenal of applications: a CRS, GDS connectivity, connections to "alternate" distribution systems, and Internet reservations. Hotels simply subscribe to the system, and all property-specific data is stored off-property in ASP-maintained warehouses (see Exhibit 5–4).

Numerous benefits are associated with ASP applications. Hotel chains do not have to make large capital investments in hardware and software. Nor do they have to employ a fleet of specialized software engineers to maintain the system and program new applications. Because every hotel uses the same software, new software enhancements are implemented immediately at the ASP site and available to all users instantaneously.

Single-Image Inventory.   The biggest benefit associated with ASP applications is single-image inventory. Similar in concept to last-room availability, single-image inventory allows all users to feed from the same database. One inventory—price and availability—is viewed by the GDS, central reservations call centers, and Internet-based distribution systems. The result is a lower error rate in reservations bookings and a resulting improvement in overall customer service.

Although last-room availability and single-image inventory (also known as *true integration*) appear quite similar, they are fundamentally different. The difference is that last-room availability uses property management system inventory for its information. Historically, CRSs have interfaced with property management systems to determine availability and pricing. With single-image inventory, all reservations applications as well as property management system applications look at the same database and draw from the same well of information.

As such, the rooms inventory can become available for others to access. One result of having an accessible inventory is an overall savings on reservations commissions. Imagine negotiating a special corporate rate with Pepsi, for example. Rather than having Pepsi book its special rates through a travel agent (and paying commissions to the travel agent and fees to the GDS and other distribution system providers), the hotel could provide Pepsi a unique access code. All reservations booked against the inventory using this special code would be virtually commission-free to the hotel!

Similarly, access to inventory can be made available to corporate or tour and travel group room blocks, giving groups the ability to develop their own rooming lists. Groups can then manipulate their room blocks, change names as often as needed, and simply send the hotel a completed rooming list at the touch of a button.

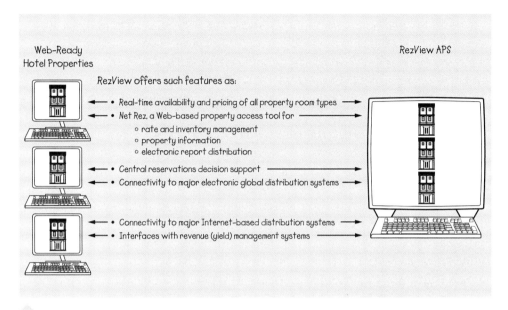

Exhibit 5–4   Features Provided Through an Application Service Provider—The Pegasus Solutions' "RezView" Model. Pegasus Solutions is the lodging industry's oldest (and most popular) provider of ASP Central Reservations software. Its ASP application, known as RezView, is utilized by more than 10,000 hotels, representing 71 brands and 2 million rooms worldwide. Its popularity rests on the features listed. *Source: Hotel & Motel Management.*

Traditional Reservation Channels

The explosion of the Internet, advancements in airline global distribution systems, and the increasing sophistication of switch technology have all played a role in changing the hotel industry's reservations landscape. As Web sites and online bookings grow in reservations volume (see Exhibits 5–1 and 5–5), other traditional channels have decreased in revenues and altered the traditional manner by which rooms are sold.

The Changing Role of the Travel Agent.   On August 30, 2001, just days before 9/11, almost every travel agent office in America closed for part of the day as a symbol of protest. The travel agents' National Day of Awareness was designed to alert consumers to the substantial airline commission changes impacting the travel agent industry. Until just a few months before their day of protest, travel agents were generously paid by the airline industry. They enjoyed a mutually beneficial relationship that created a market in which travel agents were the number one option for consumer airline ticket purchases. Those days are gone forever.

Travel agents previously received a 10% airline commission. That was gone by August 2001. Historical commissions on a $1,500 round-trip, first-class domestic ticket had been $150. That commission eroded slowly. In 1995, Delta Airlines started the trend with a $50 cap on its 10% domestic commissions. Two years later, the airlines cut the commission rate to 8%, and then in 1998, instituted a first-ever $100 commission cap on international tickets. In 1999, most airlines cut domestic and international commissions to just 5%. Then, in August 2001, American Airlines (and its subsidiary, TWA Airlines) reduced the $50 cap on domestic ticket commissions to just $20. Within days other fleets followed with their own reduced commissions.

Online Sales Revenues By Category/Industry	
Category	**Year 2005 Online Sales ($ in billions)**
Travel industries	$63.7
Computer/peripherals/PDAs	$23.7
Apparel and accessories	$11.0
Office supplies	$ 7.6
Consumer packaged goods	$ 5.0
Consumer electronics	$ 4.3
Books and magazines	$ 3.5
Computer software and games	$ 2.9
Event tickets	$ 2.9
Furniture, appliances, and equipment	$ 2.9
All other	$17.4

Exhibit 5-5   In the late 1990s online travel purchases outpaced online personal computer purchases, for the first time. Travel became the leading Internet sales category. Travel bookings continue to grow at a rate faster than any other. That's because online travel bookings make sense. According to Internet experts, the travel industry is a natural for online bookings. Through the Internet, clients are readily able to compare prices, amenities, and other features before making their purchase decision.

But hotel bookings lag behind airline bookings in terms of online purchases. This is due, in part, to the fact that hotel bookings are more complicated for the average consumer. Air is the simplest online purchase, followed by rental cars, with hotels coming up third for "ease of use." As such, just one out of every three or so Internet air bookings is accompanied by a related hotel booking. *Source: Jupiter Research, Inc., Darien Connecticut.*

This was devastating for the travel agent industry. Its bread and butter has always been airline ticket commissions, and now (using the $150 commission example above), commissions had been reduced from $150 to just $20. In 2002, they lost even that paltry sum when most major airlines simply stopped paying commissions altogether.

Why Airline Commissions Changed?   Increased operating costs have squeezed airline profitability. Rising fuel costs have done the same. Competitive pressures among carriers and the ability of consumers to comparison shop fares have kept airline ticket prices relatively low. To stay profitable when prices are low and operating costs are high requires saving money wherever possible. The 10% travel agent commissions were a logical cost-saving measure.

Whatever the reasoning, certainly the airline industry has been successful in moving consumers away from travel agent bookings toward self-directed Internet bookings. Attractive and easy-to-use airline Web sites have helped simplify the do-it-yourself process. Discounts, double frequent flier miles, and Internet-only specials have also played a critical role in motivating consumers to visit airline Web sites.

Changes Still to Come.   Once there were 500,000 travel agencies across the world. In the past decade, and with increasing frequency, the travel agent industry has experienced numerous bankruptcies and going out of business signs. The biggest change for consumers has been an increased fee structure exclusively on commission. Consumers now pay travel agents $10 to $25 per airline ticket booking fee.

In a move similar to the elimination of travel agent commissions, most airlines also reduced or eliminated commissions to Internet travel sites (Travelocity, Orbitz, etc.). Where airlines had generally been paying travel sites a 5% commission (maximum $10 cap per ticket), most now pay none at all. Internet travel sites now add a surcharge similar to the booking fees charged by travel agents.

It is hard to predict what such changes will mean to travel agents, consumers, travel Web sites, the airline industry, and the hotel industry, but we can make a few conjectures. Travel agents will attract consumers from higher economic strata. These consumers will appreciate (and pay for) higher levels of service. The travel agents' expertise, the ease and convenience of one-stop shopping, and familiarity with the customer's unique needs and wants are the products that TA's sell. As the travel agent industry evolves, larger agencies will absorb smaller ones. The resulting few mega-agencies will undoubtedly carry more clout then we see today in terms of price/fee negotiations, wholesale travel prices, Internet Web sites, and more.

The Hotel–Travel Agent Relationship.   Although some experts predict that hotel commissions to travel agents will go the way of airline commissions, that appears unlikely. There are simply too many hotels competing with each other. Even hotels within the same chain or brand are in competition with each other. Hotels cannot afford to limit their chances of selling rooms by limiting their exposure to the global distribution system.

Travel agents are a major source of hotel reservations. Travel agent bookings represent about 15% of all hotel rooms booked. Hotels pay a 10% commission—more in off-seasons to generate volume—for all rooms booked by an agency. Fees are not governmentally regulated. Amounts paid vary from property to property and even within the same property over time. *Overrides*, additional points of 10 to 15%, are paid to encourage high levels of business from one agency. Guests used to pay no fee to the travel agency for its services. That is almost unknown today. Most agencies charge a service fee for all bookings, not just commissionless airline tickets.

Many hoteliers believe they are in direct competition with travel agents, fighting for the same business and paying a commission to boot. That kind of thinking is being supported by the appearance of powerful mega-agencies and consortiums of agencies. Large-volume dealers stand toe to toe with national hotel chains. By securing the travel contracts of small and large corporations, these mega-agencies squeeze discounted rates from the national hotel chains anxious to get or retain a piece of the business. This has become especially true with the rapidly growing demand for hotel rooms the industry has experienced in the last few years. Certain major markets, New York City for example, have such high demand during select periods of the year that corporate buyers are using travel agency room blocks as one approach to guaranteeing room availability.

Travel Agent Commissions.   The classic argument between hoteliers and travel agents revolves around commissions. Travel agents argue that hoteliers are slow in paying commissions and when the check does arrive, it is often inaccurate. Studies show that from 15% to 50% of all hotel commissions are inaccurate. Hoteliers argue that certain travel agents provide so little business, the commission check costs the hotel more in processing fees than the value of the check.

The advent of travel management software tools (a popular one is Kalypso, by ECommissions Solutions) have deflated most of these arguments. Hotels are better able to track business from travel agencies, choosing to accept business from those with which the hotel has a better relationship and possibly denying business from low producers. Travel agents are paid quicker and with more accuracy. Furthermore, both the hotels and the travel agents are able to evaluate annual business levels and choose with which operators they prefer to do business.

Central Reservations Center.   Although there is a distinction between the terms central reservations system (CRS) and central reservations office (CRO), today's jargon has made them virtually interchangeable. Technically, the CRS is the electronic system, including the last-room availability interface with individual chain properties. Included are the switch technology connections and the GDS, and the chain's Internet Web sites and linkups. The CRO is the actual office site(s) at which chain reservationists reside (see Exhibit 5–6). Most hoteliers simply refer to all these activities as the CRS.

The Midwest—especially Omaha, Nebraska and Kansas City, Missouri—developed into a major central reservations hub in the late 1960s. The Bell System had unused telephone line capacity in this area due to the massive defense grid it built to accommodate the armed forces. With the support of the telephone system, hotel companies began opening CRSs in the Midwest, creating a specialized labor force which made the area even more attractive.

Exhibit 5–6   The Beardsley Operations Center is one of three remaining international reservations centers operated by BWI. As call volume has dropped, so have the number of call centers worldwide. At its peak, Best Western operated five call centers, including Beardsley (shown above), and call centers in Glendale, Arizona (on the campus of Glendale Community College); Dublin, Ireland; Milan, Italy; and Sydney, Australia. Today, Best Western operates just three call centers; Beardsley, Milan, and Manila, Philippines. *Courtesy: Best Western International, Phoenix, Arizona.*

Although the Midwest still plays a critical role in today's CRSs, it is no longer the whole story. Technology has made the world a smaller place. Add increasing domestic employment costs, and it is not hard to see why many of today's CRSs are located overseas. India and the Philippines, with their relatively inexpensive skilled labor, have become major markets for worldwide call centers.

Outsourcing Call Centers.   Central reservations offices reached their peak demand in the mid 1990s. Today, even though many chains have grown in size and volume, their CRSs see less business than a decade ago. The result has been a reduction in CRS staffing and the closing of select central reservations offices around the globe.

Reduced CRS staffing has created a new trend in call centers—*outsourcing*. Outsourcing the CRS means rooms reservations are sold through call centers or reservationists not directly staffed by the chain. Two techniques are proving quite popular. The first is outsourcing to a complimentary, noncompetitive industry. An excellent example of this relationship is Choice Hotels' outsourcing arrangement with 1-800-Flowers.com. Choice overflows CRS call volume to 1-800-Flowers.com and vice versa. The two organizations find their business cycles to be very complementary. Choice is busiest in the summer season, posting its largest call demand between the months of May through September. This is the slowest season for the flower industry. Flower demand is highest between October and May, with surges in call volume from Thanksgiving to Mother's Day. By training operators at each company to handle double duty, each chain benefits from the relationship. The operators/reservationists benefit as well, because their job has more variety, there are fewer slow periods, and the two products are widely disparate.

Another outsourcing technique takes advantage of the work-at-home revolution. Driven by expanded broadband access to the Web, cheaper computer technology, improved call-routing systems, and increased dependence on ASP providers, CRSs are beginning to find their answer to overflow call demand in at-home workers. Flexibility is the primary attraction for at-home workers. Access to skilled labor, often without the need to pay costly employee benefits, is the draw for the hotel chains.

Some 70% to 80% of at-home reservationists have a college degree, compared with 30% to 40% of reservationists working CRS call centers. The employee turnover rate is lower with at-home workers as well. There is still the boredom of taking call after call, but at-home reservationists temper the monotony with the benefits of staying home every day. The result is a growing dependence on stay-at-home reservationists, approaching one-fourth of all reservationists on the job today.

Processing the Call.   Reservation agents receive incoming calls and process them in 2 to 3 minutes. They are assisted with sophisticated telephone switching equipment. To save labor, automated telephone systems answer the call and segregate the caller according to a variety of options. The caller listens to the options and selects a specific number on the telephone keypad. Large chains use the telephone system to segregate callers according to the hotel brand in which they are most interested. Another common way to separate callers is according to whether their reservation is for a domestic hotel property, a European hotel, an Asian property, a Latin American operation, and so on.

Once callers have been properly routed, they may be placed on hold for the next available reservationist. During the holding period, a recording provides information about the chain, special discount periods, new hotel construction, and the like. In recent years, more and more recordings recommend callers visit the Web site to save time and view special Internet-only discounts. Automatic call distributor equipment eventually routes the telephone call to the next available reservationist.

Time is money, with labor and telephone lines the primary costs of CROs. Reservations management constantly battles to reduce the time allotted to each call. A sign in the office might read: "Talk time yesterday 1.8 (meaning minutes). During the last hour, 2.2. This hour, 2.1." Actually, more sophisticated devices are available. Some computer-management systems monitor each agent, providing data on the number of calls taken, the time used per call taken, and the amount of postcall time needed to complete the reservation.

However, employee evaluations must not be judged on time alone. Systems often evaluate the percentage of the agent's calls that result in firm bookings and the relationship of the agent's average room rate to the average being sold by the entire center. Remember, CROs charge a fee for each reservation booked. Since the CRO is usually a separate subsidiary of the corporate parent, even company-owned properties pay the fee of several dollars per room-night booked. Franchisees pay more than just the booking fee, including a monthly fee on each room, a percent of gross rooms sales, and other national and regional marketing costs (see Chapter 2). Though franchisees may complain about the fee schedule, the CRS and its interface to the global distribution system and other channels of distribution is the major attraction of franchising.

Inhouse Reservations.   Whether large or small, affiliated or independent, corporate or transient, all hotels accept direct or inhouse reservations. In many properties, the number of inhouse reservations is minimal. Others—especially nonaffiliated, independent hotels without a CRS (see Exhibit 5–7)—may sell the bulk of their rooms through inhouse reservationists. Inhouse reservations are also handled in quantity by hotels with large sales departments. Such business is generated by the hotel's own sales department, and those bookings often bypass the CRS. Bypassing the CRS via direct, inhouse reservations improves the profitability of each room sold by eliminating one of the fees associated with the reservation. Where group rooms are deeply discounted, this small savings on each reservation amounts to a boost in annual earnings.

Experienced shoppers often call the hotel directly. The inhouse reservationist is more informed about the property. He or she has one hotel, whereas the CRS agent has hundreds or even thousands. If the hotel is full, reservations might be refused by the central reservation office but still be accepted on site.

Unfortunately, reservation calls direct to the property are being discouraged by, of all entities, the property itself. The hotel, which should encourage bypassing the CRS, is often too poorly staffed to accept the inhouse reservation. The caller, waiting on hold to speak with an inhouse reservationist, is unknowingly re-routed to the CRS. This can be especially frustrating when the caller has made the effort to look up the individual hotel's telephone number, called the operator and asked for reservations, only to have the line redirected to the corporate CRO. This approach makes sense during busy or understaffed periods. But systems which send all reservations to the CRS are doing both the property and the guests a disservice

Internet- and Web-Based Reservations.   Internet users have a staggering array of options for booking hotel rooms. Travel-related bookings make up the largest category of Internet transactions (see Exhibits 5–1 and 5–5). And each year, the Internet attracts a larger share of reservations away from more traditional sources—growing at a rate four times faster than the rest of the industry (see Exhibit 5–8).

Over its relatively short business cycle, Internet travel bookings have experienced significant changes and increasing sophistication. One of the most vital factors to the success

Exhibit 5-7　Hotels pay numerous commissions on each hotel reservation booked. In an effort to save commissions, hotels are looking to the Internet and developing their own Web sites. Attracting customers directly to inhouse reservations bypasses costly commissions. A great idea, but not all hotels take reservations directly through their independent Web sites. Instead, their Web sites either link to the chain's CRO (resulting in a commission), to an independent reservation service (again resulting in a commission), or the hotel's Web page provides information only without online reservations capabilities.

This exhibit shows a popular independent resort in Arizona. In spite of the attractiveness and sophistication of the Web page, you'll notice the guest cannot check availability or book a room online—this still requires a call (or email) to the property. *Courtesy: Rio Rico Resort and Country Club.*

> ➤ Over two-thirds of all Internet hotel bookings are for rooms selling below $100 per night.
> ➤ While the ADR for hotel rooms has been growing at roughly 7% per year, online Internet hotel room rates have been growing more slowly—only 5% per year.
> ➤ Hotel rooms booked over the Internet sell for an average 21% lower rate than hotel rooms booked through other GDS channels.
> ➤ For rooms selling for $301 and higher, the Internet actually sells a higher ADR than for hotel rooms booked through other GDS channels.
> ➤ The average length of stay for Internet hotel room bookings is 2.1 nights. Hotel rooms booked through other GDS channels have an average length of stay of 2.2 nights.

Exhibit 5-8   Some interesting facts related to Internet hotel bookings. *Source: Lodging Magazine's Lodging Trends/Pegasus Report.*

of a hotel's online marketing performance is search engine optimization. The use of search engines by guests seeking accommodations is growing at a rate of roughly 50% per year.

Search Engine Optimization.   Some 80% of all Web visits start in a search engine. Search engines such as Google, Yahoo! Search, and Ask.com scour or *mine* the Web for a list of sites which match the search criteria requested by the user. The search criteria is a key word or words, or a phrase, such as "Hotels at LAX." The user hopes that search phrase will identify hotels located at or near Los Angeles International Airport. In fact, a quick search on Google with the phrase "Hotels at LAX" actually turned up 4,520,000 results!

The goal of search engine optimization is to juggle all the components of a search strategy so the hotel's Web site migrates towards the top of the search. Even the top 1% of a search with 4 million plus results isn't good enough. For the hotel to be found by potential buyers, it needs to make its way into the top 5 to 20 listings. Statistically, that means, for this example, making it into the top-listed .0005% of all results! Most users will view the first page or two and then revise their search if they haven't found what appeals to them.

The hotel's search engine strategy will usually have both a paid and an organic component. Organic searches are the purest and most trusted kind. When the user looks up "Hotels at LAX," one or more paid listings will appear at the very top. These are usually distinguishable to the experienced user because they are a different color, have added graphics, or are listed on the sides of the top page. Experienced users often ignore these paid commercials and opt for organic results.

Organic results are different from results based on who paid the most to be listed at the top of the page. Organic, sometimes called "pure" or "natural," search results, are based on which Web sites appeared most relevant based on the nature of the content search. Organic results boast a higher reservation conversion rate than paid results because users trust organic results more. Organic results are often very accurate and detailed—for example, adding words like swimming pool, free breakfast, and free airport shuttle to the original search of "Hotels at LAX" dropped the 4 million plus results to under 100,000. A few more criteria—free parking or club room—and the search will be further refined.

Paid searches can be costly. Hotels pay both for keyword placement and for each customer click on the search engine to the hotel's Web site (called click-throughs). Software packages are available to help hoteliers compare costs for Internet placement versus increased returns in room sales. If the reservation is the final goal, and the manager knows what each reservation is worth, the software will estimate the profitability of the search strategy. It calculates two variable components: the click-through rate of each search engine and hotel's Web site's reservation conversion rate.

Search engine optimization strategies employ a blended mix of paid and organic results. But search is only half the battle. The hotel's Web site needs to be attractive and user-friendly enough to get the potential guest to open it, linger a bit, and ultimately book the reservation. The Web site should be up to date with regard to photographs and video images that showcase the property's ambiance. Information should be updated frequently and detailed enough to explain amenities and provide seasonal information. Information should be written in a variety of languages which parallel languages used by the hotel's guests. And the Web site should enable guests to make other on-site reservations (golf and dining, for example). No wonder the hotel's Web site is being called the front desk of the new millennium.

Hotel Web Sites.   Hotel managers realize the importance of spending marketing dollars on the Web just as they spend on billboards, print media, brochures, etc. A realistic goal for a property is to spend approximately 40% of its annual marketing budget in online products. A worthy goal, though today's industry is not yet there. In a recent study (see Exhibit 5–9), most hotels stated they were spending only $1,000 to $35,000 annually in online marketing. That approaches only 10% of the average property's annual marketing budget.

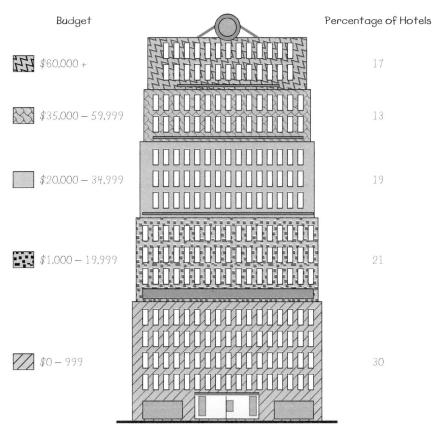

Exhibit 5–9   The weighted average annual expenditure by hotels for online marketing is just $26,400. This correlates to only about 10% of the average hotel's overall annual marketing and advertising budget. Online expenses are projected to grow as a percentage of a hotel's overall marketing budget for years to come. *Source: HSMAI Foundation.*

Spending online in such areas as search optimization, regularly updated content, rich imagery, and interactive maps can return substantial profits. When a guest books directly into a hotel's proprietary Web site, profits rise because the reservation has lower, if any, associated costs or fees. A $100 room booked through the property's Web site is worth $100 (less nominal pay-per-click fees charged by the search engines). A $100 room booked through an Internet travel site (Expedia, for example) may be worth just $60 or less!

Chain Web Sites.   In the early years of the Internet, lodging chains lost ground quickly to third-party travel sites and lodging aggregators like Expedia, Orbitz, Hotels.com, and Travelocity (see Exhibit 5–10). Early on, these third-party travel sites attracted greater demand from Internet users than chain Web sites. By establishing certain inventory and room rate pricing rules that all hotels were required to follow, heavily promoting low-price guarantees, and investing substantially in attractive and easy-to-use Web sites, the travel sites were running before the chains could react.

Exhibit 5–10

➤ Expedia	➤ Hotwire
➤ Travelocity	➤ VIPfares
➤ Orbitz	➤ Priceline
➤ Yahoo Travel	➤ ITN.net
➤ Cheap Tickets	➤ TravelNow

The top 10 Internet travel sites by gross annual revenues. New competitors with unique ways of scouring the Internet for lowest rates are constantly threatening these proven brands. Watch for the following two examples to gain popularity over the coming years:

➤ Priceline (regularly promoted by William Shatner who played Captain Kirk on Star Trek), is being targeted by search engine SideStep. SideStep has hired Patrick Stewart, who plays Captain Picard on Star Trek: The Next Generation, to promote its Web site.

➤ A recent study found that newly designed AAA.com offered the lowest rates more often than Expedia, Travelocity, or Orbitz. *Source: Travel Industry Association of America.*

Times have changed, however, as third-party travel companies have begun losing Internet demand back to the chain Web sites. The catalyst for this change was a gutsy move by Intercontinental Hotels Group in November 2004. Intercontinental announced it would provide the best room prices on its own Web site. Shortly thereafter, most of the other major lodging chains followed suit, undercutting the biggest attraction for third-party travel sites, lowest rate guarantees (see Exhibit 5–11).

Chain Web sites have other improvements ahead of them if they hope to challenge successfully the third-party travel sites. Hilton Hotels Corporation, for example, recently enhanced each of its various brand Web sites to enable users to search for all hotels on one page and then compare them side by side. Marriott International, Incorporated has enabled its Web sites to track Marriott's Rewards points in real time. And Westin's Website allows users to search by interest or amenities with such terms as "spa" or "family" (see Exhibit 5–12).

Check Rates and Availability

The Shangri-La Hotel, Beijing
Address: 29 Zizhuyuan Road
Beijing, China, 100089
Tel: (86-10) 6841 2211
Fax: (86-10) 6841 8002/3
Email: slb@shangri-la.com

Arrival Date:	April	5
Departure Date:	April	6
Number of Rooms/Suites:	1	
Number of Adults:	1	(per room)
Rate Plan Code:		(optional)

Professional Identification (Optional Information)

Corporate Rate ID:
Travel Agency: (IATA/ARC/TIDS)

[Clear Form]   [Check Availability]

Exhibit 5–11a   Making reservations online is as easy as it is widespread (see Exhibits 5–1 and 5–5). This Shangri-La Hotels & Resorts online reservation form walks the guest through the process step by step. First we pulled up www.shangri-la.com. Then we selected Beijing, China and clicked on "reservations." At that point, an availability screen popped up (Exhibit 5–11a). Once availability was assured, we were given a choice of many different room types and rates. Each room type was described, including rate; room description; bed type; and amenities, such as computer Internet connections, hairdryer, minibar, voicemail, even shoe shine availability. Once we selected our room type, a "required fields" screen pulled up for us to complete and send the reservation (Exhibit 5–11b). *Courtesy of Shangri-La Hotels & Resorts, Hong Kong.*

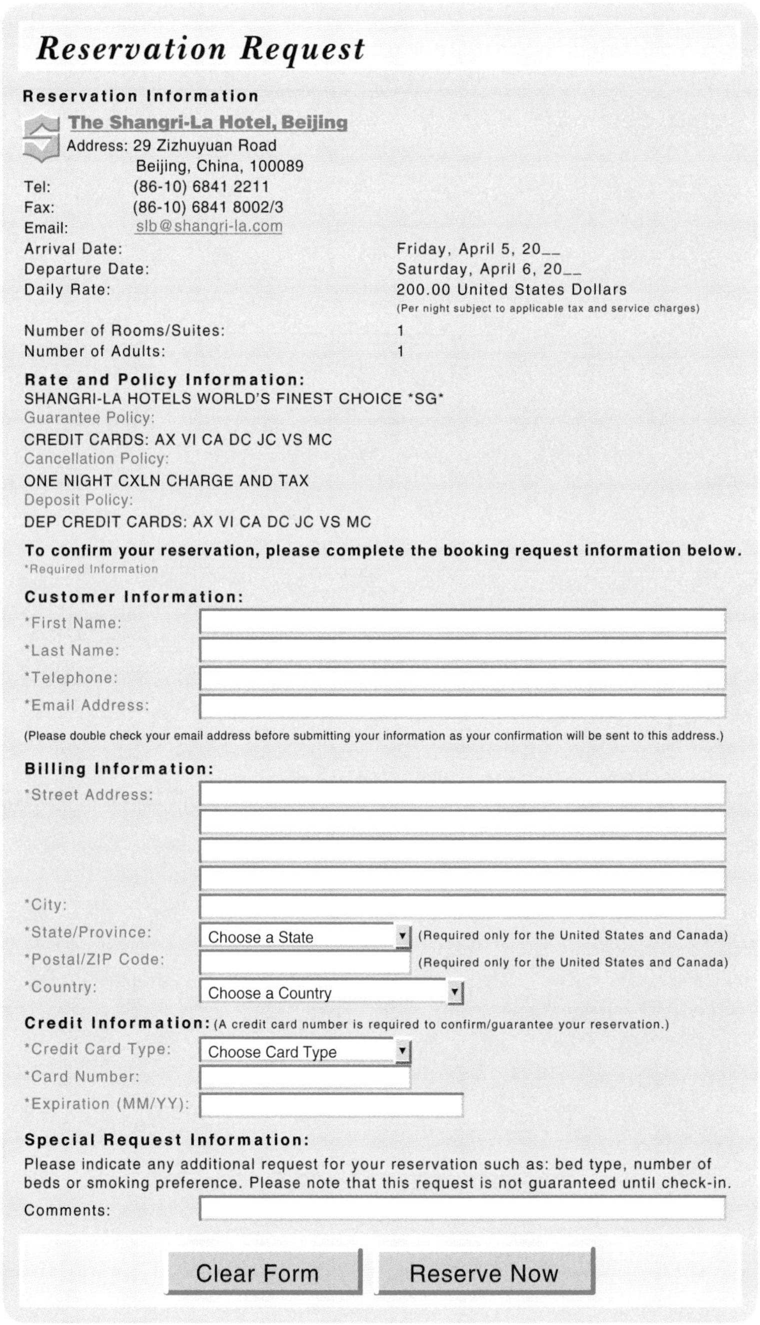

Reservation Request

Reservation Information

The Shangri-La Hotel, Beijing
Address: 29 Zizhuyuan Road
          Beijing, China, 100089
Tel: (86-10) 6841 2211
Fax: (86-10) 6841 8002/3
Email: slb@shangri-la.com

Arrival Date: Friday, April 5, 20__
Departure Date: Saturday, April 6, 20__
Daily Rate: 200.00 United States Dollars
                                       (Per night subject to applicable tax and service charges)

Number of Rooms/Suites: 1
Number of Adults: 1

Rate and Policy Information:
SHANGRI-LA HOTELS WORLD'S FINEST CHOICE *SG*
Guarantee Policy:
CREDIT CARDS: AX VI CA DC JC VS MC
Cancellation Policy:
ONE NIGHT CXLN CHARGE AND TAX
Deposit Policy:
DEP CREDIT CARDS: AX VI CA DC JC VS MC

To confirm your reservation, please complete the booking request information below.
*Required Information

Customer Information:
*First Name:
*Last Name:
*Telephone:
*Email Address:

(Please double check your email address before submitting your information as your confirmation will be sent to this address.)

Billing Information:
*Street Address:

*City:
*State/Province: Choose a State ▼ (Required only for the United States and Canada)
*Postal/ZIP Code: (Required only for the United States and Canada)
*Country: Choose a Country ▼

Credit Information: (A credit card number is required to confirm/guarantee your reservation.)
*Credit Card Type: Choose Card Type ▼
*Card Number:
*Expiration (MM/YY):

Special Request Information:
Please indicate any additional request for your reservation such as: bed type, number of
beds or smoking preference. Please note that this request is not guaranteed until check-in.
Comments:

[Clear Form]   [Reserve Now]

Exhibit 5–11b

Third-party travel sites aren't standing still. They have added many unique enhancements themselves.

Third-Party Travel Web Sites.   Even as online travel continues to rise, bookings through third-party travel sites has slowed in comparison with the growth in direct bookings to hotel proprietary Web sites. This has caused concern for third-party travel

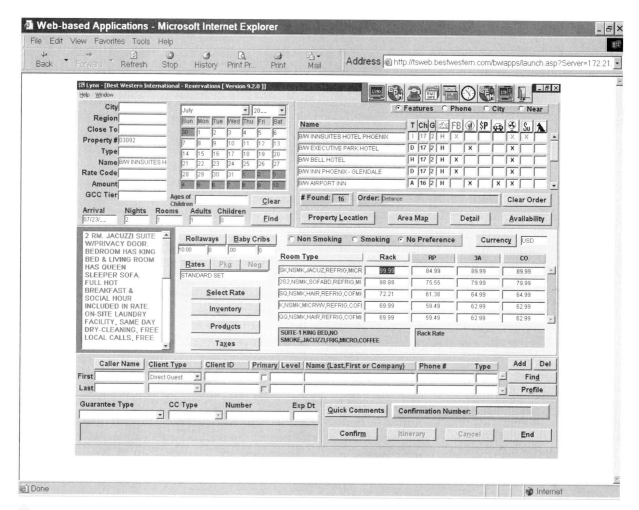

Exhibit 5–12   A sample reservations screen from Best Western International's proprietary Lynx reservations system (version 9.2.0). Exhibit 5–6 shows individual reservations work stations at Best Western International's Beardsley Operations Center in Phoenix, Arizona. *Courtesy: Best Western International, Phoenix, Arizona.*

vendors and a renewed commitment to making their sites the best for consumers in terms of usability, price, selection, and attractiveness.

Although business models will certainly change in the coming years, third-party travel sites continue to use a proven approach. Contract with the hotel for a set number of rooms (*inventory aggregation*) at a deeply discounted rate and then resell those rooms online at Web sites known for giving consumers the best rate. One variation has third-party travel vendors actually purchasing the blocks of rooms to resell rather than merely contracting for their availability. In either case, this was a winning concept—selling a product the travel sites don't own (and have no control over), for a price which is lower than the hotel would ever sell rooms on the open market. So why did hotels flock to partner with these third-party travel sites? Because hoteliers hoped this concept was their answer for selling distressed inventory. They believed it was a sure-fire method of enhancing occupancy during slow periods. It gained credence during the post 9–11 period when occupancies plummeted.

Hotels with rooms available most nights were prime candidates to sign with one or more travel sites. Even successful properties with high occupancies contracted with third-party vendors, because they still had nights with unoccupied rooms. The travel sites had some basic rules and rooms commitments, but at first glance these policies seemed reasonable to the hotel operators. Each third-party travel site had its own proprietary rules, but two standards were fairly common across all vendors. The hotel was required to commit at least 5% of its entire rooms inventory for the year, and the hotel could not—through any of its numerous channels of distribution—advertise its rooms at a rate lower than the rate on the travel Web site. In exchange, the travel Web sites provided a steady source of occupied rooms the hotel could readily depend upon.

What the hotels did not consider, until it was too late, was how this concept impacted the consumers' view of their product. There is an old adage in the lodging industry: "Once a customer has experienced a discounted rate, it is hard to get him to return to regular price." This was the case with Internet-savvy users who found it easier and less expensive to shop with third-party sites than to visit hotel or chain Web sites. It has taken the lodging industry the better part of a decade to change that trend and to regain the confidence of customers that chain Web sites do, indeed, offer the lowest available rates.

The 5% room commitments were also hard on properties. Those hotels that contracted with multiple third-party vendors (Expedia, and Hotwire, for example) were sometimes committing 20% of their inventory to deeply discounted rates. Although the travel Web sites allowed hotels to black out certain dates for which the property anticipated sold-out occupancy, the number was limited to somewhere between 5 and 15 dates per year. For low-season periods, this might make sense. But on an annualized basis, hotels were experiencing increased occupancy at the expense of profitability. With such deep discounts, even when a hotel was only reaching 80% occupancy, these significant room commitments were eating into profitability, ADR and RevPar statistics.

Today's industry managers have come full circle. Third-party Web sites, initially viewed as saviors, then later scorned, are now seen for what they are: another channel of distribution. If used wisely they do provide an avenue for unloading distressed inventory. So long as the hotel operator considers this as just one arrow in a quiver of online reservation channels, it makes sense.

Meta-Search Technology.   The newest category in the arena of third-party travel sites are the meta-search sites, led by SideStep, Kayak, Mobissimo, and TravelZoo. These sites employ a unique technology which uses advanced search techniques to find all the links on the Internet where hotel prices lurk. This includes third-party travel sites, the GDS, the hotel's own proprietary Web site, and the chain's Web site. The lowest prices are then presented to the potential guest, along with a rate and features comparison against other hotels in the area.

The growth in meta-search sites is potentially hazardous to unwitting hotels. Meta-searches exploit rate differences in those hotels which have not ensured rate integrity across all channels of distribution. And meta-searches have substantially increased the number of hits on hotel Web sites. This increase in hits not only degrades the speed of the Web site response, but also substantially increases marketing costs through search engines which charge on a "look-to-book" basis. At one time, hotel look-to-book ratios were as low as four to one. For every four users viewing rates on the hotel's Web site, the hotel averaged one booking. Today, thanks in part to meta-search sites, the look-to-book ratio is thousands to one. To shield the hotel's Web site from increased hits, hotels and lodging chains are beginning to create separate, but parallel, systems which maintain and continuously update property data. The parallel system carries room type, rate, and availability data for every hotel in the chain. As long as third-part travel sites are confident that these parallel systems are up to date, they can program their proprietary software to search these parallel systems, thereby leaving the Web site without costly hits.

Independent Reservation Services.   Membership in a CRS is one of the major advantages that chain-affiliated properties have over independent operations. The CRS provides each affiliated property access to the GDS, chain Web sites, professional assistance with the hotel's own Web site, a convenient toll-free telephone number for potential customers, automated rate and inventory data, and a wealth of other automated benefits. Yet CRSs are extremely expensive. Costs reach tens or hundreds of millions of dollars, prohibitive for most small chains and independent operations.

Smaller chains can provide better guest service at a lower cost by leasing the reservation service. For hotel rep companies—Utell International is the world's largest—this is a natural extension of their primary role and provides economies of scale for hotel clients. UtellVision is a computerized reservation system for Utell member hotels. The system displays two screens simultaneously. The top screen is a series of high-resolution pictures of the member hotel and maps of the surrounding areas; on the bottom is an online reservations availability screen.

Independent hotels and small chains that join a private reservation service generally experience a number of money-saving benefits. They save in hardware and software. They save operating and training costs. Reservation processing is more efficient due to the massive computer capacity of the independent reservation service. And salesmanship is enhanced by joining a group of professionally trained agents. If the independent reservation service is also an ASP, even more benefits are available to the small chain—the property management system database is Web accessible. Single-imaging allows all users access to the same information. Yield management decisions can be made on a chainwide basis—refer to the discussion on ASPs earlier in this chapter (see Exhibit 5–4).

Hotel Representative Services.   Hotel representative services take the independent reservation service one step further. Providing valuable tools to member hotels, hotel rep organizations also provide access to membership for independent, noncompeting hotels. By banding together to market the membership under one flag, the independent hotel garners many of the same benefits which accrue to franchise- or referral-affiliated operations. Preferred Hotel and Resorts and Leading Hotels of the World are two good examples of such memberships.

Utell International is the world's largest hotel representative service, handling thousands of reservations each day for more than 4,000 member hotels. Utell provides member properties with instant global connectivity (through parent company Pegasus) to a telephone reservation network, the Global Distribution System (GDS), and the Internet. Member hotels appear on more than 450,000 reservation terminals, where users gain immediate access to hotel information, rates, and availability.

Other Trends in Electronic Reservations

They say that in just one day, the average American adult is exposed to more information than a person living 100 years ago might have been exposed to in a lifetime. That statistical analogy speaks volumes in terms of the speed and quantity of information available today. And the trend will certainly continue. For example, the average processing power of a personal computer is expected to grow 1,000-fold over the next five years. In addition, information storage and retrieval capabilities of PCs are anticipated to grow at a compounded rate of 60% per year for the next five years. With these rapid advancements, CROs are facing increasing opportunities for unique and more effective ways of performing their businesses. From voice recognition to "mapping" software, the future is anyone's guess.

Voice Recognition.   Amazing progress has been achieved in the area of automated voice recognition. Currently there are systems in place that can recognize tens of thousands of words spoken by a host of various users. Dragon Systems' NaturallySpeaking and IBM's Via Voice are the two leading personal computer applications. Each can recognize more than 50,000 words with 99% accuracy.

We are closing in on the time when straightforward rooms reservations will be routinely handled electronically by voice-recognition and voice-synthesis (talking) systems. Thousands of voice-recognition systems are now at work across myriad other industries. The biggest argument in favor of such a laborsaving system is the overall repetitiveness of the reservationist's job. As unique as each reservation might seem, there are more commonalities than differences. Each reservation communicates the city, date, room rate and type, and other basic data. These are functions that a computer system can logically handle. In fact, the simplest of all voice-recognition software applications utilizes a "command" system. This system recognizes several hundred words from a preprogrammed list of possible commands. On what day of the week a guest is traveling (7 possible words), the date of departure (31 possible words), type of credit-card guarantee (roughly 6 to 10 possible words), and credit-card number (10 possible words) are some of the common reservations commands a computer might easily recognize.

The voice-recognition reservations program generates a series of questions for the guest to answer. With each response, the program acknowledges the answer, allows the guest to make changes as necessary, and generates a new series of questions based on the previous response. In those situations where the computer cannot recognize the guest's voice due to a strong accent or other impairment, a fail-safe system is in place. The guest might press the zero button twice on the telephone keypad, for example, to alert an operator that personal assistance is needed. An excellent voice-recognition CRO is operated by American Airlines—give it a try at 1-800-433-7300. When American's reservationists are busy, the system probes the key elements of the guest's flight information. It does a fantastic job of understanding originating airport, destination airport, day of travel, time of travel, and so on.

Such computer systems can check availability, quote rates, suggest alternative dates, and thank the guest in a manner similar to the reservationist. Of course, such a system would be significantly less personal than dealing with an actual reservationist. On the other hand, it would surely be less expensive in terms of labor costs, and the computer system would never call in sick!

Mapping Capabilities.   As CRSs gain sophistication, options that were previously unavailable (or manually performed) are increasingly being automated.

Commonplace requests such as a hotel's physical address, its distance from a popular destination, or specific travel directions were once manual tasks. Central reservations agents, representing chains of hundreds or thousands of hotels, were required to look up such information in databases provided by member properties. This was a slow and generally inefficient method.

Today, modern mapping functions provide comprehensive geographical, pictorial, and textual information about every member property. Best Western was the first company of its size to offer a mapping feature with its new CRS. Now central reservations agents across the industry have immediate access to geographically related questions about property locations, mileage, travel times, and so on.

Guest History Databases.   Another benefit of an increasingly sophisticated CRS is the ability for hotels to share guest history information. This is especially true if the chain utilizes an application service provider (ASP). Database information is currently utilized only within chains. With ASPs, guest history data could actually be shared across chains.

Even within the chain, hotels rarely take advantage of their wealth of data. Even though all property management systems allow a guest history function. Standard information required for the reservation becomes a marketing tool, if properly administered. After all, the hotel already knows the guest's name and address, the dates of the last visit, the rate paid, the room type, the number of guests, and the method of payment. Add a bit of marketing information such as the type of discount package purchased, the special rate or promotion used, and whether the reservation was midweek or was a weekend getaway package, and the manager has an enormous amount of marketing data. For a more thorough understanding of guest history, refer to Chapter 6.

AUTOMATED REVENUE MANAGEMENT SYSTEMS

An increasingly sophisticated lodging and technological industry has changed the way hoteliers sell available rooms. Rather than the old goal of simply "placing heads in beds," today's hoteliers need to selectively place the right heads into the right beds at the right price. Despite the large number of rooms that are available on an annual basis, every reservation request is not accepted. The decision depends on space and rate ranges available for the specific dates. An occupancy forecast determines the space availability for the day or days in question. Even if only one day of the sequence is closed, the reservation may be refused and an alternative arrangement offered. This is unfortunate if the declined reservation represented a request for a number of days. It is especially unfortunate if the period in question has only one sold-out date. Then the hotel is essentially trading a profitable, long-term reservation against a potential over-booking situation for one sold-out date. In many cases, the reservationist may override the system to book this type of reservation. Obviously, such a decision would be considered on a case-by-case basis.

In other scenarios, salesmanship by the reservationist comes into play. The telephone provides a two-way conversation during which the reservationist can gauge the behavior of the guest. Some guests can be convinced to reserve their chosen date at a slightly higher nightly rate. Other guests can be changed toward a slower occupancy period with the offer of reduced rates. Guests who cannot be accommodated represent lost revenues. The reservationist attempts to salvage lost reservations in a number of ways—offering premium rates during almost sold-out periods, offering different dates when rates are not as high, or even offering another sister property of the same chain in a nearby community. When all else fails, the reservationist can only thank the caller and ask him or her to try again another time.

Requests for accommodations are sometimes denied even if the house is not full. Most of the hotel's advertised packages are refused if the forecast shows that the house is likely to fill at standard rack rates. Reservationists must be taught to sell discounted packages or other reduced rates (weekend, commercial, governmental) only on request or when encountering rate resistance. With a full house, the hotel may *regret* (deny) requests from travel agents, to whom the hotel pays a commission. Busy hotels give preference to higher-paying multiple-occupancy requests over single occupancy.

Casino hotels give preferential treatment to those who are likely to gamble, even to the extent of granting them free accommodations in preference to paying guests who don't play. Noncasino hotels do the same, allotting their scarce space to reservations from certain areas or markets that the hotel is trying to develop.

The Yield Management Revolution

Revenue management, the act of controlling rates and restricting occupancies in an effort to maximize gross rooms revenue, is most commonly referred to as *yield management*. In its simplest form, yield management has been around for decades. Any seasoned manager who increased room rates as occupancy rose, or who quoted higher rates for holidays and special event periods, or who saved the last few room nights for extended-stay reservations was using yield management. It is not the practice of yield management that is new, it is the incorporation of revenue managers into dedicated senior staff positions and the automation of yield management into complex property management systems that is new.

Organizations were downsized and labor costs reduced during the low cycle of the early 1990s. Despite the squeeze on profits, many hotels added revenue managers (or yield managers) to their organizations (see Exhibit 3–1). The move was easily justified by the revenue offset. Some 15% to 25% of recent ADR growth has been attributed to yield management, the specialty of these new managers. Thus, a 400-room property with an overall 10% increase in ADR from, say, $118 to $129.80 could attribute about $2 of the nearly $12 increase directly to the new yield team. Assuming 70% occupancy, that produces some $200,000 annually (400 rooms $\times$ 70% 365 days $\times$ $2). That's a wonderful return on the costs of yield management hardware, software, and related wages!

A Brief History of Yield Management.   As with other businesses, price (hotel room rate) is a major factor in the decision to purchase one product over another. That is especially true in light of the sharper guest segmentation the industry has experienced over the last decade. Yield management works best when there are distinct market segments to attract. It is the price sensitivity of these market segments that made yield management practices successful in the first place.

The Airlines' Role.   Just as it did with GDS and CRS technologies, the lodging industry adopted yield management from the airline industry. Airline rate discounting was widespread in the early 1980s, and that contributed to the array of prices airlines found difficult to track. They began experimenting with adjusted rates based on demand forecasts. Discounted tickets purchased far in advance were used to establish a minimum level of seat occupancy and to forecast overall demand. Low and seasonal periods were also discounted. As the plane filled and departure time neared, higher and higher fares were charged. Full price was eventually charged for the remaining seats—a price that would have been virtually impossible to charge when the plane was empty.

Airlines and hotels are much alike. Both have a relatively fixed supply of product (seats and rooms), and both have products that perish with the passage of time. In the 1980s, airlines had one extra edge—large computer capability. It takes the capacity of these large systems to simultaneously track occupancy (seat or room) and the variety of price options that both industries market.

Price-sensitive concepts have been employed by hoteliers for a long, long time. Refining the practices and developing them into a computer program with *rules and triggers*, with a historical database and a strategy, awaited the superior computer capability of the airlines. Today, most major lodging chains have developed automated yield management systems that rival the best of the airline systems.

Market Demand.   Airlines and hotels did differ in one respect—their view of the guest. Hotels had previously operated on the belief that their customer was not a discretionary traveler. The guest who stayed, hoteliers felt, was someone who had to stay. Guests did not visit merely because the price was reduced enough to lure them in. Urban hotels, which cater to the least flexible guest, the commercial traveler, first evidenced the change. In desperate need of weekend business, these properties began to successfully market weekend specials to discretionary buyers. The yield management revolution had begun.

Yield management has an economic rationale. It assumes that all customers are price conscious—that they are aware of the existence of and the significance of price variations. It also assumes that customers are price sensitive—that their buying habits respond to increases and decreases in price.

All things being equal, the guest is motivated by lower prices. Theoretically, when a similar room type is available for a significantly lower rate at an otherwise equal hotel, the guest will select the lower-priced accommodations. In addition, guests who might not have left home at the rack rate are inclined to visit hotels when rates are low. That explains why low-occupancy periods are generally accompanied by lower average room rates.

Each customer class has different degrees of price consciousness and price sensitivity. Earlier discussions on segmentation (see Chapter 2) indicated the wide range of guests to whom the industry appeals. In simple categories, these are the business (corporate) class, the leisure (transient) guest, and the group (tour) buyer.

Corporate Guests.   The business or corporate customer is less sensitive to price—not unaware of price, just less sensitive to it. Businesspersons must travel when the need arises; they do not travel merely because the price is reduced.

Business arrangements may be made only a few days or hours before arrival (see Exhibit 5–13). Location is critically important, both to save travel time and to present the proper image. Business travelers need to be near the business district, which means high-priced real estate and high room rates. These travelers are away from home a good deal. They seek and probably merit a higher level of comfort than the occasional leisure traveler. In summary, business guests pay higher rates because they are less price sensitive. They have to stay in a specific location at a given time, and that arrangement is often made suddenly, with little advance planning, and therefore little opportunity to obtain discounted rates.

Leisure Guests.   The leisure guest, as the name implies, is 180 degrees removed from the corporate traveler. With leisure guests, lead time is long. Reservation bookings are well planned, with adequate time to shop for the best room rates. This class of guest is flexible as to the time of the trip, the destination of the trip, and stopping points along the way. These guests may not even use a hotel. High prices might drive them into camping or park facilities. Poor price value might send them to the homes of friends or family. When prices of accommodations, fuel, toll roads, and gasoline are too high, this guest may just stay home.

Leisure travelers have been the major beneficiaries of the yield management approach offered by both the airline and the hotel industries. The leisure travelers' flexibility with regard to travel dates and itineraries allows them to take advantage of deep discounting during off-season and slow demand periods. It is not uncommon to find hotel rooms discounted between 50% and 80% during slow periods. A $250 hotel room in Australia's Kakadu National Park in the tropics, for example, may cost only $100 or

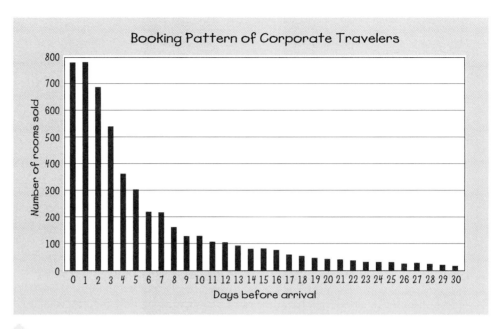

Exhibit 5-13   A 30-day booking pattern for corporate travelers. Although some corporate guests book 30 (or more) days in advance, the majority reserve rooms within a few days of arrival. This 275-room hotel receives approximately 60% of its business from corporate guests.

so during the rainy season; a $400 golf package in Palm Springs may be discounted to $175 in the heat of the summer.

Group Guests.   Group business, the last of the three general classifications, exhibits characteristics from both of the other two categories. That's because the group market forms from components of the business and leisure classifications. From the leisure category come social, fraternal, and hobby associations. (Recall the previous discussion of SMERF, social, military, educational, religious, and fraternal). From the business segment come professional, union, and governmental groups.

Both types of groups—leisure and business—have their own idiosyncracies. Generally, business-oriented groups are sensitive to date and place while being less sensitive to rate. That is because business groups usually meet the same week every year. Leisure-oriented groups are more rate sensitive and therefore tend to be somewhat flexible with regard to date and place. Profits can be increased if the sales department, based on good forecasting, can steer the business to the right (right for the hotel) time, place, and rate.

Yield management has changed the interface between the sales department and the group buyer. Based on information from the yield management program, the sales department and/or the revenue manager must decide to take the business, reject the business, or try to negotiate a different time at a different rate. Saturday arrival for a group might actually prove more profitable at $90 per night, for example, than a Monday arrival (which replaces high rate corporate guests) at $115 per night. A well-programmed yield management system should provide the answer. (A more detailed discussion of group business and related automation is available in Chapter 6.)

At issue is whether the discounted room rates requested by the group, plus the value of the group's meeting room and banquet business, is valued at more or less than the forecasted income (room and incidentals) from normal guests who will be turned away.

Yield management systems can answer that question. The discretionary decisions still remain for the salespersons to evaluate. For example, is other new business likely to spin off from this meeting? Is this a single event, or are we doing business with a meeting planner who controls 100 or more meetings per year? Will this disrupt regular corporate guests on whom the hotel depends?

Yield management means that function rooms are no longer booked on a first-come, first-served basis. Neither are guest rooms; there must be a price–occupancy mix.

Price–Occupancy Mix.   Yield is calculated by multiplying occupancy (assume 65% for a 250-room hotel) by average daily rate (assume an ADR of $75.00). In this example, yield is $12,187.50 per day. Yield can be increased by raising rates when occupancy (demand) is high. ADR is also raised by refusing packages, requiring minimum lengths of stay, and charging groups full rate without discounts. When occupancy (demand) is low, prices are dropped by promoting packages, seeking out price-sensitive groups, and creating special promotional rates. That's the dichotomy of the lodging industry. When times are good (high occupancy), they are very good because with high occupancy comes high rate. Conversely, when times are bad (low demand), times are very bad because all of the hotel's competitors are also lowering their prices.

Since yield is the product of these two elements, equilibrium is obtainable by increasing one factor when the other decreases. Exhibit 5–14 illustrates the mathematics. Yield in all three cases is identical. To earn the same room revenue, management must choose between high ADR or high occupancy.

All managers will not view the values in Exhibit 5–14 as being equal. Some would prefer the higher occupancy over the higher rate. Higher occupancy means more persons. More guests translate into more food and beverage revenue, more telephone use, more calls for laundry and dry cleaning. More guests mean more greens fees, more amusement park admissions, or more money spent in the casino. For these reasons, some hotels charge the same rate for occupancy by one or two persons.

A different group of operators would prefer to strengthen their ADR. These managers feel that ADR is the barometer of a property's service and quality levels. With the lower occupancy that accompanies higher ADR, hotels save on variable costs like utilities, wear and tear on furniture and equipment, and reduced levels of staffing.

Clearly, price–occupancy mix is not a simple, single decision. Dropping rates to increase occupancy might not be the choice of every manager. Indeed, the manager might take that option at one hotel but not at another. Variations in the facilities of the hotel, in its client base, and in the perspective of its management will determine the policies to be applied.

Hotel	Average Daily Rate	Percent Occupancy	Monthly Gross Revenue[a]	Potential Revenue	Yield Percentage
A	$ 75	65.00	$377,812.50	$620,000	60.9
B	100	48.75	377,812.50	620,000	60.9
C	50	97.50	377,812.50	620,000	60.9

[a] Revenue or Yield.

Exhibit 5–14   Price–occupancy mix: Yield is the product of occupancy times rate. Management decides whether a higher rate (ADR) or a higher occupancy is preferable. This Exhibit assumes 250 rooms and a 31-day month. Potential revenue assumes 100% occupancy at an $80 rate: 250 rooms × 100% occupancy × $80 × 31 days.

Revenue per Available Room.   Yield is usually expressed in terms of gross revenue per day, per month or per year (see Exhibit 5–14). However, there is a special advantage to quoting yield in terms of revenue per available room (RevPar). RevPar (see also Chapter 1) combines occupancy and average daily rate into a single number. Continuing the illustration: A 250-room hotel at 65% occupancy and $75 ADR produces revenue per available room (RevPar) of $48.75 (65% × $75).

Before the popularization of RevPar in the mid 1990s, hotel managers tended toward one of the two camps described above. They migrated either toward higher occupancies or toward higher ADRs. Managers who work toward maximizing RevPar, strive toward a balance or equilibrium between occupancy and rate (see Exhibit 5–15).

The only difference between calculating yield and RevPar is that yield incorporates the number of hotel rooms into the calculation, whereas RevPar looks at revenue per available room. In fact, if you take RevPar for any given day and multiply it by the number of rooms available in the hotel, the product is that day's yield. To demonstrate, take the $48.75 RevPar found above in our ongoing example and multiply it by the 250 rooms available. The product is the same $12,187.50 yield calculated several paragraphs above in the price–occupancy mix discussion and shown in Exhibit 5–15.

The RevPar calculation is also beneficial to management as a quick glimpse into the hotel's success on any given day. If the hotel knows its fixed costs on a per room per day basis (fixed costs include administrative salaries, mortgage debt, fixed franchise fees, and insurance, to name a few), it can quickly gauge how much, if any, of the RevPar can be contributed toward variable costs and profits. In our ongoing example, if RevPar is $48.75 and fixed costs are $23.25, then $25.50 per available room can be contributed toward variable costs and profit. Management can readily see how well the hotel performed on that given day.

Exhibit 5–15

Referring to the 250-room hotel of Exhibit 5–14, this graph demonstrates the infinite number of points that make up the daily yield curve.

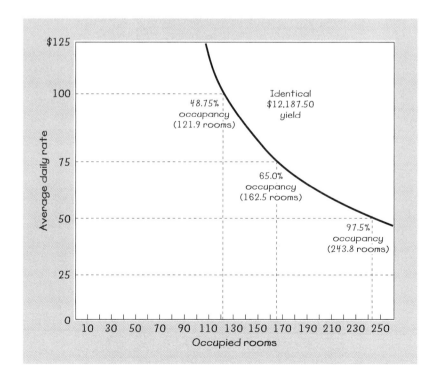

Ideal Conditions for Yield Management.   Not all industries are successful with managing yield. Unique conditions exist in the lodging and airline industries which set them apart. Perishability of inventory is foremost among these differences. Unlike manufactured goods, which can be inventoried for long periods before being sold, hotel rooms, airline seats, cruise ship berths, ferryboat stalls, and theater and movie seats are all examples of products which perish with time. Hotel rooms, berths and seats which aren't sold tonight are lost forever.

Some unique characteristics of yield management are embodied in the lodging industry.

➤ *Fixed supply.*   Altering the number of rooms available for a given hotel requires substantial lead time, planning, design, and construction. Hotels cannot change their inventory as quickly as a factory, which can add a second or third shift to match high demand.

➤ *High fixed and low variable costs.*   The lodging industry is capital intensive, requiring substantial fixed investment in real estate, automation, furnishings, and salaries. Yet there are relatively low variable costs associated with selling one more room. Aside from housekeeping wages, utility usage, a complimentary breakfast (if included), and some wear and tear, it costs hotels little above their high fixed costs to sell another room.

➤ *Interchangeability of products.*   Although hotels differentiate themselves through service levels, amenities, marketing, and brand, the basic product they offer is much the same across the entire industry. Guests are only willing to pay a certain premium for these differences (real or perceived). Too high a markup, and guests can easily find a competing product at a lower rate.

➤ *Segmented markets with differing price sensitivity.*   Yield management would not work if all travelers had the same sensitivity to price and date. When demand was high and resulting room rates were high, no guest would be willing to pay such rates (but corporate guests do). When rates were high for certain dates but other dates were less expensive, no guest would be willing to alter their plans to a different date (but leisure guests will).

➤ *Seasonality of demand.*   Hotels are able to gauge demand through advance reservations sales and historically based projections. And there are clear demand patterns across seasons.

Tools for Measuring Results.   The revenue manager's daily task is a formidable one. Both average daily rate (ADR) and occupancy percentage must be maximized internally and ranked against competitive performances. There are two parts to this *competitive market set*. Some hotels are geographic competitors (close by) while others compete on the basic measures discussed in Chapter 1: size, class (rate), and type (see Exhibit 5–16).

Gone are the days when the competitor's performance was measured by counting cars in the parking lot during the day or lighted guest rooms at night. Gone are the days when the staff made telephone calls to competing properties to gauge availability and rates. Today's hoteliers have a large assortment of reports and subscription services that provide a wealth of information. Facts that were just not available to earlier executives. Almost all of the data originates in the global distribution systems. Statistics are the byproduct of inventorying and selling rooms through the GDS. It follows that the biggest providers of subscription and information services are the very ones selling millions of rooms–the GDS.

Exhibit 5-16   The inviting main pool of the Doubletree La Posada Resort. This three-star and three-diamond property operating in Scottsdale, Arizona, includes in its competitive set such Scottsdale properties as Hilton Scottsdale Resort and Villas, Sunburst Resort, Doubletree Paradise Valley Resort, and Millennium at McCormick. Its competitive set ranges over many square miles and, interestingly, includes two other properties (Hilton Scottsdale Resort and Villas and Doubletree Paradise Valley Resort) licensed by the same Hilton Hotels Corporation that licenses the Doubletree La Posada Resort. *Courtesy of Doubletree La Posada Resort, Scottsdale, Arizona.*

Let's look at some of the most popular reports.

PHASER Complete Access Reports.   Provided by TravelCLICK, the *PHASER Report* is one of several formats available through this company. TravelCLICK is the preeminent provider of digital media and data solutions to the travel industry. By offering hotels and other travel suppliers detailed competitive reports, TravelCLICK helps hotels position themselves more aggressively within their marketplace.

TravelCLICK pulls its competitive information directly from Global distribution systems (from Sabre and other GDSs), which is used by more than 480,000 (about 98%) of the world's travel agents. The report breaks hotel rates into two categories, GDS and CRS, and reports the lowest available rate in each area. *PHASER Complete Access Reports* provide hotel managers with a custom-designed look at their own hotel as it compares with the competitive market set. Hotel managers can select the competing hotels they wish included in their market set and set the length of time they wish covered in each particular report.

Other features of this report include highlighted rates that have risen or dropped by a user defined amount (e.g., ± $10). Hotel availability status by day in both the GDS and CRS are included. So, too, are details for every rate offered in the CRS by room type across each competitive hotel during the selected time period.

Smith Travel Research's STAR Reports.   Founded in 1985 as an independent research firm, Smith Travel Research (STR) is one of the industry's leaders in providing accurate information and analyses to the lodging industry. With the most comprehensive database of hotel performance information ever compiled, STR has developed a variety of products and services to meet the needs of hotel revenue managers.

Although many reports used by revenue managers display future data (rates for a set of dates in the near future), *STAR Reports* are based entirely on historical data. This report answers the following questions: How well did I do in terms of average daily rate, occupancy, and RevPar against my competitors? Another key distinction is that *STAR Reports* do not share specific performance data for each competing property. Rather, all data are couched in aggregate, summary findings. In other words, a hotel can see how well it performed against the competitive market set of hotels, but cannot see how well each competing hotel performed individually (only as a set of hotels).

There are actually a series of *STAR Reports* providing a variety of ways of looking at historical data. The *STAR Trend Report,* for example, compares occupancy, ADR, and RevPar for a manager's property against the competitive market set for a series of months in the past. This report also provides an index (a measure of market penetration) that shows how well a manager's property performed against the competition. On a scale where 1.0 is performing exactly "on market," a manager would hope to see numbers like 1.2 or 1.3, suggesting his or her property performed 20 or 30% better than the market average.

The *STAR Competitive Set Positioning Report* shares the data listed above, but places the manager's property in rank order against competing hotels. The *DaySTAR Weekday/Weekend Report* compares competitive hotels by their success in filling rooms during the midweek and weekends. A number of other *STAR Reports* are available as well. Revenue managers are excited about a new report recently released which compares how well their hotel performs against the competition in terms of transient versus group room bookings.

Travel Information Management Services (TIMS).   The *TIMS Report* also pulls its data directly from Sabre. Rates are gathered through the CRS, and the report displays discounts and lowest available rates for all hotels in the competitive market set.

Hotelligence Report.   This is another popular report available through Travel-CLICK (see *PHASER Complete Access Reports* above). This report (see Exhibit 5–17) provides a wealth of information unavailable in other reports. It compares a given hotels available rooms with those available in the competitive market set. This establishes market share, and much of the report then compares actual history with theoretical market share. Data for the *Hotelligence Report* comes directly from Galileo, Sabre, and Worldspan—and the information from these three sources can be viewed both individually and in aggregate.

Specifically, the report compares room-nights sold for the manager's hotel against room-nights sold across the competitive set. Again, if the manager's hotel exceeds the theoretical market share, the report will show a market penetration of greater than 1.0. Similar statistics are available comparing overall revenue (yield) in the competitive set of hotels as well as average daily rate. Another thing this report does quite well is to show growth trends for current periods against similar periods the previous year.

Expedia Competitive Price Grid Report.   For hotels that sell rooms through Expedia, this has become a valuable report. Rates advertised in Expedia and its competitors

THE HOTELLIGENCE REPORT

Data Solutions for the Digital World

Subscriber	Vendor Code	GDS	Total Rooms	Data Exists													Fair Share
				Jan	Feb	Mar	Apr	May	Jun	Jul	Aug	Sep	Oct	Nov	Dec	Jan	
The Premiere Hotel	TC	Galileo		Y	Y	Y	Y	Y	Y	Y	Y	Y	Y	Y	Y	Y	
First Avenue	TC	SABRE	168	Y	Y	Y	Y	Y	Y	Y	Y	Y	Y	Y	Y	Y	11.4%
Chicago, IL 60601	TC	Worldspan		Y	Y	Y	Y	Y	Y	Y	Y	Y	Y	Y	Y	Y	

Competitive Set																	
Luxury Suites	AM	Galileo		Y	Y	Y	Y	Y	Y	Y	Y	Y	Y	Y	Y	Y	
392 Hampshire Blvd.	AM	SABRE	121	Y	Y	Y	Y	Y	Y	Y	Y	Y	Y	Y	Y	Y	8.2%
Chicago, IL 60601	AM	Worldspan		Y	Y	Y	Y	Y	Y	Y	Y	Y	Y	Y	Y	Y	
Presidential Towers	PS	Galileo		Y	Y	Y	Y	Y	Y	Y	Y	Y	Y	Y	Y	Y	
6457 Washington Square	PS	SABRE	154	Y	Y	Y	Y	Y	Y	Y	Y	Y	Y	Y	Y	Y	10.4%
Chicago, IL 60601	PS	Worldspan		Y	Y	Y	Y	Y	Y	Y	Y	Y	Y	Y	Y	Y	
Executive Suites	EX	Galileo		Y	Y	Y	Y	Y	Y	Y	Y	Y	Y	Y	Y	Y	
893 Circle Bend	EX	SABRE	370	Y	Y	Y	Y	Y	Y	Y	Y	Y	Y	Y	Y	Y	25.0%
Chicago, IL 60601	XE	Worldspan		Y	Y	Y	Y	Y	Y	Y	Y	Y	Y	Y	Y	Y	
Capitol Towers	RR	Galileo		Y	Y	Y	Y	Y	Y	Y	Y	Y	Y	Y	Y	Y	
3000 Wilson Avenue	RR	SABRE	140	Y	Y	Y	Y	Y	Y	Y	Y	Y	Y	Y	Y	Y	9.5%
Chicago, IL 60601	RR	Worldspan		Y	Y	Y	Y	Y	Y	Y	Y	Y	Y	Y	Y	Y	
The Tower	TT	Galileo		Y	Y	Y	Y	Y	Y	Y	Y	Y	Y	Y	Y	Y	
4101 Hurst Avenue	TT	SABRE	237	Y	Y	Y	Y	Y	Y	Y	Y	Y	Y	Y	Y	Y	16.0%
Chicago, IL 60601	TT	Worldspan		Y	Y	Y	Y	Y	Y	Y	Y	Y	Y	Y	Y	Y	
Regal Plaza	RQ	Galileo		Y	Y	Y	Y	Y	Y	Y	Y	Y	Y	Y	Y	Y	
632 Forbes Avenue	RQ	SABRE	288	Y	Y	Y	Y	Y	Y	Y	Y	Y	Y	Y	Y	Y	19.5%
Chicago, IL 60563	RQ	Worldspan		Y	Y	Y	Y	Y	Y	Y	Y	Y	Y	Y	Y	Y	

Exhibit 5-17(a)   TravelCLICK's Hotelligence Report helps hotel executives make both strategic and operational decisions to improve revenue management. These reports are useful for developing effective sales and marketing programs based on competitive information, for evaluating the impact of promotional offers, and for conducting performance benchmarking to fine-tune products and services.

The Hotelligence Report is 13-pages long—shown here are the first two pages. The first page (a) displays both the subscriber hotel (the fictitious Premiere Hotel), and the competing hotels (Luxury Suites, etc.). Information is shown for each property across the dates indicated by Y, as in Yes.

The second page displays the Premiere Hotel's fair market share (11.4%) as compared with its competitive set. However, you'll notice it sold far more rooms (market penetration) than suggested by its fair share—it sold 1.549 rooms for every one room it "should" have been able to sell against its competition. However, you will also note that the Premiere Hotel did less well when it comes to average room rate (bottom left corner of 5-17(b). *Courtesy of TravelCLICK.*

Notes: Galileo figures include reservations made through Galileo and Apollo. Sabre figures include reservations made through Abacus and Axess. Total rooms are used from the TravelCLICK hotel database. All reservations displayed on the following pages are net of cancels in each GDS. Each reservation represents a stay which occurred during the month shown on the report (date of arrival). "Y" signifies that the hotel received at least one booking from the respective GDS during the month. Fair Share is calculated using the Total Rooms from the TravelCLICK hotel database.

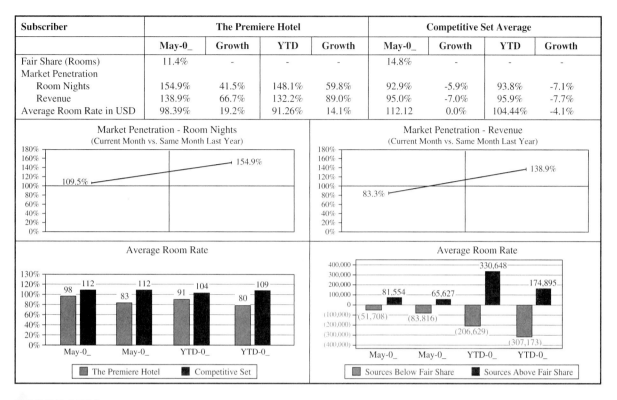

Subscriber	The Premiere Hotel				Competitive Set Average			
	May-0_	Growth	YTD	Growth	May-0_	Growth	YTD	Growth
Fair Share (Rooms)	11.4%	-	-	-	14.8%	-	-	-
Market Penetration								
Room Nights	154.9%	41.5%	148.1%	59.8%	92.9%	-5.9%	93.8%	-7.1%
Revenue	138.9%	66.7%	132.2%	89.0%	95.0%	-7.0%	95.9%	-7.7%
Average Room Rate in USD	98.39%	19.2%	91.26%	14.1%	112.12	0.0%	104.44%	-4.1%

Exhibit 5–17(b)

help the hotel manage its own Web site. The revenue manager must be certain best available rates listed on Expedia are not substantially lower than best available rates listed on the hotel's Web site. If Expedia is significantly lower, the hotel is encouraging guests to visit other Web sites as opposed to visiting the hotel-direct Web site. Remember, the hotel saves commission fees when guests book rooms through its Web site.

Other Reports.   Listed here are several other popular reports used by today's revenue managers:

Sabre.Net Reports
Hotel Information Service (HIS) Reports
CheckRate
TrendFx

Automated Yield Management Systems

As far back as 1998, a study of hotel sales and marketing departments found that 80% of hotels were using yield management technology to assist their decision process when booking group business. That figure approaches 100% adoption in recent years. By today's standards, yield management is an expense worth incurring.

Automated yield or revenue management systems are tools that aid management decision making. In the absence of management, these systems can automatically change rates, restrict rooms availability, and monitor reservation activity. Here's a brief list of the functions generally attributable to yield management systems:

➤ Establishes and monitors the hotel's rate structure
➤ Continually monitors reservations activity and sets inventory controls as needed (even in the absence of management approval)
➤ Aids rate negotiations with travel wholesalers and group bookings
➤ Monitors and restricts the number of reservations that can be taken for any particular room night or room rate/room type
➤ Allows reservationists the tools necessary to be salespersons rather than mere order-takers
➤ Matches the right room product and rate with customers' needs and sensitivities

Profits increase in all hotels that implement automated yield management systems. Certain properties, however, fare better than others. Generally, a property needs to have several characteristics in place to experience high returns on its investment in a yield management system. Some of these characteristics include a demand for rooms that can easily be segmented into distinct markets, a long lead time for some types of reservations, a variety of room types and associated rates, and high-occupancy/low-occupancy periods throughout the year.

Artificial Intelligence.   Yield management systems allow for instantaneous response to changing conditions. Seven days a week, 24 hours a day, the system compares actual performance with forecasted assumptions and adjusts rates accordingly. To make these changes, advanced computer systems utilize either standard logical functions or state-of-the-art artificial intelligence operations. Artificial intelligence (AI) or expert systems use stored data that has been developed over a period of time to form rules that govern yield management decisions.

Today's expert systems are truly artificial intelligence. They literally think through demand, formulate decisions, and provide the user with an opportunity to talk with the computer. Below is a list of the special features generally found in an expert yield management system:

1. Is able to deal with quantitative facts, and qualitative data
2. Includes an analysis of incomplete data when formulating a decision
3. Explains to the user how a given conclusion was reached
4. Allows a two-way communication interface with the user
5. Applies programmable rules and triggers to its set of facts
6. Can override basic rules and triggers when additional criteria warrant
7. Maintains a database of historical facts, including:

➤ Demand for similar periods over a number of past years
➤ Room-nights lost (regrets) through both in-house reservations and chain (toll-free) sources over a number of past years
➤ Changes to demand (by various market segments) as forecasted reservations dates close in
➤ Demand for and ratio of transient (leisure) room-nights versus corporate room-nights over a number of past years
➤ Demand for group room blocks (and the ratio of group room block "pick-ups") over a number of past years

Rules and Triggers. The computer compares actual reservation activity with budgeted forecasts. When a particular date or period falls outside the rules for that time frame, the computer flags it. Once flagged, most systems print a management report identifying periods that are exceptions to the forecast. In addition, expert systems will automatically change rates and other sales tools. The immediacy of the expert system is a major advantage. Hundreds and even thousands of dollars may be lost in the time it takes management to approve a given rate change. The expert system acts first and takes questions later.

To establish rules or triggers for the system to use, management must first segment demand into market types. A typical 250-room property might block 25 rooms for discounting to government guests or IT packages, 50 rooms for transient (leisure) guests, 100 rooms for business (corporate) customers, and the remaining 75 rooms for sale to tours, conventions, or rack rate.

Different guidelines are then placed on each of these market segments. To illustrate, assume management expects 25% of the transient room block to fill by, say, 181 days out (days before arrival). It also expects that 91 days before arrival, transient rooms will be 60% sold, and by 61 days out, the entire block will be 90% reserved. These are the parameters that management has forecasted for transient rooms. Its expectations for business rooms would be quite different. Once these triggers are identified, they are programmed into the yield management system. The computer then evaluates the effects of changing demand and acts accordingly. If, for example, 181 days out the transient room block is already 35% reserved, the computer would flag the date as a potentially busy period and increase rates for all remaining rooms. How much the rates increase is also subject to advanced programming.

Centralized Yield Management. As the trend toward seamless connectivity, single-imaging, last room availability, and centralized property management systems (ASP's) becomes more prevalent, so too is the trend toward centrally driven corporate yield management systems. Initially, centralized yield management systems look much the same. As rooms are sold through in-house reservations (at the property) or the CRO, changes in inventory are automatically reflected in the centralized yield management system. As room types or dates begin to fill, the centralized system changes rates and inventory restrictions for the individual property. Similarly, nothing prevents the property-level management to tap into its own yield statistics and manually alter rates or restrictions.

What appears quite similar on the surface actually affords the chain and individual property unique advantages. Through centralized yield management, the entire GDS becomes a yield management tool. In essence, the in-house property management system, the CRS, and the GDS are all reading from the same page. The chain can run a whole series of reports, which improves its understanding of certain market segments, lodging categories, dates, and trends (see Exhibit 5–17). Price-sensitive group room blocks can be moved to sister properties across the chain rather than being lost because one hotel in one particular city was not able to meet their price on a given date.

Yield Management Controls. Aside from simply adjusting room rates, hotels have several other tools with which they work. One common tool is *boxing* the date. Reservations on either side of the boxed day are not allowed to spill into that date. If Wednesday, April 7, is anticipated as a heavy arrival date, reservations might box it. Rooms sold for Monday or Tuesday must check out by Wednesday; rooms sold for Thursday or Friday cannot arrive a day earlier. Dates are blocked in anticipation of a mass of arrivals, usually a convention or group movement, that could not be accommodated through the normal flow of departures. With such heavy arrivals, no one is permitted to check in before that day and stay through the boxed day, even though there is more than enough space on those previous days.

Another tool available to the reservations department is closing a specific date to arrival. Dates that are *closed to arrival* allow the guest to stay through by arriving on a previous date. Closed to arrival (CTA) is utilized as a technique for improving occupancy on preceding nights before a major holiday or event.

A final example of reservations sales tools is the *minimum length of stay* (MLOS). This technique is designed to improve occupancy on nights preceding and following a major event or holiday by requiring guests to book a minimum number of nights. For example, if New Year's Eve has a three-day minimum length of stay, the hotel will probably improve occupancies on December 30 and January 1.

Nests and Hurdles.   Also known as *bid pricing, hurdle pricing,* or *inventory nesting,* this sophisticated yield management approach takes normal room allocations to a new level. Referring to Exhibit 5–18, let's assume that the Hurdle Hotel is experiencing an unusually high demand for corporate rooms and has sold out of the $120 rate (Monday) while still offering discounted and rack rate rooms. It would make little sense to turn down a corporate reservation request at $120 while still accepting discounted rooms at $60 but that is exactly what might happen if rooms allocations are not continually monitored. That's where inventory nesting comes in. By incorporating a set of nesting rules, the property can ensure that high-rate rooms are never closed for sale when lower-rate rooms are still open.

The newest trend in nesting does away with the old concept of rooms allocations by market segment. Instead, a minimum rate, or *hurdle point,* is established for each day. Reservations with a value above the hurdle are accepted, reservations with a value below the hurdle are rejected. If the hurdle point were set at or below $60 in Exhibit 5–18 all room types would be available. If the hurdle were raised to $100, the discounted rooms would be closed while corporate and rack rates remained available.

Rather than selling rooms according to unreserved market segment allocations, the hurdle concept sells rooms based on total property demand. When demand is low, the

Data for the 250-Room Hurdle Hotel			
	Discounted Rooms	Corporate Guests	Rack Rate
Normal rate structure	$60	$120	$150
Normal room allocations	75	100	75
Current rooms demand			
Monday (hurdle price is $150)	60	100	57
Tuesday (hurdle price is $120)	53	82	48
Wednesday (hurdle price is $60)	34	51	22

Exhibit 5–18   Inventory nesting prevents higher-priced categories of rooms from being closed when lower-priced categories remain open. Hurdle pricing assumes that each business day has a theoretical rate floor against which reservation requests must be evaluated.

hurdle price is low. When demand is high, the hurdle price is high. In essence, the hurdle price represents the theoretical price of the last room expected to sell that day. If the hotel expects to fill, the hurdle point might be set at full rack rate. A person making a reservation who is only willing to pay a lower rate is worth less to the hotel than the future value of the last room, and therefore such a reservation would be denied.

The real beauty of hurdle pricing is that hurdles can be added for subsequent days. For example, in Exhibit 5–18, let's say that the hotel is close to full on Monday (hurdle point $150), somewhat less full on Tuesday (hurdle point $120), and wide open for Wednesday (hurdle point just $60). A guest wishing to stay Monday for one night only would need to pay $150 to get a reservation for the night. However, a guest checking in on Monday for three nights would get the benefit of averaging the hurdles for those three nights. By adding $150 for the first night plus $120 for the second and $60 for the third night, this three-night reservation would pay a rate of $110 per night or possibly a different rate for each of three nights ($150, $120, and $60, respectively). Try explaining that to a guest!

Fenced Rates.   A relatively new addition to the list of reservations sales tools has recently migrated to hotels from the airline industry. Fences or *fenced rates* are logical rules or restrictions that provide a series of options to the guest. Guests are not forced to select these options; their rate is determined by which (if any) options they choose.

As with yield management systems themselves, the airlines originated fenced rates. Examples of airline fenced rates might include the passenger who chose a lower but nonrefundable fare, a customer who purchased the ticket at least 21 days in advance to receive a special rate, or someone who stayed over on a Saturday night to take full advantage of the best price.

Fenced rates are relatively new to the lodging industry. However, the few chains using them seem quite satisfied with their results. It will probably be standard practice in the future to offer discounts for advanced purchases and nonrefundable and non-changeable reservations. All of which have been tried.

SUMMARY

Sophisticated automation is changing the method by which reservations are requested and accepted. Never before have hotels had reservations coming into their properties from so many varied directions. The introduction of last room availability technology has started a revolution in hotel reservations management.

Last room availability is real-time communication between CROs and property-level reservations systems. With last room availability, the CRS can identify room types and rates at a member hotel and can sell to the very last available room. Electronic switch technology has afforded the industry increased access to member hotels. Travel agents, airlines, and subscription online services are all able to access electronically a property's reservations system.

With yield or revenue management (yield equals average room rate times the number of rooms sold), room prices change as a function of lead time and demand. Vacationing families, tour groups, and seniors often know as far as one year in advance their exact date and location of travel. These customers generally book early enough to take advantage of special discounts or packages. Yield management works to their advantage. Conversely, corporate travelers frequently book accommodations at the last moment. In their case, yield management works against them and for the hotel by charging maximum rates to last-minute bookings when the hotel is nearing full occupancy.

RESOURCES AND CHALLENGES
Resources

WEB SITES

http://www.hedna.org (Not-for-profit trade association formed by hoteliers to promote the booking of hotel rooms through the Global Distribution System.)

http://www.travelclick.net (A company which helps hotels maximize profits through electronic distribution.)

http://www.sabretravelnetwork.com/products_and _services/travel_suppliers/tour_operator/s1 _001198.htm (The Sabre Global Distribution System is the world's largest electronic travel reservation system.)

http://www.starwoodhotels.com/stregis/agents/agents _faq.html (A basic information site for one of Starwood's brands complete with GDS participation and GDS chain codes listed.)

http://dmoz.org/Business/Hospitality/Software/ Central_Reservation_Systems/ (An electronic directory of all sorts of resources related to Web-based central reservations systems.)

Web Assignment

Prepare two interesting facts about the Global Distribution System by reading articles and descriptors contained in these websites. They all have one thing in common, they promote business through the Global Distribution System or they utilize the GDS for development of electronic reports and research.

INTERESTING TIDBITS

➤ Holiday Inn's Holidex was the industry's first Central Reservations System (1965). Sheraton Hotels introduced its own CRS later that same year, but with one substantial difference: Sheraton was the first major chain to offer a toll-free telephone number to its customers.

➤ With the explosion of the blogosphere in the virtual universe, it isn't surprising that travel blogs are a big hit. Sites like TripAdvisor.com and Concierge.com carry blog writeups of many hotel experiences. Not all reflect positively on the hotel experience. To combat this, many hotel managers are creating fictitious traveler identities and spinning positive stories on the Web about their recent "stays."

➤ Internet taxation is an issue worth revisiting every few months. Though the government has passed federal moratoriums on Internet taxation at the state and local level, times may change as Internet sales continue to grow tax free.

➤ There are 500 million empty hotel room-nights per year in the United States. This provides huge opportunities for mass discounters and last-minute Web site purchases. *Source*: *Lodging Magazine*.

➤ A big trend with online bookings is something known as *opaque* pricing (pioneered by Priceline.com). This trend appeals to price-sensitive shoppers who are more interested in steep discounts than in specific hotel brands. Hoteliers also like this trend because it does not compromise their rate integrity. *Source*: *Lodging Magazine*.

➤ Although they've been a longtime holdout, luxury hotels are finally starting to offer shopper deals on the Internet. With savings of 50% or more below rack rates, try such sites as http://www.allluxuryhotels.com or http://www.LuxRes.com.

Challenges

TRUE/FALSE

Questions that are partially false should be marked false (F).

___1. The airline industry was smart, waiting until the hotel industry (primarily Holiday Inns in the early years) developed central reservations systems and worked out all the problems. Then the airline industry "borrowed" the existing technology and developed their own automated reservation systems.

___2. The concept of last room availability (saving the last room until at least midnight each night) was initially started in Washington, D.C. There, hotels catering to Congressional leaders were paid a small nightly fee to keep accommodations available for VIPs until at least midnight.

___3. As of the year 2002, travel agents were no longer paid a commission (of any size) for booking domestic air travel on most of the major airline carriers.

___4. Central reservations offices have experienced higher and higher call volume in recent years. Most experts suggest this is partly due to the Internet. Guests first check the Internet for prices and then call the CRS to book the rooms.

___5. In terms of yield management, experts generally consider leisure (transient) guests to be more rate sensitive while corporate guests are generally considered to be more date sensitive.

PROBLEMS

1. On busy nights, it is not uncommon for a front-office manager to remove several rooms from availability. Usually, the manager creates a fictitious reservation, thereby "selling" the rooms and removing them from availability. By holding onto a few rooms, the manager feels in a better position to accommodate a special guest or request when the hotel is sold out.

   Granted that the reason management holds rooms may be very honorable, do you believe this practice undermines the very basis of last room availability technology? Explain your answer.

2. Central reservations systems are extremely expensive. Research and development, equipment, and staffing can easily run into hundreds of millions of dollars. How has this prohibitive cost structure changed the hotel industry? How will it change business in the future? And what options are available to the smaller and startup chains in the industry?

3. Several studies indicate quite clearly that reservation calls made to a travel agent, or to the res center, or directly to the hotel may result in three different rate quotes for the same accommodations at the same period of time. Explain.

4. Discuss the merits of higher rates with lower occupancy versus lower rates with higher occupancy if you were the manager of (a) a budget economy property, (b) a commercial convention property, or (c) an upscale resort property.

5. Yield management programs often discount rates to the benefit of one segment of guests but charge full rack rate to others who book at the last moment. With attention to the rewards and penalties that such policies carry, discuss a proposed policy that (a) deeply discounts rates for noncancellable reservations made 30 days in advance and (b) discounts rates for standby guests who are willing to wait until 7 PM for vacancies.

6. Develop a list of fenced rate restriction possibilities. This list may include those currently used by airlines, or create your own possible restrictions.

AN INCIDENT IN HOTEL MANAGEMENT

Take Me Out to the Ball Game

The hotel's Web site and brochure contain this statement, "... we are close to the ballpark, which is also served by shuttle service...." The Central Reservation Office said, "The ballpark wasn't far," so the reservation was made.

In response to their inquiry, the couple, both senior citizens, is told by the desk that the ball field is about 1.5 miles northwest. The guest-service agent plots the direction on a map. "Oh, yes, there is a shuttle. A city-operated trolley car services the entertainment area and the park. The stop is a short, half-block east. Let me show you on the map."

The couple leaves the hotel in plenty of time and takes the shuttle by a roundabout course to the game. They arrive 15 minutes after the first pitch thrown out by the governor. They also miss the singing of the national anthem by a well-known Hollywood star. The departing crowd is so large that they are unable to get onto the trolley. The few cabs are booked quickly so they walk back at night through a very unpleasant neighborhood.

When they complain softly the next day to the assistant manager in the lobby, she says, "I'm so sorry! You know, of course, we have no control of the public trolley. Why didn't you take our shuttle?"

Questions: Was there a management failure here; if so, what?
What is the hotel's immediate response (or action) to the incident?
What further, long-run action should management take, if any?

ANSWERS TO TRUE/FALSE QUIZ

1. False. This statement is exactly the opposite of the right answer. It was, in fact, the airline industry that first developed central reservations systems.

2. False. Last room availability refers to online communication between each property and the CRS. In such systems, the central reservations office can access real-time rooms inventory for each property in the chain.

3. True. The airline industry began reducing their customary 10% commissions in 1995. By 2002, most major U.S. carriers suspended all domestic commissions. Travel agents now look elsewhere for income.

4. False. Central reservations offices have seen a substantial drop in call volume. The Internet is certainly responsible. Internet hotel bookings have been growing at a compounded rate, year after year.

5. True. Corporate guests need to travel when they are scheduled, and will therefore pay the prevailing rate. Leisure guests are more flexible and will book with further lead time in the hope of finding a less expensive date.

CHAPTER 6

Individual Reservations and Group Bookings

The discussion in the previous two chapters suggests that the telephone is growing less important as a source of hotel reservations. As a ratio to all other methods of booking reservations, that is true. Telephone reservations continue to represent a smaller portion of the reservations landscape. Today, the majority of business travelers use the Internet to plan some aspect of their business travel; the percentages for leisure travelers are quite similar.

While the number of telephone reservations has declined, the industry has made substantial adjustments to the way it operates call centers. Even as central reservations centers are experiencing numerous layoffs and closures (see Exhibits 5–6), the industry is renewing its focus on the all-important telephone. Studies show that busy people make hotel reservations by telephone rather than their keyboard. Although the Internet is the best way to shop for distressed inventory, a large contingent of guests (especially the older demographic) still appreciate talking with a reservationist—an experience which provides the caller a sense of place, human interaction, and confidence in the reservation.

Training telephone reservationists to be fast, efficient, and sales oriented, coupled with continued investment in telephone call systems will prove valuable strategies for the future. The role of the telephone may be more critical than ever as lodging chains seek ways to differentiate their products and to maintain rate integrity in the face of rampant discounting through third-party vendors.

COMPONENTS OF THE RESERVATION

As telephone call volume drops over time, it is easy for a chain to relegate its central reservations office to second-class status. Changes for the worse, such as understaffing on heavy-call-volume days, closing the CRO during evening and early morning hours, and installing a poorly devised automated phone system can lead to customer frustration and dissatisfaction (see Exhibit 6–1).

Automated Phone Systems

Many CROs have addressed their decreased call volume by reducing labor costs, at the same time increasing the amount of self-service required of the caller. Focusing only on the bottom line makes it easy for a central reservations office to lose sight of its basic task—customer service. After running the potential guest through a gauntlet of automated

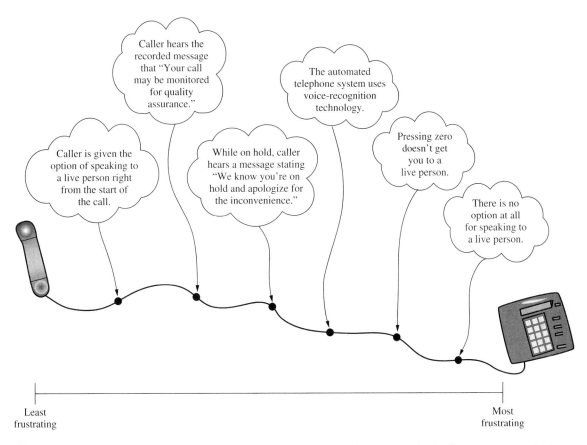

Exhibit 6-1   Results of a recent study showing the features of automated telephone systems which are the most (and least) frustrating to the caller. *Source: Customer Care Management & Consulting, June 2006.*

telephone queries, telephone keypad number punching, recorded instructions, and on-hold background messages/music, the reservations agent can easily forget there is someone on the other end of the telephone. To avoid this oversight, one chain actually pastes pictures of real customers on the office walls. It is a wonderful reminder that real people are on the other end of the line.

Certainly there is good reason for utilizing automated telephone systems. Asking the guest to select instructions in English (press "1"), Spanish (press "2"), or some other language (press "3") segregates callers to language-specific reservationists. Further instructions may separate callers by domestic reservations (press "1") versus international reservations (press "2"). Sophisticated voice-recognition systems are capable of understanding more than 100,000 words, and able to separate spoken words from coughs and background noise. Electronically, they ask callers for their cities of choice, date(s) of travel, and number of guests in the party.

Well-designed automated phone systems have met with growing appreciation from most segments of the lodging market. Over time, customers have come to trust the efficiencies offered. Guest self-service has steadily gained acceptance in the lodging industry. Some of that acceptance comes from a change in demographics; younger callers accept change more readily. Mostly, however, the change comes from substantial improvement in automated telephone system technologies. The improvement is so dramatic that many callers prefer the automated system over a live reservationist.

Chains love automated phone systems too. Research shows that for every $1 investment in an automated phone system, the lodging company will return better than $2.25 in direct savings. That savings comes from reduced labor, shorter call duration, and call self-service.

Importance of Training.   For all the benefits of telephone technology, one axiom is abundantly clear—the fastest reservation is not always the best reservation. In a study of a major lodging chain's reservation office, agents experimented with changing their initial telephone greeting. The rushed monotone so often associated with call centers was changed to a warmer, friendlier greeting. The results were astounding. Customers responded positively to the inviting greeting they received, and their perceptions of the CRO improved dramatically. (The reservations booking rate improved as well.) It took very little extra time for the reservationist to be nice and to "smile" through the telephone. The friendlier greetings added a mere 300 extra seconds (5 minutes) to each reservationist's day.

Today's hotel guests, whether corporate, leisure, or group, face more lodging choices than ever before. With so many options available, central reservations offices and inhouse reservations centers are realizing that a well-trained reservationist makes a significant difference in guest satisfaction and booking rates.

Seasoned reservations managers realize that effective communication skills are more important than basic computer skills. Poorly trained reservations agents miss potential sales by failing to understand the guests' needs. Taking a step away from the rushed script allows the agent to develop a communicative information-gathering posture. Uncovering personal information (needs) can lead to a successful closing. Reservationists must realize that price is not the only factor that guests use in determining where to stay. Patiently answering questions, skillfully diffusing objections, and building personal rapport with the customer may prove as important to the decision process as the price of the room.

Training reservations agents to be salespersons is the key to success in the new millennium. That's because collecting the guest's reservation data is pretty much the same for all lodging chains. It's easy, too: Basic reservation content and each question that needs to be asked is right there on the reservations agent's computer screen. The computer literally prompts the agent through each step of the reservation (see Exhibit 6–2).

Information Contained in the Reservation

The computer prompts the reservationist to ask essential questions. As one question is completed, the computer cursor automatically moves to the beginning of the next question. In this way, essential information cannot be overlooked. If the reservationist attempts to enter an incomplete reservation into the system, the computer beeps audibly and the cursor blinks at the beginning of the incomplete information field.

This text refers to system-mandated data as "required fields." Required fields must be completed before the computer system will accept the screen and move the reservation to the next stage. Nonmandated data is called "optional," because the system does not absolutely need this information in order to continue with the reservation. Examples of optional data include high floor versus low floor for a city center hotel, guest telephone number, and smoking versus non smoking room preference. Smoking preference is

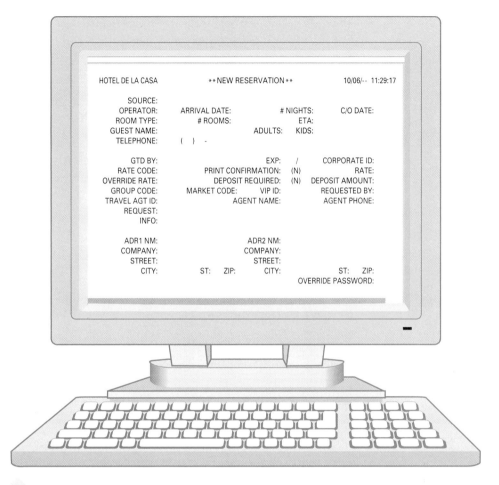

Exhibit 6-2 Reservation screens are basically the same. The system prompts the guest (or the reservationist) with the same guest information, in roughly the same order. Some are required fields and other are "nonessential." Decide which information is required and which is "nonessential." (ADR is an abbreviation for address).

generally not mandated by computer systems, yet it is certainly considered of paramount importance to those guests averse to cigarette smoke. Therefore, though data may technically be optional in the computer reservations system, it is not necessarily unimportant to arriving guests. Exhibit 6–2 is a sample reservation screen.

Required Fields. The reservation and the information obtained during the procedure are designed to improve the effectiveness of the front office. Facts communicated through the reservation form a valuable starting point from which the front office comes to understand the guest's needs. Corporate guests may be placed away from the lobby in a quieter area of the hotel, while guests traveling with children may be roomed near the swimming pool. Late arrivals are noted on the reservation screen so the front desk is better informed should it need to make difficult overbooking and walked in guest decisions. Address information is collected so the hotel can contact the guest for marketing or billing purposes or in the event the guest leaves behind a personal item (see Exhibit 6–2).

Arrival and Departure Dates.   In the chain reservations centers, the questions of arrival and departure dates come third, after "What city?" and "What hotel?" Telephone time is not used to gather the details that follow unless the clerk is certain that space is available at the time and place requested.

Number of Nights.   This bit of redundancy forestalls later problems if the guest's count of nights is not in agreement with the time between the arrival and departure dates. A common miscommunication occurs when the guest counts the departure day in the number of nights. Many systems ask simply for the date of arrival (say, October 2) followed by a question related to number of nights (say, four nights). Then, the reservationist verifies information with the guest by replying, "So we have you checking out on October 6, is that correct?"

Number of Persons.   The number of persons in the party and its structure help to clarify the type of accommodations required. Two unrelated persons need two beds; a married couple generally prefers one bed. Are there children? Is a crib required? A rollaway bed? Many hotels charge an extra fee for the second, third, and fourth persons in a room. This extra revenue contributes to the bottom line and is easily justified when one considers the added utilities, linens, breakfast, etc. See Chapter 9 for an additional discussion of double occupancy rates.

Number of Rooms Required.   Based on the size of the party and the types of rooms the hotel has available, additional rooms may be required. Most reservationists are authorized to handle requests for up to 10 rooms or so. As the number of required rooms increases above 10, the hotel's group sales department takes over.

Type of Rooms Required.   The question of room type is closely linked to the rate the guest is willing to pay. As the room type increases in luxury, the rate increases as well. Although the specific rate the guest wants to pay is the real question, the reservationist can't simply offer a series of rates. That would be gauche. Instead, the reservationist offers a series of room types.

Reservationists attempt to sell from the top down. This is accomplished by offering the guest the most expensive room first and then waiting for the guest to agree or decline before moving down to the next most expensive room type (see Chapter 8).

At this stage in the reservation, the guest may ask for a specific package or alert the reservationist to a promotional rate. It is also at this stage that the reservationist attempts to upsell the guest to more expensive accommodations (see Exhibit 6–3, as well as Chapter 8, which offers a discussion of front office sales techniques).

Corporate Affiliation.   Commercial hotels are very concerned with identifying all corporate reservations. The typical corporate guest represents far more room nights than does the average leisure guest. In addition, corporate guests usually book their rooms with less lead time (and as such pay a higher average rate) than do leisure guests (see the yield management discussion in Chapter 5). Therefore, reservation data related to the guest's corporate affiliation is essential to commercial properties. Asking the guest's corporate affiliation is often the first step in determining the rate to quote. Many corporations negotiate a prearranged nightly room rate.

Price.   The reservation (the sale) could be lost by the rate quote. The agent may have no negotiating room if the yield management system has eliminated lower-priced options. Quoting the price is not enough. Distinctions between the prices must be accompanied by descriptive matter intended to entice the buyer to the better rate.

Exhibit 6-3   Mandarin Oriental is among the finest lodging groups in the world. This package shows that.
- Mandarin Oriental calls it their Fantastic Jet Set Journey Package.
- The package includes nine room nights: three nights each at Mandarin Oriental hotels in Miami, New York, and Washington, D.C.
- At each property and between cities, guests are treated to limousine and helicopter transfers, private jet service for two, and a host of special activities. Activities include:
  ○ In Miami, guests receive two days' use of a private beach cabana, spa treatments, and a four-hour shopping spree with a personal stylist.
  ○ In New York, guests are treated with tickets to the Metropolitan Opera, Lincoln Center, and an award-winning Broadway Show. They also enjoy a pre-theater dinner at Chef Nori Sugie's Asiate Restaurant.
  ○ And in Washington, D.C., guests are provided with a private escort through the National Gallery of Art. Now, imagine trying to sell this package. The cost is a mere $220,000! *Courtesy: Mandarin Oriental Hotel Group.*

Name.   The guest's name has become more important in recent years. In the past, the name was used for alphabetical filing of the reservation and was one of several means (confirmation number, date of arrival, etc.) by which the reservations agent or front-desk receptionist could access the guest's reservation record.

Sophisticated reservation systems now use the customer's name as a means of gaining efficiency, saving time, and generating guest loyalty. Many systems integrate guest history into the reservations system. As the guest's name is entered into the reservation, a screen pops up for repeat customers. It shows the guest's address and phone; rate, room type, and number of nights stayed during the last visit(s); and other related information.

With most information already in the system, the reservations agent simply verifies that this is the same guest and asks if the information is still accurate. (Refer to the discussion of guest history databases later in this chapter.)

Quality of the Reservation.   Reservations have three quality types—nonguaranteed, guaranteed, or advance deposit. Determination is made either by the guest or the reservationist. The reservationist, for example, may be restricted from accepting nonguaranteed reservations as a function of policy or unusually high business levels. Similarly, the guest may not have a credit card with which to guarantee the reservation or may have a card but not be inclined to use it. In either case, the reservation may fail to materialize because of disagreement at this stage in the process. See Chapter 4 for a complete discussion of the quality of the reservation.

Optional Reservation Data.
Depending on the reservation system in place and/or the amount of reservation activity occurring in the reservation center, certain reservation information may not be required. This less important information is categorized as optional or "nice-to-know" data. Examples of optional information include estimated time of arrival, special guest requests or needs, discounts or affiliations, and smoking or nonsmoking room preference.

Although required fields must be complete for a reservation to be accepted into the computer system, optional information is not required. The computer will allow the input of a completed reservation into the system when nonessential data is missing. In fact, some computer screens display required fields in one color while displaying optional fields data in a secondary color. If time permits, the reservationist may request this additional data. Otherwise, it is often overlooked.

Just because the reservations system doesn't mandate certain data before accepting the reservation does not mean the data is unimportant. Remember, nonmandated information (smoking preference, for example) is still of critical importance to guest satisfaction.

Estimated Time of Arrival.   By knowing the guests' estimated time of arrival (ETA), the hotel can properly schedule front-desk receptionists to assist with check-in, van drivers to retrieve guests from the airport, and bellpersons to room them. More important, hotels that are filling to capacity can be certain to save rooms for guests who are going to be especially late.

ETA plays its most critical role in overbooking. When the hotel is oversold, front-desk receptionists refer to the incoming guests' ETAs. A room is usually held for those who provided late arrival information. But later in the evening, guests with no ETA (or guests with an early ETA who arrive late) are declared no-shows, and their rooms are released to cover overbooked reservations. See Chapter 4 for a complete discussion of overbooking.

Special Requests.   Guest requests or needs run the gamut from simple requests to essential guest needs. That is why most reservationists provide guests with an opportunity to request any other items of importance before the close of the reservation process. If the request is critical (a handicapped guest requesting a specially equipped room), the guest is usually certain to state the need. In other cases, the request (ocean view, near the Smith's room, below fifth floor) may be forgotten by the reservationist and the guest. Then it becomes the responsibility of the front-desk receptionist. Each request is handled on a case-by-case basis at the time of check in. Indeed, reservationists generally explain, "I'll note your request on the reservation, but I cannot promise you will get it." See Exhibit 6–4 for a lighter look at guest requests.

A Room With a View

It's not easy to understand travel professionals these days. And I'm not just talking about the conductors squawking gibberish over the tin-speaker public-address system on the New York City subway. Their messages are crystal clear compared to travel-brochure creators . . . Savvy travelers understand that far-flung lands don't always share the same standards.

Unfortunately, it's hard to plan a journey when you don't really know what you're getting yourself into. Before that next trip, you may want to consult this carefully researched glossary of international travel terms:

At The Hotel:

- Panoramic View: you can see the entire wall of the hotel across the alley.

- Deluxe Accommodation: end of toilet paper roll has been neatly folded to a point.

- All-Night Room Service: that's how long you'll wait for your order.

- Award Winning Hotel: has been awarded several citations from the health department.

- International Calling Available from Room: available yes, for about $12 per minute.

- Cooled by Ocean Breezes: the window is broken.

- Unrivaled Location: requires a two-hour taxi ride from the airport.

On Tour:

- Must-See: should be called might see, if the other tourists in front of you get out of the way.

- Within Walking Distance: can be reached by foot by elite Kenyan runners in less than a day

- Quaint Village: tourists outnumber locals 9 to 1.

- All-Inclusive: all except drinks, snacks, excursions, activities, and tips.

- Rain Jacket Recommended: Averages three days of sunshine per year.

Shopping and Dining:

- Where Are You From: do you come from a country with a strong currency?

- Special Price: triple what locals pay.

- Bureau De Change: will probably not charge a commission higher than the amount of money you are trying to exchange.

- Establishment Frequented by Locals: locals will try selling you roses for $5 each while you dine with other tourists.

- Tourist Menu: one meal for the price of two.

- Fully Air-Conditioned: no matter the temperature outside, the air-conditioner will be set on "turbo blast" so you can deep-freeze during your meal.

Getting Around:

- Your Luggage Will Arrive on Carousel 3: some of your luggage will arrive on carousel 3.

- Courtesy Shuttle: if it ever arrives.

- Tourist Facilities Available: gift shops within 20 yards.

- Experienced Driver: hold onto your lunch, he's been to traffic court numerous times.

Exhibit 6–4   Be careful what you ask for . . . you just might get that room with a view. Here's a spoof on travel industry euphemisms. *Reprinted from* Last Trout in Venice: The Far-Flung Escapades of an Accidental Adventurer *by Doug Lansky, copyright 2001 by Doug Lansky. Reprinted by permission of Travelers' Tales, Inc. and the author.*

Discounts or Affiliations.   Corporate, AAA (American Automobile Association), AARP (American Association of Retired Persons), or similar discounts are handled during the rate discussion earlier in the reservation process. Many of these organizations require the guest to state his or her discount in advance. The discount is void if the guest forgets to request it at the time of reservation. See Chapter 9 for a complete discussion of room-rate discounts.

Smoking Preference.   What was once merely a special request has become required reservation input on many systems. Smokers and nonsmokers alike are committed to their particular preferences. As such, practically all domestic hotels offer smoking and nonsmoking rooms. Some properties offer entire nonsmoking floors, and some chains are even experimenting with complete nonsmoking properties.

Given the amount of guest satisfaction and comfort riding on the smoking preference, it is curious that hotel reservations departments do not guarantee the smoking status of the reserved room—yet that's the standard in the lodging industry. The guest's smoking preference is noted and the hotel tries to accommodate the request, but there are no guarantees that a smoking guest will get a smoking room, or vice versa!

Address.   The guest address and/or phone number are requested by some hotels as a matter of record. Other hotels utilize the information to mail a confirmation card or confirmation letter (see Exhibits 6–5 and 6–6) when there is sufficient lead time. In the case of third-party reservations (as when a secretary or travel agent makes the reservation), the address and phone number of the person making the reservation is also requested.

Confirming the Reservation.
A letter of confirmation or a confirmation card is usually printed by the computerized property management system (or central reservations system) using the information collected during the reservation (see Exhibits 6–5 and 6–6). There is a field on the reservation screen that asks "Print Confirmation? Yes or No." The system probably defaults to "No," requiring the reservations agent to actually enter "Yes" if a confirmation needs to be mailed (see Exhibit 6–2). Some properties ask the guest "Would you like us to mail you a confirmation?" Others do it as a routine activity when there is sufficient leadtime. Over half, however, do not mail a confirmation. Instead, the reservationist closes the conversation by furnishing the caller with a confirmation number generated by the computer.

There is actually order to what appears to be random reservation numbers. First on the screen might be the scheduled arrival date, from 1 to 365. February 5, for instance, is 36. Then the individual hotel of the chain might be identified by its own code. The agent's initials sometimes follow, and identification of the reservation concludes with the next confirmation number in sequence. The number, with the pieces set apart, may appear as 36 141 ABC 2366.

However, that is only one possibility. Not every company follows this sequence. The reservation code might start with the first three letters in the guest's last name, and the clerk's identity might be dropped: VAL 36 141 2366. Or the number may be nothing more than the next digits in the sequence (Exhibit 6–6), accumulated by the month or year. In still other systems, the confirmation number is either completely random or is so complex it is almost impossible to decode.

Reservation Information Flow

Once entered into the system, the reservation appears electronically in myriad formats and printouts until the date of arrival. On that date, the reservation changes from a future reservation to an arriving reservation. On the date of arrival, the overall responsibility for incoming reservation changes from the reservations department to the front-office staff (see Chapter 8).

night's room and tax. For any amendments or additional information, please contact the reservations department at (602) 555-4400.

We look forward to welcoming you to the Wyndham Garden Hotel-LaGuardia Airport and hope to make your stay a pleasant one.

Yours Sincerely,

Colin Forres

Reservations Sales Agent

WYNDHAM GARDEN HOTEL
LaGuardia Airport

April 30, _ _ _ _

Ms. Margaret Wilson
1020 1st Avenue, Northeast
Anytown, Texas 77001

Dear Ms. Wilson:

Thank you for choosing the Wyndham Garden Hotel-LaGuardia Airport for your next visit to our community.

We are delighted to confirm your reservation details as follows:

Confirmation #	75747 Guaranteed
Arrival Date	05/09/_ _
Departure Date	05/11/_ _ An early departure may result in additional charges.
Number of Guests	1 Adults 0 Children
Number of Rooms	1
Rate	$169.00

Please take a moment to review the following: Nonguaranteed reservations will be held until 4 PM on day of arrival. Guaranteed reservations can be canceled until 4 PM day of arrival. Failure to do so will result in a charge of one night's room and tax. For any amendments or additional information, please contact the reservations department at (555) 555-4400.

We look forward to welcoming you to the Wyndham Garden Hotel-LaGuardia Airport and hope to make your stay a pleasant one.

Yours Sincerely,

Colin Forres

Reservations Sales Agent

Exhibit 6-5   A letter of confirmation provides the same reservation detail as a confirmation card. Such letters are not individually written—this one was prepared as an automatic function of the hotel's Fidelio PMS. *Courtesy of Wyndham Hotels & Resorts, Dallas, Texas.*

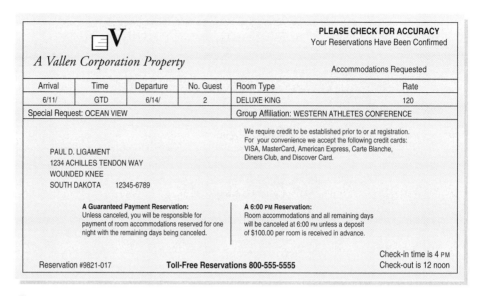

Exhibit 6–6   As with a letter of confirmation (see Exhibit 6–5), the "confirmation card" above is prepared from information collected during the reservation. Confirmation cards, however, are sometimes pre-printed with hotel information. Blank spaces are then filled in by the computer system (blank spaces include name and address, room type, etc.). Confirmation cards may be mailed as postcards. This one is designed to be stuffed into a windowed envelope.

An arrival list (Exhibit 6–7) is printed by the property management system each night for the following day's anticipated check-ins. The transfer of data is delayed until registration. Computerized reservation systems generally do not have a supporting correspondence file. Almost all supporting data is electronic in nature. Only under unusual circumstances will there be hard-copy support. Examples of these circumstances include reservation requests by mail or fax rather than telephone.

With computerized property management systems all the reservation information is stored in computer memory. It can be recalled for viewing on the computer screen if the guest name and the date of arrival are known. In a perfect world, the reservation or confirmation number would be known, and that also will bring the information forward.

Although the majority of reservations remain undisturbed until the date of arrival, a number of reservations are changed. Common alterations include a changed date of arrival or length of stay, a changed guest name (as when an existing corporate reservation is to be claimed by a different employee), a changed room type or discount request, or a cancellation.

No matter what the alteration may be, the reservationist cannot make a change without first accessing the preexisting reservation. Only under unusual situations is the existing reservation difficult to locate. Difficulty in finding an existing reservation occurs when either the guest or reservationist has made a clerical error. Common clerical errors include incorrect date of arrival or incorrect spelling of the guest's name.

In many cases, these errors are found and rectified. In other instances, the existing reservation cannot be located. If, for some reason, the reservation cannot be found, the reservationist may actually take a new reservation. This is risky, because chances are there will now be duplicate reservations in the system.

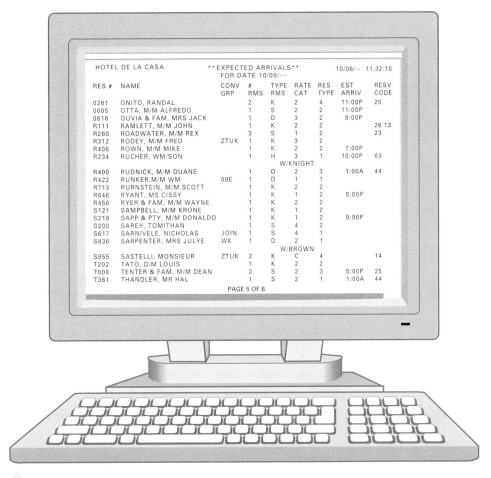

RES #	NAME	CONV GRP	# RMS	TYPE RMS	RATE CAT	RES TYPE	EST ARRIV	RESV CODE
	HOTEL DE LA CASA			**EXPECTED ARRIVALS** FOR DATE 10/08/--			10/06/-- 11:32:10	
0261	ONITO, RANDAL		2	K	2	4	11:00P	25
0005	OTTA, M/M ALFREDO		1	S	2	2	11:00P	
0616	OUVIA & FAM, MRS JACK		1	D	3	2	8:00P	
R111	RAMLETT, M/M JOHN		1	K	2	2		26 13
R260	ROADWATER, M/M REX		3	S	1	2		23
R312	RODEY, M/M FRED	ZTUK	1	K	3	2		
R406	ROWN, M/M MIKE		1	K	2	2	7:00P	
R234	RUCHER, WM/SON		1	H	3	1	10:00P	63
	W/KNIGHT							
R400	RUDNICK, M/M DUANE		1	D	2	3	1:00A	44
R422	RUNKER, M/M WM	00E	1	D	1	1		
R713	RURNSTEIN, M/M SCOTT		1	K	2	2		
R646	RYANT, MS CISSY		1	K	1	2	5:00P	
R456	RYER & FAM, M/M WAYNE		1	K	2	2		
S121	SAMPBELL, M/M KRONE		1	K	1	2		
S216	SAPP & PTY, M/M DONALDO		1	K	1	2	9:00P	
S200	SAREY, TOMITHAN		1	S	4	2		
S617	SARNIVELE, NICHOLAS	JOIN	1	S	4	1		
S836	SARPENTER, MRS JULYE	WK	1	D	2	1		
	W/BROWN							
S855	SASTELLI, MONSIEUR	ZTUK	2	K	C	4		14
T202	TATO, D/M LOUIS		1	K	2	2		
T008	TENTER & FAM, M/M DEAN		2	S	2	3	5:00P	25
T361	THANDLER, MR HAL		1	S	2	1	1:00A	44

PAGE 5 OF 6

Exhibit 6-7   Computer display of expected arrivals (reservations) list. Identical hard copies are provided on the day of arrival to the desk, the uniformed services, and even to the dining room if it is an American plan hotel. Note the estimated times of arrival and reservations codes (see Exhibit 6–8). W means with.

Guest History Databases.   One of the benefits associated with today's electronic systems has been increased data storage capabilities. Customer information, collected during the normal flow of the room reservation, can be stored in guest history databases, manipulated, and used for marketing and guest service/recognition purposes. It makes sense that the hotel's increasing use of guest history data has correlated with increasing computer capacity.

The importance of guest history was first realized at the individual property level. Until recently, centralizing guest history information at the corporate level was too unwieldy to justify. Guest history utilization at the property level was more manageable.

Guest history improves the most basic component of guest service: recognition. Hotels have always known that guests appreciate personal recognition. Imagine the unwavering loyalty that can be gained, then, if the guests' basic needs and requests are recognized in advance. That is the promise of guest history.

In its most common form, guest history is applied during the reservation process. The guest history function is first utilized when the reservations agent pulls up a guest's previous stay information and saves them both the burden of repeating address, credit card, and room type/rate preferences. However, guest history can accomplish far more than that. In upscale corporate and luxury properties, guest history databases inform front-office personnel of the various likes and dislikes of the guest. Simple preferences such as ground-floor room, feather as opposed to foam pillows, extra pears in the fruit basket, and so on, go a long way toward generating loyalty and a sense of belonging.

It makes good business sense, too. Not only does the hotel gain the benefits of enhanced guest loyalty and repeat visitation, but guest history databases are valuable marketing resources as well. Imagine the potential a mailed marketing campaign might have when focused on certain historical parameters. For example, a hotel facing a slow autumn might mail a special promotion to those corporate guests who visited their property at least two times last year during September and October—now *that's* pinpointing the market.

Centralized Guest History.   In the past decade, the industry has seen increasing centralization of guest history information. What one property in Washington, D.C. knew about a particular frequent corporate traveler has now become available through the chain's central reservations system to, say, a sister property in Olympia, Washington.

Corporate travelers have been demanding improved guest service (recognition) to compensate for rising room rates. Chains such as Marriott Hotels and Resorts, Ritz-Carlton, Preferred Hotels and Resorts, and Carlton Hospitality Worldwide saw the need to centralize guest history databanks and took an early lead in this area of automation. These chains banked on the premise that when frequent guests at one property are recognized like family in another of the chain's properties, the increased guest satisfaction translates into increased brand loyalty.

Chain guest history databases have been developed from a variety of directions. Marriott's, for example, was designed around their existing Marriott Rewards frequent guest program. Since this program was already in place, Marriott thought it made sense to use it as the starting point. As such, when Marriott rolled out its original guest history program, it already had guest profiles from more than 9 million members. However, Marriott's guest history database system initially stored only basic guest information such as bed type and smoking preference.

Smaller chains had an initial operational advantage over Marriott because of their relative size. Ritz-Carlton, for example, took the complete encyclopedia of guest history information it had developed at individual properties and integrated it into a centralized database. Ritz-Carlton calls this database its Customer Loyalty Anticipation Satisfaction System, or CLASS. Before the implementation of CLASS, regular Ritz-Carlton guests who were visiting a different Ritz-Carlton hotel for the first time would have been treated like first-timers. Now, repeat customers at one property are repeat customers at all the Ritz properties. Any front-desk receptionist at a Ritz-Carlton can call up the guest's latest visit (say, last month at the Laguna Niguel), and say, "I see in Laguna Niguel you requested a 6:30 AM wake-up call with a pot of decaffeinated coffee, skim milk, and a bagel delivered at 7 AM. Shall we provide the same for you tomorrow morning?" Wow!

Guarantees and Cancellations.

The most common method for holding a reservation is a guarantee against the guest's credit card. The procedure requires the reservation agent to input the guest's credit card number and expiration date into the appropriate fields in the reservation screen. Nothing is processed or charged at this time. The card will only be charged if the guest is a no-show. Assuming the guest arrives as expected, credit will be established at registration.

Experienced travelers soon realize how much of a game the reservation process has become. Busy properties almost always insist on credit-card guarantees rather than on a 4 PM or 6 PM hold. Credit-card guarantees reduce the number of no-shows.

At the same time, guests know that properties do not actually charge the card at the time of the reservation. If the guarantee is not processed until the expected night of arrival, unethical travelers can take advantage of the practice. They provide the hotel with an inaccurate credit-card number. In this way, if they fail to show, the hotel cannot actually charge them. On the other hand, if they do arrive and their false credit-card number is challenged, they can blame it on poor communication or a clerical error: They invent the false credit-card number by changing the sequence or transposing two digits on their real credit card, which makes for a fairly believable excuse. For example, if their VISA card number were 4567 890 123 456, they could simply change the number to 4567 809 123 456. Now they have a workable excuse in the event they do show up for their reservation—but a fictitious number in the event of a no-show.

Most hotel chains and individual properties are wise to this game and intercept "errors" at the time of the reservation. They accomplish this by interfacing the reservations system with a credit-card clearing center. During the several minutes the guest is on the telephone with the reservationist, the credit-card number is input and an approval verification is received. If the approval is denied, the reservationist gives the guest another opportunity to read the correct credit-card number.

Advance Deposits.   Advance deposit reservations are most readily used by properties which have either a high ratio of no-shows or a hotel cancellation policy that is more restrictive than the norm (e.g. 48- or 72-hour cancellation as opposed to 6 PM same-day or 24-hour cancellation). The advantages to an advance deposit reservation are clear—the hotel has the guest's money days or weeks in advance, and there is a higher certainty of guest arrival with advance deposit reservations.

Advance deposit reservations have some disadvantages as well. For one thing, they require a longer amount of the reservation agent's time because of the added step of collecting the deposit. This issue is exacerbated in those properties which experience high cancellation rates. Not only does the advance deposit add time on the front end when making the reservation, it requires that a cancellation be processed with a credit to the guest's card or a check cut in the unlikely chance the advance deposit was mailed in by check or money order.

In spite of the added costs associated with charging the guest credit card for payment of the advance deposit, this is the preferred method for the vast majority of properties. A 2 to 4% fee (merchant discount fees are discussed in greater detail in Chapter 12) is viewed as a reasonable tradeoff to requiring guests to mail money orders or checks. Handling cash or checks requires a disproportionate amount of both the hotel and the guest's time and postage relative to the slight economic gain.

Cancellations.   Cancellations require a change to the existing reservation. This is not necessarily a problem unless somehow it is improperly handled. Handling anything at the front desk in an improper manner generates problems as well as bad public relations. This is especially true with cancellations—imagine yourself in the shoes of a guest who previously cancelled the reservation. The hotel improperly recorded the cancellation and your credit-card statement now reflects a $150 no-show charge for the unoccupied room night. That is exasperating!

Encouraging cancellation calls is in the best interest of the hotel. Such calls reduce the no-show rate. Fewer no-shows generate more room revenue from walk-in guests and reduce complaints from the antiservice syndrome of overbooking (Chapter 4).

The cancellation number, which is formulated like the confirmation number (discussed earlier), is the only major difference between a cancellation call and any other reservation change. Even then, its importance is limited to guaranteed reservations. The system must protect the guest who has guaranteed the room with a credit card (or advance deposit) from being billed if the reservation is canceled in a timely manner. Nonguaranteed reservations are not generally provided with a cancellation number.

Reservation Coding

The reservation's journey ends at the front desk (see Chapter 8). Sometimes the journey is long, as when the reservation was made a year in advance. In other cases, the reservation lead time is extremely short, as with reservations made minutes before arrival. In any case, the front desk is the final stopping point in the reservation's journey.

The first step in linking the reservation with the front desk is to change the status of the reservation from future reservation to arriving reservation. In a computerized system, this change occurs automatically as a step in the night audit process.

It is at this moment that guests' special requests and needs become the concern of the front desk. Armed with the knowledge of which rooms are clean and vacant, which rooms are due to check out, and which rooms are staying over, specific room assignments are developed in accordance with guest requests. Even in an automated property, the assigning of special rooms to match special requests is a manual operation. It is the clerk, operating with good judgment, who ultimately determines which requests can be met and which requests will be declined.

Special Coding.   Certain reservations are different from the rest. They may be different in their method of payment, in the guests' specific requests, in the fact that they are *commissionable* to a travel agent, in their time of arrival, or in their affiliation. Whatever the case, the front-desk clerk needs to be alert to unique circumstances.

The difference is generally highlighted somewhere on the reservation where a numerical coding scheme is used. In this case, advance-deposit reservations will be indicated with one code number (see Exhibit 6–8, code 40) and travel agent reservations with another code (say, code 55). Following is a brief discussion about some of these special codes. For a more complete understanding of their impact on the guest check-in process, refer to Chapter 8.

Advance Deposits.   Reservations with an advance deposit need to be specially noted, because establishing guest credit at check-in is handled differently.

Late Arrivals.   If front-desk personnel know that a given reservation is due to arrive late, they will be less likely to assume it is a no-show as the evening progresses.

Corporate Guarantee.   The right to guarantee rooms with a corporation's good credit must be prearranged with the hotel. In case of a no-show, the room charge is billed to the corporation's city ledger account.

Travel Agents.   Special-coding of travel agent (TA) reservations expedites the internal office procedure. After the guest departs, the hotel pays the travel agent's commission. (When the travel agent owes the hotel—an *account receivable*—the hotel bills the balance less the travel agent's commission.) When the reservation is placed, the agent identifies the agency, providing name, address, and *International Association of Travel Agents (IATA)* code number.

Reservations are confirmed to the agency, not to the guest. In some cases, the hotel lacks the guest's address until registration time. To maintain accountability with the agency, the hotel sends a notice whenever one of the TA's clients fails to appear.

Computer Code	Internal System Meaning	Actual Printout on Guest Confirmation
11	VIP	
12	Group buyer	
13	Honeymooners	
14	Comp	
20	Connecting rooms	*Connecting rooms, if possible*
21	Adjoining rooms	*Adjoining rooms, if possible*
22	Rooms on same floor	*Same floor, if possible*
23	Need individual names	*Please advise names of individuals in your party*
24	PS	*Petit suite*
25	RS	*One-bedroom suite*
26	LS	*Two-bedroom suite*
30	Send liquor	
31	Send champagne	
32	Send flowers	
33	Send gift	
34	Send fruit	
40	Require deposit	*Please send one night's deposit to guarantee your reservation*
41	Due bill	
42	No credit, require advance payment	
43	Walk-in	
44	Late arrival	*Anticipated late arrival of guest*
50	Special rate	*Special rate*
51	Airline rate	*Airline rate*
52	Press rate	*Press rate*
53	Convention rate	*Convention rate*
54	Nonconvention rate	*Convention rate applies to convention dates only*
55	Travel agency	*Travel agency*
60	Cot	*Cot will be provided*
61	Crib	*Crib will be provided*
62	Bedboard	*Bedboard will be provided*
63	Wheelchair	*Wheelchair will be provided*
70	Casino guest	
80	See correspondence for very special instructions	
99	Print special message	*(Whatever that message is)*

Exhibit 6-8   Actual listing of reservations codes from a major hotel/casino. Code numbers correspond to an internal system description, policy, or abbreviation. Some codes (for example, code 54) print onto a special "comments" section of the confirmation form sent the guest. Other codes (for example, code 11) are designed for inhouse use only.

VIPs. Very important persons (VIPs) are generally coded. These may be well-known dignitaries, celebrities, other hoteliers, or important members of an association that the hotel hopes to book later. VIP designations are made by a member of management or by the sales department. *Star reservation* is also used. A *contact reservation* is a VIP that should be met (contacted) and escorted to his or her room by management.

Riding Reservation. Reservations for which the date of arrival is vague may be allowed to "ride." The probable date is booked and then the reservation is carried until the guest shows or an allotted period of time passes, usually less than one week. Seldom used, riding reservations are almost exclusively set aside for VIPs, celebrities, influential guests, or senior managers from the hotel's corporate offices.

Convention Delegate. *Group affiliation* is a better term than *convention delegate* because the members of a group need not be part of a convention. Hotels cater to tours, company delegations, wedding parties, and other groups that need to be identified. Several codes are needed when different groups are booked at one time. The next section of this chapter discusses groups in detail.

CONVENTION AND TOUR GROUP BUSINESS

The term *group business* represents a variety of options. Group business can range from major conventions and expositions (trade shows), to midsized corporate meetings and conferences, to smaller incentive travel packages, tour groups, and corporate retreats (see Exhibit 6–9). From large to small, group business is a major player in today's lodging industry.

For some properties, group business is almost nonexistent. Such hotels or motels may have limited or no meeting facilities, may be located in remote areas and face difficult group travel logistics, or may be so busy with leisure travel that there is no room for discounted group business. Conversely, major convention properties may derive upward of 90% of all hotel revenues from group activities. Although different types of properties have varying degrees of dependence on group business, the industry as a whole derives a significant portion of its revenues from this growing segment (see Exhibits 6–10 and 6–11).

Exhibit 6-9 About two-thirds (66.0%) of all group room revenues come from conventions and expositions. The remaining one-third is composed primarily of corporate meetings (30.5%), with incentive travel (3.5%) making up the difference.

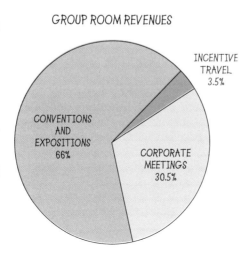

GROUP ROOM REVENUES

INCENTIVE TRAVEL 3.5%

CONVENTIONS AND EXPOSITIONS 66%

CORPORATE MEETINGS 30.5%

Hotel rooms and Incidentals:	$449.82 (47.6%)
Community Food and Beverage:	$177.66 (18.8%)
Retail stores	$103.95 (11.0%)
Hotel Food and Beverage	$ 93.56 (9.9%)
Transportation (Rental Car, Gas, Parking, etc)	$ 89.78 (9.5%)
Recreation (Sightseeing, Sporting Events, etc)	$ 30.24 (3.2%)

Exhibit 6-10   The average expenditure per delegate per convention for all conventions in the United States is $945.00 per event ($266 per day). The average length of stay for delegates is 3.6 nights. This exhibit shows how the average delegate spends his travel dollars. *Source: International Association of Convention & Visitor Bureaus.*

Incentive travel, tour groups, conventions, and trade shows have become mainstays of hotel sales in the United States and abroad. Such gatherings are clearly defined as group business. Business meetings and corporate retreats, though smaller in scale, are included in this broad definition.

Depending on the hotel, smaller gatherings lose the distinction of being classified and tracked as group business. A small wedding party requiring only five or seven rooms, for example, may be considered an individual rather than a group reservation. Several executives meeting in a conference room for a few days are often handled through the hotel's inhouse reservations department as individual rooms. Indeed, even a convention meeting planner visiting the property several weeks before the convention is probably handled as an individual (although complimentary) room. Technically, the meeting planner's accommodations should be tracked as part of the overall convention count.

Group reservations are handled differently from individual reservations. One difference is the central reservations office (or any of the GDS link-ups) may not be entitled to

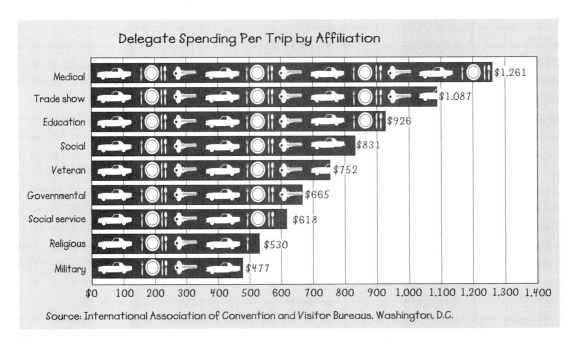

Exhibit 6-11   Convention delegates historically have spent more per trip than corporate or leisure travelers. Depending on the type or purpose of the convention (e.g., medical vs. military), certain delegates spend more than others.

handle the group. Many chains require that group accommodations deal directly with the specific hotel property. Even at the hotel property, midsized and larger operations usually remove group reservations from the responsibility of the inhouse reservations department.

Most midsized and larger properties have a group sales department designed to handle (among other tasks) group rooms reservations. Depending on business levels, policies, and property characteristics, large groups may be granted special rates and discounts. These special deals are negotiated between the group's representative and the hotel's sales manager, with final approval granted by the general manager of the property.

Because of differing policies and definitions, group business is handled and characterized differently across various hotels and chains. Therefore, it is difficult to know exactly the impact of group rooms activity on the lodging industry. A fairly large number of group activities are never counted. However, the convention industry (including conventions, expositions, corporate meetings, incentive travel, and trade shows) is conservatively estimated at close to $175 billion annually in the United States alone. According to the U.S. Department of Commerce, that places the convention industry in the top 20 of all industries in the United States.

The Group Rooms Contribution

The contribution of group rooms revenues to total rooms revenues depends on the type of hotel. Some properties—conference centers, for example—are exclusively group oriented (see Exhibits 6–12). Other operations choose to accommodate groups during slow periods and off-seasons (Exhibit 6–13). There are very few hotels that refuse to accommodate group business altogether.

Exhibit 6-12   Convention and meeting facilities come in all shapes and sizes. These two examples range from a cozy roundtable conference room at the Adam's Mark Hotel in St. Louis to the 26,680-square-foot Plaza International Ballroom at the Peabody Orlando. This ballroom can seat 2,420 guests for a banquet. *Courtesy of the Adam's Mark Hotel, St. Louis, Missouri and the Peabody Orlando, Orlando, Florida. Used with permission.*

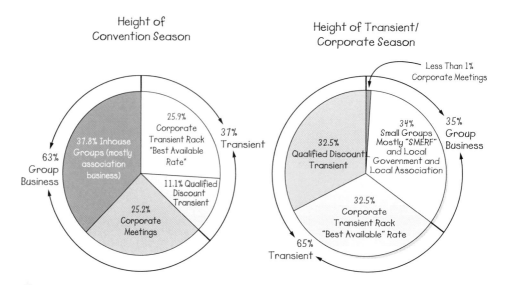

Exhibit 6-13   The Montelucia Resort (formerly the Doubletree La Posada Resort) reopened in 2008 as both a convention property and a transient resort. Depending on the time of year, this "hybrid" shifts its focus from group and convention business to transient travel.

The pie chart on the left shows the operation in the height of its convention/group season (January through March). The pie chart on the right shows the opposite demographic, when the hotel will be busiest with transient travel (June through August). *Courtesy: Doubletree La Posada Resort, Scottsdale, Arizona.*

Benefits of Group Business   Group business has three positive characteristics that make it appealing to the hotel industry: (1) The market is large; (2) Groups provide economies of scale; and (3) Group delegates spend more dollars than individual travelers. These macro characteristics only marginally impact the hotel's sales team when it decides to accept or reject the business. The offsets are what is important. Total income from guest room sales, F&B banquet sales, meeting room rentals and audiovisual equipment use is estimated. Next is the question of displacement. Is the group's dollar total, including the usual room discounts, greater than or less than the displaced corporate and transient business?

The yield management team (Chapter 5) helps to make the evaluation, but there are other considerations. If the answer seems to be "no," can the dates be changed? Is there potential for further business from the group and/or its individual members? Has the inquiry come from a meeting planner who holds the potential for other business? The GM, the sales manager, the rooms manager and the F&B manager huddle to decide.

The first characteristic, group business as a sizable market, was addressed earlier in the chapter (see Exhibits 6–9 to 6–11). There is no question that group business, an almost $175 billion industry, is "sizable." And depending on the type of hotel and the market in which it operates, some properties get more than their share of group business (see Exhibit 6–13).

The second characteristic addresses the incredible economies of scale associated with group business. *Economies of scale* is a term that denotes the economic benefits of mass production. Most items produced in mass quantities benefit from reduced per-item production costs. The same is true for the hotel industry. Selling a bulk of group rooms provides the operator with specific economies of scale. The sales department benefits from the reduced work in booking one large group as opposed to booking numerous smaller visits. The reservations department benefits from having a block of rooms set aside for the group. Even the front office, housekeeping, and uniformed services benefit from group room bookings.

With group arrivals and departures, business levels are clearly understood. With a five-day convention, for example, the front office is especially busy on the first and last days: During the first day, the front office is busy with heavy check-ins; on the last day, it is busy with check-outs. The middle days, however, are relatively slow for the front-office staff. During these slower middle days, the hotel saves labor costs by reducing its normal staffing levels. The same is true with the housekeeping and uniformed-services departments. In most cases, the housekeeping department spends less time cleaning stay-over rooms than it does cleaning check-outs. Similarly, the bellstaff is busiest when assisting guests with luggage at check-in and check-out. Uniformed-service positions are very slow during the middle days of a convention with the exception of the concierge desk.

The third reason hotels like group business is that group delegates have a higher worth than individual guests. No one understands this quite as well as the casino hotels. Interacting with other conventioneers puts group delegates in a festive mood. The trip is not just business—in many cases there is fun and excitement in the excursion. And what better way to have fun than with an all-expenses-paid trip (see Exhibits 6–10 and 6–11)?

Many convention, exposition, and conference attendees are visiting the event at no personal cost. Their company or business has funded most or all of the trip. Once at the hotel, delegates have a high likelihood of spending additional money. After all, their basic expenses (meals, lodging, transportation, and convention registration) have been paid. Therefore, they buy a round of golf that they might not ordinarily purchase. They may have an extra cocktail and buy more expensive "call" or "premium" liquor brands. They may select a souvenir from the gift shop or even a painting from the gallery. And, of course, they might gamble a few extra (or a lot of extra) dollars. Even when delegates attend a convention at their own expense, there are favorable tax deductions that reduce the real cost of the trip.

Casino/Hotels.   Casino/hotels are an interesting breed. Casino/hotels generally accept only groups that have a high likelihood of gambling. All things being equal, the casino manager may prefer a group of sanitation engineers, police officers, or morticians over a group of doctors, lawyers, or schoolteachers. In fact, the hotel may prefer a few empty hotel rooms over a hotel full of nongamblers. Therefore, even when space is available, certain groups will be refused by casino hotels.

Assuming that the sanitation engineers are considered to be good gamblers, the casino must decide how much they are worth. The question asked always is: Will the group produce more casino revenues than the individual tourists the group is displacing? If the group has a strong reputation for casino play, it will be able to negotiate a better discount than a group with a lesser (or unknown) gaming reputation.

Research shows that different delegates have different spending habits (see Exhibit 6–11). Industries in which delegates have higher annual salaries (say, physicians) usually see more spending per person during annual conventions than industries with lower annual salaries (say, military officers). This is not always the case with casino gaming. With casino gaming, lower-income delegates often spend more on the casino floor than do wealthier delegates.

The reason for this dichotomy can be found in such socioeconomic factors as education, aversion to risk, and moral perceptions among other reasons for which a delegate may or may not gamble. From Exhibit 6–11, a casino operator may prefer the military group over the physician group if the military has a higher propensity to gamble.

Why Some Hotels Refuse Groups.   Not too many years ago, select resort operations were less inclined to accept group business than they are today. They refused group bookings because the group alienated nongroup guests staying at the property. That is still often the case. Staying in a hotel that is almost entirely occupied by a large group can be disconcerting to the individual, nongroup guest. Walking the halls, eating a meal, or sitting in the lounge can be self-conscious activities when the nonaffiliated guest is surrounded by loud and boisterous group delegates. Some exclusive resorts will not subject their individual guests to such an uncomfortable situation.

Hotels may be less interested in group business for several other reasons. Group business requires a substantial investment from the hotel. The investment is not limited to construction of the hotel meeting facility. Other investments in group business include kitchen and food service equipment, audiovisual and technology software and hardware, tables and chairs, dance floors, stages and risers, and the like (see Exhibit 6–12).

Even existing hotel conference facilities are continually investing in new equipment and technologies. To remain state of the art, convention and conference facilities are taking technology to the next level. Not only do guests expect to find Wi-Fi, fax, copier, and printer equipment in every hotel room (see Chapter 14), they expect similar offerings in the conference center. These features might include dedicated amphitheaters in which every seat offers power outlets and Wi-Fi, Blue-Tooth, or similar technologies which enable attendees to log onto the Web and even download presentations. Sound systems, Internet-ready audiovisual carts with dedicated projectors, computers, and control consoles (to control lighting, projections screens, and even HVAC systems and window coverings) are all investments being made by today's conference centers.

Facilities and equipment investment aside, there is the requirement of additional labor to service the group business. Group hotels require a sales department staffed with corporate, national, and tour group sales managers. They require convention setup persons, banquet coordinators, chefs, food servers, even conference concierges.

Segments of Group Business

The need to communicate an ever-increasing amount of information has given extra strength to the convention market. Meeting and speaking with other delegates face to face offers certain benefits that the impersonal computer, telephone, or Internet cannot provide.

The continued growth for group tour and travel market looks especially strong in light of the ever-increasing numbers of Americans over the age of 55, retired, in good health, and with plenty of discretionary dollars. Lacking the expense account and tax advantages of the conventioneer, the group tourist seeks economy above all else. Group tour and travel rates are often substantially lower than rack rates.

Whereas convention business is sold as a group and guests are handled individually, tour business is sold as a group and guests are handled as a group. One sale, one reservation, one registration, one service, and one billing provide the savings on which the tour concept is built.

Tour Groups.   Tour groups are very convenient for the hotel, but that convenience comes at a price. Tour operators demand deep discounts. They get them because the entire burden is on the tour operator, with only minimal risk for the hotel.

The hotel deals with one party, the group tour company or wholesaler. The wholesaler leases the bus or plane, books the rooms, commits land transportation and entertainment, and then goes out to sell the package. Historically, travel agents have been the travel wholesaler's major sales outlets. However, as the travel landscape is changing, so are the distribution systems and sources from which end users (tourists) are finding their information. The travel wholesaler then combines all purchasers (no matter what the source of their business) into one cohesive group. In so doing, the workload of the front office is reduced considerably.

As much as 40% of the tour operator's original room estimate may be lost between the start of negotiations and the date of arrival, perhaps as long as one year later. Consequently, tour operators may be given the right to continue selling rooms up to 7 to 14 days before arrival. Specific dates are closed when the hotel is full and others may be closed to arrivals. Within the terms of the contract with the wholesaler, the hotel's team can alter the closeout date for the tours, asking for the final rooming list one week, four weeks, or even five weeks before arrival. Nowhere in this process is the hotel's inhouse reservation office involved. The wholesaler does all the selling. The deals are negotiated by the sales office, and the CRO is not generally involved.

Convention Groups. Arrangements for the convention are made by a representative, meeting planner, or committee of the organization and confirmed to the hotel with a contract of agreement. Large associations have permanent, paid executives in addition to the annually elected officers. These account executives are so numerous that they have their own organization—ASAE, the American Society of Association Executives.

If the organization is large enough to have a paid executive, he or she negotiates the arrangements with the hotel's sales staff. Details focus on many areas, including housing, meals, and meeting facilities. The organization (club, association, union) contracts with the hotel to buy meeting space (see Exhibits 6–12), banquet facilities, and rooms to house its own staff. It negotiates with the hotel for a block of guest rooms, but it does not pay for those rooms. Members deal individually with the hotel for accommodations.

The association sells function tickets to its membership for banquets, cocktail parties, and luncheons. The money collected from these events is paid to the hotel at the negotiated price. If the association charges a higher ticket price, it makes a slight profit over the hotel's charge.

In addition, the group benefits from breakage (see Chapter 2) if it sells more tickets than the number of delegates who actually show for the event. On the other hand, if it guarantees a number higher than the number of delegates who show, the hotel will reap the benefit of breakage.

The organization is responsible for its own entertainment (although it may hire people through the hotel or use a destination management company, DMC), its own speakers, films, and so on. For this, it charges the attendees a registration fee. Although some of the fee goes toward the costs of the program, the association usually profits here again.

Further gains may be made through the room rate arrangements. Sometimes organizations require the hotel to charge the attending members more than the negotiated room rate and to refund that excess to the group treasury. This raises many ethical concerns, particularly if the convention guest is unaware of the arrangement.

In no way does the association contract for rooms, except for those directly related to association headquarters, such as officers' and speakers' rooms. Room reservations are individually contracted between the hotel and each delegate. Billing is handled the same way, and collections become a personal matter between the conventioneer and the hotel.

The Threat from Discount Travel Sites.   The popularity of the Internet has made travel information more readily accessible than ever before. Broad availability of such information has affected the group travel side of the industry far more than anticipated. In the past, the group meeting planner negotiated with the hotel for the best possible convention rate, shared the headquarters hotel information—including rates—with association members and convention delegates months in advance, and assumed reservations against the group block would simply materialize. But the old way is certainly not the current way.

Discount travel sites (e.g., PriceLine.com, Expedia.com, Orbitz.com, and LastMinuteDeals.com) have provided savvy delegates several new options. Let's create a hypothetical situation. Say the fictitious Imperial Arms Hotel at a shore town in New Jersey has the American Billiards Club (ABC) convention visiting from August 3 to August 7. Delegates to the ABC convention likely made their room reservations many months ago at the group-negotiated rate of $139 per night. However, in mid-July, delegates discovered that the same rooms could be purchased over discount Internet sites for just $79 per night. It is a small sacrifice to stay outside of the convention block. Internet-booked rooms sold outside the convention block will not be identified with the convention and therefore will not receive turn-down service, a daily convention newsletter, or the nightly conference gift. Nevertheless, many delegates canceled their $139 convention room reservations and booked over the Internet at $79.

But the story does not end there. If rooms at the convention headquarters hotel are $79 on the Internet, there are almost certainly other rooms in town at substantial savings as well. It turns out that the fictitious William Penn Hotel (just across the street) has rooms for only $49 on the Internet. Other delegates decide to cancel rooms at the headquarters hotel in favor of an even better rate (although they'll have to walk across the street every day) at the William Penn Hotel.

At this point, the meeting planner faces several serious issues. The availability of substantially lower rates makes not only for an embarrassing situation, but a potentially costly one as well. The cost comes through group attrition. If the convention does not generate a certain number of room nights, the difference is billable to the convention. The ABC group may be liable for thousands of dollars in attrition costs because of the bargain-hunting antics of its delegates.

So what is to be done? Maybe the meeting planner should simply talk to the hotel sales department, explain what has happened in the last few days before the convention begins, and ask for a new contract and better rate. That action has been tried—it does not work. The hotel will stick to its guns and insist on maintaining the negotiated rate and the negotiated attritions clause.

Today's meeting planners therefore must negotiate several clauses into their contracts to combat this growing problem. One clause counts all members of the group against the guarantee. Even if members choose to stay at the hotel as unidentified delegates, if the group (ABC) can prove the members were registered with the convention, the group will receive credit against the room-night guarantee. Another response to the problem of discounted rooms is a clause in the contract stating, "No lower rates shall be offered by the hotel, through any distribution vehicle, during the contracted meeting dates, unless offered to all attendees as well."

Expositions and Trade Shows.   Expositions and trade shows have many characteristics similar to conventions. In fact, trade shows are often held in conjunction with large conventions. The association (or trade-show entrepreneur) acquires space from the hotel or convention center and leases that space to exhibitors. Those managing the trade show invite guests, exhibitors, and shoppers.

The average guest stay is longer with a show because the displays, which are costly and elaborate, require setup and teardown time. Otherwise, reservation and front-office procedures are the same as for a convention or an individual guest. More city ledger charges (direct bill accounts) may occur because the exhibitors are usually large companies that request that type of settlement.

Booking the Convention

Associations book conventions and expositions as many as 5 to 10 years in advance. Extremely large conventions (100,000 delegates or more) such as the National Association of Home Builders (NAHB) or the National Restaurant Association (NRA) Trade Show may have unconfirmed bookings as far out as 20 years in advance. For small to midsized conventions, two to three years is the norm.

Initially, a blanket reservation is committed by the hotel and a rate is negotiated. For large conventions requiring more than one hotel, a citywide convention and visitor bureau (CVB) negotiates the blanket reservation on behalf of participating hotels (see "Convention and Visitor Bureaus" below). The blanket reservation is little more than a commitment for a set number of rooms at a set rate for a set date. There is little additional detail until a year in advance.

Adjusting the Room Block.   As the date approaches, some six months to a year in advance, the hotel begins to examine the blanket reservation or room block. After discussions with the association, the hotel may adjust the number of rooms required if the association predicts its convention size to grow or shrink that year. Meetings with neighboring hotels or the CVB may shed light on their management strategies with regard to the room block and the convention's ability to deliver the rooms committed. Finally, communication with other hotels where this group has previously been housed will give some sense of the group's attrition or casualty factor.

Convention hotels usually cooperate by furnishing each other historical information about the group—numbers, no-shows, and the like. They do this because conventions usually move annually. A hotel in one section of the state or nation is not competing with another if the organization has already decided to meet in another city. Similar information is available through local convention or tourist bureaus, which report to and have access to the files of the International Association of Convention and Visitor Bureaus (IACVB). The IACVB gathers data about the character and performance of each group handled by the member bureaus.

Reservation problems occur despite the best predictive efforts of the marketing and reservations departments. Association memberships change over time, and certain cities prove more or less appealing than previous sites. The casualty factor (cancellations plus no-shows) also varies from group to group, reducing the value of generalized percentage figures.

Convention and Visitor Bureaus.   Convention and visitor bureaus are publicly funded, quasi-governmental agencies found in all large and most midsized or small cities. CVBs (sometimes known as convention and visitor authorities) are a centralized entity designed to represent the city's hospitality industries. Usually, CVBs are funded by local lodging or room taxes (see Chapter 9); they may also receive some government funding and some membership dues. Because the vast amount of funding comes from lodging taxes, hotels are viewed as paying "customers" of the CVB and the CVB is, in essence, working for the betterment of the hospitality industry.

SCHEDULED CONVENTIONS

	Hotel	Date	Attendance
Western Carwash Association	Las Vegas Hilton	October 25–October 27	2,500
Insitute for Advanced Medical Education	Venetian	October 26–October 29	350
World Wings International	Las Vegas Hilton	October 26–October 29	1,000
Amsoil, Inc.	Texas Station	October 26–November 1	25
NAHB Custom Builder Symposium	Hyatt Regency Lake Las Vegas	October 27–October 29	400
Nevada Parks and Recreation Society	Summerlin Tech Center	October 27–October 29	400
Universal Passing Over	Alexis Park Resort and Spa	October 27–October 29	60
Washington Society of Certified Public Accountants	Caesars Palace	October 27–November 2	300
Farm Equipment Manufacturers Association	Mirage	October 28–November 3	1,000
American Management Association International	Flamingo	October 29–November 1	25
National Association of Certified Valuation Analysts	Westin Casuarina	October 29–November 4	40
National Association of International Educators	Flamingo	October 29–November 4	650
Dairy Management, Inc.	Caesars Palace	October 29–November 11	1,200
Bridgestone/ Firestone, Inc.	Bellagio	October 30–November 1	3,000
Western Energy Institue	Red Rock Resort Spa & Casino	October 31–November 2	40
Automotive Aftermarket Products Expo	Sands Expo Center	October 31–November 3	130,000
Specialty Equipment Market Association	Las Vegas Convention Center	October 31–November 3	120,000
The Friedman Group	Alexis Park Resort and Spa	October 31–November 3	80
National Association of Foreign Student Advisors	Flamingo	October 31–November 3	550

Exhibit 6–14   A glimpse at this convention calendar (randomly started with October 25th) gives a sense of the wide variety of conventions, associations, and affiliations that meet. Note the numbers of delegates and headquarters hotels listed.

Three large convention centers are located in Las Vegas and host many of the top 200 largest conventions in the world. According to the Las Vegas Convention and Visitors Authority, conventions and trade shows bring in over 5 million delegates a year and generate in excess of $6 billion in nongaming revenue. *Source: Las Vegas Convention and Visitors Authority, Las Vegas, Nevada.*

The CVB represents the city in numerous group rooms bids each year (see Exhibit 6–14). Many of these bids are made directly to the ASAE or a regional counterpart of the same. Hotel sales managers from some of the larger properties (or key properties bidding on a particular piece of business) often accompany CVB representatives on national sales trips.

Expanded Services. In recent years, CVBs have begun vertically integrating more and more group services. Such areas as transportation services (moving delegates to and from the airport and daily to and from the convention center), on-site registration assistance (temporary staffing of booths), database marketing (identifying who attended and from where they came), telemarketing (swaying potential delegates to attend the convention), promotion assistance (developing videos and print materials), and even special event or off-site banquet planning (managing extracurricular activities outside the convention center) are now being offered by some CVBs.

Meeting planners are generally pleased with the trend toward expanded bureau services. After all, any value-added service included with the price of convention space will ultimately make for a better convention and might save the association money. But at what cost? Though meeting planners are happy about the trend toward vertical integration of CVBs, independent meeting suppliers and destination management companies (DMCs) are less pleased. They argue that CVBs are stepping outside their defined roles as convention and visitor bureaus. The job of the CVB, according to many meeting supply companies, is to bring business into the city. Once the CVB secures the business, independent meeting suppliers should be allowed to handle the details from there.

Certainly the CVBs' expanded role encroaches upon the independent meeting suppliers. When the CVB offers transportation services, that affects the ground-handling companies. When the CVB offers on-site registration assistance, that affects the temporary employment agencies. Others who may be affected by these expanded services include independent research and marketing consultants, video production and media print services, caterers, regional tour operators, and DMCs.

The CVBs understand the problem but often opt for the greater good to the greatest number of persons. You see, if a convention threatens to be lost to a competing city because that city is including additional services, like it or not the CVB will have to match the bid. The alternative is to let the convention, and all its associated community revenues (see Exhibits 6–10 and 6–11), slip away. With conventions of 10,000 delegates representing some $7,000,000 to hotels, restaurants, transportation services, theaters, and shops in a community, CVBs cannot afford to lose business for the sake of a few independent meeting planners (see Exhibit 6–15).

The Meetings and Conventions Industry			
	Number of Annual Meetings	Total Meeting Attendance	Total Meetings Expenditures	Average Expenditures per Delegate
Corporate	1,020,300	79.7 Million Delegates	$ 31.8 Billion	$ 399.00
Association	210,600	37.9 Million Delegates	$ 41.8 Billion	$1,102.90
Conventions	12,700	18.9 Million Delegates	$ 33.6 Billion	$1,777.78
Total	1,243,600	136.5 Million Delegates	$107.2 Billion	$ 785.35

Exhibit 6-15   The meetings and conventions industry is healthy and dynamic, with aggregate annual U.S. spending topping $107 billion.
While the corporate market holds far more meetings each year than association and convention markets, the average spending per delegate ($399.00) is far less than that of associations ($1,102.90) and conventions ($1,777.78). *Source: Meetings and Conventions Report.*

The Housing Bureau.   An important division or office within the CVB is the housing bureau (or housing authority). When the CVB is successful in bidding and committing citywide rooms to groups too large to be housed by one hotel, the housing bureau becomes involved. The San Francisco CVB's housing bureau, for example, handles well over one-quarter million room nights per year. It offers its services once a convention reaches 1,000 delegates in three or more hotels.

Each hotel commits rooms toward the blanket reservation and a citywide commitment is made to the association. Rates remain the prerogative of the individual properties.

Reservation request cards (Exhibit 6–16) are returned to the CVB's housing bureau rather than to the individual hotel. The bureau relays the guest's reservation request to whichever hotel still has space. The hotel replies to the guest and sends copies of the confirmation to the housing bureau and to the association's headquarters.

Two properties may join forces if the convention is too large for one hotel but does not need a citywide commitment. The property that booked the business becomes the headquarters site and the booking office, with the second hotel (the overflow hotel) honoring the negotiated convention rate. This practice is now considered a violation of the antitrust laws. Joint housing of delegates is permissible, but each property should negotiate its own rates.

Overflow Hotels.   Some hotels request an advance deposit from convention delegates. This is especially true of isolated resorts where there is little chance that walk-ins will fill no-show vacancies. It is also true of overflow hotels.

Conventions are often too large to be housed in just one hotel. Therefore, the association finds additional properties to supplement the rooms available at the headquarters hotel. These supplemental properties are commonly referred to as overflow hotels.

Overflow hotels often require an advance deposit sufficient to cover the cost of all nights booked. This is because overflow properties may lose occupancy to the headquarters hotel during the second or third day of the convention. Because of cancellations and no-shows, the headquarters hotel often has vacancies at the outset of the convention. Rooms available at the headquarters hotel are very appealing to delegates housed at overflow properties. After all, for roughly the same rate, they can conveniently stay in the main hotel with all of the exciting hospitality suites and activities it has to offer.

Advance deposits help overflow properties protect themselves against delegates who check out the second day and move to the headquarters hotel. Overflow properties sometimes protect themselves by charging full advance deposits equal to the entire number of nights the delegate initially planned to stay. They may also change their cancellation policy to reflect 48 or 72 hours' advance notice.

Negotiating Convention Rates

Convention pricing is unique because convention organizers bargain hard to obtain the best rates they can. Yet it is the individual convention delegate who actually reaps the benefit of the discounted rate when he or she pays the room bill. The association executive or meeting planner negotiates with the hotel(s) on behalf of the convention and all its delegates. The sales manager, the director of sales, or even the general manager negotiates on behalf of the hotel.

For most conventioneers, the hotel room is the largest expense item (see Exhibit 6–10). Therefore, the convention attempts to negotiate a favorable rate so as to attract the most delegates possible. Conversely, the hotel needs to keep its profitability and yield management policies in mind as it sets rate parameters with the group.

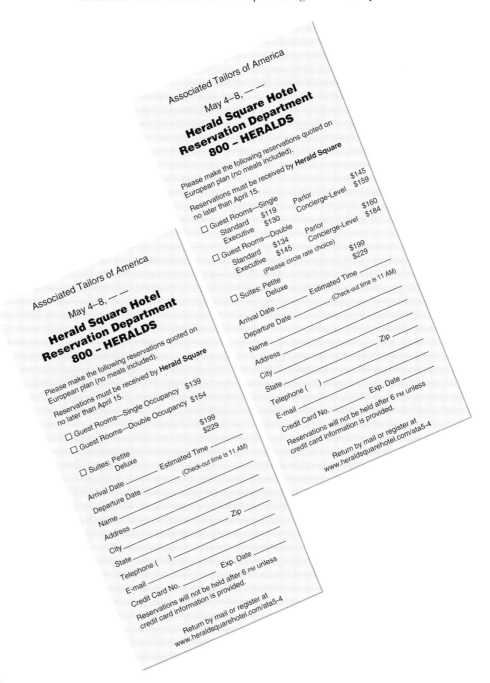

Exhibit 6-16   Here are two sample reservation request cards for individual reservations against the "Associated Tailors of America" (ATA) group room block. Note the card on the left quotes run-of-the-house (flat) rates while the card on the right offers spread rates—one or the other would be mailed to potential delegates depending on contracted arrangements made with ATA. In either case, rooms are quoted European Plan (no meals). On the opposite side is the hotel's mailing address for insertion into a window envelope before mailing (this ensures privacy/security of guest information). Similar cards would be available for each hotel housing delegates in the city-wide convention. Electronic procedures are replacing this manual system.

If the convention is planned during a slow season for the hotel, the sales department is willing to negotiate. The agreed-upon room rate is also dependent on the number (and profitability) of food and beverage functions planned in association with the convention. Other factors for the hotel to consider are the makeup or demographics of the convention, whether delegates have the potential to return as regular guests, and for casino hotels, whether delegates have a propensity to gamble.

Another variable the hotel considers is the *attrition factor*. Through contacts with other properties that have housed this group in the past, the sales manager gains an understanding of the attrition or *pickup rate* for this particular group. It makes no sense for the hotel to plan 800 rooms for five nights for the Associated Tailors of America conference (see Exhibit 6–16) if they'll be lucky to actually sell 650 rooms for an average of four nights. Associations have a tendency to exaggerate the number of rooms needed by delegates. Hotels must ascertain the attrition factor or pickup rate before committing to a specific room rate.

Attrition.   The group's attrition factor and the group's pickup rate are actually mathematical reciprocals of each other. They both provide the sales department with a measurement of the number of rooms actually reserved, in comparison to the number initially set aside in the reservation room block. They just derive this measurement in slightly different ways.

The pickup rate looks at the actual number of rooms sold to convention delegates divided by the number of rooms originally blocked. For an example, let's look back to the Associated Tailors' convention. Assume that the blanket reservation blocked 800 rooms for five nights—that's 4,000 room-nights. However, at the close of the convention, the hotel discovered it sold only 650 rooms for an average of four nights—that's 2,600 room-nights. The pickup rate was just 65.0% (2,600 room-nights sold divided by 4,000 room-nights blocked).

Conversely, the attrition factor looks at the number of rooms that were not sold or not picked up. The attrition factor measures the remaining unsold delegate rooms by the number of rooms originally blocked. Again, let's look to the Associated Tailors' convention. If 2,600 room-nights were actually picked up against a block of 4,000 room-nights, 1,400 room-nights went unsold to convention delegates. These 1,400 room-nights may have ended up being sold to corporate or leisure guests, but only after the agreed-upon closeout date for accepting convention reservations (April 15 in Exhibit 6–16). The attrition factor for this group was 35.0% (1,400 room-nights unsold divided by 4,000 room-nights blocked).

Hotels Get Serious About Attrition.   Hotel attrition policies are more prevalent (and taken more seriously) than ever before. Groups that fail to fill their contracted room block (usually a 90% pick-up rate is considered acceptable—see Exhibit 6–17) are charged attrition fees ranging from a few hundred dollars to hundreds of thousands of dollars! After all, when the hotel offers reduced group room rates, it is discounting them against the group's promise to fill them. If the room nights do not materialize, the hotel's bottom line suffers.

Although attrition policies were rarely enforced a decade ago, today's attrition policies are more serious business. One of the reasons for this increased focus on attrition is the increasing availability of information to meeting planners and association executives. Email marketing and Web-based group registration provide a great deal of information in readily usable form. With online registration, attendees book their own rooms and answer their own housing questions. This releases the meeting planner from these administrative duties—time that can be used to ensure higher pick-up rates.

Group Room Block Attrition Calculation

	Day #1	Day#2	Day #3	Day #4	Grand Total
Rooms available for sale (this is a 400-room inventory)	395	398	396	394	
Group room block	165	210	225	195	
Net room block (allows for 10% attrition-factor per contract agreement)	149	189	203	176	
Sold against group block	152	167	177	144	
Other non-group rooms	240	194	205	224	
Total rooms sold	392	361	382	368	
Vacant rooms	3	37	14	26	
Group rooms attrition Liability (smaller of net block less group rooms sold **or** vacant rooms)	0	22	14	26	62
Times contracted (negotiated) profit margin per unsold room	$129	$129	$129	$129	
Total attrition liability	0	$2,838	$1,806	$3,354	$7,998

Exhibit 6–17   An example of a room attrition calculation. This example assumes a 400-room hotel is holding a four-night group room block ranging from 165 rooms to 225 rooms per night at a negotiated $169 flat rate. It also assumes each occupied room has a variable production cost of $40, so $129 is the profit margin from each group room night. Please note the contract provides the group a courtesy 10% attrition factor before charges accrue. Also, the contract allows any group rooms sold by the hotel (to transient business) to reduce the attrition liability. Thus, the group is responsible for the lower of unsold group rooms or total hotel rooms unsold each night.

Automated attendee registration (systems like b-there.com, passkey.com, and 123sign-up.com) can alleviate costly attrition fees in several ways:

➤ Email marketing—You're attending the convention, but are your friends? Please send this email reminder to 10 of your closest associates.

➤ Targeted marketing—Which attendees who registered last year have failed to reregister this year?

➤ Cancellation tracking—Who cancelled in the past 10 days, and are any worrisome trends developing?

➤ Hotel balancing—The Omni is filled to 94% of its block (no attrition fees above 90% pick-up), yet the Radisson sits at just 74%.

Comp Rooms.   Complimentary (comp or "free") rooms are one part of the total package. Complimentary rooms for use by the association or convention are usually provided at a rate of one comp unit per 50 sold. The formula applies to tour groups as well.

Many hotels are beginning to take a hard look at how comps are earned and used. Attrition factors, no-shows, and cancellations are no longer counted in the computation. Credit is given only for the number of rooms actually sold; understays do not contribute to the count.

The use of comps is also being restricted. Comps are meant to be used by convention executives and staff during the dates of the convention and possibly several days immediately preceding or following the event. Comps are not designed for use months later as a personal vacation for the convention executive!

Rate Quotes.   Rates are quoted as flat or spread (see Exhibit 6–16). Under the *flat rate*, sometimes called *single rate*, all guests pay the same convention rate, which is usually less than the average rack rate. Except for suites, rooms are assigned on a best-available basis, called *run-of-the-house.* Some pay more for the room than its normal price, and others pay less. Run-of-the-house implies an equal distribution of room assignments. If half the rooms have an ocean view and half do not, the convention group should get a 50–50 split with a run-of-the-house rate. One Hawaiian hotel advertises "run-of-the-ocean" rates. A fair distribution includes an equitable share of standard, medium, and deluxe accommodations.

A *spread rate,* sometimes called a *sliding rate,* uses the standard rack rate distribution already in place. The level is reduced several dollars below the rack rates. Assignments are made over the entire rate spread according to individual preference and a willingness to pay. The range of wealth and interest among the attendees makes spread rates more attractive to larger groups.

Managing the Room Block.   As individual room requests arrive at the hotel, they are booked against the group room block. The hotel and the association reexamine the room commitment several times in the weeks leading up to the convention. Reservations received after the closeout date, 20 to 30 days before the convention starts, are accepted only if space remains—on an *availability basis only.*

Privacy of information provided with the delegate's reservation—either an electronically submitted reservation or a returned reservation request card (see Exhibit 6–16)—has received increased attention in recent years. When consumers read stories like the recent fiasco involving Hotels.com, where a company auditor's stolen laptop compromised the personal information of thousands of customers, the issue becomes increasingly important.

Personal information of meeting attendees is available not only to the hotel(s) involved, but to any vendors servicing the meeting and the association itself. The growing popularity of electronic name badges, scannable name badges, and imbedded name badges has increased the availability of information to many parties. Imbedded name badges, those featuring radio frequency identification (RFID) technology, track the steps of each delegate. Although there is much to be gained by knowing which delegates attended which seminars, when each arrived, how long each stayed, etc., there is also much controversy surrounding the use of this personal information.

Competitive Clauses.   Most attendees carry laptop computers and camera-capable cell phones. Consequently, no information, personal or corporate, is safe at meetings or conventions, especially where wireless technology is used. This is one reason the industry has seen an increase in the number of competitive clauses in meetings contracts. A competitive clause essentially limits who can book rooms or meetings at the same hotel during a period overlapping with the group in question. A corporation rolling out a new product or technology wants its users to see the product, but wants to keep its competitors from seeing it and potentially stealing it.

Unidentified Delegates.   Some delegates slip through the carefully planned system and appear to the hotel as regular guests unaffiliated with the convention. This is often accidental, but some guests deliberately trick the hotel to gain rate or room advantages (see earlier section entitled The Threat from Discount Travel Sites).

One of two things may happen with these unidentified conventioneers: (1) The reservation might be denied (the convention block is open, but general reservations are closed), and the guest goes elsewhere; or (2) the reservation might be accepted as a non-convention guest (both the convention room block and the nonconvention categories are open). This second option leaves the hotel with duplicate count.

The situation takes a different twist when the conventioneer accepts space outside the blanket count because all the convention spots have been filled. Once housed, this guest argues to get the special, reduced, convention rate. Too many situations like that, and the carefully balanced yield management system goes awry.

IT Packages.   The inclusive tour (IT) package (Chapter 2) is the hotel's move into the lucrative group market. The hotel combines housing, food, and entertainment but no transportation to offer an appealing multiple-night stay at greatly reduced rates. The IT package affects group bookings, but it is not a type of group business.

IT packages can and do compete with convention reservations. For large conventions, the yield management committee closes the remaining rooms to all but high-priced rates. When relatively few rooms of the hotel are assigned to the convention, all rate classes remain available, including the package, priced at less, and offering more, than the convention rate. Keen convention shoppers book the IT package.

Handling Tour Group Reservations

The workload of the reservations department is affected relatively little by the demands of tour groups. Both the initial sale and its continuing followup rest with the hotel's marketing and sales department. That department may have a division called the *tour and travel desk*, which gets involved once the buyer is satisfied with the facilities (see Exhibit 6–18).

Yield management coordination is the major role for reservations during the time before the group arrives. Hotels doing a large tour and travel business maintain four-month horizons. Sell-and-report parameters are adjusted as forecasted demand equals, exceeds, or falls short of historical expectations.

Tour groups are almost always given shares-with rooms, since a premium is charged for single occupancy. The hotel gets a rooming list that shows each pairing. The entire block of rooms is preassigned. If the tour company brings in back-to-back groups, the very same rooms may be used again and again. Keeping the block together

SITE INSPECTION CHECKLIST

ACCOMMODATIONS

Number of Rooms on Property:

	Smoking	Non		Smoking	Non
Doubles	____	____	Queens	____	____
Kings	____	____	Parlors	____	____
Suite	____	____	Other	____	____

Total Number of Rooms Available for Group:

	Smoking	Non		Smoking	Non
Doubles	____	____	Queens	____	____
Kings	____	____	Parlors	____	____
Suite	____	____	Other	____	____

ADA Rooms for the Physically Impaired:

Doubles_____ Queens_____ Kings_____ Parlors_____ Suite_____ Other_____:

Complimentary room policy_____

Sprinklers and smoke alarms in rooms?   ≅ **Yes**   ≅ **No**

Emergency speakers in rooms?   ≅ **Yes**   ≅ **No**

Room amenities (list) _____

Emergency lights?   ≅ **Yes**   ≅ **No**

Hall lighting adequate and exits well marked?   ≅ **Yes**   ≅ **No**

Walls soundproof?   ≅ **Yes**   ≅ **No**

Concierge/VIP Club level   ≅ **Yes**   ≅ **No**

Concierge room amenities (list) _____

Guest phone charge policy/cost_____Long Distance_____

Data port on phone or in room?   ≅ **Yes**   ≅ **No**

How many telephones in room? _____

Is there a desk with lighting?   ≅ **Yes**   ≅ **No**

Room Service? (open from_____ to_____)   ≅ **Yes**   ≅ **No**

Vertical tab labels (right side): Accommodations · Dates of availability · Front desk · Public space · Meeting and banquet space · Food and beverage outlets · Services and parking · Other hotel information · Sports and recreational facilities · Facilities near property · Vendor recommendations · Meeting requirements and history · Site inspection evaluation · Negotiations

Exhibit 6-18   Association executives, professional meeting planners and tour group operators evaluate numerous hotels before selecting the right property. Each hotel is evaluated for price, availability, size, ability to meet the group's unique needs, and so on. Here is one sample page (Accommodations) from a site-inspection checklist. This particular checklist has 14 pages covering a variety of categories and observations. *Courtesy of Jennifer Brown, CMP; Strategic Site Specialist, Meeting Sites Resource, Newport Beach, California.*

in the same floor or wing expedites baggage handling and reduces noise and congestion elsewhere.

Special group arrival sections, even special lobby entrances, reduce the congestion as the group arrives or departs. Transportation is by bus, even if only to the airport. These transfer costs are part of the fee and are arranged by the tour company. Bell fees for luggage-in and luggage-out are also included, levied by the hotel over and above the room charge.

SUMMARY

Reservations are contractual agreements, so the hotel or corporate reservationist must be careful to document all pertinent information. Some data, such as the date of arrival, number of persons, type of room, guest's name and rate, are required fields for this reservation. Other information, such as estimated time of arrival, special requests, and discounts, is less important to the reservation and may only be collected in certain cases or by request of the guest.

Once the reservation has been agreed upon between the customer and the hotel or the central res office, its journey begins. In some cases the journey is short, as with those reservations made a few hours or days before arrival. Other times it is a long journey, as with reservations made months—even years—in advance.

Group business means different things to different hotels, but almost all properties generate some percentage of their revenue through group contracts. Group business is especially beneficial because it is a sizable market (close to $175 billion in annual sales). There are certain efficiencies (economies of scale) associated with group arrivals and departures. Moreover, group delegates generally spend more than individual guests.

Group room blocks may be negotiated years in advance and managed down to the day of arrival. Careful management of group blocks assures a high pickup rate and little or no attrition charges accruing to the meeting planner or association executive. However, the prevalence of discount Web sites has made this task substantially more difficult.

RESOURCES AND CHALLENGES
Resources

WEB SITES

Online registration and convention delegate rooming services are growing in popularity. They provide meeting planners and association executives with important tools for ensuring high convention occupancy rates. Attendees register for the convention, sleeping rooms, and other services on line. Meeting planners track registrations and manipulate a variety of data designed to assist with maximizing head counts and minimizing attrition.

The following Web sites are vendors of registration and housing software solutions:

➤ Event411.com
➤ Eventbookings.com
➤ Eventregistration.com
➤ Register123.com
➤ Seeuthere.com

Web Assignment

What tools and information do these services provide the meeting planner that would be substantially more difficult to develop without online registration?

INTERESTING TIDBITS

➤ According to a recent survey, 64% of travelers are verbally informed of the hotel's cancellation policy while booking the reservation. Additionally 44% of hotels go a step further and actually mail a written confirmation. *Source: American Express Travel Trends Monitor.*

➤ Videoconferencing and Web conferencing have been growing in popularity as "travel alternatives." Indeed, they gained substantial popularity in the year immediately following the September 11, 2001 (9/11) terrorist attacks. Video (and Web) conferences save companies on travel, per diem, ground transportation, and lodging costs by keeping participants at home or nearby in conference-enabled facilities. But a recent survey found an added bonus: Video (and Web) conferencing usually do not utilize the costly services of meeting planners. Instead of being professionally arranged, such conferences are handled internally by the conference users (attendees), creating a substantial cost savings. Specifically, 69% of companies never use a meeting planner to assist with the hosting of video (Web) conferences. Another 20% of companies "rarely" use a meeting planner with video (Web) conferences. Some 5% range from "sometimes" to "often" in their use of meeting planners, and the remaining 5% of companies "always" use a meeting planner with video (Web) conferences. *Source: Business Travel News.*

Challenges

TRUE/FALSE QUIZ

Questions that are partially false should be marked false (F).

____ 1. Some reservation information is required, essential to the reservation. The guest's date of expected arrival is one such example. Other information is optional. The guest's date of departure is an example.

____ 2. As part of the cancellation process for a guaranteed reservation, the reservationist should provide the caller a cancellation number (sometimes a similar number to the confirmation number).

____ 3. With centralized guest history databases, a chain hotel in New York City can actually retrieve personal information (address, room type and rate, number of nights stayed, etc.) for a guest who last stayed at one of the chain's hotels in Los Angeles.

____ 4. Meeting planners or association executives who book group business are no longer responsible for room attrition due to the government's Room Attrition Act of 1999.

____ 5. A hotel that offers delegates this choice—$129 standard is available at the group rate of $99; the $169 deluxe is available at the group rate of $129, and the $199 executive parlor is available at $149—is quoting flat rates (run-of-house).

PROBLEMS

1. Many hotels are apprehensive about charging the corporation if a business traveler fails to arrive. Even though a room was held and revenue was lost, the hotel is reluctant to charge the no-show back to the corporation for fear of alienation, and loss of future business.

Develop a series of strict—but fair—reservations policies that protect the hotel's interests while minimizing conflicts with corporate accounts. In what instances would you charge the corporate no-show? When would you not charge?

2. The use of computerized reservations is far more efficient than the use of manual, hand-written reservations. Compare the manual reservations approach to the automated collection of guest reservation information. List five benefits (efficiencies) created by automated reservations systems.

3. As a follow-up to Problem 2, are there any disadvantages associated with automated reservations systems?

4. Guests generally prefer the choice associated with spread rates. Hotels find it easier to manage rooms inventory when they use flat rates. Which would you use as a hotel manager? Explain your response.

5. As a prominent hotelier, you have been asked by the CVB to appear before the county commissioners during a CVB budget-review session. The commission is angry that the local CVB spends public funds to maintain a convention housing bureau and that those services are provided without a fee. Do the necessary research to provide hard facts to support your testimony in favor of the CVB.

6. The reservation of an unidentified convention delegate is treated like a corporate or leisure guest reservation. How might this failure to identify the guest as a conventioneer affect the hotel? Could it benefit the guest? Could it hurt the guest? How will it factor into the meeting planner's attrition/pick-up rates?

AN INCIDENT IN HOTEL MANAGEMENT

Don't Box Me In!

A convention exhibitor has shipped display goods to many hotels throughout the years. He knew full well the likelihood that valuable goods *shipped* to the convention through the hotel's receiving dock may not show up on time, or even ever. So he *mailed* two medium-sized boxes to himself marked, "Hold for Arrival" in large print.

Steve, the guest-service agent "sorta remembers" the packages coming about a week back. "They weren't large enough to store with receiving; yeah, I think they went to housekeeping."

Convention Exhibitor: Could you call and find out?

Steve (pointing): The house phones are over there.

The guest returned to report that housekeeping sent them to the desk yesterday so they would be on hand for his arrival. "Well, they're not here; that's for sure!" With hands on hips, Steve waited, slowly chewing his gum.

A second guest-service agent had finished with another guest and realized there was an adjacent *situation*. "The boxes, yes, they're on the mail table in the back room."

> **Convention Exhibitor speaking to the GM's secretary:** "When I asked for his name, he glared at me, shook his head and pointed to his badge."

> *Questions:*   Was there a management failure here; if so, what?
> What is the hotel's immediate response (or action) to the incident? What further, long-run action should management take, if any?

ANSWERS TO TRUE/FALSE QUIZ

1. False. Both examples are required. It would be impossible to effectively sell a hotel if we only knew arrival dates and never knew the number of nights intended for the reservation.

2. True. Cancellations for guaranteed reservations should always be provided a distinct cancellation number as proof the cancellation was made.

3. True. In fact, the New York chain hotel could look at the guest's most recent (Los Angeles) stay history and ask him if he wanted the same wake-up call and the same breakfast.

4. False. Room attrition (usually calculated as less than 90% of the rooms initially blocked for the group actually having sold) has become a more critical issue for meeting planners and association executives. Hotels are serious about charging groups for low occupancy. P.S., there is no such thing as the Room Attrition Act of 1999.

5. False. This hotel is quoting spread rates. If all rooms (standard, deluxe, and executive parlor) were available for a flat rate of, say, $129, then the hotel would be quoting flat rates (run-of-house). But a range of rates, as shown in the question, means the hotel quoted spread rates.

PART III
Guest Services and Rate Structures

CHAPTER 7

Managing Guest Services

Outline

The organizational structure of Chapter 3 illustrates the top-down design that is the reality of hotel organizations. This supervisor–supervised relationship is not going away, but it is changing: It's softening. Everyone has come to realize that guest service, not amenity creep, is the essence of great hotel management. Guest service relies on and is delivered by those supervised, the line workers.

Guest service doesn't just happen; it must be managed—and it must be managed close to the action, not from afar. Accomplishing the shift from the traditional management-imposed culture to an employee-participative culture takes all of management's talent. It's slow, hard work. Many workers and even their immediate supervisors are not interested in taking on the job. They see guest service as management's job, not theirs. But today's innkeepers cannot be the guest's personal hosts, as they were once seen to be (see Chapter 3). The task has sifted down through several organizational levels to the staffer on the floor. Getting those employees to recognize the importance of the task and the mutual interests that result from performing them is the role of managing for guest service. No easy task, that.

TOTAL QUALITY MANAGEMENT (TQM)

The model for actively managing guest relations originated in another broader idea, *Total Quality Management (TQM)*. TQM's initial focus was manufacturing, producing products with zero defects. Why not adopt that idea—the idea of zero defects—and apply it to customer–employee interactions? Thus, total quality management included customer relations management (CRM) as the application of zero defects shifted from manufacturing to service.

CRM gets special attention when business slumps. As Chapter 1 noted, hotelkeeping slumps in cycles. The 1980s was one such period. Another was the years following New York City's World Trade Center trauma. Attention to the service-deliverer, the hotel's line employee, gained ground during these two difficult periods because hoteliers tried to differentiate their properties from their competitors. Evidence of the change has been the expansion of the lodging industry's departments of human resources (HR). In 25 years, hoteliers have seen the introduction, maturation, and influence of HR departments where none had been before (see Exhibit 7–1).

Sensitivity to customer needs is not special to hotelkeeping. Quality service should be a basic commodity of all service industries. In that respect, lodging is similar to banking, medicine, and sales. But it is also dissimilar, because lodging's service is in-your-face. That distinguishes it from other service enterprises and separates it completely from manufacturing.

> We are in the people business. Not the hotel business, not the real estate business. Instead of machinery, we have people. Instead of automated conveyor belts, we have people. Instead of computers that hum and print stuff, we have people. We have not come to grips with this basic concept.[1]

Total Quality Management in Innkeeping

An American, W. Edwards Deming, was a central figure in bringing TQM to heavy industry. His initial work took place in Japan, but then jumped the Pacific to be taken up by American manufacturers. Ford Motor Company signaled the shift by its slogan, *Quality*

---

[1]Steven J. Belmonte, president and CEO, Ramada Franchise Systems, Inc. Talk delivered at several annual conferences of Ramada, including Orlando, Florida, December 1999.

WHY
HUMAN RESOURCE MANAGEMENT
HAS COME OF AGE

Cultural diversity in the general public and, hence, in the hotel workforce.

Expectations of equality in both public and private sectors.

Increased empowerment vested in the workforce.

Legal, legislative and government agency requirements.

Loss of supervisory (middle-) managers from organizational downsizing.

Need to balance high touch with high tech.

Recognition of staff's importance to guest satisfaction.

Refocusing on operations after an era of financing and investments.

Shortage of good job applicants at lodging's traditional levels.

Simply a good business decision.

Turnover among hotel staff that may exceed 100% annually.

Exhibit 7-1   Hotel managers shuffle priorities over time. The front desk received the most attention before World War II. Food and beverage gained importance after the war, in the 1950s and '60s. Sales and marketing expanded throughout the 1970s and '80s, before giving ground to finance and real estate as the 20th century closed. Improved customer relations through human resources management is the current theme.

is Job One.[2] Deming urged his followers—that term is warranted because of the intensity of his adherents—to follow the 14 points that he promulgated. His concern with product and process included both human and technological resources. Deming's attention, say, to the size of a worker's shovel has a counterpart in the weight of a housekeeper's vacuum cleaner. So some of his points focused on the process and some on the workers and their environment.

Check-In, Check-Out does the same. First, it is a process text, dealing with the how-to: how to track reservations, how to set rates, how to implement yield management. Second, it is a human resources text, dealing—especially in this chapter—with the workers and the environment in which they work. To get on with *Job 2*, this chapter (which consists of the two components of quality service, guests and staff) is located right smack in the middle of the book. Doing so balances the how-to with the means-to. Executive attention to the employees of the hotel and through them to the guests of the hotel is essential to the successful management of the entire enterprise.

Total quality management is made of several pieces, including quality assurance (QA) and customer relations management (CRM). The essence of these terms is simple. Every person in the organization has an opportunity to impact positively on the guest. Consider that special terminology. Retailers speak of *customers*; professionals refer to *clients* or *patients*; economists cite *consumers*; galleries talk of *patrons*; the corner outlet uses *regulars*. Only the hotel industry references *guests*!

Management must make certain that employees have the opportunity to impact the guest just as it has done with other operational innovations. At first, these innovations (elevators, radios, television) were viewed as unique. They're standard products now. To the credit of the hotel industry, TQM is beginning to be viewed similarly. Quality management and customer relations management were once innovations too. Like the

---

[2]Trademark of the Ford Motor Company.

TV, QM and CRM are basic accommodations that no hotel can do without. Thus, the standard of the whole industry moves upward, as it does when every hotel has wireless computer connectivity.

Examples of Quality Management.   Attending to guest needs has always been part of the industry's buzz, although management's concern about it waxes and wanes. QM grabs management's attention when the economic cycle hits bottom (see Chapter 1) and the search is on for improving profits. And that's what's new: recognizing the role of the staff in reaching profit goals.

Interest in guest service peaked in 1992 when the Ritz-Carlton Company won the first of its two (1999) Malcolm Baldrige National Quality Awards. The award itself was new, having been established by Congress just five years earlier. It recognizes U.S. companies that achieve excellence by emphasizing quality. As the first hotel company to win the award and one of the first companies in the whole country, the Ritz-Carlton reawakened the entire industry to one of its basic tenets: Service the guest. The great hotelier, Ellsworth Statler, said it differently, "Life is service. The one who progresses is the one who gives his fellow men a little more, a little better, service."

Other hotel companies followed the pace set by the Ritz-Carlton. The AH&MA (now the AH&LA) led by holding the first QA conference in 1988. That same year, the Educational Institute of the AH&MA published a text on the subject.[3] From these beginnings, much of the industry came on stream.

Sheraton was among the earliest converts. The Sheraton *Guest Satisfaction System* (SGSS) was launched before Starwood acquired the chain. As do many QA programs, it fell into disuse and then was revitalized post-Starwood as Sheraton's *Service Promise*. The fundamentals of many QM programs are the same. They begin with an emphasis on hiring the right people. SGSS called the hiring procedure *HireVision*; Ritz-Carlton, *TalentPlus*. All programs emphasize four elements: hiring, training, delegating, and rewarding.

Sheraton's revitalization took place when Starwood rolled out a companywide initiative. It was designed "to integrate the company spiritually and to brand a [Starwood] culture."[4] Not an easy task, because Starwood has the upscale St. Regis Hotel at one end and Sheraton's Four Point Hotels at the other. Starwood uses Six Sigma as its QA base, keeping QA's industrial origins in sight because Six Sigma is a creation of Motorola, a manufacturing company.

The Ritz-Carlton Hotel Company, like its Sheraton cousin, is no longer a freestanding chain. It's a division of Marriott, which also has a mix of brands (see Exhibit 2–1). Although Marriott has not blended the QA programs of its several chains, some of the Ritz's acclaim may be tarnishing. It must now fit into a larger community both as a Marriott subsidiary and as a competitor of brands striving to out-Ritz it,[5] such as the Four Seasons.

Marriott's Renaissance Hotel Company has coined its own QA program, *Savvy Service*. Included are 20 principles that employees—Marriott prefers "associates" rather than "employees"—agree to work toward and to recite aloud during training sessions. Most interesting is the Ritz-Carlton's recent reduction of verbal and written principles from 20 to 12.

---

[3]Stephen J. Shriver. *Managing Quality Service* (East Lansing, MI: Educational Institute of the American Hotel & Motel Association, 1988).

[4]Christina Binkley. "Starwood Sets Effort to Enhance Quality and Improve Cash Flow." *The Wall Street Journal*, February 5, 2001, p. PB-4.

[5]A new word, "ritzy," entered the English language when London's elite flocked to the Hotel Savoy, operated by Cesar Ritz, ca. 1889.

Radisson was another early convert to QM. It began a well-structured effort to implement a guest-service training program. Called *Yes I Can*, the program was installed in all Radisson-owned and Radisson-franchised properties. Radisson is a member of the Carlson family. More recently, Carlson created an entirely new division called customer relations management (CRM). According to its *Global Report*, Carlson is trying to move customers beyond the point of simple transactions. Radisson wants a relationship that is lifelong. To achieve this, the company has introduced a single guest recognition program, *Gold Point Rewards*. By using this companywide currency in all of its outlets (hotels, restaurants, cruise ships, travel management, and resorts), Radisson hopes to cement permanent guest loyalty.

The early Radisson program stretched its definition of QM beyond the guest. It asked each employee to extend the same guest-oriented service to every other employee. Whether greeting or servicing a colleague, each staff member was to behave as if other staff members were guests.

Each chain gives the basic idea its own twist (see Exhibit 7–2). All aim to improve guest service by recruiting line employees to the cause and empowering them to act. Better guest service is not the only positive of empowerment. Fewer supervisors are

---

A SAMPLE
OF QUALITY ASSURANCE PROGRAMS
IN INNKEEPING

<u>Company</u>	<u>Concept</u>

Arizona Biltmore
  Architecturally Awesome
	Every employee has a budget with which to
	  implement their empowerment.

DoubleTree Hotels
  A Division of Hilton
	Both the concept and the name are
	  Continuous Improvement.

Lane Hospitality
  A Management Company
	Employee Entrepreneurship encourages
	  resolutions at the operative level.

Marriott Hotels
  Spirit to Serve Our Guests
	"The way hospitality acts, not just looks."
	  Covers five customer interactions.

The Opryland Hotel
  Awards Individuals and Teams
	Stars – Smiles; Teamwork; Attitude;
	  Reliability; Service.

Peabody Orlando
  Part of the Peabody Hotel Group
	Service Excellence is developed through a
	  train-the-trainer buddy team system.

Preferred Hotels
  A Referral Organization
	A long list to ensure employee understanding
	  of guests wants and needs.

Ramada
  A Division of Wyndham
	You're Somebody Special (1987) was
	  recently reinvented to *Personal Best*.

South Seas Island Resort
  Formerly South Seas Plantation
	Steering committee using teams of 6–8
	  members.

Union Square Hotel
  Part of Handlery Hotels
	Early adherent from AH&MA's efforts;
	  uses staff input for purchasing.

Exhibit 7–2   Ten sample programs illustrate the range, variety and content of Quality Assurance (QA) efforts within the lodging industry.

needed if staff members have the authority to make decisions. It's a round robin. Flatter organizations force decisions onto line associates and these decision-making associates reduce the need for supervisors. Finding and holding workers capable of doing the job requires extensive search and higher salaries. There is no evidence yet that the industry has implemented those steps.

The Real Components of TQM

Guests come to hotels to sleep. Hotel managers must not forget that, even as they focus on staff–customer relations. Guests will overlook missing amenities and poorly decorated lobbies if the products they are buying are delivered. So total quality management begins in the guest room. Dissatisfaction with the basic product cannot be redressed by a CRM program that has smiling guest-service agents wearing happy-face buttons.

The search is on—there are plenty of ongoing surveys—for the room that best meets guest expectations. Hilton tested Travel Lifestyle Centers, a takeoff of TLC: tender, loving care. A second phase, health-fit and stress-less guest rooms, followed a few years later. Slogans and gimmickry accoutrements are no substitute for sleep-enhancing designs. So Hilton's rooms also provided blackout curtains, improved mattresses and dual wake-up systems. (To rest well, travelers must be confident about the following morning's alarm clock.[6]) Gilding the lily, these experimental rooms added massage chairs, live plants, and aroma therapy. And there's more, as Exhibit 7–3 outlines.

Chains regularly announce dramatic changes in their guest rooms. Remodeling boomed between 2004 and 2008, when the industry topped its economic cycle. Mood lighting, ergonomic chairs, mirror TVs and more have been touted as part of the modern room. Out-with-the-old has meant altering the traditional room "box" to high style. New language reinforces the change. Renaissance Hotels touts its rooms as the "body of a

---

ENHANCING THE SLEEP EXPERIENCE BY MEANS OF . . .

Air purifiers
Calming pools using running water
Cups of specially brewed tea
Ear plugs
Eye discs containing aromatic oils
Eye masks
Hot (or cold) pillows to ease neck pain
Mattresses using air to adjust firmness
Nightlights
Printed guides with tips to better sleep
Quiet floors (no groups or children)
Sleep CDs
Sound machines with ocean noises

Exhibit 7-3 Sleep is the primary product of hotelkeepers, who have adopted new sleep-enhancing amenities to prove the point. (See also Amenities and Amenity Creep, Chapter 2.)

---

[6]Survey after survey ranks late or missed wake-up calls near the top of guests' pet peeves.

full-service hotel with the soul of a boutique." For other examples, see Interesting Tidbits at the end of the chapter.

None of which changes the needs of good hotel rooms. Less dramatic amenities such as full-length mirrors and in-room coffee makers also add to comfort, provided the room has met its basic commitment. To achieve minimum expectations, high standards must be set for bedding, cleanliness, noise, and temperature.

Bedding. The proverbial good night's rest begins with a comfortable bed. Chapter 3 provided information on bed sizes, mattress rotations, and comfortable chairs. The larger beds described there provide the extra six inches of mattress (six inches longer than the average height of the sleeper) that experts recommend.[7] The number of beds in each room and their configuration varies with the type and the class of property (see Exhibit 7–4), but every hotel offers a choice.

Beds were replaced at an amazing rate during the last renovation period. Estimates suggest that for several years hotels purchased 1,500,000 beds annually! Marriott alone reported 625,000 beds. A top-quality queen mattress plus bed frame (although many hotels have done away with frames) costs about $2,250. That level of quality assures a mattress life of 12 to 15 years. The big replacement surge last time around was triggered by design and renovation, not by mattress wear. It makes good sense to buy longer-lasting mattresses and matching springs. Even spread over 10 years, a $2,250 set costs about $0.60/night. Mattress quality is measured, in part, by the number of steel coils and the method of tying them down. A 900-coil, pillowtop mattress has been Westin's choice. Wyndham uses 992 coils on its king beds. Marriott has opted for a seven-inch foam mattress with a quilted top. Everyone is using fire-resistant bedding because smokers often fall asleep in bed.

Linens and Pillows. There is more to a bed than a mattress. Upgrading the sleeping experience requires close attention to the bed coverings (called the soft goods) and especially to the linen count. The standard is 180 count: 80 threads in one direction, 100 in the other. This is a durable product for the hotel and an acceptable one for the guest,

Hotel Bed Configuration by Type of Hotel				
Hotel Type	**Type of Bed (Percent)**			
	Double	**Twin**	**Queen**	**King**
All-suite	21	3	32	44
Bed & breakfast	26	7	38	29
Convention	44	1	14	41
Casino	28	0	36	36
Extended-stay	21	6	53	20

Exhibit 7–4 Guest rooms grow larger and rates rise higher as king and queen beds, which take extra floor space and larger linens, gain favor in all types of hotels. The single bed has disappeared; twin beds are close behind. (See also The Bed, Chapter 3.) *Source: RealTime Hotel Reports, a division of Smith Travel Research, Henderson, Tennessee.*

---

[7]Thomas J. A. Jones. *Professional Management of Housekeeping Operations*, 4th ed. (New York: John Wiley & Sons, 2004). Also, "Longer beds began creeping onto college campuses some 25 years ago. . . . today's average American male is about 5 feet 9 inches tall." *The Wall Street Journal*, September 6, 2002, p. A6.

who is probably using about the same count at home. Jumping to a 250-count, or even 300, as some upscale chains have done for their top sheets, makes a noticeable difference. Sheets of that count are silky smooth and luxurious. Despite the moves of upscale competitors, the 180–200 count remains the choice of most hotels.[8] But even the midscales have upgraded one critical level: a third sheet. Unlike a bedspread, sheets are laundered regularly. Guests are delighted to find triple sheeting in place of unwashed bedspreads.

Three sheets of 300 count impact laundry weight (cost) that has long been based on two sheets of 180 count. Introducing fitted bottom sheets, a household favorite, adds another laundry issue. Ironing machines are designed for flat sheets. Fitted sheets are folded by hand, adding labor costs to laundering costs. Less frequent linen change is the offset. It reduces both laundry loads and the housekeeper's time. To accomplish this, guests are encouraged to use "green" tent cards, which tell housekeeping to keep the linen for more than one night (see Exhibit 8–20).

Crawling into a bed of 250- to 300-count bottom and top sheets, plus a third sheet of 180 count to cover the blanket, is a memorable experience. But there's more. No longer will one pillow do. Several pillows, each with distinctive characteristics, including hypoallergenic ones, are on the bed or available on call. Some hotels now offer "pillow menus," with feathers and down (see Interesting Tidbits) at the top of the list. Even wedge-shaped pregnancy pillows that lift and support the abdomen are offered. The Benjamin Hotel in New York City offers 11 specialty pillows, all delivered and explained by a sleep concierge! (See Exhibit 7–5.)

Lighter, down blankets or comforters, which have been borrowed from Europe, add another dimension to lodging's "new" beds. Cross-ocean borrowing goes two ways.

Exhibit 7–5   Improving the sleep experience has prompted a range of bedding upgrades and innovations, including a sleep concierge. *Courtesy of The Benjamin, New York, New York.*

---

[8]Thread count is only one aspect of evaluating linen. The quality of the yarn, the source of the cotton, the finish, and the blend (of cotton/polyester) all address durability and luxury. A thread count of T-180 is more durable and might be better for high-occupancy properties. Durability is increased further if the linen supply is adequate. Low linen inventory requires the immediate reuse of sheets, but linens wear out less rapidly if they rest a day or two between uses. Recommended "par" inventory is three times the bed count. One set is on the bed, one set is in the laundry, and one set is in the linen closet.

European hotels are introducing king beds—their rooms will be getting larger, too. Comforters/*duvets* (another European adoption) are used in place of the third sheet, and are enclosed in pillowcase-like covers. Like the third sheet, duvet covers are washable and, if needed, are washed daily. Traditional bedspreads are dry cleaned two to four times a year. Reduced dry-cleaning costs help make up for higher laundry costs.

The Public Relations of Bedding.　　Bedding is as much a war of advertising/publicity as an issue of design/guest comfort. Westin advertises its Heavenly Bed with pillow-top mattress and its Heavenly Bath with five adjustable jets (see Exhibit 3–19). Accor's Sofitel Hotels offer MYBed, "a sea of comfort" in a feather bed with down comforter. Sheraton has a Sleigh Bed. Hyatt's is the Grand Bed. Marriott has, what else, the Marriott Bed.

Every chain is in the bed-promotion business. They're not just promoting beds in advertising and weekend packages (see Exhibit 7–6), they're actually selling them. Westin (a Starwood hotel) sells several a day through its bed catalog. Chicago's Ritz-Carlton delivers a complete bed to the home of a guest who has stayed several nights in its luxury suite. Everything in the room is for sale (there's an itemized chart) at the Mondrian Hotel, Los Angeles.

Cleanliness.　　No architectural design is more attractive than a sparkling bath. A survey of American Automobile Association members who use the AAA's *Tour Book* ranked cleanliness as their top concern. Cleanliness was ranked ahead of price, location, and amenities. A study done by Wyndham ranked stale, smelly rooms at the top of their guests' pet peeves. For those with allergies, perfumed housekeeping smells and mists are as bad as animal dander.[9] A triple sheet, which increases laundry costs by 50%, is the first sign of a hotel's attitude toward cleanliness.

Cleanliness is most noticeable in the bath; guests are sensitized to the quality of the housekeeping there. Tub/showers, toilets, sinks, and bathroom floors demand housekeeping vigilance to remove hair and dirt. Room corners and the areas behind the toilet take extra care. Chrome fixtures, particularly drains in sinks and tubs, must be cleaned daily. Long-term cleanliness may actually begin at construction. Marble countertops, porcelain tile, and latex-enhanced grout are easier to maintain.

Excessive clutter cancels out even the cleanest accommodations. A few simple changes can bring order to a bath. Removing nonessentials such as the coffeemaker is a first step. Putting amenities in an attractive container or simply having fewer amenities tidies the scene. A vanity of at least four feet with an off-center sink holds everything and leaves an impression of order.

Floor attendants must do more than clean. They will do so if taught to report security issues and guest-room repairs. A leaking toilet or a nonfunctioning tub stopper must receive attention. If quality assurance is in place, a simple reporting system will be created for non-English-speaking attendants. Otherwise many minor, but irritating, repairs will go unreported.

Vacuuming, the final step in cleaning the guest room, may take place only between guests. Stayover rooms are not normally vacuumed in some hotels. Elsewhere, rooms are vacuumed every day, check-out or not.

Cleanliness, inside and outside, guest rooms and public space, is taken for granted. Few guests ever compliment sanitation standards on guest-comment cards, but they do complain when it's lacking.

---

[9]Hypoallergenic rooms are available in some upscale properties. Hypoallergenic amenities include bedding, pillows, linens washed with chlorine, special room filters, and central vacuuming systems.

Exhibit 7–6   The quality of hotel beds has become a major advertising strategy. Here it is combined with the hotel's inclusive tour promotion. (See also Inclusive Tour Brochure, Exhibit 2–10.) *Courtesy of The Benjamin, New York, New York.*

An Old Enemy Has Checked In.   An old guest that the industry hasn't seen for years has checked in: bedbugs (*cimex lectularius*). The pest nests in mattresses, waiting to feast at night on unsuspecting sleepers. Bedbugs blow in with hurricanes and with international travel, riding on baggage and clothing. They can live almost anywhere and go for long periods without food. Bedbugs hide from light so they might rest during the day in dark, protected areas other than the bed. This makes cleanup very difficult. Housekeepers are reluctant to use chemical pesticides, especially in beds. Besides, DDT, which was the bedbugs' nemesis, was banned in the 1970s. A costly solution is destruction; furniture and bedding are burned or otherwise disposed of.

Housekeeping's lack of experience may be part of the cause for the spread. Floor and laundry attendants must look for the telltale signs: tiny, rust-colored blood spots on the linens. But the floor attendant herself may be the carrier as she goes from one room to the next. Hot water (155 degrees) in the laundry handles the linens, but that's preventative more than curative since the bug's habitat is not limited to the bed. Bedbug control should be part of an integrated pest management program designed to prevent and monitor all types of pests and rodents.

Noise, Temperature and Darkness. Even "road warriors" (travelers who sleep away from home a great deal) complain about noisy rooms. Poor initial construction, which is not easily fixed after the fact, is high on a list of causes. Budget limitations force builders to ignore adequate sound barriers between rooms and in the utility and plumbing shafts. Back-to-back baths make for easy construction and maintenance, but wreak havoc in transmitting noise. In very bad cases, the plumbing is strapped inadequately, so noisy vibrations follow the opening of every faucet.

Poorly insulated rooms bring the neighbor's television set resonating into the sleeper's dreams. Everyday sounds, from simple conversations to children playing, come from rooms close by. Hallway noises, which include the whirr of ice-making machine motors, ice falling into buckets, ringing telephones, elevator doors, and late-to-bed revelers, add to the din. The worst noise offenders are right in the room. Fans on heating/air-conditioning systems and mini-bar compressors sing all night. They are almost as annoying as one's inability to control the room temperature.

Central heating and air-conditioning systems are far superior to individual room units. Cost is, again, the determining factor. But some window units are not even temperature sensitive. They run all the time unless they're turned off completely. It's up to the sleeper to decide which is worse. Occasionally, the units don't run at all. Maintenance on the systems is minimal and on demand rather than preventative. Guests may be housed in rooms with nonworking units. Encountered occasionally are systems that deliver either heating or cooling, depending on the time of the year. No choice is available during swing months; guests get either heating or cooling, regardless of their own body temperatures.

Construction noise and street noise—try commuter buses running by an urban hotel—join in-room noise to test the QM challenge. QM's toughest trials come when guests are roomed near ongoing construction, either in-house or in the neighborhood. Whichever, work begins early in the morning. Management must forestall the complaint. Install double-pane windows. Alert the caller at reservations. Remind the arriving guest at registration. Above all, reflect the circumstances in the rate and make that accommodation known.

In-room lighting is another comfort gauge. One that takes on special meaning for an aging population. Rarely do guest rooms have architectural lighting, relying instead on lamps and hanging sconces. Specifications for these fixtures must include high wattage. Otherwise, the room is poorly lit, even for young eyes. The same holds true for the bath, where downlights over sinks and vanities are applauded as men shave and women apply makeup.

These same eyes like darkness for sleeping. Blackout curtains must block both the morning light and the evening's flashing neon. To counter light leaks between the drapes and noise from within, Crowne Plaza and other properties include ear plugs and eye masks as standard room equipment (see Exhibit 7–3).

Exhibit 7–3 also notes that air purifiers are offered in some guest rooms. Companies have responded to the national nonsmoking movement. Guests who violate the terms of no-smoking rooms are subject to fine, but it takes a brave hotelier to collect. Nonsmoking rooms have migrated to nonsmoking hotels (Westin), but the retrofit is difficult. Smoke lingers in drapes and carpets and bedding. Some hotels have taken an extra step toward allergen-free rooms by attacking molds, dust, and chemicals.

Each issue, noise control, cleaner air, better light and proper temperature, focuses on customer relations management. Ritz-Carlton's "Care Program" is a preventative approach, anticipative management. It inspects before the guest arrives to make certain there are adequate hangers, pillows, and towels. That everything is working: no drips in the bathroom fixtures, and no issues with HAC, heating/air-conditioning.

Total Quality Management Defined

Defining QM is as difficult as delivering it. Some approach the task through oft-told tales. Here are four of the regulars: A guest-service agent types a guest's important letters after hours. A bellperson delivers a lost attaché case to the airport just in time. A housekeeper launders clothes at home in order to meet a deadline. A door attendant lends black shoes for a formal affair.

Despite the difficulty, everyone gives formal definitions a try. The authors attempt it several pages ahead. *Managing Quality Services*, cited earlier, says, "QA is a management system that ensures consistent delivery of products and services." Another suggests that "TQM . . . is defined by and supports . . . customer satisfaction through an integrated system of tools, techniques, and training. . . . [that] involves the continuous improvement of organizational processes, resulting in high-quality products and services."[10] Both descriptions represent the general run of TQM definitions. Like most descriptions, each omits the duality of QM. Total quality management involves two parties, the buyer-receiver and the seller-giver.

Part I explained how segmented are both the lodging industry and its customer base. Each of the numerous buyers and each of the numerous sellers sees issues from different perspectives. A single, satisfactory definition of quality is just not possible with so many variations in both service-delivery and service-receipt. Quality service and the management of quality service really have no objective measures. Definitions are broad and imprecise; delivery is inexact. How fortunate that everyone "knows it when they see it."

The Buyer's View.   Guests measure quality by comparison. To what degree does the level of service actually delivered compare to expectations? If surprised by a better stay than anticipated, guests perceive quality to be high. If the visit fails to meet expectations, the property is downgraded.

Advertising, word-of-mouth comments, price, previous visits and publicity create a level of expectation within the guest. Of course, that barrage of communications is received differently with different perceptions by almost every guest. Moreover, those expectations change over time and place, even within the same guest. Influencing the guest's expectations are components that may be outside the hotel's control: a late flight, a rude cabdriver, a bad storm.

Guests hold different expectations about different hotels, even different hotels within the same chain. Quality is measured against the expectation of that particular property at that particular time more than against different hotels in different categories.

---

[10]Marshall Sashkin and Kenneth J. Kiser. *Putting Total Quality Management to Work.* (San Francisco: Berrett-Koehler Publishers, 1993), p. 39.

Driving up to an economy property with a loaded family van and a pet but without a reservation carries one expectation. Flying around the world to an expensive resort—a trip that a couple has planned for and saved for over many years—creates a much different level of anticipation. Coming to a busy convention property with a reservation made by the company's travel desk evokes still a third level of expectation. Each expectation must be met by the hotel with delivery at the highest level appropriate for the circumstances. Quality assurance attempts to do just that. It is a big, big order.

Consider two hypothetical properties. The first, an economy hotel offering minimal services, charges half its neighbor's rate. The neighbor, an expensive, upscale property and not a true competitor, has it all.

The economy hotel offers the following conveniences:

➤ No bellservice, but parking is convenient and many luggage carts are in the lobby.

➤ No room service, but the hotel is located near a well-known restaurant chain and has an exceptional choice of vending options.

➤ No health club, but the swimming pool is clean, open at convenient hours, and has a good supply of towels.

➤ No concierge, but the room clerk is knowledgeable and affable.

The upscale neighbor offers the following conveniences:

➤ Bellpersons, whom guests are urged to call on. But this hotel never schedules enough staff, resulting in long delays.

➤ Room service, but it is offered at limited times. This hotel suggests a pizza delivery company as an alternative.

➤ A well-reputed health club, but it is on lease, which means there's a charge for admission.

➤ A concierge, but a recorded message puts the guest on hold.

Extreme as these illustrations are, the point is obvious: Quality in the service industry is in the eyes of the beholder. Service lacks the established and measurable specifications used in manufacturing. How, then, could an agreement on the definition of service be reached if the product isn't created until it's delivered? Managing for quality, therefore, must include standards derived from the consumer's perspective. Doing so gives credence to the buyer's view of what quality service is all about. Management must first establish the systems and then the measurement standards for those systems—both to be based on the buyers' expectations. Management must also fix the procedure for achieving those standards. Successfully implemented, TQM matches the buyers' standards with the sellers' ability to deliver. When done right, the guest/buyer knows that the hotel delivers quality guest service.

The Seller's View.   Like every policy created and every practice put into operation, TQM originates with management. Executives either make deliberate decisions to implement particular ideas or they passively accept ongoing practices. So it is with quality management. Management creates and implements a program of enhanced guest services, or there is none.

Delivering quality requires management to focus on both employees and guests. The two are intertwined. Increasing guest services to satisfy the buyer's side of QM requires special attention to operational issues, the employees' side of QM. Staying close to the customer means stressing customer wants, ensuring consistency, remedying the mistakes that do occur, and concentrating on the whole with a passion that hints of obsession. But all of these are also operational concerns. Nothing can be accomplished without attention to the employees entrusted with the delivery.

Leadership.   Adopting TQM as a company philosophy forces major changes in the definition of management. Traditionally, management is said to be a series of functions. Planning, organizing, staffing, directing, and reviewing is the classic list. Quality management adds another element—leadership. Managing as a leader requires change in both the style of management and the composition of the workforce being managed. When both components—management and workforce—focus on delivering quality, the company is said to have a *service culture*.

With a leadership style, managers shift from their traditional position of review, which requires corrective action after mistakes are made, to a proactive style of supervision. Errors must be corrected, of course, but a proactive stance aims at error avoidance. Minimizing errors, whether on a production line or a registration line, is what TQM is all about.

Total Quality Management is a pervasive term. It has come to mean almost any action designed to improve the operation. And that's just what it is: A series of small steps taken within an organizational culture that has the customer's experience as its central focus. Developing that culture requires a fundamental shift in management style. Binding employees, supervisors, and management into closer relationships takes a committed leader. Success will depend upon the degree of entrepreneurship that is created. Employees must accept their contribution to the success of the enterprise and have the power to make it happen. It will happen if management leads by balancing its authority and discipline with delegation and flexibility.

Part of the sharing of responsibility and credit is the sharing of information that once was considered confidential. Staff members must be knowledgeable about the activities of their own departments and those departments whose functions overlap.

Overlapping interests are reinforced through quality circles (Q⊙s), employee committees. Representatives from each department and/or from several departments meet to work on problems. A quality circle at the front desk may have representatives from sales, housekeeping and accounting. Then each member sits in a Q ⊙ within his or her own department. Soon a hotelwide network exists. Quality goals and standards will then reflect the realities and limitations of the whole enterprise. Such broad input establishes fair standards to reward those who beat expectations. And, as we know, expectations are part of the buyer's view.

Empowerment.   After so much of management's once-guarded interests have been opened to the committees, the next step is anticlimactic. Some of management's power is also given away, delegated down the line to associates. Operative employees are authorized to make on-the-spot decisions about problems that fall within the scope of their job assignments. Entrusting the associate to act requires management to delegate authority to act. Giving the workforce authority to act is called *empowerment* (see Exhibit 7–7). Empowering employees creates leaner/flatter organizations. This pancake-like structure makes each department operate as a small company, with full responsibility and authority remaining under the umbrella of general management.

Empowerment doesn't happen by accident one day. It is based on knowledge and direction acquired through training and experience. Limits may apply at first. Limited empowerment allows the guest-service agent to choose from a range of established guidelines (see Exhibit 7–15). More experienced and more senior associates are given wider discretion and may be consulted by other staff members. Whichever, empowerment provides a quick response to uncertainty.

Dear Guests:

Welcome to Guest Quarters Suite Hotels and Guest Quarters Magazine — an informative guide to this hotel's community, as well as interesting and entertaining reading on a variety of subjects.

I would like to take this opportunity to share something with you that is new and exciting at all Guest Quarters Suite Hotels. It's not a new amenity or special promotion — in fact, you can't touch or see this at all. But, when you stay at any Guest Quarters, you will sense what we are calling employee empowerment.

Employee empowerment means that at Guest Quarters, all of our employees have been trained and authorized to handle your inquiries on-the-spot. Whether it be a concern over our quality levels or a special request, Guest Quarters employees have been given the tools to make your stay flawless, without having to find a supervisor. (Of course, there are special situations which require the attention of a manager.)

Employee empowerment takes our award-winning service levels one step higher. It provides you with a more efficient and effective staff that is eager to serve you. Just as importantly, empowerment further demonstrates our confidence in our company's most valuable asset — our employees.

The results? I can't express how proud I am of how our employees have utilized empowerment. Rather than just exercise their decision-making privileges to address negative guest situations, Guest Quarters employees are going "above and beyond the call of duty" to provide unexpected touches and unanticipated acts of kindness. This is the true meaning of hospitality.

As we move forward in this decade which has been designated the "Decade of Customer Service," I am confident that Guest Quarters will continue to be one of the hotel industry's shining stars. I invite you to visit any of our 30 locations nationwide to experience impeccable service, coupled with the luxury of a suite.

Sincerely,

Richard M. Kelleher
President Guest Quarters Suite Hotels

Exhibit 7-7   The letter says it all: Top management's support of empowerment is critical. With it, results are better than a host of amenities or expensive advertising campaigns. (Mr. Kelleher is no longer with Guest Quarters, which merged with Doubletree [1993], which merged with Promus [1997], which merged with Hilton [1999].) *Courtesy of Promus Hotel Corporation, Memphis, Tennessee.*

Initially, empowerment involves action by an individual. A misquoted rate is resolved by the cashier as the guest checks out. Apologies for an unmade room are reinforced with a free drink coupon in the bar. Certainly, empowerment involves thoughtful guest services like these, but it means more than that. It means empowering quality circles. At first Q☉s are asked merely to identify problems. Step two, circles suggest possible solutions. Fully empowered, Q☉s implement their own decisions. They tackle two kinds of problems. One deals with guest relations, how-to's: how to speed check-ins; how to reduce reservation errors; how to expedite group baggage within security guidelines.

The second class of problems also impacts guest services, but less directly. Attention is on in-house procedures (moving linens without tying up the elevators); cost reductions (reducing chargebacks by credit-card companies); or operational irritants (maintenance's slow response to guest-room repairs). None of which involves guest interaction, all of which improves TQM.

The Employee.   TQM requires supervisors to adopt a leadership style of management. But that's just half the battle. Employees, the other half, must be won over as well, convinced to accept the empowerment offered. Just as some managers oppose empowering line employees, some line members reject the added responsibility. They decline to take on what they believe to be management's job.

Similarly, the employer's willingness to share information about the business may not be matched by the employees' interest in receiving it—or receiving it, having the capacity to understand it, or the interest to use it. Even highly motivated employees may not comprehend what is offered or what is expected. Leadership requires followers; great leadership requires inspired and motivated followers. Quality management is burdened with the development of both leaders and followers; and that must be done within a workforce of great diversity in language, education, and cultural expectations (see Exhibit 7–8).

DIVERSITY AND TURNOVER.   The lodging industry faces two labor challenges: workforce diversity and labor turnover. They are often treated as one problem because finding and retaining competent staff requires management to look across the great diversity of America's workforce. Moreover, as Exhibit 7–8 shows so clearly, lodging relies on a nonwhite, non-Anglo workforce. Within the hotel industry, diversity is a business necessity, not a hot social issue.

Hotels are searching for staff continuously. Employees, and that term includes supervisors and managers, come and go at a costly pace. Many workers are in dead-end jobs. Boredom and repetition are blunted temporarily by moving to another hotel, even though the new job has the same tasks. The loss is especially costly if the individuals who move do so because they are motivated, the very people one wants to keep.

Turnover at the lowest level of the organization, the spots where QM must shine, exceed 200% annually in some jobs in some hotels. Said another way: Every employee is replaced twice per year! Less dramatic, but equally disturbing turnover occurs among managers and supervisors. Turnover feeds upon itself. Missing workers mean heavier loads for those remaining. Discontent grows so that establishing, maintaining, and improving TQM is put aside as resources are assigned to searching, finding, and replacing a turnstile staff.

Retaining workers is far less costly than replacing them. That's why retention plans, tools long used in other industries, are now finding their way into lodging. Training qualified staffers for career enhancement is one technique. Financial incentives is another—and one that has broader application. Retirement plans, year-end bonuses, and employee stock ownership are relatively new concepts for this old industry. Financial rewards such as these

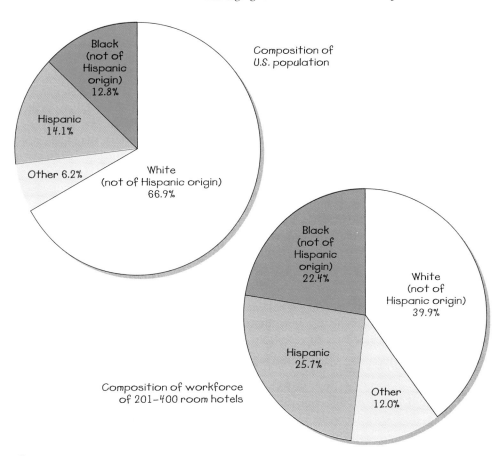

Exhibit 7–8   The workforce in America's hotels differs ethnically and culturally from the makeup of the national population, which is the likely composition of the industry's customers. (Figures are estimated for 2008.) Sensitive to different expectations, most hotels have adopted *diversity programs*, which embrace the various cultures. (*Affirmative action* is the legal protection against discrimination.) The National Association for the Advancement of Colored People (NAACP) annually ranks the hotel industry for its diversity efforts. Typical grade is C, which the authors feel is low. *Adapted with the courtesy of the American Hotel Foundation, Washington, D.C.*

enable workers to build savings even though they remain in lower-end jobs. Several chains, Marriott for one, recognized this and adopted employee-participation plans years ago. Now, a shortage of applicants for low wage positions has accelerated the introduction of financial incentives throughout the industry.

Rewards, financial and otherwise, must be part of any TQM retention plan. Incentives are especially important at the front desk where TQM demands a great deal from moderately paid personnel. Chapter 9 suggests some. Although dollars and cents remain strong incentives at the operative-level, imaginative noncash rewards can be used throughout the hotel. Among them are invitations for employees to join Q⊙s, where their ideas can get a hearing. Special cross-training sessions or second-language classes on company time go far toward retention. Building language skills adds credibility to the hotel's diversity program.

Every success should be celebrated, and every means to do so should be employed, from simple recognition such as a thank-you from the manager to incentives that bind the company and reward the individual. Employee-of-the-month is a widely used recognition. It is more effective if it carries a cash stipend and perhaps a special parking space along with a plaque on the wall and a photo in the newspaper. Some departments can accommodate flexible working hours, which may prove the best of all rewards for working parents. So, too, might job-sharing, which need not be limited to executive-style jobs. Larger hotels and local hotel consortia have taken further steps to accommodate working parents: They operate nursery schools.

Although managers, especially supervisory managers not protected under wage-and-hour laws, are not above cash rewards, the hotel industry has another incentive to offer: time off. Long hours on the job cause hardships in personal lives for many non-hourly (so-called exempt) workers. Incentives for them may simply be an extra day off.

Good staff at all organizational levels is the thread of the quality management weave. The commitment to finding and holding those persons is reflected in the salaries paid, the training offered, and the incentives rewarded. A company that concentrates on better human resources ensures a better delivery of quality service. The effort begins with selecting and retaining the right persons.

SELECTING AND RETAINING THE RIGHT EMPLOYEE.   Managing guest services by empowering employees and enlisting their help requires a broad effort. It reaches beyond the immediate delivery of services, stretching backward to employment and forward to retention. Delivering quality service begins at the selection decision. How else can the right person be in the right place when the CRM situation requires? Hoteliers knows this, so the personnel office has been the launch site for most TQM programs (see Exhibit 7–1).

Selecting the right employee—and TQM programs emphasize that it is *selection*, not *hiring*—is where good service begins. Imagine the impression when new hires meet the general manager who repeats that mantra: You've been "selected" because of your enthusiasm and your ability to smile when things go wrong. The industry has come to believe that it can teach technical skills, but it needs to select sensitive staff. Good service is actually intangible, not measurable, so the burden of delivery falls upon the employee who is on hand at that moment. Friendly, interactive applicants who have a sincere wish to help will solve problems of quality deficiency faster than do experienced technical workers who lack those qualities. Indeed, there are far more guest complaints about poor employee attitudes than about broken TV sets.

"If you don't have the right people, then you are the dummy that hired them."[11] Selecting the right person begins with finding the right pool of applicants. Personnel departments don't always clear that hurdle, because hotel job vacancies are frequent and difficult to fill. Too often, the first applicant to come is the one hired. Recruiting during good economic times takes imaginative work. Hotel companies begin with nominations from their own workforce, paying cash incentives when friends and relatives of current workers remain through a given period. Web sites are also widely used. They're great for college recruiting, but may not reach prospective applicants for the lower-end jobs that are the most difficult to fill. Success as well as a greater diversity comes from advertising in the numerous ethnic newspapers that are available in large, urban areas. However accomplished, recruiting is costly. Turnover costs have been estimated at $2,000 for hourly workers and $6,500 for exempt supervisors/managers. No wonder everyone agrees that retention is far less costly than recruitment.

---

[11]Horst Schulze, former president and chief operating officer, The Ritz-Carlton Hotel Company.

Retention improves if new hires clearly understand what the work entails. Some companies ask the applicant to spend an hour observing the job before accepting it. Others go a step further. Applicants are interviewed by the very associates with whom they'll work. The practice, called *peer-group hiring,* strengthens the TQM program and improves the hiring process.

Once hired, retaining the right worker, like retaining the right guest, would seem to be of the highest priority. Strangely, despite the spread in costs, retention sometimes gets less attention than the original search. Yet retaining both the recruited guest and the recruited worker is at the very heart of TQM. Induction, helping the new hire ease into the company, is a common pitfall. After a company spends many recruiting dollars, a new employee may be alienated in the very next step: entering the work door. Disenchanted, new hires sometimes leave within a day or two of employment

LABOR UNIONS.   Labor unions are another resource. In fact, some labor contracts require hotels to first try the union hiring halls. Hotel and culinary unions are strongest in the big hotel cities. From east to west, they are New York, Chicago, Las Vegas, San Francisco, and Honolulu. Not all hotel–union relations revolve about employment. The union of Hotel Employees and Restaurant Employees (HERE) periodically faces off with the hotel industry over wages, right to wear union buttons, fringe benefits and work rules.

Hotel chains have multiple properties in the same cities that unions have *locals* (regional divisions). At new contract time, unions bring pressure in cities that are not up for renegotiation. Thus, hotels of the chain in, say, San Francisco may find pickets because the Chicago contract is under negotiation. So far, the lodging industry has averted a single national contract. Contracts expire on different dates in different cities. Industry watchers believe the national unions are working toward a common contract date. This would increase the union's clout immeasurably.

TRAINING.   TQM views training as an investment, not as a cost. Continuous training can be likened to a program of continually upgrading the physical plant. Both the facilities and the employees are critical to guest satisfaction. Trained staff is able to do a better job for the house and the customer. This provides personal satisfaction for the employee and develops opportunities for both long-run promotions and short-run gratuities.

Training has different purposes. One type of training improves work skills—better use of reservation computers, for example. Another type, security training, for example, widens the workers' scope of understanding beyond their immediate jobs. A third type of training enhances interpersonal skills—meeting and greeting a guest in the hall, for example. Still another purpose emphasizes the worker's personal needs: cleanliness, retirement savings, language skills. The Ritz-Carlton chain has/had a well-known motto: "We are ladies and gentlemen serving ladies and gentlemen." Training makes it so, since we are not all born ladies and gentlemen. Managing for service requires training in all four areas.

Employees are held responsible for their own actions. TQM doesn't overlook mistakes, but it does replace negative discipline with positive training. New directions and positive suggestions (coaching) for the next time move the system toward error avoidance. Avoiding mistakes rather than correcting them is the essence of guest service. Pledging the costs to coach and train on a continuous basis is a measure of management's commitment to a philosophy of quality service.

The Authors' View.   A brief phrase (an aphorism) has been used to summarize the culture of total quality management: "The answer is 'Yes'; now ask me the question."[12] Such a can-do/will-do attitude represents the best that TQM can instill. Applications of the adage apply equally well to employee–guest interactions (CRM), employee–management contacts and employee–employee relations. Under so broad an umbrella, the adage offers a strong definition of TQM.

The adage also suggests a strong alignment between the culture of quality management and the culture of the concierge. Both cultures express Radisson Hotel's adage of, "Yes I can!" Hotels that promote QM understand that the concierge is neither an individual nor a department. It is an attitude that one hopes all employees will grasp. Hence, the first part of the authors' definition of TQM: *Quality Management is an attitude that has every associate acting like a concierge. . . .*

The duality of quality assurance has been emphasized throughout the chapter. The guest's side, called the buyer's view, is balanced by the house side, called the seller's view. This operational side is reflected in the second phrase of the authors' definition: *. . . and thinking like a manager.* Thus:

> QUALITY MANAGEMENT IS AN ATTITUDE THAT
> HAS EVERY ASSOCIATE ACTING LIKE A
> CONCIERGE AND THINKING LIKE A MANAGER.

CUSTOMER RELATIONS MANAGEMENT (CRM)

Unlike the individualized attention that was once the norm, modern hotels now serve mass markets. Responsive individuals, working in a democratic culture, have replaced the white-gloved authoritarianism of an era long past. It follows, then, that hotel companies have shifted from the formal to the informal; from pretense to expedited service; from rigid procedure to empowerment.

The shift has been well received because the traveling public's attitude toward service has also changed. Aware of labor costs, functioning in a self-service environment themselves, sensitive to the employees' expectations of equality, today's guests no longer expect a servile attitude. And employees no longer deliver it. Guests do expect—and are entitled to receive during each encounter—a friendly face, an attentive ear, and a twinkling eye. After all, quality service, as previously defined, is an attitude that shines through.

Customer Relations Denied

Hotelkeeping is part of a vast industry whose trade is part service, part entertainment, part recreation, and part commerce. Hoteliers offer a product called hospitality. They consider their customers to be guests. And, above all, they deliver service. Because these positions have been verbalized so often, hotel patrons get confused by the antihospitality-antiguest-antiservice syndrome that is also part of the industry.

Guest expectations, one component of quality delivery systems, were reviewed earlier. Guests recognize that every property is not charged with the same level of product despite its grouping under the common umbrella of lodging. But guests do not understand why minimal service means antiservice, and why a lack of personnel means a lack of courtesy. Management's failure to distinguish minimal service, justified

---

[12]Rick Van Warner, one-time editor of *Nation's Restaurant News,* attributes the aphorism to Keith Dunn, restaurateur, who cites Don Smith, restaurateur and one-time faculty at Michigan State University, as the source. *Nation's Restaurant News,* October 26, 1991.

by minimal rates, from antiservice, shown by employee negativism, has led to the antiservice syndrome that some hotels demonstrate and many guests experience.

Customer relations management must be the industry's response to antiservice. CRM must ferret out the problems, train for the solutions and reward those who demonstrate the right responses. Sometimes, however, the very structure of the operations thwarts the best intentions.

Who Knows Why?   Every organization develops standard operating procedures, SOPs. SOPs are to business routines what personal habits are to individual routines. Some are new and meaningful; some are bad, in need of change. Along with the new and the good, guests encounter the old and useless. Like all bad habits, the old and useless are hard to discard. Hotels that insist on keeping them irritate guests unnecessarily and undermine the concept of service. Some practices seem intentional, as if inconveniencing the guest is easier than fixing the problem.

Who knows why – Sleepers are aroused from their beds by:

    Alarm clocks set by previous occupants?

    Computerized calling systems asking for breakfast orders?

    Housekeepers knocking on the door, "Never mind, just checking?"

    Running water in the neighbor's shower?

Who knows why – Guests are charged for:

    Leaving a day earlier than their four-day reservation?

    Incoming faxes, although incoming telephone calls are free?

    Late check-outs even when occupancy is low?

    Unannounced "service fees" that duplicate the very essence of the rate?

Who knows why – Guests find:

    The pool/workout facility closed when they are there and open when they're away?

    Dining dress codes more rigid than accepted social standards?

    That requests cannot be met because of some "company policy?"

    Hotel managers taking the best parking spots?

Who knows why – Hotels:

    Sell double occupancy rooms but offer only one key?

    Require bell service for individual arrivals, but not for those in groups?

    Have lobby coffee stands that refuse service four minutes before opening?

    Impose service charges on telephone calls made with credit cards?

Who knows why – Policies dictate:

    Different rate quotes from travel agents, reservationists and Web sites?

    No towels to be taken from the room, but there are none by the pool?

    No clean linen for stayovers? Is it really ecological concerns?

    Loud, behind-the-desk discussions when arriving guests lack luggage?

Measuring Guest Services

Chapter 1 explained the several measures used by the lodging industry to evaluate its economic health. Percentage of occupancy (%) and average daily rate (ADR) are the most widely used ratios. Their values rise and fall for several reasons. Some are macroeconomic: the state of the world's economy; the strength of the national currency. Other explanations include the chain's level of advertising or the owner's commitment to maintenance. Management's contribution is the workforce. Employee attitude and productivity cannot be ascribed to any distant cause, but only to management. Startlingly good statistics come from satisfied guests served by positive employees. Poor results originate in unhappy guests served by negative employees. But waiting for low occupancy and poor ADRs to warn of problems may be a matter of waiting too long. Management must look constantly for breakdowns in guest service.

Moments of Truth. A study measuring the cost of poor service was undertaken about the time that TQM was introduced to the industry.[13] The amount of dollars lost was calculated for each missed opportunity in each department. For example, overbooking, lost reservations, and discourtesy were charged against the front office. Although one incident doesn't cause bankruptcy, poor service is insidious. Single episodes mushroom from minor, miscellaneous costs to staggering totals, per week, per month, per year. Antiservice comes at a high cost.

Guest–staff interactions are more frequent in hotel settings than in other businesses. Each day, hotel associates are asked to deliver an exceptional level of service over and over and over again. Exhibit 7–9 emphasizes the cumulative impact of having one's customers in residence. A 300-room hotel with 70% occupancy and 33% double occupancy generates 2,800 guest–employee contacts per day! The figure soars to over 1 million per year. Full-service hotels face a double whammy. Not only do more departments mean more contacts per day, but service expectation are higher. Plenty of opportunities for mistakes.

Opportunities for meeting guest expectations—or failing to meet guest expectations—have been called "moments of truth."[14] It is during these encounters, when the service provider and the service buyer meet eyeball to eyeball, that the guest's perception of quality is set. Some say the first 10 minutes are the most critical.

How does the staff respond? Does the final guest of the shift receive the same attention as the first arrival? For many, only a smile and an appropriate greeting are needed. More is expected by the next guest: the one with the problem, the one with the complaint, the one with the special need. If the employee is empowered to act, to respond with alacrity, to evidence concern, it is a shining moment of truth.

Total quality management requires similar moments of truth between supervisors and staffers. Employees will not shine outwardly unless there is an inner glow. Supervisors will not get positive moments of truth if they always second-guess subordinates who have been empowered. Supervisors will not get positive moments of truth if staffers are irritated, say, by late work-schedule postings that frustrate personal plans. Good results from service encounters begins with a good working environment. Shining moments of truth come best from a total quality program.

Controlling Quality. Management use several tools, including review and evaluation, in its oversight of operations. That's equally true whether it's customer relations management or, say, cash management. Cash management requires standards and procedures to account for and control money. Service management employs similar standards and procedures. It's that very quality control, enforced by periodic inspections, that enables chains to maintain standards across broad holdings. Guests, too, rely on these standards, picking their destinations through company logos.

---

[13]Stephen Hall, *Quest for Quality: Cost of Error Study*. American Hotel & Motel Association and CitiCorp Diners Club, n.d.

[14]The term "moment of truth," has been attributed to Jan Carlzon, former chairman of SAS Airlines.

Counting the Moments of Truth

Number of rooms in the hotel		300
Percentage of occupancy		× .70
Number of rooms occupied each night	210	
Percentage of double occupancy		× .33
Number of guest-nights	280	
Moments of Truth		
Arrival	1	
Inquiry at the desk	1	
Bellperson	1	
Chambermaid	1	
Telephone operator	1	
Coffee shop host(ess)	1	
Server/busperson	2	
Cashier	1	
Newstand	1	
Total encounters per guest-night	× 10	
Daily number of moments of truth		2,800

Exhibit 7-9 Moments of truth are the points at which the service provider and the service buyer meet eyeball to eyeball. They may number in the thousands per day. Customer Relations Management (CRM) makes certain associates don't blink because each mistake impacts the bottom line.

Controlling Quality Through Inspection.   Reinforcing standards through inspection is a critical element of TQM. Inspectors rate both the physical plant and the staff's responses to moments of truth. Some companies use their own inspectors. Others, Preferred Hotels & Resorts for example, employ third parties. Visits may be preannounced or not. Whichever, verbal reports are usually given to the unit manager before written documents are filed with headquarters.

Although they come for different purposes, inspectors from AAA, *Mobil Travel Guide*, and others are also on the road (see Exhibit 1–9). Meeting planners are there as well, anonymously checking on staff and looking at the facilities before committing their groups.

Each chain has its own set of standards, and each decides its own number of inspections. Both are part of the franchise contract. Choice Hotels makes two annual visits; Hilton aims for three; Super 8, four. Cendant (now Wyndham) published its ratings by assigning one to five sunbursts in its directory. Depending on the contract, franchisees have 30 to 180 days to remedy serious defaults before the franchise is canceled. And they do get canceled. Radisson culls from the bottom up using, among other criteria, the guest comment cards that will be discussed shortly.

Quality control has many parts, including the physical facilities. This involves issues from maintenance of the grounds, to general cleanliness, to the condition of FF&E (furniture, fixtures and equipment). Are there holes in the carpet? burns on the bedcovering? paper in the stairwell? Check sheets used by the inspectors deal with details: working blow-driers, cleanliness of air vents, number of hangers in the closet (see Exhibit 7–10).

Inspection Report

Auditor _____   Hotel _____

Identification no. _____   City _____

Date(s) _____

	Excellent	Good	Fair	Poor	Comments
Registration					
1. Waiting time		×			About 2 minutes
2. Greeting	×				Used my name in conversation
3. Friendliness		×			
4. Efficiency			×		PMS was slow
5. Staff on hand	×				Other clerks handled telephone
6. Grooming		×			Except for Grace's hair
7. Accuracy	×				
Rooming					
1. Bellperson offered				×	No, had to call housekeeping
2. Elevator wait	×				3:00 P.M.
3. Floor signage	×				
4. First impression			×		Not too clean; stale odor
Guest Room					
1. Hangers	×				
2. Paper products			×		Facial tissue box nearly empty
3. Sanitation			×		Shower curtains need attention
4. Desk	×				
5. Telephone and book	×				Displayed card with fees listed
6. Bed and linens		×			
7. Lighting				×	Bulb burned out, standing lamp
Services					
1. Call housekeeping		×			Delay in acquiring extra pillow
2. Send fax to self	×				Prompt, no charge to receive
3. Get maid to let in				×	Took $3 tip and let me in
4. Ask for second key		×			Clerk remembered me, or said so
5. Ask for toilet repair			×		38-minute delay

Exhibit 7-10 Mystery shoppers make unannounced quality-control inspections to uncover and report (using forms similar to the illustration) weaknesses that need management's attention. Some shoppers are sent by the company; other represent rating agencies; still others are convention-service companies making unannounced inspections.

Inspections like these must not be left to external agents only. Daily reports from housekeeping inspectors and periodic walkthroughs by managers of all levels must be part of the team's control of quality.

Mystery shoppers, a euphemism (nice word) for inspectors, eat in and report on all F&B outlets, including room service. They check sales techniques as well: Does the foodserver push desserts? Does the room clerk sell up? Does the telephone operator know the hours of the the cabaret? Good inspectors always visit the housekeeper's office. A neat and tidy office means a neat and tidy hotel, but an office that looks like a dormitory room raises a red flag.

Security is another quality point. Both guest security (keys, locks, chains, and peepholes)[15] and internal security (pilferage from the hotel and theft from guests) come under scrutiny during the visit. Still, mystery shoppers are neither police nor consultants. They are reporters of the scene. Quality control is maintained and improved when management acts on the reports. Good results are reinforced through rewards and recognition. Weak results bring increased training and review of procedures. Findings from the inspections must be made available to everyone. How else would management's standards be known?

Controlling Quality Through Guarantees.   Quality Guarantees (QGs) are simply assurances that the hotel will deliver on its promise of quality. If not, it will make amends; it will pay.

With QG, the company puts its money where its advertising mouth is. Guaranteeing satisfaction takes gumption because it accepts responsibility. It flies in the face of the popular excuse, "that's-not-my-fault." Quality guarantees announce unequivocally to customers and staff alike that management is confident standing behind its TQM program.

Quality guarantees must not be confused with discounted room rates, which are offered or discarded as occupancy changes. QGs become part of the company's operating philosophy. As such, they must be introduced slowly, evolving from a successful TQM effort. Guarantees are not the beginning of a TQM program. They should not be started because of an advertising idea. They must be the culmination of a proven, ongoing TQM program. Otherwise, they backfire badly.

Several years ago, a well-known chain announced a quality guarantee of "complete satisfaction." No modifiers or limiting exceptions—just "complete satisfaction." A guest, citing the guarantee, asked for a reduced rate one morning when there was no hot water. Request denied because a malfunctioning boiler was "beyond the hotel's control." Is it? Obviously, quality guarantees need to be defined narrowly. The industry found that out after many incidents of the boiler type. A different guarantee can now be found on in-room tent cards. It reads, "We promise immediate action before you leave the hotel." If guests complain, there's a quality assurance guarantee that the hotel is listening, something quite different from the open-ended promise of "complete satisfaction." Nothing on the card says anything about payments.

Implementing guarantees in small steps as capabilities come on line announces to guests and staff that service quality is in place. Many hotels take the first step with room-service breakfast. It's free if not delivered within "x" minutes. Wrapped up in that simple promise is an advertisement, a departmental promotion, an employee empowerment, an assurance of quality, and a willingness to be measured. Time parameters are easier to measure than is "complete satisfaction." So guarantees might be: ten minutes to deliver the car from the garage, or breakfast coffee served within two minutes of being seated.

Meeting planners have begun asking for and receiving guarantees. Groups have always guaranteed the number of guest rooms they will take and the number of covers for cocktail parties and banquets. Now they're asking hotels to do the same. Guarantee there will be no noise from adjoining meeting rooms; guarantee that coffee will be served

---

[15]To be included in AAA's lodging guide, hotel rooms must have deadbolts, automatic locking doors, and peepholes. AAA has also expanded its coverage of accessibility for the disabled.

within five minutes after the session breaks. Just as the group's missed guarantees carry monetary penalties, so must the hotel's.

Quality guarantees take on real meaning if staff members are empowered. Forcing a disgruntled guest to stew while searching for a manager intensifies the issue even if the resolution favors the customer. Similarly, failing to pay off after announcing a guarantee alienates the guest far more than the incident itself. Guarantees should be unambiguous, limited in scope, and focused on objectives that are easily understood. Then there is no quibbling about payment, which—when made promptly—leads to guest loyalty and positive word-of-mouth advertising.

Nothing highlights operational weaknesses more than paying off guarantees arising from legitimate complaints. Failure to deliver is evident to all. Guarantees are meant to forestall complaints, but they have fallen out of favor. Now, as we see a few pages ahead, the search is on for better methods of resolving complaints. Obviously, resolving complaints follows the incident, whereas a quality guarantee tries to avert it.

Americans with Disabilities Act

The Americans with Disabilities Act (ADA) is a quality guarantee of a special nature. This federal law was enacted in 1990 and became effective in 1992. Although it has been tweaked in the interim, it is now up for serious revision. The lodging industry faces the very same concerns that plagued it during the 1990s.

ADA requires changes in physical structures and hiring practices to accommodate the disabled, be they guest or employee. Title III of the law covers lodging, but the legislation applies to all industries. Unlike the quality guarantees of hotel companies, stringent penalties are levied under civil-rights legislation for failure to comply. Far worse than governmental oversight, civil suits, some filed for less-than-reputable reasons, have plagued the hotel industry.

Several years were allowed to pass before there was enforcement. Then the court cases began because so much was left undefined in the law. It took time for everyone—the disabled, the government, and the hotel builders—to understand and to implement the provisions. After a time, what had previously been resolved informally found its way to the desks of the U.S. attorneys. Court rulings were far reaching, holding, for example, that a franchisor was responsible for the failure of a franchisee to build according to ADA specifications. Savvy hoteliers worked with private groups (Society for the Advancement of Travel for the Handicapped, for example) to identify and correct barriers.

Both government's ADA and lodging's TQM treat identical issues. One legislates; the other practices good business. The hotel industry was aware of the issue years before the government got around to legislating. Radisson was an early employer of the disabled. So was the Ritz-Carlton Company. Holiday Inn hired many handicapped persons, especially in its Worldwide Reservation Center.

Compliance with ADA standards is not the same as accommodating the handicapped within a quality assurance profile. Hotels can be accessible but not be hospitable. So chains refocused their training after ADA's passage. Embassy Suites called its ADA segment "Commandments of Disability Etiquette." Staff members across the industry were taught what to do and what not to do to help handicapped travelers.

Training differs in each operating department. Housekeepers learn to leave personal belongings exactly in place. Cashiers count aloud, announcing which denominations are being returned. Folios and registration cards are enlarged to further help the visually handicapped. Similar alterations in procedures and space accommodate handicapped workers. Equipment might be modified or even totally replaced. Enhanced lighting, power to recharge wheelchair batteries, or other alterations are sometimes warranted. Hiring practices and other personnel procedures are often more difficult to change than the equipment or work area. Included in these special human resources needs are revised approaches to hiring, testing, job structures, position descriptions, and more.

Physical Accommodations.   Federal and state ADA laws have been confusing and contradictory. California and the federal government took seven years to reconcile conflicting legislation. Federal law had open-ended language. Specific rules and their meanings were to come later. Until then everyone fought about the meaning of *undue hardship* as it applied to implementation. Equally ambiguous was the very meaning of *disability*.

Innumerable and often frivolous lawsuits hammered out, one case at a time, the meaning of all the terms, including *reasonable accommodation, readily achievable*, and *undue burdens*. Interpretations fell to the courts because Congress failed to be specific—intentionally so, many claimed. Congress did add one quirky provision. Attorneys are able to collect fees, although the plaintiffs who are suing may not recover damages. With such an invitation, lawyers launched a host of pesky lawsuits on all business, but especially hotels.

Many dollars in construction and training have been invested to meet ADA guidelines. Many more were wasted defending frivolous lawsuits. Finally, the courts slowed the breakneck pace of litigation. Proposed new guidelines now threaten to start the process anew. Hotels that invested time and money to meet previous standards would be in compliance no longer. Particularly upsetting are proposed guest-room guidelines. For example: A 300-room hotel is now required to have eight handicapped guest rooms. The proposed figure is 12. Yet, even the 8 are not fully used according to the AH&LA's response to the proposals.

Reaction to the 1990 act concentrated on physical barriers at first. Because they are measurable, they seemed less controversial. The legislation didn't provide the following values, they came from subsequent regulations. There are many examples: Three parking spaces plus one van space was legislated per 76–100 parking spaces. (Van spaces will increase about 25% under the new proposals.) Door thresholds must be less than 0.5 inches high; roll-in showers must be no less than 36 × 60 inches; drinking fountains no higher than 36 inches from the floor. Exhibits 7–11 and 7–12 are samples of the requirements.

Innkeepers were not pleased with the passage of the original legislation. They are equally unhappy with the pending changes (www.usdoj.gov/crt/ada/hsurvey.pdf). Meeting architectural standards has been costly despite assurances from the bill's original supporters that they wouldn't be. Small offsets have been obtained because handicapped individuals represent both a new supply of workers and a new source of guests.

Guest baths topped the failure-to-act list because bath renovations are expensive. Each wheelchair-accessible vanity being proposed under the latest regulations is estimated to cost $750. Moreover, the original law stated that hotels standing before January 1993 did not need to comply with all the bath regulations. These hotels could delay changes until *major* renovations were planned. Missing was the definition of "major." Newer hotels needed to make changes but only if they were—here are those words again—*readily achievable* and *without undue burden*. Exhibit 7–12 summarizes some of the regulations mandated for baths.

Many executives viewed the Occupational Safety and Health Act (OSHA) of 1970 as a major intrusion of government into business. ADA's legislation appeared to be more

Exhibit 7–11   The Americans with Disability Act (ADA), 1990, improved accessibility for disabled guests and staff. Regulations interpreting the act have been ongoing. Lodging leaders fear that the major changes being proposed, but not yet implemented (a few examples are in different type), will be very costly for the industry. Numerous lawsuits and major construction expenses followed the first phase, which was implemented in 1992.

Communications

Telephones for the hearing impaired

Public telephones at proper wheelchair height

Telecommunication devices for the deaf (TDDs)

Guest-room telephones

Visual alert to a ringing telephone

Easy dialing for those with reduced muscle control

Large telephone buttons or replacement pad

Voice-digital phone dialing

All customer devices touch-screen

Safety Equipment

Visual alert to smoke detectors

Visual alert to door knocks, bells, and sirens

Visual or vibrating alarm clocks

Low viewports on doors

Low location of room locks

Lighted strips on stairwells

Contrasting color on glass doors and handrails

Dual handrails on ramps

Automatic door openers

Slower times on elevator door closures

Emergency alarms in work areas

Access

Handicapped parking spaces

Ramp access to and within the building

Minimum thresholds

Adequate door access

Levered hardware, or adapters

Saunas to accommodate wheelchairs

Bathroom access (see Exhibit 7–12)

Lowered drinking fountains with accessible controls

Closed-caption decoders for TV and VCR

Assisted listening systems for meetings

Mattresses on frames rather than pedestal beds

Lower light switches and thermostats

Two-level reception desks

Curb cuts in sidewalks

Eliminate high pile carpeting

Accommodating Seeing Eye and Hearing Ear animals

Closet rods and drapery controls accessible

Extension cords for recharging wheelchairs

Lifts: elevators, vertical and incline platforms

Portable devices when facilities are not permanent

Eggcrate cushions for arthritics

Increased accessible entrances

Graphics

Size, color, and illumination

Braille and raised lettering in elevators

Braille and raised lettering behind guest-room doors

Recessed or projected graphics where appropriate

Verbal recitation of bill denominations when making change

Building roll-in showers with folding seats
Replacing faucet knobs with lever hardware
Installing grab bars in tub and toilet areas
Elevating sinks to accommodate wheelchairs
Insulating pipes on the underside of the sinks
Raising toilet seats
Lowering towel bars
Enlarging bathrooms to provide turnaround space
Additional enlargement to accommodate turnarounds
Adding vanity countertops
Providing transfer seats at the tub
Designing clearance space to get through the door
Lowering mirrors
Including hand-held showers with adjustable height bars

Exhibit 7-12   The ADA requirements outlined in Exhibit 7–11 do not include the very special and mostly costly changes of the 1990 law, bathroom designs. Costs are expected to climb still higher under the 2005 proposals, which may take 5-plus years to implement. The Department of Justice has received over 1,000 comments from concerned hoteliers and trade associations.

of the same. Both laws have been around long enough so compromise and compliance has replaced confusion and anger. Some fear the new regulations will reopen the wounds.

Signage.[16]   The ADA made innkeepers look more closely at their signage. Compliance required both Braille and raised lettering. (Only 25% of the visually impaired read Braille.) The law brought attention to the whole issue of signage. Poor signs or the complete lack of them irritate every visitor, not only the handicapped. The American Automobile Association joined the push by adding sign requirements to its rating system.

Signage for the handicapped must be provided inside and outside of elevators, adjacent to handicapped rooms, and on keys. Specifications are very exact: wall mounted on the latch side of the room (to avoid being hit by an opening door while reading the number), 60 inches above the floor. Audible elevator signals, once for up; twice for down supplement elevator signs. Some properties have tried audio signals that broadcast from small transmitters to the handicapped guests' receivers. The signals tells guests where they are and how to proceed to their destinations.

Signage—whether for elevators, exits, fires or other purposes—is an issue of safety as well as convenience. Elevator locations are not always evident, even to the sighted. Well placed signs point the way and encourage the elderly and children to use the safer elevator rather than the escalator. Strategically placed signs are critical for properties with many buildings, especially if they are named and numbered differently (see also Chapter 3, Floor Numbering).

Handicapped, but sighted, guests also rely on signs. The wheelchair symbol used by tour books indicates the availability of special accommodations, including ramp access and accessibility to the desk, to guest rooms, to at least one food-and-beverage outlet,

---

[16]Interior signs consume between 0.75% and 1.5% of casino/hotel construction budgets. *H&MM*, January 10, 2000, p. 38, according to Wayne Hunt Design Associates.

and of course to parking. (Police cannot enforce handicapped parking unless the international access symbol is in place both on the pavement and at eye level.)

Good signs and directions are not special to handicapped guests. Managers must "walk" their properties, get out from their offices, and note—not just see—what guests encounter as they enter and proceed through the property as strangers. Are there fire-exit signs? If the exits are alarmed, a sign should say so. Are no-smoking rooms and floors marked? Is the ambiance of the hotel destroyed by a bunch of supplemental handwritten signs? Can one actually find a guest room following the posted directions? Are some rooms named rather than numbered? Are all the bulbs in electric signs functioning? Exterior signs on the building are often forgotten and lack maintenance and repair.

The alert manager should question the staff at the desk, in uniform, or on the guest floors about the location of certain sites. Employees who have no reason to be in particular areas of the hotel are often unable to direct guests to a banquet facility, the swimming pool, the spa, or the guest laundry.

Every cloud has a silver lining, and ADA's requirements have focused attention on signs as part of the overall picture of guest service.

Complaints

Complaints, like quality guarantees, should direct management to troubled service areas. Unfortunately, too few guests complain and too few managers look below the surface of the rare complaint. Most guests and most (secretly thankful) managers mumble quietly and let the matter slip by. That's why those complaints that are registered must be resolved quickly and correctly.

How Much Do Complaints Cost?   Measuring guest unhappiness is like measuring the value of the "moments of truth." Putting dollar amounts on them requires estimates and assumptions. Neither contains real mathematical accuracy, but one hears them over and over because they make believable points.

It is said that 10% of guests would not return to the property of their most recent visit. Using the same values as Exhibit 7–9, a hotel would lose 21 possible repeats each day (300 rooms at 70% occupancy times the 10% loss). With just 21 rooms lost nightly, the annual total is a whopping 7,665 guest nights. Make another assumption: The ADR is $70. Then the total cost of 10% of one's guests not returning is over $500,000 annually. The cost stretches into the stratosphere ($5 million) when hotels of 3,000-rooms, such as those in Exhibit 1–6, are involved. Now add the cost of finding new guests in order to retain 70% occupancy.

Some maintain that labor-intensive industries such as lodging increase productivity only by improving the service encounter. The failure to do so, goes the argument, represents not merely additional labor costs but costs from lost business. Here, too, there is little empirical evidence to support the idea. Complaints do impact profits but not every complaint takes dollars to resolve. One investigation reported just the opposite: Only one-third of written complaints were about money. Exhibit 7–13 offers another suggestion if money is the issue: Better to spend a bit to hold the guest than to invest five times that to solicit another.

Still Another Calculation.   Exhibit 7–13, like other calculations, uses widely quoted but vaguely grounded assumptions. Still, the conclusions are startling.

Premise 1: Some 68% of nonreturning guests stay away because of indifferent service. (Deaths, relocations, competition, and poor products account for the other 32%.)

Cost of Lost Guests

Loss of Guests

68% of nonreturning guests quit because of indifferent service.

32% is lost to death, relocation, competition, and poor products.

Complaints

Less than 5% of dissatisfied guests speak out—so for every one that does there may be twenty who do not.

Over half of the silent majority refuse to return—an iceberg floating beneath the surface.

Noncomplaining guests do complain to friends and acquaintances.

10 to 11 others will hear of the mishap.

13% of the group will gripe to 20 others.

Two-thirds of the iceberg could be won over if they were identified—about half of these could become boosters.

Costs

It costs over $10 to answer a complaint by letter (including the cost of writing time, follow-up time, and postage).

It costs five times more to get a new customer than to keep an existing one.

Exhibit 7-13   Guest complaints are costly; few managers dispute that. Widely quoted but never documented values reinforce the concept and emphasize the importance of a proactive approach.

Premise 2: About 2.5% or less of dissatisfied guests actually voice their unhappiness. There is an iceberg effect here. Below the surface floats the vast bulk of complaints, never voiced and never resolved. Of this silent majority, it is said that well over half will not patronize the hotel again. Worse yet, they will tell 10 to 11 others not to do so; some tell as many as 20 others. This fact is so irrefutable in the view of many that a "rule" has been created, the 1–11–5 rule. One unhappy guest will tell 11 others, and each of the 11 will tell 5 more.

Premise 3: About two-thirds of the icebergs can be warmed and won over by resolving the complaint. About one-third of complainers can be converted from blasters to boosters if their complaints are handled quickly and properly. Implicit here is the guest's willingness to speak up. Guests will when they are very angry, or when management creates an environment that encourages guests to register complaints.

Identifying the Complaint. Identifying unhappy guests can be more challenging than resolving their problems. For certain, the rote question, "How was everything?" will elicit no meaningful reply. Desk personnel and managers from all operational and organizational levels must ask direct and specific questions. That means talking to guests, whether in the lobby, by the pool, or wherever. The dialogue may start with pleasantries such as a comment about the weather; an introduction; or the frequency of the guest's visits. Then, the conversation must elicit the negatives, if there are any. "Do you like our new bedding?" "Have you ever tried room service?" "Did you know we have a special lounge drink this month?"

Comments that flow from these solicitations are not complaints. They give management direction for improving service and, thus, preempting real complaints. Informal conversations highlight hidden issues that require no immediate action, no settlement costs, no allowances on the folios (see Chapter 10). Informal chats suggest grounds for operational changes and, secondarily, build guest relations, especially if followed with a letter of thanks.

Management must be knowledgeable if it hopes to prevent complaints. Executives who don aprons and actually work the floor, say, once a month, create more than a public-relations photo-op. They learn, for example, that the location of the dish-machine is the cause for high chinaware breakage, that the housekeeper's vacuums really don't work, and that customer service warrants the front desk's purchase of umbrellas for guest use. Managers who telephone their own hotels test departmental procedures and the disposition of their staff.

Preventing the Complaint: Early Warning.

Complaints can be forestalled if the staff is trained to tell it like it is. Alerting guests to bad situations allows them to participate or not. Of course, it may also cost business. So the reservations department must explain that the pool is closed for repairs during the dates of the reservation. A request for connecting rooms is impossible to promise. The request is noted but no guarantee can be made. A no-guarantee with apologies is stated by the reservationists, not merely implied.

And so it should be across the hotel. Early warnings about other large parties in the house must be made by sales executives before finalizing the new booking. Likewise, room service would report elevator delays as it takes a breakfast order. Guest-service agents should offer reduced rates in the wing that's under renovation.

Complaints may evolve around the prompt attention paid to the "squeaky wheel." Managers know that oiling the squeak out of turn may better serve everyone in the long run. Observant guests often side with the hotel when an obnoxious squeaker rolls up to the desk. They give away their priority in line to get the pest put away. Similarly, handling families with tired, irritable children outside the sequence actually improves overall service.

Preventing the complaint by anticipating the problem and providing unsolicited accurate information is far preferable to quieting angry guests after the fact. Explaining the circumstances makes guests feel better about the situation and forestalls their complaints. "Housekeeping will not get to the room before luncheon, so we can accommodate your early arrival, but not before 1 o'clock."

If a policy of candor works wonders in reducing complaints, the opposite is also true. Misleading information, either directly or by implication and omission, enrages guests who feel they have been cheated—as they have.

Preventing the Complaint: Comment Cards.

The effectiveness of comment cards is argued over and again. Distractors say the questions are tilted toward the hotel's strengths. Hotel managers grumble because guests use the questionnaires to gripe. Guests don't balance the good and the bad, managers say, but concentrate on operating weaknesses. Executives explain away negative comments by claiming the guest is simply wrong. Poor comments hurt managers doubly when results from the cards are part of bonuses or promotion decisions.

Management's complaints aside, improving service requires every weapon to be mustered. Comment cards are one of those weapons, and like others, they have strengths and weaknesses. The better the questionnaire, the better the information obtained. Uncovering and remedying shortcomings is what managing for quality is all about. Anonymous guest cards help overcome the iceberg effect, the reluctance of guests to speak out.

Critics attack the statistical validity of comment cards. Responses are low, typically 1% to 2% of the guest population. Long questionnaires account for some of the low returns. Guests take the time only when they're really angry. Cards with a narrow focus get better responses. Short, one-themed questionnaires—cleanliness, for example—could be used throughout the property. Specialized, equally brief forms are then used within each department. Although not a guest comment card, guests do respond when asked for help with inroom repairs (see Exhibit 7–14).

Comment cards are typically static, left in guest rooms or on coffee-shop tables. Returns increase greatly when guests are invited to participate. Guest-service agents do this by handing a pencil-paper questionnaire to the guests at check-out. There's a better response if a computer-screen questionnaire is close by. Requests can be made on arrival accompanied by some incentive. How about lottery tickets? Carlson Hospitality has tried that. Giving dessert coupons or wine with dinner doubles the benefits by drawing guests into the dining room. Lottery drawings are the best incentives. Guests complete the survey after the stay when they have had time to evaluate the property. Prize drawings, done monthly perhaps, identify the guest by name, which facilitates a followup thank-you letter. (*Careful*: Some states outlaw lotteries no matter how innocent.)

Before the Web, toll-free telephone numbers supplemented comment cards. Now, telephones are rarely staffed. Besides, angry guests get angrier when the call is answered by a machine or a foreign outsourcer whose diction is, well, foreign. As guests have replaced their snail mail with email, so hotels have replaced their telephones with software platforms that correlate the electronic responses and highlight the areas that need special attention.

Exhibit 7-14
Enlisting guest participation improves the quality of the room and of the guest's experience. It adds another source of information to guest comment cards, input from quality circles, inspections, and conversations. Management can forestall complaints with good record-keeping provided it leads to corrective action.

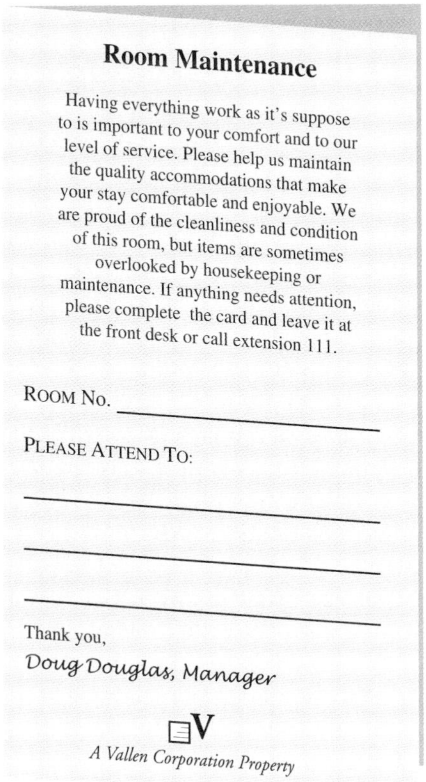

Room Maintenance

Having everything work as it's suppose to is important to your comfort and to our level of service. Please help us maintain the quality accommodations that make your stay comfortable and enjoyable. We are proud of the cleanliness and condition of this room, but items are sometimes overlooked by housekeeping or maintenance. If anything needs attention, please complete the card and leave it at the front desk or call extension 111.

ROOM No. _____

PLEASE ATTEND TO:

_____

_____

_____

Thank you,

Doug Douglas, Manager

▢**V**

A Vallen Corporation Property

Less formal, but equally helpful, are the "comment cards" by bloggers. Unlike real comment cards, blogs are seen by everyone, not just by management. Blogs are helpful. Good reviews reinforce the quality assurance effort. Bad ones require management to respond more quickly than they might with confidential comment cards.

Different information is treated differently. Feedback from guests supplements feedback from staff, which come through quality circles or suggestion boxes. Management's response will not always be immediate, and that must be explained. Some issues are operational and response is quick: placing an emergency telephone in the exercise room. Other issues are slower; they're strategic or involve large costs: building another elevator.

Information from quality circles, from guest comment cards, from employee suggestion boxes, from computer programs, and from direct conversations need to be analyzed. A simple spreadsheet highlights areas that get repeated comments. Management must analyze the input for trends in operating weakness and strength. Good systems identify both functions that are working and those that are not. Previous face-to-face encounters from agitated guests add immeasurable value to the analysis.

Handling the Face-to-Face Complaint.
Guest-service management aims for error-free service, but that is a goal more than a fact. Experience keeps a tight rein on reality, making complaint-free environments desirable but very unlikely. Only the number, timing, or place of the complaint is uncertain, not whether one will occur. As QM programs reduce the number, the remaining complaints gain in importance. Besides, not all complaints are subject to QM solutions. Systems, procedures, and training aside, the unexpected will happen. Door attendants do lose car keys!

Preparing for Complaints.   Preparing for complaints begins by acknowledging their likelihood. Training programs must emphasize the probability of a complaint. Employees with a proper mindset gained through training are not caught unaware. They recognize the importance of attitude in receiving and resolving complaints. Proper preparation minimizes the impact and cost of the complaint. Preparing properly means making the best of the worst. Readying employees to receive and resolve complaints has become an integral part of QM programs.

Although the specifics differ, complaints follow a theme in each department. This gives Q⊙s an effective role in training. Within the circle, members share their individual experiences and solutions, and the group adopts the best ideas—best practices—as departmental standards. Employee empowerment, the authority to accept responsibility and to remedy the situation, is implicit.

For front-desk employees, common themes spring from specific encounters. What is the proper response to a departing guest who protests a folio (guest bill) charge? What should be done with an irate arrival whose reservation has been sold to another? What accommodations can be made if the guest tenders a travel agent's coupon that is not acceptable to the hotel? Common situations all, playing themselves out time and again in a fixed pattern if not an exact duplication. None are rare, unexpected encounters. A series of options must be readied and employed as needed (see Exhibit 7–15).

Directing employees to kick the problem upward is an option required by certain circumstances. Even empowerment programs limit employee authority to certain decision levels. Preparing employees for the complaint must include information about when and why and to whom to refer the matter. Rarely do the sessions train for the next (frequently necessary) step: What is to be done when the next level of authority is not available? Leave the fuming guest to wait ... and wait ... and wait?

Hotel Anywhere, U.S.A.
Internal Memorandum

To: Guest-Service Agents

From: Holly Wood, Rooms Manager

Subject: Empowerment Guidelines   □**V**

Date: January 1, 20- -   *A Vallen Corporation Property*

Effective this date, all guest-service agents who have completed the four training hours have authority to make the following adjustments using their own discretion. Managers and supervisors are always available for consultation.

An Apology is the First Response! Apologies are free; we give away as many as necessary, but be sincere and listen carefully.

Where appropriate, verify information before acting.

Issue	Intermediate Response*	Maximum Response*
Noisy room	Relocate, if stayover	Upgrade now or next visit; gift to the room
Incorrect rate	Correct the paperwork	Allowance for the difference; ticket to club or spa
Engineering problems: Heat and AC, TV, plumbing	Send engineer; change rooms	Upgrade; up to 25% off rate
Protested charges: Telephone	Allowance for local	Allowance for LD
In-room film	Allowance	One per day
Valet parking	Allowance	Full amount

*Awarding up to 500 frequent-guest points is always an alternative.

Exhibit 7–15   Empowering employees requires an understanding of what can and cannot be done. Supplementing training with guidelines structures the procedure. Associates must be instructed in the next step: What action to take when higher management is not available.

Complaints may arise because the spread between guest expectations and service delivery widens dramatically after arrival. But complaints are not always of the hotel's doing. Hotel staff may just be the most convenient recipient of the guest's bad day. Tired and grumpy travelers, those who have done battle with family members or business associates, who have fought canceled flights and lost luggage, may find the hotel employee—especially an inexperienced one who dither and dathers—an ideal outlet for a week of frustrations. Preparing for the complaint means understanding this.

Preparing for the complaint means putting up with drunks and being tolerant of the show-off and the braggart performing for the group. Preparing for the complaint allows one to overlook exaggerations, sarcasm, and irony. Preparing for the complaint recognizes that senior persons sometimes berate younger persons, replaying parent–child relationships. Preparing for the complaint means understanding that some persons can never be satisfied, whatever the staff may try.

Responding to Complaints.   No complaint is trivial in the eyes of the guest. What the hotel's representative perceives as trivial often originates from a series of small, unattended-to issues that smolder until management's casual attitude fans the fire of dissatisfaction. Suddenly, the trivial explodes into a major conflagration.

BY LISTENING.   To bring about change, the complaint must be received and understood. Complaints are communicated only if the complainer speaks and the listener listens. It is not enough for the complaint-taker to hear passively; he or she must listen actively. Careful listening is fundamental to resolving every complaint. Full attention to the speaker moves the problem toward prompt resolution even before the explanation is complete. Experienced complaint-handlers never allow other employees, guests, or telephone calls to distract them from hearing out the complainant.

Complainers do not always begin with the real issue—which is true, of course, with many conversations. Questions are appropriate provided that they are not judgmental, but interrupting unnecessarily angers the speaker and pushes the conversation to another level of frustration before all the facts are in hand.

Listening requires good eye contact and subtle supportive body movements. Appropriate nodding, tsh-tshing, mouth expressions, and hand movements encourage the speaker and convey attention, sympathy, and understanding. It is important to remain in contact with the speaker and empathetic toward his or her experience throughout the recitation.

Guests do not like being rushed along; they want the whole story to come out. The listener must be sensitive to his or her own body language, careful that negative signals are not halting the complainer or dropping a cold blanket over the encounter. Watching for the guest's nonverbal signals helps interpret the guest's readings of one's own signals.

Attentive listening is particularly important in the resolution of accidents. Small mishaps end in court cases when the listener makes short shrift of the incident and of the person involved in the accident. Aggrieved guests want management's attention and evidence of its concern. They want a sympathetic audience to hear them out. Lawsuits are the invariable results of leaving the entire situation to the security staff. Management's representative should handle the public relations while security completes the required investigation. Together, the team must summon help and attend to any injuries. Then the investigation follows, but not in the presence of the injured party. Managers and security agents must admit no fault and promise no medical or insurance coverage. Neither should they discuss details nor quiz others staffers at the scene.

IN A PROPER VENUE.   Complainers who grow hostile or overly upset, loud, or abusive must be removed from the lobby. Shifting to a new venue should be done as quickly as possible. Don't wait for the issue to intensify or the time committed to the situation to outgrow the lobby discussion. Perhaps the pretense can be that of comfort: Let's sit down in the office; we'll be more comfortable there, and there will be no interruptions.

Walking to the new location offers a cooling-off period. It provides an opportunity to shift the topic and to speak in more conversational tones. Walking changes the aggressive or defensive postures that one or the other might have assumed in the lobby. The office location adds to the manager's authority and prestige.

The louder the guest growls, the softer should come the response, which usually brings an immediate reaction: Loud complainers quiet down to hear replies that are given in near whispers. A harsh answer to abuse or to offensive language only elevates the complaint to a battle of personalities. Above all, the hotel wants the guest to retain dignity. Divorcing the interaction from personalities helps do that. The facts are at issue, not the persons; certainly not the employee, who may be the original target of the guest's ire.

Ultimately, the manager may refuse to discuss the issues further unless the guest modulates language and tone. The hotelier tells the complainer that he or she is being addressed politely and the listener expects the same courtesy. In a worst-case scenario, say with a drunk or drug-crazed guest, police are called.

By Making a Record.   Asking permission to record the complaint by taking notes indicates how seriously management views the matter. It also allows the guest to restate the issue and have it recorded with accuracy, at least from the guest's point of view. The hotel's representative gets an additional opportunity to express concern and sympathy as the issues are restated aloud. It also slows the conversation, helping to cool emotions. Contributing to the written report makes the complaining guest sense that already something is being done. Thus, the stage is set for resolving the problem.

Front offices maintain permanent journals of the day's activities, including complaints. These logs improve communications with later shifts since the issues often carry over. The documentation helps the participants recall the incident later, provides a basis for training, and supports legal proceedings if the matter goes that far. Serious accidents are documented again by security and by the hospital or the police, depending on circumstances.

The recordkeeping goes further. Getting the guest's folio, registration card, or reservation data helps the manager understand what happened. Calling an employee into the office or on the telephone in the guest's presence broadens the investigation, clarifies the facts, and mollifies the complainer. Employees should get as much courtesy as the guest. Training or discipline, if appropriate, is done elsewhere in private. Both the staff member and the guest should be addressed with civility, certainly using surnames and appropriate titles: Mr., Mrs., Dr., Ms.

With a Settlement.   Once registered, the complaint must be settled, resolved somehow and closed. The complainant expects some satisfaction or real restitution for the embarrassment. The hotel wants to keep the customer, strengthen the relationship, if possible, and send the guest forth as a booster who tells the world how fairly he or she was treated. Still, the hotel doesn't want to give away the house by atoning for mistakes that caused no harm and little damage.

Apologies are free—we can give away as many as needed; and indeed, only an apology may be needed. Apologies are in order even if the complaint seems baseless or unreasonable. The effectiveness of the apology depends on the guest's reading of the manager. And that reading often reflects the importance of and the guest's involvement in the delivery of the service. A transient family views situations differently than a family celebrating an important anniversary. A business traveler's anger increases directly with the importance of the message that wasn't delivered.

Does the unhappy guest see the hotelier as truly contrite or merely mouthing niceties? There are different ways of apologizing, but none are effective unless they ring true. "I am sorry, and I apologize on behalf of the hotel," goes a long way toward settling minor issues quickly and satisfactorily. "I am sorry" can take on different nuances with different levels of emphasis—"I *am* sorry"—additional words—"I am *so* sorry"—or deleted words—"I'm sorry."

Guests listen for subtle connotations in words and voice. Voices can be shaped and honed through practice to carry just the right intonations and emphases. Concern, belief, and self-disparagement can be communicated irrespective of the words. Other standbys, although often repeated, have a proper place in the list of apologies: "I know how you must feel"; "Yes, that is distressing"; and "I would have done the same."

Although it is not necessary to fix blame for the incident—and doing so may be counterproductive—the hotel's staff clearly may be at fault. When pertinent, admitting as much helps to set the tone, as long as the admission doesn't include minimizing the incident or offering lame excuses. Use a simple statement about "our" mistake.

Managers who want to go beyond the apology send gifts to the room. The traditional fruit basket, or a tray with wine and cheese, or even a box of amenities serve this function. Apologies appear on the card once again.

Complaints that are settled with apologies are the least expensive kind and often prove to be the most satisfying for both sides. Subsequent telephone calls or letters reinforce the apologies that were expressed during the face-to-face encounters.

After hearing out the guest, quieting down the situation, and offering appropriate sympathy, the hotel manager must provide restitution and lay the issue to rest. The quicker the problem can be resolved, the better. That is what happens with most complaints. But serious items are not settled that easily. Smashed fenders, dentures broken on a bone, or snagged designers' dresses are not remedied on the spot. Insurance companies, or law firms in more serious instances (a fall in the tub), work their wares slowly. Nevertheless, sympathy, concern, and prompt, on-the-spot action reduce the longer-run consequences and costs.

More concrete solutions are needed when apologies are not enough. A list of options should be identified for the hotel's representative as part of the preparation process (see Exhibit 7–15). Heading the list are items that cost the hotel little or nothing, as would an upgrade. Even here, there are degrees: Should we upgrade to another level? To the concierge floor? To an expensive suite? The upgrade is offered for this visit or for another. If for another, the manager's card with a direct number—"call me personally and I'll arrange it"—reinforces the special nature of the solution. Some managers preface every offer by hinting that the arrangements are special. By implication, deviating from standard procedure recognizes the guest's importance and the hotel's desire to make things right.

Annoying but inconsequential incidents can be handled with small gifts. Tickets to an event that is being held by the hotel are welcome. Athletic contests (tennis tourneys), presentations (distinguished speakers), theater-style entertainment, and the like are almost without cost if seats are plentiful.

Admission to the hotel's club or spa, tickets to local activities such as theme parks or boat rides, or transportation to the airport in the hotel's limousine are other options. Cash refunds are the last choice, but they may be the only appropriate response. Damage to property requires reimbursement, and extraordinary circumstances necessitate an allowance against folio charges.

Usually, the situation is less serious. The guest has twice before reported an inoperative television set. Or, the guest's request to change rooms has been ignored. Or, the long delay in getting a personal check cleared for cashing is irritating and embarrassing. Complaints of this type need fast and certain action. Once the solution is resolved, a wise manager explains what is to be done and how long it will take. Better to overestimate the time—then a more rapid turnaround will impress the guest with the hotel's sincerity.

By Asking the Guest.   Guest demands soften if the episode is handled well and if the guest feels that the treatment is fair. To get that kind of response, the hotelier needs to get into the guest's head, to view the situation from the other side. If the interview appears to be moving favorably, the guest can be brought into the decision loop. Carefully, the hotel's agent elicits the guest's expectations, which often are less than the hotel's, and draws the guest into formulating the remedy. The complainer becomes part of the solution, and the process gains momentum toward a quick and satisfactory conclusion.

All of which is easier said than done. Standing near an experienced complaint-handler—listening to what is said and how it is said—is the best learning experience the manager can have. It is especially helpful if the claim is denied.

Customers are always right! Except sometimes they aren't. The first reference is to the attitude with which management hears the guest's complaint; the second reference is to the context of the complaint. Management can listen attentively, sympathize completely, and communicate caringly, but still *say no* to outrageous requests based on nonevents.

Refusing compensation—remember, apologies are always in order—may cost the customer's patronage. It is a fine judgment call, as repeat patronage may already be lost. In denying restitution, inexperienced managers resort to "company policy" as the reason. Company policy is a great turnoff! Better to explain the answer in terms of fairness, of safety, of service to other guests, of economic reality, or of past experience.

Unhappy guests may request the intervention of higher authority. If that is appropriate, the next manager must be formally introduced and the issue recapped aloud to expedite the meeting. Thereafter, the first interviewer remains silent unless questioned and allows the second conversation to progress without interruption.

Complaints that are resolved quickly and equitably make friends for the hotel. Resolved or not, management's attitude, as expressed in words and movements, goes far toward minimizing (or aggravating) the damages.

SUMMARY

Service is what the hospitality industry is all about. But service has a broader meaning than someone serving breakfast or opening the door of an arriving car. Service means providing what is needed. Above all, guests need the industry's basic product, sleep. The real meaning of service is providing guest needs within a cordial atmosphere generated by employees, by associates committed to the service concept. Although the facilities of hotels differ across a broad range, the essence of the delivery remains the same: "Every staff member thinking like a manager and acting like a concierge."

So broad a definition needs an equally broad conceptual base. That comes under the heading of *total* quality management (TQM). Every aspect of the operation is managed at the peak of quality. No easy job, that, because management's scope of responsibility is broad and varied. For one, there is the physical hotel, which the chapter discusses briefly in topics such as room size, linens, and the ADA. It is the other,

the attitude displayed by the staffers, that is the thrust of the chapter's discussion and the real meaning of service.

Each hotel delivers its product within its individual identity of type, class, and size. Those limitations notwithstanding, every organization can deliver a high standard of service if its members are imbued with customer relations savvy. Instilling and installing customer-relations management (CRM) is part of the industry's drive toward TQM.

Guest satisfaction (and employee satisfaction, too) is at its highest when service is delivered by courteous, empowered staffers. Opportunities to do so occur often during the many "moments of truth" generated at busy hotels. Recognizing the associates' critical role and facing labor shortages, management is changing its methods of supervision. Winning the staff's commitment is an ongoing process that has redefined the role of everyone employed. Part of the change is management's empowerment of workers within their individual levels of authority. Part of the change is a flatter organization with fewer middle-management levels. Part of the change is a greater level of diversity within the industry and part of the change is the introduction of new language.

TQM, itself a term of recent origin, has introduced other language into human-resources management.

Fads in management come and go like other fashions. The language of CRM and of quality circles will soon fade away. Hotel management must retain the vision behind the language, even as the actual terms disappear. Operating in a fast-changing society, innkeepers must hold onto the industry best practices. Total quality management ranks high among them.

RESOURCES AND CHALLENGES
Resources

WEB SITES

http://www.access-able.com (Private, family-based organization supported by various travel companies)—(Wheat Ridge, CO. Tips for mature and handicapped travelers.) And http://www.sath.org (SATH, Society for Accessible Travel & Hospitality)—New York, NY. What handicapped travelers need to know.

http://www.sleepfoundation.org (Sleep research and sleep aids)—Washington, D.C.

http://www.westin.com (Westin Hotels—A division of Starwood Hotels)—White Plains, NY. Offers its Heavenly Bed for sale with its accoutrements.

http://www.usdoj.gov (U.S. Department of Justice)—Washington, D.C. Information about the Americans with Disabilities Act, past legislation, and anticipated changes.

Web Assignment

Use *Google* or other search engines to seek out "Hotel Jobs." Submit a paper outlining what sources you might pursue to find a career in (1) a given geographic area; (2) a specific career path; (3) a minimum salary level; (4) a particular company; and (5) comment on general availability.

INTERESTING TIDBITS

➤ Hotels have taken wholeheartedly to "buzz," the marketing term that started with the Internet. Four examples: (1) Marriott created mSpot, a glass-enclosed guest room first displayed in Times Square, New York City; (2) Westin Hotels ran full-page ads in *The Wall Street Journal* describing its "insanely comfortable bed that envelops you"; (3) Starwood promoted its aloft hotels at festivals and sports events using an old-fashioned trailer outfitted like an aloft hotel room; (4) Hampton's "bed-head" mobile featured the messy hair that comes from a good night's sleep.

➤ Stylized hotel names are another part of the industry's buzz. There's *aloft hotels* (see above); Hilton's new Embassy effort, *Creativity Suites*; and Le Méridien's offering, *Art + Tech*.

➤ Down, which some upscale hotels use in pillows and blankets, is the soft, first underplumage of birds, usually geese (very expensive) or ducks (expensive).

➤ One division of Hilton Hotels is unsure about its own name. Often the company identifies itself with a capital "T," Double-Tree, but other references use the lowercase "t," Doubletree. Sometimes both spellings appear in the same release.

Challenges

TRUE/FALSE

Questions that are partially false should be marked false (F).

___ 1. A 180-thread count sheet, 100 threads in one direction and 80 in the other, is popular with high-occupancy hotels, especially those in the midscale range.

___ 2. "Road warriors," who protect travelers against mishaps, are more evident in the U.S. since the attack on the World Trade Center.

___ 3. As one would expect, the racial and cultural balance of the hotel industry's workforce is the same as the cultural and racial diversity of the national population.

___ 4. Hotel labor unions are strongest in the largest hotel cities, best represented by the cities of the South: Orlando, New Orleans, and Memphis.

___ 5. A "moment-of-truth" is a term used during employee interviews, when sensitive questions are posed by the interviewer, who watches how the job applicant responds.

PROBLEMS

1. Using the computer, create a simple spreadsheet showing the form and functions that management can use to summarize and analyze complaints originating within departments of the rooms divisions.

2. Prepare and briefly discuss a list of three quality guarantees that are defined narrowly enough to be communicated easily and achieved successfully: for example, room service breakfast delivered within 30 minutes. Be certain to include the penalty to be paid by the hotel if the guarantee is not met.

   a. Explain why Marriott's guarantee of breakfast is, in the words of the authors, "an advertisement, a departmental promotion, an employee empowerment, an assurance of quality, and a willingness to be measured."

3. Compute how many moments of truth occur in a full-service convention hotel of 630 rooms during a typical month. Comment.

4. From readings and personal experience, discuss six of the most difficult elements of resolving a complaint.

5. You are the hotel's liaison with the architects designing guest rooms for a new tower. Present them a list of the 10 most important items that must be provided if the hotel is to meet its obligations under the Americans with Disabilities Act.

6. List five incentives that a hotel might offer to get guests to complete a guest comment card. Make a special effort to have the incentives encourage cross-advertising, by which one department awards incentives for use in another department.

AN INCIDENT IN HOTEL MANAGEMENT

Force Majeure

How to attract more customers from companies in the local business park was the topic of this month's meeting of departmental managers. The group was confident of its ability to deliver, so they adopted and widely advertised a quality guarantee for local businesses. "If anything goes wrong, the room rate is on us!"

An out-of-town representative of Allied Manufacturing, a nearby industry, has been in the hotel for two nights. There was no hot water last night or the morning of the third day. The guest mentions this to the guest-service agent as he goes through the check-out procedure. "I think I'll take advantage of your quality guarantee."

"Yes sir; please wait while I get the manager."

It was almost 15 minutes before the hotel manager appeared. "Good morning. The agent has told me about your request and I would like to comply. There's no hot water because the boiler is down. It's an act of God, a *force majeure*, so, as I have told other guests, the situation isn't covered by our guarantee."

Questions: Was there a management failure here; if so, what?

What is the hotel's immediate response (or action) to the incident?

What further, long-run action should management take, if any?

ANSWERS TO TRUE/FALSE QUIZ

1. True. Higher thread counts are used in many upscale hotels. They are more costly and do not wear as well as 180 counts. So hotels in the midprice range with high occupancy (and therefore heavy linen wear) have stayed with the industry's old standby, 180 count.

2. False. "Road warriors" is a term for identifying guests who do a great deal of required business travel with all the pressures and discomforts associated with long and frequent stays away from home.

3. False. The hotel workforce is not a cross section of the U.S. population. Therefore, recruiting and retaining a great number of less educated workers in routine, low-wage jobs is a difficult task for lodging's human resource management.

4. False. Unions, in general, are not strong in the southern states. Hotel unions, in particular, are strongest in the northern, urban areas such as New York and Chicago, and in major hotel cities such as Las Vegas, San Francisco, and Honolulu.

5. False. "Moment-of-truth" is a reference to the important moment when a hotel associate offers service to a hotel guest; that point when all the talk and training is applied, or not.

Arrival, Registration, Assignment, and Rooming

Outline

Previous chapters, but especially Chapters 4, 5 and 6, built the backdrop behind guest arrivals. Those earlier discussions—about forecasting and reservations, about individuals and groups—concentrated on attracting guests, selling them to come. Chapters 1, 2 and 3 first structured the issue from the guest's side, explaining the options behind each guest's personal choices. Next, Chapter 7 explained the quality of the reception that newcomers are apt to receive. Now, finally, our guests are arriving. Let's follow them and learn how they're greeted, registered, assigned, and roomed.

ARRIVAL

The arrival procedure appears routine and standardized. And it is, although a wide choice of sizes, classes, and types of hotels means no two arrivals are exactly the same. Guests also contribute to the range of expectations. Some are seasoned travelers, some novices. Some know the brand well and some are first-timers. The arrival procedure mixes the personalities of each property, with its range of services and levels of training, with the personalities of each individual, both those of the arrivals and those of the reception staff.

At one extreme are the road warriors. They may arrive, register, and take occupancy without any staff interaction. First-time travelers fall at the other end. They need guidance, coddling, and reassurance. Both types arrive and register; both types must be greeted and roomed. So the arrival procedure is everywhere the same, even if it isn't.

Arrival is the guest's first encounter with the hotel. It is, therefore, one of the critical "moments of truth." There can be but one opportunity to make a first, good impression. If all front-office functions are running smoothly and all systems are working in unison, the arrival is an auspicious one. The guest's car is handled promptly. Uniformed services pose the initial greetings. Reception (guest-service agents) processes the registration quickly but hospitably. Baggage is unloaded and taken to the room. The guest is settled in, ready to buy the services and incur the charges discussed in the following chapters.

Moments of Truth

Arrival time signals the sharpest distinction between the industry's many levels of service. Limited-service properties have one representative, the guest-service agent, between the guest's arrival and his or her occupancy of the room. Indeed, limited-service guests who use self-check-in terminals may see no one at all!

Full-service hotels make the arrival procedure part of the guest's experience, one of many moments of truth. Several ranks of associates stand behind and give emphasis to the arrival experience (see Exhibit 8–1). Each contributes to the reception and creates a moment of truth, a separate opportunity for the hotel to excel. Initial ranks are all from the uniformed services: valet parking attendant (or airport shuttle driver); doorperson; and bellperson.

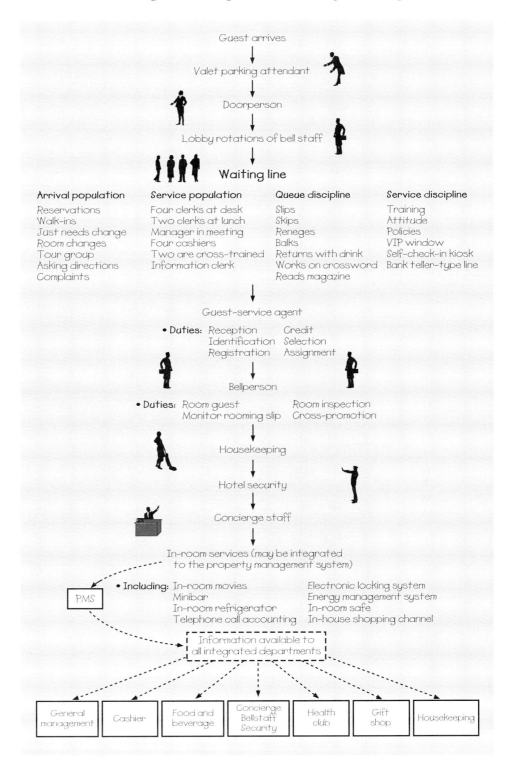

Exhibit 8-1   The arrival process is an exacting choreography of departments working together to make a seamless, positive experience for the guest. Luxury hotels add even more to this flow pattern; limited-service properties much less.

Valet Attendant.   Parking attendants greet guests arriving by private auto. If there is no door attendant, they'll open car doors, greet arrivals, and assist with luggage. Taking control of the guest's vehicle, providing a receipt, and parking the car is the essence of the job. Valet parking is both an amenity and a necessity. Center-city hotels rarely have attached parking. Space is at a premium, and self-parking can be confusing and usually unattainable for new arrivals. The parking facility may be some distance from the hotel's porte-cochère.[1] Urban hotels, including luxury properties, even lack the convenience of a porte-cochère. Instead, arrivals park temporarily on the street (see Exhibit 8–2). Street parking, even temporarily, requires a special relationship with the police department's traffic-control division.

Urban parking is a revenue center for the hotel. This is so even if the hotel does not own and operate the garage. Parking fees either offset the cost of maintaining and insuring the hotel's own garage or help pay the rent if the hotel leases space in a public facility. Public facilities are more often the case and may be privately held or city-owned. Downtown parking fees are high, sometimes greater than the room rate of hotels in small towns![2] Nightly

Exhibit 8-2   Arriving guests are met by a smiling doorperson, especially at urban properties. This doorkeeper also acts as parking attendant (note sign to the right of the entry). Without a porte cochère, guests and cabs unload on the street by the curb. The doorperson needs to juggle traffic control, guests, baggage, walk-up inquiries, taxis, and parking. *Courtesy of the Wedgewood Hotel, Vancouver, British Columbia, Canada.*

---

[1]Pōrt-kō-shār', French for coach gate. A covered drive-through on hotel property, not part of the public thoroughfare, that accommodates arrivals out of traffic and under shelter. May be heated or cooled. Porte-cochère is a modern version of the horse-and-carriage courtyard where guests disembarked within the shelter of a U-shaped inn.

[2]In 2007, hotel parking fees in New York City were $60 per night plus a $10 charge for each in-and-out time.

fees of $50 and up are added directly to the guest's folio (see Exhibit 13–1). In addition, guests often tip the valet attendants, who may need to run between the hotel and the garage.

Parking arrangements may be reversed with the parking company paying the hotel for the right to pick up guests' cars. This outside company takes responsibility, pays the insurance, and staffs the position. Hotels must be careful because the valet attendants are then the parking company's employees, not subject to hotel control. Parking contracts need thorough legal scrutiny because guests are rarely aware of this third-party intervention, especially so because charges are posted to the folio. It certainly appears to be a hotel facility. Hotels then remit collections less commission to the parking company.

Motor inns and resorts usually have ample parking and guests attend to their own vehicles. Even so, arrivals often find valet attendants at upscale properties and casino/hotels, even those with convenient on-property parking.

The Doorperson.   Door attendants produce no direct income for the hotel. Unlike parking attendants, this position falls early to the budget ax. (Many Asian hotels offer a contrasting view. Several employees staff the entryways, including some who spin the revolving doors for arriving and departing guests.) The presence of a door attendant makes a strong statement about the hotel, its concern for guests, and its level of service.

The doorperson is part concierge, part bellperson, part tour guide, part host, and part friend. Guests and nonguests alike look to this person for suggestions, directions, and advice and, not incidentally, for taxicabs.[3] They work closely with parking valets (see Exhibit 8–2). They keep the entry free of ice and snow and loiterers. They serve as an early-warning system for hotel security. Watching the comings and goings of regulars and strangers, doormen build an inner sense of who is who. Their antennae pick up the signals of something amiss, from lurking strangers or suspicious packages. Without question, doorpersons in their splendid uniforms make an impressive impact and a comforting presence at the hotel's entry.

REGISTRATION

Just as the organizational structure discussed in Chapter 3 is not applicable throughout the industry, so Exhibit 8–1's sequence of arrivals is not applicable to every property. Guests may be greeted at the curb, or not. Guests may have help with baggage to the lobby, or not. Guests may find long lines at registration, or not. Large properties such as those listed in Exhibit 1–6 staff the desk, which may be hundreds of feet long, with numerous guest-service agents (see Exhibit 8–3). Smaller properties get along nicely with one clerk (see Exhibit 3–8).

Segments of larger front desks handle arrivals and departures separately. Arriving guests are guided by one of several signs: RECEPTION, or REGISTRATION, or ARRIVALS or CHECK IN. (See Exhibit 8–3, above the desk.)

Arriving guests may or may not hold reservations. Those with reservations are handled quickly because the information is already in the computer. The guest-service agent confirms the accommodations, has the guest sign the registration card, secures a credit-card imprint, selects a room, transfers a key, and exchanges pleasantries. The entire reception is handled in a matter of minutes.

---

[3]Clubs and restaurants may make "referral" payments to taxi drivers, who share with the door-persons when tourists are directed to their properties. Many localities outlaw the practice.

Exhibit 8-3   A fully staffed front desk is needed to service this 2,884-room, 220-suite property, among the largest independent hotels in the world (see Exhibit 1–6). Waiting lines are managed, in part, by directing guests to the right line. Note the signs above the desk. *Courtesy of the Opryland Hotel, Nashville, Tennessee.*

Provided rooms are available, registration is delayed but a short time, even if the desk has no record of the reservation. Basic information needs to be recaptured as unobtrusively as possible, but there is no reason to tell the guest that the reservation is missing. Registration is handled as if the guest were a walk-in.

Guest-to-agent interaction changes dramatically when the house is full: 100% occupancy. "You mean there aren't any rooms?" Then speedy/cordial registration changes to angry/tension-filled reception. Little can be said to assuage an angry guest with a valid reservation. Guest-service agents must display great composure and immediately implement previously developed plans. Chapter 4 outlined those procedures. A quick and caring response from the hotel staff might convert a traumatic experience into a positive moment of truth.

Walk-Ins

Registering walk-ins takes more time than registering reservation-holders. Guest-service agents collect the same information from walk-ins that is captured through reservations. To make the assignment and quote a rate, the agents need to elicit the number in the party, the length of stay, and the accommodations desired.

Sales to walk-ins boost the hotel's bottom line. Walk-ins are the final tier of the yield management system. Motor hotels rely on walk-ins for a greater portion of their occupancy than do urban, commercial hotels. Yet the industry could do a better job of seizing the opportunity. The potential sale is standing in the lobby. It's not on the telephone; not on the Web; not with some third-party that takes a commission. An inviting lobby is the first means of capturing the sale (see Exhibit 8–4). A cordial, knowledgeable guest-service agent

Exhibit 8–4 An inviting lobby, which includes bellhops posted in critical locations ready to serve in any capacity, helps capture walk-in guests and helps service arriving and departing guests. Bell service is essential to this hotel because it is adjacent to Orlando's Convention Center. Rosen Hotels was the first Orlando hotel company to offer baggage delivery to and from the airport. *Courtesy of Rosen Hotels & Resorts, Orlando, Florida.*

with the right message is the second. Prompt attention to the walk-in might be the real answer. Motor-inn guests run into the lobby while the car idles, the kids fidget, and the spouse smolders. Given the right reception, these walk-ins will take the offer. Otherwise it's back to the tension in the car and another try elsewhere. Rate is a major factor in such decision. So while the motor inn's level of occupancy, its yield system, plays a role, so does the time of day and the likelihood of additional walk-ins.

Registered, Not Assigned (RNA)

Early arrivals, especially those who appear before the check-out hour, may need to wait until a departure creates a room vacancy. Waiting guests are offered baggage-check service and sometimes a complimentary beverage. The registration card is completed but marked RNA, registered but not assigned. An actual room number is assigned only after someone checks out. Even then, the guest is kept waiting until housekeeping has finished its job; the room is *on change*. Guests are never sent to unmade rooms.

Early arrivals who come after rooms have been vacated are assigned immediately, but not given the key while the room is on change. That's a slightly different procedure than the RNA. Occupancy takes place once housekeeping releases the room. Wait-time is usually less for these early arrivals.

RNAs occur when hotels are full with simultaneous arrivals and departures such as large conventions or overlapping tour groups. Busy holidays cause RNAs at resorts because arrivals like to come early and departures try to stay late. The problem is less critical at commercial hotels. Businesspersons are happy to check in, leave their luggage, and go about their workday. They return later to a room that's ready, with their baggage delivered.

Waiting for a room is a distressing experience; time ticks by so slowly. In extreme cases, guests may be roomed in accommodations that are not appropriate and moved later when the right room becomes available. Costly duplication is always avoided unless no other option is appropriate for the circumstances. Handicapped guests might warrant such an exception. Checking guests in as RNAs allows them to incur charges and use the hotel's facilities until their rooms open. Having breakfast helps pass the time.

Early Arrivals.   RNAs are not frequently used because a full house, 100% occupancy, is rare even in very good times. Furthermore, no-shows (see Chapter 4) create a mathematically full house that may still have empty rooms. Last night's no-shows are charged for rooms they never occupied. That room is ready the next morning for an early arrival.

Room charges are the real issue with early arrivals. Almost unknown a few years ago, most hotels now advertise both a check-out hour and a check-in time. Check-in times vary, but usually range between 1:00 PM and 4:00 PM. An argument could be made to merely charge the regular nightly rate to, say, an 11:00 AM arrival. Does that also hold true for a 9:00 AM arrival? or a 7:00 AM arrival if the published arrival time is, say, 3:00 PM? The answer has varied with the industry's cycle. When occupancy is low, almost anything goes. At the cycle's peak, guests can expect additional charges. Special fees such as these are examined further in Chapter 9. Exceptions to the charge are granted to members of frequent-guest programs. Crowne Plaza's Priority Club, for example, accommodates members for 7:00 AM arrivals and 3:00 PM departures.

Waiting Lines

Few check-ins occur early in the day, so the early arrivals of the previous paragraph get prompt attention. The busiest times vary with the type of hotel. Commercial arrivals peak between 4:00 PM and 7:00 PM. Their busiest check-out time is 7:00 AM to 9:00 AM.

Arriving guests want in as quickly as possible. They have waited in innumerable lines and experienced delays ranging from bad weather to lost baggage. Security travel procedures have exacerbated the experience. Frustrated with travel, some arriving guests are quick to explode. Management must forestall arrival incidents through careful scheduling and sensitive hiring. It must balance budgets and sick calls; meal times and labor laws; inexperienced agents and staff shortages. All that, while checking in thousands of arrivals across the industry one guest at a time. Several innovations have helped offset these difficulties. One technique, queuing theory, has made the wait more acceptable. Other ideas, kiosks and pods, have changed the procedure altogether.

Better Lines Through Queuing Theory.   A 20th century mathematician, A. K. Erlang, introduced a theory known as queuing ("q-ing") theory. It was quickly dubbed *waiting line theory* because of its application to customer lines at toll booths, 911 calls, traffic lights, and more. Queuing theory attempts to balance costs against waiting time. For lodging, the wait is on the telephone reservation line, the Web window, or at the registration line.

> Too much service increases operating cost;
> Too long a wait, and revenues are lost.

Hotel executives must balance the four elements of waiting lines: arrival population; service population; and queue and service disciplines (see Exhibit 8–1).

ARRIVAL POPULATION—like so many variables within lodging—varies with the type and class of hotel. Arrival configurations form around the hours of the day, the days of the week, and the months of the year. Tour and group hotels have different arrival dynamics than do motor inns or exclusive resorts. Preregistration options also impact the desk's workload; so does the hotel's size. Besides, there is no purity to "registration" lines. Some guests are waiting to ask questions; others need directions. Some are in line to complain; others need keys or mail. Many are in the check-in line in order to check out (see Exhibit 8–1).

SERVICE POPULATION is best exemplified by the number and capability of guest-service agents. Cross-trained staffers, who support the regulars as needed, improve the service dynamics. Central to this component is the blueprint of the desk. Some designs limit the ability of guest-service agents by fixing the scope of their work, either as receptionists or cashiers. Better if everyone can respond to every guest request. Further improvements result from shuffling tasks. Simple modifications of longstanding procedures can produce quick upgrades to service. Two examples: Shift stamp sales from the desk to the gift shop and install change-making machines to reduce desk traffic (and the size of front-office banks as well).

QUEUE DISCIPLINE, the behavior exhibited by waiting guests, changes waiting-line theory from a mathematical process to a behavioral one. Queue discipline considers the guest's reaction to the line itself. Some guests will balk and refuse to join the line. Some will switch multiple lines as their respective lengths change. Others will renege and drop out after waiting a while. If so, do others permit their return? and at what place? Skips and slips in the line push each member back a turn. Do guests cry "foul," rebuke the sinners and force them out? What is the line's reaction when a late arrival is served first?

Little is known about queue discipline in hotel lines; the subject needs research.

SERVICE DISCIPLINE examines employee attitudes as queue discipline does for guests. Is there a rationale for agents to service guests out of sequence? How are interruptions fielded from a "one-quick-question" interloper? Do VIPs, distinguished guests, and frequent-guest members receive special attention? Are they supposed to? Who answers the telephone? Does an agent stop servicing guests to help another agent who has problems? Many questions await management's attention.

Creative Solutions.   Check-in time might well be the guest's first encounter with the hotel and its staff. Management's failure to attend to the four parts of queuing theory creates negative moments of truth. Guests become agitated when the wait times exceed expectations. Long waits, especially when there are just a few in line, translate to a poorly run hotel in the minds of the standees. Wait time angst can be mitigated. Empty minutes flow faster when the guest's time is filled with activity—so distract and entertain! Not knowing increases frustration—so communicate the estimated length of wait, even if the wait is long.

Line management is an issue for all service businesses. Banks respond with one line; that's *queue discipline*. Grocers advertise a *service discipline* by opening new lines whenever three customers are waiting. Airlines send an agent to the rear of the line (*service population*), and restaurants solicit *arrival populations* with their "early-bird specials." Hotels have used some of these ideas and made up some of their own (see Exhibit 8–5).

The Mirage Hotel and Casino created one spectacular solution: a 20,000-gallon, saltwater aquarium behind the desk (see Exhibit 8–6). Hundreds of flashing fish and lurking sharks distract those waiting, create conversations between strangers, and serve as one of the very best solutions to the irritating queue.

Better Lines Through Innovation.   Queuing theory treats the line. Other techniques approach the problem by eliminating it. Registration can be handled on the bus from the airport with radio-assisted techniques. Or it can be done right in the lobby by catching new arrivals at the door or working the back of the registration queue. The information is captured by the computer. Guests are directed to a special desk to sign in and collect a key.

HOTELIERS MANAGE THE
DISTRESS OF LONG QUEUES WITH . . .

... Animals: household pets and exotic creatures exhibited by qualified handlers

... Interactive participation: guests decipher codes; draw graffiti; converse with robots (actors in robot dress)

... Live entertainers: comedians; jugglers; magicians; ventriloquists

... Meet the people: hotel executives; entertainers playing the hotel; mimes

... Preshows: informative videos describing the property (rooms, spas,) and events (entertainment venues and convention activities)

... Quiz shows: pose questions about the area or nonargumentive issues

... Rewards to guests: with complimentary drinks, reduced rates, or room upgrades

... Segmented queues: allow guests to see only small segments of the line in order to create an illusion of shorter lines

... Snaking the line: back on itself if lobby space allows

... Tasting: cookies, snacks, house favorites, and special wines or liquors

... Themed environment: something to see and wonder at (Exhibit 8–6)

... Time signs: estimated wait time is _____ minutes

... Video screens: entertaining video clips; national news; inhouse channel

Exhibit 8–5   Managing the line is not the critical issue that it once was. The stress of long queues has diminished as self-check-in terminals (see Exhibit 8–7), including mobile units, have gained favor with both guests and innkeepers.

Exhibit 8–6   Wait-time complaints are lessened by managing both those who wait and those who service the line. Directing the guests' attention to a 20,000-gallon saltwater spectacle with sharks circling a coral reef is memorable, whether it's for line management or word-of-mouth advertising. *Courtesy of MGM MIRAGE, Las Vegas, Nevada.*

Separating certain guests from the regular line speeds the line even as it acknowledges the special nature of those selected. Frequent-guest members, important persons, and premium corporate accounts are registered in a different area by the concierge or a hotel executive.

Registration pods don't eliminate lines, but they make the experience more cordial. Pods may actually slow the process, but they generate a less institutional feeling and create a warmer environment. Guests are more relaxed. Exhibit 3–10 illustrates the pod and reflects the more intimate nature of that arrival procedure.

Self-Check-in Kiosks.   Broad acceptance of self-check-in–check-out kiosks belies the call for more and more personal attention. Guests are happy to bypass greetings from the desk in favor of speed and efficiency (see Exhibit 8–7). Self-service check-in is viewed as a special accommodation rather than a reduction in service. Seasoned travelers see it as an extension of similar capabilities at the nation's airports. They are pleased, not displeased, to find these ATM-cousins in the lobbies of even four- and five-star hotels.

Not only does self-registration save line-waiting time, it's actually faster than a manual check-in. Estimates put self-check-in times between 30 and 45 seconds in contrast to some 210 seconds required at the desk—that is, after one finally gets there. Walk-ins require extra time to input the information, so the registration is slower. But then it also is with traditional desk registration.

The check-in kiosk is an extension of the property management system (see Exhibit 13–6). Guests select room types and rates from an online inventory of clean, ready rooms. It is the same inventory offered by the desk. Over time, the equipment has become portable and wireless. It can be located anywhere in the lobby to accommodate

Exhibit 8-7   Self-check-in, check-out terminals are in widespread use. Updated versions serve up to eight languages, accept walk-ins, reduce waiting time, and enable departing guests to print airline boarding passes. Hyatt Hotels encourages their use with 1,000 bonus points for Gold Passport® holders, Hyatt's frequent guest program. *Courtesy of NCR Corporation, Dayton, Ohio.*

large group arrivals. It can be moved to an airport baggage area to register a group while its members wait for their luggage. For security, room keys are issued later at the hotel.

Initially, self-check-in terminals required the arriving guest to hold a reservation and a payment card, either credit or debit. Newer modifications accommodate walk-ins, accept cash, and "speak" foreign languages. Newer terminals are also more consumer-friendly, activated by touch screens rather than by slower keyboards. Terminal options now go beyond check-in. They accommodate speedy check-outs, provide community information and advertise hotel services such as food and beverage.

The terminal displays an electronic map of the property showing the new arrival where to find the assigned room and where to park. Guests can opt for a different room or try for a different rate. The computer counters: It tries to upsell. A room key and a printed receipt are dispensed once the assignment is finalized. With some systems, it's a blank key card that guests swipe through an electronic key writer adjacent to the terminal. Still newer systems direct guests to use their credit cards as the key.

A full house, almost 100% occupancy, when all rooms are taken and only a few suites are available, challenges the terminal's capability. An arriving guest will not find an available room and will be referred to the desk. Rather than walk the arrival, the desk clerk will likely upgrade the reservation to one of the suites. That's not something an electronic terminal can do—not yet.

Every hotel chain has joined the trend. Hyatt Hotels has a system called *Touch and Go.* Wyndham built *AutoCheck* into its Wingate Inns. Choice Hotel's MainStay Suites, whose rates are on the high end, encourage computer check-in by providing language options and downsizing the desk. Choice's system prompts by electronic voice. It asks for the same credit card that made the reservation. Guests also supply a personal identification number (PIN), which they use thereafter to access the system.

The Registration Card

Guest-service agents greet arriving guests with pleasantries and a registration card. Like the arrival procedure itself, registration and registration cards vary little across the United States. Other countries have other requirements, however.

Registration begins with a welcome. Pleasantries are part of all desk training, but the length of the greetings varies with the volume of business. A smile and a warm welcome are delivered when other guests are waiting; longer chats are appropriate when desk traffic is slow.

Timing applies to the registration cards as well. Guests with reservations are accommodated quickly because registration cards are preprinted as part of the previous night's audit (see Chapter 13). The property management system (the computer) transferred the reservation information into the registration format (see Exhibit 8–8). Front-office clerks ask guests to scan the cards for accuracy and sign. Walk-in guests take longer because the agent must determine who the guest is and what is wanted. The new arrival then completes and signs the card.

The guest's signature is not essential for the creation of a legal guest–host relationship in common law. It is required, however, by most state laws. In contrast, other countries view the card as a police document (see Exhibit 8–9), so guests must provide a great deal of personal information. Some countries require arrivals to surrender passports to the desk. Brazil asks registering guest to furnish the names of both parents. Age, birth date, nationality and itinerary are required in many jurisdictions outside the United States.

```
2059                M/M Paul D. Ligament    6/14/      PL        RATES DO NOT INCLUDE TAXES
Room                Name                    Depart
                                                               Account # 1229821
DLX K (N/S)         Western Athletes        6/11/             Group # WA
Type                Firm or Group           Arrive

ABC                 2A/1K                                      Deposit
Clerk ID            Party


            Address        Rate Plan
                            (160)
Street 1234 Achilles Tendon Way
City/State Wounded Knee, SD 00000-0000                    ⚡ HOT WIRE HOTEL
Company Horsn Around, Inc.                                  Shocking Behavior Drive
Date Departure 6/14/                                        Electric City, Washington
Signature  Paul D. Ligament                                   77777-7777

I agree that my liability for this bill is not waived and I agree
to be held personally liable in the event that the indicated      NOTICE TO GUESTS:
person, company, or association fails to pay for the full          This hotel keeps a fireproof safe and will not
amount of the charges.                                             be responsible for money, jewelry, documents,
                                                                   or other articles of value unless placed therein.
I would like to handle my account by:                              Please lock your car.
  ☐ Cash/Check  ☐ MasterCard ☐ VISA
  ☐ Diners Club  ☒ American Express
  ☐ Discover Card
```

Exhibit 8-8   Computer-prepared registration cards speed the arrival process. Unless there are changes from the reservation, the guest merely signs in and arranges payment, a credit card usually. The guest may be asked to initial the card (PL upper center) as acknowledgement of the rate, the date of departure, and recognition of the several stipulations. They include an agreement to be responsible for the debt and an acknowledgement of the availability of a safe.

Exhibit 8-9   International registrations require a surprising amount of personal information. Age, sex, travel plans, and parent's names are questions not posed at U.S. hotels. Arrivals overseas may also be required to surrender their passports to the desk. Changes may be coming to domestic hotels if the Anti-Terrorism Act is enlarged. Currently, registration is regulated by state laws as Exhibits 8–11 and 8–12 illustrate.

Release of Registration Information. U.S. hotels may not have as much information as their foreign counterparts, but they have quite a bit. Included are names, addresses, company affiliations, times of arrivals and departures, telephone and Internet records, credit-card data and more. Guest-history and frequent-guest memberships add information about previous visits and personal preferences.

Heretofore, innkeepers have released sensitive information to federal and local authorities only by subpoena or warrant. Time-sensitive emergencies—a heart attack, for example—were exceptions, of course. The conflict that hoteliers faced—help authorities or protect guest privacy—was resolved by the 2001 Anti-Terrorism Act. The law was passed immediately after the attack on New York City's World Trade Center. Law-enforcement authorities were given streamlined procedures to access information from private entities, hotels included. Hotelkeepers who respond to the written orders are protected from litigation arising from an invasion of privacy. The dilemma for hoteliers—help authorities or preserve guest privacy—seems to have been resolved.

Contents of the Card. Exhibit 8–8 illustrates the content of a typical registration card. Readers should reference it as the discussion continues.

Name and Address. Complete name and address are needed for identification, for credit verification, for billing, and for marketing through mailing lists. The information must be legible and complete, including ZIP codes, apartment numbers, city, and state. Commercial hotels also request business affiliation, organizational title, and company address. Guest-service agents must clarify nonlegible scribbles by printing the information above the scrawl.

Greater credit can be extended when the guest's address has been verified by an exchange of reservation correspondence. Unfortunately, few hotels are actually doing that. Whereas those intent on fraud use false addresses, including vacant lots and temporary box numbers, honest guests who inadvertently leave unpaid folios can be traced and billed.

Number in the Party. Although not always, the number of persons in the room generally determines the rate to be charged. Adults and children are identified separately, especially at American-plan and all-inclusive resorts which charge less for children. As Chapter 1 explained, the number of registered guests and the number of occupied rooms are important for statistical computations.

Room Number. Within the hotel community, guests are identified by room number. Once the registration is complete, staff members reference the room number rather than the guest's name. The room number is the major means of locating, identifying, tracking, and billing. Reservation numbers (or preassigned folio numbers) are used before the guest's arrival to locate reservations and record advance deposits. If the party is large, the "reg" card might have several room numbers. If the guests are unrelated, more than one card is used.

Date of Departure. The expected date of departure is critical to the hotel's forecasting model and its yield management system (see Chapter 5). Verifying that date is an important step in the registration procedure. This is especially true during periods of high occupancy when departures create the vacancies needed to accommodate new arrivals. Plans change; emergencies arise; business takes more or less time than anticipated. Such is the challenge of rooms forecasting. Many guests really don't know what their plans are or what they told the desk on arrival. Exhibit 8–10 illustrates one

A Vallen Corporation Property

Just a Reminder

Mr M.T.Wallet   Room *3308*

Thank you for staying with us. I hope you have had as pleasant a time with us as we have had serving you.

As you requested when your arrived, we are reminding you that tomorrow is your check-out date. Check-out time is 12 noon. The room is reserved for an arriving guest so it will not be possible to extend either the check-out hour or the day of departure.

If you need an additional time in the city, our assistant manager will be happy to help you search for accommodations nearby. All of our rooms have been reserved for tomorrow.

The assistant manager has a desk in the lobby, or call extension 123. The desk will also help with future reservations here or at another property in our group.

Joona Carr
Reservations Manager

Exhibit 8–10   Check-out reminders may be placed on the bed or included with folios slipped under the door (see Chapter 10) the night before the guest's anticipated departure. Reminders are used only when the hotel anticipates an overbooking the following night.

of the tools that hotels employ when they face a full house.[4] Exhibit 8–11, paragraph 72-1, is special to North Carolina. Codes in other states do not address this situation (see Exhibit 8–12).

Rate.   Room rate—the daily amount to be charged—is another line on the registration card. It is determined by the number of persons and the number of rooms recorded on the card as well as the type of room(s) assigned.

---

[4]Hotels take a large risk if they eject guests who overstay their reservations because guest stays are "indeterminable" under the legal definition of a hotel.

Affiliation, if any, is another component of rate. Corporations negotiate rates with the hotel's sale department. The desk charges the negotiated figure and tracks the number of arrivals because these special rates are based on annual sales volume. Leisure guests such as AAA and AARP members also get discounted rooms. Other "special" rate classes include the clergy, persons in uniform, and government employees traveling on business, called per-diem rates. Chapter 9 discusses rate at length.

Agent's Identification.   Registration cards always identify the guest-service agent who registered the arrival. Exhibit 8–8 illustrates this with the clerk's initials, ABC. Property management systems identify the clerk from the password used to log into the computer. Management can then return to the source if issues about courtesy, rate, or clerical questions arise later. Better still, it's used when guests compliment the agent.

Folio Number.   Guests' accounts carry identification numbers (see the upper right sides of Exhibits 10–1 and 10–2). Folios can be accessed by this ID number, by the guest's room number or, of course, by the guest's name. Sequential numbering also serves as an accounting control device when one staff member is clerk (and sells the room), cashier (and takes the money) and auditor/supervisor (prepares the control records, the night audit).

Folios and reg cards must be stored for seven years. Computerized records make that job easier because they are downloaded daily during the night audit onto disks or tapes (see Chapter 13). Everyone complies so the old files are rarely disposed of: simply forgotten after seven years and numerous staff turnovers. However, if necessary (as discussed in Release of Registration Information), computerized and numbered documents make retrieval easier.

Disclaimer of Liability.   State statutes, not federal laws, control the innkeeper's liability for guest's luggage and personal belongings. If the innkeeper meets the provision of the state's law, liability for property loss is greatly reduced. Without statutory limitations, innkeepers would be liable under common law with an open-ended amount of damages. To gain this special protection, innkeepers must inform their guests of the hotel's limited liability and do so in the manner prescribed. The "manner" is not consistent state to state (see Exhibits 8–11 and 8– 12).

Two legislative components are similar in every state: The hotel must maintain a safe for guest valuables and give notice of that safe (see Exhibit 8–8, lower right corner). Also, notices must be "posted," along with the excerpts of the code.[5] One invariably finds that posted notice on the inside of the guest-room door. Liability limitations have been extended by many states to include checkrooms, inroom safes, spa facilities, and goods too large to fit into the safe—salesman's samples, for example. In some states, hotels may simply refuse to accept guest valuables (see Exhibit 8–12, paragraph 509.111).

Posted notices that list the room rates (see Exhibit 8–12) contain a trap for the unwary. Hotels can put any value they want on that posting, but they exceed that amount at risk. Once a maximum rate is posted, as required by law, it is the maximum. Exceeding that figure invalidates the notice and makes the hotel liable under common law. Statutory limits are a safeguard no longer. Too frequently, old notices are left despite inflationary increases in room rates.

---

[5] "Posted" means just that. Notices laid on the bureau top—not hung, not posted—have been declared invalid and the protective dollar limits of the statutory law were lost.

Welcome to North Carolina

LAWS OF NORTH CAROLINA

LAW GOVERNING INNKEEPERS   (From General Statutes of North Carolina)

72-1. MUST FURNISH ACCOMMODATIONS: CONTRACTS FOR TERMINATION VALID. (a) Every innkeeper shall at all times provide suitable lodging accommodations for persons accepted as guests in his inn or hotel. (b) A written statement setting forth the time period during which a guest may occupy an assigned room, signed or initialed by the guest, shall be deemed a valid contract, and at the expiration of such time period the lodger may be restrained from entering and any property of the guest may be removed by the innkeeper without liability, except for damages to or loss of such property attributable to its removal.

72-2. LIABILITY FOR LOSS OF BAGGAGE. Innkeepers shall not be liable for loss, damage or destruction of the baggage or property of their guests except in case such loss, damage or destruction results from the failure of the innkeeper to exercise ordinary, proper and reasonable care in the custody of such baggage and property and in case of such loss, damage or destruction resulting from the negligence and want of care of the said innkeeper, he shall be liable to the owner of said baggage and property to an amount not exceeding one hundred dollars. Any guest may, however, at any time before a loss, damage or destruction of his property notify the innkeeper in writing that his property exceeds value the said sum of one hundred dollars, and shall upon demand of the innkeeper furnish him a list or schedule of the same with the value thereof, in which case the innkeeper shall be liable for the loss, damage or destruction of said property because of any negligence on his part, for the full value of the same. Proof of the loss of any such baggage, except in case of damage or destruction by fire, shall be prima facie evidence.

72-3. SAFE KEEPING OF VALUABLES. It shall be the duty of innkeepers, upon the request of any guest, to receive from said guest, and safely keep money, jewelry, and valuables to an amount not exceeding five hundred dollars; and no innkeeper shall be required to receive and take care of any money, jewelry or other valuables to a greater amount than five hundred dollars. No innkeeper shall be liable for the loss, damage or destruction of any money or jewels not so deposited.

72-4. LOSS BY FIRE. No innkeeper shall be liable for loss, damage, or destruction of any baggage or property caused by fire not resulting from the negligence of the innkeeper or by any other force of which the innkeeper had no control. Nothing herein contained shall enlarge the limit of the amount to which the innkeeper shall be liable as provided in preceding sections.

72-5. NEGLIGENCE OF GUESTS. Any innkeeper against whom claim is made for loss sustained by a guest may show that such loss resulted from the negligence of such guest or of his failure to comply with the reasonable and proper regulations of the inn.

72-6. COPIES OF THIS ARTICLE POSTED. Every innkeeper shall keep posted in every room of his house occupied by guests, and in the office, a printed copy of this article and of all regulations to the conduct of guests. This chapter shall not apply to the innkeepers, or their guests, where the innkeeper fails to keep such notice posted.

72-8. ADMITTANCE OF PETS TO HOTEL ROOMS. (a) Innkeepers may permit pets in rooms used for sleeping purposes and in adjoining rooms. Persons bringing pets into a room in which they are not permitted are in violation of this section and punishable according to subsection (d) of this section.

(b) Innkeepers allowing pets must post a sign measuring not less than five inches by seven inches at the place where guests register informing them pets are permitted in sleeping rooms and in adjoining rooms. If certain pets are permitted or prohibited, the sign must so state. If any pets are permitted, the innkeeper must maintain a minimum of ten percent (10%) of the sleeping rooms in the inn or hotel as rooms where pets are not permitted and the sign required by this subsection must also state that such rooms are available.

(c) All sleeping rooms in which the innkeeper permits pets must contain a sign measuring not less than five inches by seven inches, posted in a prominent place in the room, which shall be separate from the sign required by G.S. 72-6, stating that pets are permitted in the room, or whether certain pets are prohibited or permitted in the room, and stating that bringing pets into a room in which they are not permitted is a misdemeanor under North Carolina law punishable by a fine not to exceed five hundred dollars ($500.00), imprisonment not to exceed 30 days, or both.

(d) Any person violating the provisions of this section shall be guilty of a misdemeanor and upon conviction shall pay fine not to exceed five hundred dollars ($500.00) or be imprisoned for not more than 30 days, or both.

(e) The provisions of this section are not applicable to assistance dogs admitted to sleeping rooms and adjoining rooms under the provisions of Chapter 168 of the General Statutes.

Exhibit 8–11 Every state has special innkeeping laws, but many of them have been standardized (see also Exhibit 8–12). North Carolina has two unique provisions: Paragraph 72-1 requires the guest to sign or initial the check-out date; 72-8 regulates pets in guest rooms.

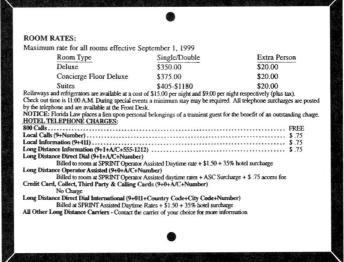

Exhibit 8-12   Posting notices about the availability of a safe and the maximum room rate are standard provisions of most state laws. Innkeepers who comply with all the provisions of the code have limited liability for the loss of guest's belongings. Limitations do not apply to harm of the guest's person. Fire-conscious states and localities also required fire-safety directions. *Courtesy of Rosen Hotels & Resorts, Orlando, Florida.*

Points of Agreement.   New legal language is being added to reg cards even as hotels work to speed up the registration process. These notices meet legal niceties, but few harried guests actually read them during registration. So hotels highlight the issues again: on rooming slips (see Exhibit 8–19); on key-card envelopes; and verbally by desk clerks.

To minimize misunderstandings, the agent repeats several facts as the registration closes. Among them are the date of departure and the room type that was just assigned. Room rates have always been high on the list of after-the-fact protests. To forestall later complaints, clerks close the registration process by circling the rate and asking the guest to initial the card (see Exhibit 8–8 with the guest's initials, *PL*). Now is the time for guests to raise issues about room charges, special rates, and ultimate liability for their bills.

Guests are expected to settle their folios at check-out time, but almost no one pays with cash. Credit cards and other third-party payers (companies, agencies, associations) are the norm. Guests assign their debts to these third-parties, but sometimes the intermediaries won't pay. Credit-card companies, for example, occasionally chargeback claims (see Chapter 11). So still another disclaimer appears on all reg cards. Arriving guests may not read the statement, but they agree to ultimate responsibility for their own folios (see Exhibit 8–8, lower left).

New social issues have added to the guest-service agents' responsibilities. Where appropriate, *Points of Agreement* have expanded to include no-smoking rooms, pets, and "green" facilities.

ASSIGNMENT

Many things are going on during registration. Exhibit 8–13 presents them in an alphabetical listing, but events do not flow in any particular order, even in the same hotel. Nor are all the items applicable to every arrival. Special handling is required for the rare due bill (advertising contract) that is presented. Travel-agency vouchers are more common, but not an everyday event. Even rates may need adjusting. Pre- and post-convention rates often differ from the convention rate. Clarification is especially needed for guests assigned to no-smoking rooms.

No-Smoking Rooms

A decade ago, no-smoking rooms were rare. Gradually, as calls for no-smoking grew, hotels set aside entire floors or wings for nonsmokers. Today, some hotels are entirely smokefree. Public contention between smokers and nonsmokers has spilled over to hotel rooms. Nonsmokers want a fresh room without the stale odor of smoke or the sweet scent used by housekeeping to mask the smell. Smokers want matches and ashtrays and less harassment. Hotels supply both, but are designating more and more rooms as nonsmoking. The issue comes to a head when space limitations require that smokers be assigned to nonsmoking rooms. The politics of smoking aside, economics is the issue for innkeepers.

Nonsmoking rooms are very expensive to reconstruct once a smoker has lit up. Wall coverings, bed linens, and carpets absorb the smoke. Opening a window—and that isn't possible in many hotel rooms—does not remedy the foul air. Smokers assigned to nonsmoking rooms must be alerted to the cost. Hotels typically add $200 or so to the folio after housekeeping alerts the desk. This contentious issue must be foreclosed by the desk clerk when a guest is assigned a nonsmoking room. Otherwise, every bit of a manager's skill will be required to answer an irate smoker who faces this hefty "fine." Guest-service agents circle the N/S letters to confirm their no-smoking discussion with the guest. Guests

---

THE STEPS IN
ARRIVAL, RECEPTION, REGISTRATION, AND ROOMING

. . .	Accommodations reviewed or revised
. . .	Anticipated departure date verified
. . .	Bellservice called
. . .	Clerks sell up
. . .	Coupons, packages, and due bills processed
. . .	Credit cards accepted and verified
. . .	Greeting, welcome and smalltalk take place
. . .	Guest is roomed
. . .	Handicapped facilities assigned
. . .	Keys and rooming slip passed
. . .	Mail and messages handed over
. . .	Names and spellings reviewed
. . .	No-smoking-room rules explained
. . .	Other hotel services highlighted
. . .	Pet registration and regulations reviewed
. . .	Rate (regular or special; full or discounted) quoted
. . .	Registration card completed
. . .	Reservation information retrieved
. . .	Room assigned is blocked from later sale
. . .	Room requests checked against available inventory
. . .	Travel agency records processed and completed
. . .	Valuables accepted for the safe
. . .	VIPs processed appropriately

Exhibit 8-13   Walking guests through the four parts of the arrival process requires a great deal of one-on-one attention. Each arrival is different, both from the guest's side and the hotel's side. Every item on this alphabetical list is not applicable to everyone and may be incomplete for others.

such as Mr. Ligament in Exhibit 8–8 initial the card for nonsmoking as well as for rate. His room assignment is a deluxe, no-smoking king (upper left on the exhibit: DLX K (N/S)).

Pets

Strangely, as the hoopla over smoking has accelerated, hotels have welcomed more pets into guest rooms. Forget the smoker–nonsmoker issue; many guests are allergic to pet dander! Pet-friendly rooms should be separated and designated with signs on corridor doors just as hotels do with no-smoking rooms. It isn't done and although hotels charge special cleaning fees, housekeeping may not expend the extra effort needed to–or know how to–desensitize the room.

Denver's most famous hotel, the Brown Palace, has had a welcoming bed and bowl for nearly a century. During that time, pet-friendly hotels have developed into a sizeable U.S. market. AAA reports that some 13,000 hotels accept pets.[6] And well they should

---

[6]*Traveling with your Pet: The AAA PetBook.*® 8th edition, 2006.

because catering to pets can be a profitable decision. A pet-friendly policy attracts not only new, human business, but also adds to the revenue stream through special pet fees. A $100 nonrefundable charge is not unusual. Then there are the extras: The Soho Grand (New York City) charges $20 for pet toothpaste and $20 more for a pet pillow! Other properties increase the animal's registration fee and then deliver pet goodies (beds, bowls, pet-walking services) without special charge.

Almost every chain has some type of pet accommodation. Loews offers "puppy pagers" to call pet owners when barking disturbs other guests. Sheraton's Four Points chain has launched a pet-friendly program. Marriott's Residence Inns and some Inter-Continental properties have joined the march. All have recommended or established rules (see Exhibit 8–14).

Pets are not welcomed everywhere. Innkeepers who are sensitive to the noise, to the appearance of unclean accommodations, and to guest allergies arrange for local pet hotels—and these are everywhere—to accommodate the animals. Only seeing-eye dogs and other animals that meet that purpose are welcomed. If the hotel has pet-designated rooms, they would be part of the assignment process, discussed next.

The Assignment Process

Each morning and throughout the day, the desk estimates the number of rooms available for sale. Reference is made to the housekeeper's report (see Exhibit 13–16) and to the dates of departure that guests furnished during registration. Obviously, last night's unoccupied rooms are available immediately. Check-outs, if they actually vacate (see Exhibit 8–10),

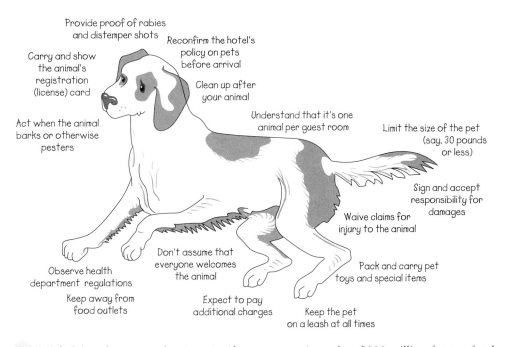

Exhibit 8-14   The pet market is a significant one, estimated at $300 million for pet food advertising alone. Petswelcome.com lists 25,000 hotels soliciting pet-owner business. Notwithstanding figures like these, there are many non–pet lovers among the industry's clientele. Established rules that are strictly enforced accommodate both groups. North Carolina's provision (see Exhibit 8–11) for guests with animal allergies strikes a balance for hotels that cater to this growing market.

become available throughout the day. Tying daily information to the hotel's historical experience for this day and date, the desk forecasts the number of walk-ins to accept. That decision is revised several times throughout the day, as Chapter 4 explained.

Matching arriving guests with the proper accommodations is what guest-service agents do best. The better the agent knows the room inventory, the better the assignment. Every room has its own features. Some have better views; some are larger. Certain rooms are noisier because they are closer to the elevator or overlook an alley. Renovations with new baths and new bedding are done floor by floor. So even rooms in the same category are not the same.

Desk clerks are not clairvoyant. They cannot know the order of arrivals relative to the order of departures. Guests are not kept waiting in the lobby for someone to vacate a particular room if other rooms are open. But there are circumstances that require the desk to assign rooms to reservation-holders who have not yet arrived.

Blocking the Room.

Rooms are *blocked*, *preassigned*, to make certain the hotel can honor special requirements. Hotels match specific rooms against pending arrivals whenever the room count is tight, as it would be with an approaching full house. Assigning specific rooms to anticipated arrivals minimizes the chance of overselling to walk-ins.

Special cases are preassigned whether the hotel is full or not. Handicapped rooms are an obvious need. Careful room managers also block early arrivals and connecting rooms. Attention is paid especially to management-made reservations and VIP arrivals. Guest-service agents also "play solitaire" with the room rack. They shift this or that room block as the arrival sequence, mixed with walk-ins and check-outs, becomes apparent. Changes are needed if an arrival comes early and the designated room has not been vacated. Or, perhaps, the arriving party is larger or smaller than the original reservation, or there's been a change in length of stay.

Constant changes to the rooms profile holds a degree of danger. Reassignments must be entered promptly into the property management system. Any delay at a busy desk, where each agent is acting independently, could cause two assignments to the same room.

Choosing—Selling—the Room.

Front-office members have an old saying: The fewer rooms available, the easier the assignment. The same is true about knowledge. The better one knows a subject, the better one deals with it. Front-office managers must be certain that agents know their products. Lessons begin with detailed floor plans that can be referenced on computer screens or printed charts. Frequent inspections of guest rooms during slow periods at the desk offer the best means of knowing the room that the agent is selling. And agents should sell rooms, not merely choose them.

Agents should sell up: Convince guests to take higher-priced rooms. Agents will upsell if they have been trained how to, if they know their products, and if there is a cash incentive system in place (see Exhibit 9–21a). Showing the room is an aid to selling it. It is an especially good technique for selling walk-ins at resorts. Prospective shoppers can be shown the actual room, or images can be displayed either at desk monitors or far earlier across the World Wide Web. Photo albums at the desk serve nicely for smaller properties that lack the technology.

Algorithms and Property Management Systems. Algorithms, a series of if–then statements, structure the property management system. Algorithms are at the core of the many computer displays that management relies upon: an over-the-credit-limit report, for example. The computer also uses this function as it searches for appropriate room assignments.

Suppose the agent is looking for a double-double assignment. The system can be programmed in several ways. One method displays a single choice, programmed into the PMS based on management's criteria. Or, at the agent's prompting, the screen displays a broader selection of ready rooms, on-change rooms, and out-of-order rooms (see Exhibit 8–15).

Without the algorithmic function, available rooms would always be displayed in sequence. In which case, the first room would most likely be sold over and over. With algorithms, management controls the display and achieves several goals. Room use is rotated equally; assignments can be concentrated on newly furnished facilities at higher rates; wings, floors, and exposures can be restricted or enlarged to save energy, reduce wear and tear, and concentrate labor.

Upgrades.   Upgrades—rooming guests in better accommodations than their rates warrant—are part of the assignment process. Members of frequent-guest programs are automatically upgraded, space permitting. "Space permitting" is the operative term for all upgrades: Better rooms have to be available. Business guests from companies with negotiated rates or other business relationships with the hotel get upgrades. "Regulars," guests who return on a recurring cycle, are recognized with an upgrade. Upgrades are used to settle minor complaints or to thank guests who have waited patiently in the queue.

Upgrades are automatic if no rooms are available at the rate reserved. Unless the agent can upsell to a higher rate, guests get better rooms but pay the reserved rates. Guests are always told about their upgrades. Otherwise, they will expect the same assignment on the next visit. These guests may be moved to the original rate on the following day, "space permitting," but only if the rate spread is huge or the better facilities are essential for new arrivals. Guests are not moved if their stay is brief. Moving is costly to both the guest and the hotel. Sometimes the move is made while the guest is away. At least two individuals (a bellperson and a supervisor from some other department) inventory the guest's belongings, pack them up, and move them to the new assignment. There are no happy road warriors then. Moving is bad enough; worse if it's done while one is away; unacceptable if done without the guest's knowledge.

VIPs are almost always upgraded, and often comped.

VIPs.   Hotels identify special reservations and registered guests by flagging them as VIPs (Very Important Persons), DGs (Distinguished Guests) or SPATT (Special Attention). STAR GUEST is also used. VIPs represent good publicity or major business for the hotel. Meeting planners, company and association presidents, and celebrities get VIP treatment. So do travel writers. Each represents some business gain for the hotel. DGs are recognized because of their accomplishments rather than their economic impact. DGs include politicians, heroes, prize-winners, and distinguished persons of every discipline.

Management walks these special arrivals to their rooms, which have been upgraded and/or comped. Registration may take place there, away from the glare of the front desk. Fruit baskets, cheese trays, and wine or champagne are awaiting the arrivals.

Did Not Stay

In very rare instances, the arriving party may register and leave immediately. Dissatisfaction with the hotel or an incident with a staff member may precipitate the hasty departure. The guest may or may not seek remedy. More likely, the hotel is not the issue. Either an emergency message is waiting at the desk or comes soon after the guest is

THE LODGE AT RIVER'S EDGE

Room Status Report

Date: 06/06/___ 10:37

Room Number	Discrpncy	Room Type	Clean Sectn	Hskpg Credits	# of Guest	Room Status	Description
102		DDSN	R1	1	0	VACANT, CLEAN	RIVER N/S CONNECT 103
103		DDSN	R1	1	2	OCCUPIED, CLEAN	RIVER N/S CONNECT 102
105		KEX	R1	1.5	0	VACANT, CLEAN	RIVER S
106		KKEX	R1	1.5	2/2	OCCUPIED, CLEAN	RIVER S
107		KN	N1	1	2	OCCUPIED, CLEAN	POOL N/S
108		DDN	N1	1	0	VACANT, DIRTY	POOL N/S
109		KK	N1	1	2	VACANT, CLEAN, BLOCKED	POOL S
110		KEX	N1	1.5	0	VACANT, CLEAN	POOL S
111		PEXN[a]	S1	2	0	VACANT, DIRTY	MTN VIEW N/S CONNECT 112
112		DDN	S1	1	0	VACANT, CLEAN	MTN VIEW N/S CONNECT 111
115		QSN	S1	1	0	VACANT, CLEAN	MTN VIEW N/S
116		DDSN	S1	1	2/3	OCCUPIED, CLEAN	MTN VIEW N/S
117		K	S1	1	3	VACANT, CLEAN, BLOCKED	MTN VIEW S
118		QS	S1	1	0	VACANT, CLEAN	MTN VIEW S
119		K	S1	1	2	VACANT, CLEAN, BLOCKED	MTN VIEW S
120		DD	S1	1	1	VACANT, CLEAN, BLOCKED	MTN VIEW S
121		PEXN	P1	2	1	OCCUPIED, CLEAN	SPA N/S
123		PEXN	P1	2	2	OCCUPIED, DIRTY	SPA S CONNECT 125
125		PEX	P1	2	1	VACANT, DIRTY, BLOCKED	SPA S CONNECT 123

MORE

Due check out: 30	Dirty: 67	Occupied: 114	Occupied/dirty: 52	Occupied/clean: 62
Blocked: 24	Clean: 193	Vacant: 146	Vacant/dirty: 15	Vacant/clean: 131

[a] PEXN indicates a no-smoking, executive parlor with a Murphy bed.

Exhibit 8–15 Computerized room-status reports can be displayed in a variety of predetermined formats. Here, the display is in room-number sequence. Other options include a listing by status (clean, vacant, occupied, etc.); by room type (double-double, connecting rooms, suites, etc.); or by other parameters (view, no-smoking, concierge floor, etc.). Rooms can be displayed in reverse numerical order to assure equal wear on all rooms.

roomed. Typically, no charge is made if check-out takes place within a reasonable time, even if the room was occupied briefly.

The completed reg card is marked DNS and given over to a supervisor. Management wants to make certain the issue does not rest with the hotel's reservation system or its employees.

Establishing Credit and Identity

Guests with reservations have already established a preliminary level of credit and identification. Both the guest-service agent and the registration card (see Exhibit 8–8, bottom left) prompt the next step by asking how the bill will be settled. Hotels, for certain, and most guests, usually, prefer a credit-card payment. Guests sometimes offer several cards. Desk clerks should take the card that charges the smallest discount (processing) fee (see Chapter 11), even if the reservation used a different card.

Credit cards help establish the guest's identity, but some jurisdictions require additional identification. Driver's licenses, passports, or state-issued ID cards are used. Required by law or not, asking for extra ID dissuades prostitutes and other undesirables. Identification is critical in case of guest injury or death, in recovering stolen items, and in collecting unpaid accounts or losses from room damage. Knowing the guest's identity facilitates the return of lost items, but *only after* the guest inquires. Lost items are never returned unsolicited!

The credit card is entered into the hotel's property management system through the credit-card terminal (see Exhibit 11–5), which reads the encoded strip. Back comes the approval (or denial) with an authorization number. Chapter 11 explains the process in detail, including the credit limits (called floors) that apply.

A small number of guests still prefer to settle with cash. In which case, the hotel offers two options. Pay in advance or provide a credit card and settle with cash at check-out. Either one works. Hotels have the legal right to collect in advance and guests may always settle with cash. Guests must understand upfront that a check, be it personal or business, is not cash.

The second option is the better one. Guests can charge services throughout the hotel when a credit card is on file. The PMS closes that option if payment is made in advance with cash. Guests cannot then charge in the dining rooms and lounges, and cannot use the room telephone for outside calls.

This cash-or-credit option is needed with other methods of payment as well. New arrivals might have prepaid the room, or paid through a travel agent, or offer a trade account, or assign the bill to a third party, say, the traveler's company. These are all acceptable billing arrangements. Still, the desk needs a credit card on file if the guest wants to charge services in other departments.

Associates throughout the hotel must be vigilant if the paid-in-advance system is to work. Guest-service agents must disconnect outgoing telephone service for paid-in-advance rooms. And cashiers in spas, restaurants, lounges, and clubhouses must use the PMS to verify the guest's status before accepting payment by signature. Without a card on file, all services must be paid in cash.

ROOMING THE GUEST

Registration and assignment completed, the new arrival is ready to be roomed. And someone from the uniformed services is standing by (see Exhibit 8–16).

Exhibit 8-16   Bellhops rotate tip-generating assignments, called fronts, in a predetermined sequence. The next front stands by the desk, close to the bellstand, ready to service the guest who has just finished registering. In some hotels, baggage (shown on the cart) is taken to the guest room via the service or rear elevator, while the guest rides the guest or front elevator. *Courtesy of the Fairmont Hotel and Tower, San Francisco, California.*

The Uniformed Services

Many guests prefer to room themselves and few hotels insist otherwise. Upscale hotels may prefer, and a few might actually require, a bellperson to accompany each new arrival. The escort handles the luggage, serves as guide, acts as host, promotes other hotel services, and makes a quick inspection of the guest room before leaving. With a bellperson present, the occasional error of sending a new arrival to an already occupied room is tempered.

Members of the bell staff are in a unique position to improve communications between management and guests. After "visiting" on the elevator and down the corridors, guests often develop a rapport with the bellhop who roomed them. Experienced bell staffers sense and respect a guest's preference for silence. But there can be a quick intimacy during the 10 or 15 minutes of the rooming process when the guest and the staff member are isolated in a one-on-one setting. Later, the staff reinforces the previous familiarity by smiling, greeting, and conversing with the guests during their stay. This guest–staff connection can serve well the hotel's quality assurance program (see Chapter 7). Serious operational problems can be forestalled if management keeps open a communication channel with the uniformed personnel.

Bellpersons are the hotel's most mobile employees. They can and should play a key role as the eyes and ears of hotel security. That's one of the advantages of outfitting the staff with inconspicuous earpieces, voice-activated mouthpieces, and attached belt packs. Wiring the crew improves communication between the desk and the individual employee wherever he or she is in the building. Several well-known companies have installed talk-about equipment as a means of improving both service and security. The Breakers, a five-star

Florida property, was one of the first. Hyatt Hotels and the Ritz-Carlton chain have been advocates as well, confident that outfitting all members of the unformed department has proven well worth the investment.

Rotation of Fronts. Bellpersons, if they exist at all, take on a variety of duties, especially in small properties. They drive the shuttle, watch for arrivals at the door, deliver room service, serve cocktails in the lobby, and relieve the desk for meals. Taking guests to their rooms—*rooming* them—remains their principal duty.

Uniformed service personnel are minimum-wage workers, but are at the top of all hotel wage-earners because gratuities—tips—comprise their main income source. They zealously guard access to that income flow by regulating turns at tip opportunities. The one who comes forward to take the key and rooming slip from the desk clerk is called the *front* (see Exhibit 8–16). Fronts rotate in turn. The one who has just completed a front is called a *last*. Lasts are assigned errands that are unlikely to produce tips. They would move luggage for lockouts and deaths or for room changes when guests are not present. They kept the lobby clean and neat.

Between the front and the last, bellhops rotate assigned positions in the lobby (see Exhibit 8–4). Each position has a purpose. The station by the entrance catches the incoming luggage of new arrivals. The elevator position assists departures and strengthens security. The belldesk might assign several posts throughout the lobby, depending on the size of the crew. Staffing requirements depend on the class of hotel. A general range of one bell position for every 40–65 estimated check-ins contrasts greatly to the 1 for 20 ratio of San Francisco's Fairmont Hotel, shown in Exhibit 8–16.

Bell service is much less formal today than it was 25 years ago. Fronts rarely need prompting with bells, hand signals, and verbal calls, "Front," that were standards a generation ago. Remote printers at the bell (captain's) desk provide the front with the arriving guest's name. Guest identity is also made from the rooming slip, discussed shortly, or even the tags on luggage. Also helping is an expected-arrivals list that was prepared during the previous night audit (see Chapter 13).

A record of fronts assures each bellperson his or her proper turn. The sequence is broken only if a guest requests a particular person, or if the next front has not returned from a previous errand. Missing turns are recovered because a record is maintained. The old pencil-and-paper journal has been replaced with a computerized record. It tracks the members of this very mobile department with times in and out, destinations, and purposes. Reference to the journal tells who was where and for how long. Each journal entry explains a bellperson's presence on a particular floor if some issue arises. Obviously, there is a role here for the talk-about equipment that was suggested previously.

Group Luggage and Other Income. Group business is important both to the hotel's bottom line and the income of the bell department. Almost universally, but especially where the hotel is unionized, each suitcase of a tour group is assessed an in-and-out fee. The charge is added to the group's master bill (see Chapter 10), collected by the hotel, and paid to the bells.

Baggage is unloaded from the bus and processed either in a group lobby or the regular reception area. Colored tags, previously fixed to the bags, help with identification throughout the tour. Each tag has the guest's number, which corresponds to that person's identity on the master rooming list (see Exhibit 8–17). Copies of that list, provided by the tour company, are distributed in advance. Numbers are used because they are easier than names to read when matching baggage with the room assigned. Another technique uses preprinted adhesive-backed tags with the name and previously assigned room number. The tag is peeled from the list and slapped onto the bag.

| HMS32G | FINNERMAN | VAIL SKI MEADOW'S LODGE | | | | | 2/05/ |
REFER #	GUEST NAME	ROOM	GROUP	ARRIVAL	DEPART	COMPANY LINE	# PERS
1	ADAMS ADAM	609	NEWMEX	2/05	2/08	NEW MEXICO ST. SKI TEAM	1
2	BURTON BOB	607	NEWMEX	2/05	2/08	NEW MEXICO ST. SKI TEAM	1
3	CURTIS CHARLES	612	NEWMEX	2/05	2/08	NEW MEXICO ST. SKI TEAM	1
4	DILARDO DALE	612	NEWMEX	2/05	2/08	NEW MEXICO ST. SKI TEAM	1
5	ELAN EVAN	616	NEWMEX	2/05	2/08	NEW MEXICO ST. SKI TEAM	1
6	FEINSTEIN FRED	613	NEWMEX	2/05	2/08	NEW MEXICO ST. SKI TEAM	1
7	GRAY GARY	604	NEWMEX	2/05	2/08	NEW MEXICO ST. SKI TEAM	1
8	HARRIS HARRY	606	NEWMEX	2/05	2/08	NEW MEXICO ST. SKI TEAM	1
9	INGOLS IAN	616	NEWMEX	2/05	2/08	NEW MEXICO ST. SKI TEAM	1
10	JEFFREYS JEFF	606	NEWMEX	2/05	2/08	NEW MEXICO ST. SKI TEAM	1
11	KASTLE KRIS	604	NEWMEX	2/05	2/08	NEW MEXICO ST. SKI TEAM	1
12	LANGE LOUIS	605	NEWMEX	2/05	2/08	NEW MEXICO ST. SKI TEAM	1
13	MORRISON MORRIS	602	NEWMEX	2/05	2/08	NEW MEXICO ST. SKI TEAM	1
14	NORDICA NEWT	605	NEWMEX	2/05	2/08	NEW MEXICO ST. SKI TEAM	1
15	OLIN ORSON	609	NEWMEX	2/05	2/08	NEW MEXICO ST. SKI TEAM	1
16	POWELL PAUL	607	NEWMEX	2/05	2/08	NEW MEXICO ST. SKI TEAM	1
17	QUAIL QUINN	618	NEWMEX	2/05	2/08	NEW MEXICO ST. SKI TEAM	1
18	ROSSIGNOL ROBERT	602	NEWMEX	2/05	2/08	NEW MEXICO ST. SKI TEAM	1
						TOTAL PEOPLE:	18

Exhibit 8–17   A group arrival list, another computer-generated report (see Exhibit 8–15), is prepared before the group arrives. The rooming arrangement is sent earlier to the hotel by the tour operator or meeting planner. The list serves the desk for individual identification because group members do not usually register individually. It serves the bell staff, which assigns the individual's reference number (extreme left column) to lobby baggage for prompt delivery to the room assigned (third column). Group arrivals are housed on the same floor close to one another to facilitate baggage handling. Back-to-back groups are assigned to the very rooms occupied by the previous group.

Baggage is moved en masse to the group's floor and delivered to each room. Hopefully, the desk has done its job by assigning rooms that are close together. Hotels that do large groups back to back use the same floors and the same rooms for successive arrivals.

Tour guests room themselves. The master rooming list has preassigned room partners using instructions from the tour operator. Envelopes, marked with room numbers and containing keys (see Exhibit 11–7) and instructions, are distributed to the tour members. Meal tickets and freebies (gaming coupons, for example) would be included. Information that would otherwise be covered during the rooming process is communicated by these instructions or orally on the bus before the group has disembarked.

Group luggage is the bell department's bread and butter. Each bag is worth between $1 and $3 each way, in and out. Payroll records reflect these in-and-out earnings because the contracts flow through the hotel's sales and accounting offices. Tips earned from other fronts are not handled by the hotel; they pass directly from the guest to the bellperson. Bells earn other incomes as well. How much, depends on the services offered and the presence of a concierge or not. Auto rental companies, event venues, and local tour operators pay commissions of 10% to 15% for business booked through the bell desk. The same arrangement may apply if the hotel sends guests' laundry and dry cleaning to an outside company. Commissions are paid to the bellcaptain, but sometimes the whole department shares. Rarely does the hotel get a cut, although it furnishes the space, the labor, and the utilities.

Rooming Slips

Through the rooming slip, the front desk communicates with the bells and the bells with the guest. Without bell service, the guest-service agent hands the rooming slip directly to the guest. With bell service, the slip passes to the guest after he or she has been roomed.

Rooming slips ask the guest to verify three bits of information: name and spelling, date of departure, and the rate. Disclaimers that appear on the registration card may be repeated on the rooming slip: the availability of a safe, for example.

The bellperson uses the slip to obtain the guest name and the room assigned, their destination. Other information may be used en route to make conversation and act as host. The guest's city or state and the weather are good starting points for welcoming the new arrival. Other nonthreatening topics are athletic events and the convention in town. Performers in the hotel or the gourmet restaurant/chef on premises are other conversational openers.

Some items that the bellperson promotes verbally may also be on the rooming slip. Whereas, foreign rooming slips contain some outside advertising, U.S. slips focus inward. They provide a range of information and product promotions (see Exhibit 8–18). Although the guest is just arriving, rooming slips include check-out instructions. Safety alerts and recreational features are highlighted and sometimes special promotional items are included.

Rooming slips have been used as identification cards. Guests are asked to show them when signing for services throughout the hotel. Color-coding the slips adds extra value. VIPs have one color, all-inclusive guests another. Different colors distinguish American-plan guests; tour-group guests; paid-in-advance guests, and so on. Both service and accounting improves when the staff knows who is who.

Informative
  Floor plan of the property
  Aerial view of the property
  Emergency and fire exits
  Telephone directory of services
  Kinds of lobby shops
  Foreign language capabilities of the staff
  Airline, taxi, and limousine telephone
    numbers
  Local sites to see and things to do
  Airport bus: times of operation and rates
  Currency exchange capabilities
  Map of the city with highway
    designations

Marketing
  List of restaurants: prices, hours of
    operation, and menu specialties
  A message of welcome or a note of
    appreciation
  WATS number for other hotels in the
    chain
  Recreational facilities: tennis, golf, pool,
    sauna
  Discount coupons to area retailers and
    attractions

Regulatory
  Check-out hour and check-in hour
  Rate of gratuity applied to the room charge
  Regulations for visitors
  Limitations on pets

Dress code
Availability of the safe for valuables
Settlement of accounts
Expectations for guaranteed reservation
  holders
Deposit of room keys when leaving the
  property
Fees for local, long distance, and 1-800
  calls
Other hotel fees and surcharges

Identification
  Clerk's identifying initials
  Identification of the party: name, number
    of persons, rate, arrival and departure
    dates
  Room number
  Key code—where room access is controlled by
    a dial system key

Instructional
  Express check-out procedure
  Electrical capacity for appliances
  What to do in case of fire
  How to secure the room
  Notification to the desk if errors exist on
    the rooming slip
  How to operate in-room movies, Internet,
    and games; their cost
  How to operate the in-room refrigerator;
    cost
  Rate of tax applied to the room charge

Exhibit 8–18   The size and content of rooming slips varies with the size and content of the hotel. Small properties provide a slip of paper and a key. Period. Large hotels, anxious to market in-house attractions, to supply safety information, and to defend against legal issues, may include all sorts of information, as this rooming slip illustrates.

The Internal Revenue Service (IRS) has given the slips an unexpected use. Service employees must report gratuities as income. To verify the accuracy of the reported figure, the IRS estimates tip income from the bell department's call book or from copies of the individual rooming slips. Reported incomes are then compared to IRS estimates. It's the same approach that the IRS uses with bars and dining-rooms. Check values provide estimated tip incomes, which are then compared to tax payments made by food-and-beverage servers.

Rooming slips range from a simple piece of paper with the basic information scribbled by hand to a full spread of facts and advertisements (see Exhibit 8–19). Management's biggest hurdle: Get the guest to read them.

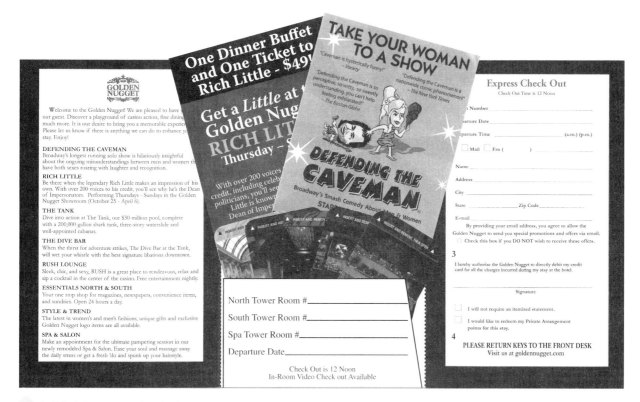

Exhibit 8–19   Example of a key envelope and welcome packet provided to arriving guests. Rooming slips are important vehicles for cross-promotions. Full-service hotels such as the Golden Nugget use the material to promote restaurants; shows; lounges and amenities, including spas, and salons, and, here, a $30 million pool. *Courtesy: Golden Nugget Hotel and Casino, Las Vegas, Nevada.*

Arriving at the Room

Registration completed, the bellperson moves toward the elevators with the guest in tow. At some locations, baggage is carried on the service (or rear) elevators while guests take the guest (or front) elevators. The party reunites on the assigned floor and proceeds to the room. Bellhops always knock on the guest-room door and announce themselves. The party enters only after a reasonable wait. Walking in on a half-clad guest is anywhere from awkward to extremely serious.

Guests precede their guide into the room. The bellperson usually blocks the automatic door with a suit case. Then he or she enters, hangs loose clothing, sets the suitcases on the baggage racks (not the bed) and checks the room. Special features such as temperature control, emergency equipment, and the minibar are explained. The room is inspected for cleanliness, towels, tissues, and hangers. Connecting rooms are unlocked if the party is taking more than one room. Unless there is a final request for service, the bellperson leaves the key and the rooming slip and accepts the proffered tip, if any, with thanks.

Hotels have gone "green," so explaining the sign on the bathroom mirror (see Exhibit 8–20) may become another commentary for the bellperson.

Exhibit 8-20   Typical notice hung on hotel doors, posted in the bath or laid under the glass on the bureau top. Some 87% of guests support "green" travel, according to the U.S. Travel Data Service. The results are good for the hotel industry as well as the public. Savings in water, detergent, energy, and housekeeping time can be traced directly to the notice.

Green Hotels

Lodging's early efforts at "greening" the industry were chiefly cosmetic. Innkeepers posted appropriate statements about saving water and the environment (see Exhibit 8–20). "Towels on the rack" and "cards on the bed linen" meant guests were willing to use both for another day. Doing both made guests feel better and produced a dollar-and-cents surprise for the hotels. Savings in water and energy were measurable.[7] These savings have been reinforced now by environmental awareness and new products. Together, they have driven lodging toward the next environmental stage. Hotels, big (such as Taj and Starwood) and small (such as Auberge and Grand Teton Lodge), have launched a range of new and real environmentally perceptive programs.

Ecotourism.   The greening of the American lodging industry is recent, but ecologically sensitive tourism, carrying an *ecotourism* label,[8] has been around for 25 years. Most of it has taken place outside the United States. Ecotourism's major attractions have been endangered animal life, rain forests, and other natural phenomena such as the Red Rock of Australia or the Karsts of China's Pearl River. Critics see successful ecotourism as an eventual failure! The more visitors participating, the faster the environment degrades. The more tourists using showers and toilets and consuming local foodstuffs, the less pristine grows the environment and the greater the need for imports. Ecotourism brings desperately needed foreign funds into economically poor locations but without care, success may destroy the very attraction. A worrisome theme of ecotourism: It is successful only so long as it doesn't succeed.

Very little of the total lodging industry is ecosensitive. Rather than selling the ecology, the industry has worked to reduce the impact of its operation on the environment. Some efforts are marginal and some are spectacular (see Exhibit 8–21).

Some Specifics.   Terminology is an important part of innovation and change. An early, but derogatory ecoterm, "tree-huggers," was replaced with "green." Green, which still carries some political baggage, has morphed to "sustainable." Whatever the term, hotels that display sensitivity to the environment have come to the attention of LEED (Leadership in Energy and Environmental Design). LEED certifies environmentally desirable buildings. To win LEED endorsements, hotels have tested and installed a range of products, including bamboo floors, bamboo sheets and towels (at twice the cost of cotton), recycled carpeting, and chemical-free cleaning supplies. And that's just the beginning of a long list.

To achieve LEED accreditation, the building must also save energy. Two of many standards are rooftops covered with sod or white reflective toppings, and windows that open. Real savings come from gadgets that turn off lights and energy when guests or employees leave an area (see Chapter 14). Equally important has been the switch to energy-efficient light bulbs. Big hotels have thousands of bulbs! An unexpected bonus comes from utilities, which rebate dollars when energy is reduced, water consumption drops, or natural landscaping replaces water-hungry grass.

Storm water and some effluent water can be biocycled for landscaping and golf courses. Where location allows, ecosensitive hotels buy power from wind- and thermal-generated

---

[7]By washing bed linens every other day, a 291-room hotel saved 6,000 gallons of water and 40 gallons of detergent each month. The program was voluntary, so the results came without the participation of every guest.

[8]The International Ecotourism Society defines ecotourism as "responsible travel to nature areas that conserve the environment and improve the well-being of local people."

Exhibit 8-21   Mandarin Oriental has 400 rooms and 227 condo units planned for MGM MIRAGE's $7 billion project called City Center. City Center (Las Vegas) boasts the largest certified LEED project (Leadership in Energy and Environmental Design) in the history of the United States. All buildings associated with this project feature low-flow water systems, energy-efficient lighting, shaded design to reduce heat, underground parking to reduce "heat island" effect, and natural gas cogeneration plants to provide 10% of the electricity and 100% of the hot water. (Sales tax relief from both the state and the county gave impetus to the project.) Mandarin Oriental, which has won awards for operating green hotels elsewhere, is a logical tenant. Shown here is the Mandarin Oriental, New York. *Courtesy: Mandarin Oriental, The Hotel Group.*

sources to provide a secondary level of support. Form turns into function when onsite thermal ponds are used for energy as well as for mud baths or landscaping.

Three components structure the greening of lodging: energy and resource management; maintenance and operations; and design and construction. Moving sustainable development from a novelty to a workable commodity requires a large commitment of capital, especially for the design and construction element. *CityCentre*, an 18-million-square-foot project, is a $7 billion venture of the MGM Mirage. The company received an unexpected surprise as it followed LEED recommendations. Initial estimates suggest that the construction costs of its green design will have an operational payback of just a few short years. Economies of scale have driven down costs as hotels and their suppliers invest in long-range planning. Innkeeping is not likely to be the leader of sustained development, but it has begun to do its share.

The new designs and exciting architecture of recently built hotels have become attractions in and of themselves. *Courtesy of the Westin Diplomat Resort & Spa, Hollywood, Florida.*

Urban hotels serve several markets, but chiefly business and convention guests. Location, location, location is critical to the commercial hotel. If not downtown—the illustration is New York City at 45th and Broadway; the hotel has 1,919 rooms—commercial hotels favor business parks or research centers. *Courtesy of New York Marriott Marquis, New York, New York.*

Resorts have expanded their markets beyond the "social guests" that persisted through the middle of the 20th century. Amenities, including executive conference centers, spas, tennis clubs, marinas, and more—even a private island—appeal to groups as well as to leisure guests. *Courtesy of the Sagamore, Bolton Landing, New York.*

Bed and breakfasts (B&B) operate under a variety of names. *B&B inns* are popular on the west coast; *Country B&Bs* are popular in New England. In between are many wonderful stopping places with award-winning breakfasts and distinctive guest rooms. *Courtesy of The Inn at 410, Flagstaff, Arizona.*

Boutique hotels, which started as a fad, have become a distinct segment of the American hotel market. They achieved this by breaking the stereotype of the chain property. This California example well represents the genre. *Courtesy of the Georgian Hotel, Santa Monica, California.*

Conference centers blend pleasant surroundings with high-tech facilities and dedicated meeting space. Hotels that compete for this market segment do so with multiuse space. *Courtesy of Barton Creek Resort, Austin, Texas.*

The versatile space of convention hotels accommodates meetings and banquets, trade shows and weddings, proms and seminars, and more, in contrast to the dedicated space of the conference center. *Courtesy of Radisson Hotel Orlando, Orlando, Florida.*

Spas are new, profitable amenities that both resort and nonresort properties have added. Modern spas no longer rely on the curative waters from which the term originated. Health, exercise, massage, diet, and stress reduction are today's attractions. This new profit center may be leased (outsourced) to third parties. Spa etiquette preserves the quiet: Cell phones are prohibited. *Courtesy of Hotel Hershey, Hershey, Pennsylvania.*

Public convention centers solicit and service trade shows whose delegates might number in the tens of thousands. What is good for the local hotel business has a major economic impact on the whole community. That value approximates $800 daily for each delegate. *Courtesy of Las Vegas Convention and Visitors Authority, Las Vegas, Nevada.*

The Sofitel is a commercial hotel that has its business center and banquet/meeting facilites on the 3rd floor. Extra elevators and an additional stairwell service the banquet floor. *Courtesy of the Sofitel Water Tower Hotel, Chicago, Illinois.*

The large square footage of all-suite facilities is appealing both to the transient traveler and to the long-stay guest to whom the concept was originally marketed. Either a fold-out chair or a sofa bed in the parlor provides extra sleeping accommodations. All-suites are the fastest growing segment of the hotel market. *Courtesy of Candlewood Hotel Company, Wichita, Kansas.*

To assure accessibility, this concierge is located in the lobby. Some hotels limit this service to concierge floors, which offer other extra services at a higher room rate. The pleasant working conditions and the aura of confident service are highlighted in this lobby photo. *Courtesy of the Wynfrey Hotel, Birmingham, Alabama.*

The once sterile and uninviting lobby has been revitalized as a dining spot and social center. Hyatt Hotels pioneered the movement with its atrium concept. *Courtesy of Hyatt Regency Atlanta, Atlanta, Georgia.*

Below is a sample reservations screen from Best Western International's proprietary Lynx reservations system (version 9.2.0). Illustrated above are reservations workstations at Best Western International's Beardsley Operations Center in Phoenix, Arizona. This is one of five international reservations centers operated by BWI. It also operates centers in Glendale, Arizona (on the campus of Glendale Community College); Dublin, Ireland; Milan, Italy; and Sydney, Australia. *Courtesy of Best Western International, Inc., Phoenix, Arizona.*

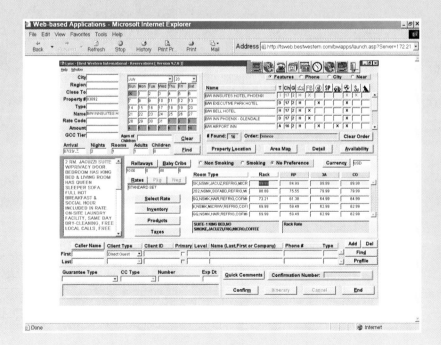

The inviting main pool of the Doubletree La Posada Resort. This three-star and three-diamond property operating in Scottsdale, Arizona, includes in its competitive set such Scottsdale properties as Hilton Scottsdale Resort and Villas, Sunburst Resort, Doubletree Paradise Valley Resort, and Millennium at McCormick. Its competitive set ranges over many square miles and includes two other properties (Hilton Scottsdale Resort and Villas and Doubletree Paradise Valley Resort) licensed by the same Hilton Hotels Corporation that licenses the Doubletree La Posada Resort! *Courtesy of Doubletree La Posada Resort, Scottsdale, Arizona.*

New attention to the hotel's basic product, the bed, has prompted a range of bedding upgrades, even a sleep concierge. *Courtesy of The Benjamin, New York, New York.*

The quality of hotel bedding has become a major advertising point as the industry recognizes the importance of sleep, and works to communicate that understanding to its guests. *Courtesy of The Benjamin, New York, New York.*

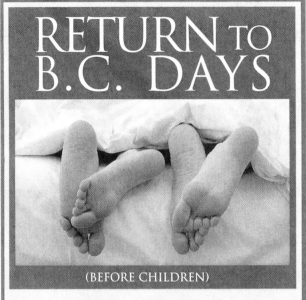

Above: example of a hotel offering both doorperson and valet parking services (note the sign to the right of the doors). At the Wedgewood Hotel, doorpersons and parking attendants are one and the same. Although most small four-diamond hotels would probably not offer both services—the Wedgewood has just 51 luxury standard and executive rooms, 34 one-bedroom suites, and 4 penthouse suites—their average rate ($220–$498) is sufficient to warrant it. *Courtesy of The Wedgewood Hotel, Vancouver, British Columbia, Canada.*

Below: The front desk of one of Orlando's busiest convention properties—The Rosen Centre Hotel. On slow check-in days, this desk works well with just one or two front-desk agents; on busy days, the desk can accommodate as many as 22 agents. Rosen Hotels & Resorts is a small chain (just seven properties, all in Orlando) with big properties (6,387 rooms in just seven hotels).

For convention business, this is one of the best places to be. Orlando's Orange County Convention Center (OCCC) boasts 1.7 million square feet of space and is ranked as one of the nation's top convention centers by *Tradeshow Weekly*. Rosen Hotels & Resorts is well positioned with major convention properties flanking both sides of the OCCC! *Courtesy of Rosen Hotels & Resorts, Orlando, Florida.*

Here's a look at the busy front desk of the Opryland Hotel in Nashville. The Opryland is among the largest independent, unaffiliated hotels in the world. It boasts 2,884 rooms, 220 suites, and over 30 specialty shops. *Courtesy of the Opryland Hotel, Nashville, Tennessee.*

The Mirage Hotel and Casino in Las Vegas takes hotel front-desk design to the extreme! Hard to grow impatient waiting in line when a 20,000 gallon saltwater tank replete with full-sized sharks circling a coral reef sits just a few yards away. *Courtesy of MGM MIRAGE, Las Vegas, Nevada.*

Advanced ATM machines offer many more features than the standard ATM cash machines, including check cashing for personal, corporate, and payroll checks with no risk to the hotel or merchant. Risks are minimized by the Mr. Payroll ATM, which uses a security system based on facial recognition. With biometrics technology, the ATM "never forgets a face." *Courtesy of Mr. Payroll Corporation, Fort Worth, Texas.*

A manual room rack, circa 1960. With one glance, the guest-service agent determines which rooms are vacant and which occupied; who the occupants are and their home towns; rates paid; arrival and anticipated departure dates. It takes several computer screens to obtain the same information. Colors furnished additional facts: members of a tour group; paid-in-advance; permanent guest and so on. (*For ease in reading, all illustrations use small dollar values, which may not seem realistic.*)

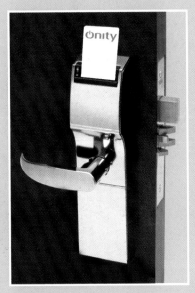

Major providers of ELSs, such as Timelox, Onity, ILCO Unican, and SAFLOK, offer automatic deadbolt features on their current systems and some even offer inexpensive upgrades to existing systems.

Cordless in-room telephones are the latest high-end guest amenity. Designed for use in high-density hotel settings where hundreds of such cordless telephones may be operating in limited transmission space, they usually offer a multitude of features. Most, for example, provide state-of-the-art channel security (to prevent crosstalk and channel-hopping), up to 10 preprogrammed guest-service buttons, three-way conference calling, volume control, base/handset message waiting, and a readily accessible data port. Teledex cordless phones (like the one displayed here) offer one additional feature, an exclusive lifetime warranty! *Courtesy of Teledex Corporation, San Jose, California.*

SUMMARY

The guest and the hotel come face to face for the first time during the arrival sequence. There's plenty of opportunity for the hotel to make an impression, good or bad, during the several parts of the arrival process, including the greeting, the registration, the assignment, and the rooming. Each of several different associates has a critical role to play. There are moments of truth for members of the uniformed services and for the desk agents who process the paperwork and the reception. Small hotels blend all these staffers into one individual, the agent.

Check-in time is a sensitive moment when the front-office staff communicates with the arriving guest in an unscripted interchange. Experienced guest-service agents balance business with reception. Some of the encounter is structured by waiting lines but long queues are disappearing as guests turn to kiosks and electronic registrations. Whatever the mechanical techniques, a great deal of information must be taken from each new arrival. Identification, preferences and needs, length of stay, and method of payment are the most critical. Guests with reservations are processed quickly because the hotel's computer has already captured most of the information. Simultaneously, the hotel needs to communicate its own information, some of which is mandated by law. During very busy times, the check-in process can be an intense several minutes. During slower times, it can be a relaxed bit of hospitality.

Many guests now room themselves. They do because it can be faster, because guests are experienced travelers, and because they prefer privacy. Property management systems have enhanced the assignment part of the arrival. The role of the bell department has withered as self-registering guests take the machine-dispensed keys and room themselves. Fewer calls for bell support has reduced the size of that staff and thus weakened the security, inspection, and reception capability of the individual hotel and the whole industry. Simultaneously, but not as a replacement, comes a new trend, sustainable development—the "greening" of the industry.

RESOURCES AND CHALLENGES
Resources

WEB SITES

http://www.greenlodgingnews.com (Division of Hasek Communications, L.L.C.)—Middleburg Heights, OH. The firm specializes in hotel public relations, but offers the industry a service through its publication about environmental issues.

http://www.ehow.com/how_1974_tip-bellhop.html (eHow, Inc)—Bellevue, WA. A Web site that attempts to explain (ehow) things. This site offers insight from actual bellhops speaking about their job functions.

http://www.passkey.com (Passkey International, Inc.)—Quincy, MA. Specializing in online group reservations and group rooming lists; an independent company working as a partner with individual hotels and chains.

http://www.petswelcome.com (Petswelcome.com, Inc.)—Referred to as "PWI." Offers a large Web site with a range of services for both the pet owner and the lodging establishment, including a "Pet Welcome Sign of Approval" logo.

Web Assignment

Reference the current Web site of *Green Lodging News* and identify two specific efforts by hotel companies to save in (1) energy and two efforts to save in (2) water. Comment in some detail about one of your picks.

INTERESTING TIDBITS

➤ Looking for a pet-friendly hotel? Sheraton's Los Angeles Airport Hotel was asked to furnish frozen rats to feed a visiting eagle as part of Alaska's tourism promotion!

➤ In 2006, Marriot Hotels and its owners followed earlier moves by other big players (Westin, for example) by banning smoking in its 2,500 hotels, about 400,000 guest rooms. The ban extends to all public spaces as well as all guests rooms. There is an immediate savings in housekeeping costs. The longer-run savings in avoiding law suits over second-hand smoke can only be guesstimated.

➤ Do Not Disturb signs hang in the inside of the guest-room corridor door until needed. Guests who want privacy move the sign to the outside knob to alert housekeeping.

Guest: (Telephoning the desk): Help! I can't get out of my room, 1422.

Desk: I don't understand, sir. What's wrong? Just open the door.

Guest: There are three doors. One opens into the bath; the second into the closet. And the third door has a "Do Not Disturb" sign hanging on it.

Challenges

TRUE/FALSE

Questions that are partially false should be marked false (F).

___ 1. "On-change" designates the 10-minute rest period that guest-service agents must take every three hours under most union contracts.

___ 2. "Upgrades" are promotions given to guest-service agents who meet specific selling targets, especially upselling higher room rates.

___ 3. Hotels have a legal right to require payment in advance whether the guest tenders a credit card or not, and whether the guest has baggage or not.

___ 4. "Rooming a guest" is the process used by the guest-service agent when assigning a room to an arriving guest who holds no reservation.

___ 5. How to register a line of dozens of group members, all arriving at the same time in the same bus, is one waiting-line issue that hoteliers have not yet solved.

PROBLEMS

1. Reorganize the following jumbled list of events, persons, and job activities into a logical flow, from start to finish, of the guest arrival process:

a. Room selection

b. Establishing guest credit

c. Registered, not assigned

d. Bellperson

e. Valet parking attendant

f. Rotation of fronts

g. Room assignment

h. Obtaining guest identification

i. Rooming slip

j. Upgrading and/or up-selling

k. Rooming the guest

l. Preblocking rooms

m. Doorperson

n. Ice bucket filled

o. Guest queue

p. Registration card signature

q. Check-out reminder

r. Room status report

s. AAA discount

t. Pet deposit

2. Foreign registration cards often require significantly more personal information than is required for domestic registration cards. Some management personnel feel that this extra data amounts to an invasion of the guest's privacy. Other managers, however, believe this extra information aids the hotel in providing better security and service levels to the guest. With whom do you side? Why might a hotel legitimately need to know your future and past destinations, your mother's maiden name, and your date of birth?

3. Intentional bias can be programmed (through computer algorithms) into the room-selection sequence of a property management system. Rooms will then appear in a prescribed order rather than in sequence or at random. Certain rooms can be offered first, or not, depending on management's criteria. Give examples explaining why management might wish to decide which rooms appear in which sequence in order to direct the clerk's selection.

4. A local merchant, whose attempts to service the hotel's guest laundry and dry cleaning business have been frustrated, visits with the new rooms manager. (The laundry of this 600-room, commercial hotel does not clean personal guest items.) The conversation makes the rooms manager realize that she has never seen commission figures on any of the reports. She learns that the bellcaptain, who doesn't seem to do any work—that is, he doesn't take fronts—gets the commissions.

The rooms manager initiates a new policy. All commissions from car rentals, bus tours, ski tickets, laundry, balloon rides, and so on, will accrue to the hotel. An unresolved issue is whether or not the money will go into the employee's welfare fund.

A very angry bellcaptain presents himself at the office of the vice president of the rooms division. Explain with whom you agree (the rooms manager or the bellcaptain) and prepare an argument to support your opinion.

5. Some hotels upgrade corporate guests to nicer rooms when space is available. Usually, the guest need not even ask for this courtesy—it is offered as standard operating procedure. Managers of such properties believe that the corporate guest appreciates the courtesy and the nicer room. And since the room is not likely to sell anyway, why not make someone happy?

The reverse side of this argument, however, suggests that the guest comes to expect this treatment and even feels slighted if only standard rooms are available. In addition, hotels that give upgrades away free are doing themselves a disservice in terms of upselling corporate guests to a higher rate. After all, why should corporate guests ever select higher-priced rooms (or concierge floor rooms) when they are given at no extra charge as a matter of standard practice? How would you respond to these arguments?

6. Ten weary, footsore travelers,
   All in a woeful plight,
   Sought shelter at a wayside inn
   One dark and stormy night.
   "Nine beds—no more," the landlord said,
   "Have I to offer you;
   To each of eight a single room,
   But number nine serves two."
   A din arose. The troubled host
   Could only scratch his head;
   For of those tired men, no two
   Could occupy one bed.
   The puzzled host was soon at ease—
   He was a clever man—
   And so to please his guests devised
   The most ingenious plan:

   | A | B | C | D | E | F | G | H | I |

   In a room marked A, two men were placed;
   The third he lodged in B.
   The fourth to C was then assigned.
   The fifth went off to D.

In E the sixth he tucked away.
    In F the seventh man;
The eighth and ninth to G and H.
    And then to A he ran.
Wherein the host, as I have said,
    Had lain two travelers by.
Then taking one—the tenth and last,
    He lodged him safe in I.
Nine single rooms—a room for each—
    Were made to serve for ten.

And this it is that puzzles me
    And many wiser men.
        —Excerpted from *Hotel
        News*, Winnipeg, 1935.

Does it also puzzle you? How was the ingenious host able to lodge ten men in only nine rooms?

AN INCIDENT IN HOTEL MANAGEMENT

Barking Up the Wrong Lobby

A friend of a registered guest met with that guest in the lobby to get money to buy theme-park tickets for the two of them. The friend—and supposed visitor—had a large dog on a leash and was feeding it dog bones. Housekeeping had called the desk earlier to report evidence (dog bones and dog hair) of animal occupation in room 606.

When the guest came to the desk for change of a large denomination bill, she was told there would be a $50 cleaning fee for the dog and an additional $40 plus tax for a second occupant of the room. She denied that the dog had been anywhere but the lobby. This was contradicted by several complaints about loud barking that the desk had received from other guests. The staff had found those entries in the log left by the night shift.

Questions: Was there a management failure here; if so, what?
    What is the hotel's immediate response (or action) to the incident?
    What further, long-run action should management take, if any?

ANSWERS TO TRUE/FALSE QUIZ

1. False. "On change" is a housekeeping term that refers to the condition of a guest room. Rooms go on-change between the time the previous guest checks out and housekeeping readies the room for the next occupant. Housekeeping notifies the desk when an on-change room goes to "ready" (for occupancy) status.

2. False. "Upgrade" refers to the quality of a room assignment made by the guest-service agent. Guests assigned to a room with a higher room rate than the guest is being charged, is said to have been "upgraded."

3. True. Under common law (traditional law based on previous court rulings) hotels may require guests to pay in advance. Statutory law (passed by a legislature) could change the common law, but that has not been so in this case.

4. False. "Rooming a guest" refers to the sequence by which a bellhop escorts a guest to, and settles the guest in, his or her room.

5. False. It need not be solved because group members do not register individually. The hotel is provided a list of roommates before the group arrives so the hotel knows the party's identity and affiliation.

The Role of the Room Rate

Outline

Room rates communicate a great deal about a hotel. Higher than average rates indicate a well-run property. One that is better than the norm because of superior service, a premium location, a newer property, or, most likely, a superior management team. It has a cadre of managers who understand the elasticity of demand within the yield management concept.

THE ROOM RATE'S IMPACT ON GUEST DEMAND

In the aftermath of September 11, 2001, the lodging industry faced a slowdown in overall travel demand. This slowdown caused a momentary reduction in the relentless growth of annual hotel room rates. According to some analysts, the industry's average room rate for 2001 was $85.38, or about 1% less than the rate experienced for the year 2000 ($86.24). The impact of 9/11/01 continued into 2002, causing the industry's annual average room rate to fall to $83.67. By 2003, however, rates were back on track and again growing faster than the nation's rate of inflation. The rate of growth in room prices has held roughly steady at 5.8% per year for more than 30 years (see Chapter 1). The average room was selling for just $17.29 in 1975. It was selling for $94.57 in 2005, 30 years later. Thirty years from now (assuming room-rate growth remains steady at 6.8% annually), the average hotel room will run about $517.26 per night!

Hotel Room Demand

Today, there are more hotel rooms available in the United States than ever before, (see Exhibit 9–1), but room demand is higher than ever before too. The result is a form of inflation—inflation at a microeconomic level, affecting just the travel industry. Inflation occurs when too many dollars are chasing too few goods. The result is a rise in consumer prices. The entire travel industry (hotels, air travel, rental cars, and restaurant meals) has experienced an inflation of prices over the past decade.

The amazing thing about the economic boom of the late 1990s, the economic slowdown in the early 2000s, and the steady economic engine (supported by stable interest rates) characterized by the years 2002–2008 is that most other industries demonstrated extremely low inflation. The national Consumer Price Index (CPI) reflected low single-digit inflation during most of these years (generally 2% to 3%). Most products, the travel industry excepted, cost little more today than they did, say, five years ago—but not so with hotel rooms. Hotel rooms represent a microcosm of the overall economy—and a unique microcosm at that.

Unique, because no matter what direction the nation's economy, room rates continue to rise. In the economic boom of the late 1990s, room rates rose because increasing room demand created upward pressure on rates. When the economy is strong, salespeople travel; companies host more lavish retreats; and conferences boast record attendance. The leisure travel market, flush with its own sense of wealth, is also traveling more.

In slower economies, as experienced in the early 2000s, there is often a different type of pressure on room rates. Faced with lower corporate profits and depressed stock prices, public hotel companies continue to push room rates as a critical means of retaining earnings even when the market seems to be slowing. How else can one account for the continued growth of room rates through the lean years?

That's the uniqueness of the situation—other industries are experiencing small price increases, while the lodging industry is averaging better than twice the national rate of inflation (see Exhibits 9–2 and 9–3). The thing about "averages," however, is that there are highs and lows. Some markets (mostly major urban areas) are seeing rate increases even higher than those described. Other markets are stagnant in terms of room rate inflation.

A Ten-Year Comparison of Hotel Company Growth: By Number of Hotel Properties			
Hotel Company	Number Hotel Properties, 2005	Number Hotel Properties, 1995	Percent Growth in Number Hotel Properties
Wyndham	6396	4208	52%
Choice	4987	3358	49%
Best Western	4097	3409	20%
Accor	3973	2265	75%
InterContinental	3532	1925	83%
Marriott	2564	874	193%
Hilton	2226	226	885%
Carlson	890	349	155%
Starwood	733	425	72%
Hyatt	355	167	113%

By Number of Hotel Rooms			
Hotel Company	Number Hotel Properties, 2005	Number Hotel Properties, 1995	Percent Growth in Number Hotel Properties
InterContinental	532,701	356,800	49%
Wyndham	520,860	413,891	26%
Marriott	469,218	184,995	154%
Accor	463,427	256,607	81%
Choice	403,806	293,706	37%
Hilton	354,312	92,452	283%
Best Western	308,131	280,144	10%
Starwood	230,667	132,477	74%
Carlson	147,093	79,482	85%
Hyatt	111,651	77,512	44%

Exhibit 9-1   At first glance, this exhibit suggests that growth in the lodging industry has been booming. It hasn't. Much of the growth listed above (Hilton grew by 283% and Marriott by 154%) has come from mergers and acquisitions, not new construction. Real growth from new construction has ranged between 1 and 1.5 percent per year, not enough to keep up with surging demand. *Source: Business Travel News.*

Competition.   Just as operating costs dictate the minimum a hotel can afford to charge, competition sets the maximum it can expect to get. External competition from neighboring facilities prescribes the general price range. Internal physical differences within the rooms determine the rate increments.

Breakdown of 2006 U.S. Corporate Per Diem Dollars

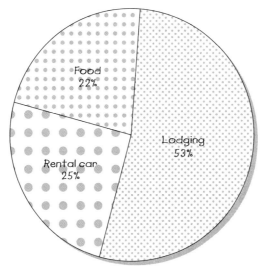

Average Daily Cost = $309.58

Exhibit 9-2   The national average daily cost of lodging, ground transportation, and food (per-diem travel costs) was $309.58 in 2006. The same national average per-diem travel costs was just $231.36 four years earlier, representing a 7.5% growth per year! *Source*: 2006 *Corporate Travel Index*, <u>Business Travel News</u>.

Supply and demand, the degree of saturation, and the extent of rate cutting in the community fix the rate parameters. Customers comparison shop, and hotel management should do the same. Differences in both the physical facilities and the range of services offered justify higher rates than the competition. The physical accommodations are easier to compare; they are there for the looking. Swimming pools, tennis courts, meeting rooms, restaurants, and lobby bars head a long list of differences that give one property a competitive advantage over its neighbor. Room size, furnishings (bed and bath types), location, and exposure further differentiate the product.

The condition of the facilities can offset their competitive advantage. "Clean and neat" sends an important subliminal message. Hotels with burnt-out bulbs in exterior signage, wilted flowers in the planters, and litter at the entry lose out to hotels with lesser facilities that look fresh and new.

Differences in service are more difficult to discern, but they add to the room rate as substantially as other components. Twenty-four-hour room service, pool guard on duty, and an extensive training program for employees begin another, less visible list of competitive advantages. Like capital outlays for physical accommodations, these costs must be recaptured in the room rate as well.

Room Rate Elasticity.   Elasticity is defined as the change in demand (rooms sold) resulting from a change in price (room rates). If demand increases with a drop in price (or decreases when price is raised), demand is elastic. If demand appears unaffected by drops or increases in price, demand is inelastic. Hotel room rate reductions in an elastic market generate new business (higher occupancy). Hotel room rate reductions in an inelastic market generate little or no new business.

The hotel industry has always believed that reductions in rate produce less new revenue than is lost from lowering the unit price. This suggests that room demand is

City	Lodging	Rental Car	Food	Total
New York	$504.50	$117.25	$99.53	$721.28
Boston	$296.93	$103.47	$81.56	$481.96
Washington, D.C.	$274.61	$103.83	$85.09	$463.53
San Francisco	$276.85	$79.98	$79.40	$436.23
Philadelphia	$259.56	$90.22	$67.49	$417.27
Newark, NJ	$229.02	$114.73	$72.87	$416.62
Honolulu	$258.91	$77.87	$79.43	$416.21
San Diego	$258.28	$72.25	$71.91	$402.44
New Orleans	$242.76	$79.37	$73.29	$395.42
Las Vegas	$236.79	$75.10	$70.77	$382.66
Miami	$219.35	$79.38	$80.57	$379.30
Fort Lauderdale	$195.36	$89.96	$84.80	$370.12

Nation's Dozen Most Expensive Travel Cities in Terms of 2006 U.S. Corporate Per-Diem Dollars

Exhibit 9-3   In 2006, 86 of the nation's top 100 cities saw per-diem rates above $250. Five years before (2001), just 16 of the top 100 cities were above the $250 threshold. By the way, the least expensive city in the nation's top 100 is Akron, Ohio, where lodging ($106.63), rental car ($59.11), and food ($46.73) total just $212.47 per day. *Source: 2006 Corporate Travel Index, Business Travel News.*

somewhat inelastic. The supposition is supported by actual experience. Room income (occupancy multiplied by average daily rate) actually rose during the low-occupancy periods of the late 1980s and again in the early 2000s. Increased room rates did not drive away significant amounts of sales (occupancy). It did not, goes the reasoning, because room demand is inelastic (see Exhibit 9–4).

Elasticity of demand for hotel rooms is complex. An inelastic property or market can actually increase rates during an economic slump with profitable results. Rate changes can be disastrous—or very beneficial—depending on the elasticity of demand for the property and market in question.

Different markets have different degrees of sensitivity. Tour properties are more elastic, and commercial demand is more inelastic. Hotels experience different degrees of elasticity throughout the year. That is what the demand pricing behind seasonal rates is all about. A given hotel may have numerous "seasons" throughout its annual cycle.

Elasticity of demand was the catalyst for major change throughout the travel industry between the 1970s and 1990s. During this period, customer profiles began to form into distinct buyer segments. The airlines—after deregulation—were the first to capitalize on the emerging distinctions between corporate travel and the leisure market. The hotel industry wasn't far behind.

This parameter shift was the beginning of a conscious attempt to segregate buyers by their price sensitivity, the concept behind yield management. Both industries discovered that demand was elastic for the leisure market and inelastic for the business segment in terms of both time and price. The group-rooms market seems to share some of the characteristics from both corporate and leisure travelers.

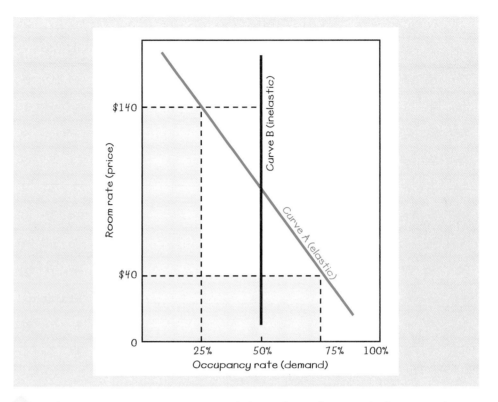

Exhibit 9-4   Curve A represents a normal elastic demand curve. The leisure market is generally considered to have elastic demand. As room rates fall, room demand from the leisure market increases. In the example diagram, when the rate is reduced from $140 to just $40, occupancy jumps from 25 percent to 75 percent. The corporate travel market, on the other hand, is considered relatively inelastic (curve B). Corporate travelers have historically been little concerned with rate, and a reduction in room price will not create much increased demand. Change may be coming, however, as corporate travelers experiment with booking the last-minute discounted rooms found on a number of Internet travel sites.

There is an art as well as a science to managing two distinct markets. Success from discounting rates for elastic (leisure) markets will not carry over to the inelastic (business) market. Similarly, leisure groups may respond positively to alternative (lower-rate) dates, that prove useless with corporate groups, who travel on a need-to-go basis. Discretionary (leisure) buyers may even change location to save the lodging budget, while corporate guests are last-minute shoppers with little flexibility (see Exhibit 9–4).

Complicated as this may seem, group business adds yet another dimension. Price sensitive tour groups take on the characteristics of the leisure segment—elastic in terms of rate, flexible with regard to date. Conventions, trade shows, conferences, and corporate retreats generally demonstrate the characteristics of the corporate market—inelastic with regard to rate, inflexible in terms of dates. But even an inelastic market becomes elastic at some point. There may be little or no difference in corporate occupancy when the rate fluctuates between $80 and $160. But if the rate becomes too high, say $260, some sensitivity will result. A growing trend—corporate guests finding last-minute bargains via Internet travel sites—is adding a new twist to the old formula.

Elasticity of Lodging Taxes.   One rate component over which hotel managers have little or no control is local lodging taxes. Also known as bed, room, or hotel taxes, these guest charges often provide significant revenues for the local municipality (see Exhibit 9–5). Operating with increasingly tight budgets, cities are lured into the easy money available from taxing out-of-towners. After all, it appears politically correct to increase the tax revenue base without actually raising the taxes charged to local citizens.

But the reality of the situation is not so straightforward. Several concerns are not apparent initially. First is the ethical debate. Antagonists of the hotel tax believe it is wrong to charge out-of-town visitors for city services that are not tourism related. How does one justify a bed tax that's earmarked for new schools and local sports complexes (as shown in Exhibit 9–5)? The visitor clearly does not benefit from the taxes paid—it is taxation without representation.

Studies have demonstrated that an increased lodging tax may actually hurt the local economy. More revenue may be lost in other taxes than is actually gained in room tax. For example, at one time, New York City had the highest lodging tax in the United

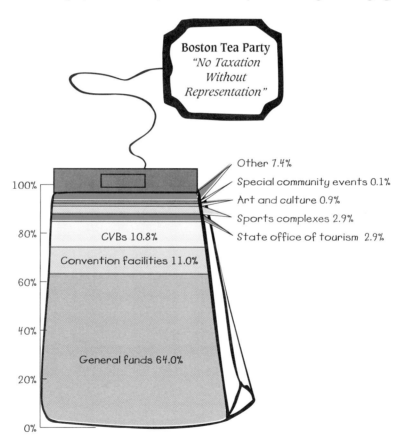

How Travel-Related Sales Taxes Are Used

Exhibit 9-5   Someday, tourists may complain "No taxation without representation" as loudly as at the Boston Tea Party. That's because travel-related taxes generate about $11 billion a year for local municipalities. Yet little of these visitor-paid taxes find their way into improved tourist-related facilities (see the illustration). The bulk of lodging tax revenues is deposited into community general funds and then used for urban projects with little or no relation to tourism (maintaining a prison, as is the case in Phoenix!).

States (an effective 21.25% rate). In large part because of this tax, the city suffered a decrease in convention business by as much as 30%. With 30% fewer convention visitors, that was 30% fewer purchases of souvenirs, arts and crafts, meals and drinks, clothing, and related purchases. Each of these purchases generated revenue sales tax in its own right. The increase in the lodging tax decreased related sales tax revenues for New York City. Today, New York City's lodging tax (13.25% + $2 per night) doesn't even rank in the top five U.S. cities (see Exhibit 9–6).

Taxing Demand. Although the individual traveler rarely considers the rate of local taxes, group business has become increasingly conscious of this vexing premium. Carefully negotiated group rates seem purposeless and inconsequential if the city then slaps an additional 15% to 20% levy on rates that have been shaved by just five to ten dollars. Bed taxes have become deterrents to the marketing efforts of numerous convention and visitor bureaus. Taxes in the 10% to 12% range seem acceptable to most consumers. Rates above 14% meet resistance among some groups and associations. Yet, Washington, D.C., Houston, and San Antonio—well recognized destinations for groups—struggle with room taxes close to 17% or higher (see Exhibit 9–6).

The trend may be changing. Hotel managers are battling rising bed taxes in their cities. By forming one cohesive and vocal group, hotel managers represent a formidable opponent to city councils bent on raising the tax. It is not difficult to garner additional support from local merchants when fewer visitors come to the city.

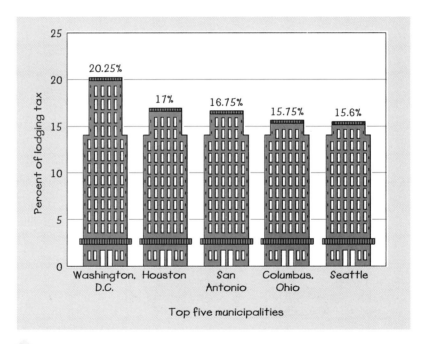

Exhibit 9-6 In rough economic times, when cities and other municipalities face budget shortfalls, hotel occupancy (lodging or bed) taxes offer an easy solution. By taxing tourists, city governments avoid the fight that would likely ensue if they raised citizens' property taxes or sales taxes.

This exhibit shows the five communities with the highest bed taxes in the United States. Across the country, the average lodging tax is 11.65%. High tax rates, yes, but not as bad as many foreign countries—Hungary charges hotel guests some 59 separate taxes totaling a whopping 39% of the hotel bill!

To fight increasing taxation, industry associations have begun conducting research and educational campaigns aimed at local politicians. This research has generated some interesting findings. Twenty-five years ago, total room taxes (state and local sales and bed taxes) were just 3% to 4% of the room charge. Today, the national average is 11.65%—a threefold increase (see Exhibit 9–6). The rise in bed taxes may be the highest increase in taxation of any industry in the United States, except possibly the gaming industry. The lodging industry pays about twice the tax rate imposed on most other goods and services.

Looking at 50 destinations around the globe, the World Tourism Organization (WTO) concluded, "taxes on tourism are proliferating ... in some cases they can stifle tourism and cause a net loss in revenues for a destination." According to the WTO, roughly 73% of the destinations studied had raised tourism-related taxes over the past several years. Indeed, governments are finding creative ways to levy new taxes against tourists—more than 40 different kinds of taxes were identified, including many new ones (environmental taxes) that had never before existed.

Similar research by the American Hotel Foundation discovered that an increase in the bed tax has negative repercussions on rooms demand. Elastic rooms demand declines when the total room rate including tax increases. A decrease in rooms demand doesn't just affect the hotel industry. A hypothetical 2% increase in the lodging tax results in a 5.1% reduction in room sales and associated visitor spending.

Dynamic Pricing in Negotiated Coroporate Rates. Corporate travel managers often negotiate favorable rates for their corporate travelers. Hotels have been willing to lock down fixed, discounted rates with corporate buyers, because the corporation promises to use the hotel. Sometimes the corporation even guarantees the hotel a certain number of room nights for the coming year.

The corporation likes the arrangement as well. Not only does the company receive guaranteed access to hotel rooms, but the fixed rate makes the job of budgeting annual travel expenses much easier for the corporate travel manager. The fixed rate is especially desirable during busy times when the hotel—through its revenue management system—is quoting rates substantially higher than the norm.

The status quo is about to change, however. Hotel chains are adopting new dynamic pricing strategies. Dynamic pricing differs from the traditional approach. The negotiated corporate rate is no longer a fixed, flat annual rate. Rather, dynamic pricing provides the corporate traveler a negotiated discount from prevailing rates. During normal business periods, the discount rates provide corporate travelers the same price they've come to expect from the hotel. But during high-demand periods, when the revenue management system drives rates to new highs, the corporate traveler's discounted rate is calculated against the higher prevailing rate. This provides a higher net rate to the hotel and leaves the corporate travel manager perplexed in terms of how to establish an annual travel budget (see Exhibit 9–7).

Some of the questions corporate travel managers are asking about dynamic pricing include:

➤ Will the dynamic pricing discount include all room types in the hotel(s)?

➤ Will the discount apply across all expenses for the trip, including breakfast, Internet access, telephone calls, etc.?

➤ Will the rate fluctuate by night for a multinight stay?

➤ Will there be a floor or ceiling limiting how low or high the rate can fluctuate?

Hotel Companies Interested in Establishing Dynamic Pricing Contracts	Percentage of Travel Managers Asked by the Hotel Company
Hilton	12
Marriott	12
Starwood	10
Hyatt	6
InterContinental	5
Radisson	5
Four Seasons	3
Loews	3
Omni	3
Ritz-Carlton	2

Exhibit 9-7   Dynamic pricing, though still in its infancy, is destined to become the norm in a few years. Travel managers are facing more requests from hotels in key cities to establish dynamic pricing contracts rather than fixed negotiated rates. This exhibit looks at a recent survey where travel managers were asked which hotel chains had requested dynamic pricing deals with their companies. Some 24 percent of all travel managers who responded to the survey said they had been asked by at least one chain to establish a dynamic pricing arrangement. *Source: Mastering T&E Expense Management.*

Discounts off Rack Rate

All hotels have a rack rate against which other pricing structures are designed (see Exhibit 9–8). A hotel's rack rate is the quoted, published rate that is theoretically charged to full-paying customers. The rack rate is the full retail rate. However, just as customers rarely pay the sticker price for a brand-new automobile, guests rarely pay the rack rate for a hotel room.

Although reservationists try to offer the customer full rack rate, shrewd guests never accept it. Corporate discounts, affiliation discounts (AAA and AARP, for example), frequent-travel discounts, advanced and nonrefundable purchases, and a host of other possibilities have all combined to erode the hotel's ability to charge full price.

Proof of discounting is most evident in the average daily rate computation. Hotels with an average rack rate of, say, $78 probably never actually attain a $78 ADR. Instead, the property's ADR is a reflection of the vast discounting taking place throughout the property. Corporate meetings, tour groups, discounted transient travelers, and corporate guests negatively affect the hotel's ability to sell rooms at rack rate. As a result, a hotel with an average rack rate of $78 probably receives an ADR closer to $68.

The Discounting Dilemma.   In those markets where demand is strong, competing hotels continue to push rates to new ADR heights. Hotels find it easier to sell expensive rooms, and price-sensitive guests find few properties willing to bargain on rate. This is not the case in all markets. In soft markets, the industry tears down the very prices it works so hard to build. And like anything else, it is easier and faster to destroy than to build. In markets where discounting is rampant, the only sure winner is the customer who buys a quality product for a fraction of the price. If and when occupancy demand finally catches up to rooms supply, the industry finds itself dug into a deep hole. After becoming accustomed to discounted rates, customers perceive full rates as very poor value.

Discounting Profitability.   Room discounting is designed to increase occupancy at the cost of a lowered room rate. If the resulting occupancy increase is sufficient, it covers the lost revenues from reduced rates. In such a situation, both parties are

⊟V

A Vallen Corporation Property

NO ONE CAN OFFER OUR ROOMS AT A LOWER RATE. WE GUARANTEE IT!

Next Four Month Calendars >>

MAY (Hotel A)						
S	M	T	W	T	F	S
		1 $230	2 $230	3 $260	4 $380	5 $430
6 $160	7 $230	8 $230	9 $260	10 $260	11 $270	12 $270
13 $ 90	14 $ 90	15 $230	16 $260	17 $230	18 $290	19 $390
20 $300	21 $360	22 $360	23 $300	24 $270	25 $390	26 $430
27 $280	28 $ 90	29 $ 90	30 $200	31 $200		

MAY (Hotel B)						
S	M	T	W	T	F	S
		1 $ 79	2 $ 79	3 $ 79	4 $149	5 $149
6 $ 59	7 $ 79	8 $ 79	9 $ 79	10 $ 79	11 $ 79	12 $ 79
13 $ 59	14 $ 59	15 $ 79	16 $119	17 $	18 $119	19 $149
20 $119	21 $149	22 $149	23 $149	24 $119	25 $149	26 $149
27 $119	28 $ 59	29 $ 59	30 $ 79	31 $ 79		

ARRIVAL & ROOM TYPE | Help   Rates valid for single or double occupancy.
$25.00 additional charge for each additional person.

Exhibit 9-8   In volatile markets, such as Las Vegas, rates fluctuate widely based on occupancy projections, in-house groups, citywide conventions, weather and other variables. Hotels in such markets do not print rates cards or rate brochures showing rack rates! Changes in rates are available to reservationists, guest-service agents and guests (on the Web) in configurations such as these.

Two actual properties–not identified–but of different rate classes in this competing locale illustrate the wide range of daily rates around the rack rate. Readers can test this for themselves by visiting the Web of several Vegas properties.

happy—the guest pays less for the room and the hotel makes a higher profit from having created more room demand.

However, rate discounting has a negative side as well. In fact, the whole idea of discounting rates to increase demand is somewhat suspect. Let's assume that a given hotel property was operating at an annualized occupancy of 60% with a $70 ADR. To increase occupancy, the property establishes a rate discounting program. Exhibit 9–9 shows that for this example, a 10% rate discount (second column of Exhibit 9–9) requires occupancy to rise to 66.67% in order to gross the same revenues as previously earned. That's an 11% increase in occupancy required to offset a 10% discount in price to gross the same revenues.

Rate Cutting.   According to many industry experts, there is a distinct difference between rate cutting and discounting. Rate cutting functions in an inelastic market. Unwarranted rate cuts generate new business for one property only by luring the customer away from another property. Discounting, on the other hand, attracts new customers to the industry, benefiting all properties. Discounting seeks out the stay-at-home customer, the visit-friends-or-family customer, and the let's-camp-out customer. Rate cutting aims at the guest already staying in a competitor's hotel across the street.

Competitors, who lose business, counter with rate cuts, and the price war is on. A decline in price per room and in gross sales, rather than the hoped-for increase in occupancy, is the net result. Some resort localities outlaw price wars by making it a misdemeanor to post rates outside the establishment. Printed rate schedules are permitted; it is advertising on the marquee that is not allowed. Conversely, other communities actually require room rates to be posted outside the property. In such cases, the lowest and highest posted room rates on the marquee establish the rate parameters that the customer can expect to pay. This reduces the unsavory practice of "sizing up" the walk-in guest before quoting a room rate.

The long list of special rates (discussed next) proves that not all rate variations are viewed as rate cutting. The family plan, in which children staying with their parents are accommodated without charge, caused dissension when it first appeared (see Exhibit 9–13). It is today a legitimate business builder. So, too, is the free room given to convention groups for every 50 or 100 paid rooms. Like any good sales inducement, special rates should

Current Occupancy (%)	Percent of Rate Discount			
	10%	**15%**	**20%**	**25%**
50	55.56	58.82	62.5	66.67
55	61.11	64.71	68.75	73.33
60	66.67	70.59	75.00	80.00
65	72.22	76.47	81.25	86.67
70	77.78	82.35	87.5	93.33
75	83.33	88.24	93.75	100.00

Exhibit 9-9   Shown is a rate-discounting equivalency table. Figures in columns two through five (listed as 10% through 25%) reflect the new occupancy percentages required in order to produce the same gross revenues the hotel was generating before the rate discount. For example, a hotel that discounts rates by 20% must increase occupancy from its current 65% level to 81.25%, or room revenue will fall.

A well-known comment from Randy Smith, founder and chairman of Smith Travel Research, says it all: "It's starting to dawn on the industry that reducing room rates isn't going to bring more people into the market—[reducing room rates] is just stealing the existing customers from down the street."

create new sales (elasticity), not make the product available at a lower price. For once sold at a lower rate, it is almost impossible to get the buyer to pay the original price.

Examples of Discounted Rates. Discounted or special rates come in a variety of shapes and sizes. Some provide a slight discount from the rack rate, as is the 10% price reduction for AAA or AARP members. Other special rates, such as volume discounting programs and seasonal price reductions, are quite significant, reducing the posted rate up to 50%, 75%, or even more.

The list of those entitled to special rates is limited only by the imagination of the marketing department. One hotel chain has special rates for teachers, another for students. Most have discounts for senior citizens; almost all allow children in the room with their parents at no charge (see Exhibit 9–13). The *Worldwide Directory* of Holiday Inns advertises a sports rate for U.S. amateur and professional teams. Special introductory rates are a common tactic for launching a new hotel. The same tradition that gives police officers discounts in the coffee shop gives other uniformed groups such as the clergy and the military discounts off the room rack. And so the list grows.

Travel agents and travel writers usually get free accommodations while they are on familiarization (fam) trips. At other times, the special rate is a standard 50% discount, unless, of course, they come during the height of the busy season.

Hawaii's *kama'aina* rate (literally, kama means "person"; aina means "land"; translation is "native-born") is an interesting case of special rates. A class-action suit was filed by a Californian on the grounds that the 25% discount granted to Hawaiian residents was discriminatory. The argument was denied by the court. The judge found that "offering a discount to certain clients, patrons, or other customers based on an attempt to attract their business is [not] unlawful." The decision is important because it shows the other side of the issue. Rates that are raised to discourage business from certain persons might well be judged as discriminatory. Rates that are lowered to attract certain persons are viewed quite differently.

All rate discounts should be aimed at the development of new markets and should be phased out as that market stabilizes. It does not work that way in practice. Over time, many special rates become part of the established rate structure. Here are some of the more common examples of discounted rates found in most hotels:

Seasonal Rates. Posted rack rates can be changed, or they can include seasonal variations. Season and off-season rates are quoted by most resort hotels, with incremental increases and decreases coming as the season approaches and wanes (see Exhibit 9–10). The poor weekend occupancy of urban hotels has forced them to offer a seasonal rate of sorts—a discounted weekend rate.

Hotel capacity in many resort communities is vast, able to handle great numbers of tourists during periods of peak demand. Because of this glut of hotel rooms available for high-season demand, low-season rates are often deeply discounted—so steeply in fact, that many resort properties once closed their doors during low-occupancy seasons. This practice changed some 15 or 20 years ago. Today, very few resort properties actually close for the off season. The expense of reopening the facility, training and hiring new staff each year, and operating a skeleton crew to maintain the closed facility combined to change the economics of closing the property. Instead, resorts remain open, steeply discounting rooms to value-conscious guests.

Weather-Related Discounts. When it comes to negotiating group rates, even nature gets involved. A growing trend designed to reduce the length of the low or shoulder season at certain resorts is a weather discount factor. Credits or discounts against the rate are offered guests for each day it rains or stays unseasonably cool.

Nestled in the high Sonoran Desert foothills north of Scottsdale, the Boulders offers the enchantment of a dramatic location created by the forces of time. Spectacular rock outcroppings that captivate everyone who steps within their spell. Ancient saguaros silhouetted against the clear Sonoran sky. And a world-famous resort which blends so easily with nature that the local wildlife might never notice it was there.

The private country club features two 18-hole championship golf courses built right into the desert, as well as a tennis garden and the new Spa... which offers a variety of signature body treatments using the natural herbs of the desert along with a fully equipped cardiovascular and weight room, aerobics classes, and a variety of nature hikes and other stimulating programs.

Just a short stroll from the resort is el Pedregal, a festival-style marketplace of intriguing shops, restaurants, and galleries. And all around the Boulders is the enticing tranquility of the lush Sonoran Desert with its breathtaking natural views.

RESORT CASITAS

At The Boulders there's no such thing as a typical guest room. Instead there are 160 guest casitas shaped into the dramatic terrain, each decorated with natural wood and Mexican tile. Among the pleasures of these individual casitas are fully stocked mini-bars, a woodburning fireplace for cozy evenings, and a private patio or balcony overlooking the spectacular desert terrain.

CASITA DAILY RATES

Oct 1–Dec 8	$429	April 28–May 26	$495
Dec 9–25	$305	May 27–Sept 7	$205
Dec 26–31	$575	Sept 8–Dec 7	$495
Jan 1–Feb 14	$550	Dec 8–25	$290
Feb 15–April 27	$625	Dec 26–31	$575

PUEBLO VILLAS

Ideal for families or groups of friends who want to make themselves at home in a spacious setting, the Pueblo Villas offer all the same services and amenities as the casitas. Each Southwestern-style patio home features a fully-equipped kitchen, spacious dining area and living room, fireplace, private patio, laundry facilities and garage, with a choice of one, two or three bedrooms.

PUEBLO VILLA DAILY RATES

	1-Bedroom Plus Den	2-Bedroom	2-Bedroom Plus Den	3-Bedroom
Oct 1–Dec 8	$515	$675	$775	$1195
Dec 9–25	$365	$480	$550	$749
Dec 26–31	$690	$902	$1040	$1450
Jan 1–Feb 14	$660	$865	$995	$1095
Feb 15–April 27	$750	$985	$1130	$1245
April 28–May 26	$595	$780	$895	$985
May 27–Sept 7	$245	$320	$370	$405
Sept 8–Dec 7	$595	$780	$900	$990
Dec 8–25	$350	$455	$525	$575
Dec 26–31	$690	$905	$1040	$1145

All rates are per accommodation, subject to limited availability and do not include tax or daily service charge.

Exhibit 9-10   The Boulders Resort & Golden Door Spa in Carefree, Arizona, publishes the year's high-, mid-, and low-season rates on one brochure. (*This is not a current brochure.*) Notice the wide price disparity between seasons. Add in the fact that such hotels are often more restrictive to certain discounts during high season and less restrictive during low season, and the disparity grows even wider. To illustrate the point, a low-season Resort Casita at $290 is more than twice as expensive in high-season at $625. The disparity is even more exaggerated with Pueblo Villas (high-season 3-bedroom at $1,245 is more than three times the price of the low season's $405). *Courtesy of the Boulders Resort and Golden Door Spa, Carefree, Arizona.*

Obviously, this is risky business, and few resorts are yet offering such plans. But select Hiltons and Marriotts are currently on the bandwagon, and others are sure to follow. Indeed, at least one Marriott resort offers a "temperature guarantee" package that they have insured through Lloyd's of London!

Weekly Rates.   Weekly rates, which are less than seven times the daily rate, are offered occasionally. Improved forecasting and increased revenues in all the other departments compensate for the reduction in room revenue.

Both the daily rate—assume $170—and the weekly rate—assume $1,050—are documented by the clerk. The $170 rate is charged daily until the final day, when a $30 charge is posted. In this way, the daily charge is earned until the guest meets the weekly commitment. If one-seventh of the weekly charge were posted daily, the hotel would be at a disadvantage whenever the guest left before the week was up, as frequently happens. One variation on weekly rates leaves the daily rate intact but discounts services such as valet, laundry, and greens fees.

Corporate Rates.   America's corporations do a great deal of business with the nation's hotels. Corporations and hotel chains are synergetic. Corporations have offices and plants worldwide. Employees at all levels (management, personnel, sales, engineering, accounting) travel in vast numbers. They visit the very countries and cities in which the hotel chains have opened their properties worldwide. The synergism works when the employees of a certain corporation stay in the hotels of a given chain. By guaranteeing a number of room-nights per year, the corporation negotiates a better rate, a corporate rate, from the hotel chain.

Reducing room rates is only part of the discount. Reducing the number of rooms needed to close the deal is a more subtle form of discounting. Not many years ago, corporate rates required 1,000 room-nights per year. Recent figures place the level as low as 50 for some chains. The figures were pushed lower by the appearance of third-party negotiators. Corporations with numbers too small to negotiate on their own can be included under the umbrella of room consolidators: Third-party volume buyers who are in no business other than negotiating discounts with hotels (and airlines) represented numerous companies. Hotels have responded by dealing directly with the smaller corporate accounts, bypassing the travel agents and the consolidators.

Technology has altered the corporate discount picture as well. In the past, major corporations negotiated favorable rates by promising a large annual room volume with a given chain. However, no one really counted, and room volume (actual or anticipated) was never verified. With the increasing sophistication of CRS systems, most major hotel chains are now able to track accurately a corporation's total room volume chainwide. Corporate room activity at franchised properties, parent properties, and through the CRS are all combined into a quarterly volume report. Renaissance Hotels, for example, produces quarterly reports for more than 1,800 of its major corporate accounts. These reports take the guesswork out of room rate negotiations and give both the hotel chain and the corporation an accurate picture of utilized volume.

Commercial Rates.   Commercial rates are the small hotel's answer to corporate rates. Without the global chain's size to negotiate national corporate contracts, smaller hotels make arrangements with small commercial clients. Such understandings might account for 5 or 10 room-nights per year for a manufacturer's representative or salesperson traveling on a personal expense account.

Under the commercial rate plan, a standard low rate is negotiated for the year. This standard rate provides the commercial guest with two advantages. First, the rate is guaranteed. Even during periods of high occupancy, most small hotels honor the commercial rate. Second, when demand is mild, the commercial guest is granted an upgraded accommodation at no additional charge. This small courtesy costs the hotel nothing, yet generates substantial loyalty on the part of the guest. Few hotels actually distinguish between corporate and commercial rates. The two terms are effectively synonymous.

Government Per-Diems. Federal, state, and local governments reimburse traveling employees up to a fixed dollar amount. This per-diem (per day) cap is made up of two parts: room and meals (and may include a third component—car rental). Reimbursement is made on the actual cost of the room (a receipt is required) but no more than the maximum. Anyone traveling on government business is reluctant to pay more than the per-diem room allowance, since the agency will not reimburse the excess. Meal reimbursement is a given number of dollars per day and generally requires no receipts (see Exhibits 9–2, 9–3, and 9–11).

 GSA   **U.S. General Services Administration**

Domestic Per-diem Rates
Utah-FY 07

(October 1, 2006 through September 30, 2007)

Cities not appearing below may be located within a county for which rates are listed. To determine what county a city is located in, click here for the National Association of Counties (NACO) website (a non-federal website).

NOTE: If neither the city nor the county is listed, the location is a standard CONUS destination with a rate of $60.00 for lodging and $39.00 for meals and incidental expenses (M&IE).

State Tax Rates & Exemption Forms
Properties at Per-Diem (FedRooms)

Primary Destination (1)	County (2,3)	Max Lodging (exc. taxes)	+	M & IE Rate	=	Max Per-Diem Rate (4)	First & Last Day (72% if M&IE)
Ogden	Weber	61		44		105	33.0
Park City (October 1 - November 30)	Summit	68		64		132	48.0
Park City (December 1 - March 31)	Summit	135		64		199	48.0
Park City (April 1 - September 31)	Summit	68		64		132	48.0
Provo	Utah	69		49		118	36.75
Salt Lake City	Salt Lake And Tooele	90		54		144	40.5

Exhibit 9–11A   The General Services Administration (GSA) of the U.S. government prints annual per-diem tables for official travel within CONUS (Continental United States). Annual adjustments are made to per-diem rates each October. The state of Utah is shown as an example.

Major cities and counties are listed. Travel in the rest of the state uses the standard CONUS destination per-diem rate. Per-diem travel is broken into two components; maximimum allowed lodging (must provide a receipt), and meals and incidental expenses (M&IE) paid at a flat daily rate (no receipt required). Note that the first and last day of travel pays only 75% of the M&IE. See www.gsa.gov for more information. *Source: GSA, Washington, D.C.*

Key cities, those with higher costs of living, are given higher caps (see Exhibit 9–11). The General Services Administration (GSA) of the federal government publishes the per-diem rates that apply to federal employees. The distinct market segment covers all federal civilian employees, military personnel, and recently, cost-reimbursed federal contractors.

Difficulties may arise when the per-diem guest encounters the desk. Some chains accept the government rates, but individual properties may not. And if they do, the yield management decision may reject these heavily discounted rates for that particular period. Moreover, since per-diems, like some other special rates, are on a space-available basis, some central reservations systems will not quote the rate for confirmation. *Space available* means that rooms are not confirmed until close to the date of arrival. Over all these hurdles, the guest must then prove per-diem entitlement. Without a standardized form, letter, or procedure, the individual room clerk makes a discretionary call based on whatever evidence the guest can provide.

In recent years, a controversial repeal of a previously mandated government regulation has left the lodging industry wondering what is fair in terms of per-diem rates. The debate revolves around the Hotel and Motel Fire Safety Act of 1990. This act was proposed after a U.S. Treasury agent perished in a fire at the Dupont Plaza Hotel in San Juan, Puerto Rico, on New Year's Eve 1986.

Per-Diem Footnotes

1. Unless otherwise specified, the per-diem locality is defined as "all locations within, or entirely surrounded by, the corporate limits of the key city, including independent entities located within those boundaries."

2. Per-diem localities with county definitions shall include "all locations within, or entirely surrounded by, the corporate limits of the key city as well as the boundaries of the listed counties, including independent entities located within the boundaries of the key city and the listed counties (unless otherwise listed separately)."

3. When a military installation or Government-related facility (whether or not specifically named) is located partially within more than one city or county boundary, the applicable per-diem rate for the entire installation or facility is the higher of the two rates which apply to the cities and/or counties, even though part(s) of such activities may be located outside the defined per-diem locality.

4. Federal agencies may submit a request to GSA for review of the costs covered by per-diem in a particular city or area where the standard CONUS rate applies when travel to that location is repetitive or on a continuing basis and travelers' experiences indicate that the prescribed rate is inadequate. Other per-diem localities listed in this appendix will be reviewed on an annual basis by GSA to determine whether rates are adequate. Requests for per-diem rate adjustments shall be submitted by the agency headquarters office to the General Services Administration, Office of Governmentwide Policy, Attn: Travel Management Policy Division (MTT), Washington, DC 20405. Agencies should submit their request to GSA no later than 12/31 for the city to be included in the annual review. Agencies should designate an individual responsible for reviewing, coordinating, and submitting to GSA any requests from bureaus or sub-agencies. Requests for rate adjustments shall include a city designation, a description of the surrounding location involved (county or other defined area), and a recommended rate supported by a statement explaining the circumstances that cause the existing rate to be inadequate. The request also must contain an estimate of the annual number of trips to the location, the average duration of such trips, and the primary purpose of travel to the location.

Exhibit 9–11   *(continued)*

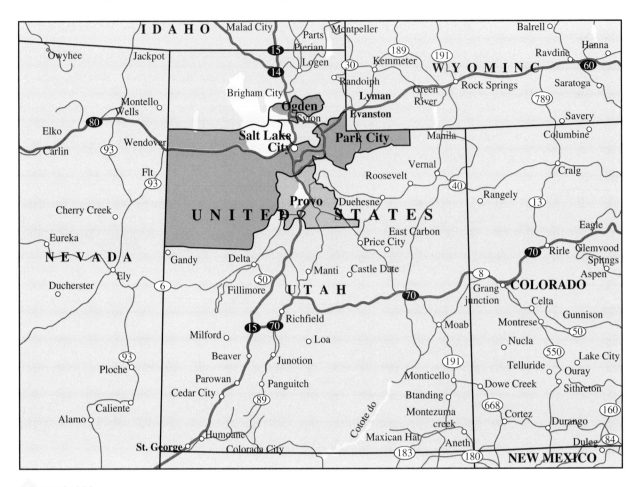

Exhibit 9–11B

In an effort to protect government employees traveling on business, the 1990 act mandated that hotels must comply with certain smoke detector and sprinkler regulations if they wished to sell rooms to government employees traveling on per-diem. Complying with this act cost the lodging industry over $1.2 billion per year! Some 17,000 hotels and motels across the country (about 38% of all hotel and motel rooms nationwide) complied with the Fire Safety Act.

These hotels made the fire safety investment because they believed that compliant properties would be the only ones allowed a piece of the lucrative government market. In late 1996, however, the government—just as it was about to begin auditing all hotels to verify their compliance with the act—pulled the plug on the policy by removing the audit requirement. Today, hotels are still urged to provide adequate fire safety protection, but the government is not auditing their actual compliance—a move that has been deemed unfair by the thousands of hotels who spent billions of dollars bringing their fire safety systems up to code in the early 1990s.

Employee Courtesy Rates. Most hotel chains extend special rates to their employees when they travel within the chain. Indeed, for the large chains, this is actually a market segment. Substantial discounts from the hotel's minimum rate plus upgrade whenever possible result in a very attractive bargain. Special rates are always provided on a space-available basis. Employee-guests are accepted only if rooms are vacant when they present themselves (some chains allow reservations a few weeks before arrival if projected occupancy is below 75% or so). The Federal Deficit Reduction Law of 1984 reinforced this by taxing the employee for the value of any free room if paying guests were turned away.

Offering complimentary or discounted employee rooms is an inexpensive way for chains to supplement their employee benefits packages. Because such rooms are provided on a space-available basis, there is little associated cost (aside from housekeeping) to providing the employee a free or deeply discounted rate. And many chains find some real benefits in increased morale and motivation as employees take advantage of the chain's discounted rooms.

In fact, some chains actually listen to their employees. They request visiting employees to fill out evaluation forms complete with comments and suggestions for improvement. If carefully monitored and tracked, such a "secret shopper" program can have enormous advantages to the chain.

It Pays to Pay Rack Rate.   Although not really a discount, some upscale chains are experimenting with added perks for guests who actually pay full rack rate. The perks include such valuable amenities as free use of a cellular telephone, limousine service to the airport and nearby shopping, free dry cleaning, and even free food items. Several Ritz-Carlton properties allow full rack–rate guests an extended check out until 6 PM. Four Seasons hotels give deluxe accommodations (a free upgrade) to rack rate guests.

Senior Citizen Rates.   Every 7 seconds, another person reaches age 50. There will be close to 100 million Americans over the age of 50 by the year 2010. In addition to these age-related statistics, it is important to note that senior citizens (defined as 50-plus years of age by some organizations) represent the fastest-growing travel market.

Although seniors are by no means a homogeneous group, they have certain features and expectations in common. First, people over the age of 50 are the best money savers in the world. As such, when they travel (and they love to travel), they're careful with money. They try to find travel bargains, and they can find them, because they have such flexible travel schedules.

When asked about their preferences, seniors listed discounted buffet breakfasts, complimentary newspapers, and free cable television as their top lodging amenities. They also seem to appreciate hotels where grandchildren stay free, low-cholesterol and low-sodium menu items are offered, bathtub grab bars are provided, and large-digit alarm clocks and telephones are available. Chains such as Ramada Inns, Howard Johnson's, and Hilton are among the leaders in marketing to senior travelers.

Infinite Other Discounts.   There are an unlimited number of additional rate discounting possibilities. Large groups such as AAA, Discover Card members, or the like no longer have a monopoly on special rates. Any sized group that can produce even a few room-nights per year is negotiating discounted rates.

One growing midsized market is bank clubs. Members of credit unions or banks and holders of numerous credit cards now find discounted rates part of their incentive package. Some of these groups charge for the service; others provide it free as a means of attracting and holding bank customers.

The Entertainment Card, Quest International and other travel clubs carry more clout today than ever before. By providing members with deep discounts (usually about half of rack rate) for traveling during off-peak periods, such clubs provide a win–win–win product. The travel club wins because it charges members a fee to join, members win by gaining access to substantial travel discounts, and hotels win when rooms fill (albeit at discounted rates) during less busy periods.

Auction Travel Sites. Auctioning is a form of discounting that has gained popularity with the individual traveler. Auctioning allows hotels, airlines, and rental car agencies to enter a product-available database marketed directly to the traveler through technology available to the average person (see Exhibit 9–12). The guest—say, Carl Jones—decides where he is traveling to, the dates and times he wishes to travel, and any specifications (must be a four-star property, a midsized car, etc.) related to the trip. He is then asked to quote his own rate!

If a hotel, airline, and/or rental car agency informs the database that this is a reasonable offer, Jones gets the deal as bid. He never knows until the offer is accepted which airline he will fly, which hotel will accommodate him, or which rental car he will drive. If the bid is too low, Jones places a time limit on his offer and waits to see

Exhibit 9-12 Since its introduction in 1998, priceline.com has become the largest online seller of hotel rooms and the leading travel service for value-conscious leisure travelers. Here is how the process works:

Every night, thousands of hotel rooms go unsold throughout the country. That's lost revenue for the hotels, and a great opportunity for priceline customers! Tell us where and when you want to go, select the hotel quality level (1–5 stars), tell us how much you want to pay, and guarantee your request with a major credit card. We'll take your offer to all the participating hotels in the city or area you select (with priceline, you'll always stay in a nationally recognized, name-brand or quality independent hotel). If your offer is accepted, we'll immediately book the room(s) you requested, at the price you want to pay! *Courtesy of priceline.com, Stamford, Connecticut.*

over the next few days whether the various travel components in question will respond favorably.

In recent years, companies such as priceline.com (see Exhibit 9–12), Bid4Travel, LuxuryLink.com, and skyauction.com (to name a few) have taken inventory auctioning to new levels (see Related Discussion in Chapter 5). By matching millions of potential buyers with millions of vacant rooms (and available rental cars, empty airline seats, etc.), travel auction companies have created a growing niche for themselves. To qualify for deep discounts, travel auction companies often require a degree of flexibility on the part of the customer (non–prime-time flight schedules and less popular travel dates are the norm). As the popularity of travel auction Web sites continues to grow, and their contribution to total rooms and other services sold continues to rise, customers will find their purchasing clout rising as well. The result will be more peak-time and high-demand travel bookings.

Complimentary Rooms. Hotel managers should be as reluctant to give away complimentary (comp) rooms as automobile sales managers are to give away free cars. But both the perishability of the room and the low variable cost of housing an occupant change this reality. Comps are used for business promotion, as charitable giveaways, and as perks.

By custom, complimentary rates are extended to other hoteliers. The courtesy is reciprocated, resulting in an industrywide fringe benefit for owners and senior managers. Such comps rarely include food or beverage (costs are too high) even in American plan hotels. As mentioned earlier, another portion of the travel industry—travel agents and travel writers—are comped during fam trips. Deregulation permitted fam trip comps by the airlines, which have now joined the hotel industry in developing site inspection tours for the travel industry.

Site inspections are also made by association executives, who are considering the property as a possible meeting place. Site visits are comped even though some association executives have been known to abuse the industry standard by using site inspection opportunities to vacation with their families. Comp rates as part of the group's meeting were discussed previously, and these are considered to be acceptable standard practice.

Comps are given to famous persons whose presence has publicity value. Comps are used as promotional tools in connection with contests in which the winners receive so many days of free accommodations. In gambling casinos, comps extend to rooms, food, beverage, and even airfare from the player's home. Parking is so difficult in Atlantic City that it too has become part of the high-roller's comp package. After all, in a brief period of table play, a high-roller can lose many times the cost of these promotions, which on close inspection prove to be surprisingly inexpensive.

Posting the Comp. Internal control of comps is crucial. The night auditor submits a report of comps granted each day and by whom. To that end, the actual room rate is recorded on the registration and marked "COMP." Daily, or at the end of the stay, the charge is removed from the folio with an allowance (see Chapter 10). Under this procedure, a daily room charge is made so that the room and the guest are both counted in the room and house counts. The total allowances at the end of the accounting period provide statement evidence of the cost of comps.

Some casino hotels have the comp paid by a paper transfer to another department (sales, casino, entertainment). The departmental manager has accountability, and the amount of comps appear on that departmental budget.

Recording no value at all is another method for handling free accommodations. No dollar value is charged each day and, therefore, no allowances are required to remove the charges. Neither is a permanent dollar record of comps available. Comps are not usually recorded in room and house counts under this procedure.

Additional Rate Factors

Not all variations to the rack rate involve discounting. Some factors actually raise the room charge to a premium level above the posted rack rate or charge additional fees of some form or another. Special, high-demand, premium dates (New Year's Eve, for example) may find rooms selling for rates substantially higher than the hotel's normal rack pricing. Likewise, many hotels charge extra for each additional guest occupying the room. Another example of room prices rising above rack rates can be found in long-term group room negotiations. When the group is contracting for rooms to be delivered years into the future, inflationary issues need to be factored into the quoted rate. Other fees or additional charges increasingly evident in the past several years are the energy surcharge, "resort charges," and other nonroom fees.

Energy, Resort Fees and Other Nonroom Surcharges.   Imagine spending several lovely days at a resort only to find at check-out a $20 per-day "resort fee" on your guest folio. "What is this fee?" you ask the cashier.

She replies, "We add that fee to each room for your convenience. It blends a number of services into one simple price for all rooms." As you wonder what kind of convenient services you're paying for, she continues, "Rather than add a daily fee for the newspaper, health club, pool towels, and energy your room used, we simply charge $20 to all rooms."

Wow. That seems a bit underhanded—and it may well be. Several states' attorneys general have examined such hidden fees and surcharges under their Deceptive and Unfair Practices Acts. In spite of the perception that these are deceptive practices, many hotels have adopted such charges in recent years.

Most hotels entered the guest-room surcharge arena with energy surcharges starting in early 2001. You may remember certain states, California especially, were hit with substantial energy price increases during the winter of 2000–2001. For many such hotels, the rapid increase in energy prices was a financial nightmare resulting in 100% and 200% increases in monthly energy expenses. The Hotel del Coronado, for example, saw its $50,000 to $60,000 monthly energy bill rise to more than $200,000 per month. As another example, the Wyndham Hotel in San Diego received a $46,000 energy bill for the month of January 2001. That was substantial when taken in context—the hotel's entire energy cost for all of 2000 was just $96,000! What else could hotels do but pass these charges onto their guests?

Wyndham responded by adding a $3.50 per room-night energy surcharge for California-based hotels and $2.50 for many other Wyndhams across the country. Similarly, Starwood Hotels & Resorts Worldwide implemented a $2 per room-night energy charge across its west coast properties. A month later, it began charging such fees across all its brands (Westin, Sheraton, Four Points, St. Regis, Luxury Collection, and W Hotels) in many of its U.S. locations. Hilton, Crowne Plaza, Holiday Inn, and other chains have similarly added energy charges to guest-room folios across the country.

The Consequences of Hidden Charges.   Hidden fees are not going away. They have become an industry staple with record revenues from surcharges and fees during each of the past several years. The industry has reported $1.6 billion in annual U.S. sales of resort fees and surcharges. Among them are:

➤ Use of the inroom safe
➤ Unlimited local calls service fee
➤ Minibar restocking fee (the minibar items aren't included; this is a fee for the labor to enter your room and restock the minibar)
➤ Swimming pool towels
➤ Swimming pool maintenance
➤ Complimentary newspaper
➤ Inroom coffee
➤ Administrative fee
➤ Cable television
➤ Internet usage
➤ Suite attendant gratuity
➤ Discretionary services fee (read: tips)
➤ Health club and/or spa access
➤ Business center usage
➤ Fax machine usage

Although fees provide a new and substantial revenue source wise hoteliers should realize that the incremental revenue does not offset the loss of customer goodwill. Complaints usually come at check-out, the last guest experience before exiting the property. Guests have become increasingly aware of these deceptive charges and vocalize their distaste by asking for them to be removed from their folios. Additionally, groups, aware of these hidden fees, ask they not be included in group rooms pricing.

After weathering a storm of lawsuits, Wyndham settled a suit in Florida, Hilton settled a suit against 11 of its resorts. Starwood was involved in a $100 million class-action suit. The industry learned how to disclose these charges legally: train employees to fully disclose, in advance of the guest's arrival, the amounts and types of resort fees and surcharges. Starwood's suit, for example, claimed that employees were misrepresenting the resort fee as a type of occupancy tax.

Imagine how guests must have reacted to a now-defunct policy at Westin Hotels & Resorts to add a dollar donation for charity to every guest's folio at check-out. Although the program was ostensibly "voluntary," many guests complained that they did not know it was being added and therefore were not able to request the dollar be removed from the folio. The campaign, Check-Out for Children, was a substantial source of revenue to UNICEF.

According to the Federal Trade Commission, mandatory fees must be disclosed at the time the room is purchased—at the time of reservation. Hotels which fail to disclose the fee in advance or which only provide information about the fee at the time of check-in are required to make such fees nonmandatory, voluntary, or "opt-in" fees. In other words, once the guest is told about the fee at check-in, the guest can decide to agree with the fee or not; to opt in if so desired. The fee cannot be charged unless the guest says "Okay."

That is how Hilton got into so much trouble with its 11 resorts several years back. Hilton charged all guests a resort fee, disclosing it at check-in (not at time of reservation) but only removing it if the guest complained. According to the Federal Trade Commission, that was an incorrect procedure, because it required the guest to "opt out," or to specifically request it not be included on the bill. That is much different from agreeing to have it placed on the bill. Opt-out fees are considered mandatory, and therefore must be disclosed at the time of reservation. It is too late for the consumer to make an informed purchase decision when standing at the desk for check-in.

Double Occupancy.   Double occupancy refers to the use of the room by a second guest. Traditional rules increased the single-occupancy rate by a factor (normally not twice) whenever the room was double-occupied. Today one rate for one or two persons is used just as frequently because the major costs of a hotel room are fixed (debt service, taxes, depreciation). Having a second or third occupant adds relatively few incremental costs (linen, soap, tissue). As such, one charge for both single and double occupancy is the norm in higher-end properties.

Convention rates are almost always negotiated with double occupancy at no extra charge. The more persons in the hotel, the more the hotel benefits from sales in other departments: banquet, bar, casino. Suite charges have also followed that pattern. The room rate is the number of rooms that comprise the suite, not the number of guests who occupy it. The room, not the guest, becomes the unit of pricing.

Several arguments support the movement toward a single room price (see Exhibit 9–13). The fewer the rate options, the less the confusion, and the more rapidly the telephone reservationist can close the sale. Price is a critical issue in package plans or tour bookings, and rates can be shaved closely because the second occupant represents a small additional expense. A third occupant adds a still smaller incremental cost. The incremental cost is almost unnoticed if the extra person(s) share existing beds. That is what makes family-plan rates attractive. An extra charge is levied if a rollaway bed, which requires additional handling and linen, is required. Suite hotels are popular because the extra hide-a-bed is permanently available as a sofa bed in the room.

With rollaway beds, the used bed is returned to the housekeeping office, where linens are changed and the bed is stored for its next use. With sofa beds, however, the housekeeping department must remember to look at the sofa bed linens after each guest check-out. Guests often use sofa beds during their stay and then fold the sofa bed back up before check-out as a means of straightening the room and creating more floor space. Without careful followthrough by housekeeping, new guests find the sofa bed has been used previously.

Unless the family-rate plan has been quoted, a charge is generally made for the third and subsequent occupants to a room. Even in hotels where single and double occupancy is charged the same rate, a third or fourth guest often pays an additional fee. Usually, that added charge is a flat fee—say, $20 per extra person.

Many hoteliers find a flat $20 fee illogical in light of the numerous room types available at the property. Where $20 may be fine for a $100 standard room, it does not seem high enough for a $150 deluxe or a $200 executive parlor. Indeed, if the hotelier can make the argument that we charge for extra guests because they cost the hotel incremental expenses, that argument is doubly true in premium rooms.

In a standard room, extra guests cost the hotel in a variety of ways, including extra water and electricity, additional amenities, more towels and linens, and of course some wear and tear. These costs are not identical from a standard room to a deluxe accommodation. Hotels outfit deluxe rooms with larger bathtubs, more expensive personal amenities, heavier-quality linens, and higher-quality furnishings. An additional person in a deluxe room has a higher incremental cost to the hotel than does an additional person in a standard room.

A flat $20 rate represents a declining percentage of the rate as the quality of the room increases. In the $100 standard, $20 reflects a 20% surcharge. Yet in the $200 executive parlor, $20 reflects only a 10% surcharge. If the $100 standard guest is willing to pay

Controversy is growing among American hotelmen about the family rate plan method of basing hotel rates upon occupancy by adults only. Children of 14 years or less, accompanying their parents, are not charged for occupancy of rooms with their parents. For example, one adult and a child are charged a single rate for the double occupancy of the room. Two adults and children are charged a double rate for a room, or two single rates if two rooms are engaged. There are various other modifications of the plan, but fundamentally it represents complimentary accommodation of children below a certain age level.

At least three leading hotel chains have adopted the plan and report great success from the higher occupancy attributable to it. Why, then, the controversy? Certainly when hotel chains of the stature of the Statler, Eppley, and Pick chains favor the family rate plan, it is well on its way to becoming a standard practice for most other hotels in the country.

The controversy rests on the issue of whether this plan is a form of rate cutting—the most disagreeable word in the hotelman's language. In this era of downward adjustment from high wartime levels of occupancy, naturally hotelmen are sensitive to any indirect methods of reducing rates. No hotelman wishes to see any kind of repetition of the rate-cutting practices of the 1930s.

In an attempt to evaluate the plan in its rate-cutting connotation, we believe that most hotelmen would be hardpressed to define a rate cut in exact terms. For example, is the commercial rate to traveling men a type of rate reduction? Does a convention rate involve a hidden discount? We can remember the time when it was standard practice to compliment the wife of a traveling man, when a week's stay at a hotel resulted in having the seventh day free of charge, and when the armed forces, clergy, and diplomats got lower rates.

In our opinion, rate cutting is practiced only when hotels depart from their *regular* prices and tariff schedules in order to secure patronage from prospects who are openly shopping for the best deal in room rates. If, therefore, it is regular practice for hotels to have special rates for group business, this does not seem to represent rate cutting; and the same principle should apply to the family rate plan. If this plan becomes widely adopted—as seems very likely—then it falls into the category of any other special type of rate for special business.

In some respects the plan is a form of *pricing accommodations by rooms instead of by persons*. In many resort hotels a room is rated regardless of its occupancy by one or two persons, and a similar concept is used in apartments and apartment hotels.

Although the arguments for or against the family rate plan must be decided by hotelmen themselves, a strong point in favor of the plan is found in its adoption by other vendors of public service—the railroads and airlines. Family rates, weekday rates, seasonal rates, special-type carrier rates, etc., have been in vogue for several years. If the hotels adopt the family rate plan, it seems that they will be falling into line with a national trend rather than venturing alone into a new and untried experiment in good public relations.

Exhibit 9–13   A circa-1958 article discusses the controversy surrounding the family-rate plan. The article states "the plan is a form of pricing accommodations by rooms instead of by persons." Note in the third paragraph that rate-cutting (i.e., discounting) is referred to as "the most disagreeable word in the hotelman's language." Also note the names of old chains that are no longer in business. *Source: The Horwath Hotel Accountant.*

$20 for an extra occupant, the $200 executive-parlor guest should be willing to pay, say, $40 for an extra guest.

Time is Money

While the actual date of arrival and departure is the primary consideration for establishing the guest charge, the number of hours of occupancy may someday play more of a role in rate determination than it does today.

Arrival Time.   The day of arrival is listed on the reservation, the registration card, and the guest folio. The exact time of arrival is also indicated on the folio by means of an internal electronic clock operating in the property management system.

The time of arrival is more critical to the American plan hotel, where billing is partially based on meals taken, than to the European plan operation. American plan arrivals are flagged with a special meal code.

The hour of arrival at a European plan hotel is less critical. An occasional complaint about the promptness of message service or a rare police inquiry might involve the arrival hour. Very, very late arrivals, such as a guest who arrives at 5 AM, are the exceptions. Somewhere in the early morning hours (5 to 7 AM) comes the break between charging for the night just passed and levying the first charge for the day just starting.

Check-in hours are difficult to control, although most hotels have established check-in hours. The termination point of a night's lodging is more controllable, so every hotel posts an official check-out hour (see Exhibit 9–14).

Departure Time.   Check-in and check-out hours are eased or enforced as occupancies fall or rise. Setting the specific check-out hour is left to each hotel. The

CHECK-OUT TIME: 1 PM

We would like to ask your cooperation in checking out by 1 PM so that we may accommodate travelers who are beginning their stay. If you require additional time, you may request a two-hour grace period (until 3 PM) from the assistant manager or the front-office manager. If you wish to check out later, we regret that there must be a $12-per-hour charge, from 3 until 5 PM, for this added service. An additional half-day rate will be charged to guests who delay their departure until between 5 PM and 8 PM. After 8 PM, a full-day rate will be charged. Of course, you are then welcome to remain until the following afternoon at 1 PM.

As an incoming guest, your comfort and convenience depend on these stipulations. We hope you will visit again soon.

□V
A Vallen Corporation Property

Exhibit 9–14   Permanent night-stand tent card left in each guest room. Many hotels place a similar statement on the registration card.

proper hour is a balance between the guest's need to complete his or her business and the hotel's need to clean and prepare the room for the next patron.

Seasoned travelers are well aware that check-out extensions are granted by the room clerk if occupancy is light. Under current billing practices, the effort should be made cheerfully whenever the request can be accommodated. If anticipated arrivals require enforcement of the check-out hour, luggage should be stored in the checkroom for the guest's convenience.

Resorts are under more pressure than commercial hotels to expedite check-outs. Vacationing guests try to squeeze the most from their holiday time. American-plan houses usually allow the guest to remain through the luncheon hour and a reasonable time thereafter if the meal is part of the rate. Some 90% of the resorts surveyed in an AH&LA study identified their check-out hour to be between noon and 2 PM, in contrast to the 11 AM through 1 PM range used by transient hotels. These same properties assigned new arrivals on a "when-available" basis.

Special techniques in addition to that shown in Exhibit 9–14 have been tried to move the guest along. On the night before departure, the room clerk, the assistant manager, or the concierge calls the room to chat and remind the guest of tomorrow's departure. Even today, this task could be assigned to a computer. A more personal touch is a note of farewell left by the room attendant who turns down the bed the night before. A less personal touch can be seen in Exhibit 9–15.

The 24-Hour Stay.   Recently, some hotels have been experimenting with true 24-hour stays. There is no official check-in time and no posted check-out hour. Rather, guests explain their travel plans at the time of reservation and identify their estimated times of arrival and departure. They are then welcome to stay at the hotel an entire 24-hour period for one set room rate.

To qualify for these 24-hour programs, guests make advance reservations and identify their estimated hours of arrival and departure at the time they make the reservation. Additionally, guests must pay rack rate—discounted packages do not qualify for the 24-hour programs. Rate/time programs such as these are most likely found at airport properties. Guest arrivals (and departures) are predicated on flight schedules. A hotel that will accommodate guests' unique 24-hour stays may develop a favorable reputation and earn higher market share.

It makes sense to view these 24-hour day programs as marketing tools. They drive higher rates and hopefully attract unique customer segments who appreciate the unusual policy. Today, these programs are viewed as marketing "gimmicks," but so are any policies that differentiate a hotel from its competitor. Only time will tell if these programs are ushering in a new era of room pricing.

Incentive Rate Systems.   Incentive rate systems have been suggested as a means of expediting check outs. First, the check-out period for a normal day's charge would be established—say, between 11 AM and 1 PM. Guests who leave before 11 AM are charged less than the standard rate, and those who remain beyond 1 PM are charged more. Flexible charges of this type require a new look at the unit of service, shifting from the more traditional measure of a night's lodging to smaller blocks of time.

Unlike other service industries, hotels have given little consideration to time as a factor in rate. Arrival and departure times establish broad parameters at best. We can expect these to narrow as hotelkeepers become more concerned with the role of time in rate structuring. Taken to the other extreme, it is conceivable that the hour will eventually become the basic unit for constructing room rates. Under current practices, a stay of several hours costs as much as a full day's stay (see Exhibit 9–16).

Recently, while staying at one of the San Antonio Marriotts, I had occasion to make this request. I would be in meetings all morning, and I wasn't scheduled to leave until 3 PM. I figured I could have lunch, go back to my room and dig out my winter coat and boots, then check out.

The night before I was to leave, I made my request. The clerk asked me what time I wanted to check out. "Three o'clock," I answered.

"You can stay until three, but we'll charge you for a half-day," he said.

At first, I was stunned by the sheer greed this response implied. When I recovered, I asked whether this was an arbitrary decision on his part or a policy of the hotel.

"It's our policy," he said, defensively.

"Is it a *new* policy?" I responded, trying to keep a smile on my face, "because I've never heard of such a thing."

"No, it's not new, and I don't know what kind of hotels you've been staying in, but it's very common."

First deny my simple request, then try a subtle insult. Good thinking.

This kind of treatment would probably have bothered me in any hotel, but it seemed terribly out of place at a hotel with an otherwise extraordinarily friendly and accommodating staff.

The next day, I visited the front desk, posed the same request—hypothetically—to a different employee, and asked how he would handle it. He said he would ask how late, check to see if the room was booked, and possibly okay it based on whatever information he got from the reservations system. If he wasn't sure, he would check with someone in the back office, and they would most likely okay it. Standard operating procedure, in my experience.

Exhibit 9–15   This excerpt from "The Late Check-Out" in the March 1997 issue of *Lodging Hospitality* plays off a vague set of policies that plague our industry. Is it okay to check out late—certainly. But not too late. In most hotels, permission to check out a bit later, say 2 PM, is readily forthcoming. But 3 PM, and worse yet, 4 PM, are somehow far more difficult to attain in almost all hotels! When asked why, front-desk receptionists often respond, "Our housekeeping department goes home at that hour," or "We have your room reserved for another arrival," or similar such comments. *Written by Megan Rowe, Senior Editor, and used with permission.*

Guest	Rate Paid	March 15th Arrival	March 16 Departure	Total Hours Occupied
1	$225.00	1 AM (March 16)	Until 6 AM	5
2	225.00	2 PM	Until 11 AM	21
3	225.00	8 AM	Until 3 PM	31

Exhibit 9-16   Shown are three different hotel room utilization schedules. Three guests, facing substantially different travel schedules, have three unique hotel experiences, even though each pays the same $225 rate.

The first guest flies in very late (1 AM) and is forced to check out early the next morning (6 AM) to catch a connecting flight. The second guest exactly parallels the hotel's standard check-in and check-out times by arriving at 2 PM and checking out the next day at 11 AM. The third guest has nothing but time on his hands. By taking advantage of light occupancy and normal front-office courtesies, he asks for an early check-in (at 8 AM) and an extended late check-out (3 PM—see Exhibit 9-15).

No wonder hotels are looking more closely at hours occupied as one variable in establishing rate. These three guests paid the same rate, yet one guest occupied the room 620% more hours than another!

The total length of stay may also be an issue in the guest's level of satisfaction with the hotel. Guests with few hours to visit scarcely get enough time to sleep and bathe. It is the guest with sufficient leisure hours who truly enjoys the property by taking advantage of relaxation and recreational activities.

A popular journalist once observed facetiously that the length of time one spends in a hotel room is inversely proportional to the quality of that hotel room. When one arrives at, say, 1 AM and needs to get some rest for a 7 AM flight the next morning, the room will be lavish—there will be vases of roses, trays of food and drink, soft music, a Jacuzzi tub, and candlelight. Conversely, when one has no time commitments and all day to spend in the hotel, the assignment is invariably an establishment with no restaurant or lobby, fuzzy TV reception, and a drained swimming pool!

The American Plan Day.   Meals are part of the American plan (AP) rate, as they are with the modified American plan (MAP). Accurate billing requires an accurate record of arrival and departure times. Arrivals are registered with a meal code reflecting the check-in time. For example, a guest arriving at 3 PM would be coded with arriving after lunch but before dinner.

A complete AP stay technically involves enough meals on the final day to make up for the meals missed on the arriving day. A guest arriving before dinner would be expected to depart the next day, or many days later, after lunch. Two meals, breakfast and lunch, on the departing day complete the full AP charge, since one meal, dinner, was taken on the arriving day. MAP counts meals in the same manner, except that lunch is ignored.

Guests who take more than the three meals per day pay for the extra at menu prices, or sometimes below. Sometimes, guests who miss a meal are not charged. That is why it is very important to have the total AP rate fairly distributed between the room portion and the meal portion. Meal rates are set and are standardized for everyone. Higher AP rates must reflect better rooms, since all the guests are entitled to the same menu.

AP and MAP hotels have a special charge called *tray service*. It is levied on meals taken through room service. European plan room service typically contains hidden charges or inflated prices as a means of recovering the extra service. Menu charges are greater than the usual restaurant prices when the food is delivered to the room. This device is not available to the American plan hotel because meals being delivered to the room are not priced separately. Instead, a flat charge is levied as a tray service charge.

Day Rate Rooms.   Special rates exist for stays of less than overnight. These are called *part-day rates*, *day rates*, or sometimes *use rates*. Day rate guests arrive and depart on the same day.

Day rates obviously make possible an occupancy of greater than 100%. Furthermore, the costs are low. Nevertheless, the industry has not fully exploited the possibilities. Sales of use rates could be marketed to suburban shoppers and to small, brief meetings. Airport properties have promoted their locations as central meeting places for company representatives coming from different sections of the country.

A new day rate market is becoming evident. Motels near campsites and along the roadways are attracting campers as a wayside stop during the day. A hot shower, an afternoon by the pool, and a change of pace from the vehicle are great appeals when coupled with the low day rate.

Check-in time is often early morning. Corporate guests prefer to start their meetings early, and truck drivers like to get off the highway before the 8 AM rush hour. If clean rooms remain unsold from the previous night, there is little reason to refuse day rate guests early access to the room—they may order room-service coffee or breakfast as an added revenue bonus.

Since rooms sold for day use only are serviced and made available again for the usual overnight occupancy, the schedule of the housekeeping staff has a great deal to do with the check-out hour. If there are no swing-shift room attendants, the day rate must end early enough to allow servicing by the day shift. On the other hand, low occupancy would allow a day rate sale even late in the day. Nothing is lost if an additional empty room remains unmade overnight.

There are no rules as to what the hotel should charge for the day room. Some purists suggest that it must be half the standard rack rate. Others appreciate the extra revenue and are willing to charge whatever seems appropriate. Corporate hotels must remember that their day rate rooms compete with their convention and meeting facilities. A small group of executives might prefer meeting in a day rate suite room with its attached bathroom and access to room service rather than the larger impersonal convention meeting room. This can prove detrimental to the hotel if the meeting room sells for two or three times the day rate room.

DETERMINING THE PROPER ROOM RATE

Because a sound room rate structure is fundamental to a profitable hotel operation, every manager is sooner or later faced with the question of what is the proper room charge. Room rates reflect markets and costs, investments and rates of return, supply and demand, accommodations and competition, and not least of all, the quality of management. Determining the proper room rate can be a complicated undertaking.

Divided into its two major components, room rates must be large enough to cover costs and a fair return on invested capital, and reasonable enough to attract and retain the clientele to whom the operation is being marketed. The former suggests a relatively objective, structured approach that can be analyzed after the fact. The latter is more subjective, involving factors such as the amount of local competition and the condition of the economy at large. There is little sense in charging a rate less than what is needed to meet the first objective. There is little chance of getting a rate more than the competitive ceiling established by the second limitation.

Yield management, the balancing of occupancy and rate, has emerged as the number one component of rate making. Yield management has attracted attention because it introduces two new concepts to room pricing: (1) the industry is selling rooms by an inventory control system, and (2) the pricing strategy considers the customer's ability and willingness to pay. This discretionary market, with a sensitivity to price, is itself a new phenomenon (see Chapter 5).

In years past, the rate structure was built around internal cost considerations. Yield management has not eliminated that focus. Important as they are, customers are not the only components of price. Cost recovery and investment returns, depreciation and interest, and taxes and land costs are outside the hotel–guest relationship but not external to the room charge.

The more traditional components of rate deal with recovering costs, both operating and capital. They deal with profits and break-even projections. Mixed into the equation are competition, price elasticity, and rate cutting. And the average daily rate earned by the hotel is also determined by the ability of a reservationist or room clerk to sell up.

Traditional Rate Calculations

Hotel room rates are derived from a mix of objective measures and subjective values. Expressing room rates numerically gives the appearance of validity, but when the origins of these numbers are best-guess estimates, the results must be viewed with some measure of doubt or uncertainty.

Facts and suppositions combine together when hotel managers calculate the required room rate. As useful and respected as the following mathematical formulas may be, they are still merely an indication of the final rate. Fine-tuning the formula, establishing corporate and double occupancy prices, and adjusting the rate according to the whims of the community and the marketplace are still the role of management.

The Hubbart Room Rate Formula.   The Hubbart room rate formula offers a standardized approach to calculating room rates. The Hubbart formula establishes rates through the costs of operating the enterprise, not the price sensitivity of the guests. The average rate, says the formula, should pay all expenses and leave something for the investor. Valid enough—a business that cannot do this is short-lived.

Exhibit 9–17a illustrates the mechanics of the formula. Estimated expenses are itemized and totaled. These include operational expenses by departments ($1,102,800 in the illustration), realty costs ($273,000), and depreciation ($294,750). To these expenses is added a reasonable return on the present fair value of the property: land, building, and furnishings ($414,000). From the total expense package ($2,084,550) are subtracted incomes from all sources other than room sales ($139,200). This difference ($1,945,350) represents the annual amount to be realized from room sales.

Next (continuing Exhibit 9–17b), an estimate of the number of rooms to be sold annually is computed. Dividing the number of estimated rooms (22,484) to be sold annually into the estimated dollars ($1,945,350) needed to cover costs and a fair return produces the average rate to be charged ($86.52).

Shortcomings of the Formula.   Like many forecasts, the Hubbart room rate formula is only as accurate as the assumptions on which it was projected. Several assumptions come immediately to mind for the Hubbart formula: What percentage is "reasonable" as a fair return on investment? What occupancy rate appears most attainable? What are the cost projections for payroll, various operating departments, utilities, and administrative and general?

The formula leaves the rooms department with the final burden after profits and losses from other departments. But inefficiencies in other departments should not be

	Example
Operating Expenses	
Rooms department	$467,400
Telecommunications	60,900
Administrative and general	91,200
Payroll taxes and employee benefits	178,200
Marketing, advertising, and promotion	109,800
Utility costs	138,900
Property operation, maintenance, and engineering	56,400
Total operating expenses	$1,102,800
Taxes, Insurance, and Leases	
Real estate and personal property taxes	67,200
Franchise taxes and fees	112,200
Insurance on building and contents	37,200
Leased equipment	56,400
Total taxes, insurance, and leases	$ 273,000

Depreciation (Standard Rates on Present Fair Value)	Value		Rate		
Building	$_____	at	____%	168,750	
Furniture, fixtures, and equipment	$_____	at	____%	126,000	
Total depreciation					$ 294,750

Reasonable Return on Present Fair Value of Property	Value		Rate		
Land	$_____	at	____%		
Building	$_____	at	____%		
Furniture, fixtures, and equipment	$_____	at	____%		
Total fair return					$ 414,000
Total					$2,084,550

Deduct—Credits from Sources Other Than Rooms		
Income from store rentals	14,850	
Profits from food and beverage operations(if loss, subtract from this group)	131,400	
Net income from other operated departments and miscellaneous income (loss)	(7,050)	
Total credits from sources other than rooms		$ 139,200
Amount to be realized from guest-room sales to cover costs and a reasonable return on present fair value of property		$1,945,350

Exhibit 9–17   (a) Although the Hubbart Room Rate Formula was first introduced in 1952, it is still the most widely used means of computing zero-based room rates. By dividing annual fixed costs, variable expenses, and a reasonable return on the property by the estimated number of rooms projected to be sold for the year, the Hubbart formula provides a fairly reliable minimum average rate calculation.

		Example
1. Amount to be realized from guest-room sales to cover costs and a reasonable return on present fair value of property [from part (a)]		$1,945,350
2. Number of guest rooms available for rental		88
3. Number of available rooms on annual basis (item 2 multiplied by 365)	100%	32,120
4. Less: allowance for average vacancies	30%	9,636
5. Number of rooms to be occupied at estimated average occupancy	70%	22,484
6. Average daily rate per occupied room required to cover costs and a reasonable return on present fair value (item 1 divided by item 5)		$ 86.52

Exhibit 9–17   (b) Computing the denominator, the estimated number of rooms to be sold for the year, requires an occupancy projection. This example is based on an 88-room full-service resort. One of the biggest challenges with the Hubbart formula is projecting occupancy before fully understanding the average rate to be charged. *Courtesy of the American Hotel & Lodging Association, Washington, D.C.; used here with the Association's permission.*

covered by a high, noncompetitive room rate. Neither should unusual profits in other departments be a basis for charging room rates below what the market will bring.

There is some justification in having rooms subsidize low banquet prices if these low prices result in large convention bookings of guest rooms. (Incidentally, this is one reason why the food and banquet department should not be leased as a concession.) Similar justification could be found for using higher room rates to cover unusually high dining-room repairs and maintenance, or advertising costs. The tradeoff is wise if these expenditures produce enough other business to offset lost room revenue resulting from higher room rates.

Additional shortcomings become apparent as the formula is studied. Among them is the projected number of rooms sold. This estimate of rooms sold is actually based on the very rate being computed. How can a hotel estimate the number of rooms it will sell before first knowing the average rate for which it will sell each room—yet that is exactly what the Hubbart formula requires! The ADR is also dependent on the percent of double occupancy. Yet the increased income from double occupancy is not a component of the Hubbart formula.

The average rate that is computed ($86.52) is not the actual rate used by the hotel. Hotels use a number of rate classes, with various proportions of the total number of rooms assigned to each classification (see Exhibit 9–10). The actual average rate will be a weighted average of the rooms occupied, reflecting the range of accommodations the hotel is offering and the guest's purchase of them based on nearby competition.

Square Foot Calculations.   To compensate for the fact that the Hubbart room rate formula provides no rate detail by room type classification, some managers use a square foot calculation. The basis for this is the fact that more expensive and higher-quality guest rooms are invariably larger than standard rooms at the same property. Therefore, rather than calculating the Hubbart room rate per room sold, this variation calculates the rate on a per-square-foot basis.

To illustrate, assume that the small, full-service resort hotel presented in Exhibit 9–17 has a total of 27,250 square feet of space in its 88 guest rooms. With occupancy of 70%, there would be an average of 19,075 square feet sold per day. With an annual required return of $1,945,350, the daily required return is $5,329.73 ($1,945,350 divided by 365 days). Therefore, each square foot of rented room space must generate $0.27941 per day ($5,329.73 divided by 19,075 square feet sold per day) or almost 28 cents in daily revenue. As a result, a 300-square-foot room would sell for $83.82 (300 square feet times $0.28) and a 450-square-foot room would sell for $125.73. Assuming that the hotel sells all room types in equal ratios to the number of rooms available in each type, this square foot calculation offers another means for determining individual room type rates.

The Building Cost Room Rate Formula.

Time and repetition have created an industry axiom saying that rate can be evaluated by a simple rule of thumb: the building cost rate formula. The average room rate should equal $1 per $1,000 of construction cost. For a 200-room hotel costing $14 million (including land and land development, building, and public space but excluding furniture, fixtures, and equipment), the average rate should be $70 ($14 million ÷ 200 rooms ÷ $1,000).

The building cost yardstick is about as reliable as an old cookbook's direction to the chef: "Flavor to taste." Despite some very radical changes throughout the years, the rule is still being quoted on the theory that rising construction costs are being matched by rising room rates. Higher construction costs are due, in part, to larger room size as well as building materials and labor. This generation of rooms is 100 to 200% larger than rooms of 25 or 30 years ago.

Cost of construction (including the costs of land and land improvement) includes other factors: type of construction, location, high-rise versus low-rise buildings, and the cost of money (interest rate on debt). Luxury properties can cost five or six times as much per room as economy hotels. Land costs vary greatly across the nation. Comparing California and Arkansas is a lesson in futility. New York City may be stretching toward a $600 per-night room rate, but that is not the expectation of the manager in Dubuque, Iowa.

Economy chains have stopped advertising a minimum national rate. Each locale has its own cost basis for building, borrowing, taxing, and paying labor. Budgets aim only for a percentage rate below that of local competitors. Advertising a single rate as part of the national company logo is no longer feasible.

Increases in room construction costs are startling. Marriott's typical room cost runs between $200,000 and $250,000 today. Its figure was $8,000 in 1957. Consider what has happened in Hawaii over 20 years. Twenty years after the Mauna Kea was built at $100,000 per room, it was sold at $1 million per room, and the hotel was two decades older by that time!

The situation is the same in New York. Regent Hotels, a superluxury chain, built a 400-room hotel in New York with an average cost of $750,000 per room. With an actual average daily rack rate in the $550-range, the hotel is far from the $750 ADR dictated by the rule-of-thumb standard.

The Hotel Bel-Air in Los Angeles is another hotel that broke the mold. With only 92 rooms, the property sold in 1992 for a record $110 million (or approximately $1.2 million per room) to a Japanese hotel concern. Despite its incredibly high average daily rate for that time (about $400), the hotel earned far less than the $1,196 per average room-night that the building cost rate formula dictates.

These examples are special cases of "trophy hotels." Viewing the trophy as an art asset, which gives satisfaction and pleasure to the owner, offers some perspective on the price. Like an art piece, these eyebrow-raising prices are justified as long-term investments and by their uniqueness (location). In retrospect, the excessive prices of a generation ago have proven to be good deals—no one actually expected the Japanese hotel company that purchased the Hotel Bel-Air to make an operating profit. Profit, if any, would come from selling the resort several years down the road. The Japanese buyer was one of four interested parties willing to bid in excess of $1 million per room for the Hotel Bel-Air. And Rosewood hotels, which sold the hotel made an enormous profit, having purchased it just seven years earlier for $22.7 million, $247,000 per room.

Trophy hotels are extreme examples that do not set the rule for the remainder of the industry. With economy hotels costing about $70,000 per room, and standard properties over $250,000-plus per room, advocates of the rule take heart. The building cost formula, a standard whose first known reference was in 1947, is still as roughly accurate today as it probably was back then.

The Cost of Renovation. The costs of additions, property rehabs, or new amenities such as swimming pools fall within the scope of the $1 per $1,000 rule. First, the cost of the upgrade is determined on a per-room basis. The installation of an in-room air-conditioner might be priced at $1,500 per room. A general-use item such as a sauna would need a per room equivalent. The cost (assume $150,000) would be divided by the number of rooms (100) to arrive at the per unit cost. Exhibit 9–18 shows the impact on room rates from management's decision to undertake a propertywide remodel.

The Ideal Average Room Rate.

The firm of Laventhol & Horwath designed the ideal average room rate as a means of testing the room rate structure. Although the L & H accounting firm is no longer in business, its ideal average room rate lives on. According to this approach, the hotel should sell an equal percentage of rooms in each rate class instead of filling from the bottom up (least expensive rooms selling first). A 70% occupancy should mean a 70% occupancy in each rate category. Such a spread produces an average rate identical to the average rate earned when the hotel is completely full—that is, an ideal room rate.

Exhibit 9–19 illustrates the computation used to derive the ideal rate. This formula assumes each room type (standard, executive, deluxe, and suite) fills to the same percentage of rooms sold as every other room type. At 70% occupancy, 70% of the standard rooms will be sold, 70% of the executive rooms will be sold, 70% of the deluxe rooms will be sold, and 70% of the suites will be sold.

Once calculated, the manager is armed with a valuable figure, the ideal average room rate. If the actual average rate on any given day or week is higher than the ideal average rate, the front-office staff has been doing a great job of upselling guests. Either that, or the hotel has failed to provide a proper number of high-priced rooms. Such a hotel's market may be interested in rooms selling above the average, so room types and rates may need to be adjusted upward.

An average room rate lower than the ideal, and this is usually the case, indicates several problems. There may not be enough contrast between the low- and the high-priced rooms. Guests will take the lower rate when they are buying nothing extra for the higher rate. If the better rooms do, in fact, have certain extras—better exposure and newer furnishings—the lack of contrast between the rate categories might simply be a matter of poor selling at the front desk (discussed later in the chapter).

Check-in at the front desk represents the last opportunity to upsell the guest to a more expensive room accommodation. Good salesmanship coupled with a differentiated

1. Renovation Project Parameters

	Guest rooms: Cost per Room	Hallways: Cost per Door	Meeting Space: Cost per Square Foot	Lobby: Cost per Square Foot	F&B Outlets: Cost per Seat	Total Project
Soft costs[a]	$ 515	$ 194	$ 2	$ 3	$ 212	N/A
Hard costs[b]	3,305	755	5	18	1,342	N/A
Subtotals	$764,000	$189,800	$105,000	$73,500	$170,940	$1,303,240

2. Basic Hotel Information
- A 200-room full-service airport hotel
- 15,000 square feet of convention space
- 3,500 square feet of lobby space
- One 110-seat restaurant and bar
- 12% cost of funds interest rate
- Total renovation cost $1,303,240

3. Project Cost per Average Guest Room
- $1,303,240 project divided by 200 rooms equals $6,516.20 per room.
- Assume that the $6,516.20 project cost per average room is to be repaid over 15 years at a 12% cost of funds rate.
- The combined principal and interest charge is $956.74 per room per year.

4. Impact of the Building Cost Room Rate Formula
- The $956.74 annualized cost per average room divided by $1,000 rule-of-thumb formula equals $0.96 increase per average room night sold.

[a] Soft costs include professional and contractor fees, sales tax, and shipping fees.

[b] Hard costs include construction costs, labor, materials, and all FF&E.

Exhibit 9–18 Figures developed in this exhibit come from applying the $1 per $1,000 building-cost room-rate formula. The project results in an added $0.96 in required per-room revenue.

Room Type	Number Rooms by Type	Percent of Double Occupancy	Single Rate	Double Rate
Standard	140	30	$ 80	$ 95
Executive	160	5	105	105
Deluxe	100	25	120	140
Suite	75	70	160	160
Total rooms	475			

Calculation Steps

1. Multiply all standard rooms (140) by their single rate ($80) to get a product of $11,200. Then take the double occupancy percentage for standard rooms (30%) times the total number of standard rooms (140) to get 42, the number of double-occupied standard rooms. Next, take the 42 double-occupied standard rooms times the differential between the single and double price ($95 double rate minus $80 single rate equals $15 differential) to get $630. Finally, add the room revenue for standard rooms calculated at the single rate ($11,200) to the additional room revenue received from standard rooms sold at the double rate ($630) to get the full-house room revenue for standard rooms, a total of $11,830.

2. Follow the same procedure for executive rooms: 160 rooms times $105 equals $16,800. The differential between single and double occupancy for executive rooms is zero, so there is no added revenue for double occupancy. The full-house room revenue for executive rooms is $16,800.

3. Follow the same procedure for deluxe rooms: 100 rooms times $120 single rate equals $12,000. In terms of double occupancy, there are 25 deluxe rooms (25% double occupancy times 100 rooms equals 25 rooms) sold at a $20 differential ($140 double rate minus $120 single rate equals $20 differential) for a total double occupancy impact of $500. The full-house room revenue for deluxe rooms is $12,500.

4. Follow the same procedure for suites: 75 rooms times $160 equals $12,000. The differential between single and double occupancy for suites is zero, so there is no added revenue for double occupancy. The full-house room revenue for suites is $12,000.

5. Add total revenues from standard rooms ($11,830), executive rooms ($16,800), deluxe rooms ($12,500), and suites ($12,000) for total revenues assuming 100% occupancy—ideal revenues. That total ($53,130) divided by rooms sold (475) is the ideal average room rate of $111.85.

No matter what the occupancy percentage, the ideal average room rate remains the same.
Try this problem again, assuming, say, 70% occupancy. The end result will still be an ideal average room rate of $111.85.

Exhibit 9–19   Although Laventhol & Horwath, the firm which first developed the ideal average room rate, is no longer in business, the formula remains viable. Follow these steps to develop an ideal average room rate for any hotel. *Courtesy of Laventhol & Horwath, Philadelphia.*

product gives the hotel a strong chance to increase middle- and high-priced room sales. Such comments as "I see you have reserved our standard room; do you realize for just 20 more dollars I can place you in a newly refurbished deluxe room with a complimentary continental breakfast?" go a long way toward satisfying both the guest and the bottom line.

A faulty internal rate structure is another reason that the ideal room rate might not be achieved. The options, the range of rates being offered, might not appeal to the customer. Using the ideal room rate computation, the spread between rates could be adjusted. According to the authors of the formula, increases should be concentrated in those rooms on those days for which the demand is highest. That begins with an analysis of rate categories.

Rate Categories.   The discrepancy between the rates the hotel offers and those the guests prefer can be pinpointed with a simple chart. Guest demands and the hotel offerings are plotted side by side.

Guest demands are determined by a survey of registration card rates over a period of time. The survey should not include days of 100% occupancy when the guest had no rate choice. Special rate situations would also be excluded. Using elementary arithmetic, the percentage of total registrations is determined for each rate class. Exhibit 9–20 illustrates the contrast between what the guest buys and what the hotel offers. It also points to the rates that need adjustment.

Exhibit 9–20 assigns 40% of the hypothetical hotel to the median room rate. Two additional categories of 20% and 10%, respectively, appear on both the lower and upper ends. It is the sad history of our industry that hotels fill from the bottom up. Lower-priced rooms are in greatest demand. This means that low occupancy is accompanied by a low average daily rate. It is felt, therefore, that hotels should offer more categories at the lower end of the price scale. These lower categories would be bunched together, while the higher rates would be spread over fewer categories. That might be the reason that Hilton advises its franchises to concentrate on the minimum single rate as the key in competition.

Upselling Premium Accommodations.   The room rate policy faces a moment of truth when the front-office employee and the buying public come face to face. Fashioning a room rate policy is a futile exercise unless management simultaneously trains its staff to carry out the plan. The selling skills of reservationists and clerks are critical to the average daily rate until the house nears capacity. Since full occupancy is less common, earning a consistently higher ADR on the 60 to 70% day is achieved only when a program for selling up is in place.

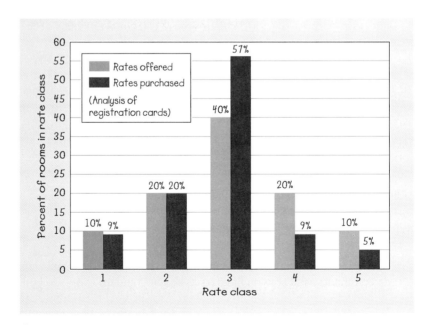

Exhibit 9-20   An analysis of registration cards, over a period of time, will reveal which room rates are purchased most regularly. This sample hotel has five rate classes, representing 10%, 20%, 40%, 20%, and 10% of all hotel rooms, respectively. However, an analysis of rates purchased suggests that a disproportionate percentage of guests opt for class 3 (and fewer guests than expected choose classes 4 and 5).

The hardest sell comes from the guest-service agent. A guest who approaches the desk with a reservation in hand has already decided to buy. Already committed, the new arrival is susceptible to a carefully designed and rehearsed sales effort (see Exhibit 9–21). The hardest job comes from the reservationist, who doesn't even see the buyer. Too hard a sell, too firm a price, and the guest is lost early on. Teamed up, the reservationist and the guest-service agent deliver a one–two punch to the ADR, although they could be 1,000 miles and 30 days apart.

Mastering the Basics of Selling

1. Impressing the Guests
- Maintain an appealing physical appearance, including good posture. Don't lean or hang over the front desk. Bring to the job your own sense of spirit and style.
- Organize and keep the front-desk area uncluttered.
- Get to know your property's every service and accommodation type thoroughly. Make frequent forays around the property to learn firsthand about each kind and category of room so that you can better describe the facilities to potential guests.
- Memorize or keep close at hand an up-to-date list of the locations and hours of operation of all food and beverage facilities; entertainment lounges; recreational and sports rooms; and banquet, meeting, exhibit, and other public areas.
- Learn the names and office locations of the general manager and all department heads, including directors of marketing, sales, catering, convention services, and food and beverages.
- Be friendly to guests, greeting them warmly and, whenever possible, by name and title. For instance, when requesting a bellperson's service, ask him or her to take "Mr. Smith to room 340." (To ensure the guest's privacy, be discreet in mentioning the room number to the bellperson.) Call the bellperson by name as well.
- Give guests your undivided attention.
- Answer all questions completely, but concisely and accurately, based on your in-depth knowledge of hotel operations. Refrain from boasting about accommodations and services; instead, offer simple, to-the-point descriptions of features.
- Assume a polite, patient manner in explaining the various options available—for example, the size of rooms, kinds of reservations (confirmed or guaranteed), and the terms *American, European,* or *modified American plan.*

2. Winning the Guests
- Expand prospects' accommodations horizons with descriptions of the room and service possibilities awaiting them. Potential guests may think of a hotel as simply a building filled with bedrooms, but you know better. So inform them about rooms with views, rooms near the health spa, twin-bed rooms, suites, rooms furnished according to a certain historical period, or ultramodern accommodations with Jacuzzis. Lay everything out for prospects, dwelling on the positive, distinctive appeals of each choice. Throw in the tempting intangibles associated with each type of room; for instance, the prestige of having a room on the same floor as the hotel's exclusive club for special guests, or the pleasure of staying in a room equipped with a VCR or a fireplace.

Exhibit 9–21   Mastering the basics of selling. Commonsense advice from the Foundation of the Hospitality Sales and Marketing Association International's pamphlet entitled *The Front Office: Turning Service into Sales. Courtesy of Hospitality Sales and Marketing Association International, New York.*

- Attempt to sell a room to suit the client. Observe people and try to read their particular hankerings. If a guest is new to the hotel, a room with a nice view might be impressive. Business travelers might prefer a quiet room at the back. Guests with children, people staying for an extended visit, honeymooners, and celebrities are among those who might be interested in suites.
- Sell the room, not the rate. If a guest asks flat out for rates, avoid quoting a minimum or just one rate, instead, offer a range, portraying in detail the difference in accommodations that each rate affords.
- Should a prospect look unsure or reluctant to book a room, suggest that the guest accompany a hotel employee on a walkthrough. A tour of the premises gives guests a chance to settle any doubts they might have and demonstrates the hotel's policy of goodwill and flexibility.
- Keep abreast of special sales promotions, weekend packages, and other marketing strategies, and dangle these offerings to prospects. (To make sure you're informed, you might ask your sales department to hold regularly scheduled presentations to front-office staff on their latest schemes.)
- Look for opportunities to extend the sale—there are many. If a guest mentions that he or she is hungry or arrives around mealtime, promote the hotel's dining facilities; if a guest arrives late, talk up the entertainment lounge or room service. As the person most in contact with guests throughout their stays, you are in the enviable position of being able to please both your guest and hotel management. You can delight guests merely by drawing their attention to the multitude of services your hotel offers, whether it's quick dry cleaning or a leisurely massage. And you can thrill the boss by advancing a sale and hotel revenues through your promotion of in-house features.

3. **Wooing the Guests**
- When a guest arrives, upgrade the reservation to a more luxurious accommodation whenever availability allows, ask whether the guest would like to make a dinner reservation, and ask whether he or she would like a wake-up call.
- Record and follow through on all wake-up call requests.
- Deliver mail and messages promptly.
- Avoid situations that keep guests waiting. For instance, if you're unable to locate a guest's reservation and a line is beginning to form on the other side of the counter, assume that the hotel has plenty of the desired accommodations available and go ahead and book the guest. Finish registering anyone else who is waiting, and then search for the missing reservation.
- Should mishaps occur, whether a reservation mix-up or a housekeeping error, handle the matter with aplomb without laying the blame on any individual employee or department.
- Dispatch each departing guest with a favorable impression of the hotel. In other words, treat the guests with care and courtesy during check out. Regardless of whether guests enjoyed their stay, they will remember only the hassles experienced at check out if you allow them to occur. Therefore, don't. That is, be sure there are useful, comprehensive procedures for dealing with guests who dispute postings and payments, and follow those procedures with assurance and professionalism.

Exhibit 9–21   *(continued)*

A firm sale begins with product knowledge. That's why good sales executives travel to the central reservation office to brief the operators there. On property, both the reservationists and the guest-service agents need continuous training about the facilities and accommodations of the hotel. This is rarely done. Few hotels ever assign 15 minutes per day for staff visits and inspections. Hotels spend millions of dollars upgrading rooms and modernizing facilities, but the guest-service agents never see the changes. A simple and consistent training program assures management that employees know their product.

If the desk staff knows the product, a repertoire of reasons can be developed to upsell. A 10% upsell of $10 to $20 is not a large increment in terms of today's rate (see Exhibit 9–3). Since every dollar of the increment goes to the bottom line, it represents a large annual figure, even if only a portion of the attempts are successful. The focus might be to sell the commercial guest from standard service to a concierge floor. The leisure market needs a different approach. These discretionary buyers may turn away if the rates quoted at check-in fail to reflect the package plan originally booked at the time of reservation.

Each guest looks at the incremental dollars differently, and so does the employee. Management must be cognizant that the basic room rate and especially the incremental upsell seem excessive to employees working for an hourly wage. Part of the training must attend to the employee's frame of reference. Having some type of incentive plan for the employee does help change attitudes.

Incentives to Upsell.   Motivated guest-service agents are better selling tools than cut rates and giveaways. They are less expensive, too, even with an incentive-pay plan. And it takes a good incentive plan coupled with proper training to make the system work.

Incentive systems stimulate interest and emphasize the goals of management. Rewards are especially important during heavy discounting periods, when guests know that low rates are available and sales resistance is high. Unlike some other places of the world, clerks in the United States do not share in any mandatory service charge. Therefore, a special cash pool is needed for incentive distributions.

Incentive systems require an accurate and easily computed formula. Flat goals can be established, or the focus can be on improvement from last year, or last month, or last week for that matter. Most front-office incentives are keyed to average daily rate. Occupancy is a factor in total revenue, which suggests other bases for setting goals.

Most systems establish a pool that is shared by the team: the reservation office, telephone operators, bellpersons, and others. That's why the pool, with its spinoff in morale and teamwork, is preferred.

The cash pool is generated from a percentage—say, 10%—of room sales that exceed projections. Management projects either the total room sales or the average daily rate. Management projections might be based on the ideal room rate (see Exhibit 9–19) or the budget forecast. If actual sales exceed target sales, the bonus becomes payable. The bonus period is important. It must be long enough to reflect the true efforts of the team but short enough to bring the rewards within grasp.

Higher ADRs are a win–win–win situation. The employee wins by receiving increased payroll as an incentive for upselling. Management wins because upselling contributes proportionately higher profits to the P&L Statement. And the guest wins by receiving exactly the room desired. The clerk isn't forcing anything on the guest that the guest doesn't want. Guests are more than ready to pay top dollar for better accommodations. That's been demonstrated time and again as room rates and room quality continue to rise.

SUMMARY

A proper room rate is as much a marketing tool as it is a financial instrument. The room rate needs to be low enough to attract customers (marketing), while being high enough to earn a reasonable profit (financial). Easier said than done. Even in this day of sophisticated computer technology, calculating the room rate still involves guesswork and gut instincts. There is an unquantifiable psychology involved in the room rate. An attractive rate for one guest may appear too high or too low to another. For some, high rates suggest a pretentious operation; for others, a low rate suggests poor quality.

Searching and working toward the perfect rate is difficult. Even after the rate has been determined and established, it is changed immediately. Rates fluctuate by season, they change according to room type, they vary with special guest discounts, and they shift as a function of yield management.

Although there are some well-established methods for calculating the proper rate, these should never

be used to the exclusion of common sense and market demand. The Hubbart room rate formula and the building cost rate formula are two common means for determining the rate. In addition, the ideal average room rate formula adds a dimension of retrospection to understanding the appropriateness of a rate in terms of the local marketplace.

RESOURCES AND CHALLENGES
Resources

WEB SITES

http://www.policyworks.gov/org/main/mt/homepage/mtt/perdiem/taxesr (The General Services Administration (GSA) of the U.S. government, a site with lodging taxes across the country).

http://www.runzheimer.com (Runzheimer International offers a number of products and links related to travel costs. Try their *Runzheimer Guide to Daily Travel Prices*).

http://www.traveltax.msu.edu (An economic index report that tracks lodging taxes in high-traffic destinations worldwide. Try their tax barometer. Unfortunately, this partnership between The World Travel & Tourism Council and Michigan State University has come to an end, so this site will gradually become outdated).

http://www.tia.org (The Travel Industry Association of America researches lodging taxes and their impact on state economies).

http://pods.dasnr.okstate.edu/docushare/dsweb/Get/Document-2975/F-883web.pdf (Oklahoma Cooperative Extension Service. Explains the impact of lodging taxes on local municipalities in Oklahoma: *"Hospitality or Lodging Taxes as a Source of Revenue for Tourism Economic Development Efforts)."*

Web Assignment

With tax rates of 20.25% and 17% respectively, Washington, D.C. and Houston are the highest in the nation. Milwaukee and Cleveland, secondary cities, are both nearly 15%. In contrast, Boston, which has the nation's second highest ADR, is 38th in terms of lodging taxes, less than 10%. Report and compare the total cost of lodging taxes (state and local) for your home town to three domestic or international cities other than those cited above.

INTERESTING TIDBITS

➤ According to a study recently published by the Center for Hospitality Research at Cornell University's School of Hotel Administration (*Revenue Management in U.S. Hotels 2001–2005*), the use of revenue management is more prevalent in hotels which

outperform their competitive market set. In other words, hotels which charge more than their competitors are those most likely to use revenue management strategies more frequently and with greater success than their competitors.

➤ The 11 Hilton resorts which improperly charged resort fees (a case which was settled in 2006) included;

> Doubletree Golf Resort, San Diego
> Doubletree Surfcomber, Miami
> Doubletree Guest Suites Walt Disney World Resort, Orlando
> Embassy Suites Hotels Deerfield Beach, Florida
> Hilton Sedona Resort & Spa, Sedona, Arizona
> Pointe Hilton Squaw Peak Resort, Phoenix
> Pointe Hilton Tapatio Cliffs Resort, Phoenix
> Hilton Waikoloa Village Resort, Hawaii
> Hilton Walt Disney World, Orlando
> Hilton Myrtle Beach, South Carolina
> Hilton Palm Springs, California

➤ Few convention delegates realize that part of their expensive room rate is actually a profit center for their convention's treasury. Rebates from headquarter hotels that are housing convention delegates are very common. The negotiated room rate for the convention often includes a percentage or flat amount earmarked by the hotel as a rebate to the convention's treasury. Such rebates make sense if they help fund continental breakfasts, expensive speakers, or elaborate theme parties. Such rebates are suspect if they are kept confidential and held in secret from delegates.

➤ An August 1995 letter to the editor of the *Cornell Hotel and Restaurant Administration Quarterly* stated that the earliest reference the author (Bjorn Hanson) could find for the building cost room rate formula was a 1947 publication of the *Horwath Accountant* (a newsletter from a now-defunct accounting firm). The author of this newsletter (Louis Toth) stated that for the $1 per $1,000 rule of thumb to work, several things needed to be in place: (1) The rule referred only to the cost of the building, not the entire project; (2) the hotel needed to receive rents from concessionaries to cover debt service and taxes on the land itself; (3) the hotel needed a 70% occupancy; (4) the cost of FF&E could be no more than 20% of the cost of the building; and (5) income before fixed charges must be at least 55% of room sales.

Challenges

TRUE/FALSE

Questions that are partially false should be marked false (F).

___ 1. Hotel room rates have a floor and a ceiling. The floor is the minimum needed to cover variable costs. The ceiling is the maximum amount that can be charged and still remain competitive in the marketplace.

___ 2. The fact that hotel rates continue to rise at a pace faster than the rate of inflation suggests there is some level of inelasticity in terms of the lodging industry as a whole.

___ 3. Assume a brand new 200-room hotel has $15 million in construction costs, $3 million in land and land improvement costs, and $2 million in furniture, fixtures, and equipment (FF&E) costs. The building cost rate would be $90 per room, because we do not include FF&E when looking at brand new construction.

___ 4. The most expensive community in the United States in terms of lodging taxes is Los Angeles (Los Angeles County) with a 24.25% lodging tax.

___ 5. Hotels and resorts often charge additional fees (sometimes called resort fees or service fees) to help defray the costs of newspapers, health clubs, in-room coffee, and so on.

PROBLEMS

1. Assume that the ideal average room rate for a given property is $87.25. Month after month, however, the hotel consistently outperforms its ideal average room rate by at least $5 to $10. Based on the fact that the hotel's actual ADR is consistently higher than its ideal average room rate, what do you know about the front-office staff's ability to sell rooms? What do you know about the price sensitivity of your customers? And what do you know about rate tendencies in the surrounding marketplace? Armed with this data, what type of action might you now consider?

2. Upselling at the front desk is paramount to enhancing hotel profitability. Yet upselling also has the potential to cause the guest discomfort and to appear pushy or aggressive. There is a fine line between professionally upselling the room and appearing as if you are "hustling" the guest. How might you attempt to upsell each of the following types of guests? Acting as the guest–service agent prepare a professional upselling dialogue for each of these situations (make up your own room types and rates as necessary):

   a. Standing before you is an executive on your corporate-rate plan. He is stretching and yawning from a hard day of air travel and local meetings.

   b. About to check in is a mother with her three young children. She is alone—her husband doesn't arrive until tomorrow. The kids are obviously excited about the prospects of swimming and running around the courtyard.

   c. Two gentlemen from a recently arrived bus tour are standing in front of you. Even though the rest of the tour group is housed in standard queen doubles, these men are commenting that their room is much too small.

   d. A female executive with an extended-stay reservation is currently checking in.

She comments on the fact that she must stay in your hotel for at least 10 days. How can she possibly survive 10 days away from home?

3. A commercial hotel offers a deeply discounted rate on Friday, Saturday, and Sunday nights. Discuss what should be done or said in each of the following situations:

   a. A guest arrives on Saturday but makes no mention of the special rate and seems unaware of the discount possibilities. The desk clerk charges full rack rate. On check out Monday morning, the cashier notices the full rate charged for two nights, but the guest (after reviewing her folio) says nothing.

   b. The situation is the same as that in (a), but this time the guest does comment that she thought a discounted rate might apply.

   c. A corporate guest stays Wednesday through Wednesday on company business. He receives a slightly discounted commercial rate for all seven nights, but his rate is still much higher than the special weekend rate available to anyone off the street. He knows about the special rate and asks that his three weekend nights be reduced accordingly.

   d. Create a fourth scenario of your own.

4. Explain why hoteliers differentiate between discounting practices and rate cutting. Create a list of similarities and differences between discounting and rate cutting. Then conclude whether you believe they are substantially different activities or really two different statements for describing exactly the same practice.

5. The Hubbart room-rate formula calls for an average room rate that will cover expenses and provide a fair return to the investors. Compute that rate from the abbreviated set of data that follows:

Investment (also fair market value)

Land	$ 3,000,000
Building	25,000,000
Furniture and equipment	6,000,000
Nonappropriated expenses, such as advertising, repairs, etc.	$ 1,200,000
Income from all operating departments except rooms, net of losses	$ 3,200,000
Rooms available for sale	563
Nonoperating expenses, such as insurance, taxes, and depreciation	510,000

Desired return on investment	16%
Interest on debt of $25,000,000	14%
Percentage of occupancy	71%

6. Using the data from Problem 5, compute what the typical room charge should be according to the building cost rate formula.

AN INCIDENT IN HOTEL MANAGEMENT

So What Does FSG (Frequent-Stay Guest) Stand For?

Occupancy has been so high this year that the hotel has "regretted" a large number of reservation requests.

A registered couple was scheduled to leave at 6:00 AM on the morning of March 31. A family emergency with their seven-month-old child called them home on March 30 at about 3:00 PM. The airline accommodated the couple on a red-eye flight without charging for the ticket change, typically $100. They ask the desk for a late check-out, 9:00 PM, and a half-day rate of $110.

The hotel was full—Sunday—when the business crowd usually arrived. The manager on duty denied the request because of the late hour and the unlikelihood of servicing and reselling the room.

In his letter of complaint, the husband asks to be reimbursed and questions the meaning of being a FSG. He notes that "I am not a big customer of yours." Adding, "You'll probably see me even less frequently now." The FSG profile shows three stays from the family since their membership was launched almost three years previous.

Questions: Was there a management failure here; if so, what?
What is the hotel's immediate response (or action) to the incident?
What further, long-run action should management take, if any?

ANSWERS TO TRUE/FALSE QUIZ

1. True. The floor (lowest point in the rate range) is the minimum the hotel can charge and still be able to recover variable costs and some additional amount toward fixed costs and profitability. The ceiling (highest point in the rate range) is the maximum the hotel can charge and still remain competitive in the marketplace.

2. True. As a whole, the lodging industry is relatively inelastic. This can be seen when all hotels in a given community raise their rates. But remember, a single hotel is relatively elastic in terms of its competitors.

3. True. The building cost rate formula does remove the cost of furniture, fixtures, and

equipment when calculating the rate. So, construction ($15 million) plus land and land improvements ($3 million) total $18 million. Divide that by 200 rooms to get $90,000 in costs per average room. Divide that by the $1,000 constant to arrive at a $90 average rate.

4. False. The most expensive community in the United States in terms of lodging taxes is actually Washington, D.C., with a 20.25% lodging tax.

5. True. Hotels and resorts do charge resort or service fees. This practice has come under growing scrutiny. Some hotels have decided to eliminate these hidden charges. Others have a liberal refund policy for any complaining guests.

PART IV

The Hotel Revenue Cycle

C H A P T E R   1 0

Billing the Guest Folio

Outline

There's a rhythm to the flow that marks the guest's passage through the hotel. Reservations sound the first drumbeat (Chapter 4), followed by arrival and registration (Chapter 8). The tempo of the visit ends with the guest's departure (Chapter 10). Between check-in and check-out, guests enjoy the services of the hotel. Selling those services is what hotelkeeping is all about. Recording those sales is what this chapter is all about.

WHAT THE CHAPTER IS ALL ABOUT

Sale of Services

Hotels sell rooms, food, and beverage along with other services depending on the size, class, and type of hotel. Just as some hotels (budgets) offer room sales only, others (full-service properties) have many operating departments ranging from room service, to wedding chapels, to spas. The more offerings, the more detailed the system of recordkeeping.

Recording Sales

Hotels and their customers (guests) have a different relationship than do other retailers and their customers. Guests register as they arrive. Names, addresses, business associations and—most important—credit-card numbers are known to the innkeeper. Having this information allows the sale of services without immediate payment. Unlike other retail merchants, the hotel merchant waits for payment. The wait may be a few hours or even an entire week. In the meantime, guest purchases are recorded on a bill, which hotel professionals call a *folio*. The folio is presented as the guest checks out. But, as we shall see, it may not be paid even then.

Preparing the Folio

The folio is a current, accurate record of what the guest owes. It is available on demand to both the guest and the hotel's management. Whereas other retailers—department stores for example—send monthly statements, the hotel's statement is ready at a moment's notice. The folio is ready even though the exact moment of departure is unknown, even unknown to the guest. Of course, the hotel is as anxious as the guest to have an accurate accounting available. Incorrect bills delay the check-out procedure and create ill will. Charges (amounts the guest owes) not on the folio are difficult to collect after the guest has departed. Collecting these *late charges* by mail is costly in both clerical expenses and guest relationships.

Recording (Accounting) for Each Transaction

> *Understanding accounting rules is not essential to a clear understanding of the three other components of the chapter. Hereafter, accounting rules are set in a box like this one. Students unfamiliar with the debits and credits of accounting may choose to read these accounting fundamentals or not. The text will make good sense even if the accounting information is skipped.*

ACCOUNTS RECEIVABLE

Except at the retail level, most commerce is carried on without immediate payment. Businesses buy and sell to one another without a direct exchange of money. Payment is delayed until a more convenient time in order to complete the sale as quickly as possible. Hotels also work that way. Guests are not disturbed during their sleep in order to collect the room rates! Instead, charges are made to the folio and collections are made later. Guests usually settle at check-out time. During the period between the sale (room, food, beverage, etc.) and the payment (at departure), the guest owes the hotel. A customer who owes a business for services that have not been paid is known as an *account receivable*.[1]

Definition of Terms to be Used

Accounts Receivable (A/R)	Customers who owe for services already rendered
City Receivables	Accounts receivable who are not registered
Transient Receivables	Accounts receivable who are currently registered
Charge	The amount that the hotel asks for its service
Late Charge	Service charged to the folio after the guest has left
Folio	Guest bill; also called account card; an A/R
Ledger	Group of folios
City Ledger	A ledger of city receivables
Transient Ledger	A ledger of transient receivables; also called a rooms ledger, a front-desk ledger, a guest ledger
Posting	The process of recording a charge or credit on the folio

Types of Accounts Receivable (A/R)

Hotels have two types of accounts receivable because there are two types of hotel guests. The most obvious guest (or account receivable) is one who is currently registered and occupying a room. Oddly enough, this most visible class of guest is not the largest dollar debt (accounts receivable) that the hotel is owed. More money is owed by the second type of accounts receivable: persons or companies that owe the hotel for services but are *not* registered and *not* occupying a guest room. Registered guests are called *transient guests*; non-registered accounts receivable are called *city guests*. Both owe the hotel for services rendered and sold. One group, the city receivables, are not even in the hotel and may never have been.

---

[1]Remember the spelling rule for rec*ei*vable: Place *i* before *e*, except after *c*, or when sounded like *a*, as in n*ei*ghbor and w*ei*gh.

Guests can and do change categories; transient accounts receivable usually become city accounts receivable. When guests check out, leaving their transient classification, they usually settle their folios (that is, pay the bill) with a credit card. The amount owed is now a debt of the credit-card company. The hotel will be paid by a city-ledger receivable: Visa, MasterCard, or other credit card. Credit-card companies obviously are not registered guests occupying a room. The credit-card debt is owed by an account receivable who is not registered: a city account receivable.

The Ledgers.   There are numerous individual accounts in both the registered and city-guest categories. Hotels as large as those in Exhibit 1–6 have several thousand registered guests and about the same number of folios. Accountants call a group of folios *a ledger*. (Any group of records can be called a ledger.) Since all the parties are registered, that is, transient guests, the folios at the front desk are viewed as one record, *a transient ledger*.

City accounts receivable are similarly combined. The total of individual city accounts, debtors who are not currently registered (Visa, for example), is viewed as one record, *a city ledger*.

In the preelectronic age, ledgers were actual piles of paper with each folio on a separate form, such as Exhibit 10–2. Today's folios are in computer memory. We still call them folios and their location is still identified as transient folios (transient ledger) or city accounts (city ledger). The language has carried over although the format is no longer used.

Professional Lingo: The Transient Ledger.   Transient ledger is shorthand for the transient accounts receivable ledger. Hotel professionals use other jargon to identify this particular ledger. Because the ledger (that is, the total record of debt to the hotel by registered guests) is available at the front office, it is frequently called the *front-office ledger*. Since it is made up of registered guests, it is also called the *guest ledger*. Room rates are the largest source of charges to guest folios, so *rooms ledger* is still another term used for the transient ledger.

The variety of terms used to identify the transient ledger spills over to the folios that make up this ledger. Thus, the single transient folio may be called the *folio*, or *guest folio*, or *front-office folio*. Since the folio is a record of the guest's account with the hotel, the folio is also called an *account card* or *guest bill*.

Professional Lingo: The City Ledger.   There are numerous subcategories of the city ledger; Chapter 11 explains them. But only one general term is used: city ledger. So a city-ledger reference is easier to remember than the transient ledger with its variety of names: guest ledger; rooms ledger; front-office ledger.

The guest ledger is located at the front desk, the city ledger in the accounting office. With computerization, ledgers have no real physical location. They can be accessed wherever a control terminal allows. Timing is the major difference between the two ledgers. Charges, which are the records of services rendered, are *posted* (recorded) immediately to the guest ledger since the guest might choose to leave at any time. City guests, who must establish credit in advance, are billed periodically. This permits some delay in posting city-ledger charges. Like many other businesses do, hotels bill city accounts monthly. Often, a three-day cycle is used for the first billing. These variations in timing are accommodated by different ledger forms as well as by different posting and billing procedures.

What Is and Isn't Accounted For.   Each folio is a record of the guest's debt to the hotel. Folios deal only with accounts receivable. Persons who pay cash for services, as they might in cocktail lounges and restaurants, are not billed at the front desk. It makes no difference whether the buyer is a registered guest or a stranger.

There is no hotel debt, hence no account receivable, when settlement is made immediately with dollars.

Strangers, nonguests without front-office folios, can still purchase on credit. They do so with credit cards. A credit-card purchase creates an account receivable within the city ledger, not with the guest ledger (front-office ledger). Using the credit card means the credit-card company will pay the hotel. The credit-card company is a nonregistered account receivable. That's the definition of a city-ledger account. If services are purchased with a credit card by anyone, guest or nonguest, the purchaser owes the credit-card company and the credit-card company owes the hotel.

In summary, both registered guests and nonguest customers use the hotel's dining rooms and lounges. These persons pay by one of two methods. Either they pay with cash (Chapter 12 treats that) or they pay with a credit card (Chapter 13 treats that). This chapter concentrates on the third method of settlement, available only to registered guests. Such guests sign for services when delivered. That debt is recorded on the folio. During check-out, the guest settles all the charges on the folio.

The Folio: The Individual Account Receivable

Folio, bill, guest account, account card, guest account card, and guest bill are used interchangeably. Some parts of the world use *visitor accounts*. All refer to the single folio that is opened for each guest. "For each guest" is not entirely accurate, because one folio may serve several persons, as it does with a family.

Definition of Terms to Be Used

Account	A guest's transient folio, or a city-ledger record
Asset	Something owned by the hotel (building, A/R, furniture)
Balance of the Account (or Account Balance)	The net difference between charges and credits
Cashier's Bucket (or Well or Pit)	A front-office file, sometimes recessed in the desk
Charges	Amounts owed by guests for services received
Credits	Amounts by which guests settle the charges they owe
Direct Billing	Bill goes to the entity that created it, not to a credit card
Incomes	Earnings that the hotel enjoys from the sale of services
Master Account	Front-office folio for group charges and credits
PMS	Property management system, the hotel's computer
Sales	Same as incomes, although technically not exactly
Split (Billing or Folios)	Distribution of charges between master account and folio

---

Location and Filing of Folios. Without exception, modern hotels use the computerized folios (see Exhibit 10–1) that property management systems (PMSs) create. There are no physical folios because the records are in computer memory. Folio information can be viewed on computer screens, by guests on their inroom television sets, or by a printed copy, a *hard copy*. Guest-service agents need skills on keyboards, scanners, display screens, and printers in order to record and access folio information.

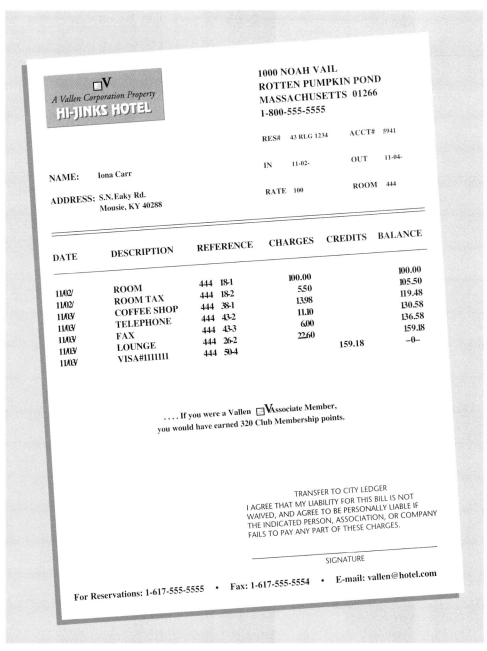

Exhibit 10-1   Standard format and presentation of a computer-prepared folio (guest bill) printed at the end of the guest's stay by a property management system (PMS). Information above the double line (reservation number, rate, arrival and departure dates) is obtained from reservation and/or registration data. Services rendered to the guest are recorded below the double lines, and their meanings are the focus of this chapter.

Unlike computer-prepared folios, hand-prepared, pencil-and-paper folios (see Exhibit 10–2) are actually stored at the desk. They are kept in a *cashier's well*, also called a *bucket* or *pit* (see Exhibit 10–3), because many are recessed in the desk top. Folios are maintained there in room number sequence separated by cardboard dividers. Room numbers are used because room numbers, more than names, are the chief means of identifying guests. Not all hotels have done away with the buckets. They are a convenient means of filing paper records whatever the system being used.

Pencil-and-paper folios generated large quantities of paperwork so billing clerks (or posting clerks) supported the front-office cashier. Almost all posting is now done electronically, much of it by the departmental (restaurant, bar, etc.) cashier on site, not at the desk. As front-office jobs are combined (see Chapter 3), guest-service agents have taken over the duties of front-office cashiers and billing clerks.

Number of Folios.   One folio is the norm for each occupied room. There are exceptions. A room with several unrelated persons would need several folios if each is to pay an equal share. Moreover, each would have signed in on a separate reg card. On the other hand, just one folio would be used for a single occupant in a two- or three-room suite. Likewise, one folio would do for a family of four assigned to a queen double.

There is no relationship between the number of city-ledger accounts and the number of occupied rooms. City-ledger accounts are opened for nonregistered guests (individuals, companies, associations) who want credit privileges, not room occupancy. Before credit cards were adopted, large hotels had upward of a thousand city-ledger accounts. Individual accounts are not needed today because almost everyone carries a credit card. Now the bulk of the city ledger can be accounted for in a half-dozen credit-card accounts. Electronically tying city-ledger accounts to the computers of credit-card companies and banks speeds processing and reduces administrative costs.

The Folio: The Group Account Receivable

Master Accounts.   Master accounts accommodate tour companies, trade associations, convention organizations, and single-entity groups (see Chapter 2). The master account (master folio) is its own person, much like a corporation has a legal identity separate from its individual owners. Charges that are incurred by the group—not billable to any one person—are accumulated on the master account. Master accounts are transient accounts receivable, not city-ledger accounts. So long as the group is in the house, the master account is a front-office account. It uses a standard folio (see Exhibit 10–4).

As with all folios, master accounts are settled at check-out. Settlement involves a joint review of the many charges by representatives of the hotel and the organization. Then the folio is transferred to the city ledger for direct billing. Obviously, then, the city ledger has more than just credit cards. Individual accounts receivable with billing to be made to the person, company, or organization (rather than through credit cards) are also part of the city ledger.

Master accounts are complex. They may number 25 pages and more. It takes telephone calls and faxes and emails to resolve what the hotel believes it is owed and what the association believes it owes. Conflicts arise over the number of persons at each function, over who signed for services, over the number of comp rooms, over sales taxes due, and so much more. Chapter 11's discussion of the city ledger explains the final billing and settlement.

How Master Accounts are Structured.   Decisions about master account billing are made well in advance of the group's arrival. Service details, credit terms, and authorized signatures are part of the negotiations between the hotel and the organization. How charges are to be distributed between individual folios and the master account is the group's decision, not the hotel's. The hotel is responsible for billing as instructed.

ROOM NO.	409						E69080		CLERK

m M/M Art E. Fishal

SB

86 Bates Boulevard
Hitchcock, Texas 01020

ARRIVED	RATE	PERSONS	COT	REG. CARD #	PREV. INV. #	CLERK
12/23/	78	2	N/A	69080	N/A	SB

DATE	12/23/		12/24/											
BROUGHT FORWARD			99	24										
ROOM	78	–												
TAX	6	24												
RESTAURANT	15	–												
"														
TELEPHONE-LOCAL														
-LONG DISTANCE														
TELEGRAMS														
LAUNDRY & VALET														
CASH ADVANCES														
"														
NEWSPAPERS														
TRANSFERS *from 407* #69081			84	24										
TOTAL DEBIT	99	24	183	48										
CASH														
ALLOWANCES														
CITY LEDGER:														
-ADVANCE DEPOSITS														
-CREDIT CARDS			183	48										
-TRANSFERS														
BALANCE FORWARD	99	24	0											

ALL ACCOUNTS ARE DUE WHEN RENDERED

Exhibit 10–2a   Standard format and presentation of two, pencil-and-paper folios (guest bills) with attached carbon copies. They are no longer in use, replaced by Exhibit 10–1. Their purpose, explaining the meaning of *credits* and the mechanics of *transfers*, is explained later, under the chapter heading "Transfers."

Single-Entity Groups.   Employees gathering for company business or groups traveling together, say, to perform, are examples of single-entity groups (see Chapter 2). Charging all the room rates to a single master account is one method of billing such closely related groups.

Convention Groups.   Unlike single-entities, convention delegates hail from many locations and companies. Delegates pay their own room and personal charges. No master account would serve for room rates, since delegates have no relationship other

ROOM NO. _____ 407 _____   **E69081**

m ___ *Benny Fishal* _____

12345 *Education Avenue*
Reading, Pennsylvania 98765

ROOM NO. _____ 407 _____   **E69081**

m ___ *Benny Fishal* _____

CLERK

SB

12345 *Education Avenue*
Reading, Pennsylvania 98765

ARRIVED	RATE	PERSONS	COT	REG. CARD #	PREV. INV. #	CLERK
12/23/	78	2	N/A	69081	N/A	SB

DATE	12/23/		12/24/											
BROUGHT FORWARD			84	24										
ROOM	78	–												
TAX	6	24												
RESTAURANT														
"														
TELEPHONE-LOCAL														
-LONG DISTANCE														
TELEGRAMS														
LAUNDRY & VALET														
CASH ADVANCES														
"														
NEWSPAPERS														
TRANSFERS														
TOTAL DEBIT	84	24	84	24										
CASH														
ALLOWANCES														
CITY LEDGER:														
-ADVANCE DEPOSITS														
-CREDIT CARDS														
-TRANSFERS TO 409	#69080		84	24										
BALANCE FORWARD	84	24	-0-											

ALL ACCOUNTS ARE DUE WHEN RENDERED

Exhibit 10-2b *Continued*

than their mutual attendance. However, the association staging the event has a master account for banquet costs, cocktail parties, and meeting expenses. Other general costs, such as telecommunications and room charges for employees or speakers, also go onto the master account (see Exhibit 10–4). Such charges must be authorized by the signature of the person or persons identified during the prenegotiations.

Many master accounts are created during a large convention. Participating companies in attendance at the convention may have exhibits, employee rooms, hospitality suites, and other services that require charges to that subgroup. As affiliated or allied members, they may see public relations benefits from sponsoring a meal. Each, then, has

Exhibit 10-3   A *cashier's well*, also called a *bucket* or *pit*, separated pencil-and-paper folios (see Exhibit 10–2) by heavy cardboard dividers. Folios were kept in room-number sequence. Buckets are still used at some front desks for filing vouchers and correspondence.

its own master account. There is no accounting relationship to the association's master account. The hotel tracks and bills each separately.

Tour Groups.   Master accounts for tour groups differ from master accounts for convention groups. Convention attendees pay their own bills. Tour-group participants pay the tour company in advance, and the tour company negotiates with the hotel. So the tour company is responsible for payment of all charges included in the package. The tour company's master account includes the room charges for everyone in the group, plus whatever else was sold with the package: meals, drinks, shows, golf, and so on. Personal expenses—those not within the package—are charged to the guest's personal folio.

Split Billing.   The distribution of the charges between the master account and the guest's personal folio is called *split billing* or *split folios*. Both the master folio (often called the *A folio*) and the guest or *B folio* are standardized forms of the types illustrated throughout the chapter. A and B are used merely to distinguish the group entity from the individual person. The A folio is the major folio where the large charges of the association, tour company or business are posted. Sometimes, the hotel itself is the A folio. Such is the case with casino comps and frequent-stay customers.

Casino Comps.   Casino hotels sometimes provide complimentary (free) accommodations to "high rollers" (big players). Split billing is used to account for the comps. To the A folio is posted all the charges that the hotel/casino will comp. Depending on the size of the guest's credit line, the comp could be for room only, or

DATE	DESCRIPTION	REFERENCE	CHARGES	CREDITS
5/14	BD DIRECTORS LUNCHEON	2323 38-3	550.00	
5/14	AUDIO/VISUAL	2323 50-1	100.00	
5/14	COCKTAIL RECEPTION	2323 26-2	12,000.00	
5/14	ROOM 2323	2323 18-1	200.00	
5/14	ROOM 2325	2323 18-1	200.00	
5/14	ROOM 1618/1620	2323 18-1	600.00	
5/14	ROOM TAX	2323 18-2	80.00	
5/15	BREAKFAST BAR	2323 38-4	800.00	
5/15	ROOM RENTALS	2323 38-1	1,500.00	
5/15	BUFFET LUNCHEON	2323 38-3	10,500.00	
5/15	FLAG RENTALS	2323 50-4	250.00	
5/15	ROOM 2323	2323 18-1	200.00	
5/15	ROOM 2325	2323 18-1	200.00	
5/15	ROOM 1618/1620	2323 18-1	600.00	
5/15	ROOM TAX	2323 18-2	80.00	
5/16	FULL-SERVICE BREAKFAST	2323 38-3	3,500.00	
5/16	ROOM ALLOWANCES 1/50	2323 18-6		2,000.00
5/16	ADJUSTMENT FOR FLAGS	2323 50-8		250.00
5/16	DIRECT TRANSFER	2323 C/L		29,110.00
5/16	THANK YOU			-0-

.... If you were a Vallen ▢VAssociate Member,
you would have earned 58,220 Club Membership points.

TRANSFER TO CITY LEDGER
I AGREE THAT MY LIABILITY FOR THIS BILL IS NOT WAIVED, AND AGREE TO BE PERSONALLY LIABLE IF THE INDICATED PERSON, ASSOCIATION, OR COMPANY FAILS TO PAY ANY PART OF THESE CHARGES.

SIGNATURE _____

For Reservations: 1-617-555-5555   •   Fax: 1-617-555-5554   •   E-mail: vallen@hotel.com

Exhibit 10–4 Folios are used for both individual guests and master accounts. Master accounts, such as this one accumulate charges for groups. Nightly charges for rooms 2323, 2325 and 1618/1620 are for the association's use, probably for staff members or guest speakers. The folio is settled with "credits." The $2,000, fourth line from the bottom, represents a typical group allowance: One free room night for each 50 room nights sold. There was also some issue with flags that warranted a second adjustment (allowance) of $250. The folio was brought to a zero balance at check-out (as must all folios) by transferring the balance to the city ledger for direct billing. (Figures are rounded for clarity.)

for room, food, beverage, and telephone. Even the airfare might be reimbursed. Items not covered are posted to the B folio, which the guest pays at departure.

Preferred-Guest Programs. Preferred-guest (or frequent-traveler) programs employ the flexibility of split billing. Two different folios are opened when a guest checks in with frequent-traveler points. The full rate of the room is charged on the A folio. On departure, the guest pays the nonroom charges, which have been posted to the B folio. The A folio is transferred to the city ledger, and either the parent company or the franchisor is billed. According to the frequent-traveler contract, one of them is now the account receivable obligated to pay the room charge.

The actual amount paid to the hotel under the preferred-guest program is always less than the rate quoted to the guest. Most programs pay full rack rate only if the occupancy of the hotel is above a given figure—90% perhaps. Below that figure—and the hotel is usually below that figure—the program reimburses the participating hotel for its operational expenses: linen, labor, and energy. So the reimbursement may be set anywhere from $20 to $50. No provision is made for recovering fixed costs such as taxes, interest, or fair wear and tear.

The burden falls heaviest on resorts. Frequent travelers go to resorts to spend the points that were earned at commercial hotels. Resorts are reimbursed from the parent company based on their previous months' ADRs. Resorts discount room rates during both the off season and the shoulder season. The result: Reimbursement for frequent-guest stays during the high season is often based on the months when ADR is at its lowest.

Understanding Charges and Credits

Familiarization with accounting and with its system of charges and credits gives guest-service agents a big assist in handling folios. This knowledge is especially helpful in understanding the interface between front-office records (the transient ledger) and back-office records (the city ledger). Nevertheless, folios are designed for use by anyone, with or without an accounting background.

Bracket materials are used hereafter to repeat the same discussion using accounting terminology. Explanations are complete even if the bracketed paragraphs are skipped. Students are urged to read the bracketed content for a broader understanding of the folio and its relationship to the hotel's accounting system.

Charges for services rendered *increase* the guest's debt to the hotel. The ISLANDER (restaurant) posting on the folio of Exhibit 10–5 is an example. *Credits reduce* the guest's debt. ADJUST PHONE of Exhibit 10–5 is an example. Credits must offset charges when the guest checks out. At departure, the guest's folio must always be zero (see Exhibit 10–5).

Charges and credits are identified with separate columns in Exhibits 10–5 and 10–6. Another technique, illustrated in Exhibit 10–13, uses plus (+) for charges and minus (−) for credits. Exhibits 10–10 and 10–15 illustrate still a third approach, which uses only one column. Credit values are marked CR. Since most folio postings are charges, there is no need to mark them. Charge is understood with the one-column folio.

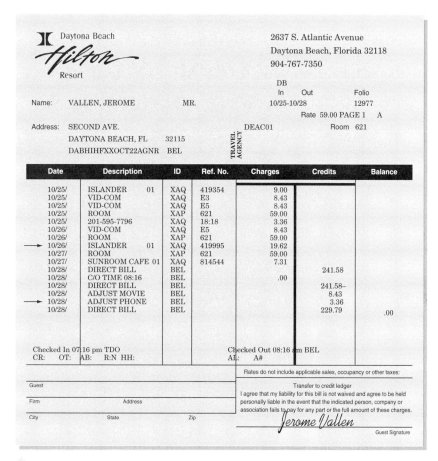

Exhibit 10–5 Another example of a modern folio. The final entry is similar to that of Exhibit 10–4. "Direct bill" or " Direct transfer" indicates the folio balance is moved from the transient ledger to the city ledger for direct billing to the client's headquarters. The heavy vertical line between charges and credits is designed to show accountants the similarity between the folio and a simple T-account. *Courtesy of Daytona Beach Hotel Resort, Daytona Beach, Florida.*

THE MEANING OF DEBITS AND CREDITS

Accounting language speaks of debits and credits instead of charges and credits. Debits (or charges) increase the values of certain accounting records. In this chapter, the focus is on folios, which are accounts receivable. Other accounts, cash for example, are also increased with debits. Cash and accounts receivable are among the many assets (things that hotels own) that follow the same accounting rules. Accounting records, assets among them, that are increased with debits are decreased by credits.

> Increases in assets, including *accounts receivable* and *cash*, are made with debits. Decreases in assets, including *accounts receivable* and *cash*, are made with credits.

Accounting students will recognize the folio as a T-account, where debits are on the left side and credits on the right. Exhibit 10–5 is highlighted with horizontal and vertical lines to reinforce the visual similarities between an account receivable folio and an account receivable T-account.

Radisson Hotel Ottawa Centre

100 Kent Street, Ottawa, Ontario, Canada K1P 5R7 Telephone (613) 238-1122

LA RONDE FINE CUISINE   **CAFE TOULOUSE**   *Lautrec's*

ROOM / CHAMBRE	NAME / NOM	RATE / TAUX	DEPARTURE / DEPART	TIME / HEURE	
2228	STEIN, FRANK N.	75.00	14/10/		ACCT# 20539

ROOM / CHAMBRE	FIRM OR GROUP / COMPAGNIE OU GROUP	PLAN	ARRIVAL / ARRIVEE		
1K1A	AMERICAN		09/10/	12:29	GROUP 6566

54	P.O. BOX 1211 DB LANSING MI 90125-0012				

| CLERK COMMIS | ADDRESS / ADRESSE | | METHOD OF PAYMENT MODE DE PAIEMENT | | |

DATE	REFERENCE/RÉFÉRENCE		CHARGES	CREDITS / CRÉDITS	BALANCE DUE / SOLDE DÛ
09/10	ROOM	2228, 1	75.00		
09/10	ROOM TAX	2228, 1	3.75		
10/10	TOUL POS	000000	17.12		
10/10	LNG DIST	315-386-	.57		
10/10	ROOM	2228, 1	75.00		
10/10	ROOM TAX	2228, 1	3.75		
11/10	ROOM	2228, 1	75.00		
11/10	ROOM TAX	2228, 1	3.75		
12/10	LNG DIST	315-386-	1.14		
12/10	LNG DIST	315-386-	1.14		
12/10	ROOM	2228, 1	75.00		
12/10	ROOM TAX	2228, 1	3.75		
13/10	TOUL POS	000000	9.86		
13/10	TOUL POS	000000	16.58		
13/10	ROOM	2228, 1	75.00		
13/10	ROOM TAX	2228, 1	3.75		
					440.16

FIRM / COMPAGNIE   ADDRESS / ADRESSE

CITY _____ PROV. _____ POSTAL _____
VILLE   POSTALE

ATTENTION _____

GUEST SIGNATURE X _____
SIGNATURE DU CLIENT

I AGREE THAT MY LIABILITY FOR THIS BILL IS NOT WAIVED AND AGREE TO BE HELD PERSONALLY LIABLE IN THE EVENT THAT THE INDICATED PERSON, COMPANY OR ASSOCIATION FAILS TO PAY FOR ANY PART OR THE FULL AMOUNT OF THESE CHARGES.

IL EST CONVENU QUE MA RESPONSABILITÉ DE CETTE FACTURE N'EST PAS ABROGÉE ET JE CONSENS A L'ASSUMER DANS L'ÉVENTUALITE OU LA PERSONNE INDIQUÉE, SOCIÉTÉ OU ASSOCIATION REFUSE DE PAYER LE MONTANT EN TOTALITÉ OU EN PARTIE.

Courtesy: Radisson Hotel Ottawa Centre, Ottawa, Canada.

Exhibit 10–6   Another group folio. This one identifies the group by name, American, its identification number, #6566; the identification of the guest-service agent who registered them, #54; the group's account (folio) number, #20539, which could be the same as the room number; and the assumption of liability (bottom right). There's a folio balance so the account is not yet checked-out. *Courtesy of Radisson Hotel Ottawa Centre, Ottawa, Canada.*

Assets.   An asset is something a business owns. Hotels own many assets, including land, buildings, furniture, and kitchen equipment. Only two of the numerous assets owned are important to the front office and its folio responsibilities. Accounts receivable, which are debts that customers owe the hotel (the hotel owns the debt), is one of those assets. Cash is the other. Cash is money: money in the bank, money at the desk, money in the bar till. Cash has become less important to the records of the front office because both guests and hotelkeepers prefer folios to be settled with credit cards: accounts receivable.

Be they guests or strangers, customers who buy services with cash in the lounge, the coffee shop, the newsstand, or other hotel departments increase the hotel's cash asset. There is no record on the guest's folio, but there is an increase (debit) to cash according to the accounting rule:

> Increases in assets, including accounts receivable and *cash*, are made with debits.
>
> Increases in incomes (sale of rooms, *food*, beverage, spa, etc.) are made with credits.

> Debit: Cash   33.00
>   Credit: Proper Department (room, *food*, beverage, spa, etc.)   33.00
> *Explanation*: Sold coffee-shop meal for cash.

Hotel guests may make the same purchases by signing for the charges. That requires an entry on the folio, a debit to the asset accounts receivable.

> Increases in assets, including *accounts receivable* and cash, are made with debits.
>
> Increases in incomes (sale of rooms, *food*, beverage, spa, etc.) are made with credits.

> Debit: Accounts Receivable/Guest's Folio   33.00
>   Credit: Proper Department (room, *food*, beverage, spa, etc.)   33.00
> *Explanation*: Sold coffee-shop meal on account (to registered guest).

Sales or Incomes.   Hotels are in the business of selling services. It's those sales that produce incomes and, eventually, profits for the business. The sale of rooms is the hotel's major product. Depending on the size, class, and type of property, income is also earned from the sale of other products and services. Guests pay for these services by charging them to the folio (establishing an asset called account receivable) or paying for them with cash. Sometimes they use credit cards. The delivered product or service is the same, they're just paid for differently. The record of service is different from the record of payment, although the two records take place simultaneously, as we shall see next in the discussion of equality.

Debit/credit rules are different for sales (incomes) than for assets. Just as all assets follow one asset rule, so all incomes follow one income rule. It is an opposite rule.

> Increases in assets, including *accounts receivable* and cash, are made with debits.
>
> Increases in incomes (sales of *rooms*, food, beverage, etc.) are made with credits.

> Debit: Accounts Receivable/Guest's Folio   100
>   Credit: Proper Department (*room*, food, beverage, spa, etc.)   100
> *Explanation*: Guest occupied room.

Sometimes, but not too often, incomes are decreased. Go back mentally to the guest-management contents of Chapter 7. Assume that as a result of a serious mistake on the hotel's part, the guest's room charge is waived. The room income, which was recorded yesterday with a credit (see previous page 387) must now be reversed. Allowances, which are the opposite of sales, are used to do that.

Decreases in incomes (sales of *rooms*, food, beverage, etc.) are made with debits.

Decreases in assets, including *accounts receivable* and cash, are made with credits.

Debit: Proper Departmental (*room*, food, spa, etc.) Allowance   100
    Credit: Accounts Receivable/Guest's Folio   100
Explanation: Room allowance because of housekeeping failure.

The room-sale debit offsets the original room-sale credit. The net result is no charge in the guest's folio. Both postings, the sale and the sale adjustment (an allowance), appear on the folio.

Every accounting event has two parts. This dual accounting system always requires equal dollar amounts of charges and credits. For example, two things happen when a bar bill is paid with cash. One, the hotel has more cash in the till. Two, bar sales, or bar income, has also increased. Both increase by the same dollar amount. The $33 food example several paragraphs back illustrates that equality.

If the bar drinks are charged to the room, the accounting entry changes somewhat, illustrated by the second $33 example, but the equality of debits and credits remains the same.

Reexamine the room sale and then the room adjustment discussed above, giving special attention to the equality of charges and credits—first, when the room sale was recorded, and then when the room was adjusted because of the complaint.

POSTING TO THE FOLIO (THE ACCOUNT RECEIVABLE)

Hotels readily extend credit to guests because guest identities have been confirmed through reservations, registrations, and credit cards. Guests charge goods and services to their front-office accounts, their folios. Folios are accounts receivable, debts *owed by the guest* and *owned by the hotel*. Posting to the folio means recording the event, usually a sale (the charge), or a payment (the credit).

Guests may also buy goods and services by paying cash or using a credit card at the time the service is rendered. Paying for a bar drink or a breakfast buffet with cash or credit card does not impact the folio. The cash goes into the till and the credit-card charge appears eventually on the credit-card mailing sent to the guest's home or business. Most registered guests sign for such services. Then the debt appears on the folio to be settled at some later time, usually at check-out.

Certain services, room charges, and telephone calls made from the room, must appear on the folio. There is no practical way for the hotel to collect when those services are rendered. No one expects collection for the room occupancy in the middle of the night. Telephone calls are posted (recorded) on the folio automatically, electronically. So both room sales and telephone sales are made to the guest on credit, charged to the folio.

Cash and credit cards do have a role at the front desk. They are used by the guest to settle (pay for) the folio charges. That discussion appears at the end of the chapter.

Definition of Terms to Be Used	
Allowance	Reduction of the debt owned by an account receivable
Departmental Control Sheet	Pencil-and-paper record of departmental (food, beverage, etc.) charges made to various guest rooms
Transfer	Movement of a folio balance between ledgers or guests
Zero Balance	After check-out, every folio has a balance of zero

Overview of the Billing Procedure

Electronic folios gained favor from the mid-1980s and on. Paper-and pencil folios were the norm during the previous half-century. That period produced, first, better carbon paper and then duplicating paper without messy carbons. Stationery companies introduced packaged forms that reduced the need to write and rewrite the same information for duplicate copies, say, a folio for the guest and a copy for the hotel. Property management systems (PMS) reduced the paperwork still further. Records are retained in computer memory and printed on demand.

Preparing the Folio. The property management system formats the folios as guests arrive and register (see Exhibits 10–5, 10–6 and others.) The data for the folio comes from the registration card. Some hotels use the reservation information instead. Those hotels preprint the reg cards as part of the previous night's audit so they await the guests' arrivals. Preprinted cards speed up registration.

Many bits of information appear on the folio, including the times of arrival and departure (Exhibit 10–5, on the bottom). There are no rules, so information may appear anywhere or not at all. Exhibit 10–6 shows arrival time of 12:29 at the folio's top. Group affiliation is also shown there. Exhibit 10–6 indicates membership in the *American* group, whose billing code is 6566, right side above the center.

There is common information in every folio exhibit of the chapter. Exhibit 10–6 can serve as the source. Illustrated are the room assigned (2228); the rate charged ($75); and dates of arrival and anticipated departure (9/10 and 14/10).[2] Included, of course, is the guest's name, Frank N. Stein, and address. The number of persons is usually shown, but not in Exhibit 10–6 (see Exhibit 10–9).

Folios are numbered sequentially as a means of identification and accounting control. The folio account number of Exhibit 10–6 is 20539. Folio numbers are especially important for internal control when the hotel uses pencil-and-paper folios, and almost always appear in the upper right corner, Exhibit 10–2.

---

[2]In many nations, the day of the month is written before the month of the year. So it is on this Canadian folio. 9/10 is the 9th of October, not the 10th of September.

As society grows more litigious, information of all kinds is being added to the folio to protect the hotel from unwarranted lawsuits. Notice of the availability of a safe for the protection of the guest's valuables is one such disclaimer. This fits better on the registration card (Chapter 8), which the guest sees on arrival, rather than on the folio, which the guest normally sees at departure.

Nearly every folio now carries at the bottom of the page a statement about liability for the bill (see Exhibit 10–1 and others). With so many persons (employers, associations, credit-card companies) other than the guests accepting the charges, hotel lawyers want to make certain that eventually someone pays. The odd part about the statement is how rarely the guest is asked to sign it.

Presenting the Bill.   Common law protects the innkeeper from fraud. Guests who are unwilling or unable to pay may be refused accommodations. Extending credit, as most hotels do, is a privilege that may be revoked at any time. Nervous credit managers do just that whenever their suspicions are aroused. The folio is printed and presented to the guest with a request for immediate payment. Even the traditional delay of paying at check-out is revoked. The entire industry has gone one step further by collecting in advance with cash (rare) or by obtaining credit-card identification.

Since most guests are not credit risks, bills are normally presented and paid at check-out time. It works that way for the vast majority of guests who stay for several nights. A folio is printed on demand as the guest departs. If there are any adjustments, an amended copy is printed for the guest to take away. Many hotels deliver the customer's initial copy under the guest-room door sometime during the previous night. If a hard copy is not needed, the folio can be viewed on a front-office monitor or more leisurely on the television in the guest room.

Long-term guests are billed weekly, and they are expected to pay promptly. Regardless of the length of the stay, folios are also rendered whenever they reach a predetermined dollar amount. The class of hotel, which reflects room rates and menu prices, determines the dollar figure that management sets as the ceiling. No charges are allowed beyond that value.

Communicating the Charges.   Guests buy services—that is, incur charges—throughout the house. Perhaps there's a drink by the swimming pool, a dinner in the grill, or laundry for overnight service. Getting the information (name, room number, and dollar value) about the charge from the point of origin to the folio requires some type of communication.

Before the Age of Electronics.   Paper-and-pencil systems required close cooperation and fast footwork between departments. The department making the sale had to communicate manually to the desk where the folio entry was entered. And it had to be done quickly. To illustrate, assume a guest takes breakfast in the coffee shop. By signing the $15 guest check, the guest ordered the meal charged to the folio.

{*Reminder*: Folios are not used if payments are by cash or credit card!}

The signed check, now called a *voucher,* was used to communicate with the desk. As a precaution against its loss (it's just a piece of paper) the coffee-shop cashier recorded the

DEPARTMENT CONTROL SHEET

NAME

VOUCHER NO.	ROOM NO.	GUEST NAME	AMOUNT	MEMO
11370	409	*Fishel*	$ *86*	
11371	1012	*James*	*27*	

THIS REPORT MUST BE SENT TO NIGHT AUDITOR BY 12 O'CLOCK EACH NIGHT.

Exhibit 10–7   Segment of a departmental control sheet. Guest checks (called vouchers) are recorded as a precaution against loss. They are then dispatched to the front office for pencil-and-paper posting to the folio. This system has been replaced by electronic posting at the point of origin as illustrated in Exhibit 10–8.

information on a *departmental control sheet* (see Exhibit 10–7). Both the voucher and the control sheet showed the guest's name and room number, the amount of the charge, and the voucher (coffee-shop check) number. The cashier retained the control sheet.

Sending the voucher to the desk was easier said than done. Hand-carried vouchers moved slowly because the coffee-shop cashier had to wait for a runner: a busperson, a bellperson, or a foodserver. Several vouchers were accumulated before a runner was summoned. That minimized the inconvenience of frequent calls; after all, the cashier had no authority over these runners. Busy runners sometimes forgetfully pocketed the voucher as they ran off to perform their regular duties.

Vouchers were often late in arriving at the desk. Charges that appear on a folio after the guest has checked out, called *late charges*, are difficult to collect. If the amount is small, the hotel doesn't even try.

With the voucher in hand, the guest-service agent began the posting (recording) sequence. A search was made for that particular guest's folio, filed in room-number sequence in the cashier's well (see Exhibit 10–3). The folio was removed and the $15 was posted (see Exhibit 10–2). Each posting had to be located in the correct vertical column (the date) opposite the proper department, "RESTAURANT," as Exhibit 10–2 illustrates.

With Electronic Systems.   The hotel's property management system (PMS) has done away with vouchers, control sheets, runners, and late charges. Communication is electronic and instantaneous. The distant department is tied to the folio electronically. Cashiers throughout the hotel enter the charge onto the folio by means of an electronic cash register, called a *point-of-sale terminal (POS)*. The system bypasses the front desk and the guest-service agent altogether (see Exhibit 10–8). Folios are always current; late charges are practically unknown. There's an extra: Information furnished through the POS terminal enables the departmental cashier to verify the guest's identity, if that is an issue.

POS installations are costly. Management might make an economic decision to leave certain minor departments, which generate small revenue streams, without POS capability. Then the property operates with a mix of the old pencil-and-paper system and the new electronic system.

Exhibit 10-8   Point-of-sale (POS) terminals are located in revenue centers (restaurants, bars, gift shops, etc.) throughout the hotel. The POS interfaces with the hotel's PMS, permitting cashiers at distant locations to post electronically to guest folios, eliminating control sheets and vouchers. The screen shown in Chapter 13, Exhibit 13–2 appears in the window of this exhibit.

Recording Charges to Accounts Receivable

Charges (increases in accounts receivable) and credits (decreases to accounts receivable) are posted (entered on the folios) to keep guest accounts current. The discussion now focuses on posting those charges and on the meaning of each. Credits are discussed next.

   Understanding the Line of Posting.   Each *charge* line on the folio represents two things. One is the change in the value of the folio. The amount owed by the guest grows larger with each charge posting. The more services the guest buys, the more dollars are owed.

   Each folio line has a second message. It tells the reader the source of the charge, the department providing the service. Hence, the second meaning reflects the income that the hotel earns from the delivery of the service. Exhibit 10–9 illustrates several of these departmental charges. Among them are room sales (Exhibit 10–9, lines 1 and 7); restaurant sales (Woodlands Restaurant, line 5); and telephone sales (lines 4 and 6).

   {*Reminder:* The folio would not be used if the Woodlands' charge was paid with cash or credit card. Folios are accounts receivable, guests who *still* owe the hotel.}

   Each folio illustrated in this chapter and each used in reality have the same format. There is a single line entry for each activity. The printed information in the center of the folio identifies a source of income for the hotel. The fact that there is a posting means that the guest (the account receivable) has purchased some service from the hotel and owes the same amount that is recorded as departmental income. That amount is added automatically to the previous balance.

STOUFFER WESTCHESTER HOTEL
80 WEST RED OAK LANE
WHITE PLAINS, NEW YORK 10604
(914) 694-5400

	ARRIVAL	3/11/	
TOWNS, SEYMOUR	DEPARTURE	3/13/	
	NO. IN PARTY	2	
123 NORTH STREET	RATE	89.00	
WHITE PLAINS, NY	RESERVATION#	NR	
10601			

ACCT. NO.   801936   ROOM NO.   346

#	DATE	DESCRIPTION	AMOUNT
1	3/11/	ROOM/346/2/2/4	89.00
2	3/11/	SALES TAX/346/2/2/4	6.19
3	3/11/	COUNTY OCCUPANCY TAX/346/2/2/4 OCCUPANCY TAX	2.67
4	3/12	LOCAL/LOCAL TOLL/346/3120XX4006/1/4 09:56/6987991	.75
5	3/12/	WOODLANDS/346/736334/1/4/113355	24.03
6	3/12/	LOCAL/LOCAL TOLL/346/312CXXX011/1/4 11:41/6987991	.75
7	3/12/	ROOM/346/2/2/4	89.00
8	3/12/	SALES TAX/346/2/2/4	6.19
9	3/12/	COUNTY OCCUPANCY TAX/346/2/2/4 OCCUPANCY TAX	2.67

* BALANCE DUE *   221.25

ACCOUNTS PAST 30 DAYS SUBJECT TO SERVICE CHARGE OF 1 1/2% PER MONTH (ANNUAL RATE OF 18%)

PRINTED ON RECYCLED PAPER ✪

COMPANY   STREET   ZIP

CITY / STATE

I agree that my liability for this bill is not waived and agree
to be held personally liable in the event that the indicated   SIGNATURE _____
person, company or associations fails to pay for any part of
these charges.

Exhibit 10–9   Electronic folios are all much the same. This one isn't. Previous illustrations contain two columns, charges and credits. This illustrations has but one, leaving the user to distinguish charges from credits. Note the sale tax posting on lines 2, 3, 8 and 9. (The guest is a walk-in. There's a NR [no reservation] on the top right.) Alert hoteliers will recognize that Stouffer is no longer a hotel chain! *Courtesy of Stouffers Westchester Hotel, White Plains, New York.*

Examine Exhibit 10-9 or any of the other folio exhibits. Each line is read as a two-part accounting entry. One is a debit, the other the balancing credit. Since folios are accounts receivable, every folio line represents either an accounts receivable debit or an accounts receivable credit! With charges, each line is an accounts receivable debit, and the credit is to the department printed on the horizontal line.

Increase in assets, including *accounts receivable* and cash, are made with debits.
Increase in incomes (sales of *rooms, food, telephone*) are made with credits.
Increase in liabilities (debts owed to banks and *governments*) are made with credits.

Line 1   Debit accounts receivable, credit room sales for $89.
Line 2   Debit accounts receivable, credit sales taxes payable for $6.19.
Line 3   Debit accounts receivable, credit occupancy taxes payable for $2.67.
Line 4   Debit accounts receivable, credit telephone sales for $0.75.
Line 5   Debit accounts receivable, credit restaurant sales for $24.03.
Line 6   Debit accounts receivable, credit telephone sales for $0.75.
Line 7   Debit accounts receivable, credit room sales for $89.
Line 8   Debit accounts receivable, credit sales taxes payable for $6.19.
Line 9   Debit accounts receivable, credit occupancy taxes payable for $2.67.

Reference Numbers.   Exhibits 10–5, 10–6, 10–9, and 10–10 display reference numbers on each line of posting. These numbers identify departments in the hotel's chart of accounts. A chart of accounts is a coded numbering system by which the hotel classifies its records. Each department within the hotel is identified by code, but it isn't a secret code. Having codes makes recordkeeping easier. There is no uniform coding system among hotels, but there is consistency within the individual property and the chain.

Consider the reference numbering of Exhibit 10–10. In the second column under the "description," the number 2315 appears on lines 2 through 11. That's the room number, the number of the account receivable being charged. In the third column is a second series of numbers, which represent the departments generating the postings. Lines 2, 3, and 4 contain the numbers 518, 519, and 520 respectively. The rooms department is identified by the number 5. Hence, 518 is room sales, 519 is room tax, and 520 is room tax for a second governmental agency.

Increases in assets, including *accounts receivable* and cash, are made with debits.
Increases in incomes (sales of *rooms*, food and other) are made with credits.
Increases in liabilities (debts owed to banks and *governments*) are made with credits. Values for Exhibit 10–10:

Line 2:   Debit accounts receivable, credit room sales for $125.
Line 3:   Debit accounts receivable, credit excise taxes payable for $5.21.
Line 4:   Debit accounts receivable, credit room taxes payable for $6.25.

HAWAII PRINCE HOTEL

W A I K I K I

⊙ *PRINCE HOTELS*

Hawaii Prince Hotel, 100 Holomoana Street, Honolulu, Hawaii 96815
Telephone: (808) 956-1111   Facsimile: (808) 946-0811

A-STANDARD

DECAT, M/M BILL
1234 PENNSYLVANIA AVENUE
WASHINGTON, DC
56789-0000

ARRIVAL DATE	6/21
DEPARTURE	6/22
NO. IN PARTY	2
RATE	125.00

ACCOUNT NO. 67877   ROOM NO. 2315

NUMBER	DATE	DESCRIPTION		AMOUNT
1	5/31	ADV DEP VISA MASTER 4000 0000 0000 0000		$130.21CR
		1NT RM/ST TAX 67877		
2	6/21	ROOM	2315 518	$125.00
3	6/21	EXCISE TAX	2315 519	$5.21
4	6/21	ROOM TAX	2315 520	$6.25
5	6/21	LOCAL PHONE 3:57	2315 621XXX9005	$.75
6	6/21	PROMENADE DECK	2315 5996	$23.00
7	6/21	PROMENADE DECK	2315 5996	$3.00
8	6/21	PROMENADE DECK	2315 5996	$.96
9	6/22	PRINCE COURT	2315 1382	$18.00
10	6/22	PRINCE COURT	2315 1382	$2.00
11	6/22	PRINCE COURT	2315 1382	$.75
				$54.71
		* Balance Due *		

SIGNATURE

I AGREE THAT MY LIABILITY FOR THIS BILL IS NOT WAIVED AND AGREE TO BE HELD PERSONALLY LIABLE IN THE EVENT THAT THE INDICATED
PERSON, COMPANY OR ASSOCIATION FAILS TO PAY FOR ANY PART OR THE FULL AMOUNT OF THESE CHARGES.

Exhibit 10-10   Line 1 of the folio indicates an advanced deposit made with a credit card; a very unusual entry. Under "description," this folio references the chart of accounts that the hotel maintains. Each record (posting) has two parts! One is always a charge to the account receivable, room 2315. Equal and opposite credits are recorded in their respective departments. The code tells us that the 500s (518, 519 and 520) are rooms; the 5900s are beverage and the 1300s (1382) is food. The balance still due is net of the $130.21 deposit (one night's stay plus tax) and will be settled in all likelihood with the same credit card. *Courtesy of Hawaii Prince Hotel, Honolulu, Hawaii.*

The number 5996 appears on lines 6, 7, and 8. In this case the number 59 indicates beverage sales and 96 indicates the Promenade Deck, so 5996 is beverage sales on the Promenade Deck. The number 5997 might be beverage sales in the Prince Court, 5998 might be beverage sales through room service, and 5999 might be beverage sales in banquets. Line 6 is the actual sale of beverages, line 7 is the tip that the guest added to the bill, and line 8 is the tax due.

Increases in assets, including *accounts receivable* and cash, are made with debits.

Increases in incomes (sales of rooms, *beverage* and other) are made with credits.

Increase in liabilities (debts to *employees* and *governments*) are made with credits.

Line 6:   Debit accounts receivable, credit beverage sales for $23.
Line 7:   Debit accounts receivable, credit tips owed to employees for $3.00.
Line 8:   Debit accounts receivable, credit sales taxes payable for $0.96.

Food sales are similarly referenced in Exhibit 10–10 using number 13. The number 1382 is food sales in the Prince Court. Just as beverage sales had several divisions, so might food sales: coffee shop, banquets, room service, pool snack bar, and buffet, 1383 . . . 1387.

Exhibit 10–9 follows the same concept although the presentation differs. The account receivable is identified on each line by its room number, 346, immediately after the department name. Then, just as with Exhibit 10–10, comes a series of numbers identifying the departments that generated the charge. Code 2/2/4 (lines 1, 2, and 3) represent room department charges (rooms sales and room taxes) corresponding to code number 5 of Exhibit 10–10.

The references of Exhibit 10–5 do not follow the same pattern. The ID column is the person doing the posting. The Ref. No. column may refer to the number on the voucher that gave rise to the charge. That idea is supported by the sequential numbering of the two Islander postings, 419354 on 10/25 and 419995 two days later, on 10/27.

Posting Room Charges.   Room charges are posted differently from charges from all the other departments. Charges for food, telephone, and bar sales may appear several times daily. Depending on the type and class of hotel, charges also originate in other departments. They, too, may appear more than once, or not at all. Among them are laundry and dry cleaning, garage and parking fees, saunas and health clubs, inroom safe and inroom bar charges. Inroom films may also be charged (see Exhibit 10–5, lines 2 and 3). Full-service resorts have sports and recreational charges for greens fees, watercraft, ski tickets, skeet, horseback riding, and the like. All of these are posted as previously explained: either directly through the departmental POS or by runners carrying pencil-and-paper vouchers to be input by the desk.

Room charges are different. They are posted just once, at night. Room charges originate at the desk so communications from distant departments is not an issue. Room charges are posted by the night auditor, not by the guest-service agents during the day.

With the old pencil-and-paper system, the night auditor removed each folio from the well (see Exhibit 10–3); wrote the room charge and tax on each folio; and totaled the account (see Exhibit 10–2). This was a time-consuming, error-prone procedure.

Property management systems keep the room rates in memory, compute the taxes automatically, post and total electronically, and print on demand. With a PMS, the night auditor initiates a program that posts the room rates and taxes to all the folios, as illustrated in Exhibit 10–10, lines 2 through 4, and in other illustrations throughout the chapter.

Four exceptions, all infrequent ones, require room rates to be posted during the day rather than by the night auditor. Exception one is the day rate: Guests arrive and depart the same day—leaving before the night audit even takes place. Late check-outs are another example. The previous night's room charge is posted in the normal manner by the auditor, but the premium for staying beyond the check-out hour is added by the cashiers/guest-service agents as the guest departs. Situation three is a recent innovation that has caused industrywide angst and is not likely to be retained. Guests who leave earlier than their original reservation are penalized. Where inflicted, these outrageous charges are also posted by the cashiers/guest-service agents.

Paid-in-advance guests, usually those without luggage, are the fourth and final exception to who-posts-the-room-rates. Here again, it is the cashiers/guest-service agents. They also collect for the night before the guest is roomed. Payment is night by night and no other charges are allowed against the folio. Without a cumulative folio balance, paid-in-advance guests must use cash or credit cards in the bars and restaurants. Guests are given receipts when they pay for the room, so they rarely come to the desk to check out.

In each of the four cases (day rate, late check-out, reservation overstay, and paid in advance), the night auditor finds the room charge has already been posted just as other charges (food, telephone, etc.) have been.

Although posted at a different time and in a different manner, room sales have the same impact as sales in other departments. All increase the amount owed by the guest, the account receivable. Most folio postings do that: increase the amount owed by the guest. The critical posting is the guest's settlement of the account. That's when the debt is paid and the account receivable is reduced to zero. *It is* always *reduced to zero*. Before examining account receivable settlements, let's review sales taxes as another of the charges (increases) to accounts receivable.

Sales Taxes.   Taxes levied on room sales by local, county, and state governments are universal to hotelkeeping (see Chapter 9). Government finds taxing visitors easier than taxing residents. Making the hotel collect the tax adds insult to injury. With rare exceptions, every jurisdiction requires each room charge to be followed by one or more tax charges. The amount owed by the account receivable increases with each room sale, which belongs to the hotel, and with the room tax, which the hotel collects for the government.

Taxes collected (taxes payable) make the hotel an account receivable to the government just as the guest is an account receivable to the hotel. Logically enough, an account receivable becomes an *account payable* when situated on the other side of the owe–owed relationship. The government considers the hotel's debt as an account receivable. The hotel, which owes the amount collected from guests, considers the government an account payable. So, the amount due is labeled *taxes payable*. Exhibits 10–6, 10–9, and 10–10 reflect those tax entries.

Periodically, perhaps quarterly, the hotel pays the governmental agencies the taxes due.

WHEN TAXES ARE LEVIED ON THE GUEST

...For Exhibit 10–9:

Increases in assets, including *accounts receivable* and cash, are made with debits.

Increases in incomes (sale of *rooms*, food, beverage, spa, etc.) are made with credits.

Increases in liabilities (debts to employees and *governments*) are made with credits.

Debit: Accounts Receivable/Guest's Folio   97.86
    Credit: Room Sales   89
    Credit: Taxes Payable   8.86
Explanation: Collected taxes on guest's room charges.

WHEN TAXES ARE PAID BY THE HOTEL TO THE GOVERNMENT

Decreases in liabilities (debts to employees and *governments*) are made with debits.

Decreases in assets, including accounts receivable and *cash*, are made with credits.

Debit: Debit Taxes Payable   8.86
    Credit: Cash   8.86
Explanation: Paid government sums collected from guests.

Recording Credits to Accounts Receivable

As the guest folio (an account receivable) is increased by charges (room sales, food sales and so on) so it is decreased by credits (payments). It's simple: Paying the bill reduces the debt.

Although charges occur and are posted numerous times throughout each day, settlement of the account usually waits until check-out time. Of course, guests can and do make payments during the stay. With reservations, payments are often made in advance, prepaid. Irrespective of when and how the payment is made, the transient folio (the guest bill, the front-office account) *must* always have a zero balance at check-out! That is, total charges posted throughout the stay and total credits, whenever posted, must be equal at departure. Departed guests can have no transient folio balance if they are no longer registered. The first few pages of the chapter made clear that only registered guests can have accounts in the transient ledger.

Three Methods of Settling Accounts.   Unlike the many charges itemized earlier (from room charges to bar charges, to green fees, to saunas), there are only three ways to "pay" the bill. They can be applied separately or in combination.

1. Cash is one method, but it is used infrequently. Cash means any kind of money: bills and coin; foreign currency; domestic and international traveler's checks; personal checks; bank checks; cashier's checks; even casino chips. Payment with cash is discussed thoroughly in Chapter 12.

2. Allowances, reductions to the amount owed, are a second method of settlement. One study suggested that billing errors that require allowance adjustments may occur as often as one in four postings!

3. Transfers—shifting the amount due to someone else—is the third method, and the most frequently used one. Credit-card transfers are the best examples. Departing guests shift their folio balances in the front-office ledger (the transient ledger) to the credit-card company's account in the city ledger. Earlier, the chapter pointed out that front-office ledgers (with their folios) are for registered guests only. Similarly, the city ledger is for nonregistered accounts receivable. When the guest leaves—is no longer registered—the charge must be moved to the city ledger, to the credit-card account. The credit-card company eventually settles with the hotel.

Settling with Allowances.   Just as retail stores permit the return of unsatisfactory goods, hotels give credit for poor service, misunderstandings, and mathematical errors. The retailer's exchange of goods is the hotel's allowance. Part or all of the folio settlement (by which the guest pays the bill) can be made with an allowance. Legitimate adjustments to guest complaints are high on management's radar. So much so that hotels often retain authority to grant allowances against privately owned concessionaires renting shop space in the hotel.

A record of every allowance highlights the issue for both the hotel and the guest. Using a pencil-and-paper allowance voucher (see Exhibit 10–11) provides guidance for the company anxious to avoid future errors in guest service. Improving weaknesses in the operation starts with knowing what the failures are.

Allowance reports summarizing the day's experience are prepared as part of the night audit. Reports to management take on extra significance because employees are now being empowered (see Chapter 7). Granting allowances could become abusive. Employee empowerment aside, good fiscal management requires a supervisor's signature (see Exhibit 10–11, bottom line) when the allowance exceeds a certain value. That limit would vary with the class of the hotel.

Allowances are given to adjust the folio after the fact. The first step is to correct the problem if possible. Allowances are warranted only if it is too late to rectify the situation. *Rebates*, another name for allowances, are also used to correct errors on the folio and are the means of accounting for comps.

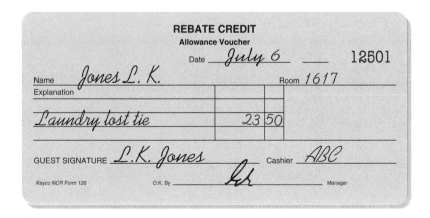

Exhibit 10–11   Allowance (or rebate) vouchers, which are credits to the guest folio, are issued to settle guest claims. They are numbered for internal control and serve to alert management to the quality of guest service. A nightly allowance report highlights company errors and areas of guest complaints (see also Chapter 7).

Comp Allowances. The authority to compliment rooms or other services—professional lingo calls it "the power of the pen"—should be restricted and carefully monitored. Because comps, like allowances in general, are subject to abuse, management requires a comp report (see Chapter 13) as an adjunct to the allowance report. Misuse of comps starts when comp guests are not registered. With no record, there is no room count, no house count, and no dollar income. Proper handling of room comps starts with a daily posting of the full room rate. To allay the guest's concern, the rate is flagged on the rooming slip, "$189 COMP," for example. An allowance, valued for the total of the daily room charges, is granted as the comp guest checks out.

This allowance illustration builds on the previous illustration on 398 dealing with room taxes and using the same values. Assuming the comp guest stayed for two nights, the room and tax posting would appear twice. (See Exhibit 10–9 for the actual folio postings.) Here the folio entries appear in accounting form.

> Increases in assets, including *accounts receivable* and cash, are made with debits.
>
> Increases in incomes (sales of *rooms*, food, beverage, etc.) are made with credits.
>
> Increases in liabilities (debts owed to banks and *governments*) are made with credits.

Debit: Accounts Receivable/Guest's Folio   97.86
    Credit: Proper Department (*room*, food, beverage, spa, etc.)   89
    Credit: Sales Taxes Payable   8.86
Explanation: Comp guest occupied room.

Reversing the room sale (or any other sale) with one allowance results in no charges to the guest and no room (or other) income earned by the hotel. However, a clear record of what occurred is now on the books. Some jurisdictions require room taxes to be paid on comp rooms. Sometimes the hotel pays; sometimes the comped guest pays, as illustrated next.

> Decreases in incomes (sales of *rooms*, food, beverage, etc.) are made with debits.
>
> Decreases in assets, including *accounts receivable* and cash, are made with credits.

Debit: Proper Departmental (*rooms*, food, beverage) Allowance   178.00
    Credit: Accounts Receivable/Guest's Folio   178.00
Explanation: Comped two nights (leaving guest to pay the $17.72 tax bill).

Allowance for Poor Service. Accidents happen: A shirt is scorched in the laundry; a skirt is torn on a rough cocktail table. And service delivery fails: A foodserver spills coffee on a guest; a child's crib is never delivered. Service mishaps are bound to occur when servicing hundreds of visitors each day.

If the problem is caught immediately, management remedies the mistake (delivers the crib). If not caught immediately, or if the problem has no remedy (the shirt is burned), there is little to do but reimburse with an allowance. Every allowance, whether for comps or adjustments, results in reductions of both the account receivable (the guest's folio) and the departmental income. If the original charge was made to a credit card (as it might be in the lounge where the skirt was torn), the adjustment would be made to the credit card, not to the folio.

> All allowance entries follow the same format as the room comp allowance. The specific departmental allowance is subsitituted for the room allowance of the illustration on page 400.

Allowance to Correct Errors.   Handling small late charges is one of several clerical errors requiring correcting allowances. A late charge is posted to the folio of a guest who has already checked out. If the charge is large enough to pursue by mail, a transfer—soon to be explained—is used. If the late charge is too small to warrant the costs of collection, including guest annoyance, it is wiped off. Accounts receivable is credited and the hotel absorbs the error.

Some errors are just carelessness in posting. Exhibit 10–12 shows the allowance for $0.99 that was inadvertently posted as part of the room charge by the night auditor. Exhibit 10–5 (third line from the bottom) adjusts for a dual posting of an in-room film (lines 2 and 3).

Many errors originate in misunderstandings or lack of attention. For example, a couple arrives for several days but one spouse leaves early. Although the desk is aware of the situation, the double occupancy rate continues for the entire stay. An allowance is needed to reduce the charges by the difference between the single and double rates multiplied by the number of nights overcharged.

In theory, it should not happen, but sometimes a guest folio is carried one night beyond the actual departure day. An allowance corrects the error. This happens most frequently with one-night, paid-in-advance guests who do not bother to check out.

Every protested charge is not the hotel's error. This is why having old vouchers accessible to the cashier is helpful. (New PMS programs display vouchers from previous days, reducing the time needed to otherwise search manually.) When shown a signed voucher, guests often recall charges that they had vehemently protested only moments earlier. Large bar charges fall into this category when viewed with a sober eye the following day. This also happens when two persons share a room and one makes charges but the other pays. Especially when the first guest has already checked out is it necessary to prove to the remaining guest that the charge was made.

Although computers reduce the number of errors, they do not compensate for guest forgetfulness or for honest misunderstandings or mistakes.

Extended-stay Allowances.   Some resorts and extended-stay properties allow a rate reduction if the guest remains an extended length of time. To make certain of the guest's commitment to remain, the full daily charge is posted and not the prorata charge of the special rate. Either an allowance is given on the final day to adjust the weekly rate or the charge of the final day is reduced to meet the special weekly total.

Recording the Allowance.   Allowances as well as the other two means of settlement, cash and transfers, are usually resolved as the guest departs. Once the amount has been

V
A Vallen Corporation Property

MR. STERLING SILVERS

STATEMENT DATE
12-23-

FOLIO NUMBER
98141 (304)

CO-NRL 7:42 AM

ACTIVITY DATE	CHARGE CODE	DESCRIPTION	CHARGES	CREDITS
12-22-	R#304	ROOM CHARGE	59.99	
12-22-	RT304	ROOM TAX	3.60	
12-23-	ARNRL	ALLOWANCE/ROOMS		.99
12-23-	MC7:43AM	MASTER CHARGE/VISA		62.60

I agree that my liability for this bill is not waived and agree to be held personally liable in the event that the indicated person, company or association fails to pay for any or the full amount of these charges. All accounts are due and payable upon receipt.

Signature: ______________________

BALANCE DUE
0.00

ORIGINAL

Exhibit 10–12 At check-out, all folios must have a zero balance (see lower right corner). This folio is balanced with two credits: an allowance and a transfer of the balance to a credit-card company. Exhibit 10–14 illustrates the third possible credit, payment with cash. Note the sequential folio number on the top right and the charge codes in the second column.

settled, a voucher is completed (see Exhibit 10–11). As Chapter 7 explained, empowered employees are authorized to sign off within a given dollar range. The allowance is used with either or both other methods of payment to settle the bill. Exhibit 10–12 illustrates settlement with an allowance and a credit-card transfer. Cash, not illustrated here, is the third method of settlement.

> Using the vouchers and computer records, the accounting department, not the front desk, will charge (debit) each allowance against the sales of the department from which it originates.

Settling with Transfers.   Allowances, cash payments, and transfers are usually—but not always—recorded as the guest checks out. A transfer simply moves the balance of one record (say, a front-office folio) to another record (most often, a city-ledger credit-card account). The balance of the front-office folio gets smaller, usually falling to zero. The balance of the other record gets larger by the same amount.

All or part of a folio balance can be transferred. Transfers can be made between accounts in the same ledger (registered guest to registered guest in the transient ledger) or between accounts in two ledgers (registered guest in the transient ledger to city account in the city ledger). The first transfer type, registered guest to registered guest, is easier to track because both folios are available to the front-office staff. Transfers between transient folios and city accounts, usually credit-card companies, may appear incomplete to the front-office staff because the city ledger may not be accessible to the front desk. It is the accounting office's responsibility.

> Every accounting event (entry) must have equal dollar debits and credits.

Folio Transfer of Registered Guest to Registered Guest.   The two pages of Exhibit 10–2 illustrate how transfers were recorded on the old pencil-and-paper folios. Note that both parties have folios and both stay one night, December 23 (the first vertical column). Both folios reflect room and tax charges of $84.24 ($78 + $6.24). When the new day starts, December 24 (column 2), both have beginning balances, BROUGHT FORWARD. The BROUGHT FORWARD value is larger in Room 409 than in 407 because of the previous day's restaurant charge. As the second day unfolds, Room 407 *transfers* its balance to Room 409. Both check out before the second day ends. Room 409 pays the total of both folios.

At check-out, the balance on each folio is zero. Room 407 has paid by transferring the balance to another front-office folio, 409. That's the topic of this chapter segment.

At check-out, Room 409 also has a zero balance. Room 409 has paid both folio charges. by transferring the balance to the city ledger. That's the topic of the next segment. In both cases, the balances of the departing guests are zero. Closing balances must always be zero!

The same sequence and results can be seen in Exhibit 10–13, on modern PMS folios. Guest Berger, room 301, settles his account by transferring his folio to another folio, Meade's, room 723. Berger's folio falls to zero at check-out and Meade's increases by the same value, $230.80. Then Meade departs, transferring his account including Berger's balance to the American Express card's city-ledger account. His front-office balance is now zero also.

Transfer of Folios to the City Ledger: Credit Card.   Most guests pay by transferring their folio balance to a credit-card account in the city ledger. That's what Meade did in the paragraph above. The cashier/guest-service agent sees Meade's front-office folio

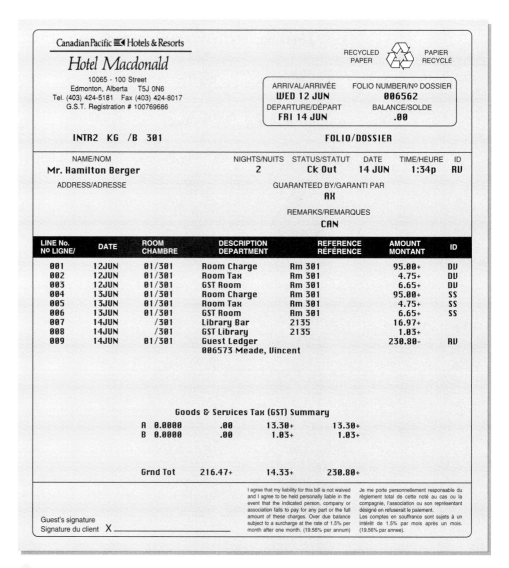

Exhibit 10–13a   Line 9 of both folios illustrates a transfer from room 301 (left page) to room 723. That transfer zeros room 301 and the guest checks out. Room 723 also checks out after making a second type of transfer, one from the guest ledger to the city ledger using an American Express credit card. Two items to note: Sales taxes (GST in Canada) are summarized on each folio and charges and credits are indicated by + and − signs instead of two columns. (A folio-to-folio transfer is also illustrated in Exhibit 10–2.) *Courtesy of Hotel McDonald, Edmonton, Alberta, Canada.*

settled, brought to zero. Collection from the credit-card company is left to the accounting office. And that story is picked up in Chapter 11.

Three exhibits in this chapter illustrate the folio-to-city-ledger transfer. Exhibit 10–2a, room 409 and Exhibit 10–13b, room 723 have been reviewed several times. Exhibit 10–12 offers another example, employing two of the three means of settlement. An allowance is granted in conjunction with the credit-card transfer. The two credits balance the total charges, the guest departs, and the accounting office is left to collect from the credit-card company.

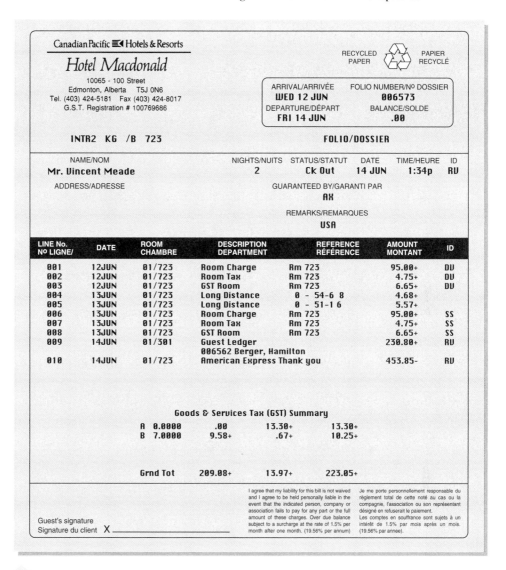

Canadian Pacific ⊫◄ Hotels & Resorts

Hotel Macdonald

10065 - 100 Street
Edmonton, Alberta   T5J 0N6
Tel. (403) 424-5181   Fax (403) 424-8017
G.S.T. Registration # 100769686

RECYCLED PAPER   PAPIER RECYCLÉ

ARRIVAL/ARRIVÉE	FOLIO NUMBER/No DOSSIER
WED 12 JUN	**006573**
DEPARTURE/DÉPART	BALANCE/SOLDE
FRI 14 JUN	**.00**

INTR2 KG /B 723   **FOLIO/DOSSIER**

NAME/NOM	NIGHTS/NUITS	STATUS/STATUT	DATE	TIME/HEURE	ID
Mr. Vincent Meade	2	**Ck Out**	**14 JUN**	**1:34p**	**RV**

ADDRESS/ADRESSE

GUARANTEED BY/GARANTI PAR
AX

REMARKS/REMARQUES
USA

LINE No. No LIGNE/	DATE	ROOM CHAMBRE	DESCRIPTION DEPARTMENT	REFERENCE RÉFÉRENCE	AMOUNT MONTANT	ID
001	12JUN	01/723	Room Charge	Rm 723	95.00+	DV
002	12JUN	01/723	Room Tax	Rm 723	4.75+	DV
003	12JUN	01/723	GST Room	Rm 723	6.65+	DV
004	13JUN	01/723	Long Distance	0 - 54-6 8	4.68+	
005	13JUN	01/723	Long Distance	0 - 51-1 6	5.57+	
006	13JUN	01/723	Room Charge	Rm 723	95.00+	SS
007	13JUN	01/723	Room Tax	Rm 723	4.75+	SS
008	13JUN	01/723	GST Room	Rm 723	6.65+	SS
009	14JUN	01/301	Guest Ledger 006562 Berger, Hamilton		230.80+	RV
010	14JUN	01/723	American Express Thank you		453.85-	RV

Goods & Services Tax (GST) Summary

A	0.0000	.00	13.30+	13.30+
B	7.0000	9.58+	.67+	10.25+
Grnd Tot		209.08+	13.97+	223.05+

Guest's signature
Signature du client   X _____

I agree that my liability for this bill is not waived and I agree to be held personally liable in the event that the indicated person, company or association fails to pay for any part or the full amount of these charges. Over due balance subject to a surcharge at the rate of 1.5% per month after one month. (19.56% per annum)

Je me porte personnellement responsable du règlement total de cette noté au cas ou la compagnie, l'association ou son représentant désigné en refuserait le paiement. Les comptes en souffrance sont sujets à un intérêt de 1.5% par mois après un mois. (19.56% par année).

Exhibit 10–13b   *Continued*

Transfer of Folios to the City Ledger: Direct.   By far the greatest number of transient ledger transfers are those just discussed, transfers to credit cards. But there are other transfers, too. The obsolete pencil-and-paper folio had one major advantage. It showed these other transfers, and that's significant enough for the text to reproduce the otherwise outdated example.

Exhibit 10–2 lists the several options that guests can use to settle their folios. Six credit lines appear below the TOTAL DEBIT (total charge) line. One is CASH (treated in the next chapter). One is ALLOWANCES (previously discussed), and one is CITY LEDGER (meaning transfers). There are three city-ledger choices. Exhibit 10–2 lists them in sequence: ADVANCE DEPOSIT (the final topic of this chapter); CREDIT CARDS, discussed immediately above; and TRANSFERS (meaning transfers other than credit cards).

Two transfer types have already been discussed at length: transferring one folio to another (Exhibits 10–2 and 10–13), and moving the folio to a city-ledger credit-card account (also Exhibits 10–2 and 10–13). Now a third is highlighted: transferring a folio to the city ledger but not to a credit card. The form and procedure are no different than the credit-card transfer. The difference is the destination in the city ledger. *Recall:* The city ledger is made of accounts receivable not now registered. Among those "persons" may be credit-card companies, business enterprises, associations, airlines, travel agents, individuals, and others. Creditworthiness is not an issue with credit-card companies in the city ledger. Since it may be with the other accounts receivables, hotels usually require city-ledger credit to be established beforehand.

MASTER ACCOUNTS.   Master accounts are a good example of the direct city-ledger transfer. And they're quite common in hotels doing a large group business. Exhibit 10–4 illustrates a transfer in which the Alumni Association shifts its transient folio to a city account of the same name. Billing is direct—not to a credit-card company, but to the headquarters of the Alumni Association. Exhibit 10–5 is exactly the same, but the billing is to an individual. In both illustrations, payment comes from the source, not a third party (credit-card company) where payment is assured. Credit is not extended lightly. Exhibit 10–14 illustrates a form that initiates the hotel's verification of the organization's credit credibility.

COUPONS.   Direct city-ledger transfers may involve coupons. A guest whose reservation was made by a travel agent or airline may settle the front-office folio with a coupon. A coupon is a receipt by which a third party, the travel agent, acknowledges that it has already been paid by the guest. By accepting the coupon, the hotel agrees to bill the travel agent or other third party. This is accomplished by transferring the front-office folio of the guest to the city-ledger account of the agent. Then the agent is billed by mail. Obviously, the agent must have previously established credit with the hotel (see Chapter 11).

SKIPPERS.   Despite increased credit vigilance, hotels sometimes get stuck by skippers, persons who leave (*skip*) the hotel without paying. Some skippers are accidental or the results of a misunderstanding. Since honest guests leave a trail of reservation and registration identification, collection takes place without difficulty.

Real skippers make their living by skipping. Their moves are deliberate, even though states have legislated skipping to be a prima facie case of intent to defraud the innkeeper. Because it is a crime, a police report should be filed.

It often takes a day or two to verify the skip. Charges for additional nights are added to the folio. It makes little difference, actually, since collection is very rare. Once discovered, the room is checked out and the folio balance is transferred to a section of the city ledger called *Skippers*. After a while, the account is written off as a bad debt.

Transfer from *the City Ledger* to *the Guest Ledger: Advance Deposits.*   This interledger transfer differs from anything previously considered. The transfer flows in the opposite direction from earlier discussions. The balance is moved *from* the city ledger *to* the guest ledger. Earlier discussions were just the opposite; the balance flowed *from* the guest ledger (the folio) *to* the city ledger.

For this to happen, there must be some balance in the city ledger to be transferred. Guests may be asked for a prearrival deposit. This is not very common because rooms are usually guaranteed with a credit-card number, but the charge is *not* processed. Some hotels, resorts especially, may want cash in advance of arrival (see Exhibit 10–15) or may wish to process the credit-card guarantee (see Exhibit 10–10).

☐**V**

A Vallen Corporation Property

VALLEN CORPORATE REQUEST FOR MASTER BILLING

Date(s) of the Function(s)   _____

Hotels/Cities That Might Be Used _____

_____

Thank you for choosing the Vallen Hotel Company. To better serve you, we shall quickly process the credit information furnished. Extension of credit requires accounts to be settled within 30 days or be subject to a charge of 6% per annum. Your signature below grants us authority to verify the information provided.

NAME OF THE ORGANIZATION OR
PERSON REQUESTING MASTER BILLING _____

ADDRESS _____
         Street   City   State   Zip
CONTACT _____
         Telephone   Fax   Email

CREDIT REFERENCES: (PLEASE PROVIDE NAMES, ADDRESS AND TELEPHONE NUMBERS)

COMPANIES _____

BANKS   _____

           _____

PREVIOUS   _____
HOTELS   _____

DOES YOUR ORGANIZATION REQUIRE A PURCHASE ORDER?   Yes/No _____
WHICH CHARGES WOULD BE AUTHORIZED FOR THE ACCOUNT?

_____ All room charges and incidentals   _____ Organization's functions only

_____ Room charges only for identified persons   _____ Other _____

_____
Authorized Signature   Title   Date

Sales Manager's Estimate of Charges: Rooms_____   F&B_____

Approved Yes_____   No_____   Credit Manager _____

Exhibit 10-14 Companies and associations that request direct billing of their city ledger accounts must first establish their creditworthiness. First, the hotel sales executive estimates the cost of the event(s). Then the credit manager reviews the application by checking references with other agencies, especially previous hotels, before giving the applicant an OK. Credit is one of the topics of Chapter 11.

What is to be done with the money when it arrives? It cannot be posted to a front-office folio. Front-office folios are for registered guests, and the guest has yet to arrive. Accounts receivable who are not registered are recorded in the city ledger. So a city-ledger account called *Advanced Deposits* is opened for the yet-to-arrive guest, who has already paid for one or more nights. Actually, of course, the guest isn't a receivable; the guest owes nothing. The hotel owes the guest; so the guest is a negative account receivable, in other words, an account payable.

The situation is similar to the tax issue raised earlier. The hotel collects taxes from the guest (taxes payable) and eventually pays the government. Here the hotel collects from the guest and eventually applies it to the account receivable.

When a cash deposit (check) is received,

> Increases in assets, including accounts receivable and *cash*, are made with debits.
> Increases in liabilities, including *debts to guests* or governments, are made with credits.

Debit: Cash
    Credit: Accounts Payable/Advanced Deposits (City Ledger)
Explanation: Cash deposit received for future arrival

The record of the hotel's liability to the guest remains in the city ledger until the guest arrives days or weeks later. Then the balance is moved (transferred) from the city ledger to the arriving guest's newly open front-office folio (see Exhibits 10–10 and 10–15). These two illustrations show the transfer *from* the city ledger *to* the guest ledger on the first line. Actually, they could appear any place, depending on how many services the guest buys before the transfer is made.

The deposit is applied to the arriving guest in the following accounting entry, which appears in folio format on line 1 in Exhibit 10–15.

> Decreases in liabilities, including *city-ledger debts to guests*, are made with debits.
> Increases in liabilities, including *front-office folio debts to guests*, are made with credits.

Debit: Accounts Payable/Advanced Deposits (in City Ledger)
    Credit: Accounts Receivable/Guest's Folio (in Guest Ledger)
Explanation: Guest with advance deposit arrives; liability is transferred.

The hotel still owes the guest; the transfer has not changed that. Purchases during the guest's stay (rooms, food, and so on) are applied against the original deposit. Either the hotel still owes the guest at the end of the stay, or the guest has charged more than the original deposit. With the former, a refund is necessary, and that is explained in Chapter 11. More likely, the guest checks out owing an additional amount because deposits are usually one night's room rate only. Then the cycle begins again with payment at check-out.

Exhibit 10-15 A credit balance, a cash advanced deposit transferred from the city ledger, is the first line of this folio. Another cash payment closes the account as the guest checks out. Cash payments like these are one means of settling a folio balance, but are rarely used. Exhibit 10–12 illustrates the other two methods, allowances and credit cards. *Courtesy of Sydney Renaissance Hotel, Sydney, New South Wales, Australia.*

30 PITT STREET
SYDNEY NSW 2000 AUSTRALIA
TELEPHONE: (02) 259 7000
FACSIMILE: (02) 252 1999
TELEX: AA127792
A.R.B.N. 003 864 908

SYDNEY
RENAISSANCE
HOTEL

GUEST		
VALLEN, M/M J	ROOM	2003
EASTER PACKAGE	RATE	170.00
2ND AVE BEACHSIDE APPTS	No. PERSONS	2
BURLEIGH HEADS QLD 4220	FOLIO No.	152490
	PAGE	01
	ARRIVAL	04/12/
CH-A BUNNY	DEPARTURE	04/16/
	DEPOSIT	$680.00

DATE	REFERENCE No.			DESCRIPTION	CHARGES / CREDITS
		00754		DEPOSIT	680.00CR
APR12	401	01859	99	LOCAL CALL	.70
APR12	011	02003	00	ROOM CHG	170.00
APR13	131	04071	61	BRASSERIE	22.00
APR13	401	02145	99	LOCAL CALL	.70
APR13	011	02003	00	ROOM CHG	170.00
APR14	181	02003	43	MINI BAR	2.50
APR14	011	02003	00	ROOM CHG	170.00
APR15	401	01736	99	LOCAL CALL	.70
APR15	011	02003	00	ROOM CHG	170.00
APR16	001	00001	23	PAID CASH	26.60CR
				TOTAL-DUE	.00

TRAVEL AGENCY
LOVE   TRAVEL
JENN
SH8 HIGH ROAD
SOUTHPORT   QLD   4215
CHARGE TO

I AGREE THAT MY LIABILITY FOR THIS BILL IS NOT WAIVED AND AGREE TO BE HELD PERSONALLY LIABLE IN THE EVENT THAT THE INDICATED PERSON, COMPANY OR ASSOCIATION FAILS TO PAY FOR ANY PART OR THE FULL AMOUNT OF THESE CHARGES.

SIGNATURE

SYDNEY RENAISSANCE HOTEL · INSPIRED BY THE PAST, DESIGNED FOR THE FUTURE. sm
FOR RESERVATIONS: AUSTRALIA (008) 222 431, IN SYDNEY (02) 251 8888 ● BANGKOK 02 236 0361
HONG KONG (852) 311 3666 ● JAPAN (0120) 222 332, IN TOKYO (03) 3239 8303 ● KUALA LUMPUR
(03) 241 4081 AND (03) 248 9008 ● SEOUL (02) 555 0501
AUSTRALIA ● CANADA ● CARRIBEAN ● CENTRAL AMERICA ● CHINA ● EUROPE ● HONG KONG ● INDIA
INDONESIA ● JAPAN ● KOREA ● MALAYSIA ● MEXICO ● MIDDLE EAST ● PAKISTAN ● SRI LANKA
THAILAND ● UK ● USA   FORM No FO 001 12/92

Payment at check-out brings us back to the beginning of the chapter. Guests settle their transient accounts (the folios) in the front-office ledger by one of three methods: cash, allowances, or transfers. Most settlements will be by transfer because departing guests usually shift their folio balances to credit cards in the city ledger.

SUMMARY

Hotels sell services to strangers and to registered guests. Whereas strangers must pay immediately for services like food and beverage, guests may delay payment until check-out. In the interim, guests owe the hotel; they are accounts receivable (A/R). A record of that debt, called a folio, is maintained in the front office. All the folios together are called a ledger. Hence, the billing records of registered guests are in a front-office (or transient) ledger. Nonregistered parties—credit-card companies, for example—may also owe the hotel. Their records are maintained in a different ledger, the city ledger, by the accounting office.

Usually, guests settle their individual folios as they check out. That's the time they pay for all of the services (room, room taxes, food, beverage, spas, golf, etc.) that have been charged to them. Payment is by cash (rare), by allowances (for service adjustments), and by credit cards (the usual method). Credit-card settlements transfer the balance of the front-office folios to the records of the credit-card companies in the city ledger. The accounting office bills and collects from credit-card companies.

Master accounts, which track the charges of groups, are also maintained on folios. These too are transferred to the city ledger when the association or company checks out. (Every folio must have a zero balance after check out.) Master accounts are billed directly to the group's headquarters. That's different from billing credit-card companies for third-party folios. Both types of billing originate in the city ledger, having been transferred there from the front-office ledger. That discussion resumes in Chapter 11.

Hotels have not only accounts receivable, but also accounts payable. Receivables are something the hotel owns. Payables are something the hotel owes. Hotels owe governments for room taxes collected but not yet paid. Hotels owe employees for tips collected but not yet paid. Hotels owe guests with advance deposits (not common) for services not yet delivered.

RESOURCES AND CHALLENGES
Resources

WEB SITES

http://www.lansingclarion.com/pdf/dbapp.pdf (Clarion Hotel)—Lansing, MI. Illustrates a simple application for direct billing to a small hotel catering mostly to a university community.

http://www.dphs.com (Data Plus Hospitality Solutions)—North Chelmsford, MA. Property management system (PMS) with special emphasis in back-office accounting, including the city ledger.

http://www.hotel-software.com (TCS Hotel Software, Inc.)—Valley Cottage, NY. Test a version of the company's software for a PMS, from reservations to reports to call accounting (posting of telephone charges).

http://www.meetings-conventions.com (Northstar Travel Media, LLC)—Secaucus, NJ. Trade press that features stories about meeting and conventions often with articles on master accounts.

Web Assignment

Assume you are responsible for the city-ledger segment of your hotel's back-of-the-house records. Use the *dphs* Web site to identify four products that you would buy in order to update your system. Explain why you chose one of them.

INTERESTING TIDBITS

➤ Comp rooms, a traditional perk for hotel executives visiting other properties, are harder then ever to come by. One reason: There are no rooms. Occupancy is high as the industry moves toward its economic peak. Another reason: Yield management systems (see Chapter 5) force greater accountability. Still, comps are available for legitimate business reasons such as temporary employee quarters; travel writers and travel agents; and meeting planners shopping for convention space. Casino comps for high rolling "whales," those who bet $10,000 or more per hand, are still very much the norm.

➤ For guests who "record their profiles"—join frequent guest programs, FGPs—Marriott, Hilton, and others have added a third method for checking out. Heretofore, guests went either to the front desk or to their inroom TV screen to process the check-outs. Now, FGP members can access folios online for up to 90 days after departure, and even track the number of FGP points they own.

➤ Meeting planners demand a sharp accounting before settling their master accounts. They demand that folio postings be in the same sequence that the group's activities took place. They insist on resolving minor dollar-amount items before paying thousands of dollars of undisputed charges. They reject charges, even those they ordered, if the service was signed for by an unauthorized member, say an ex-president.

Challenges

TRUE/FALSE

Questions that are partially false should be marked false (F).

___ 1. Because hotels are open 24 hours a day, guest services recorded after midnight have been given a special designation, they're called "late charges."

___ 2. It is most likely that the hotel's largest accounts receivable have never been registered as guests.

___ 3. Posting room charges is a major responsibility of the night auditor because that position is the only one authorized to post room charges to guest folios.

___ 4. Guests have one of two choices in settling (paying) the folio. They use either a credit card (transferring the balance to the city ledger) or cash (there are several forms of cash: traveler's checks, coins and bills, etc.).

___ 5. The discussion of master accounts and their transfers to the city ledger could easily be omitted from the text because there are so few users of master accounts in the hotel business.

PROBLEMS

1. Differentiate the following:

a. Charge from credit.

b. Master account from split account.

c. A folio from B folio.

d. Transient guest from city guest.

e. Charge from payment.

2. Use a word processor to replicate the folio that would be produced when the Arthur Jones family checks out. Mr. and Mrs. Jones and their infant son, George, reside at 21 Craig Drive in Hampshireville, Illinois 65065. Their reservation for three nights at $125 per night plus 5% tax was guaranteed

May 17 with a $200 cash (check) deposit for one night, indicating that they will arrive late. They check in at 10 PM on June 3 and take one room (1233).

   a. Breakfast charge on June 4 is $12.90.

   b. Mrs. Jones hosts a small luncheon meeting for her company, and a $310 charge for the meeting room and meal is posted to the folio.

   c. The family decides to leave earlier than planned and notifies the desk of a 7 PM check-out.

   d. A long-distance call of $8 is made.

   e. The family checks out. They raise the issue of no clean linen—the laundry had a wildcat strike—and argue for an allowance. One is given—$25. The rooms manager then charges 30% of the normal room charge for the late departure.

   f. Payment is made with an American Express card, no. 33333333333.

3. Create a pencil-and-paper folio; use Exhibit 10–2 as a guide. Post the events of Problem 2 as they would appear on a hand-prepared folio.

4. Under which of the following circumstances would management grant an allowance? What would be the value of that allowance? What else might be done if an allowance were not granted?

   a. Guest sets the room alarm clock, but it fails to go off, which causes the guest to miss a meeting that involves thousands of dollars of commission.

   b. Same circumstance as part (a) but the guest called the telephone operator for a morning call, which wasn't made.

   c. Guest checks out and discovers the nightly room charge to be $15 more than the rate quoted two weeks earlier by the reservations center.

   d. Same circumstance as part (c), but the discrepancy is discovered soon after the guest is roomed.

5. How would the following transfers be handled? (Answer either by discussion, by offering the accounting entries, or both.)

   a. A departing guest discovers that a $60 beverage charge that belongs to another guest, who is still registered, was incorrectly posted yesterday to the departing guest's account.

   b. Same circumstance as part (a) but the $60 beverage posting was made today.

   c. Same circumstance as part (a) but the other guest has departed.

   d. Two days into a guest's four-day stay, the reservation department realizes the guest's advance deposit was never transferred to the front-office account.

   e. Same circumstance as part (d) but the discovery is made by the guest, who writes to complain about the omission one week after check-out.

6. Check your understanding of accounting by proving the debits and credits for each of the following situations, which were not discussed in the text.

   a. The hotel pays the quarterly sales taxes of $8,925.00 due the local government, the city of Popcorn, Indiana.

   b. The hotel receives a check from Diners Club for payment of credit-card balances due of $1,000.

   c. Same as part (b), but Diners Club withholds 4% for a fee.

   d. The hotel receives a check from its parent company for $1,500, representing the total payment due for several frequent-stay guests who used their points at your hotel. The amount of room charges generated by those guests was $5,500.

AN INCIDENT IN HOTEL MANAGEMENT

Just a Hole in the Wall

Last month's security report contained three items dealing with noise and heavy traffic one night in the Kit Carson suite. The following day, housekeeping reported a huge hole in the wall between two of the bedrooms. It hadn't been there four days earlier, the last time the suite was used. Other damage included a broken chair, a smashed vase, and a cracked mirror. Engineering estimated $1,300 for repairs; that amount had been posted to the folio of the 18-year-old guest. She signed the folio as she checked out. It was posted to her father's city-ledger account and billed at month's end. He is president of a large local business.

The dad stops by the GM's office after a business luncheon in the gourmet room. "Good grief! $1,300? It's only a hole in the wall."

Questions: Was there a management failure here; if so, what?

What is the hotel's immediate response (or action) to the incident?

What further, long-run action should management take, if any?

ANSWERS TO TRUE/FALSE QUIZ

1. False. A late charge is a record of guest service that is to be posted to the guest's folio, but arrives from one of the operating departments (restaurant, cocktail lounge, etc.) after the guest has checked out and the folio has been closed.

2. True. The largest accounts receivable that the hotels have are credit-card companies. Credit-card companies are city-ledger records; they are not individual persons who could occupy a hotel room.

3. False. False in part. Posting room charges *is* a major responsibility of night auditors, but several circumstances (late check-out, part-day rate, and so on) require guest-service agents to also post room charges.

4. False. There is a third method of settling a folio, an allowance. Allowances are similar to unsatisfactory goods returned to a retailer. Unhappy guests have their bills reduced because of accounting mistakes, irreparable errors in service, comp rooms, and so on.

5. False. Master accounts have widespread use. They are not found in roadside hotels and small properties. It is the large hotels with adequate rooms, and meeting and banquet facilities which cater to group businesses that require master accounts, often several for each event.

C H A P T E R   1 1

Credit and the City Ledger

Outline

Chapters 10, 11 and 12, which comprise Unit IV, flow in sequence. Chapter 10 explained the guest folio. The emphasis was guest charges (increases to accounts receivable) and guest credits (decreases to accounts receivable). Chapter 11 expands the discussion, focusing on a specific class of accounts receivable: those in the city ledger. The progression concludes with Chapter 12, which discusses cash—another, less frequently used, credit.

REVIEW: THE CITY LEDGER

Registered guests enjoy the services offered by the hotel, but don't pay for them immediately. Many businesses work that way. Customers who have not yet paid for goods and services are called *accounts receivable, A/R*. Hotels have two types. Guests who are still in the hotel are called *front-office* (or *transient*) accounts receivable. Their debts are tracked by guest-service agents at the desk. A/R who are not registered are *city-ledger* receivables. Their debts are tracked by the accounting office.

In the age of computers, the records of both guest types are maintained electronically. The term "ledger" survives, although the records are no longer in bound books. The city ledger references the accounts receivable of all nonregistered guests. Front-office ledgers are tracked through the room numbers of the registered guests. City-ledger records are assigned account numbers because these A/R are not registered in any room. Moreover, they may never have been, and may never be registered guests, although most start out as such.

As registered guests depart, they shift their account balances to credit cards. Credit-card companies, which then owe the debt, are nonregistered A/R, which means they are tracked through the city ledger. Other A/R types are also in the city ledger. The list is large: travel agents, associations, wholesalers, and client companies. Almost all of these originate in the guest ledger as the hotel sells services, but delays collection. Credit-card accounts hold the largest amount of dollar debt compared to these other categories. This chapter starts there.

CREDIT CARDS

Credit, as a means of payment, has its history in the biblical inns of Ancient Rome. Innkeepers issued negotiable tokens that were used as money. Similar coinage was used 2,000 years later during America's colonial period. The concept expanded in about 1915 when Western Union, the telegraph company, issued special cards (no longer tokens) to preferred guests. As the action heated up (see Exhibit 11–1), hotels chains joined the rush, but not for long. The financial and administrative burdens (precomputer age) were too heavy. By the 1970s, the lodging industry had come to understand that credit cards were

Chronology in the Development of the Credit Card

1936	Universal Air Travel Plan consolidated and rebranded with PassAge, AirPlus and Air Travel Card to its present-day terminology of Universal Air Travel Plan. UATP is a travel card, not a consumer card. It is accepted by virtually all the world's airlines and cobrands other segments of the travel experience with MasterCard or Visa.
1950	Diner's Club focused on wealthy clientele patronizing fashionable New York restaurants.
1958	AmEx (Green) Card launched by American Express, long-time leader (since 1850) in the travel business.
1960	Bank Americard introduced and franchised by Bank of America.
1961	The Japanese credit card, JCB, is the largest credit-card company outside of the United States. The logo of the Japanese Credit Bureau implies an endorsement of the merchant.
1965	MasterCard founded as a joint venture of Chicago banks.
1967	MasterCharge founded as a joint venture of California banks.
1970	MasterCard and MasterCharge merge and form MasterCard International.
1975	First appearance of debit cards.
1977	Bank Americard changes its name to Visa.
1978	Carte Blanche acquired by Citigroup (Citicorp/Citibank/Citi). Still in circulation but not aggressively marketed in 25 years.
1980	First appearance of affinity cards.
1981	Citi adds Diners Club to its Carte Blanche network.
1981	Frequent-flier programs introduced.
1985	Discover Card is launched as a product of Sears Financial Network, which later became Novus Services. Now, Sears' National Bank issues MasterCard, and Morgan Stanley owns Novus/Discover Card.
1990	American Telephone and Telegraph (AT&T) becomes the first nonfinancial enterprise to enter the credit-card business with its Universal Card.
1998	Citi acquires AT&T's Universal Card, adding it to its credit-card division.
2003	T&E cards battle bank card in the courts eventually gaining access to the banking system (see Exhibit 11–6).
2006/07	MasterCard and then Visa and Discover switch from joint ventures of member banks to public corporations.

Exhibit 11–1   Sixty-plus years have transformed credit cards from one person's idea (1950, Diner's Club) to a multibillion-dollar industry that has changed the way the world's commerce does business.

financial instruments and not the marketing tools that the industry had hoped. Frequent guest programs, which came later, now serve that marketing need.

Kinds of Credit Cards

Credit cards are much alike; but they didn't start out that way. Although the number of cards seems endless, consumer cards fall into only three categories. *Bank cards* are the most common, followed *by travel and entertainment cards* (T&E). All others, including *private-label cards*, would be the third category.

Each of the three types was designed initially for different consumer markets. T&E cards were for travel and business entertainment. That's the very name of the card class. Bank cards were visualized as retail cards. The distinctions hold true no longer.

➤ Bank cards now charge annual fees, although they were initially offered without charge.

➤ T&Es, which always required merchants to wait for their reimbursements, now have express deposits.

➤ Prestige cards with high spending limits for the affluent, the initial customers of the T&Es, are everyone's game today.

Bank Cards.   Visa and MasterCard[1] are the best-known bank cards. Bank cards are issued to anyone: depositors and nondepositors, locals and distant consumers, strong and weak debtors. Annual solicitations are estimated at more than 3 billion mailings. There are more bank cards in the United States than there are residents!

Recall that T&E cards, which marketed to the affluent customer, preceded bank cards by a decade (see Exhibit 11–1). Bank cards entered the market by soliciting consumers unable to qualify for the more stringent credit standards of the travel and entertainment cards. Banks are in the business of lending money for interest. Banks cards are just another form of bank loan. Lower economic groups are solicited to take cards and pay them off over time. Wise cardholders make prompt payments to avoid the high finance charges, up to 1.5% per month. The banks are lending at 18% or more annually while they borrow for far less. It's a good business to be in!

Bank cards are the products of numerous banks, each competing for the same customer. Until quite recently, the cards were franchised by Visa and MasterCard, which were joint ventures of their member banks. That's true no longer. MasterCard and Visa are now publicly traded corporations.

Discover Card has a different structure. The bank that issues the card is owned by Morgan Stanley, an investment banking company. The banking system (see Exhibit 11–2) refused to process the card since it was not a MasterCard or Visa member. That was also true for American Express (AmEx).[2] Both sued to gain access to the banking system. It was just one of many lawsuits between the two groups, and between Visa and Master-Card themselves.

---

[1]Trademark names are used throughout the chapter as they are throughout the text. Read® adjacent to each registered name.

[2]AmEx and AMEX, abbreviations for American Express, are sometimes confused with Amex, an abbreviation for the American Stock Exchange.

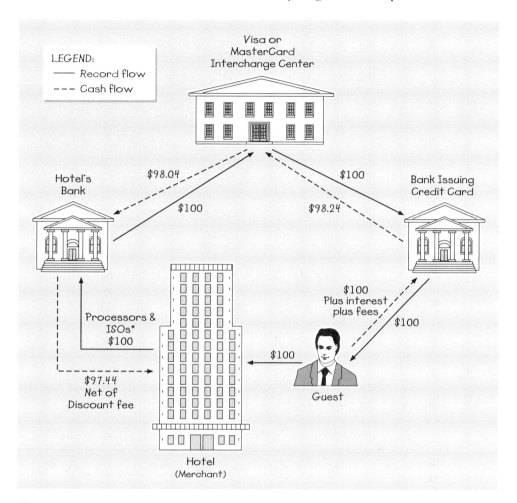

Exhibit 11-2   The full burden of interchange fees, 2.56% ($100 − $97.44) in this example, falls on the merchant/hotel. Other costs paid by merchants are listed in Exhibit 11–4. Merchants have filed numerous lawsuits (see Exhibit 11–6) against the credit-card companies and their member banks for allegedly fixing rates. *See Exhibit 11–4.

Discover Card offers the ultimate to card holders, cash refunds up to 1% of purchases. Despite that and its low merchant fee (hotels are merchants), it lacks the image of snazzier cards.

Travel and Entertainment Cards.   American Express is probably the best known T&E card. Others, including Diners Club and Discover Card, have recently joined banks to facilitate processing. Lacking the interest-earning tradition behind bank cards, T&E members are expected to settle their accounts each month. Failure to do so evokes penalties, one of which is interest. That certainly muddles the distinction, although interest is not the driver of T&E earnings. Annual fees account for more T&E earnings because yearly charges are higher than bank-card fees. T&E users also face tougher credit checks, so the issuer's bad debts are lower. The third major income source for T&E cards is the higher user fees charged to merchants.

T&E's are slower than bank cards in reimbursing merchants/hotels. This provides another means of earnings, called *float*. If collection is made from cardholders on day 1 and payment to the merchants is delayed until day 11, the credit-card company has interest-free use of the money for 10 days. What is merely aggravating to the merchant waiting for several hundreds or even thousands of dollars is big money to the T&E working with tens of millions of dollars. Everyone—credit-card company, merchant, business user, and consumer—chases the float. Float is one explanation for the increased use of credit cards by businesses. The business has interest-free use of the money for 30 to 60 days, between dates of purchase and payment to the credit-card company.

Private Label Cards.   Among the private-labeled cards (PLC) are those of department stores and even of some hotel companies still. Gasoline companies marketed their own PLCs for many years. Consumers carried multiple cards as they do today with credit cards. Just as the lodging giants left the credit-card business, so have other noncard companies. The move away was facilitated by the introduction of affinity and cobranded cards. But their actual demise had more economic causes: heavy capital costs and very limited application. No one else took their cards.

Affinity cards carry two designations: the name of the affiliated company and, of course, the credit-card company. Almost any organization that offers the credit-card company an extensive mailing list can affiliate. Charities, professional organizations, and others add their names to one of the national cards. The organization may get a signing bonus along with a small percentage of every sale made by a member using the card. The association uses the earnings to support the membership.

Affinity cards have faltered on two counts, but have not died. Banks, which give away a portion of their discount fees, haven't experienced an offsetting surge in volume. To accomplish the group's goal, individual members must use the card and forgo their own points and gifts. It is one thing to waive claim to a roadmap or such and quite another to sacrifice frequent-flier points. Enthusiasm of individual members wanes quickly and volume declines.

Another marketing device is the cobranded card. Affinity cards are associated with specific groups, but cobranded cards aim at the broadest of markets. For example, Chase Bank's Visa card might cobrand with Marriott. A second Chase card could carry Hilton's logo, and so on. The initial attraction to users was the promise of big wins. Big wins attracted big players. General Motors, Ford, and AT&T came on the scene, but quickly withdrew. Earn enough points and get a car, or at least a discounted car. Ford spent $500 million before exiting the program.

Cobranding remains popular with hotel companies. Cobranded card-users get special privileges such as check-cashing, room upgrades, and free continental breakfasts. Many are the same goodies that go with memberships in frequent–guest programs (FGP). The key to using the hotel's Visa or MasterCard is the reward structure. Points are earned in a FGP or an airline's FFP, frequent-flier program. Chapter 7 pointed out another use. Hotels sometimes resolve complaints with points instead of with cash. Marketing is one more use of FGP points. Hotels double the award to lure guests; many did that after 9/11. The industry needs to be cautious lest it piles up huge, unmanageable liabilities.

Broadening the Options.   Card competition between individual banks within the systems is keen—very keen. "New" products are introduced with much hoopla to lure the card user. Basic cards have morphed into silver cards, gold cards, platinum cards, titanium cards, and black cards. Each has different costs, different privileges, and different rewards. But the greater the differences, the more they seem to stay the same (see Exhibit 11–3).

Card Type Choices	
Airline-credit	Earn frequent-flyer miles
Bad-credit	Help reestablish credit record
Balance-transfer	Swap higher rates for lower rates
Business	Available to businesses, large and small
Cash-Back	Give cash rewards
Debit	Remove cash from bank accounts
Gift	Celebrate birthdays, graduations, newborns, etc.
Gimmick	Appeal to funky market segments[a]
Incentive	Supplement payroll cards with bonuses
Instant-approval	Come from select banks, not all
Limited-use	Restrict use; perhaps only for travel
Low-interest	Offer low fixed rates and zero introductory rates
Payroll	Allow associates to withdraw wages from ATMs
Perishable	Have limited use; perfect for Web purchases
Prepaid Debit	Put limits on spending
Procurement	Pay for company purchasing
Rewards	Reward with gifts or tee times, rather than with cash
Stored	Contain prepaid, but fixed, values
Student	Target high school and college students

[a]For example: AmEx's butterfly card; aromatic cards; cards with specialty pictures: ball teams; cards with touchy/feely materials.

Exhibit 11–3 Financial institutions have followed a general marketing trend: Give consumers choice, whether in autos, bottled water, or credit cards.

Minicards designed for key chains are a recent gimmick. So are perishable cards for one-time use with Web purchases. Special campaigns target first-time users such as college and high-school students, and senior citizens at the other end of the age spectrum.

How the System Works

Not only has the credit-card system worked, it has grown exponentially, passing the $2 trillion dollar mark in annual consumer purchases. The system works because there is something for everyone. Hotel guests are able to purchase services without cash. Card issuers profit through fees, which are discussed next. Merchants, including hotels, foot the entire cost, but make sales that might otherwise be missed, and they do so with less risk of loss. Consequently, many have been able to eliminate the position of credit manager. Processing fees are the incentive for local banks (see Exhibit 11–2), the first step in the process.

Fees. Credit-card companies charge merchant/hotels discount fees. Bank cards charge at the lower range, 1% to 2% of the transaction; T&E's at the upper end, 3% to 5%. Card fees are no different from other business expenses—they can be negotiated. Large-volume merchants such as hotel chains negotiate smaller discount fees. Competition among rival banks and their independent sales organizations (ISOs) is so keen that even the smallest hotel dickers successfully. Besides, hotels have other banking relationships that give the merchant additional bargaining leverage. Franchise systems have a competitive edge over independents because they combine the volume of their memberships. Umbrella organizations have tried to do the same for independents, but administrative costs offset the gains from quantity discounts.

Card type (bank versus T&E) and dollar volume generated are only two of many cost components. Handling, authorization, and settlement procedures add to the merchants' (hotels') costs. Before the credit-card business grew so large, banks handled all support services. Costs have now been unbundled. The jobs of selling the merchant and servicing the merchant are handled by agents other than the banks (see Exhibit 11–4). With these services come fees: setup fees, per-transaction fees, programming fees, statement fees, authorization fees, monthly minimum charges, telecommunication costs, and lease

Credit Card Terminology and Definitions	
Associations	Affiliations of member banks to form the MasterCard and Visa systems.
Card-processing company	Handles electronic transactions at the *POS*, which includes verifying the card, transferring the funds, and issuing approval codes. May also be an *independent service organization*.
Card-service provider	See *Merchant service provider*.
Chargeback fee	Credit-card company's charge added to the original value of a service when the charge is protested because of error or guest dispute.
Credit-card Companies	Technically, firms that appoint their own merchants and issue their own cards. Best known are American Express, Diners Club/Carte Blanche, and Discover. Generically used to include bank cards as well.
Discount rate	The percentage of each sale that the card companies charge the merchant; one of several fees, including a flat fee.
Handling	The method, manual or electronic, used to generate a sales slip.
Independent service organization	ISOs are contracted by banks to sell merchant status to businesses (hotels). May simultaneously be *card-processing companies* or may purchase wholesale services from one, reselling the services at retail.
Interchange fee	Charge paid by the merchant's bank that issued the card to compensate in part for the waiting time—float time—until payment is received.
Merchant service provider	Also called a *card-service provider*. Any company, including banks, *card-processing companies*, and *independent service organizations*, that arrange for and service *merchant status*.
MOTO	Mail order/telephone order; nonelectronic communications.
Merchant status	A business (hotel) authorized to process credit-card charges. Authorized merchants may not process cards (factor) for nonmerchants.
POS	A widely used abbreviation for point-of-sale.
Processor	See *Card-processing* company.

Exhibit 11–4 Continuing growth in the credit-card industry requires a host of supporting agents to sell and service the transactions. Banks can do the full job no longer. Merchants, including those in the lodging industry, pay the costs.

payments. These third-party costs add 2% to 3% or more to the discount fees. Effective rates often reach 3% to 5%, even for bank cards!

Point-of-sale terminals (see Exhibit 10–8) in F&B and other departmental outlets save processing costs. So does swiping cards through electronic scanners (see Exhibit 11–5). Costs go up if credit cards are handled manually using telephones, faxes, and surface mail. Savings from electronic processing offset somewhat the costs of owning or leasing electronic equipment.

Another fee, a chargeback fee, is collected from the hotel when the credit-card charge fails to clear. Transactions are voided if guests dispute the charges or if processing errors occur. In addition to the chargeback fee, the hotel loses income from the original sale. Losses are even greater if the chargeback contains tips that the hotel had previously paid to service employees (see Exhibit 12–1).

Similar issues arise if the hotel allows folio charges from concessionaires. Guests buy products from lobby businesses and charge them to the room folios. If the lease with the concessionaire allows for such charges, it must also cover chargebacks and chargeback fees.

Fees of all types generate as much controversy for merchants as for consumers. Fees have caused lawsuits between retailers and credit-card companies and between credit-card companies and other credit-card companies (see Exhibit 11–6). Giant retailers, Wal-Mart and Sears, have worked to establish their own banks in an effort to check the rising costs of interchange fees. Competition continues to shape the profile of the credit-card industry.

Competition.   Credit-card companies struggle to gain and hold market share. That's what eroded the initial differences between bank cards and T&E cards. Innovations by one were copied by the other. Competition is fierce because the U.S. credit-card industry, much like the U.S. hotel industry, is maturing. Growth is stronger overseas, especially in Asia. Unlike their parents, who have always favored

Exhibit 11–5   Swiping a credit card (regardless of brand) through an electronic reader brings an immediate response about its validity. It is the most recent development in card processing and security. The cost of buying or leasing electronic equipment is partly offset by savings in reduced discount fees, in faster settlement, and in reduced losses from chargebacks. *Courtesy: Hypercom Corporation, Phoenix, Arizona.*

The Credit-Card Wars			
THE ANTAGONISTS[a]			THE ISSUE
Plaintiff	vs.	Defendant	Court Case[b] or Not
MasterCard & Visa		AmEx	Right to use "Gold Card," which AmEx had named and used for years[b]
Visa		MasterCard	Battle to win Citibank's (Now Citi's) business
MasterCard & Visa		AmEx	Ongoing effort to have merchants refuse AmEx
Boston restaurateurs		AmEx	Bank cards join boycott to force fee reduction
Justice Department		Bank cards	Antitrust; heretofore, T&E cards could not use the banks[b]
Wal-Mart & Sears		Bank cards	Excessive debit-card fees[b]
Retailers		Bank cards	Dozens of law suits over collusion in setting fees[b]
Bank cards		Merchants	Require merchants who take credit cards to also take debit cards[b]
Merchants		Credit cards	Ongoing effort to have Congress impose price controls on fees
Merchants		Debit cards	Higher fees if customer signs; lower fees if pin numbers are used[b]
MasterCard		Visa	Wal-Mart's Sam's Club division picks MasterCard
MasterCard		World Soccer	Visa attempts to replace MasterCard in World-Soccer sponsorship[b]

[a]The winner of the issue or the legal suit is identified by italics; many issues are unresolved.
[b]Decided (or to be decided) by the courts.

Exhibit 11–6 An increasing number of lawsuits have resulted from increased competition among card companies and the ever-higher operating costs levied on merchants. Estimates place the annual card costs to small businesses equal to their net profits! Some fear governmental intervention will set fees; Australia has done so.

cash settlement, younger Japanese have embraced the card with enthusiasm. China, too, has fallen under the credit-card spell now that foreign banks have been able to buy into China's state-owned banks. The moves are just in time because international hotel chains, especially Best Western International and Wyndham Worldwide, are moving aggressively into the PRC.

The fight for market share has pitted the T&E's against the bank cards (expected) and bank-card Visa against bank-card MasterCard (unexpected). Visa, the larger of the two, is usually the victor (see Exhibit 11–6). Even as the internecine (battle within the group) clash continues, all credit-card companies work toward a common goal: Minimize society's use of cash and checks (Chapter 12).

Other Cards

Despite their inclusion in a chapter titled Credit and the City Ledger, debit cards and smart cards are neither credit instruments nor categories of the city ledger. They are discussed here because both card types are issued by the same credit-card companies/banks and both impact on hotel guests.

Debit Cards. Debit cards transfer funds (money) electronically. Thus comes the term EFT, electronic funds transfer. Money is switched instantaneously from the cardholder's bank account to the hotel's bank account. If payment is by EFT, there is no debt. No debt means no accounts receivable, no ledger postings, no transfer of front-office folios to city-ledger accounts, and no subsequent collections. Payment is up front and immediate. Since no actual money changes hand, cash losses from change-making mistakes, dishonest employees, and bounced checks also disappear. No wonder hotels love them, despite the high fees.

Debit cards are to merchant/hotels as automatic teller machines (ATMs) are to card-holders. With an ATM, the users gets cash in hand. With EFTs, so does the merchant/hotel. There is no time lag, no question about the user's ability to pay, and no float. No float is a negative for the consumer/guest, but a positive for the merchant/hotel, which doesn't wait for its money.

The switch to debit cards gained momentum after credit-card companies reduced grace periods for payment (reduced float time) and increased late fees for consumers. Debit cards are good for the banks too. They not only collect a processing fee, they eliminate the high costs of processing personal checks. Theft is the major debit-card negative. Imposters can clear out a victim's entire account. Debit-card issuers now cover that contingency as they do with credit cards.

Debit cards are the first step in the march toward the cashless society that futurists predict. Smart cards are the next.

Smart Cards. Smart cards were introduced in France during the 1950s, but they are just now approaching the level of success that was envisioned. Part of the delay has been a search for universal application, and part is the concern over privacy. Broader acceptance has come recently because American Express, MasterCard, and Visa have agreed on the technology.

Smart cards are miniature computers almost indistinguishable from standard cards. They have electronic chips instead of the magnetic strips of traditional cards. Hence comes the terms *chip cards* or *digital cash*. Smart cards carry a quantity of information. Their 8K memory equates to about 15 typewritten pages. Smart cards are seen to be the future because they are everything in one. They are credit or debit cards; stored-value cards; and ATM cards. Identification, electronic door keys, medical and insurance records, and more can be stored for immediate recall. They hold promise for Internet commerce and Web access.

Retailers, especially supermarkets, are already using low-level smart cards to track customer demographics and preferences. These cards provide marketers with names and addresses, purchasing patterns and income levels. The hotel industry has had much of the same information for years. Guest's identity, address, company affiliation, room preferences and more are available to every hotel with a property management system.

Privacy concerns have arisen anew as recently issued *contactless* cards containing embedded radio chips (called radio frequency identification, RFID) grow in popularity. The new cards can be swiped through traditional terminals (see Exhibit 11–5) or waved before special readers such as door locks (see Chapter 14). Merchants have signed on and guests have accepted the no-signature-required part of the transaction.

New terminal readers will add another $150 to the merchant's processing costs. The return on the investment promises speedier transactions and, theoretically, greater safety. Waved cards never leave their owner's hands, say the promoters. (That doesn't work when paying a server for a restaurant meal.) Critics fear electronic eavesdropping and encourage users to forgo the upgrades.

OTHER CITY-LEDGER CATEGORIES

Credit cards are found in every city ledger because they are one of the three methods (cash; credit cards; allowances) for settling front-office (folio) accounts (see Chapter 10). Depending on their markets, hotels may have other city-ledger accounts as well. Charges that arise from nonregistered customers (in contrast to registered guests) are recorded in the city ledger. Such charges originate in banquet room rentals (charity dances, for example) and parties such as retirement dinners.[3] Still, most city ledger records come from registered guests who settle their folios by transferring the balance to a city-ledger credit card. Master accounts are a marriage of the two types.

Master Accounts

Master accounts (see Exhibit 10–4) accumulate charges for groups, especially conventions. As Chapter 10 explained, master accounts are front-office folios. However, the "guest" is a group or an association, not an individual. Entertainment, banquets, meeting space, and special guest room charges are some of the items that master accounts accumulate. Outside vendors (florists, bands, and audiovisual rentals) are sometimes paid by the hotel and charged to the master account. Chapters 10 and 12 explain how such charges appear on the front-office folio. At the end of the stay, total charges are transferred to the city ledger from the master-account folio, but not as a credit-card charge. Billing and collection are directed to the group's headquarters, not to a credit-card company. This creates a new category of the city ledger.

Functions that involve hundreds of persons represent large sums of money. The hotel wants prompt payment. To ensure this, the master account folio is carefully reviewed by the client (the meeting planner, the association executive) and by the hotel (the sales manager and the accountant). Errors in master account folios may be substantial, but even meeting managers concede that they are not always in the hotel's favor. Even so, there are four common errors that irritate meeting planners. Attending to these beforehand expedites the billing, the settlement, and the eventual payment. Preventing the complaint is what good service is all about.

Error 1 is split billing. Meeting planners complain that charges are incorrectly split between master accounts and individual, personal accounts. Charges for group events should appear on the master folio and not on the personal folio of the executive who signs the tab. Front-office employees grow careless despite specific, written instructions from the client.

Error 2 is unauthorized signatures. Meeting and convention groups have many bosses. In addition to the elected board of directors, the officers, and the paid professional staff, there are informal leaders and past officers. Not all these persons are authorized to sign for charges. Meeting planners complain that unauthorized charges with unauthorized signatures appear on master accounts despite an advanced list of authorized signatures having been provided.

Error 3 is the sequence of posting. The breakfast charge of day 2 of the meeting should not appear on the folio before the dinner of day 1. Picky clients require the entire bill to be reposted to show each event in sequence. Comparisons to the original contract and to the function sheets are facilitated thereby. That pleases the meeting planner, but the hotel could have done it beforehand.

---

[3]Some hotels open a temporary front-office folio for such events and immediately transfer the balance to the city ledger.

Error 4 is comp rooms. Complimentary rooms are given to the group according to a widely used formula: 1 free room-night per 50 paid room-nights. Meeting planners complain that hotels deduct the lowest room rates against the free markers instead of the highest room rates. Comp rooms go either to VIPs or to staff members working the convention. Therefore, when making the adjustment, the best rates should be comped, says the client. Specifically, if the group has a secretary in one room and a keynote speaker in another, the hotel should match the one comp room allowed against the speaker's higher room rate, not the staffer's lower room rate.

Although it is best to resolve billing differences while they are still fresh, it may not be possible to do so before the group departs. Agreed-upon items should be resolved and billed promptly without waiting to reach accord on the few differences. Otherwise, a small sum keeps thousands of master-account dollars unpaid.

Groups, Packages and Company-Sponsored Functions

Master accounts are not limited to conventions. The format also holds true for group and package business. Such is the case with single entities, a traveling athletic team, or a company-planned outing. Prepaid tour packages offered by wholesalers (see Chapter 2) also use master accounts. One folio, one master account, accumulates all the room charges in both examples. The team's manager or the company's treasurer pays their master account. The wholesaler, who has collected in advance from the tour members, settles that master account.

The hotel may be instructed to post every charge to the master account. That's unlikely with single entities and tour packages, but is sometimes done with company-sponsored functions. Personal items purchased by company employees or single-entity members and services not covered by the wholesaler's package are excluded from the master account. Split folios are the answer (see Chapter 10). Major items, rooms and included meals, are posted to the master account (the A folio). Personal charges are posted to the individual's room (the B folio). B folios are settled by the individual at check out. Group members may be reminded of that arrangement while they are still on the arriving bus. If not, the alert comes at the desk when computer-generated notices are included along with the keys. Room assignments having been made before the group's arrival (see Exhibit 11–7). Master folios (A folios) are settled by the group, almost always by a transfer to the city-ledger.

The advertised package tells the buyer what is and, by inference, what is not included (see Exhibit 2–9). Colored and dated coupons are issued to the package guests. Guests use the proper coupon to pay for meals, drinks, golf, whatever was included with the package. Cashiers in the various hotel departments treat the coupons as part of their daily "turn-in" (see Chapter 12).

Coupons are charged to the tour operator's master account, so breakage accrues to the tour operator. That is, the tour operator collects from the guest for the entire tour but pays the hotel only for actual tickets returned to the master account. By not using the services they have purchased, guests create additional profit for the promoter. The hotel also creates additional profits for the promoter if it handles the vouchers carelessly. Vouchers are not just colored slips of paper that can be lost or thrown away; they are debts that the promoter must pay if the hotel can account for them.

In the hotel's own inclusive tour (IT) package, breakages accrues to the hotel. The package is sold to the guest and the money is collected in advance (minus commissions if it goes through a travel agency). If the guest fails to use the coupon, the hotel has

1. INSERT CARD
2. REMOVE CARD
3. OPEN DOOR

Exhibit 11–7   Room keys, meal coupons, and information about the distribution of expenses between the group and its members, including B folio charges, are readied for distribution to arriving members. The form in the envelope reads:

> Your tour operator has paid for your room for three nights, beginning *Sunday, May 3*, and for all meals (tickets attached) covered by the tour. You are responsible for personal purchases in the gift shop, dining rooms, and lounges, and personal services such as telephone, laundry, and dry cleaning. Here is your room key, number *1217*.

gained. The hotel distributes the single payment received from the guest among the departments, allocating a portion to room sales, food sales, bar sales, and so on.

Individual City-Ledger Receivables

The city ledger contains individual accounts, actual persons or companies, as well as master accounts. Dollar volume is small generally, but that doesn't make their management any easier.

Travel Agencies.   Hotels have a love–hate relationship with travel agencies. That antipathy springs from the industry's view that travel agents (T/As), as third parties in the reservation process, get paid for supplying hotels with the hotels' own customers. Travel agents complain about not getting paid, which lodging's spokespersons deny vehemently. If hotel payments are sporadic, at least they exist. Airlines have stopped paying commissions altogether. In contrast, hotel chains have consolidated payments to assure that individual properties honor the commission structure.[4] Some chains have outsourced commissions to payment-processing companies. Pegasus Solutions, Perot Systems, and

---

[4]*H&MM* reports that Marriott paid travel agent commission of $177 million in 2005, and that Hyatt Resorts gets 30% of its bookings from agents. *Hotel & Motel Management*, March 6, 2006, p. 4.

Utell's Pay-Com[5] are representative of these. Processors consolidate commissions from hotels and other commission-paying industries. For that, they take fees out of the travel agencies' fees.

Not all travel agents are small, corner proprietorships. American Express's travel agency volume is probably larger than that of the hotels with which it deals. But even big guys are fighting online bookings and rate-cutting competitors. Size aside, travel agents complain that they are heavily solicited when the lodging business is slow, but neglected when occupancy improves. Front-office managers do turn away commission-able business during peak occupancies, just as they increase room rates at that time. Notwithstanding industry-to-industry complaints, individual agencies and individual hotels, particularly Hawaiian hotels, develop strong profitable relationships. For the most part, hotels are pleased to take travel agency business and pay the 10% to 15% commission.

A travel agency can become an account receivable in the city ledger. The process starts if the agency collects for the room in advance of the guest's arrival. Later, the guest arrives, paying the first night's room charge with the agency's coupon. That coupon appears on the folio as a transfer and becomes a city-ledger account receivable.

Increases in assets, including *accounts receivable* and cash, are made with debits. Decreases in assets, including *accounts receivable* and cash, are made with credits.

    Debit: Accounts Receivable/City Ledger, Travel Agency Account   100.00
      Credit: Accounts Receivable/Guest ledger, Front-office Folio   100.00
    Explanation: Guest checks out and settles room charge with travel agency's voucher.

Eventually, the agency pays the hotel, less commission.

Increases in assets, including accounts receivable and *cash*, are made with debits. Increases in expenses, including salaries, *commissions*, and utilities, are made with debits.
Decreases in assets, including *accounts receivable* and cash, are made with credits.

    Debit: Cash   85.00
    Debit: Rooms Commissions   15.00
      Credit: Accounts Receivable/City Ledger, Travel Agency Account   100.00
    Explanation: Travel agency settles prepaid guest's room charge, less commission.

---

[5]Trademark names are used throughout the chapter as they are throughout the text. Read® adjacent to each registered name.

Travel agents are entitled to commission even if they don't collect in advance. Then, the agency waits for the hotel to compute the amount and forward the check. There may be delay while the hotel waits for the credit card to clear.

Increases in expenses, including salaries, *commissions* and utilities, are made with debits.

Decreases in assets, including accounts receivable and *cash*, are made with credits.

> Debit: Rooms Commissions   15.00
> Credit: Cash   15.00
> *Explanation:* Hotel pays travel agency's commission for room charge settled by the guest.

The status of the nation's travel agencies is unclear. They are threatened by Web shopping, satellite ticket purchases (convenience stores in Japan sell domestic airline tickets), and ticketless travel. Agencies must find new revenue sources or face extinction. Commissions alone no longer sustain them. Agencies are consolidating, diversifying, charging new fees to customers, servicing commercial accounts, or disappearing from the hotel's city ledger.

The Original City-Ledger Accounts. Local individuals and companies were the original nonregistered accounts receivable. That's where the term *city* ledger originated. Individual accounts still exist, but they have been replaced in the main by the widespread use of credit cards. Hotels hunger for individual city accounts with good credit because payment is made in full without credit-card fees.

What accounts there are may not be local and may not originate at the front desk. Standard city accounts include individuals and companies that preestablish credit in order to use the hotel's facilities. A distant company may send employees to the hotel on a regular basis. A local business might use guest rooms for visitors and public rooms for business meetings and social affairs. Once credit has been established, the authorized user merely signs for the charges. Bills go out monthly, sometimes more frequently.

Airline crews are a good example of the standard city-ledger account. They are much sought after by hotels as basic occupancy even though the average daily rate is very low. Layover crews charge rooms to the airline's city account, and once a month the hotel bills. Airline contracts sometimes require the hotel to accommodate stranded travelers as well as crews. Typically, the airline pays for the rooms and meals by giving the passenger a miscellaneous charge order (MCO). The stranded passenger pays with the MCO, which the hotel uses to balance the front-office folio. The account receivable is transferred to the city ledger and the airline is billed. MCOs are also used when the airline acts as a travel agency and books the guest into a prepaid room. The MCO becomes a travel agency voucher, as previously explained.

Banquet Charges. Open-book credit, nothing more than a personal signature, was once the norm for banquet sales. Party givers and banquet chairpersons signed the tab and left—left the hotel waiting for payment. Catering managers still extend this courtesy in very special instances. More likely, they charge a credit card or obtain a deposit before the event begins. Open credit charges and unpaid balances still remaining after deposits become city-ledger accounts and are billed within three days. Three-day billing is standard procedure for city-ledger banquet charges, master accounts, speedy check-outs, and late charges.

Late Charges.   Late charges are departmental charges (food, beverage, spa, etc.) that appear on the folio after the guest has checked out. The postings were late getting into the system from either the point-of-sale terminal (see Exhibit 10–8) or the front-office terminal.

Property management systems have done much to minimize the frequency of late charges. Those that slip through are irritants to both the guest and the hotel. Guests may need to modify already submitted expense accounts after the late charge arrives by mail. (But see below, Electronic Folio Update.) Hotels usually absorb the cost when guests ignore the subsequent billing. Small late charges are not even billed; they are erased with an allowance. Processing costs and the loss of guest goodwill often exceed the small amount sought.

Late-charge collection is seamless with express check-outs. Although the guest has seen a copy of the folio, the hotel has not yet billed the credit card. The late charges are added to the folio, transferred to the proper credit card in the city ledger, and billed. The final folio arrives several days later with its balance identical to the charge on the guest's credit card.

Reconciling late charges is not as easy if the guest settled at the cashier's window and left with a credit-card receipt and a folio marked "Paid." That receipt will be smaller than the figure that eventually appears on the guest's credit-card statement. In fact, most card companies do not allow changes to be added after the fact. If the late charge is substantial, the hotel will bill the the guest at the address on the folio. The hotel has a second chance at collection, but at a risky public-relations cost.

Direct billing for late charges is the only option if the guest had paid with vouchers, cash, checks, or traveler's checks. At least the hotel has the address of registered guests. There is no option at all if a nonregistered individual pays a lounge or dining-room bill with a credit card that is charged back (see Exhibit 11–10). *Nonregistered* means the hotel has no address, and credit-card companies will not release that information.

Late-Charge Procedures.   Late charges are abbreviated LC or AD (after departure). As explained, small LCs, say under $15, may be wiped off with an allowance. First, the folio of the guest who has checked out is reopened and the late charge is recorded. The balance is immediately brought to zero by means of an allowance. This sequence creates a permanent record of the charge.

Increases in assets, including *accounts receivable* and cash, are made with debits. Increases in incomes (food, beverage, spa, etc.) are made with credits.

> Debit: Accounts Receivable/Guest's Folio
>   Credit: Proper Departmental (food, beverage, spa, etc.) Sale
> *Explanation:* Late-charge income posted to reopened folio.

Decreases in incomes (food, beverage, spa, etc.) are made with debits. Decreases in assets, including *accounts receivable* and cash, are made with credits.

> Debit: Proper Departmental (food, beverage, spa, etc.) Allowance
>   Credit: Accounts Receivable/Guest's Folio
> *Explanation:* Allowance issued for late charge to zero out the folio balance.

A separate late-charge folio is an alternative approach. All small late charges are posted there rather than individually to each folio. Daily, the day's total late charges are cleared with one allowance, which is obviously less burdensome for the desk. Either way, management should get a daily allowance report, which is one of the exception reports prepared during the night audit (see Chapter 13).

Notwithstanding these provisions for allowancing late charges, efforts to collect large amounts should be pursued conscientiously. In that case, the late charge could be posted to the guest's reopened folio and immediately transferred to the city ledger for billing.

Electronic Folio Update.   A recent innovation has been introduced by the credit-card companies working with hotels and with ever-present intermediaries, third parties. It's called *e-folio.*

The text's introductory unit explained how dependent the lodging industry is on the commercial guest. It's estimated that well over 75% of all guests settle with credit cards. The figure for commercial guests is close to 100%. Business persons may use either company cards or personal cards, which are then reimbursed. Accounting for these costs has become a business in itself. Intermediary companies, such as Outtask and Extensity,[5] have teamed up with credit-card issuers and the major hotel chains to expedite record-keeping, billing, and payment. The information flows electronically from the hotel folio to the proprietary reporting systems of the credit-card companies. From there it goes to these intermediaries and then to the traveler's company. Intermediaries sort the charges electronically (rooms, food, beverage, etc.) before reporting to the guest's company. Similar procedures were introduced several years ago for businesses that use credit cards for purchasing (see Exhibit 11–3).

E-folios are in the introductory stage. Only large companies are using the intermediaries, and not all hotels are aboard yet. Even AmEx, the largest commercially oriented credit-card company, is still firing up. The concept has yet to meet critical mass.

In the meantime, guests can call up their folios by email. Other options for viewing have been guest-room TVs, lobby kiosks, and physical copies left under the door the night before departure. Extending folio accessibility has been a priority for Marriott, among others. They began with corporate accounts. Then members of Marriott Rewards (frequent guest program) were given the service. All guests now have access to getting folios via an email option. So, too, do guests at Hilton's 2,000-plus properties, and most of the other large chains.

Chapter 9 explained that hotel chains negotiate special rates for large companies that commit a fixed number of room nights per year. Therefore, the e-folio may have two serendipitous spinoffs. Both the hotel chains and their corporate clients can harvest the actual number of room nights used. That value has always been elusive. And spinoff number two: Hotels obtain the email addresses of their guests.

Delinquent Accounts.   Receivables that may not be collectible are placed in the delinquent, or bad debt division, of the city ledger. Such is the case with late charges that are too large for an allowance and too small for legal action against the offending party. Unrecoverable receivables are eventually written off as bad debts.

Returned (bounced) checks are also tracked as delinquent accounts. Rather than reestablishing the guest's old records, returned checks are viewed as new debts and maintained as delinquent accounts. Checks come back for many reasons: insufficient funds; no such account; account closed; illegible signature; incorrect date. Hotels accept very few checks (see Chapter 12), so this is no longer a major issue in the accounting office. Passing bad checks is a criminal offense. Hotels should support the police in prosecuting offenders even when restitution is made. Credit-card chargebacks (see pages 438 and 439), skippers (guests who intentionally leave without paying), and judgmental

---

[5]Trademark names are used throughout the chapter as they are throughout the text. Read® adjacent to each registered name.

errors in extending open credit make up the balance of this city-ledger division. Hotels that show significant costs in these areas should reevaluate their credit policies.

Executive Accounts.   Hotel executives can be city-ledger receivables in their own hotel. Management people use the hotel for personal pleasure as well as for house business. Company policy dictates how charges are to be made. House entertainment might be distinguished from personal charges on the guest check by an "H" (house business) or an "E" (entertainment) added under the signature. Without the symbol, the accounting department bills the person as a regular city account. Many times, though, the billing is only a percentage of the actual menu price, depending on the employment agreement.

Due Bills.   Hotels have traded room-nights for products since the great depression of the 1930s. Swaps with radio and television stations, billboards, newspapers, and magazines involve free rooms for free advertising. Trades with manufacturers for capital goods such as beds, carpets, and televisions are a later development. Evidence of the hotel's obligation to meets its half of the bargain is a contract called a *due bill* (see Exhibit 11–8). *Trade advertising contacts, trade-outs,*

VALLEN CORPORATE TRADE ADVERTISING CONTRACT

The_____ [Media or Manufacturing Company's Name and address] _____

agrees to____ [Deliver a particular product; or billboard signage, or insert advertising, etc.] ____

in the amount of $_____ to be paid for by room accommodations at any of the Vallen Corporation's member hotels. This trade contract expires on ___[Date]___. Accommodations will not be available until the product has been delivered to the hotel or until the first advertisement appears. Claims for accommodations or for advertising not used by the date above are hereby cancelled.

Charges for services in excess of this trade order or services other than those specifically identified above are the responsibility of the party using the contract and must be paid in full at departure (or more frequently if the stay is extended). The company or organization named above is responsible for full payment whether or not its owners, employees or individuals in due course actually use this due bill.

No guarantee of room availability is made or implied; reasonable advanced noticed is recommended. Every effort will be made to accommodate the dates requested.

This contract must be presented to the guest-service agent upon arrival, but neither the hotel nor the Vallen Corporation accept responsibility for identifying the validity of the user. The hotel and the Vallen Corporation retain the right to eject undesirable guests and to charge the full amount of the reservation against the contract. The hotel and the Vallen Corporation assume no liability for personal injuries or property damages to the person or persons using this contract whether or not the personal injuries or property damages were caused by the negligence of the corporation, the hotel, or its employees.

Date   _____

Merchant_____   Hotel_____
   Authorized Signature   Authorized Signature

_____   _____
   Title   Title

Exhibit 11–8   Trade advertising contracts swap hotel rooms for advertising or products such as inroom TVs. Contracts are widely used during downturns in the economic cycle and rarely used during upturn periods such as that of 2004–2008.

and *reciprocal trade agreements* are other names for due bills. Temporary accounts receivable in the city ledger are needed when the other party to the agreement checks in to take advantage of the "free" facilities.

Rationale for Due Bills.   Airlines, theaters, arenas, and the media deal in highly perishable products. There is no means of recapturing an unsold airline seat or an unused television spot for resale another day. The same is true with the lodging industry. All of these businesses have the same problem: no means of inventorying the product for resale at a later time. Once the newspaper is printed, that day's advertising space is lost. Once the night has passed, that empty hotel room cannot be sold again. Trading the lost inventory for something useful is mutually beneficial when both parties have unsold, perishable products.

The hotel would like to restrict the products it trades to its most profitable item, rooms, and have the occupant pay in cash for the less profitable items, food and beverage. This is understandable from the hotel's point of view. The cost of providing an otherwise empty room is minimal; the cost of food and beverage is high. Moreover, unused food and beverage, unlike unused rooms, can be sold the following day. The advertising media set restrictions too, making no promise as to where the hotel's ad will appear in print or at what time it will be heard on the airwaves.

Whereas the hotel would like to limit the due bill to rooms, to use by certain individuals, and to given days of the week with advance reservations required, the facts of life may be otherwise. It is a matter of negotiation.

Some due bills are so negotiable that they are traded on an open market. Discount brokers buy the bills from the original receiver, or negotiate directly with the hotel, at reduced prices. The due bills are resold to a third, or even a fourth party, each time with an additional markup. In due course, they are used at the hotel by the final buyer in lieu of cash. The hotel accepts the bills at face value, which is still greater than the price paid by the user.

The concept works, and so does the series of marked-up resales, because two prices are involved. Both the hotel and the media (or other swapping party) deliver the due bill at retail prices but deliver the goods or services at cost. If the media accepts a $100 room for a $100 TV spot that costs $40, the TV station can resell the room at $60 and still make $20. There is even greater impetus when we remember that the room and the air time would have gone unused anyway.

Due bills are favored during periods of low or moderate occupancy and are less popular during busy periods. The oil embargo of the 1970s and the poor economy of the early 1980s and early 2000s brought a rebirth of due bill usage. By 2004, the situation had turned again. Due bills were out of favor. They aren't needed during the top of the economic cycle (see Chapter 1), when occupancy is high and new room construction has yet to resume.

Processing the Due Bill.   Due-bill users must present the actual due bill agreement as they register. This enables the guest-service agent to assign the most expensive accommodations. (The hotel's cost of delivering an expensive room is almost the same as delivering an inexpensive one.) The clerk also verifies the expiration date of the agreement. Amounts unused after that date are lost to the due bill holder. When that happens—and it does frequently—the hotel gets the advertising (or product), but the media company never gets to use all of its due bill.

The due bill is attached to the registration card and the rate is marked "Due Bill" along with the dollar room charge. A standard guest folio, or sometimes one specially colored or coded, is used. The actual due bill is filed at the front desk during the guest's stay. After the value of the accommodations used has been recorded on the due bill, it is returned to the holder at check out.

The transient folio, which was used to accumulate charges during the due bill user's stay, is transferred to the city ledger in the usual manner. However, the city ledger account is treated differently. There is no billing. Instead, the account is charged off against the liability incurred by the contract. At the time of the agreement, a liability was created by the hotel's promise to furnish accommodations to the media or other trader. As hotel accommodations are furnished, that liability is decreased. It is balanced off against the city–ledger account that was created from the transfer of the guest folio at the time of check-out.

Increases in assets, including *prepaid advertising* and cash, are made with debits. Increases in liabilities, including *due bills* and taxes *payable,* are made with credits.

> Debit: Prepaid Advertising
>   Credit: Due Bills Payable
> *Explanation:* Negotiated a swap of rooms for advertising.

Increases in assets, including *accounts receivable* and cash, are made with debits. Increases in incomes (*rooms,* food, beverage, spa) are made with credits.

> Debit: Accounts Receivable/Guest's Folio
>   Credit: Room Sales
> *Explanation:* Due-bill guest occupies accommodations.

Decreases in liabilities, including *due bills payable,* are made with debits. Decreases in assets including *accounts receivable* and cash are made with credits.

> Debit: Due Bills Payable
>   Credit: Accounts Receivable/Guest's Folio
> *Explanation:* Due-bill guest pays transient folio with a trade-out via the City Ledger.

MANAGING CREDIT

This chapter first focused on the mechanics of handling credit, the records of accounts receivable. We now exam the management of credit, starting with the establishment of credit policy.

Weighing Costs Against Benefits

There is no perfect credit policy. Any business that extends credit becomes vulnerable to loss. Equally certain, any business that fails to extend credit become vulnerable to loss. Each credit decision weighs immediate, determinable gains against possible, uncertain losses. Recognizing this, the lodging industry has dramatically reduced its level of open credit. More reliance is now placed on credit cards, credit investigations, and credit denial. Personal checks are almost unknown. Open credit has been minimized, although it is still used for advances to concessionaires, outlays for employee gratuities (see Chapter 12), and even occasionally for banquet or convention sales.

Successful credit policy cannot be measured by accounting figures alone. Hotels with small amounts of bad debts (or small ratios of bad debts to accounts receivable) are not necessarily the best managed ones. A conservative credit policy will mean few credit losses, but it may also cause substantial losses from business that was turned away. Low credit losses are easily measured on the books; lost business has no entry. Profits might have been improved by taking the business that an ultraconservative credit policy denied. The conundrum is that the increase might not have been achieved; there's no way to know.

The issue is not black and white—always credit/never credit. Every full-service hotel offers some amount of credit. The question focuses on how much, when, and under what circumstances credit is offered. The answer is not always the same, even for the same credit manager in the same hotel. With different conditions, credit could be severely curtailed, moderately administered, or liberally issued, even to the same customer with the same credit standing (see Exhibit 11–9).

Good occupancy, the first item of Exhibit 11–9, permits the hotel to adopt a conservative credit policy. There is no reason to replace low-risk guests with those of uncertain credit standing. When occupancy is high, a bad debt loss is the sum of full rack rate plus administrative costs, not just the marginal cost of providing a room during low occupancy.

Food and beverage sales, which have a high variable cost, are different. Far more caution is needed to justify banquet sales during a low period than room sales during a low period. A banquet bad debt may well cost the hotel two-thirds or more of the bill (food, call-in labor, flowers, special cake, favors, etc.). Room losses are substantially less, both in percentage (about 25% marginal cost) and in absolute dollars.

Hotels reduce rates when occupancies are low. These would also be the times for a more liberal credit policy. In fact, the more liberal credit policy might allow higher room rates. Too dismal a circumstance, and the hotel will need to give both to get the business. Fighting for market share or competing with better appointed properties are additional reasons for liberalizing credit (see Exhibit 11–9).

Factors In Administrating Hotel Credit		
Credit Severely Curtailed	**Moderately Administered**	**Credit Liberally Issued**
High occupancy	...	Low occupancy
In-season	...	Off-season
No competition	...	Price cutting
Established property	...	New hotel
Interest rates are high	...	Interest rates are low
Reputable hotel	...	Disreputable hotel
Item of high variable cost	...	Item of low variable cost
Inexperienced lender	...	Low losses from debt-recovery
Hotel's credit overextended	...	Hotel has good credit rating

Exhibit 11–9   The amount of credit that a hotel extends depends on more than the guest's creditworthiness; it depends also on the hotel's circumstances. So one hotel may ease or tighten credit as another a short distance away does just the opposite.

The most obvious cost of poor credit is the out-and-out loss from nonpayment. Bank charges, attorney fees, and collection expenses are heavy additional costs. So too are several hidden expenses that are not usually added on. Rarely charged against the debtor are inhouse administrative costs, forms, printing, credit checks, postage and telephone, and employee time. To the whole package must be added the permanent loss of a customer.

Expanded sales volume is the offsetting benefit to credit risk. Hotels also gain from a spread in interest rates. If the hotel's credit rating is good, it borrows at low rates or self-finances. Extending credit at 18% (1.5% per month) represents a measurable benefit, provided, of course, that it eventually collects.

Components of Credit Management

Establishing credit policies and monitoring them is a broad-based management function. Credit managers may lead the effort, but not all hotels have one. If not, the controller takes on some of the tasks as part of a credit committee. Other members are the rooms manager, the convention manager, and the catering manager. The team operates with a credit policy that encourages a healthy marketing approach, but one that assures prompt payment and bottom-line returns. Credit must be extended with diligence and collection must be balanced with the good customer relations.

> I've never seen an organizational chart or read a job description for accounts receivable that included guest-relations and sales components. I've never heard of a director of sales and marketing routinely being invited to participate in the training of accounts receivable personnel.[6] [Implying, of course, that they should.]

Extending Credit.   Successful collection from late accounts requires information about the debtor. This must be done at registration. Fewer reservations come directly to the hotel as they once did. Prescreening to verify identification is no longer possible, and never was with walk-ins. Collecting after the fact relies on procedures that are in place during registration.

Identification was more reliable when guests had reservations that involved correspondence. Then the name and address, and perhaps even the company name, was verified by mail. This must now be done at registration with complete name, not just initials; complete address, not just post-office box, office building, or city. Scribbled, illegible signatures must be translated. Early suspicions can be confirmed quickly. ZIP code directories uncover false addresses. Some hotels have the bellstaff record car license numbers on rooming slips. Telephone calls to the guest's supposed office puts many issues in perspective.

Unheard of a generation ago, guests are expected to announce their method of settlement as they register. Strange as it seems, hotels prefer credit cards with their costly merchant fees over cash or checks. This shifts some credit issues to the credit-card companies and provides the hotel with help from their fraud divisions.

Credit procedures put stress on the clerk–guest interchange. Specific information must be elicited but done under the customer relations umbrella. Tact in selecting the right words and care in applying voice intonations—often ignored in training programs—must be taught and practiced. Many factors, such as a tired guest or a misplaced reservation, exacerbate an already awkward situation. If baggage is missing or light, the clerk will need to press for more complete details. If the guest is nervous or poorly dressed,

---

[6]Anthony Marshall, "Accounts receivable and guest relations: An imperfect mix." *Hotel & Motel Management*, March 20, 2000, p. 16.

the clerk may insist on photocopying a driver's license. The line between information gathering and invasion is a thin one, as is the line between guest understanding and anger. Front-office clerks need to be masters of diplomacy.

No magic formula separates safe risks from poor ones. But collection is possible only if the hotel can identify the person and the address. Returned checks, late charges, credit-card chargebacks, and other open accounts cannot be collected, regardless of the guest's sincerity, without these essential facts. Unlike most industries, innkeeping has the opportunity to get the data. Procedures should be in place to ensure its collection.

Because walk-ins pose additional credit risks, they are flagged with special identifications. NR (no reservation), OS (off-the-street), and WI (walk-in) are common abbreviations (see Exhibit 10–9). The reg cards of walk-ins may go through additional credit checks. Telephone directories, Web sites, city directories, credit-card companies, colleagues at other hotels, and telephone calls are used to verify questionable information. Not many walk-ins warrant this level of concern.

Any guest can be required to pay in advance, credit card or not. Guests who have already been roomed can be called back to the desk. Extreme measures like these do not build guest loyalty. Few guests, walk-ins included, are out to defraud. The extra caution used to protect against a few must not disintegrate into antiservice for all. Guests and front-office staff stand face to face in an important "moment of truth." Credit issues must be resolved promptly, courteously, and confidentially.

Minimizing Chargebacks. Hotels spend large sums to attract and service customers. Yet they fail to collect in nearly half of all credit-card challenges, called chargebacks. Chargebacks are disallowed credit-card charges or debit memos.[7] The card company bounces the charge back to the hotel until the issue is clarified. Either the guest has refused to pay or a procedural error (see Exhibit 11–10) has made the charge unacceptable to the card company. Merchant/hotels have 30 days to respond, but accounting offices often fail to do so.

Reservation no-shows are common chargebacks. Guests guarantee the reservation using a credit card. One night is charged when the guest fails to show. With a credit-card number and no record of a cancellation, the hotel can counter the guest's challenge of the charge. A successful response requires just that, a response. Of course, not demanding payment may be more about guest relations than about credit. Indeed, different responses may depend on the occupancy and RevPar on that particular day. Whatever the decision, it should be policy dictated, and not rest with an accounting clerk's disposition.

Not all chargebacks originate from unclaimed reservations. Some stem from efforts to recover room damage and property theft. Smoking in nonsmoking rooms, theft of pictures and towels, damages during conventions and prom nights account for special charges by the hotel and corresponding chargebacks by the guests.

Mistakes in procedures account for many chargebacks. Procedural snafus originate with departmental cashiers. Training programs, undertaken with help from the card companies, concentrate on the do's and don'ts of taking and processing cards (see Exhibit 11–10).

Monitoring Credit

Two special credit restrictions need extra attention. One is hotel derived; the other is a credit-card issue.

---

[7]"Debit" because hotel debt is a liability (that is, a credit) to the credit-card company. Now the charge is being reversed; the reverse of a credit is a debit. "Memo" is a another term for "notice."

Avoiding Chargebacks

1. Check credit cards for both expiration and starting dates.
2. Scrutinize credit cards signed with felt pens; they may cover original signatures.
3. Decline requests to split charges on two vouchers to avoid floor limits.
4. Remember that MasterCard begins with number 5; Visa with 4; AmEx with 3.
5. Place no telephone numbers on credit-card slips.
6. Refuse to post fictitious items in order to give cash against the card.
7. Maximize recovery by retaining original, signed vouchers.

FOR IMMEDIATE ACTION

    a. Replace the printer ribbons frequently.
    b. Replace the printer's paper roll as soon as colored streaks appear.
    c. Handle carbonless paper with care to prevent black marks.
    d. Retain the white copy of the two colored draft print-out.
    e. Store sales drafts carefully within a retrieval system

8. Issue credit-card refunds, not cash, against original credit-card charges.
9. Respond promptly to all chargebacks and furnish evidence for the charge.
10. Watch for altered cards: rearranged numbers; glue; misaligned numbers; color changes.
11. Compare suspicious card signature with driver's license signature.
12. Insure against false arrest caused by inaccurate information from the card company.
13. Exercise no force to retrieve cards or restrain users.
14. Anticipate some employee misuse such as increasing the gratuity.

Exhibit 11–10   Chargebacks and other losses from credit-card transactions can be minimized with good training that keeps employees abreast of the law and the card companies' rules and procedures.

Hotels retain the right to bill at any time. They do so whenever management becomes concerned, but especially when a guest folio nears a preset value. This predetermined amount varies directly with the class of hotel and with its average daily rate (ADR). Upscale properties set a far higher ceiling than do budget-class hotels (see Exhibit 1–8). Collection efforts begin as soon as the folio total—which includes all charges, not just room rates—creeps toward that figure. Two reports prepared during the night audit (see Chapter 13) alert management. One identifies unusually high daily charges; the other flags high cumulative values. Property management systems enable management to monitor these questionable folios throughout the day.

Credit-card companies also establish dollar ceilings. Strangely, they are called "floors." Every hotel has a floor, the maximum credit to be extended to any one guest and still retain protection from the card company. The hotel negotiates as high a floor as it can. Just as the hotel's own ceiling reflects its ADR, so does the card company's floor. If the guest's credit card is swiped at registration and accepted, the card company stands behind the charges up to the hotel's floor.

Losses are complete if floor limits are breached without prior clearance. Coverage is an issue only if the card company denies the request and the hotel extends credit nevertheless. Even then, there is no problem if the guest settles. But guests have their own floors. Credit-card holders have specific limits that also jeopardize the card's validity.

Several situations require immediate action by the hotel. Clearly, the card company's refusal to increase the guest's limit is one. Guests who have exceeded in-house limits are another. Paid-in-advance guests who have accrued charges somehow or guests who have exceeded preapproved direct billing lengthen the list. If efforts to collect immediately are unsuccessful and if the situation has grown dire, management may take extreme action. Guests' luggage may be seized and guests locked out. Common sense dictates not doing this in the middle of the night. Wait too long, however, and the guest might skip.

Credit Alerts and Skippers.   Professional skippers can often be identified by the pattern of their actions. Skipper profiles should be developed similar to the airlines' profile of a possible hijacker. The typical skipper is a 30–35-year-old male with light baggage and vague identification. He is a heavy tipper and consequently a quick new friend of the bartenders. He cannot be traced through telephone calls because he makes none. His address always proves to be false. He offers no business identification and scribbles the reg card information.

Skipper alarms begin ringing when baggage is light or worthless. Guests arouse additional suspicion when they charge their folios with small items (candy bar, tube of toothpaste) that are normally paid for in cash. Skippers compound the hotel's costs by passing bad checks or using stolen credit cards. Bad-check passers concentrate on weekends or holidays when commercial hotels are understaffed and banks are closed. With ATM machines readily available, few hotels cash checks. Those that do maintain a check-cashing record to alert other shifts of ongoing activities. Then a check-cashing report becomes part of the night-audit activities.

Skippers and bad-check passers frequently work one area before moving on. A telephone, Web, or fax network among local hotels does much to identify the culprit even before arrival. Photographs of suspects and identifying information, perhaps from the police, will undoubtedly be displayed someday on computer terminals.

Something needs to be done because crime has moved from the street into the hotel. Frustrating the criminal takes the combined efforts of all employees. Clerks, bellpersons, house police, cashiers, housekeepers, engineers, and room service waiters, too, must watch for and report the telltale signs. Large quantities of blank checks or money orders, firearms and burglary tools, keys from other hotels, unusual amounts of cash or gems, or just heavy traffic or loitering about a room indicate serious trouble is brewing.

Collecting Receivables: Billing and Chasing

Receivables are amounts owed the hotel by guests who have not yet paid for services received; *received*, hence *receiv*ables. Some enter the city ledger directly: credit-card charges from the food and beverage outlets, for example. Most come to the city ledger as transfers from front-office folios. The city ledger accumulates every category of customer debt. These have been itemized throughout the chapter and are summarized in Exhibit 11–11. How these receivables are collected and by whom reflects on the hotel's profit picture and on its critical cash flow. Having gone to the trouble of marketing, servicing, and charging the accounts, the hotel can be no less diligent in collecting what's due. Sometimes that calls for chasing the debt.

Hotels announce a three-day billing cycle for city accounts. In reality, processing and mailing usually delay the invoice. So do some master accounts whose review may be delayed a day or more. Ideally, all the direct billings of Exhibit 11–11 would meet that three-day horizon with followups in 15- and 30-day cycles. Management needs to allocate adequate resources to the job and then review the results.

List of City-Ledger Receivables and their Disposition

Source	Likely Disposition[a]
Airline crews	Direct billing
Associations	Direct billing to headquarters
Bad debts	Wipe off as an expense
Banquet charges	Direct billing of remaining balances
Bounced checks	Redeposit
Conventions	Direct billing to headquarters
Credit cards	Collection from card companies
Delinquents	Move to bad debts
Direct billings	To preapproved individuals and companies
Due bills	Offset against advertising
Executive accounts	Direct billing to hotel executives
Late charges	Credit card; direct billing; or allowance
Master accounts	Direct billing
Tour operators	Direct billing of remaining balances
Travel agency coupons	Offset against prepayments
Skippers	Move to bad debts
Wholesalers	Direct billing of remaining balances

[a]Direct billing takes place only after credit standing has been preapproved and/or contracts have been signed.

Exhibit 11-11   The city ledger accumulates a variety of accounts receivable (persons, companies, associations, and organizations that owe the hotel). The disposition of those debts vary according to their source.

Second notices should follow soon after the first bill, usually at the end of the month. The collection procedure includes routine notices twice during the next 30 days and a telephone call to make certain the statement has been received. Inquiring into the intended disposition is certainly in order. Each statement should contain notice of the additional interest charges that are accumulating and the age of the account. Earlier efforts at collection are essential because the longer a bill is unpaid, the less likely it will ever be paid (see Exhibit 11-12).

Chasing unpaid debts should not be a random assignment. It must be in someone's job description. Without followup, debtors get the impression that the hotel has forgotten or decided it isn't important. Nor should the collector be apologetic—the late payer is the wrongdoer. Settlement arrangement should be specific in both amounts and dates. Partial payments plus interest are acceptable, provided when and how much are fixed and enforced. Small payments should be avoided because they are costly to administer and tend to be overlooked as insignificant when payments are missed.

No matter how carefully credit requests are screened or how diligent the followup, some bad debts will materialize. The responsible manager must then decide to continue the internal collection efforts or employ a third party. The first step may

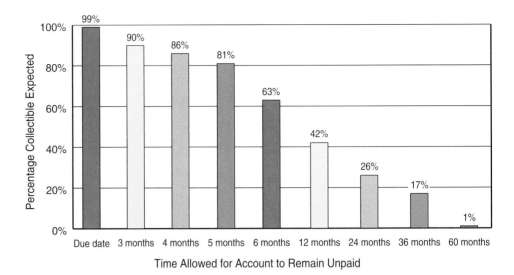

Exhibit 11-12   The likelihood of collecting debts (city-ledger receivables) decreases the longer they remain unpaid. Credit management requires prompt billing and an aggressive pursuit of late, unpaid accounts.

be an inhouse attorney, if the hotel has one. If not, collection agencies and outside attorneys are a second option. Either way, substantial collection costs are part of the process.

Hotels that choose the internal option must be prepared to invest in the process. In addition to outright fees, there are hidden administrative costs. Credit collection is not a sometime affair. To be effective, collection must be systematic and thorough, not a passing effort. It takes a flow of information and a stack of records, manual or computerized, to track debtors. Yet the job is one more task added to the office of controller when there is no full-time credit manager. Knowledge of federal and state legislation is another hurdle. If the inhouse staff is insensitive to the rights of the debtor (and they have many legally protected rights), the process might best be left to a third party that has legal expertise.

The worst of the bad debts ends up with collection agencies. Oddly enough, their basic technique is writing letters, much like the hotel does. More than 90% of their collections are generated by simple dunning letters. Still, collections are light, especially for small accounts, which have the lowest priority with the collection agencies. Less than 25% of accounts turned over are collected. If no collection is made, there is no fee, but the fee takes 30% to 40% of what is collected.

What success collection agencies have is probably due to psychological effects on the debtor as much as to techniques employed by the agency. For a start, the customer realizes that the matter has grown more serious, more intense, seeing the agency as a more relentless and threatening force than the hotel. Whatever softening existed through the customer–client relationship has dissolved with the appearance of this third party. The debtor is aware that the agency knows more about his entire credit record than the hotel knew. Credit ratings may suddenly be in jeopardy. Sometimes the debtor simply tires of the battle and willingly makes arrangements. *Arrangements* is a good word for any collector to use because it says that some kind of settlement can be negotiated and worked out. That is, after all, the intent of the collection effort.

MECHANICS OF THE ENTRY

Two procedures are used to translate guest activities to guest records in the city ledger. For now, we postpone the credit-card discussion that involves neither the folio nor the front office. Guests, registered or not, buy services in the various departments and pay for them with credit cards or cash. No charge appears on any folio.

Chapter 10 explained the second, more common, procedure. Registered guests accumulate charges on front-office folios, which are then transferred to the city ledger. These transfers from the guest-ledger folio [a receivable] to the city-ledger account [a receivable] decrease the balance of the first and increase the balance of the second (see Exhibits 10–5 and 10–12). It's the same whether the destination in the city ledger is to a credit card or to a direct bill.

Increases in assets, including *accounts receivable* and cash, are made with debits. Decreases in assets, including *accounts receivable* and cash, are made with credits.

    Debit: Accounts Receivable, City Ledger/Credit Card Company
        Credit: Accounts Receivable, Guest Ledger (Folio)/Guest Name
    Explanation: Folio settled with a credit card.

OR

    Debit: Accounts Receivable, City Ledger/Personal or Company Account
        Credit: Accounts Receivable, Guest Ledger (Folio)/Guest Name
    Explanation: Folio to be settled by direct billing.

Total debits to the city ledger must equal total credits from the guest ledger both daily and cumulatively. Once the transfer is made, billing takes place from the city ledger. When settlement is received (from an individual, company, organization, or credit-card issuer), the debt (the city-ledger account receivable) is cleared and the check (cash) is deposited. For some receivables, such as an association's master account or a bridal shower, the one-time city-ledger account is closed. Other receivables, such as the credit-card companies, are continuing records with new charges and new payments continually flowing in and out. Cash payments by check are being replaced by electronic fund transfers.

Increases in assets, including accounts receivable and *cash*, are made with debits. Decreases in assets, including *accounts receivable* and cash, are made with credits.

    Debit: Cash
        Credit: Accounts Receivable, City Ledger/Personal or Credit-Card Co.
    Explanation: Any city-ledger account receivable settled its account

> Increases in assets, including accounts receivable and *cash*, are made with debits.
> Increases to expenses, including *fees*, labor, utilities, etc., are made with debits.
> Decreases in assets, including *accounts receivable* and cash, are made with credits.
>
> Debit: Cash
> Debit: Credit-Card Fees
>   Credit: Accounts Receivable, City Ledger, Visa [or MC, etc.]
> *Explanation*: Credit-card company settled part of its account, less fees.

The city-ledger settlements just described generate cash, but not all city-ledger settlements do. Travel-agency records and frequent guest programs have different formats. The accounts are transferred to the city ledger in the normal manner, but their dispositions differ.

Travel-Agency Records

Antipathy between travel agents (TAs) and hotels can be ascribed to poor record-keeping on both sides. Hotels start the process when the reservation arrives. Commissionable reservations are flagged and that identification stays with the records. It appears on the reg card and the folio. Computer systems track the TA's reservation with ease, but so did good pencil-and-paper records. DNAs (Did Not Arrive) signal the first issue. A notice of nonarrival, perhaps just a postcard, is mailed immediately to the agency. Doing so forestalls claims and the endless correspondence that follows.

How It's Supposed to Work.   The number of hotels and the number of agencies worldwide is immeasurable. Every hotel cannot possibly know every agency, and vice versa. Therefore, it's best if the agency prepays the reservation by company credit card or check, less commission. Accompanying the payment is a reservation form similar to Exhibit 11–13. (Attempts to standardized these forms have failed.) The hotel confirms the reservation by returning one copy. Since payment was received before due, the hotel owes the agency. The cash received is less than the room rate because the agency has kept its commission, usually 10%. Commissions are incomes to the agency and expenses to the hotel, similar to credit-card fees.

> Increases in assets, including accounts receivable and *cash*, are made with debits.
> Increases in expenses, including fees and *commissions*, are made with debits.
> Increases in liabilities, including *accounts* and taxes *payable*, are made with credits.
>
> | | | |
> |---|---|---|
> | Debit: Cash | 90 | |
> | Debit: Rooms Expenses/Travel Agency Commissions | 10 | |
> | Credit: Accounts Payable/City Ledger/ABC to Agency | | 100 |
>
> *Explanation:* Received advanced payment, less commission, for reservation.

Step 1. Agency types out as much of form as it can.
Step 2. Agency faxes Parts 2 and 3 to hotel or completes form by phone.
Step 3. If Step 2 was done by fax, hotel fills out balance of form on both parts and returns

Part 3 to agency. If Step 2 was completed by phone, agency throws away Part 2.
Step 4. When form has been all filled out, remittance is attached to Part 4 and mailed to hotel.

Step 5. Part 3 is filed in client's folder and Part 1 is mailed or delivered to client.
Step 6. Part 5 is filed in date tickler for commission collection and/or is thrown out when commission has been collected.

AGENCY REQUEST FOR HOTEL/MOTEL ACCOMMODATIONS

Date_____

☐ INITIAL REQUEST   ☐ CANCELLATION   ☐ CHANGE

CONFIRM TO AGENCY VIA   ☐ RETURN FAX   ☐ E-MAIL   ☐ TELE-PHONE
CATEGORY   ☐ MINIMUM   ☐ MODERATE   ☐ DELUXE

CLIENT

AGT.
HOTEL/MOTEL

TEL. NO.

AGENCY LIABILITY SUBJECT TO CONDITIONS ON REVERSE SIDE HEREOF

CONFIRMED RESERVATIONS FOR:
_____ ROOMS _____ PERSONS _____ NIGHTS
                HOUR   DAY   DATE   VIA   FROM
ARRIVE
DEPART
_____ SINGLE _____ TWIN _____ DOUBLE _____ STUDIO _____ SUITE

☐ NO MEALS(EP)   ☐ CONTINENTAL BREAKFAST   ☐ AMERICAN BREAKFAST
☐ DEMI PENSION (MAP)   ☐ FULL PENSION(AP)

CONFIRMED FOR HOTEL BY _____ DATE _____

ROOM RATE $ _____

NO. OF NIGHTS _____

WHEN VALIDATED THIS VOUCHER HAS A VALUE OF
$
EXCLUDING TAXES AND CHARGES FOR SERVICE AND PERSONAL INCIDENTALS

PLEASE REPLY BELOW AND RETURN GREEN COPY TO TRAVEL AGENCY
☐ Quote rates in U.S. Dollars or specify currency exchange rate _____
☐ Advise cancellation date without penalty _____
☐ State if reservations are guaranteed _____ YES _____ NO
☐ May agency deduct commission if fully prepaid _____ YES _____ NO

COMM. $ _____
DEPOSIT _____
HOTEL/MOTEL TO COLLECT FROM CLIENT $ _____

Reply by Hotel/Motel:

THIS BOX FOR AGENCY USE ONLY
CK. NO.   DATE SENT

By _____ Date _____

Exhibit 11–13   Hotels and travel agencies have the best relationships when the agency prepays its request for room reservations for a client. Unfortunately, despite several major efforts, the form used has never been standardized. The introduction of corporate and business credit cards (see Exhibit 11–3) has simplified the procedure by making the credit-card company an intermediary. *Courtesy of Willow Press, Syosset, New York.*

The arriving guest presents a copy of the same reservation form (Exhibit 11–13) now called a *coupon* or *travel agency voucher*.[8] Full credit is given against this voucher, although the hotel received less from the travel agency. Everything worked perfectly: The room has been prepaid (usually for just one night); the hotel has its money; the agency has its commission. Most important, the guest has been welcomed and accommodated even if the unknown agency is located on the other side of the globe.

At check-out, the coupon-carrying guest pays for incidentals, including extra room nights and room taxes, as does any other guest. An additional commission check is mailed to the agency if the guest's stay exceeds the original deposit. As Chapter 10 discussed, settlement is with cash, allowance or credit-card transfers. This scenario requires a special transfer. The coupon used to pay for the room is transferred to the city ledger, where it offsets the liability that was created when the TA's payment arrived.

---

[8]Travel-agency coupons differ from marketing coupons (discount incentives) and tour-group coupons (used as tickets for admissions and meals).

> Decreases in liabilities, including *accounts* and taxes *payable*, are made with debits.
> Decreases in assets, including *accounts receivable* and cash, are made with credits.
>
>   Debit: Accounts Payable/City Ledger/ABC Travel Agency   100
>   Credit: Accounts Receivable, Guest Ledger (Folio)/Guest Name   100
>   *Explanation:* Prepaid room rate offsets room charges of current folio.

Why It Doesn't Always Work.   Agency reservations don't work as well in practice as in theory. First of all, the agency may not send a check; there may not be time. Even if there were time, the agency may not have the money. Corporate accounts, for example, are customarily settled after the trip, not before. So rather than being prepaid, the hotel guest tenders the agency's coupon, an IOU. The expectation is for hotel credit, even though payment has not been received and the party is unknown. Only the most naïve would expect that to work.

The hotel will refuse the voucher unless previous relationships have established the agency as a reliable risk. Otherwise, the hotel takes the guest's credit card and leaves the travel agency to resolve the situation. In extreme cases, guests may find themselves without accommodations. With a full house and without a deposit, the hotel may not have saved a room.

Equally confusing is a guest whose paperwork is in order, but who stays less than the original, prepaid voucher. There's no refund to that guest; the unused balance belongs to the agency, and is rebated there.

Vouchers from overseas agencies add to the tension. The desk is unprepared to deal with strange forms from unknown sources. Some help for identifying foreign agencies is available from trade associations such as PATA (Pacific Asia Travel Association) and IATA (International Air Transport Association). Payments from foreign travel agents need conversion to local currencies, and local currencies, need conversion for commission payments (see Exhibit 12–11). IATA will also assist in currency conversions, as will foreign-exchange companies and international banks. All require a fee as well as a foreign-exchange fee.

Helping to Make It Work.   The issues between TAs and hotels are all about upfront money. If the reservation is prepaid, the system works. If not prepaid, it works only if the hotels knows the agency and accepts its coupons (vouchers). Do guest-service agents recognize the voucher (Exhibit 11–13)? And if so, can they read it? Forms are not standardized, even in the States. Unfamiliar forms, formats, colors, designs, and languages raise questions which a busy desk can rarely answer. Attempts at standardization by companies as big as Hilton and Holiday have floundered on the second issue: the creditworthiness of the agency. Credit is not granted willy-nilly to unknown customers or unknown agencies.

Enter the credit-card companies. They interposed their financial credibility between hotels and travel agencies just as they did between hotels and guests. Before corporate credit cards were introduced, travel agencies would pay the credit-card company and receive a reservation voucher. Hotels accepted that voucher because it was backed by the credit-card company, not by some unknown agency thousands of miles away. The form was standardized, and payment was in local currency. Of course, fees were charged, but transferring accounts to the city ledger and cutting commission checks to travel agencies also involve costs. The process was short lived because corporate credit cards were introduced for travel agencies, and overseas visitors grew more receptive to personal cards.

Frequent Guest Programs

Frequent guest programs (FGP) have been discussed several times throughout the text. Guests earn points toward free accommodations and/or airline tickets by staying at any hotel within the chain.[9] Using the credits is a different matter. Given a choice, guests spend their points at resorts, not at the commercial hotels where the points were likely earned. The destination hotel accepts payment with a FGP coupon and looks to the parent company's FGP division for reimbursement.

Split folios (see Chapter 10) are used to process the awards that the frequent guests tender. B folios accumulate all incidental charges; those not covered by the award program. Guests are responsible for these and settle as they check out. Settlement is identical to any other check-out: by transfer to a city-ledger account, by allowance, or by cash.

Room charges plus any other services included in the FGP are posted to the A folio. That folio is also transferred to the city ledger for billing. Unlike other city accounts, the chain itself is the account receivable. It is charged either for the full rack rate or a lesser amount, as the FGP contract provides. Reimbursement at full rack rate is almost unknown. Everyone knows that rooms have a high profit margin. Besides, sales of food and beverage, not covered by the program, are additional income to the hotel. A room allowance reduces the amount between the rack rate that the guest was charged and the FGP rate that the parent company will reimburse. The allowance can be recorded either when the bill is sent or payment is received.

Increases in assets, including accounts receivable and *cash*, are made with debits.
Decreases in sales, including *allowances*, are made with debits.
Decreases in assets, including *accounts receivable* and cash, are made with credits.

Debit: Cash	40	
Debit: Room Allowances/Frequent Guest Program	60	
Credit: Accounts Receivable/City Ledger/FGP Account with Chain		100
Explanation: FGP account is settled at rate agreed to in FGP contract.		

The illustration shows payment in cash; that isn't always the case. Some FGP programs offset the amount *due to* the hotel with the amount *due from* the hotel. Franchise fees and FGP fees are among them. Others keep the accounts separate; hotels collect the FGP debt and pay whatever corporate or franchise fees are due.

---

[9]Starwood's Preferred Guest Program has won the Freddie Award for Hotel Program of the Year for several consecutive years. It features no blackout dates and innovative benefits.

> Increases in expenses, including credit-card fees and *other fees,* are made with debits.
>
> Decreases in sales, including *allowances,* are made with debits.
>
> Decreases in assets, including *accounts receivable* and cash, are made with credits.
>
> | | |
> |---|---:|
> | Debit: Frequent Guest Program Fee | 40 |
> | Debit: Room allowances/Frequent Guest Programs | 60 |
> | Credit: Accounts receivable/City Ledger/FGP Account with the Chain | 100 |
>
> *Explanation*: Amount due from FGP settlement used to pay FGP fees.

Electronic Draft Capture

The final segment of this chapter opened with this statement:

> For now, we postpone the credit-card discussion that involves neither the folio nor the front office. Guests, registered or not, buy services in the various departments and pay for them with credit cards or cash. No charges appear on any folio.

That's accurate, of course. Many guests, whether registered or not, use credit cards to pay for food, beverage and other services. These credit-card charges are not posted to any folio. They become part of the departmental cashier's daily turn-in of cash and credit-card sales (see Chapter 12). Cashiers report their shift's activities to the accounting office, bypassing the front desk, its folio records, and its ledger-to-ledger transfers.

The electronic highway has reduced the paperwork and delays that hampered the prompt processing of manual charge slips. Electronic terminals (see Exhibit 11–5) accept the scanned credit-card by printing receipts, one copy for the guest and one for the hotel. The "For Immediate Action" insert of Exhibit 11–10 focuses on that printer and its paper output, which is illustrated in Exhibit 11–14.

What happens during the processing is less visible but as important as what happens with the two printed slips. One of the copies goes to the guest; the other stays with the merchant/hotel as backup to any system failure and to any chargeback claims. The charge is captured electronically by the credit-card company. Simultaneously, the card's status is validated; approval to proceed is granted; and the card's ceiling is updated.

Electronic transfers eliminate paper sales drafts and all of the sorting, postage and manual posting that batch handling of paper charge slips entailed. Electronic transfers permit access to funds more rapidly than the old manual systems. Lower discount fees are an extra bonus that helps offset the cost of the equipment and lines. There is also a benefit to the credit-card companies, which now use laser imaging. Charges appear sooner on the customer's monthly statement because there is no waiting for piles of paperwork to clear. The sooner the billing, the sooner the credit-card company gets paid.

Credit-card processing has passed quickly through a series of ever-improving communication processes. First were printed lists of bad-risk credit-card numbers that guest-service agents needed to check manually. Then came telephone calls from the agent to the credit-card company's representative. Manual-dial telephones and then touch-tone terminals followed in rapid sequence. Electronic transfer is certainly not the end of the transition. But for now, it allows direct, speedy processing between the hotel's property management system and that of the card company's. The hotel's city ledger captures the charge, holding the credit-card company as an account receivable, awaiting ultimate payment.

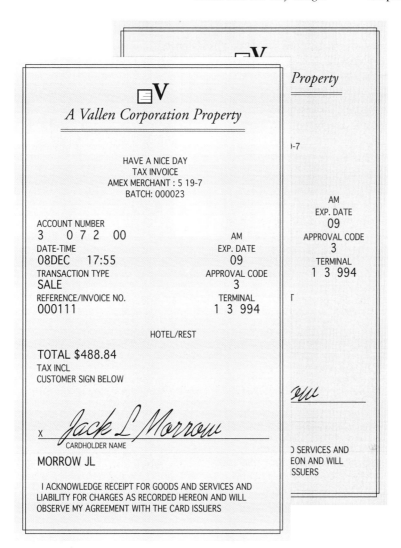

Exhibit 11–14   Although electronic terminals (see Exhibit 11–5) have replaced paper-and-pencil vouchers, paper receipts are still needed for the guest and for backup records. The printout looks similar to an old-fashioned adding machine tape. Exhibit 11–10 alerts users to problems that even electronic systems have.

SUMMARY

Today's travelers prefer credit cards over cash. So do today's hotelkeepers. They know that the gains from credit cards outweigh the costs. The goals of both (increasing sales and decreasing losses) are compatible. So, despite some operational irritations, hotels and credit-card companies work closely together.

Innkeepers also know that assigning some credit risks to the card companies does not lessen their own need for vigilance. Collecting outstanding debts must be managed just as the marketing and servicing of the customers who created that debt was managed. Chargebacks, credit cards that the card companies have sent back for processing, is one area that cries out for continuing management.

Hotels track and bill their credit guests (accounts receivable) through the city ledger. *City ledger* is an easy way of referring to a group of records that contains information about nonregistered persons who owe the hotel for services. Hotels provide rooms, food, beverages, and other services to a variety of city-ledger identities. Among them are banquet and convention groups, travel agents, companies, individuals, including the hotel's own executives, and frequent-guest participants.

Most city-ledger records start out as front-office folios. They become city-ledger accounts when guests check out and transfer the amounts owed to credit cards. Other city accounts come directly into the city ledger from credit-card charges in the hotel's various outlets.

Modern electronic communication has replaced much of the paper recordkeeping that once plagued the front desk. The development of this capability has been undertaken by a variety of third-party intermediaries. Lodging now has numerous credit partners, including national credit-card companies and banking institutions. They issue two classes of credit card. Travel and entertainment cards (T&Es) are used primarily by businesses and individuals with better credit ratings. But there are far more bank cards than T&Es. Competition has forced each type to borrow ideas from the other. Court decisions that gave T&Es access to the banking systems have further blurred the distinctions.

Credit and credit cards have been essential to the growth of the lodging industry. Debit cards are growing in popularity; smart cards have yet to make their full impact.

RESOURCES AND CHALLENGES
Resources

WEB SITES

http://www.buyerszone.com (Privately held by Bessemer Partners and others)—Waltham, MA.

Aid to buyers and sellers of numerous products. Choose "credit-card processing" or "credit-card terminals" for a range of credit-card products.

http://www.cardweb.com (Cardweb, originally a subsidiary of RAM research)—Frederick, MD.

Company offers a full menu of free and fee-based services pertaining to all types of cards (credit, debit, smart, phone) and their management.

http://www.concur.com (Concur Technologies)—Redmond, WA.

Offers "end-to-end" travel services with emphasis on corporate expense travel management. A third-party service company coordinating hotel records and corporate travel offices.

http://www.visa.com (Linked to some 20,000 financial institutions)—San Francisco, CA.

Follow its metamorphosis from institutional-member ownership to a public corporation, a process undertaken in late 2007.

Web Assignment

Differentiate between "cobranded cards" and "private-label cards" by referencing the alphabetic listing provided on the Cardweb site. Is that difference an important issue for lodging managers? If so, what?

INTERESTING TIDBITS

➤ For a few cents per mile, airlines sell frequent-flier points to banks for credit-card usage and to hotels for frequent guest programs. The buyers then use the points as gifts and promotions. Heavy demand for seats has allowed airlines to reduce the number of flights and the overall supply of frequent-flier seats while raising the price (number of miles) required.

➤ A 1963 film, *The Man From Diner's Club*, starring Danny Kaye, played off of the one-time popularity of the earliest credit-card, Diner's Club card, an icon of early credit-card history; see Exhibit 11–1.

➤ The Visa card was *BankAmericard* when it first came out (1960). The card was renamed "Visa" when it was launched internationally because the word is pronounced the same in many languages.

➤ Guests use lobby kiosks with touch screens and computer keyboards to check out and to transfer their folios to the city ledger. Four-sided kiosks date back to the Ottoman Empire, 13th century. Modern forms are found in airports and public centers for use by a range of services, from tourist agencies to street vendors.

Challenges

TRUE/FALSE

Questions that are partially false should be marked false (F).

___ 1. To avoid the high cost of credit-card fees, most large hotel chains have issued their own credit cards as part of their frequent–guest programs.

___ 2. *Split billing* uses the traditional "G" and "I" abbreviations. Folios designated "*G*" are paid by the **group** (tours, conventions, etc.); "*I*" folios accumulate individual charges; each guest pays his or her own expenses.

___ 3. A *late charge* is one posted to the folio after the "late hour" (usually midnight) has passed, so it appears under the date of the following day.

___ 4. Many due bills are negotiable, so the end user of the bill may not be the person or organization that first negotiated the deal.

___ 5. A nonregistered guest who charges a bar tab has that charge posted to a front-office folio called, naturally enough, "bar charges."

PROBLEMS

1. Write two dialogues for a training manual that is to be used by guest-service agents at the front desk. Include the questions posed by a room clerk seeking additional credit information and the responses made by a guest. What disposition does the room clerk make when (a) a walk-in guest arrives with no baggage?, (b) a *same-day* reservation arrives, but no information has been provided previously?

2. Explain how the following transfers should be handled. Be specific, citing the location of the entry, the ledger or ledgers involved, and the debit or credit requirements.

   a. A transient guest checks out using a national credit card.

   b. The president and treasurer of a small company check in for a business meeting. The hotel has been carrying the unpaid balance of a charge generated by these officers at their last business meeting about three months ago.

   c. A couple departs and requests that the balance of the folio be charged to the couple's parents, who are registered in another room. The parents concur.

   d. An association completes its meeting and the association executive, after reviewing the balance due, requests billing to the group's headquarters.

3. In terms of the front office and of the city ledger, explain the quick check-out system used by numerous hotels.

4. Many older hotels in the area in which your resort is located have suffered for years from a seasonal influx of skippers and room burglary gangs operating with stolen keys. (Few of these old properties have modern locks.) The local hotel association has asked you to draft a plan for a security network that could be implemented before the next season. Prepare the plan, providing details of the procedure by explaining the roles of the individuals or groups involved.

5. In terms of the front office and of the city ledger, explain how a reservation request from a travel agent is processed if (a) the agency has a good credit relationship with the hotel and the guest pays the agency; (b) the agency has no credit rating with the hotel, and the guest pays the agency; and (c) the guest makes no payment to the agency.

6. A noticeable squeeze on profits had brought the management team to a brainstorming session. One idea is put forth by the controller. Noting the large amount of credit-card business that the hotel is doing, the controller suggests that each tip charged to a credit card be reduced by 4.77% when paid to the employee. (That amount is the average discount fee the hotel is paying to all the credit-card companies.) The controller further suggests that an additional 1.1% be subtracted, representing the percentage of credit-card charges that prove uncollectible. What comments would the food and beverage manager be apt to make? The rooms manager?

AN INCIDENT IN HOTEL MANAGEMENT

We've Both Made Mistakes

A very late arrival is standing at the desk waiting to be roomed. Unfortunately, there are no rooms. "No, you don't seem to understand; I have a reservation. It was guaranteed with my credit card because I was going to be so late."

"Sir, you made the $90 reservation nine weeks ago on credit card number 4300 0000 0000 0003. Last month, the credit-card company dishonored that card. So we cancelled the reservation. There are no rooms here and the citywide convention means the closest accommodations are in the next town, 18 miles away. Their rate is $165; my guess is the cab will be about $60. They're on the telephone, what should I tell them?"

"I need a room. Have them hold space. I feel you should pay the cab fare and the $75 difference between the rates. Since we have both made mistakes; make it an even $100!"

Questions: Was there a management failure here; if so, what?

What is the hotel's immediate response (or action) to the incident?

What further, long-run action should management take, if any?

ANSWERS TO TRUE/FALSE QUIZ

1. False. Many years ago, lodging companies tried issuing credit cards. They lacked the financial and technical expertise to make it work. Hotels cobrand today, putting their logos on credit cards issued by financial institutions.

2. False. Split billing uses "A" and "B" folios, not "G" and "I" folios. "A" folios accumulate group charges; "B" folios, individual charges.

3. False. A late charge is one that gets posted to the guest's folio after the guest has checked out. That could happen at any time, day or night.

4. True. Due bills are negotiated between the hotel and another entity, an advertising agency or manufacturer. To make it happen, the deal often requires a "sweetener," a negotiable due bill. Negotiable bills allow the other party to resell or trade the asset, often at a higher value than the original figure.

5. False. Nonregistered guests have no folios. Folios are accounts receivable, records of debt owed to the hotel. "Bar charges" are not accounts receivable. A nonregistered guest would charge on a credit card and the card company would be a city ledger receivable, not a front-office one.

Cash Transactions

HANDLING CASH TRANSACTIONS

Due to the ease, security, and prevalence of credit cards and debit cards, departing guests rarely pay hotel folios with cash. Conservative estimates place cash payments during check-out at something less than five percent of the time. Cash payments are more common in budget or economy properties. They are less common in corporate hotels (where employer-provided credit cards are frequently used) and resort properties (where the folio from a one-week stay might easily reach $3,000 or more).

In today's electronic age, cash is simply less convenient than electronic payment. Compared with credit or debit cards, cash is bulkier, less secure, provides a less detailed transaction trail, and requires an exchange to local currencies when visiting foreign countries. For corporate guests, an added step is required when using cash. The corporate guest must either obtain a cash advance before beginning the business trip or be out of pocket until the company reimburses travel costs.

In spite of the small amount of cash that changes hands over the front desk, its relative importance to the operation of the hotel is substantial. Full-service properties monitor daily cash balances in cashiers' drawers to ensure there is enough cash on hand to manage the cash transactions that do occur. Guests expect to cash traveler's checks, even personal checks at times. They may need to change large bills. The growing number of overseas visitors to the United States and the increasing popularity of the Euro currency have created a higher demand for foreign currency exchange conversion services at hotel front-office cashiers. Cashiers also handle cash advances to guests and provide upfront money for some hotel uses. So cash is not going to disappear into a cashless society.

Even as cash grows less popular as a means of folio settlement, its security grows more problemsome. Cash is very negotiable, easily pocketed, and a continuing target of the bad guys. Counterfeiters, bad check artists, photocopiers, and short change manipulators work their wares at hotel desks. They would rather try the hotel desk than busier retail outlets. Guest-service agents handle less actual currency than most other retailers, and are, therefore, less skilled at identifying bogus paper.

Cash Paid-Outs

Cash at the front desk flows both ways; *cash receipts* and *cash paid-outs*. In every other operational department of the hotel, cash flows only one way, in to the various departmental cashiers in the form of cash receipts. Only at the front desk does cash flow in both directions.

Cashiers in the front office, as in all hotel departments, may receive cash as payment to settle a guest account. However, as already noted, cash is less frequently used at the front desk to settle the guest folio than it is in various other departments where the purchase is substantially less (e.g., breakfast in the dining room, a few beverages in the lounge, or a newspaper in the gift shop).

There is another difference between the front office and other hotel departments. Cashiers in other departments receive cash to settle purchases such as breakfast, beverages, newspaper. Cash transactions at the front office settle accounts receivable. Front-office cashiers have no product to sell. Conversely, outlet cashiers have no record of accounts receivable and are not able to accept payments from departing guests.

Here is a simple formula for understanding the relationship of cash to accounts receivables:

Increases in assets, including accounts receivable and *cash*, are made with debits.
Decreases in assets, including *accounts receivable* and cash, are made with credits.

Cash paid-outs are the exclusive right of the front-office cashier. Except for tips paid to employees (waitstaff, for example), no paid-outs are ever made by cashiers in other operating departments. Paid-outs to guests are, in fact, small loans made by the front office to or on behalf of the guest. Paid-outs are debits to the guest folio and increase the amount the guest owes the hotel (accounts receivable). Similarly, the paid-outs require a cash outlay and therefore reduce the amount of cash in the front office cashier's drawer. Again,

Increases in assets, including *accounts receivable* and cash, are made with debits.
Decreases in assets, including accounts receivable and *cash*, are made with credits.

Tips to employees are the most common paid-out, but there are others as well.

Tips to Employees.   Tips are the most common cash advance. They are paid to an employee upon request of the guest. A signed check from the dining room or bar is the usual method of request. The amount of gratuity is added to the check by the guest when signing for the service. When the room charge reaches the front-desk clerk, the departmental charges are separated from the tip. The tip is posted under the cash advance category (paid-outs), not the food or beverage category. After all, the tip is not departmental income, so it must not appear under a departmental heading. (See page 396 for Exhibit 10–10.)

Acting on behalf of the guest, the front-office cashier pays the tip to the server, who signs for the money on a cash advance voucher. At the end of the shift, this paid-out appears on the cashier's balance report in lieu of cash in the cashier's drawer.

Since the procedure is not an unusual one, a traffic problem could develop at the front desk if employees from all over the hotel came to collect their tips. To forestall this, tips are paid by the cashiers in the various dining rooms and bars. In a way, the problem handles itself. Most tips are added to national credit cards. Charges made to national credit cards in other hotel departments do not come to the front office. Only charges to the guest's folio, whether there are tips or not, flow through the front-office procedure. Even a credit-card charge (restaurant, bar) made by a registered guest will not pass through the guest's folio, but rather, will be deposited as income directly by the department involved.

Front-office cashiers still process tips to front-of-the-house employees: bell, housekeeping, and delivery persons. Most hotels pay their employees' tips on receipt or at the end of the shift. This is wonderful for the employee, but it can often result in the hotel subsidizing its employee gratuities in three common ways: float (that is, the time value of money), merchant discount fees on credit cards, and potential noncollectible accounts. Granted, it may be a minimal sum of money when considered on a per employee basis, but over time (and in large properties with hundreds or thousands of employees) it can quickly add to a significant amount.

A different procedure, not treated here, has the accounting/payroll office accumulate all employee tips. Payment is attached to salary checks. This has always been the procedure for banquet servers when a gratuity was added to the per-cover charge. The IRS, which carefully monitors income from tips, prefers the accounting office's participation. Tips are then reported at year's end on the W-2 form.

Float.   Because of the time value of money, prepaying an employee's tip before the guest's bill is paid costs the hotel money. Yet this is exactly what happens with many paid-out tips. Let's follow the payment cycle for a newly arriving guest, Diane Green.

Green asks the front desk to issue a $10 tip to the bellperson as a paid-out against her folio. Because this is the first day of a lengthy visit, let's assume that Green's folio will not be settled for nine days. In this example, the hotel has paid the bellperson with money it will not receive for nine days. Furthermore, Green's bill will probably be settled by a national credit card. Credit-card companies may take days before they pay the hotel. It is conceivable, therefore, that the hotel has paid the bellperson a tip with money it will not receive for several weeks. That is a costly employee benefit (see Exhibit 12–1).

Merchant Discount Fees.   National credit-card companies charge merchants (hotels) a fee for accepting their credit card. The merchant discount fee may range anywhere from just over 1% to just under 5%, depending on the sales volume of the hotel, the credit card in question, and a number of other variables (see Chapter 11). In Green's example, she settled the bill with an American Express card. Let's assume that the hotel pays a 2% fee for the use of American Express.

A 2% fee on all American Express card sales means that the hotel receives $98 from American Express for every $100 charged at the hotel. Therefore, American Express will only reimburse the hotel $9.80 for the bellperson's $10 tip, which the hotel has already paid in full.

Although 20 cents sounds trivial, it adds up over time and volume. After all, that's 20 cents for just one tip to one bellperson; imagine dozens of tips to possibly hundreds of employees per day (see Exhibit 12–1).

Noncollectible Accounts.   The most blatant example of subsidizing employee paid-out tips is when the guest folio becomes uncollectible. Whatever the reason for the uncollectible account, the hotel loses more than the departmental revenues. Whether the uncollectible folio was a direct bill account gone bad, a personal check with insufficient funds, or a fraudulent credit card, the hotel also loses the amount of the paid-out tip.

Some hotels attempt to recover uncollectible tips from their employees. But collecting from the employee months after the service was rendered is quite unlikely. In addition, it negatively affects morale to collect what the employee perceives as a rather trivial sum of money.

Another Look at Employee Tips.   Exhibit 12–1 demonstrates the hidden costs to the hotel of paying employee tips upon receipt. For example, while visiting the hotel, Ms. Green might charge a few meals (and tips) to her folio, she might call the front desk and ask them to pay the bellperson a tip on her behalf, and she might charge cocktails (and tip) in the lounge one evening as well. Although Ms. Green has yet to check out (and when she does, her bill might not be settled for some days), the employees will all receive their tips on the days she makes the various charges. This is a costly employee benefit for the hotel.

Schedule of Hypothetical Costs Associated
with Paying Employee Tips Upon Receipt

---

1. **Assumptions**
   - A 525-room hotel staffs 7 bellpersons per day, who average $20 per day in charged tips.
   - 22 waitpersons and room servers per day, who average $45 per day in charged tips.
   - 4 bartenders per day, who average $40 per day in charged tips.
   - Some 75% of all charged tips are paid by credit card. The average merchant discount fee for all types of credit cards is 2.25%.
   - The average time for settlement of the bill (including those who pay by credit card, those who pay by direct bill, and those who pay by cash) is two weeks past the date the charge was made.
   - Approximately 0.5% of all folios are noncollectible.

2. **Float-Related Costs**
   - Total employee tips paid out per day are $140 for bellpersons, $990 for waitpersons, and $160 for bartenders. That's $1,290 per day for 365 days equals $470,850 per year.
   - Assuming a 9.0% internal rate of return and an average 2 weeks before collection, the hotel's cost of floating employees' tips equates to $1,629.87 per year.

3. **Merchant Discount Fees**
   - Assuming $470,850 per year in total employee tips and that 75% of all tips are paid to credit cards, the total amount of tips paid by credit cards is $353,137.50.
   - If the average merchant discount fee is 2.25%, the hotel's annual cost of paying employees tips in full (rather than discounting them) is $7,945.59.

4. **Noncollectible Accounts**
   - Assuming $470,850 per year in total employee tips and that 0.5% of all folios are noncollectible, the hotel pays employee tips of $2,354.25 but never receives payment from the guest.

5. **Grand Total Annual Costs**
   - The hotel's cost of floating employees' tips equates to $1,629.87 per year.
   - The hotel's cost of paying the employees' share of the merchant discount fees is $7,945.59.
   - The hotel's cost of paying employee tips on noncollectible accounts is $2,354.25.
   - For this hypothetical scenario, the total cost to the hotel for paying employee tips in full is $11,929.71.

Exhibit 12-1   Employee tips are frequently handled as paid-outs on the same day they are charged to folios or credit cards. This costly practice is, in fact, an employee compensation benefit and should be explained that way and so treated during wage negotiations.

Yet almost all hotels conduct this practice. There really is no other way to handle employee tips without creating additional burdens. Hotels could refuse to allow guests to charge tips against their folio. Although this would save hotels the cost of the merchant discount fee, the practice would create far more ill will than it would save in expenses. Similarly, hotels could wait to pay employee tips until the guests' bills actually cleared. This would save hotels those expenses related to both float and noncollectible accounts. It would, however, create such an accounting and tracking nightmare that it would be hard to justify. Hotels look upon tip expenses as another cost of doing business, a costly one at that.

Cash Loans.   Although paid-outs against the guest folio represent money provided by the hotel on the guest's behalf (as when a tip paid to a bellman is charged against the guest's folio), they are not exactly cash loans. Actual loans to hotel guests are very rare, occurring under unusual circumstances and only to those guests well known by the hotel's management. Advancing money to the guest as a paid-out (debit) against the folio runs the same costs and risks discussed above (float, credit-card merchant discount fees, and potential losses from uncollectible accounts). However, just as no hotels charge processing fees to employees who receive tips, no hotels charge fees to guests desperate for a cash loan.

It is now more difficult to cash a check than it was to obtain a cash loan years ago. This is especially true on weekends when banks are closed. Some hoteliers believe that it is better to have a small loan skip than to have a large check bounce, so they grant the former if forced to choose. Companies that use the hotel on a regular basis may establish "loan" arrangements for their staff by guaranteeing the advances. Preferred-guest programs provide just such check-cashing privileges.

Third-Party Sources of Cash.   Over the years, a number of options surfaced due to the hotel industry's unwillingness to act as banker for the millions of domestic and international travelers. Among the options available to today's cashless traveler are automatic teller machines (ATMs), credit-card advances, person-to-person pay services (like iKobo's VISA debit card), Internet money services (like PayPal), payday loan companies, and expedited money order services. Each of these options provides cash to the guest without jeopardizing the hotel or putting it into a business for which it lacks expertise.

Credit-card advances (for example, Comcheck) and money order services (for example, Western Union's Quick Collect or Send Money) transfer the related costs and risks (float, credit-card discount fees, and potential losses from uncollectible accounts) from the hotel to the guest. In essence, guests send themselves money and pay their own costs. For example, by calling Western Union and using a national credit card, guests authorize payment to themselves. The guest gets the money, and in some cases, Western Union, not the guest, is the hotel's account receivable.

These financial services are not free. Fees paid by the guest to the third parties range upward from a low of 10%. Guests who would howl at the hotel for charging such usury pay up without a whimper (see Exhibit 12–2).

Automatic Teller Machines (ATMs).   ATMs are the most common means of accessing cash (see Exhibit 12–2). They are everywhere including hotel lobbies and casinos both within the United States and abroad. Two networks are particularly popular overseas. Cirrus (linked to MasterCard) and Plus (linked to VISA) can be accessed by over 90% of the ATM bank cards circulating in the United States. Moreover, ATMs offer foreign exchange rates that are usually lower than those of foreign banks.

Exhibit 12–2   Advanced ATM machines offer many more features than the standard ATM cash machines, including check cashing for personal, corporate, and payroll checks with no risk to the hotel or merchant. Risks are minimized by the Mr. Payroll ATM, which uses a security system based on facial recognition. With biometrics technology, the ATM "never forgets a face."*Courtesy of Mr. Payroll Corporation, Fort Worth, Texas.*

Travelers of every category depend on the ATM's worldwide accessibility (see Exhibit 12–3) to minimize the amount of cash needed. Carrying fewer dollars is not merely good economics, it reduces careless losses or frightening thefts.

ATMs in Hotel Lobbies.   Lodging chains have responded to the popularity of ATMs by installing them in lobbies all across the world from *A* (aloft hotels, New York City) to *Z* (Z Palace Hotels, Xanthi Thraki, Greece). Their popularity is more than guest convenience, the machines are a new revenue source for hotels (see Exhibit 12–4).

Prior to 1996, there was no incentive for hotels to install ATM machines, because banks did not charge the user a fee per transaction. Instead, all ATM network costs were paid internally by the banks themselves. In April 1996, VISA and MasterCard eased their restrictions on surcharging cash ATM transactions. Following this change in policy, ATM users began paying a surcharge ranging from roughly $2 to $5 per transaction (depending on card, location, bank, and amount of transaction).

A number of ATM manufacturers provide hotel service contracts. In exchange for a place to install the ATM (usually in a secure high-traffic area such as the hotel lobby) and access

Company	Number of Worldwide ATMs	Number of Countries in which ATMs are Available	Approximate Fee per Transaction
American Express	550,000+	130+ countries	2 to 5% of the transaction amount
Cirrus / MasterCard / Maestro	1,100,000+	105+ countries	Rates set by the issuing bank
Diners Club access via MasterCard/Cirrus ATMs	900,000+	105+ countries	4% of the transaction amount or $6
Plus (VISA)	1,000,000+	160+ countries	Rates set by the issuing bank

Exhibit 12–3   Corporate and leisure travelers have benefited from the growing number of available ATMs. This is especially true in foreign countries where travelers gain the convenience of local currency without the concern of exchanging just the right amount of money. Using international ATMs also allows the traveler to float the currency exchange for some 20 or 30 days.

ATM machines in hotel lobbies likely increase revenues. Some of the money dispensed to the guest through the ATM stays in the hotel. Research shows that 30% to 33% of cash is retained from ATMs located in large retail stores; 35% to 40% is retained from ATMs located in small retail stores; and 70% to 80% is retained from ATMs located in nightclubs. No research is yet available for hotel lobbies.

to thousands of guests, the service provider agrees to purchase, install, and maintain the machine; load it with cash on a regular basis; and split surcharges with the hotel. Pay telephones, soda, snack, newspaper, and cigarette machines are installed under similar contracts.

Not only does the hotel benefit from this new revenue source, but it reduces or eliminates the need for the front desk to cash personal checks. In addition, with more cash in their hands, guests may spend more in the gift shops, restaurants, bars, and casinos.

ATMs Dispense More Than Cash.   The newest ATMs are fast becoming important new marketing tools for hotels and local merchants. ATMs promote products through coupons and/or on-screen graphics. Many ATMs allow a hotel to custom-design one or more coupons for the back of the guest receipt. A coupon might be worth a free drink in the bar or a free appetizer in the restaurant. In addition to this approach, ATMs flash messages and promotional screens to the guest while waiting for the transaction to process.

Today's hottest ATMs are wired directly to the World Wide Web. Guests can pay utility bills, apply for a new car loan, or trade stocks. Indeed, the ATM can print cashier's checks, make a pitch suggesting the customer try the hotel's new credit card, even show tomorrow's weather forecast. Exhibit 12–4 provides a glimpse at some of the most likely ATM possibilities.

Paid-Outs to Concessionaires.   Full-service hotels often arrange for local merchants to provide guest services the hotel is unable to offer. These merchants may actually have a shop inside the hotel (for example, a beauty salon, florist, or gift store), or they may contract services off premise (for example, a travel agent, valet cleaning, or a printing shop). These private vendors are commonly referred to as *concessionaires;* their shops are known as *concessions.*

The concessionaire–guest relationship often mandates that the hotel act as middleman. In circumstances where the hotel relays the goods on behalf of the guest (laundry is usually delivered to the guest's room by the bellstaff, for example) or where the

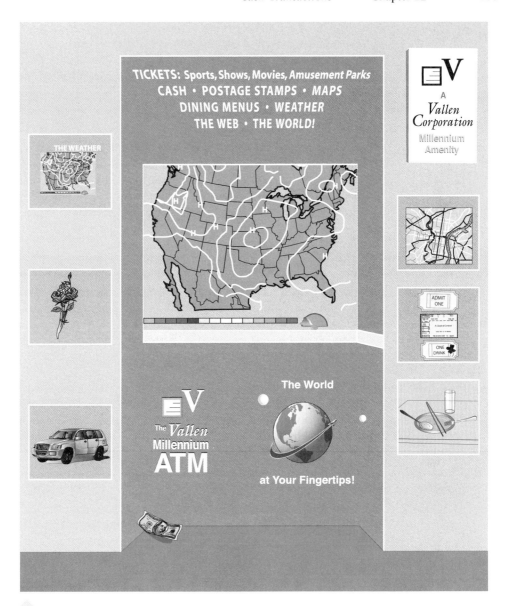

Exhibit 12-4   Many ATMs are wired directly to the World Wide Web. They provide a variety of services. Hotels need to choose which features are most appropriate for their guests and which generate the most revenue. Tickets for sporting events and nearby shows, maps, weather forecasts, and postage stamps make sense for corporate guests and the hotel's bottom line. (Ticket purchases usually have a hotel commission built into the sales price.) But when other guests are waiting in line to withdraw funds, time is of the essence—it makes little sense to show movie trailers (which also represent revenue to the hotel) at the expense of guests waiting to check in.

concessionaire looks to the hotel for collection (say, when a guest charges her hairstyling to the room folio), the hotel is acting as an intermediary and is entitled to a fee or commission for its part in the process. Hotels earn 10% to 20% of the laundry and dry cleaning revenue (the other 80% to 90% accrues to the vendor) as their share of providing laundry bags, bellstaff pickups and deliveries, storage, and collections.

The hotel also finds itself stuck in the middle when dealing with problems or complaints. When a piece of clothing has been lost or destroyed, the guest is not interested in learning that the laundry service is a private concession. A quality guest experience dictates that the hotel provide seamless service and solve the problem on behalf of the guest.

Accounting for Paid-Outs to Concessionaires.   The hotel also acts as intermediary in terms of disbursing revenues to the concessionaire. Payment is made to the merchant when the service is completed and charged to the guest's folio as a paid-out. Specifically, the clerk debits accounts receivable (a paid-out on the guest's folio) and credits cash. The clerk then removes the cash from the drawer in the amount of the paid-out. (Remember, the paid-out charged the guest may be different from the amount of cash handed over to the concessionaire, because the hotel may keep a portion of the proceeds as its share of the transaction.) The concessionaire then signs the paid-out voucher and the money is handed over.

At the end of the shift, the cashier's balance report reflects the reduction of cash in the money drawer. In essence, the hotel has loaned the money on behalf of the guest and awaits repayment when the guest checks out. Of course, all of the costs associated with float, credit-card discount fees, and uncollectible accounts are issues for negotiation between the hotel and the concessionaire.

Paying the concessionaire in cash each time the service is used is expensive and time consuming, for the merchant as well as for the hotel, since the concessionaire must wait for the cash and sign the paperwork. In larger hotels, a different plan is arranged. The hotel bills the guest just as if the concessionaire were a department of the hotel, collects on check-out, and reimburses the merchant periodically (monthly). In such cases, the guest's folio looks a bit different. Rather than reflecting a paid-out posting, the charge instead is posted to an actual department (say, laundry or valet). The net effect—the guest owes the hotel—remains unchanged.

Refunds at Check-Out.
On occasion, the hotel owes the guest a refund at the conclusion of the stay. This happens for one of several reasons. Either there was a substantial deposit with the reservation, or a large payment on account was made on (or after) arrival. If the guest shortens the stay, or the hotel adjusts the rate downward, there could be a credit balance at the time of departure. Paid-in-advance guests who make additional deposits to cover other charges to their rooms (such as for inroom movies or room service) may also show a credit balance.

At check-out, the hotel pays the guest. Zeroing the credit balance of the account requires a debit or charge entry. A paid-out voucher is prepared for the guest's signature in the amount the hotel owes. At the end of the shift, the computerized cashier's balance report subtracts the amount of the paid-out from the total cash remaining in the money drawer.

Cash is never refunded if the original payment was not made in cash! If the guest's personal credit card was the source, for example, the hotel would issue a refund against the credit card. Similarly, large cash deposits made by the guest may not be refundable on check-out. Before receiving the large cash deposit, the clerk should explain hotel policy regarding paid-outs. Some hotels restrict the size of the paid-out to, say, $100. Anything above that amount requires a check to be processed by the hotel accounting department and mailed to the guest's home. This prevents guests from depositing illegitimate traveler's checks, personal checks (discussed later in this chapter), or counterfeit money and then attempting to collect legitimate cash against that amount the following day.

Cash Receipts

We have already emphasized that cash paid-outs are limited to front-office cashiers; cashiers in other departments never make cash paid-outs. Cash paid-outs are essentially advances or loans against accounts receivable. Eventually, those advances are repaid by the guest. That normally takes place when the balance of the folio is settled, typically at check-out. Guests settle their folios, as Chapter 10 stressed, by one of three methods: with cash, with an allowance, or with a transfer (credit). Cash paid by the guest and received by the hotel is the thrust of this chapter. Again,

Increases in assets, including accounts receivable and *cash,* are made with debits.
Decreases in assets, including *accounts receivable* and cash, are made with credits.

Cash Receipts at Check-Out.   Only a small percentage of check-outs elect to settle with cash. Most guests pay by credit card or request direct billing through the city ledger. Very few use cash, traveler's checks, or personal checks.

Posting cash paid to the folio has the opposite effect from posting a cash paid-out to the folio. Whereas the paid-out increases the amount owed by the guest (debit to accounts receivable), cash receipts decrease the amount owed by the guest (credit to accounts receivable). In all cases, the amount collected from the guest is the exact amount required to reduce the folio balance to zero.

It is a quick procedure: The property management system maintains a cumulative balance, which indicates the amount due. Some hotels display the folio on the computer screen for the guest to review, others deliver preprinted hard copies to all departing guests, and still others encourage self-check-out via the television screen (see Chapter 13).

Whatever the method, all cashiers are trained to inquire about last-minute charges that may still be unrecorded. Catching unposted telephone or breakfast charges minimizes the number of *late charges*, with their high rate of uncollection and guest displeasure.

Cash Receipts on Account.   Payments may be requested at any time, not just at departure. Long-term guests are billed weekly, as a means of improving the hotel's cash flow and keeping the guest as current as possible. Guests who exceed certain credit limits or guests who generate too many charges (especially items normally paid for in cash) are billed at the hotel's discretion. Sometimes, guests themselves decide to make payments against their accounts.

At check-out, departing guests are given a copy of the zero-balance folio as a receipt for their cash payment. Similarly, guests who make cash payments on account are given a copy of the folio to serve as a receipt of the payment. The only difference is the timing: the folio given in the middle of the stay is probably not a zero-balance folio. In fact, paid-in-advance customers maintain a credit balance on their folios throughout the visit.

The desk may face a guest—especially one who hasn't traveled extensively—who tries to pay on the day before departure. Because of possible late charges, the desk tries to discourage guests from making payment too early. In fact, day-early payments require special attention by the cashier, who must be certain to collect enough to cover the upcoming room-night and room tax that will not be posted until the auditor arrives. So the employee convinces the guest to wait until the next day rather than paying in full the previous day in anticipation of an early departure. Many guests find it incomprehensible that they are dissuaded from concluding their business until the next morning. This is much less a problem in modern hotels, which provide the guest with a number of rapid automatic or self-check-out options.

Cash Receipts at Check-In.   All guests are asked to establish credit at check-in. Most simply proffer their credit card and the desk clerk verifies it for a predetermined floor limit. Direct bill guests may not be asked about credit at check-in because their company has a previously established account. The norm for direct bill guests, however, is to establish personal credit for incidental charges (room service, inroom entertainment, etc.) While utilizing the direct bill account as the means for room and tax payment. Only cash guests, then, are actually asked to pay their room charges up front. Cash guests include those paying with currency, traveler's checks, and personal checks (if allowed).

Unless an additional deposit is made, no other room charges are allowed against a paid-in-advance guest, who often departs the hotel without stopping at the desk. An additional room charge is made and collected each succeeding day the customer remains. Unless this is received, someone on the desk automatically checks out paid-in-advance guests by the check-out hour of the following day. Some limited-service properties may actually lock out guests who remain beyond the check-out hour. Less extreme measures, including telephone messages, are usually used to communicate with the paid-in-advance guest.

Automatic check-out of a paid-in-advance guest requires coordination and communication. The front desk must be careful not to prematurely show as vacant any room that was paid in advance. Prior to automatically checking the guest out, a bellperson or housekeeper is asked to inspect the room. Only after they communicate that the room is truly empty should the front desk complete the check-out.

Reservation Deposit Receipts.   Just as cash is seldom used to settle the guest folio, it is seldom used to secure a reservation. As explained in Chapter 4, most reservations are guaranteed to a guest credit card or corporate account. Even advance deposit reservations are usually charged to a credit card at the time of reservation. Few advance deposit reservations actually require the guest to mail in payment.

Some hotels, usually resorts with many weeks of lead time between reservation and arrival, prefer other forms of payment for the advance deposit as opposed to the guest's credit card. Who can blame them? When there is sufficient lead time, a mailed-in deposit (check or money order) has no merchant discount fee associated with it. For the hotel that collects an entire season's worth of advance deposits, this small distinction may represent thousands of dollars in added profits. The most common method for handling reservation deposits uses the city ledger. See Chapter 11 for a complete discussion of the topic.

House Receipts and Expenses

Although the front-office cashier is primarily responsible for handling rooms-related revenues and disbursements, other responsibilities are assigned for convenience. Due to the fact that the front desk is centrally located and accessible to all departments of the hotel, the cashier in the small hotel takes on a set of hotel-related cash responsibilities, both house receipts and house expenses.

Assorted City- and General-Ledger Receipts.   Some hotels, especially small properties that lack a full accounting staff, elect to funnel all cash and check receipts through the front office. This adds another person and record to the process, which strengthens the internal control. It also adds another set of responsibilities to the front-office cashier.

Examples of assorted city- and general-ledger receipts not affiliated with the rooms division include receipts for meetings or banquet functions, reimbursements or rebates for overpayment to vendors, refunds or credits from taxes, and lease revenues from merchants or concessionaires. In small hotels, the front-office cashier might serve as dining room or lounge cashier. Magazines, newspapers, and candy may be sold across the desk. Coin collections from vending machines or sales of miscellaneous items such as kitchen fat (to tallow-rendering plants) or container deposits may all flow through the front desk. Meal tickets in American-plan resorts are also commonly sold at the front desk to nonguests.

Depending on the accounting system in place, the cashier records a credit to some type of general account and a debit to cash on the front-office documentation. The specific detailing of the general account (each affected account must be updated) is later handled by the accounting department on an item-by-item basis.

Assorted House Paid-Outs.

Assorted House Paid-Outs.   The front-office cashier acts, on one hand, as a depository for the accounting department and, on the other hand, as the accounting department's disbursing agent. Unlike guest paid-outs, which have an impact on the cashier's drawer, house paid-outs do not. As such, house paid-outs are not posted to the property management system—guest paid-outs most certainly are. The reason house paid-outs do not affect the cashier's drawer is because the cashier treats house paid-outs (petty cash disbursements) just like cash.

The person receiving the money (say, the bellperson who just purchased $30 worth of flour for the kitchen) signs a petty cash voucher (see Exhibit 12–5). The voucher is kept in the cashier's drawer and treated as if it were cash. It is cash, because the accounting department's general cashier will buy the petty cash voucher at some later point. The purchase of this voucher by the general cashier reimburses the front-office cashier and leaves the cash drawer intact—as if the petty cash disbursement had never been processed in the first place.

The Imprest Petty Cash Fund.   If the front-office cashiers are reimbursed daily, the petty cash fund is administered by the accounting department's general cashier. If the front-office cashiers are only reimbursed when petty cash vouchers reach a sizable sum or at the end of each month, it is known as an imprest petty cash fund. An imprest fund authorizes the front-office cashier to hold petty cash vouchers in the drawer day after day.

The cashier holds the house petty cash vouchers until some predetermined point is reached. This point is usually a function of both time and amount. A cashier is assigned a limited bank from which to conduct all the day's transactions. If the cashier's ability to make change and serve the guest is compromised by a large petty cash holding, it is time to sell the vouchers to the general cashier. Some hotels have a specific policy when the total petty cash vouchers in a given cashier's drawer reaches, say $50, the amount must be turned over to the general cashier. Petty cash vouchers are also cleared from front-office cashiers at the end of each accounting cycle, usually the last day of the month.

A wide range of small expenditures are processed through the petty cash fund. Salary advances to good employees or termination pay to employees the hotel wants immediately off the premises might be paid through the fund. Some freight bills need immediate cash payment under ICC regulations. Stamp purchases, cash purchases from local farmers or purveyors, and other payments (see Exhibit 12–5) may be handled through the front office, especially in smaller hotels.

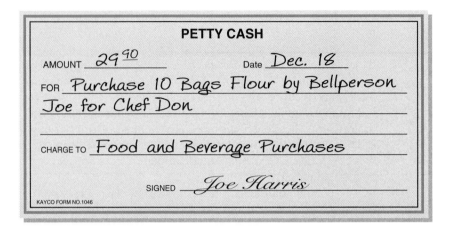

Exhibit 12-5   Petty cash vouchers are often simple, handwritten forms. When available, a store receipt documenting the exact amount of the purchase should also be attached.

THE CASHIER'S DAILY REPORT

Every cashier in the hotel, whether at the front office, the dining room, the bar, room service, or the snack bar, prepares a daily cash report. With the report, the cashier turns in the departmental monies. These combined funds (plus any that clear through the general cashier) constitute the hotel's daily deposit made to the bank.

The daily deposit is supported by a flow of cash records. The records of the front-office cashiers (see Exhibits 12–6 and 12–7) are first reviewed by the night auditor because they contain accounts receivable information. They are processed again the following day through the income audit. The income audit combines the front-office cash

CASHIER:	ARDELLE		REPORT DATE: 03/09/--			15 : 27 : 30	

CASHIER'S BALANCE REPORT

CODE	ROOM	LAST NAME	FIRST NAME	ACCOUNT	RATE	TIME	AMOUNT
→ 0001	217	JOHNSON	LINDA	CASH	RACK	06:57:23	48.52
0026	1171	VANLAND	TOM	VISA	GRP	07:11:10	179.37
0024	678	HARRISON	GEORGE	DSCV	TOUR	07:12:12	87.50
0025	456	LENNON	JOHN	MC	TOUR	07:16:44	87.50
→ 0011	319	WILSON	BILL	CHCK	DISC	07:17:17	82.50
0011	337	ADAMS	JOHN	CHCK	RACK	07:21:50	67.21
0031	902	GREENBACKS	LOTTA	P OUT	RACK	07:24:01	−17.50
0026	842	STUART	LYLE	VISA	GRP	08:10:15	161.40
0024	212	JONES	ROBERT	DSCV	DISC	08:34:20	242.59
0011	711	GREGORY	GARY	CHCK	TOUR	09:10:10	111.77
0011	315	GONNE	CONNIE	CHCK	RACK	09:44:30	96.20
0031	107	MOORE	MANNY	P OUT	TOUR	10:10:15	−20.00
0025	371	ORTIZ	RAUL	MC	RACK	10:40:29	68.57
0011	211	JACKSON	ANDY	CHCK	DISC	11:04:41	46.31
→ 0011	551	WASHINGTON	BOB	CHCK	TOUR	11:57:01	1,278.71

Exhibit 12-6   In the "account" column of this cashier's balance report are shown cash, checks, city ledger (credit cards), and paid-outs. The "code" column references the hotel's chart of accounts. Follow the arrows marking cashier Ardelle's cash guests, Johnson and Wilson, through Exhibits 12–7, 12–8, 12–9, and 12–10.

records with the records of the other departmental cashiers. This creates a support document (see Exhibit 12–8) for the bank deposit.

Preparing the Cashier's Report

The front-office cashier's report is much more complicated than standard cashier reports found in other departments. This is due to the two-way flow of the front-office cashier's responsibilities. Remember, whereas departmental cashiers only receive payment from guests, front-office cashiers both receive funds and pay them out.

The Cashier's Bank.   Each cashier receives and signs for a permanent supply of cash, called the *bank*. The amount varies depending on the position and shift that the cashier works. A busy commercial hotel needs front-office banks of as much as $10,000, but the night cashier at the same hotel might get along with $250. It is partly a question of safety and partly a question of good financial management. Excessive funds should not be tied up unnecessarily; temporary increases can be made for busy periods.

A careful review of all house banks may release sizable sums for more profitable use. One major accounting firm reported that the total of a hotel's house banks and cash on hand should be about 2% of total sales. An excessive percentage suggests that cashiers are borrowing from their banks or that daily deposits and reimbursements are not being made, which means that extra funds are required to operate the banks. There are other reasons, of course—infrequent reimbursement of the petty cash fund, for example, which makes the fund unnecessarily large.

```
CASHIER: ARDELLE          REPORT DATE: 03/09/--          15 : 28 : 41
                       CASHIER'S BALANCE REPORT BY CODE
```

CODE	ROOM	LAST NAME	FIRST NAME	ACCOUNT	RATE	TIME	AMOUNT
→ 0001	217	JOHNSON	LINDA	CASH	RACK	06:57:23	48.52
TOTAL	CASH			0001			48.52
→ 0011	319	WILSON	BILL	CHCK	DISC	07:17:17	82.50
0011	337	ADAMS	JOHN	CHCK	RACK	07:21:50	67.21
0011	711	GREGORY	GARY	CHCK	TOUR	09:10:10	111.77
0011	315	GONNE	CONNIE	CHCK	RACK	09:44:30	96.20
0011	211	JACKSON	ANDY	CHCK	DISC	11:04:41	46.31
0011	551	WASHINGTON	BOB	CHCK	TOUR	11:57:01	1,278.71 ←
TOTAL	CHECKS			0011			1,682.70
TOTAL	AMERICAN EXPRESS			0021			0.00
TOTAL	CARTE BLANCHE			0022			0.00
TOTAL	DINERS CLUB			0023			0.00
0024	678	HARRISON	GEORGE	DSCV	TOUR	07:12:12	87.50
0024	212	JONES	ROBERT	DSCV	DISC	08:34:20	242.59
TOTAL	DISCOVER			0024			330.09
0025	456	LENNON	JOHN	MC	TOUR	07:16:44	87.50
0025	371	ORTIZ	RAUL	MC	RACK	10:40:29	68.57
TOTAL	MASTERCARD			0025			156.07
0026	1171	VANLAND	TOM	VISA	GRP	07:11:10	179.37
0026	842	STUART	LYLE	VISA	GRP	08:10:15	161.40
TOTAL	VISA			0026			340.77
0031	902	GREENBACKS	LOTTA	POUT	RACK	07:24:01	−17.50
0031	107	MOORE	MANNY	POUT	TOUR	10:10:15	−20.00
TOTAL	PAID-OUTS			0031			−37.50 ←

Exhibit 12-7   Cashier's report by code (the hotel's chart of accounts). This portion of the report shows payment methods against which the cashier reconciles cash, checks, charges, and paid-outs. This report shows payment activity by room number. Other reports would also be printed showing activity by department (say, restaurant, or lounge). This exhibit is the second in a series of interrelated exhibits (12–6 through 12–10) that follow the reports of cashier Ardelle.

Cashiers lock their banks in the safe or hotel vault after each shift. The cashier's bank may not be used for personal loans. To ensure that all funds are properly held in the cashiers' bank, the accounting office randomly schedules surprise counts. When the cashier comes on duty, he or she will find the safe deposit box inaccessible—access to the safe deposit box requires two keys, one is the cashier's key and the other is the accounting office's master key. To open the box, the cashier needs to summon an auditor, who takes a few minutes with the cashier to count and verify the contents.

Unfortunately, common banks shared by several employees are not unusual. These are seen in every department from the bar to the front office. With shared banks, control is difficult to maintain, and responsibility almost impossible to fix. Custom and convenience seem to be the major reasons for continuing this poor practice, although it obviously requires less hotel funds to stock shared banks.

CASH RECEIPTS SUMMARY REPORT

DEPARTMENT	CASHIER	CASH SALES	COLLECTION TRANSIENT RECEIVABLES	COLLECTION CITY LEDGER RECEIVABLES	TOTAL CASH RECEIPTS	PAID-OUTS TRANSIENT	PAID-OUTS CITY LEDGER	NET CASH RECEIPTS	ADD: OVERAGES LESS: SHORTAGES	TURN IN FOR DEPOSIT
FRONT OFFICE	ARDELLE		452.51	→ 1,278.71	1,731.22	→ -37.50	0.00	1,693.72	-.76	1,692.96
FRONT OFFICE	BABETTE		1,171.14	622.50	1,793.64	-49.00	-25.00	1,719.64	1.20	1,720.84
FRONT OFFICE	CHARLES		850.19	1,460.51	2,310.70	-11.50	-5.00	2,294.20	0.00	2,294.20
FRONT OFFICE	DIANE		67.10	0.00	67.10	0.00	0.00	67.10	0.00	67.10
FRONT OFFICE	EDWARD		572.46	604.27	1,176.73	-12.90	0.00	1,163.83	-2.41	1,161.42
FRONT OFFICE	FRANCES		934.72	210.58	1,145.30	-18.65	-14.00	1,112.65	.87	1,113.52
GIFT SHOP	GARY	687.14	0.00	0.00	687.14	0.00	0.00	687.14	0.00	687.14
GIFT SHOP	HARRY	901.73	0.00	0.00	901.73	0.00	0.00	901.73	-1.47	900.26
LOUNGE	ILONA	1,262.85	0.00	0.00	1,262.85	0.00	0.00	1,262.85	1.01	1,263.86
LOUNGE	JEROME	2,411.59	0.00	0.00	2,411.59	0.00	0.00	2,411.59	0.00	2,411.59
RESTAURANT	KATE	816.44	0.00	0.00	816.44	0.00	0.00	816.44	-.25	816.19
RESTAURANT	LOUISE	1,017.55	0.00	0.00	1,017.55	0.00	0.00	1,017.55	-.61	1,016.94
SNACK BAR	MARC	469.68	0.00	0.00	469.68	0.00	0.00	469.68	2.71	472.39
SNACK BAR	NANETTE	371.02	0.00	0.00	371.02	0.00	0.00	371.02	0.00	371.02
DAILY TOTALS		7,938.00	4,048.12	4,176.57	16,162.69	-129.55	-44.00	15,989.14	.29	15,989.43

Exhibit 12-8   This cash receipts summary recaps records of all departmental cashiers and serves as the source document for the income auditors' daily bank deposit. Information shown for front-office cashier Ardelle corresponds with Exhibit 12–7, from which Washington, a city-ledger collection, appears in the 5th column. The total of the other cash collections, Johnson through Jackson, appears in column 4 as transient collections. Paid-outs of $37.50 originate in the bottom three lines of Exhibit 12–7. Follow the balanced cashier report of Ardelle across a continuing series of interrelated Exhibits 12–7 through 12–10.

Everyone handling money should be covered by a bond. Bonds are written to cover either individual positions or as blanket coverage, whichever best meets the hotel's needs.

The bank must contain enough small bills to carry out the cashiering function. There is no value in a bank comprising of $100 bills. Two examples follow: with a $500 bank for the text discussion, and a $1,000 bank for the separate discussion of the exhibits.

Net Receipts.   Net receipts represent the difference between what the cashier took in (receipts) and what was paid out. Since only front-office cashiers are permitted to make paid-outs, net receipts in the bar and coffee shop are the same as total receipts except when credit-card tips are paid. Net receipts at the front office are computed by subtracting total advances (paid-outs), city and transient, from total receipts, city and transient. House paid-outs and miscellaneous receipts are not included because they're counted as cash (as discussed earlier in the chapter).

For discussion, assume the totals of the front-office cashier's balance report to be:

Receipts	
Transient receivables	$2,376.14
City receivables	422.97
Total receipts	$2,799.11
Paid-outs	
Transient ledger paid-outs	$ 107.52
City ledger paid-outs	27.50
Total paid-outs	$ 135.02
Net Receipts	
Total receipts	$2,799.11
Less paid-outs	135.02
Equals net receipts	$2,664.09

The front-office cashier accesses this information through the cashier's balance report. See Exhibits 12–6 and 12–7 for examples of a cashier's balance report. Note, however, that this current example (total receipts of $2,799.11 and total paid-outs of $135.02) does not correlate to the figures shown in Exhibits 12–7 through 12–11. For an example of a net receipts calculation using the figures found in Exhibits 12–6 and 12–7, see Exhibit 12–9.

Some balance reports provide only summary data such as that described in this section—total transient ledger receipts, total city ledger (and general ledger) receipts, total transient ledger paid-outs, and total city ledger paid-outs. Other balance reports are very complete, telling the cashier exactly how much net receipts to have in the drawer.

Whether the system provides detail for net receipts or not, this figure is a simple number to compute. In this example, net receipts are total receipts ($2,799.11) less total paid-outs ($135.02) equals $2,664.09 in net receipts.

Over or Short.   No cashier is perfect. The day's close occasionally finds the cash drawer over or short. Sometimes the error is mathematical, and either the cashier finds it without help or it is uncovered later by the auditor.

Cash errors in giving change are usually beyond remedy unless they are in the house's favor. Guests may not acknowledge overpayments, but they will complain soon enough if they have been shortchanged. Restitution after the fact is possible if the cash count at the end of the shift proves this to be so.

Overages and shortages become a point of employee–management conflict in those hotels where cashiers are required to make up all shortages but turn in all overages. Better systems allow overages to offset shortages, asking only that the month's closing

Given

1. A starting bank of $1,000
2. The cashier's balance report shows:

Cash receipts (both transient and city ledger), See 12-8	$1,731.22
Paid-outs (both transient and city ledger), See 12-8	37.50

3. Count in the cash drawer at the close of the watch

Checks (See Exhibit 12-10)	$1,682.70
Currency	821.00
Coin	177.26
House vouchers (See Exhibit 12-10)	12.00
	$2,692.96

Computation

1. Net receipts (gross receipts minus advances)
    NR = $1,731.22 − $37.50 = $1,693.72. See 12-8
2. Overage and shortage (what should be in the drawer minus what is in the drawer)
    O&S = ($1,000 + 1,693.72) − 2,692.96 = $0.76 short
3. Turn-in (checks, vouchers, other nonnegotiable items, and all cash except the bank)
    TI = $1,682.70 + 12.00 = $1,694.70
4. Due bank (amount needed to reconstitute the bank)
    DB = $1,000 − (821.00 + 177.26) = $1.74. (See Exhibit 12-10)
5. Verification (the excess of the turn-in over the amount due)
    DB = $1,694.70 − ($1,693.72 − .76) = $1.74.

Exhibit 12-9 Preparation of Ardelle's front-office cashier report requires an understanding of the computations. Refer to Exhibits 12–6, 12–7, and 12–8 to understand the numbers shown under "cash receipts," "paid-outs," "checks," and so on. Remember, this exhibit is based on the figures shown in the continuing series of Exhibits 12–7 to 12–10, and is *not based on the text discussion,* which provides a look at a *different* example.

record balance. Both procedures encourage the cashier to reconcile at the expense of ethical standards. Shortchanging, poor addition, and altered records accommodate these management requirements. It is a better policy to have the house absorb the shortages and keep the overages. A record of individual performance is then maintained to determine if individual overages and shortages balance over the long run. They should, unless the cashier is inept or dishonest.

Over or *short* is the difference between what the cashier should have in the cash drawer and what is actually there. It is the comparison of a mathematically generated net total against a physical count of the money in the drawer. The cashier *should* have the sum of the original starting bank plus the net receipts. What money is on hand in the drawer is what the cashier *does* have. Over or short is the difference between the *should have* and the *does have.*

In our continuing example, the front-office cashier should have $3,164.09 on hand at the close of the shift. This is calculated by taking net receipts of $2,664.09 (see discussion) plus starting bank ($500) equals $3,164.09.

Should Have on Hand	
Net receipts	$2,664.09
Starting bank	500.00
Total of should have	$3,164.09

Once the cashier knows how much should be in the drawer, it is a simple matter of comparing that total with the actual cash on hand. The cashier's drawer could contain personal and traveler's checks, currency, coin, and petty cash vouchers. Credit cards are not included in the reconciliation of the cashier's drawer. Credit cards are handled by the accounting department as a city ledger accounts receivable. A full discussion of credit cards is included in Chapter 11.

Does Have on Hand		
Traveler's Checks		$2,704.60
Currency	418.13	356.00
Coin		62.13
House petty cash vouchers		42.50
Total cash on hand		$3,165.23

The cashier apparently has more in the drawer than there should be. In such a case, the cashier has an overage. If the amount of cash on hand were actually less than what there should be, the cashier would be short. The amount of the overage or shortage is simple enough to compute—just subtract the amount there should be ($3,164.09) from the amount of cash on hand ($3,165.23). The net total ($1.14) is the amount of overage. A positive net number is an overage; a negative net number is a shortage.

The Turn-In. When the cashier has calculated net receipts, determined the amount there should be, and counted the actual cash in the drawer, it is a simple matter to compute the turn-in. However, in many hotels, the cashier is not responsible for counting the drawer. In such operations, cashiers are not allowed to count the drawer even if they wish to.

Cashiers who are permitted to total their receipts and count their drawers know exactly how much they are over or short. Overages can be very appealing to unscrupulous cashiers. If allowed to calculate the amount of overage, some cashiers will pocket the difference. That is troublesome, but it becomes double trouble when the cashier's calculations were in error. If the cashier bases the overage amount on an error and then steals that amount, the mistake (and the theft) is likely to be uncovered by the night auditor. This is a common way in which hotels uncover employee embezzlement.

For this reason, many hotels limit the employee's access and knowledge regarding the correct amount of the day's deposit. Instead, the employee rebuilds the starting bank with currency and coin and then deposits everything else remaining. In such operations, the front-office cashier functions no differently than a departmental cashier.

The Front-Office Turn-In. The turn-in of the front-office cashier is more complicated than the turn-in of the departmental cashiers. As stated, the front-office bank is used to cash checks, make change, and advance cash as well as to accept receipts. Assume, for example, that nothing took place during the watch except check cashing. At the close of the day, the bank would contain nothing but nonnegotiable checks. It would be impossible to make change the next day with a drawer full of personal checks. So the cashier must drop or turn in all nonnegotiable items, including checks, traveler's checks, foreign funds, large bills, casino chips, cash in poor condition, vouchers for house expenses, and even refund slips for inoperative vending machines.

The objective of the cashier's turn-in is to rebuild the starting bank in the proper amount and variety of denominations to be effective during the next day's shift, and "drop" the rest of the contents of the cash drawer. Sometimes, there are enough small bills and coins in the cashier's drawer to rebuild tomorrow's bank quite easily. At other times, there are too many large denomination bills or nonnegotiable checks and paper to rebuild tomorrow's bank. In such cases, the cashier must turn in all of the large bills and nonnegotiable paper, leaving tomorrow's bank short. That's OK, because the income audit staff will leave currency and coin in requested denominations for the start of tomorrow's shift. By adding these new funds to the short bank, tomorrow's drawer will be both accurate and effective.

Our continuing example helps to illustrate the concept of turn-in or drop. Remember that the cashier has a total of $3,165.23 on hand, comprising checks ($2,704.60), currency ($356.00), coin ($62.13), and house petty cash vouchers ($42.50). The cashier must turn in all of the nonnegotiable paper, including checks ($2,704.60) and house petty cash vouchers ($42.50), which equals a $2,747.10 total turn-in.

Parts of this discussion has limited application because few lodging properties accept personal checks across the desk.

Due Bank. At this point it is quite obvious that the cashier does not have enough small bills and coin to rebuild tomorrow's $500 starting bank. In fact, tomorrow's bank will be short by $81.87. This shortage is commonly referred to as the *due bank*. It is also known as the *due back, difference returnable, U-owe-me's,* or the *exchange*.

The due bank is calculated by subtracting the amount of money retained by the cashier, $418.13 ($356.00 in currency plus $62.13 in coin) from the amount needed to open the next day's bank, $500.

Due Bank Computation		
Original bank		$500.00
Cash on hand	(See page 474)	418.13
Due bank		$ 81.87

Since the cashier always retains the exact bank, it is apparent that the turn-in includes the overage or allows for the shortage. The hotel, not the cashier, funds the overages and shortages. A due bank formula, which produces the same due bank figure as the simple subtraction computation, mathematically illustrates the hotel's responsibility for the over and short.

Due Bank Formula
Due bank = turn-in − (net receipts ± over or short)
Due bank = $2,747.10 − ($2,664.09 + $1.14)
Due bank = $2,747.10 − ($2,665.23)
Due bank = $81.87

To keep their banks functional, cashiers specify the coin and currency denominations of the due bank. There is little utility in a due bank of several large bills. For the very same reason, the turn-in may be increased with large bills to be exchanged for more negotiable currency. More often, the change is obtained from the general cashier before the shift closes, or from another cashier who has coins and small bills to exchange.

Exhibits 12–9 and 12–10 offer a second example complete with cashier's turn-in envelope, but with different values from the text discussion.

The Income Audit

Income auditors and general cashiers are members of the hotel's accounting department. They usually perform the income audit each morning to process the cashier drops made the preceding day. One purpose of the income audit is to verify that each department's (and indeed each shift's) cashiers have accurately dropped (turned in) the amount indicated on the deposit envelopes (see Exhibit 12–10). Although this function is performed

DEPARTMENT CASHIER'S REPORT			
DAY *TUE* DATE *3-9*			
CASHIER *Ardelle*			
DEPT *F.O.*			
SHIFT *8:00* A.M. ☑ P.M. ☐ TO *4:00* A.M. ☐ P.M. ☑			
		AMOUNT	✓
CURRENCY $1.00			
" $5.00			
" $10.00			
" $20.00			
" $50.00			
" $100.00			
COIN 1¢			
" 5¢			
SILVER 10¢			
" 25¢			
" 50¢			
" $1.00			
BAR STUBS:			
PAID-OUTS:			
VOUCHERS AND CHECKS:			
New York Exchange-Wilson →		82	50
Cleveland Trust-Adams		67	21
Chicago 1st Natl.-Gregory		111	77
Bank America-Gonne		96	20
Natl. Bank of St. Louis-Jackson		46	31
First Interstate-Washington		1278	71
Postage Stamp Voucher		12	—
TRAVELER'S CHECKS			
LESS SHORT (See page 473)			76
TOTAL AMOUNT ENCLOSED		1694	70
NET RECEIPTS WITH O & S		1692	96
DIFFERENCE (See page 473)		1	74

Exhibit 12–10   Cashier's envelope for preparing the "turn-in" (or "drop") at the close of the shift. Refer to Exhibits 12–6 to 12–9 to understand the source of checks enclosed, the postage stamp voucher, the "due bank" difference of $1.74, and so on. Note that the net receipts figure includes the $.76 shortage (O & S stands for "over" and "short").

in a vault or safe room, there are several general cashiers present. The audit may even be videotaped as an additional safeguard, especially in casinos.

The income audit generally has two purposes: to audit the day's incomes from cash and accounts receivable sales, and to prepare the hotel's daily bank deposit. During the income audit, every deposit envelope from every department cashier is opened, verified, and added to the growing pile of cash, checks, traveler's checks, foreign currency, house vouchers, and so on. Every form of payment except credit cards is counted, totaled, and added to the hotel's daily deposit. Credit cards are the exception because they are electronically deposited to the hotel's bank account. The income audit includes both front-office cashiers (who probably calculate the exact amount of their turn-in and know shift by shift whether they are over or short) and departmental cashiers (who may or may not precalculate their turn-in before preparing the deposit envelope). In the case of departmental cashiers who rebuild their starting bank and blindly drop the rest of their money, the general cashier merely counts and verifies the contents of the drop. Whereas the general cashier attends to the actual count of the cash turned in, the income auditor focuses on the accuracy of the amounts reported by the various departmental cashiers. Together, the general cashier(s) and income auditor(s) make up the day audit team.

Paying Off the Due Bank.   As discussed above, due banks are caused by a variety of factors: there may have been a large house paid-out that used most of the drawer's cash; there may have been too many large denomination bills and too few small ones to effectively rebuild tomorrow's starting bank; or there may have been too many checks cashed to leave sufficient money for tomorrow. Whatever the reason, the income audit staff pays each cashier's due bank from the growing pile of turned-in cash before preparing the hotel's daily deposit.

Most operations use a signature and witness system to facilitate returning the due banks to each cashier. One main cashier (often a front-office cashier) is given a series of due-bank envelopes with the name of each cashier to whom the envelope is owed. The departmental cashier then signs for the sealed envelope in the presence of the main cashier and adds the contents of the envelope to his or her's starting shift bank. The sealed envelopes were prepared during the cashier audit and were witnessed as to the correct amount sealed inside. Although simple, these signature and witness systems are generally quite effective.

Paying Off the House Vouchers.   In hotels that utilize an imprest petty cash fund, front-office cashiers are asked to hold their house vouchers until they reach some predetermined amount (say, $25). Front-office cashiers write house vouchers for a soda machine refund ($0.75), a video game refund ($0.50), and topping off gas for the shuttle van ($19.50). These are kept in the cash drawer until they exceed the predetermined amount ($25). Even at the close of the shift, as the cashier is building tomorrow's starting bank, the vouchers are still kept by the cashier. Tomorrow, however, if the cashier writes a few more house vouchers (say, a sour cream was purchased from the grocery store for $4.59), the entire sum of all vouchers will be turned in.

In this example, the sum to be turned in by the end of tomorrow's shift is $25.34. The cashier turns in all of the house vouchers, not merely the one or two vouchers that put the total over the predetermined amount. The income audit staff counts the house vouchers as cash and credits the drop envelope with the amount of house vouchers. In some cases, a due bank may be caused by an extremely large house voucher (say, a large C.O.D. shipment arrived).

Tour Package Coupons.   Hotels that operate in busy tour and travel markets often incorporate the redemption of package coupons and certificates into their cash drawer procedures. Such coupons or certificates are found primarily in departmental cashier turn-ins, but front-office cashiers may also redeem them under some circumstances.

Generally, package tours provide the guest with substantially more than just a hotel room. Breakfast each morning, two free rounds of golf, a discount in the gift shop, several free drinks, and a dinner show are all examples of products that might be included in a packaged tour. In order to identify themselves as members of the tour, guests are presented with a coupon booklet that contains redeemable certificates.

As an example, when a couple arrives at the dining room for breakfast, the wait-staff and cashier may not be aware they are tour customers. In fact, they are treated like any other customer until the end of the meal. Then, instead of paying for the breakfast in cash, credit card, or room charge, the tour couple need only present their complimentary breakfast coupons.

It's at this point accounting systems break down. Departmental cashiers forget to collect tour coupons with the same determination that they show when collecting cash. After all, the cashier thinks, the meal is complimentary; if the tour guest accidentally forgets the coupon booklet in the room, what's the harm? This overlooks the fact that someone is paying for the guest's complimentary meal (golf, drinks, or whatever). In fact, the redeemed coupon serves as documentation to the travel wholesaler for payment. Redeemed coupons are proof that goods (breakfast in this case) were exchanged and become the basis for the account receivable. That's why redeemed coupons become part of the departmental cashier's daily turn-in.

Foreign Currency.   Foreign currency (see Exhibit 12–11) is not regularly accepted in the United States. Overseas, U.S. currency is widely accepted. Even the Canadian dollar, with its stability and similarity of value, experiences exchange problems as it moves southward from the U.S.–Canadian border. But international tourism has grown at an amazing rate. A weak U.S. dollar means more to come in the years ahead. As more foreign currencies are being tendered across hotel desks, more language capability is being encouraged among front-office staffs.

Nevertheless, relatively few American hotels have followed their international counterparts into the foreign-exchange business. This is a service that many U.S. hotels prefer to have done by another agency. Thus the growth in foreign-exchange facilities has been largely outside the hotel lobby.

Cities with large numbers of foreign visitors, such as New York and Miami, have developed adequate exchange facilities to accommodate the international tourists. These currency-exchange companies, privately owned, have been supported by local tourists bureaus, chambers of commerce, and the U.S. National Tourism Organization, all of which see the importance of the international tourist to the balance of trade. Exchange agencies allow the hotels to service the currency needs of the international guest with a reasonable ceiling on costs.

Servicing the guest is all that American hotels appear to do. It is a limited service at that—limited to relatively few hotels that deal only in a handful of popular currencies because they have identified a well-defined international market segment for themselves. Overseas, foreign exchange is a profit center for the hotel. There is a profit to be made because both domestic and foreign hotels exchange currency at something less than the official rate. That's a double insult because even the official rate, which is determined by open market bidding, provides a spread between buy price and sell price.

Since it is not desirable to inventory money from all around the world, hotels do not provide for the reconversion of local currency into foreign funds as the visitor prepares to go home. Therefore, the hotel's concern is only with the bid rate. Money brokers quote both a buy (bid) rate and a sell (ask) rate. The desk buys foreign currency from the guest at a rate that is lower than the broker's bid rate, reselling later to the broker at the bid rate. The hotel might buy Canadian dollars, for example, at 8 cents less than it sells them for, although

Country	Currency	Country	Currency
North America		**Other European Currency**	
Canada	Dollar	Denmark	Krone
Mexico	Peso	Norway	Krone
		Russia	Ruble
Central and South America		Switzerland	Franc
Argentina	Peso	United Kingdom	Pound
Bolivia	Boliviano	**Caribbean, Bahamas, and Bermuda**	
Brazil	Real	Bahamas	Dollar
Chile	Peso	Bermuda	Dollar
Colombia	Peso	British Virgin Islands	Dollar
Costa Rica	Colon	Curacao	Guilder
Ecuador	Dollar	Jamaica	Dollar
El Salvador	Colon	Martinique	Franc
Guatemala	Quetzal	Trinidad	Dollar
Honduras	Lempira	**Africa**	
Nicaragua	Cordoba	Algeria	Dinar
Peru	New Sol	Egypt	Pound
Uruguay	New Peso	Ethiopia	Birr
Venezuela	Bolivar	Ghana	Cedi
		Libya	Dinar
Europe's EURO/Now	**Practice**	Morocco	Dirham
Austria	Schilling	South Africa	Rand
Belgium	Franc	Sudan	Dinar
Bulgaria	Lev	Tanzania	Shilling
Finland	Markka	Zambia	Kwacha
France	Franc	**Mideast, Far East, and Pacific**	
West Germany	Mark	Australia	Dollar
Greece	Drachma	Bahrain	Dinar
Ireland	Punt	China	Renminbi
Italy	Lira	Hong Kong	Dollar
Luxembourg	Franc	India	Rupee
Netherlands	Guilder	Indonesia	Rupiah
Portugal	Escudo	Israel	Shekel
Romania	Leu	Japan	Yen
Slovenia	Tolar	Jordan	Dinar
Spain	Peseta	Kuwait	Dinar
Vatican City	Lira	Lebanon	Pound
		Malaysia	Ringgit
European countries currently under consideration for accession to EURO		New Zealand	Dollar
Cyprus	Pound	Pakistan	Rupee
Czech Republic	Koruna	Philippines	Peso
Estonia	Kroon	Saudi Arabia	Riyal
Hungary	Forint	Singapore	Dollar
Latvia	Lats	South Korea	Won
Lithuania	Litas	Syria	Pound
Malta	Lira	Taiwan	Dollar
Poland	Zloty	Thailand	Baht
Slovakia	Koruna	Turkey	Lira
Sweden	Krona	United Arab Emirates	Dirham

Exhibit 12-11   Shown are most of the world's currencies. Conversion rates for major currencies are quoted in local newspapers and in *The Wall Street Journal*. See the text for additional discussion on the European Economic and Monetary Union's (EU) euro, and monitor the news for new member countries.

the official spread might be only 4 cents. The extra spread between buy and sell may be further enriched by a supplemental exchange fee. This fee, which currency dealers call *agio,* provides the hotel with additional funds to pay for bank charges or to offset unexpected variations in foreign currency value. The latter makes it especially important to process foreign currency quickly and to include it in the turn-in every day.

Obtaining daily quotes and avoiding banks that are not brokers themselves (that is, middlemen) will maximize foreign exchange profits. In fact, the hotel could become an intermediary broker by also converting funds for taxi drivers, bellpersons, and servers throughout the community in addition to its own personnel. Of course, this opens a whole new business with the large risks that accompany foreign exchange.

If the hotel is dealing in foreign currencies, the accounting office must furnish the cashier with a table of values for each currency traded (see Exhibit 12–11). (Several airlines quote currency rates, including rates on foreign traveler's checks, as part of their reservation system service.) If currency values fluctuate over a wide range, a daily or even hourly quote is necessary to prevent substantial losses. More likely, the hotel will just refuse that particular currency.

Canadian currency poses less of a problem than most other kinds. It is similar in form, divisions, and value to the U.S. dollar. Consequently, hotels close to the border have accepted each other's dollars at a par. Although this practice involves an exchange cost to the hotel, it has been a good advertising and public relations gimmick that more than offsets the expense.

Automated currency conversion systems. International hotel guests have experienced the antiservice syndrome for many years—they have been unable to review their guest folios in their own currency of choice. U.S. hotels have always quoted and sold rooms in U.S. dollars, simple as that. International guests were required to do their own currency conversion calculations—at least that was the mindset until recently.

In the last few years, hotels have rapidly begun implementing dynamic currency conversion (DCC) software in their property management systems. The logic for this change has been twofold: It has become required by major credit-card companies as a software enhancement for international guests; and hotels offering this service have experienced huge growth in international business—especially Web-based reservations.

Here's how DCC software works. At the time of reservation or check-in, the DCC software highlights international guests allowing them to choose the currency: U.S. dollars or their home currency. At check-out, the folios are calculated in the currency selected and presented for approval. Once approved, the transaction is complete, and the cost of the hotel stay, including conversion fees and exchange rates is shown.

The EU Euro.   In an attempt to become more competitive on a global basis and to simplify currency transactions in closely related countries, the European Economic Monetary Union (EU) created a new form of currency. As many experts predicted, the euro has become a dominant force in international tourism. In part because of a weak U.S. dollar and in part because the euro reflects the assets and GNP of the European community.

The euro has certainly simplified matters for the lodging industry. Currency exchange rates with the euro are far less volatile and are easier to track than were the currencies of 12 separate countries (there were 12 original countries converted to the euro in 2002). In addition, currency exchange rates among the EU countries have been eliminated, saving tourists the cost and inconvenience of exchanging various monies. But best of all, the new euro has made much of Europe seem almost borderless, as tourists travel country to country with little more difficulty than Americans travel from state to state (see Exhibit 12–11).

The euro (denoted by a € symbol) has eight coins and seven notes in circulation. While the reverse side of every euro coin is the same across all member states, the obverse side is unique to whichever EU member state printed that particular coin. No matter which side shows on a particular coin, it can be used anywhere inside the 12 member states. For example, a German citizen could purchase a slice of pizza in Italy using a coin depicting the imprint of the King of Spain.

In terms of the common reverse side, all coins are minted with a map of the European Union against a background of lines to which are attached the stars of the European flag. The 1, 2, and 5 cent coins put emphasis on Europe's place in the world; the 10, 20, and 50 cent coins present the European Union as a gathering of nations. The 1 and 2 euro coins depict Europe without frontiers.

The seven euro notes, in different colors and sizes, are denominated in 500, 200, 100, 50, 20, 10, and 5 euros. Unlike euro coins, the euro notes have no national side—they are uniform throughout the euro area. Designs of the notes are symbolic of Europe's architectural heritage. Interestingly, the buildings depicted on the various notes do not represent actual structures: They are all fictitious, to prevent any one country from gaining undo exposure to its monuments. Windows and gateways dominate the front side of each banknote as symbols of the spirit of openness and cooperation in the European Union. The reverse side of each banknote features a bridge from a particular age, a metaphor for communication among the people of Europe and with the rest of the world. All notes carry advanced security features (Exhibit 12–12).

Example from the Land of Nod.   Let's see what needs to be done when a guest from the Land of Nod tenders a ₦ 1,000 bill in payment of a $34 account. Each ₦ (Nod dollar) is exchanged at 5 cents U.S. money by the hotel, although the official rate may be somewhat higher—say, 5.1 cents. Therefore, the ₦ 1,000 is exchanged at $50, which is $1 less than the official rate of exchange. The cashier would return $16 U.S. in exchange for the ₦ 1,000 and the charge of $34. Change is given only in U.S. dollars even if the cashier has Nod dollars. If, on the other hand, the guest had offered only a ₦ 500 bill, the cashier would have collected an additional U.S. $9 to settle the $34 account in full. What if it were a ₦ 2,500 bill, and the cashier had on hand 1,500 Nod dollars? What would be the change? (Answer: The cashier would give U.S. $91 in change. Remember: Foreign currency is never returned even if it's available in the cash drawer. That would give away the profit earned on the exchange rates.)

Foreign traveler's checks (especially Canadian traveler's checks) are more readily accepted than personal checks. Cashiers are cautioned to use the same level of scrutiny with foreign traveler's checks as they use with U.S. traveler's checks. Foreign traveler's checks look identical to U.S. traveler's checks, with one simple difference: Instead of stating "Pay to the order of (name) in U.S. dollars," the foreign traveler's check states "Pay . . . in foreign-country dollars" (see Exhibit 12–18). Many clerks accidentally cash foreign traveler's checks in U.S. funds. This can represent a considerable loss to the hotel.

CASH AND CASH EQUIVALENTS

The busy hotel, with its hundreds of new guests daily, creates the perfect haven for crimes of forgery and counterfeiting. It is of critical importance that managers be trained in the secure handling of cash and cash equivalents.

Hotels are likely targets for professional counterfeiters and forgers for several reasons. First, guest receptionists are often rushed with numerous small transactions,

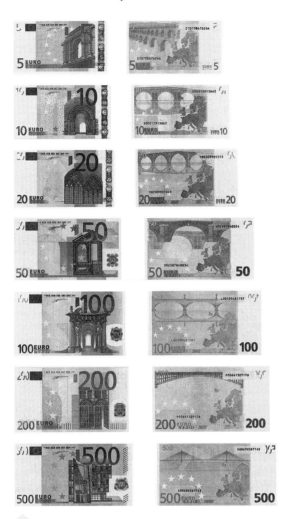

Exhibit 12–12   The observe of each of the seven Euro banknotes features architectural styles from the seven ages of Europe's cultural history. The windows and gateways are symbols of the spirit of openness and cooperation in the European Union. The reverse depicts seven different European bridges. Each bill boasts a unique color, and the size of the note increases with denomination.

allowing the professional criminal easy access and egress. Second, hotel cashiers are inundated with so many guests that they would probably have a difficult time remembering (much less describing or identifying) the professional counterfeiter and/or forger.

Finally, as discussed earlier, hotels handle relatively little cash as a percentage of all sales volume. Although that may sound contradictory, counterfeiters often seek establishments that have little cash dealings. That's because cashiers who handle lots of cash become very adept at spotting a phony.

Counterfeit Currency

According to the U.S. Secret Service, there may be as much as $1 billion in counterfeit currency in worldwide circulation. In the United States, the number is far less (under $100 million). As the U.S. dollar became accepted worldwide, the incidence of counterfeiting increased. Just as hotel front-office cashiers (who handle relatively little cash) are likely targets for counterfeiters, so are international cashiers, who probably handle even fewer U.S. dollars. According to the Secret Service, the most popular counterfeit bill in the United States is the $20 bill. Overseas the most popular counterfeit is the $100 bill! According to the Secretary of the Treasury, the top 10 overseas countries for U.S. dollar counterfeiting are:

Ranked by Seizures **($ Amount Seized)**	
Colombia	($23,311,980)
Bulgaria	($ 4,558,350)
Germany	($ 3,567,361)
Dominican Republic	($ 1,223,000)
Latvia	($ 702,200)
Russia	($ 515,600)
Yugoslavia	($ 500,000)
Moldova	($ 468,900)
Lebanon	($ 389,400)
Italy	($ 245,500)

As computer technology has improved, the counterfeiting problem has been compounded. Virtually anyone willing to spend the few hundred dollars necessary to purchase a color printer/scanner can enter the counterfeiting business. In just four short years, computer-generated counterfeit money has risen from 0.5% (half of one percent) to over 44% of all counterfeit money in circulation.

Detecting Counterfeit Currency.   Beginning in 1996, the U.S. Treasury began issuing currency with new security features. The $100 bill (see Exhibit 12–13) was the first, followed by the $50, $20, $10, and $5 bills introduced at the rate of roughly one new bill every year. In October 2003, several redesigned enhancements were added. The redesigned notes take advantage of new technologies to make them more secure from counterfeiting as well as easier to recognize when passed see Exhibit 12–13. Since the first series of notes was introduced in 1861, U.S. currency has continually evolved in an attempt to thwart counterfeit activities. Despite many previous alterations, this most recent design change is probably the most noticeable.

Exhibit 12–13 details the eight new features embedded in bills introduced since 1996. Hold a new $100, $50, $20, $10, or $5 bill to the light and notice some interesting enhancements. For example, a polymer security thread runs top to bottom down the bill, just to the left of the portrait. A watermark, to the right of the portrait, is visible from both the obverse and reverse of the bill. These two features are difficult to replicate on counterfeit bills. The most difficult of all, however, is the color-shifting ink found in the numerical denomination of the bill at the bottom right corner. Looking at it head on, the number appears green. Bringing it up under your eye and turning the bill away from you, you'll notice that the green color shifts to black or copper in the new series 2004 bills.

Supernotes.   As secure as today's currency appears to be, it is not unbeatable. Just a couple of years ago, a container ship berthed in the United States became involved in an FBI and Secret Service sting operation. When they opened one container, they discovered hundreds of thousands of dollars in counterfeit $100 bills. Just months later, the FBI and Secret Service uncovered another cache of nearly $700,000, and days later, another $3 million.

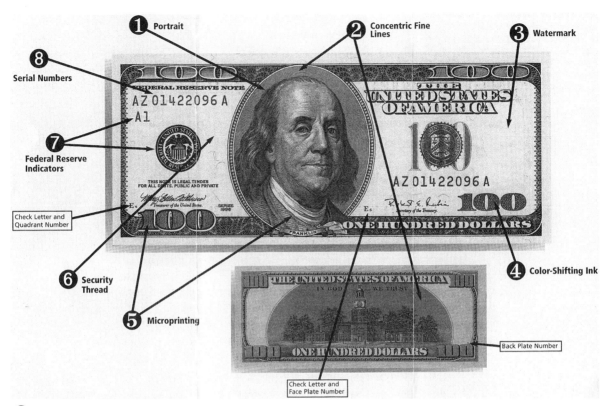

① **Portrait** The enlarged portrait of Benjamin Franklin is easier to recognize, while the added detail is harder to duplicate. The portrait is now off-center, providing room for a watermark and reducing wear and tear on the portrait.

② **Concentric Fine Lines** The fine lines printed behind both Benjamin Franklin's portrait and Independence Hall are difficult to replicate.

③ **Watermark** A watermark depicting Benjamin Franklin is visible from both sides when held up to a light.

④ **Color-Shifting Ink** The number in the lower right corner on the front of the note looks green when viewed straight on, but appears black when viewed at an angle.

⑤ **Microprinting** Because they're so small, microprinted words are hard to replicate. On the front of the note, "USA 100" is within the num-

ber in the lower left corner and "United States of America" is on Benjamin Franklin's coat.

⑥ **Security Thread** A polymer thread is embedded vertically in the paper and indicates, by its unique position, the note's denomination. The words "USA 100" on the thread can be seen from both sides of the note when held up to a bright light. Additionally, the thread glows red when held under an ultraviolet light.

⑦ **Federal Reserve Indicators** A new universal seal represents the entire Federal Reserve System. A letter and number beneath the left serial number identifies the issuing Federal Reserve Bank.

⑧ **Serial Numbers** An additional letter is added to the serial number. The unique combination of eleven numbers and letters appears twice on the front of the note.

Exhibit 12–13 State-of-the-art security features have been incorporated in U.S. currency since 1996. Here are the original 1996 features. Beginning October 2003, a new round of changes to U.S. currency began with the redesigned $20 bill Exhibit 12-14. This was followed by the new $50 and $10 bills. The new $5 bill came out in early 2008, to be followed by the new $100 bill (introduction date as yet uncertain).

Exhibit 12–14 The U.S. Secret Service refers to the newest bills, those introduced in October 2003, as Series 2004 currency. These bills have all the features of the Series 1996 currency (shown in Exhibit 12–13) along with several new complex features designed to thwart counterfeiting. These include:

- Offset-printed multicolored background
- Borderless portrait
- Iconic symbol to the right of the portrait printed in metallic pigmented ink
- New color-shifting ink: from copper to green in bottom right of bill
- Security thread of $50 bills is 50% wider and in a slightly different position

Each of these fake bills was nearly flawless. Counterfeits of this superior sort are known as "supernotes." Supernotes are generally printed on paper made with the appropriate mix of $3/4$ cotton and $1/4$ linen—the same as genuine U.S. currency. Making secure paper with this mix requires a special papermaking machine rarely seen outside the United States. Supernotes also feature the same high-tech color-shifting ink as genuine American bills. The engraved images are as fine as anything produced by the United States Bureau of Engraving and Printing.

In addition, many of these notes are manufactured using an intaglio press, the most advanced form of currency-printing technology available. Intaglio presses are far more expensive than ordinary offset, typographic, or lithograhic presses, which yield inferior counterfeits. An intaglio press actually coats the printing plates with ink and then wipes the surface clean—leaving behind ink in the recesses of the engraving. The press then brings paper and plate together under pressure, so the ink is forced out of the recessed lines and deposited on the paper in relief.

It is virtually impossible for hotels faced with criminals passing supernote-quality counterfeits to detect these fakes. Even armed with counterfeit detection equipment (discussed in the next section), hotels are still at a disadvantage. Only when subjected to sophisticated forensic analysis can such bills be confirmed as imitations.

Other Cashier Applications. Hotel cashiers are using a number of relatively inexpensive counterfeit detection devices that have hit the market in recent years (see Exhibit 12–15). Aside from the sophisticated security identification features readily

Exhibit 12–15   Detection devices like MoneyChecker supplement front-office training designed to recognize counterfeit currencies and related products. Detection devices are generally inexpensive and require minimal training. The least expensive (and least sophisticated) detection comes with special pens designed to change color when they contact the starch in paper counterfeits—real currency is made from cotton fibers. But inexpensive detection pens are easily thwarted by coating the fake bills in plastic (usually with a sprayed-on ScotchGuard-type product).

A slightly greater investment by the front office affords substantially improved detection in the form of UV lamps. UV lamps (like those found in the MoneyChecker) readily illuminate the color-coded security threads found in all $5, $10, $20, $50, and $100 U.S. currency bills (see Exhibit 12–14). A built-in template on all MoneyCheckers shows the location and color of each denomination's security thread. Additionally, the UV lamp can help authenticate credit cards, driver licenses, and travelers checks, many of which now boast logos or overprinted areas visible only under the specific wavelengths of UV light. *Courtesy of Angstrom Technologies, Erlanger, Kentucky.*

visible to the human eye found in today's U.S. currency, these inexpensive detection devices utilize two additional technologies in their search for counterfeit currency. One of the most popular devices is a detector shaped like a marker pen made by companies such as Dri-Mark Products of New York. This pen is popular with major retailers because it is simple to use. In essence, it employs a chemical reaction to indicate whether the currency in question has authentic cotton fibers. All U.S. currency is made from 100% cotton rag—there is no paper content. As such, detector pens that react with starch (found in paper products) turn counterfeit bills brown.

A second detection technology searches the bill for magnetic ink. Magnetic ink has been used by the Federal Reserve since 1932. The ink is found on the portrait and around the edges. Counterfeit currency created on copiers or printing presses lacks the magnetic ink.

Whatever their approach, hotels are urged to use caution when accepting currency. Counterfeit currency can cost a hotel a considerable amount of money in a relatively short amount of time because counterfeiters usually pass a number of bills in quick succession. Counterfeit bills are like ants—there never is just one! And when the hotel finally realizes what has happened and calls the Secret Service, they are in for another shock—the counterfeit bills will be confiscated without restitution.

Check-Cashing Safeguards

Even in the smallest hotel, management cannot make every credit decision every hour of the day. Instead, it creates the policies and procedures that will minimize losses and retain customer goodwill. A credit manual or credit handbook is the usual manner of communicating management's position. Each management team has its own approach to policies, but procedures for handling personal checks (and traveler's checks) are much alike from hotel to hotel and from handbook to handbook.

Hotels train their front-office personnel to be pleasant, courteous, and accommodating. Check scam artists are usually loud, rude, and threatening. By pushing in during rush hours, harassing the clerks who have been taught to "take it," and pressuring for service, passers of bad checks walk away with millions. Losses can be reduced when certain procedures are put in place. Risk can be reduced, but not entirely eliminated—there is no foolproof system. "If you believe you have a foolproof system, you've failed to take into consideration the creativity of fools." This advice comes from Frank W. Abagnale, a well-known check counterfeiter made famous by the movie *Catch Me If You Can.*

Procedures for Minimizing Fraud.
Hotel operations are 100 times more likely to lose money to forged and fraudulent checks than they are to armed robbery! Using proper check-cashing procedures is critical to avoid significant losses from this form of theft.

As with counterfeiting, computer technology has made check-cashing forgery a simple crime for anyone to perpetrate. Basic desktop publishing and scanning equipment is all one needs to ably copy and alter personal checks. And since checks are computer automated, the altered check will clear the bank provided the account has sufficient funds.

Unfortunately, hotels that accept forged or worthless checks have little recourse. Banks are not responsible for losses incurred from bad checks passed against them. Prevention is the only cure.

The Old "One–Two–Three."   Prevention is as easy as one–two–three. That's because the vast majority of faulty checks can be detected by front-office cashiers with three simple observations.

First, is the check perforated? All legitimate checks are perforated on at least one side (except for government checks, some checks printed on computer card stock, and counter checks). Because perforation equipment is so bulky and expensive, few check forgers bother with this detail.

Second, do the Federal Reserve district numbers 1 to 12 match the location of the issuing bank? Cashiers should compare the Federal Reserve district number located between the brackets along the bottom of the check with the restated district number printed (in smaller type) in the upper right-hand corner of the check (see Exhibit 12–16, item 9). Many check forgers change the Federal Reserve district numbers at the bottom of the check to a different district. If the numbers don't match, the check is a forgery.

Third, is the routing code printed in magnetic ink? The routing code found at the bottom of the check (Exhibit 12–16, item 8) must be printed in dull, flat magnetic ink. If the ink is shiny or raised, the check is a forgery.

Although these are the three critical questions for a cashier to observe, there are others. Refer to the comprehensive check-cashing checklist on pages 489–491. It provides management with a more thorough understanding of the check-cashing process.

Simple Deterrents.   Every weapon available must be employed in the battle against check fraud. Closed-circuit televisions and photographing procedures go a long way toward preventing fraud. Dual-lens cameras, which simultaneously record a picture of the instrument being negotiated and of the check passer, are available. Other systems allow the development of latent fingerprints without the use of ink or other messy

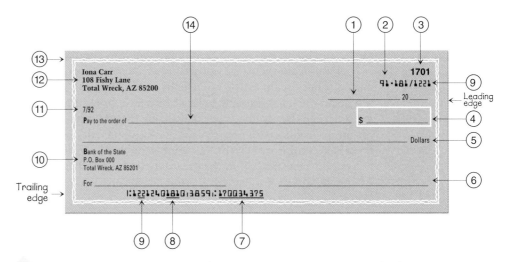

Exhibit 12–16   Fourteen locations flag a possible bad check: (1) Is the date current? (2) Do the routing numbers correspond to the magnetic numbers? (3) Has the account existed for some time? (4) Is the amount more or less than the statutory definition of grand larceny? (5) Are the values of the handwritten dollars and the numerical dollars identical? (6) Does the signature correspond to the registration card or the endorsement? (7) Are the account numbers in agreement with a bankcard that is being proffered? (8) Is the magnetic ink dull or reflective? (9) Is the number of the Federal Reserve region accurate? (10) Does the bank directory list this bank as shown? (11) When was the account established? (12) How does the maker's identity compare with the hotel's records? (13) Is the check perforated? (14) Is the payee a third party, a corporation, or cash?

substances. Just a sign explaining that such equipment is being used serves as a deterrent, as does a printed warning citing the penalty for passing bad checks.

Other hotels collect a check-cashing fee, which is used to offset worthless checks. The rationale of penalizing honest guests is open to debate. It would be better to adopt and enforce a stringent procedure, irritating as it is to the honest guest, than to collect an unwarranted fee. The procedure may include a telephone call at the guest's expense to his or her office or bank according to the circumstances and time of day. Using a check-cashing service may cost the guest a similar fee, but it puts the hotel in a better light.

Endorsements.   Procedural protection requires proper and immediate endorsement after the check is received. This is particularly true with open endorsements containing only the payee's name. The cashier should use a rubber stamp that reads as follows:

For Deposit Only
The ABC Hotel

The stamp should contain space for identification, credit-card number, room number, and the initials of the person approving the check.

Invariably, bank endorsements blot out much of the information recorded on the rear of the check. The data is unusable when needed most, if the check comes back. This issue, which was one that every industry faced, was addressed by Congress in 1988. The legislation that emerged assigned the first 1.5 inches from the trailing edge of the check to endorsements. In that space on the rear of the check go all the endorsements and whatever identification will fit into the area. The front of the check can still be used if more data is needed.

Check-Cashing Checklist.   No single set of rules covers every circumstance, but a list of limitations and restrictions is a helpful guide to those responsible for approving checks. Such a list follows. Modifications depend on the class of hotel, the source of authority, and the circumstances surrounding the particular request:

---

1. Accept checks only for the amount of the bill. Be particularly alert for the cashback technique, by which cash as well as services rendered are.

2. Allow no one to be above suspicion on weekends, holidays, and after banking hours.

3. Refuse to accept any check that is altered, illegible, stale (older than 30 days), postdated, poorly printed, or from a third party.

4. Be suspicious of checks slightly smaller than the statutory measure of grand larceny. If $500 separates petty larceny from grand larceny in the state, a $507 check is less likely to be counterfeit than is a $496 one.

5. Compare the signature and address on the check with those on the registration card: Are they similar? Should they be? Compare the signature on the front with the endorsement on the rear. Ask the same questions!

6. Compare the age of the guest with the birth date on the driver's license. Has the license expired? Compare the person's listed height and weight, hair and eye color, and the photograph, if available, to the person standing before you. More and more state driver's licenses and identification cards are being manufactured with tamperproof technology. When identification data has been altered, the card disintegrates in some conspicuous manner. For example, with Pennsylvania's driver's licenses, the state seal disintegrates if the card has been altered (see Exhibit 12–17).

7. Pay special attention to endorsements. Accept no conditional, circumstantial, or restrictive endorsements. Challenge endorsements that are not identical to either the printed name (in the case of a personal check) or the payee (in the case of a third-party check).

8. Require endorsements on checks paid to the bearer or to cash. Require all endorsements to be made in your presence, repeating them when the check is already endorsed.

9. Refuse a check payable to a corporation but endorsed by one of the officers seeking to cash it.

10. Obtain adequate and multiple identification and record it on the rear 1.5 inches of the trailing edge along with any other information that can help if the check is refused: address, telephone number, credit-card number, license plates, clerk's initials.

11. Verify business names in telephone directories or listings such as Dun & Bradstreet, Inc. Obtain military identification. Call local references. Request a business card.

12. Create fictitious information or names of company officers and see if the guest verifies them.

13. Make certain that the check is complete, accurate, and dated. Watch for misspellings and serial numbers of more than four digits.

(Continued)

---

14. Keep a bank directory and check the transit and routing numbers against it. Verify the name of the bank with the directory listing, giving special attention to the article "the" and the use of the ampersand (&) in place of the word *and*. "City Bank of Laurelwood" is not the same as "The City Bank of Laurelwood"; "Farmers and Merchants Bank" is not "Farmers & Merchants Bank."

15. Check for perforations. Almost all legitimate checks have at least one side that is perforated.

16. Remember, cashier's checks (checks drawn on the bank by one of its officers) are spelled with an apostrophe *s,* are full size, never pocket size. Watch it! These checks can be stopped at the bank of issue up to 72 hours after being validated. (Trust companies issue treasurer's checks, not cashier's checks.)

17. Be cautious of certified checks, since most persons do not use them.

18. Check the signatures on bank drafts (a check drawn by a bank on its correspondent bank) with the bank directory, and verify the bank's correspondent bank at the same time.

19. Note that because of withholding, payroll checks are almost never even dollar amounts.

20. *Read* identification—don't just look at it! Ask questions: "What does your middle C stand for?" Don't offer the answer: "Is your middle name *Charles?*"

21. Determine whether the guest is registered from the same city as the one in which the bank is located.

22. Be familiar with bank locations: The 12 Federal Reserve districts are numbered from 1 in the east to 12 in the west. Locate the magnetic code on the lower left of the check. The first two digits following the bracket (⎸:) identify the Federal Reserve bank handling the commercial paper. Numbers greater than the 12 Federal Reserve districts are fakes. This is not true of NOW accounts or similar noncommercial checks.

23. Watch the calendar: Most bad checks are passed during the final quarter of the year, the holiday season.

24. Expect the magnetic code to be dull; shiny numbers that reflect light have been printed with other than magnetic ink. Preestablish firm limits on the value of the checks to be cashed.

25. Question emergencies. If airfare is needed to fly home unexpectedly, why can't the airline take the check?

26. Ignore evidence of identity that consists of social security cards, library cards, business cards, or voter identification cards. These are easily forged or reproduced, and they generally carry no photo.

27. Personally deliver the check to the cashier without allowing the guest to retrieve it once it has been approved.

28. Watch check numbers. Low digits mean a new account where the danger is greatest. The larger the number, the safer the check. New accounts generally begin with number 101, and 90% of all "hot" checks are written on accounts less than a year old (numbered 101–150).

(Continued)

29. Look for the small date on the left upper section of the check (when available). This indicates the date the account was opened.

30. Do not write the check; insist that the check be written by the guest.

31. Machine, color-copied checks can be smeared with a wet finger; real safety-paper checks cannot.

32. Remember that bank cards do not cover cash losses, only merchandise purchased. Limit check cashing to the front-desk cashiers.

33. Note that credit managers have been known to eavesdrop on guest telephone calls.

34. Ask yourself how difficult it would be to create the identification offered.

35. Compare the numerical amount of the check with the written amount.

36. Watch the value of foreign traveler's checks. Foreign checks are issued in foreign currency. Don't cash 20 pesos or kronas as a U.S. $20 value (see Exhibit 12–18).

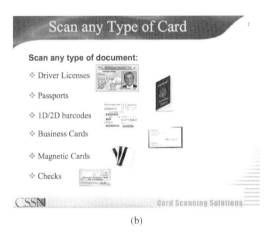

(a)

(b)

Exhibit 12–17   Card Scanning Solutions provides check-cashing security as well as guest history management applications. Their IDScan (a) can easily read and save data from guest business cards, drivers' licenses from all 50 states, personal and corporate checks, passports, and other magnetic card or barcode applications. (b) Once the information is scanned, their unique proprietary software reads the information and populates each of the data fields; name, address, telephone, I.D. number, etc. as well as scanned images. (c) Additionally, the software verifies the identification in use (it can validate the drivers' licenses from all 50 states) no matter which technology is in use: OCR, 2D barcode, or magnetic strip. *Courtesy of Card Scanning Solutions, Los Angeles.*

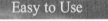

(c)

Debit Cards.   Debit cards provide the hotel with immediate payment through the guest's bank account. Rather than writing a personal check, the debit card electronically debits the guest's bank account and credits the hotel's. Payment is immediate, and the risk associated with accepting personal checks is removed.

PURCHASING CARDS.   Purchasing cards (called P-cards) have been growing in popularity as a means of controlling small payments without mailing checks to cover direct bill accounts. Here's a simple example. The SunGlow Tanning Products company sends its regional sales manager to a hotel once a month. He stays two nights, on average, at a negotiated rate of $149 plus tax. At the end of his stay, his room and tax totals $333.76. Rather than going through the process of direct billing SunGlow and waiting for them to mail a check, SunGlow provides the hotel with a P-card. After the travel purchase order was approved, SunGlow loaded the card with $333.76. At the end of the salesman's stay, the hotel simply swipes the card. The value of the purchase order is transferred to the hotel's bank account, as it is with a debit card, and the empty card is filed away (see Exhibit 11–3).

Traveler's Checks.   American Express (AmEx) pioneered the traveler's check, and it has retained its preeminent position ever since. VISA and MasterCard entered the field in the 1970s and 1980s as extensions of their credit-card business. Several banks and travel agencies round out the slate of participants. It is a competitive business. However, due to the proliferation of ATM machines, the traveler's check industry has stagnated. Travelers feel more secure carrying plastic ATM cards as opposed to dozens of bulky traveler's checks. The traveler's check industry stalled in the late 1990s at about $50 billion per year. It will probably decline in volume over the coming decades, even as the industry has found renewed popularity through the use of gift checks (traveler's checks given instead of cash for weddings, birthdays, etc.).

Generally, traveler's checks are purchased by the consumer prior to a trip. They are used as if they were cash, with the issuing company guaranteeing their replacement against loss or theft. The charge is usually 1%, but the checks are often issued without

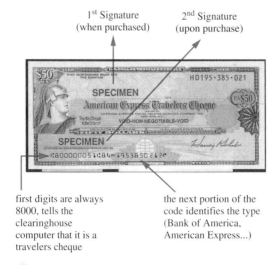

Exhibit 12–18a   This exhibit shows signature lines and clearinghouse magnetic identification codes for an American Express Traveler's check.

U.S.

Australian

Canadian

Exhibit 12–18b   This exhibit demonstrates how similarly foreign traveler's checks look to U.S. traveler's checks. Although there are variations in color, an unwary cashier can easily confuse currencies. This is especially true when the check is payable in dollars, which are used by a number of countries, including Australia, Canada, Jamaica, Hong Kong, Singapore, and the United States (see Exhibit 12–11). *Courtesy of American Express Company, Fort Lauderdale, Florida.*

charge. Even without charge, there is plenty of competition for the business. Large sums of interest-free money are available for investing. The time lag (the float) between the purchase of the traveler's check and the use of the check might be months. Some 15% to 20% of traveler's check sales are never claimed. No wonder AmEx advertising encourages buyers to hold their checks for some distant emergency.

Buyers sign the checks at the time of purchase and countersign when they cash the instruments. Signature comparison is the main line of defense against fraud. Checks must be countersigned under the scrutiny of the cashier or re-signed if they were initially endorsed away from the cashier's view. Some traveler's checks provide for dual countersignatures (usually to accommodate a husband and wife team), yet only one signature is required to cash the check.

Traveler's checks are very acceptable and some hotels will cash them even for non-registered guests. Other hotels are extra cautious and require additional identification or compare signatures to registration cards. Comparing signatures is all that's required. In fact, many issuing companies do not even want the cashier to ask for additional identification. That is because extra identification takes the cashier's focus away from the signature line. And the identification may also be invalid—in more than half the instances of stolen traveler's checks, the identification has also been stolen!

Prompt refund of lost or stolen checks is their major appeal. Hotel desks, with their 24-hour service, represent a logical extension of the issuing company's office system. Hilton entered into such an agreement with Bank of America. It is both a service to the guest and a marketing device for the chain.

Traveler's Checks Deterrents.   The best defense is to carefully watch the guest sign the traveler's check. Cautious cashiers should never remove their eyes from the check being signed. Indeed, some cashiers never even remove their hand from the check, always holding onto one corner while the guest is signing. It is a simple matter for someone to produce a stolen traveler's check, pretend to sign it while the cashier's attention is focused elsewhere, and then quickly substitute a previously signed traveler's check with a well-forged signature.

Like their commercial brothers, traveler's checks employ a magnetic code on the lower left portion of the paper (see Exhibit 12–18). In the United States, the first digits are always 8000, which tells the clearinghouse computer that it is a traveler's check. The next portion of the code identifies the type. For example, 8000001 is Bank of America, 8000005 is American Express.

Although forgers can easily alter the clearinghouse transit codes, they cannot easily copy the high-quality, high-speed laser images major companies print in their traveler's checks. These images can be seen when holding the traveler's check to the light (don't confuse these highly detailed laser imprints with simple watermarks found in paper). MasterCard and Thomas Cook, for example, show a Greek goddess on the right side of the check. Similarly, Citicorp displays a Greek god's face on the right of the check. Bank of America uses three globes (which supplement the other globes already visible). And VISA provides a globe on the left with a dove in the upper right of the check.

American Express utilizes a somewhat different safety approach. Red dots are visible in the check if held up to the light, but a wet finger is the acid test. It will smear the check when applied to the denomination on the back left side but will not smear the back right side.

SUMMARY

Even as the quantity of cash circulating in hotels declines, the need for careful cash-handling practices increases. This is especially true for front-desk cashiers because they not only receive cash but pay it out.

Front-office cashiers receive cash from a number of potential sources. Guests may pay cash on their room folio at check-in, at check-out, or in the middle of their stay. Cash is also received at the desk on behalf of other departments (as when a customer pays

for a banquet) and for auxiliary revenue centers such as soda machines or gift shop kiosks.

Cash is paid out by the front-office cashier for a number of reasons as well. On check-out, the guest who overpaid the folio may receive a refund. Employees may receive charged tips in cash, concessionaries may receive room–charge purchases in cash, and guests themselves may receive cash advances against the folio. Add to this list of paid-outs the use of an imprest petty cash account and the front-office cashier's job becomes a complicated and sensitive task.

To make the job even more difficult, cashiers must remain alert to potential check-cashing, credit-card, or cash transaction frauds. Hotel front desks are favorite targets for counterfeit currency, forged checks, or stolen credit cards. Front-office managers need to carefully train cashiers to identify situations where fraudulent practices may occur.

RESOURCES AND CHALLENGES
Resources

WEB SITES

http://www.newport-wa.org/bad%20check%20policy .html (Newport Police Department's bad check guidelines and how to handle fraudulent checks).

http://www.secretservice.gov/know_your_money .shtml (This U.S. Secret Service site is designed to help you detect counterfeit currency and guard against forgery loss).

http://retail.about.com/od/storeoperations/qt/ drawer_balance.htm (A look at how, why, and when to balance a cashier drawer and many related articles).

http://retail.about.com/od/storeoperations/qt/ drawer_balance.htm (Techniques for collecting bad debts owed by customers).

http://www.atmmarketplace.com (All the latest ATM products, services, and sources of revenue).

Web Assignment

These Web sites broaden the topics covered in this chapter: bad checks, counterfeiting, balancing the cashier's drawer, collecting bad debts, and making a profit from the lobby ATM. Take the time to visit the five sites listed and identify three suggestions, recommendations, or facts that you didn't previously know.

INTERESTING TIDBITS

➤ The average ticket costs airlines $12 in credit-card merchant discount fees. Most airlines pay more in annual credit-card fees than they do GDS fees! To combat costs, airlines are considering transparent ticket pricing, which will charge credit-card fees back to the patron. Transparent pricing will provide patrons a series of options—including PayPal and an airline affinity credit card. Choosing to use a personal credit card will increase the ticket price.

If the hotel industry follows the airlines' strategy, as it frequently does, the result will be substantial savings. A 350-room corporate hotel with an average $150 rate pays $882.00 per day in merchant discount fees, assuming 70% occupancy, 80% credit-card usage, and a 3% merchant discount fees rate.

➤ Some first class hotels operating in cities with large international markets use transient ledger paid-outs to provide exceptional service. Intercontinental Hotels & Resorts, among others, prepare small cash packets (Intercontinental calls these packets by such names as; "Little Touches," "Instant Money," or "Currency Exchange Kits") for their arriving guests who have not yet had time to secure local currencies. The cost for these packets (usually in bundles worth $25 to $50) is charged to the guest folio as a paid-out, but that small attention to detail is priceless.

➤ In contrast to the European Union's mass conversion to the euro (twelve member states introduced the euro on the same date in 1999), Central America has "dollarized" in a more quiet fashion. Today, quetzals, colons, balboas, and sucres (currencies of Guatemala, El Salvador, Panama, and Ecuador, respectively) have all been replaced by (or used in tandem with) the U.S. dollar. Similar conversions to the U.S. dollar have been taking place in South America as well.

➤ Don't forget tradeouts as a means of extending the hotel's purchasing power. While most tradeouts exchange advertising (radio, television, and print media) for hotel services, other products are known to be traded. The Washington Redskins, for example, traded red carpet from the Marriott in D.C. (to be used in their locker rooms) for a full-page ad in the Redskin's program. Another story shows a hotel trading a wedding reception for state-of-the art audiovisual equipment (see Chapter 11).

Challenges

TRUE/FALSE

Questions that are partially false should be marked false (F).

___ 1. Front-office cashiers handle cash in two directions. They receive cash (receipts) as well as pay out cash (paid-outs). This is different from cashiers in other departments where cash transactions flow just one direction. Cashiers in other departments do not make paid-outs.

___ 2. Cash settlements for hotel account balances (paid in cash) are common. This is especially true in corporate hotels where cash payments account for more than one-third of all room folio settlements.

___ 3. The front-desk cashier is often the source of imprest petty cash funds for all other departments. For example, if the restaurant was running low on butter, awaiting Thursday's delivery, it could use the front-desk cashier's imprest fund to purchase butter at the grocery store.

___ 4. To determine how much a front-office cashier might be over or short, the cashier compares her "should have" against her "do have." The amount of the cashier's "should have" is equal to the starting (opening) bank drawer plus net receipts.

___ 5. Today's U.S. currency contains a number of state-of-the-art security features designed to prevent counterfeiting. These features include, among others, a watermark visible when the bill is held to the light, a security thread whose location changes according to the denomination of the bill, and color-shifting ink.

PROBLEMS

1. Industry experts suggest the amount of cash in the banks of hotel cashiers should equal some 2% of gross revenues, or about $600 per available room. For a 100-room hotel that grosses $3 million annually, this equals $60,000 in cashiers' banks.

As a new general manager, you are concerned with the sizable amount of outstanding cash in your cashiers' various banks. You know that if it were released from the banks, the cash could return significant revenues or interest income.

Be creative as you identify three distinct methods for identifying which banks have excess cash or other means for releasing some of the $60,000. However, remember to maintain cash bank security as you brainstorm new methodologies.

2. An international guest tenders $171 in U.S. funds and #2,000 from his native land to settle an outstanding account of $206.20. #s are being purchased by the hotel for 51.50 per U.S. dollar. What must the cashier do now to settle the account? Assume that the guest has more U.S. dollars; assume that he doesn't. The hotel cashier has no foreign funds in the drawer.

3. Explain how international tourism helps balance the trade deficit of the United States. How does international tourism worsen the deficit?

4. Sketch and complete a cashier's envelope for October 11 showing the details of the turn-in and the amount of due back. (City-ledger collections are handled by the accounting office. No provisions are made for cash over or short; the cashier covers both.)

Given for Problem

House bank	$1,800.00
Advances to guests	$181.15
House vouchers	$16.20
Vending machine refunds	$0.50
Received from guests	$7,109.40
Cash in the drawer exclusive of other cash listed below	$1,721.00
Traveler's checks	$2,675.00

Personal checks:

Washington	$75.25
Lincoln	$310.00
Jefferson	$44.98
Carter	$211.90
Kennedy	$55.00
Others	$1,876.85
Bills of $100 denomination	10 each
Torn and dirty currency	$62.00
Coins	$680.14

5. Imagine that your hotel operates in a community where the incidence of counterfeiting is quite high. Develop a procedure for all front-desk cashiers in terms of accepting U.S. currency. Remember to be sensitive to the amount of time it takes to examine a bill properly and the fact that the cashier may be busy with other guests in line. Also, discuss whether the procedure should be eased for smaller denominations: $50s?, $20s? What if the cashier knows the guest from previous hotel visits? Be certain that your policy distinguishes between the newer currency (introduced in 1996 and enhanced in 2004) and the older currency (which will be in circulation for many years to come).

6. Some hotels prevent cashiers from knowing their net receipts. Without knowing net receipts, the cashier turns everything in from the day's drawer except the bank. If the drawer is significantly over for the shift, the cashier is none the wiser and is not tempted to steal the amount of the overage. Do you support such a policy? Are there any drawbacks to not allowing cashiers access to their net receipt figures?

AN INCIDENT IN HOTEL MANAGEMENT

No, a Real Train Wreck!

The passenger was happy to get away with his life. They said the train jumped the tracks minutes before the station. Emergency help arrived quickly. Mr. Rider was checked at triage and released. The police gave him a ride to the hotel. That's a story to tell the family!

"Hello, I need a room. Rider's the name. Bet I look as if I were in a train wreck."

To this very disheveled and disreputable looking individual, the guest-service replied politely, "Indeed, you do, Mr. Rider. Please sign the card. How will you be paying for the room?"

"Uh-oh, I've lost my wallet, so I have neither cash nor a credit card. The hotel will have to trust me."

"Sir, we have no provision for that. You have no reservation and you say you are not a member of our frequent-stay program. Why not use the ATM? There's one right in our lobby."

"But I really was in a train wreck."

Questions: Was there a management failure here; if so, what?

What is the hotel's immediate response (or action) to the incident?

What further, long-run action should management take, if any?

ANSWERS TO TRUE/FALSE QUIZ

1. True. For front-office cashiers, cash flows in two directions: receipts and paid-outs. For all other cashiers, cash flows one way—receipts.

2. False. Cash settlements for hotel account balances are relatively rare, probably ranging below 5%. This is especially true for corporate hotels, where almost all accounts are settled as either a transfer to the city ledger's corporate account or paid by credit card.

3. True. By signing an imprest voucher, the restaurant would secure funds to purchase the butter. The receipt and any remaining change would be returned to the imprest petty cash fund.

4. True. The starting bank plus net receipts equal the "should have." Comparing that with what is actually in the drawer (by court) at the end of the shift ("do have") determines whether or not the cashier is over or short.

5. True. These are all security features currently found on U.S. currency.

PART V
Technology

The Night Audit

Outline

THE AUDITOR AND THE AUDIT

Hotels close the business day by means of the night audit. Guest folios (accounts receivable) are balanced and reconciled. Hotel guests come and go at all hours. Their folios must be current and accurate when called up. That's the primary job of the night audit. Since hotel sales are recorded mostly on folios—guests charge purchases to their rooms—reconciling the folios enables the night auditor to also reconcile the bulk of the day's income activity. That's the second aim of the night audit. With so much data gathered, the third purpose evolves almost automatically: Present the information in reports that help management do its job.

Uncovering clerical mistakes made by the desk throughout the day was the original focus of the night audit. Its paper-and-pencil procedure (the transcript) dates to the 1920s. This chapter retains these outdated procedures as a means of explaining what takes place within the heart of the computerized audit. PMS and hand-posted records have the same goals. With tedious hand-prepared audits, balancing the folio was the main thrust. With PMSs, the emphasis changes. Folio errors are still being repaired, they just are not visible. Readers can see a pencil-and-paper folio, voucher, and transcript that makes the records. They can see only the output, the results, of a PMS audit: a printout. Readers who follow the pencil-and-paper explanations of the chapter will better understand the modern audit.

The night audit ends the hotel's day. All records of accounts receivable (A/R) are collected, corrected, and summarized by the night-audit crew—in a small hotel, no more than a single person. Closing the day's accounting records validates the work of the previous shifts and provides information for the issues of the upcoming day.

What night auditors do and how they do it have changed dramatically since the introduction of electronic data processing. EDP has altered the focus and changed the procedure. Precomputer audits concentrated on uncovering the errors of pencil-and-paper systems. Fewer errors occur with property management systems (PMSs), so management reporting has become the new emphasis.

The Night Auditor

Despite the title, the night auditor is rarely a trained accountant and is an auditor only by the broadest definition. In general terms, an *auditor* is an appraiser–reporter of the accuracy and integrity of records and financial statements. One type of auditing, internal auditing, involves procedural control and an accounting review of operations and records. Internal auditing also reports on the activities of other employees. It is this final definition that best explains the role of the hotel night auditor.

No special knowledge of accounting or even of bookkeeping's debits and credits is required of the night auditor. That's why this and previous chapters identify accounting explanations in a different format and font. Having this knowledge is helpful and desirable, but it is sufficient for the auditor to have good arithmetic skills, self-discipline, and a penchant for detailed work. Auditors must be careful, accurate, and reliable. The latter trait is an especially redeeming one because the unattractive working hours make replacements difficult to recruit and almost impossible to find on short notice.

Work Shift.   The audit crew works the graveyard shift, arriving sometime between 11 PM and midnight (see Chapter 3). The shift ends 8 hours later, at 7 or 8 in the morning. The night audit reconciles records that are needed to start the new day. Failing to reconcile keeps the auditor on the job until everything is in balance, regardless of the hour.

General Duties.   The audit staff of a large hotel consists of a senior auditor and assistants. Guest-service agents and even cashiers may also be on hand. Their presence frees the auditors to do their job without interruption. In smaller hotels, the audit team relieves the entire desk, filling the jobs of reservationist, guest-service agent, cashier, telephone operator, and auditor. Whether or not auditors assume these jobs, they must be conversant with them. It is those very duties that the night audit audits.

When the actual tasks are taken on, the night auditor is likely to be the only responsible employee on duty. The auditor assumes the position of night manager, whether the title is there or not. The same range of problems faced by the day manager is involved, but to a lesser degree. Emergencies, credit, mechanical breakdowns, accidents, and deaths are some of the situations encountered by the night manager.

Security and incident reports must be filed by either the night auditor/manager alone or cooperatively with the security staff. Without a security contingent, the auditor may be the one who walks security rounds and fire watch.

Few hotels of less than 150 rooms employ a night engineer. Yet management has generally been lax in preparing the night auditor/manager for the problems that arise in this area of responsibility. Fire, plumbing problems, power failures, elevator mishaps, and boiler troubles are matters that may take the auditor's time.

Equally time consuming are guest relations: a noisy party going into the early hours of the morning; the victorious football team shouting in the lobby; a sick guest; visiting conventioneers in the 11th-floor suite; paid reservations yet to arrive and the hotel 100% occupied. Such are the nonaccounting matters for which the night auditor might be responsible.

Mature judgment and experience are needed to carry out these nonaudit functions. The combination of audit skills, working hours, and responsibility merit a higher salary for the night auditor than for the average guest-service agent, but the spread is not noticeably larger.

The Audit

The night audit is an audit of accounts receivable, an audit of guest folios. Most hotel sales are account-receivable sales. Guests obtain services such as room, food, and beverage with a signature, a promise to pay; an account receivable. Cash sales throughout the hotel are not the night auditor's responsibility. Income auditors (day auditors in contrast to night auditors) review cash sales in conjunction with the general cashier (see Chapter 12). Folio sales (the night auditors' work) passes the next morning to the same income (or revenue or day) auditors. Then both types of sales, cash and credit, are combined. From that step comes the daily report to the manager and, ultimately, entries into the hotel's sales journal, the permanent records of the business.

Reconciling Accounts Receivable.

Every business authenticates its accounts receivable periodically. Whereas most businesses do this monthly or even less frequently, hotels do the job nightly: the night audit. The night audit verifies the accuracy and completeness of each folio each night. In so doing, it also verifies all charge sales made throughout the hotel that day.

Hotel auditors lack the luxury of time because hotelkeeping is a very transient business. Arrivals and departures keep coming and going without notice at all hours of the day and night. Each new day brings more charges and more credits whether or not the previous day has been reconciled. There is no holding a departing guest until the folio is ready. The night audit must make certain that it always is ready.

The pressure of immediacy is missing with city-ledger guests. City-ledger receivables are not registered, so their billing cycle is more like the accounts receivable of other businesses. Depending on the nature of the original charge, city receivables are billed for the first time three days—sometimes 10 days—after the charge is incurred.

The Closeout Hour.

The night audit reconciles the records of a single day. Since hotels never close, management selects an arbitrary hour, the *closeout hour* (also called the *close of the day*), to end one day officially and start the next. The actual time selected depends on the operating hours of the lounges, restaurants, and room service of the particular hotel. Each new charge changes the folio, so the audit is prepared when changes are infrequent—in the early morning hours when guests are abed. Departmental charges before the closeout hour are included in today's records. Departmental charges after the closeout hour are posted to the folio on the following date after the night audit has been completed.

A late closeout hour captures the last of the day's charges, but it puts pressure on the auditing staff, which needs to finish the job before early departures begin leaving. On the other hand, too early a closeout hour throws all the charges of the late evening into the following day, in effect, delaying their audit for 24 hours. Standardized stationery forms list midnight as the closeout hour (see Exhibit 10–7), but the actual time is set by management.

Posting Room Charges

Posting room charges during a pencil-and-paper audit is an onerous task in a large hotel. Posting room charges during an electronic audit allows the staff time for coffee.

Posting Room Charges Manually.

Posting (recording) room charges is one of the night auditor's major tasks. Before the advent of the PMS, room charges were posted manually. That required each folio to be removed one by one from the cashier's well (see Exhibit 10–3). The room charge and the room tax were recorded in pencil, the column totaled, and the folio returned to the well in room number sequence. Exhibit 13–1 illustrates the results on a manual folio: $60 recorded on the horizontal line labeled "rooms" and $3 for the tax. The $78 and $6.24 posted in Exhibit 10–2 offers a second illustration.

Once the room charge and tax are posted, the night auditor adds the column, which includes the previous day's total. (The second columns of Exhibits 13–1 and 10–2 illustrate the addition.) The new balance is carried forward from the bottom of the column to the top of the column of the following day. In this manner a cumulative balance is maintained, and the manual folio is ready at any time for the departing guest.

THE CITY HOTEL
ANYWHERE, U.S.A.

#8001

NAME _B. M. Oncampus_

ADDRESS _1 Campus Rd., University City_

ROOM NUMBER _1406_   RATE _60_

NUMBER IN THE PARTY _1_   CLERK _ABC_

DATE OF ARRIVAL _10/5_   DATE OF DEPARTURE _10/7_

CHANGES: ROOM NO. _____ TO ROOM NO. _____ NEW RATE _____

DATE	10/5	10/6	10/7				
BAL.FWD		(19)	70				
ROOMS	60	60					
TAX	3	3					
FOOD	10	12					
BAR		6					
TELEPH							
LAUNDRY							
CASH DISBR GARAGE	8	8					
TRANSFERS							
TOT CHRG	81	70					
CASH							
ALLOWANCES							
TRANSFERS	100						
TOT CRDS	100						
BAL DUE	(19)	70					

Exhibit 13–1   Pencil-and-paper folios (see also Exhibit 10–2) accumulate daily charges in separate vertical columns. Figures from the column of a given day are copied onto a transcript sheet for balancing during that night audit. Column 10/6 appears on line 1 of Exhibit 13–12. The initial value of ($19) is a credit; the hotel owes the guest. Pencil-and-paper folios are no longer used. They are included throughout the text to illustrate the relationship of the folio to the audit. That relationship is not visible with folios and audits prepared by electronic property management systems. Chapter 10 provides many illustrations of today's electronic folios. *(For ease in reading, several illustrations use small dollar values, which may not seem realistic.)*

Included in the cumulative total are departmental charges other than room. These are posted throughout the day by the front-office staff as the charges arrive at the front desk from the operating departments. Exhibit 13–1 shows these as food, bar, and garage. Garage is a cash paid-out made by the hotel to the garage for the guest (see Chapter 12).

Manual System Errors.   With a manual (pencil-and-paper) system, the same values are written repeatedly. Guests' names, room numbers, and dollar values are recorded many times by different individuals on reg cards and folios, vouchers, and control sheets. The night auditor rewrites the figures once more: room rates, departmental charges, credits, and others. Writing, rewriting, and adding columns manually create numerous human errors that PMSs avoid. Point-of-sale (POS) terminals (see Exhibit 13–2) communicate electronically, bypassing the need for written vouchers between the department and the desk.

Additional errors are inherent in the manual system. Poor handwriting is the most obvious one. When handwritten, figures 1 and 7, 4 and 9, and 3 and 8 are often confused. Recopying also causes slides and transpositions. Slides are misplaced units, which may involve decimals. Saying 53 21 mentally or aloud may result in either 53.21 or 5,321 being recorded. Transpositions are similar errors, but the digits are reordered—53.21 may become 35.21.

Even simple addition causes problems. The auditor may create errors by incorrectly totaling the folios, the control sheet, or the packets of vouchers. Adding machines help, but there is no guarantee that the figures are entered accurately. Hand audits still require adding-machine tapes to allow comparison between the actual figures and those entered into the calculator.

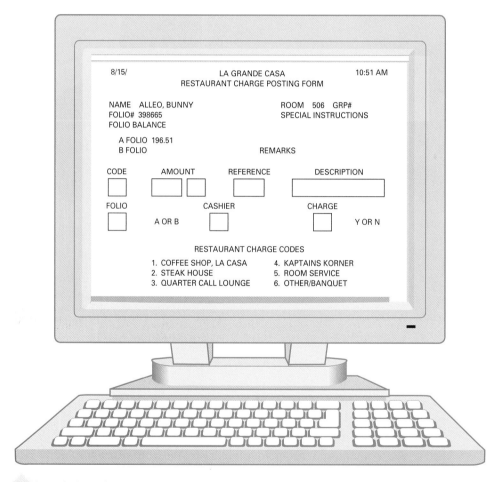

Exhibit 13–2   The display screen of the point-of-sale (POS) terminal guides departmental cashiers through the posting sequence. (See also Exhibit 10–8.) The posted charge appears instantaneously on the folio maintained in memory by the property management system. Without a POS, cashiers communicated with written vouchers, which had to be forwarded to the desk for posting, either with a POS located there or manually. Poor handwriting and frequent handling increase the number of errors when a POS is not used.

Subtracting one total from another highlights the error. Errors of addition usually appear as differences of 1 in the unit columns. If the difference in the totals is 1 cent, 10 cents, $1, $10, and so on, the culprit is likely to be an error of addition. If not an error of addition, it might be a slide or transposition. Slides and transpositions are flagged when the difference in the total is evenly divisible by 9. For example, the difference between 53.21 and 35.21 is 18, evenly divisible by 9. Searching for mistakes begins by looking for errors of addition or transpositions and slides.

Posting Room Charges Electronically.   Electronic posting is easier and faster than manual posting. There are no physical folios. Labor is saved in simply not moving 100, 500, or 1,000 folios in and out of a cashier's well (cashier's bucket). Room charges and taxes are not posted individually. Folios are not totaled arithmetically. The property management system does the work. Memory stores the room rates and taxes, updates the individual folios, and prints them on demand. Chapter 10 illustrates several such folios.

There are no errors of addition with a property management system. But they do crash! Not often, but an emergency backup is part of every night audit. Exhibit 13–3 illustrates the nightly report that is prepared at the close of each electronic audit. In form and content, it is much like the hand-prepared audit illustrated in Exhibit 13–12. Guest-service agents can work from the closing balance of each folio (available by room number) even if the PMS crashes on the following day.

THE CITY HOTEL, ANYWHERE, U.S.A.						Page 1
03/16 Guest Ledger Summary Report						
Room #	Name	Folio #	Open Bal	Charges	Credits	Close Bal
3004	Huent	0457	–0–	81.30	.00	81.30
3005	Wanake	0398	65.72	91.44	.00	157.16
3008	Lee	0431	132.00	101.01	.00	233.01
3110	Langden	0420	–0–	99.87	100.00	0.13–
3111	Nelston	0408	233.65	145.61	.00	379.26
3117	O'Harra	0461	789.75	121.10	.00	910.85
6121	Chiu	0444	32.60–	99.87	.00	67.27
6133	Valex	0335	–0–	165.30	.00	165.30
7003	Roberts	0428	336.66	109.55	.00	446.21
7009	Haittenberg	0454	19.45	87.43	.00	106.88
Totals			44,651.07	18,632.98	950.00	62,334.05

Exhibit 13–3   A hard (printed) copy of closing folio balances is prepared nightly as part of the PMS audit and left at the desk. The new day's opening balances (last night's closing balances) are then available in case the computer fails the following day. Each column of the report corresponds to a column of the pencil-and-paper audit. For example, the counterpart of the Charges column of this Exhibit is column 16, Total Debits, of Exhibit 13–12. (Charges and debits are interchangeable terms.)

Room Charges Not Posted During the Night Audit. In four special circumstances guest-service agents, rather than night auditors, post room charges. Chapter 10 discussed the four in detail. (1) *Day rates* (also called *use rates* or *part-day rates*) is one instance. (2) Extra room charges for late check outs are another special case. (3) During the heady days of the late 1990s, when occupancy was high and hotels thought they could do no wrong, a penalty rate was posted by the day shift if guests failed to stay through their reservation commitment. (4) Guest-service agents sometimes post rates for paid-in-advance guests.

Revenue Verification

Night audits have two objectives. Reconciling accounts receivable is one. Each folio (receivable) is updated nightly so an accurate bill can be presented on demand. By the time the night audit begins, hundreds or thousands of charges will have been posted to guest folios. A small highway property may have room and tax postings only. Full-service hotels have charges from dining rooms and bars; local and long-distant telephone calls; laundry and valet; greens fees; saunas; ski tows; inroom safes, films, and bars. The night audit proves the accuracy of all: that the income (the sale) has been recorded and the guest has been charged.

Chapter 10 emphasized that every departmental charge has equal debits and credits. Each service that guests buy has an offsetting income to one department or another. What takes place individually—one folio being increased and one sale being recorded—has application to the audit. A rule of mathematics—the total is equal to the sum of the parts—plays a fundamental role in balancing the audit. All the income earned by any one department, say, room service, must equal the total of all the individual room-service charges posted to guest folios. If each individual room-service event increases a guest's folio and simultaneously increases income to the room-service department, then the totals of each should agree, that is, be in balance. Since there are hundreds of posting and hundreds of folios, this simple fact is not evident immediately. The night audit reconciles the two by making evident this equality: The total income earned by each department from accounts receivable sales is the same total charged to guest folios.

The accounting rules apply:

Increases in assets, including *accounts receivable* and cash, are made with debits.
Increases in incomes (sales of rooms, *food*, beverage, etc.) are made with credits.

 Debit: Accounts Receivable/Guest's Folio 50
  Credit: Proper Departmental (room, *food*, beverage, spa, etc.) Sale 50
 Explanation: Guest charged food in the coffee shop.

RECONCILING USING A PROPERTY MANAGEMENT SYSTEM

The night audit provides the most spectacular demonstration of the PMS in action. Only those who have machine-posted using the NCR (National Cash Register) system or hand-copied pages of transcript sheets can appreciate the savings in time and efficiency. Labor savings, the often touted but seldom delivered advantage of computer installations, is certainly evident in the PMS night audit. Since a minimum crew is always needed, the greatest labor savings are at the largest hotels.

The computer has altered the mechanics of the audit, its purpose, and its scope. Traditionally, the night audit concentrated on finding and correcting errors—except the errors were caused by the system. Initial errors, transmittal errors, posting errors, and errors of addition are inherent in the hand audit. The entire thrust of the hand audit is discovery and repair. The computer audit has no such problems. The information that is input with the departmental POS appears everywhere, and everywhere it appears the same. Of course, there are errors of input, and these are discussed shortly.

Interfacing Different Systems

The property management system began life as a rooms device. Its initial purpose was limited to the front office and was seen as a replacement for the NCR audit. The NCR[1] posting machine was, in turn, a replacement for the pencil-and-paper audit. Additional tasks, called interfaces, were affixed to the PMS as its capacity grew. Linkages were added to support point-of-sale (POS) terminals in food and beverage outlets. Then came call accounting systems (CAS), a type of POS for telephone charges (see Chapter 14). These and other interfaces—linkages between equipment made by different manufacturers—created equipment issues. One manufacturer made the PMS, another the POS, and still a third created the interface linkage. The system grew willy-nilly as additional interfaces were added again and again: inroom minibars; housekeeping status; reservation programs; and more. The more the merrier, but the more frequently the system crashed.

The American Hotel & Lodging Association encouraged manufacturers to develop integration standards.[2] Improving the compatibility of different products by different manufacturers reduced the frequency of computer downtime. Minimizing computer crashes minimized service interruptions. The AH&LA's effort was effective, but the real push came from the large hotel chains and franchisors.[3] To increase seamless connectivity, particularly communications between the franchisor's reservation center and the franchisee's property, one system was installed chainwide. Common reservation equipment and programs have made last room availability (see Chapter 5) accessible across a wide range of channels, including the Web.

Technology suppliers have followed the hotel industry in more than one sense. Both are consolidating. The number of dealers has fallen dramatically from the 100 or so that initially competed to a dozen good vendors.

Verifying Basic Data

Both the manual audit (pencil-and-paper) and the electronic audit (property-management-system) summarize the day's activities at the closeout hour. Although either audit could be done at any time, preference is for the quiet hours of the business day when there is little posting activity; hence the term "night audit." The late hour is especially important for the

---

[1]NCR is the abbreviation for National Cash Register Company, manufacturer of the NCR 4200 front-office-posting machine that was once widely used by hotels and banks.

[2]The AH&LA worked with several large chains, notably Holiday and Microsoft to make it happen. Vendors were encouraged to adopt HITIS (Hospitality Information Technology Integration Standards) knowing that their bid solicitation would receive greater acceptance. The first set of standards was the interface between the PMS and the POS terminal.

[3]InterContinental Hotels chose the MICROS system for its Candlewood Suites hotels. "We realized that because of the scale (more than 75 hotels) we could save roughly $US 15,000 per hotel," said vice president Gustaaf Schrils. *HOTELS*, April 2006, p. 54.

PMS audit because departmental POS terminals are shut down temporarily. Changes to guest folios must wait until the audit is finished. Manual audits are not quite as limiting. With much erasing and rewriting, pencil-and-paper audits can accommodate folio changes during the audit process.

Closing Routine.   Every night audit has a fixed procedure for closing out the day (see Exhibit 13–4). A major part of the PMS audit requires nothing more than monitoring. Room charges and taxes are posted automatically. So is the cumulative balance on each folio. In contrast, the pencil-and-paper auditor writes the values and adds the columns (see Exhibit 13–1). The PMS audit sets the stage for tomorrow with the summary printout illustrated by Exhibit 13–3. It does so because the closing balance of one day is the same value as the opening balance of the following day. That's also true of the pencil-and-paper audit's transcript sheet (see Exhibit 13–12).

Verifying departmental revenues is another part of the audit. Each time an account receivable (folio) is charged, a counterbalancing record should appear as income for one of the operating departments. Unlike pencil-and-paper systems, PMS discrepancies are rare. POS terminals automatically record the same figure on the folio and the department revenue. Pencil-and-paper audits have numerous handwritten entries. First by the departmental cashier, then the guest-service agent who posts to the folio, then the auditor. Each permits handwriting errors, misplaced values, and mathematical mistakes.

The night auditor finishes the PMS audit with an end-of-the-day routine much like that of the hand audit (See Exhibit 13–4). A trial balance of debits and credits is made. Debits are charges to the receivable folios; credits are earnings in the several departments. The day and date are closed and the next day opened. The POS terminals are put back online. Monthly and annual totals are accumulated as part of the reporting process that follows next. The sequence varies at each hotel. At some properties, the routine is preprogrammed; at others, the update proceeds by prompts from the system to which the auditor responds.

Folios of guests who are departing the following day may be printed as part of the audit procedure. Preprinting folios speeds the check-outs. Copies are filed by room number sequence in the cashier's well and produced without delay when the departing guest appears at the desk. If subsequent charges—breakfast, for example—alter the previous night's balance, the old folio is merely discarded and a new one printed.

A copy of the preprinted folio might be left under the guest-room door for use in express check-outs. (This won't be necessary if the hotel provides express check-out by means of the TV.)

Express Check-Out.   Express check-out is one of the exciting stories of PMS installations. Standing in line to check out has been the bane of hotel guests, who are always in a hurry. Flexible terminals able to shift quickly from registration to departure status, and vice versa, were one of the first PMS innovations to focus on the problem. This increased the number of front-office stations when demand was greatest. Lines were shortened, but not enough.

Because early output printers were slow, many operations began printing the folios of expected departures during the previous night's audit. From printing them to delivering them to the room wasn't a large conceptual jump, but it created *zip-out check-out*, also called *speedy check-out, no-wait check-out*, or *VIP check-out*.

Zip-out check-out is only for guests using direct billing or credit cards—but that is almost everyone. At first, guests who wanted the service completed a request card. Later,

Closing Routine for Position of Combined Night Auditor/Guest Service Agent

Attend to Relief of the Previous Shift
    Compare late arrivals (reservations) with room availability
    Examine the front-office log
    Retrieve keys to drawers; watchman's clock; etc.
    Review issues: messages to be delivered; equipment failures; noisy revelers
    Set wake-up-call clock if equipment is not yet automated
    Verify cash drawer if cashier's banks are carried over
    Walk the first safety patrol/fire watch while previous shift is still on duty
    Witness cash turn-in of previous shift's deposit

Before the Income Audit
    Check cashier's bucket; many desks use it for special messages
    Close POS interfaces
    Post any vouchers not yet posted
    Prepare non–dollar-denominated reports such as:
        Inhouse list (night clerk's report)
        Tomorrow's arrival list
        Tomorrow's departure list
    Sell nonguaranteed room reservations

During the Income Audit
    Identify special-case folios: high balances
    Match due-bill folios with due bills, if any
    Post room and tax charges
    Print folios for under-the-door delivery
    Reconcile audit: Source documents agree with folio totals and departmental incomes
    Total and reconcile coupons

Following the Income Audit
    Back up data
    Charge no-shows who have guaranteed arrivals with credit cards
    Complete the night auditor's report to the manager
    Leave completed materials properly sequenced for the day auditor
    Prepare reverse housekeeper's report
    Prepare dollar-denominated reports
    Prepare statistical reports
    Reconcile credit cards and prepare reports
    Reconnect POS interfaces
    Reset all systems for the new day
    Verify credit-card revenues and prepare appropriate reports

Other Duties
    Coordinate with incoming shift
    Deposit cash collections with cashier's report after relief shift arrives
    Interact with guests as needed
    Maintain log
    Monitor lights and door locks
    Set up continental breakfast
    Walk a fire/security watch

Exhibit 13–4   A list of duties arranged chronologically and alphabetically for the combined position of night auditor/guest-service agent. Small hotels should support the position with a security watch. Large hotels would have a full front-office staff on duty, leaving the audit group free to do its main job.

every departure using a credit card had a folio under the door. If the folio was accurate, the guests left after completing one additional step: They either telephoned an extension to give notice, or they dropped a form with the key in a lobby box (see Exhibit 13–5). The final folio was mailed to the guest within a day or two, and the charges were processed through the credit-card company.

Express check-out leaped ahead with the interface of Spectradyne's TV pay-movie system into the hotel's PMS. Delivering folios to the room was necessary no longer. The folio appeared on the TV set any time the guest wanted it. From then on, the procedure was the same. With a click of the remote control, the guest signaled departure. As with zip-out check-out, the folio followed in the mail, and the credit-card charges were processed. An integrated PMS transfers the charges, which have been accumulated in the front-office folio, to the city ledger module.

Another great leap forward was taken when self-check-in/check-out terminals were interfaced with the ever-expanding PMS. At freestanding locations within the lobby, self-check-out terminals present guests with their folios and accept their credit cards to speed them on their way. Having guests leave using the very terminal at which they registered (see Exhibit 8–7) was once a great achievement. Chapter 11 highlights a more recent upgrade: emailing guests an electronic folio. Each innovation brings the industry a step closer to the fully electronic hotel (see Exhibit 13–6 and Chapter 14).

PMS Posting Errors.

Property management systems are not error free. Staffers make mistakes whether the system is manual or electronic. Human errors are not offset by high-priced equipment. Computerized front offices minimize errors and facilitate corrections, but they do not create error-free environments.

A detailed list of transactions is the first step in reconciling departmental charges against guest folios. A hard (printed) copy itemizes transactions by POS terminals and by reference codes. The folio exhibits of Chapter 10 illustrate these codes. Charges to the folios require a code number (automatic with many POSs) and the number of the original voucher, if there is one. Postings will not clear without that information. A second code, the guest's room number, and sometimes the first three letters of the guest's surname, are also required. Exhibit 13–2 illustrates the screen that a dining room cashier uses to post the charge.

Matching the guest-room keycard (with its magnetic strip) to the PMS's registration data file is another means of verifying a guest's identity. The guest inserts the keycard into a POS and the system verifies the identification. Implementation of this system has already begun, but it may be replaced even before it goes into general use. The smart cards of Chapters 12 and 14 suggest that one's own credit card may become the keycard for the next generation of electronic locks.

The POS reduces receivable losses by rejecting invalid postings. The guest may have checked out already; be a paid-in-advance customer with no charges permitted; or have exceeded the credit-card floor or other credit ceiling set by the hotel. Late charges are reduced dramatically when POS terminals are in place.

Departing guests sometimes challenge the accuracy of departmental postings. Denying that the charges were ever made, they ask for offsetting allowances from the front desk. Obtaining a copy of the check (voucher) signed by the guest to show its accuracy is a slow process with a pencil-and-paper system. So time consuming is it that the front-office cashier simply grants the allowance without further investigation. Until recently, the results were the same with a PMS. Now disputed charges are being met with proof in a program first introduced at the Boca Raton Resort and Beach Club. The PMS is able to display the protested voucher.

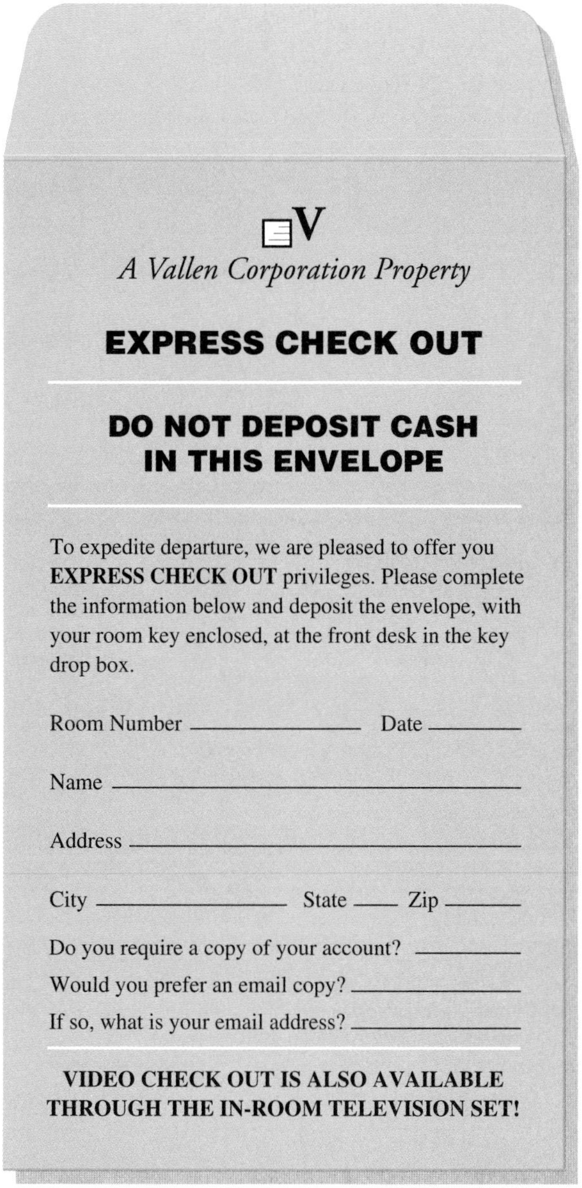

⊟V

A Vallen Corporation Property

EXPRESS CHECK OUT

DO NOT DEPOSIT CASH IN THIS ENVELOPE

To expedite departure, we are pleased to offer you **EXPRESS CHECK OUT** privileges. Please complete the information below and deposit the envelope, with your room key enclosed, at the front desk in the key drop box.

Room Number _____ Date _____

Name _____

Address _____

City _____ State ____ Zip _____

Do you require a copy of your account? _____

Would you prefer an email copy? _____

If so, what is your email address? _____

VIDEO CHECK OUT IS ALSO AVAILABLE THROUGH THE IN-ROOM TELEVISION SET!

Exhibit 13–5 Express check-out began with the envelope shown, which explains the procedure. The process shifted in sequence to under-door delivery of folios; to inroom TV screens; to front-office consoles; and, most recently, to emailed folios, as described in Chapter 10. Zip-out check-outs assure harried guests of a quick departure, but keep the desk updated on room status.

Reports from the Night Audit

An unlimited number of reports can be generated by the PMS once it captures the information. Data can be arranged and reordered in a variety of ways. The registration card is a good example. From it, several different reports can be generated: geographic origin of guests; membership in groups; credit limits; company affiliations; average length of stay; and rate level preference.

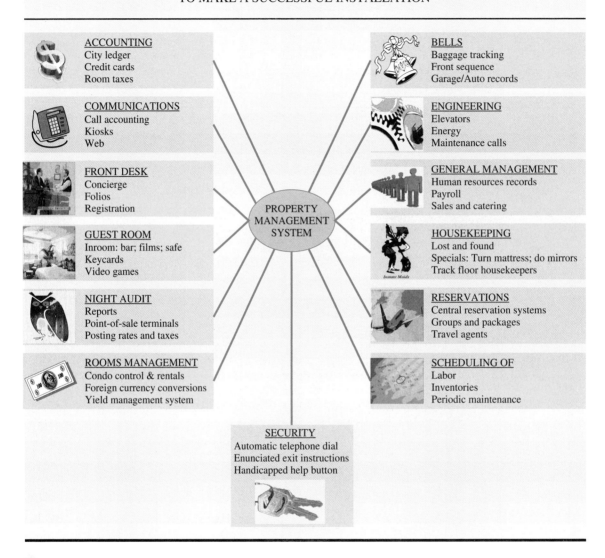

THE MANY **INTERFACES** OF THE PMS
HAVE BEEN **INTEGRATED**
TO MAKE A SUCCESSFUL INSTALLATION

ACCOUNTING
City ledger
Credit cards
Room taxes

COMMUNICATIONS
Call accounting
Kiosks
Web

FRONT DESK
Concierge
Folios
Registration

GUEST ROOM
Inroom: bar; films; safe
Keycards
Video games

NIGHT AUDIT
Reports
Point-of-sale terminals
Posting rates and taxes

ROOMS MANAGEMENT
Condo control & rentals
Foreign currency conversions
Yield management system

PROPERTY MANAGEMENT SYSTEM

BELLS
Baggage tracking
Front sequence
Garage/Auto records

ENGINEERING
Elevators
Energy
Maintenance calls

GENERAL MANAGEMENT
Human resources records
Payroll
Sales and catering

HOUSEKEEPING
Lost and found
Specials: Turn mattress; do mirrors
Track floor housekeepers

RESERVATIONS
Central reservation systems
Groups and packages
Travel agents

SCHEDULING OF
Labor
Inventories
Periodic maintenance

SECURITY
Automatic telephone dial
Enunciated exit instructions
Handicapped help button

Exhibit 13–6 Property management systems have taken on new dimensions. Rather than merely interfacing separate functions, newer PMSs integrate the whole. Separate bits of information, islands of unconnected data, characterized the PMS's development. Both users and suppliers are moving to integrate the whole. Touchscreen technology has made the adaptation easier. The computer's role in hotelkeeping is just in its beginning stages. Chapter 14 broadens the view.

The ease of obtaining reports undoubtedly contributed to the vast numbers that were demanded when PMSs were first introduced. Much of that has shaken out. Management took control and pared the numbers by emphasizing exception reports. One no longer sees piles of reports prepared by the night auditor trashed, unread by the recipient the next day.

Still, the night audit produces a wide range of reports for all departments of the front office. Many of these are day-end summaries, since unit managers use (through display terminals or hard-copy print) the same data several times throughout the day. Some reports are traditional from the days of the pencil-and-paper audit: the balancing of accounts receivable, credit alerts, and statistical reports to the manager.

Turnkey Systems.   With a turnkey installation, the buyer/hotel merely "turns the key" to activate the PMS. The vendor has programmed the system including the reports. Nothing is ever quite that easy, but it is unlikely that the industry would be so far along if the burden of development had not shifted from individual hotel companies to industrywide vendors.

Prior to the turnkey concept, each hotel shopped among manufacturers for its own hardware. Then it developed its own software by employing computer specialists, who at that time knew nothing about the business of keeping a hotel. The large data processing departments that appeared as a result of inhouse programming disappeared quickly with the introduction of the turnkey package.

Now systems are purchased off the shelf, shopping among suppliers for an existing system that is close to what the hotel needs. And systems are close to what is needed. Generic programs are much alike because hotels are much alike. What differences there are in off-the-shelf products diminish as third- and fourth-generation programs are developed. Each generation improves flow and screening, new or missing functions being added to remain competitive. Most recently, the push has been toward a Windows/Intel environment with dragged icons, touch screens, and reduced training time.

Turnkey companies now dominate the field. Single suppliers furnish both the hardware and the software. If the supplier specializes in one segment, other vendors supply the missing parts. Responsibility remains with the primary vendor, who puts together the package, gets it up and running, trains the staff, and services the installation—not without some major grief for the hotel, of course.

Vendors who adopt the Hospitality Information Technology Integration Standards (HITIS) that the AH&LA encouraged offer systems that interface with others who comply with HITIS. Hotels that specify HITIS in their bid solicitations enjoy reduced risks, lower costs, and savings in installation time. Access to the World Wide Web is changing the hotel's PMS from one with dedicated hardware to one that uses Web technology. As that happens, the front-office workstation becomes a general-purpose rather than a specific-purpose screen.

It is difficult to say whether a uniform need created the turnkey system or whether mass production created standardization across the industry. That standardization is most evident in the reports churned out during the night audit.[4]

Reports provide information for management's use. Property management systems have the data from many transactions and can arrange that data to spew out numerous reports. Many are viewed on screens throughout the day as circumstances change and decisions are needed. They are also formalized by nightly printouts covering a range of topics. Exception reports and the daily report to the manager, discussed later, are the most carefully examined.

Exception Reports.   Exception reports highlight digressions from the norm. Reporting everything that happens overwhelms the user. Reports by exception alert

---

[4]On its Web site, Micros Systems, Inc. (Beltsville, MD) advertises over 150 standard report templates.

the reader to problem areas without a time-consuming inspection of all the data. A credit-limit report best illustrates the group. Listing the folio balance of every guest requires a tedious search to uncover possible problems. An exception report lists only those folios close to the hotel's ceiling. There's no need to scrutinize pages of data to find a problem. More important, such a report grabs management's immediate attention and action. Cumbersome reports are usually put aside for later examination, which never takes place.

Allowance Report: identifies who authorized each allowance, who received the allowance, the amount, and the reasons.

Cashier's Overage and Shortage Report: pinpoints by stations overages and shortages that exceed predetermined norms.

Comps Report: similar to an allowance report; identifies who authorized each comp, who received the comp, the amount, and the reasons.

No Luggage Report: lists occupied rooms in which there is no baggage (see Exhibit 13–15).

Room Rate Variance Report: compares actual rates to standard rate schedule and identifies the authority for granting the variance (not meaningful if the hotel is discounting frequently and deeply).

Skipper Report: provides room identification, dollar amount, and purported name and address.

Writeoff Report: lists daily writeoffs, usually late charges, whose account balances are less than a specified amount.

Downtime Reports.   Downtime reports, for use when the computer crashes, provide insurance against disaster. Like a great deal of insurance, the reports usually go unused because emergencies rarely materialize. Downtime reports are dumped 24 hours later when the contingency has passed and the backup reports of the following day have been printed.

Folio Balance Report: itemizes in room number sequence the previous day's record of each account receivable (the folio) as illustrated in Exhibit 13–3; comparable to columns 1, 2, 4 and 5, 16, 20, 21, and 22 of a pencil-and-paper transcript (see Exhibit 13–12).

Guest-List Report: alphabetizes registered guests with their room numbers; computer version of a manual information rack.

Room Status Report: identifies vacant, out-of-order, on change, and occupied rooms at the beginning of the new day; a computerized room count sheet (see Exhibit 13–14).

Disk Backup: not a report, but part of the closing sequence of the auditor's shift; data is replicated onto another disk to be retrieved if a malfunction erases the working disk.

Credit Reports.   The night auditor is the credit manager's first line of defense. In that capacity, the night auditor handles both routine matters and special credit situations.

Mention has already been made of the auditor's responsibility to preprint the folios of expected check-outs. Although not nearly as numerous, folios must also be prepared for guests who remain longer than one week. On the guest's seventh night, the auditor prints the folio for delivery to the guest the next day.

The night auditor also makes an analysis of guest account balances. With a manual system, the auditor scans the last column of the transcript (see Exhibit 13–12, column 21) and itemizes those rooms with balances at or near the hotel's limit. The computer makes the same list, an exception report. If the audit team has time, additional credit duties may be assigned. All credit reports are sensitive and may be viewed as exception reports:

Credit Alert: list of rooms whose folio charges exceed a given amount in a single day. That amount varies with the class of hotel.

Cumulative Charges Report: similar to the credit alert except a cumulative figure for the guest's entire stay.

Floor Report: list of guests whose folio balances approach the maximum allowed the hotel by the credit-card company (the hotel's floor), or the maximum the credit-card allows on the guest's own card.

Three-Day Report: unpaid folios three days after billing.

Reservation Reports. Computerizing reservations added a new dimension to the process. The toll-free WATS number globalized the reservation network. Instant confirmation was given for dates that were months away to persons who were miles apart. In so doing, reams of information—fodder for reports—was generated.

Information is the power to decide. Reservation managers must know the number of rooms sold and the number available, by type, rate, and accommodations. They must know the number of arrivals, departures, stayovers, cancellations, out of orders, and walk-ins. This information comes to the reservation department in a variety of reports.

Supplemental information flows from the same database. Which rooms are most popular and at which rates? Do no-show factors vary with the season and the day of the week? If so, by how much? How many rooms in which categories are turnaways? How many reservations were walked? How many in-WATS calls were there? How many were initiated by travel agents? Questions of this type illustrate again the dual management–operations capability of the computer.

An alphabetical list of arrivals is an example of the computer in operations. It reduces the number of lost reservations and facilitates the recognition of VIPs. It helps the bellcaptain schedule a crew. It identifies group affiliation, which improves reservation and billing procedures.

Reservation data can be displayed on a monitor or preserved on hard copy for further digestion and evaluation. A permanent copy turns the data into a report. Then it serves more as a management tool than an operational one.

Arrivals Report: alphabetical list of the day's expected arrivals, individually and by groups.

Cancellation and Change Report: list of reservation cancellations for the day and reservation changes and cancellations for a later date.

Central Reservations Report: analysis of reservations made through the central reservations system, including numbers, kinds, rates, and fees paid.

Convention (Group) Delegates Report: compilation of group (and tour) room blocks; the number of rooms booked, and the number still available by rate category and name of group. Also called a **Group Pickup Report.**

Daily Analysis Report: one or more reports on the number and percentage of reservations, arrivals, no-shows, walk-ins, and so on, by source (travel agent, housing bureau, etc.) and by type of guest (full rack, corporate rate, etc.).

Deposit Report: reservations by deposit status—deposits requested and received, deposits requested and not received, deposits not requested. Could be treated as an exception report.

Forecast Report: one of a variety of names (**Extended Arrival Report, Future Availability Report**) for projecting reservation data forward over short or long durations (see Exhibit 4–7).

Occupancy Report: projection within the computer's horizon of expected occupancy by category of room.

Overbooking (Walk) Report: list of reservations walked, including their identification; the number of walk-ins denied; and the number farmed out to other properties.

Regrets Report: report on the number of room requests denied.

Rooms Management Reports. The PMS has brought major procedural changes to the front office but not to the functions that need doing. Comparisons of the old and the new are best illustrated through the room rack. Unlike manual room racks, which one can see and physically manipulate, computerized racks are in computer memory, viewable only on the monitor screen (see Exhibits 13–7 and 13–8). Whether the clerk turns to one rack type or the other, the information is the same: room rates, location, connecting and adjoining rooms, bed types, and room status.

The computer restructures the data. It separates into different windows what is visible with one glance to the user of the manual rack (see Exhibit 13–9). Separate menus (see Exhibit 13–8) are needed to view what the manual rack identifies as one class of information. With a glance at the manual rack, one sees the rooms vacant and occupied, the rooms out of order and on change, the names of the guests and their city of residence, the number in the party and their company or group affiliation, the rate on the room and the anticipated check-out date. It doesn't work that way with an electronic system, where separate programs are needed for each function. Room identification (see Exhibit 13–7) is different from guest identification (see Exhibit 13–10).

Far more information is available from the computer rack than from the manual rack of Exhibit 13–9, but the information has to be manipulated to provide the data. For example, the computerized rack can display all the vacant rooms on a given floor. All the king rooms in the tower or all the connecting rooms in the lanai building can be listed. Facts that would take many minutes to ascertain, if at all, from the manual rack are flashed onto the screen in seconds.

Information is more complete and can be processed more rapidly with the computerized rack than with the manual one. This is true for the whole, although a greater amount of time may be required for the computer to process a single fact. In a contest to identify a guest whose name begins with either "Mac" or "Mc," for example, the manual user may be able to beat out the computer user.

Change Report: identification of changes in rooms, rates and number in the party.

Convention Use Report: summary of the room use by different convention groups in order to justify the number of complimentary rooms.

Expected to Depart Report: list of anticipated departures. The converse would be a Stayover Report.

Flag Report: list of rooms flagged for special attention by the desk.

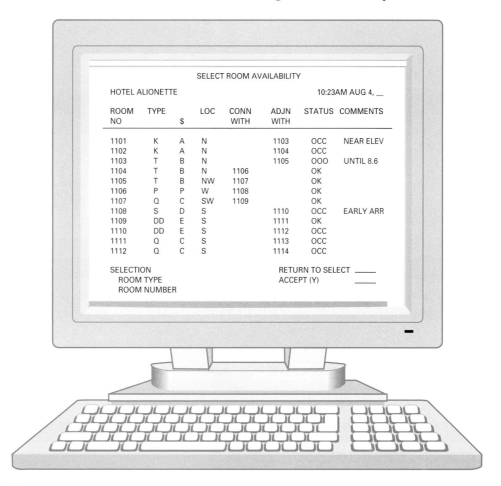

Exhibit 13–7 The computer screen of Exhibit 13–7 has replaced the metal room rack of Exhibit 13–9. Both screens and racks display the same information: availability of rooms by type, location, rate, and status. The guest-service agent completes the assignment once the selection made (lower left) agrees with the previous input of room type requested. The agent exits with a "Y" (Yes).

House Use Report: list of rooms occupied by hotel personnel.

Out-of-Order Report: list of out-of-order or out-of-inventory rooms, with reasons.

Pickup Report: names and room numbers picked up by members of a specific group against its block.

Rate Analysis Report: display of distribution of rates by sources—reservations, walk-ins, travel-agency made, res system, hotel sales department, packages, company-made.

Room Productivity Report: evaluation of housekeeping's productivity in total and by individual room attendant.

VIP Report: list of distinguished guests (DGs) and very important persons (VIPs), including casino high rollers.

Rooms Status Reports. Rooms status offers what is probably the best example of an old function with a new face. Whether the hotel uses a manual rack or a computer,

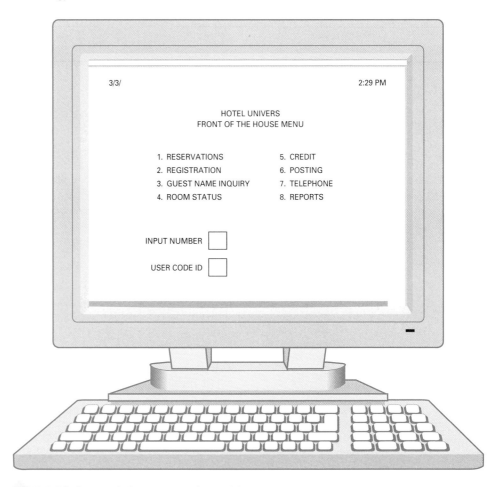

Exhibit 13-8   Each function performed by a guest-service agent requires a separate screen. The options, room availability of Exhibit 13–7, for example, is called up from this main menu. Several screens may be required in sequence before the function is completed.

room status (on change, vacant and ready, out-of-order, or occupied rooms) must be communicated between the desk and housekeeping. Clerks need to know which rooms are ready for sale, and housekeeping needs to know which rooms require attention. A room status display on the monitor is called up innumerable times throughout the day by both ends of the communication link.

The procedure hasn't changed with the computer. The cashier still puts the room on change as the guest checks out. (This is done electronically if the guest uses the speedy check-out option.) That's how the room clerk learns that a given room will be available soon. On-change status tells housekeeping that the room needs attention. When the room is clean, the housekeeper updates the system, switching the on-change room to ready. Immediately, the desk clerk has the information. The room is sold and the cycle begins anew. The faster the process goes around, the quicker the new guest is settled and the room sale consummated.

Prior to the computer, the cashier–desk–housekeeping link was direct conversation person to person; by means of paper notations; by telephone calls; and, frequently, not

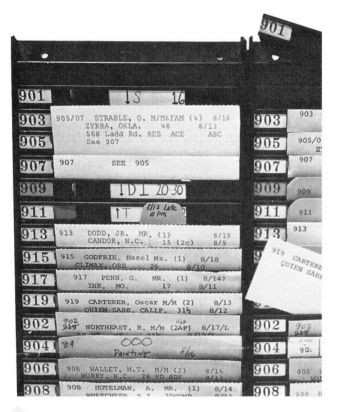

Exhibit 13–9　　The illustration is a manual room rack, circa 1960s. With one glance, the guest-service agent determines which rooms are vacant (without a room-rack slip) and which are occupied and by whom (names are typed on the slips). Also available is the guest's home town, rate paid, and arrival and anticipated departure dates (upper right corner of the room rack slip). Color (not shown) furnished additional facts: members of a group; paid in advance; permanent guest; and so on. *(For ease in reading, several illustrations use small dollar values, which may not seem realistic.)*

at all. The floor housekeeper wasn't included in the communication loop. Although the critical link, she couldn't be reached at all. Today's housekeepers communicate by telephone, not by conversation, but as an electronic input device to the computer. The message is tapped in either through the telephone or by means of a terminal located in the linen closet on each floor. PCs have been introduced into guest rooms to upgrade guest service, but they also provide the staff with another terminal.

With access to the computer, the housekeeper's office tracks room attendants as they dial in and out of the system (see Exhibit 13–11). Daily job assignments can also be computer designed. At the start of the shift, employees get a hard-copy list of rooms that each is to do. The printout also includes special assignments such as mirrors in the corridors, attention to sick guests, or messages from management to the staff.

ADA Report: Lists rooms occupied by handicapped guests. Copies to bell department and desk, but especially to security in case evacuation of the building is required.

Out-of-Order Report: special focus on out-of-order or out-of-inventory rooms, includes dates the rooms went down, expected ready dates, and the causes of

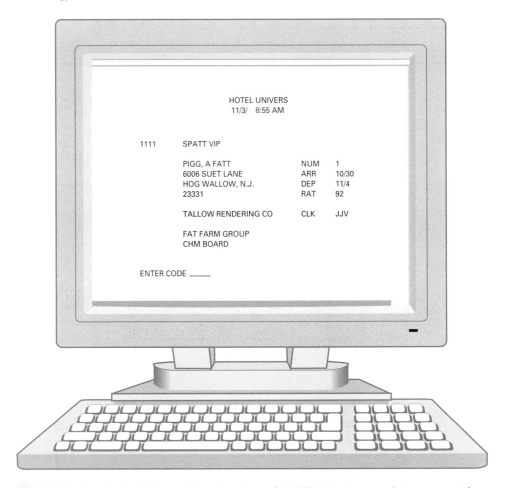

```
                              HOTEL UNIVERS
                               11/3/  8:55 AM


        1111         SPATT VIP

                     PIGG, A FATT              NUM    1
                     6006 SUET LANE            ARR    10/30
                     HOG WALLOW, N.J.          DEP    11/4
                     23331                     RAT    92

                     TALLOW RENDERING CO       CLK    JJV

                     FAT FARM GROUP
                     CHM BOARD


        ENTER CODE _____
```

Exhibit 13-10   Code 3 (Guest Name Inquiry) of Exhibit 13–8 opens this screen to identify a particular guest. Compare the information shown here with the rack slip information of Exhibit 13–9. Both contain the same facts: guest name and address, number in the party, rate, arrival and departure dates, group membership, and the initials of the guest-service agent.

each OOO or OOI room. (This report also appears among the rooms management reports.)

Permanent Guest Report: list of permanent guests by room number and name.

Room Status List: room-by-room identification of occupied and vacant rooms, made-up and not-ready rooms, out-of-order rooms, and on-change rooms. (This report also appears among the downtime reports.)

Sick Guest Report: list of sick guests by room number and name.

Accounts Receivable Reports.   The PMS prepares electronically what the manual audit prepares with pencil and paper. Both audit the same thing: front-office folios, accounts receivable. Viewed at its simplest, the night audit is nothing more than a cumulative inventory of accounts receivable. Comparing accounts receivable to food items, say, canned peas on a storeroom shelf, helps clarify the point.

| ROOM ATTENDANT'S SCHEDULE | | | | | | 01:53 PM NOV 11 | | | | | | |
| NAME | | NUMBER OF ROOMS ASSIGNED | | NUMBER | | DUTY H | | MESSAGE SIGNAL OFF BEGINNING ROOM NUMBER | | | | |
ROOM	U-R	IN	OUT	SL	HK	CO	ROOM	U-R	IN	OUT	SL	HK	CO
1200	A	9:35A	9:49A	SG	OK	SO	1209	A			SD	D	SO
1201	A	9:50A	10:14A	SS	OK	SO	1210	A	8:44A	9:02A	SD	OK	SO
1202	A	11:50A	12:12P	SS	OK	SO	1211	A	1:13P	1:48P	OK	I	OK
1203	A	9:20A	9:35A	SS	OK	SO	1212	A	9:03A	9:19A	SG	OK	SO
1204	A	10:54A	11:17A	SM	OK	SO	1213	A	1:48		OK	57	DO
1205	A	11:17A	11:50A	SD	OK	SO	1214	A			OK	D	DO
1206	A	10:31A	10:54A	SS	OK	SO	1215	A			OK	D	DO
1207	A	10:14A	10:31A	SS	OK	SO							
1208	A	12:12P	1:13P	OK	OK	OK					END DISPLAY		

Exhibit 13–11 Property management systems track each floor housekeeper. Management is able to locate and contact otherwise isolated employees as well as monitor productivity among room attendants. At the time of this display, 1:53 PM (top right), this housekeeper had serviced almost the entire assignment, 16 rooms.

Each day's computation starts with the opening balance of accounts receivable (cans of peas on the shelf). This opening balance is the amount already owed to the hotel (peas on hand). New charges (account receivable debits) made by guests (new pea purchases) that day are added to the opening balance:

	Of Accounts Receivable in Dollars	Of Peas in Cans
Opening Balance	$ 186,000.00	186
Today's Charges (Purchases)	24,000.00	24
Total	$ 210,000.00	210

From that sum are subtracted payments (credits) made by guests (cans opened and consumed) that day. The new (closing) balance is thus obtained for both accounts receivable and peas. This closing becomes the opening balance of the following day, and the sequence begins anew.

	Of Accounts Receivable in Dollars	Of Peas in Cans
Total (See Above)	$ 210,000.00	210
Today's Payments (Consumption)	60,000.00	60
A/R owed at day's close	$ 150,000.00[*]	
Peas on the shelf at day's end		150[*]

[*]Opening balance tomorrow.

Alpha List: alphabetically lists the entire guest (accounts receivable) population and the amount each owes (this would be comparable to a list of each can of peas on the shelf).

City-ledger Transfers: itemizes all the accounts transferred from the front-office ledger to the city ledger that day; a journal of city-ledger transfers. (Identifies specific cans of peas shipped to the kitchen from the storeroom).

Credit-Card Report: includes amounts and identities of credit-card charges by both registered and nonregistered guests.

Daily Revenue Report: analyzes revenue from all sources by outlet and by means of payment. (Comparable to the once-used NCR-machine D Report, and sometimes called a D Report.)

Departmental Sales Journals: report the individual transactions of each operating department. (Comparable to the vertical columns (#5–#15) of the transcript; see Exhibit 13–12).

Guest Ledger Summary: displays the daily opening balances, charges, credits, and closing balances of guests' A and B folios. Exhibits 13–3 and 13–12 contain the same information. One is a property management report (Exhibit 13–3); the other a paper-and-pencil form (Exhibit 13–12). Compare specifically 13–3's Room # column and 13–12's column 2. Similarly, 13–3's Opening Bal(ance) column equates with 13–12's columns 4 minus 5. Continuing: 13–3's Charges, Credits, and Closing Bal(ance) columns are the same as Exhibit 13–12's columns numbered 16, 20, and 21 minus 22.

Late Charge Report: identifies late charges transferred to the city ledger that day.

Posting Reports: list the postings made by each departmental POS terminal (comparable to pencil-and-paper departmental control sheets; see Exhibit 10–7).

Room Revenue Report: provides the room rates and taxes posted to each room that day. Because room revenue can be obtained floor by floor, it is comparable to a manual room count sheet (without taxes); also called an occupancy and room revenue report (see Exhibit 13–14).

Reports to the Manager

The night auditor addresses and reconciles account-receivable sales. The income auditor (day auditor) casts a wider net, auditing cash sales and credit-card sales that have not passed through the folios. Both are combined during the income audit and presented in a *daily report to the manager.* That report also becomes the basis of the daily entries into the permanent books of account. There is obviously some delay between the time the day auditor reports to work and the completion of the income audit. In the interim, the general manager relies on the *night auditor's report to the manager* (see Exhibit 13–13). Although the night auditor's report contains less information, it does reflect total room sales, the hotel's largest revenue source. That room sales figure is accurate and complete because room sales are sold only to receivables.

Exhibit 13–13 illustrates an abbreviated night auditor's report to the manager. Four items are reported. (1) Accounts-receivable sales in the several departments appear in the upper left. These values originate in the night audit. They would agree with columns 6 through 16 of Exhibit 13–12 were the hand transcript still being used. (2) The total receivable charges, $18,632.98, are entered in the lower left corner of the report to obtain a cumulative balance of accounts receivable. The earlier pea-inventory discussion reinforced this concept of a "running" accounts-receivable balance. Chapter 1 previously

DAILY TRANSCRIPT OF
ACCOUNTS RECEIVABLE

DATE __10/6__ 20 ___

1 ACCOUNT NO.	2 ROOM NO.	3 NUMBER OF GUESTS	OPENING BALANCE 4 DEBIT	5 CREDIT	6 ROOMS	7 RESTAURANT	8 BEVERAGES	TELEPHONE 9 LOCAL CALLS	10 LONG DISTANCE	11 LAUNDRY	12 VALET	13 CASH DISBURSEMENTS	14 TRANSFERS	15 ROOM TAX	16 TOTAL DEBITS	17 CASH RECEIPTS	18 ALLOWANCES	19 TRANSFERS	20 TOTAL	21 DEBIT	22 CREDIT
8001	1406	1		19 –	60 –	12 –	6 –					8 –		3 –	70 –					70 –	
8811	1817	2	63 60		30 –	5 –			4 –					60	39 60					103 20	
8123	1824	1			18 50	6 40						1 –		37	26 27	37 –			37 –		10 73
7188	1906	2	21 93		21 56									43	21 99					43 92	
7913	1907	2	39 96		30 –		6 –						47 96	60	84 56					124 52	
TOTAL 40		51	768 20	2532	2676 50	52 10	61 70	7 20	18 40		4 –	17 –	47 96	13 53	898 39	167 50	2 10		169 60	1488 70	17 03

DEPARTURES

8106	1616	3	46 20			4 40									4 40				50 60	50 60	
8007	1649	1	18 87													18 57	30		18 87	
7992	1824	2	39 96															39 96	39 96	
8282	1600	1	– 0 –			4 –	4 –	40	3 60						8 –	8 –				
TOTAL			105 03			4 40	4 –	– 40	3 60							12 40	26 57	30	90 56	117 43	

CITY LEDGER

Cum			500 –		40 –	30 –							90 56		160 56			47 96	47 96	612 60	
TOTALS 40		51	1373 23	2532	2676 50	96 50	95 70	7 60	22 –		4 –	17 –	138 52	13 53	1071 35	194 07	2 40	138 52	334 99	2101 30	17 03

Courtesy: American Hotel Register Co., Northbrook, IL.

Exhibit 13–12 This transcript is a summary of accounts receivable and was used to balance paper-and-pencil folios. The vertical column of each folio was copied here as a horizontal line. Doing so separated the folio charges by columns. Column totals were then compared to the control sheets maintained in each operating department, restaurant, beverage, etc. Discrepancies indicated an error that night auditors had to track down.

N.B.: Two methods of recording the folios are shown here. *Only one or the other would be used!* Line 1 (the folio of Exhibit 13–1) includes the opening balance of columns 4 minus 5 in the total column, column 16. The remaining exhibit illustrates a second method. Column 16 represents the total of this day's accounts receivable. The opening balance columns are *not* included in column 16's total. Both systems reflect the same cumulative balance of accounts receivable, column 21 minus column 22 of each folio and of the grand total. *(For ease in reading, several illustrations use small dollar values, which may not seem realistic.)*

explained the source and the meaning of statistics and their ratios, which are items 3 and 4 of the report, the right side. That discussion is broadened in the next section.

Room Count, House Count, and Room Income. Room count, the number of rooms sold (occupied); house count, the number of guests (persons) registered; and room income (room sales) are computed during the night audit. Done, in part, with a rooms revenue report, also called a room count sheet (illustrated in pencil-and-paper format as Exhibit 13–14).

These three values are verified again by the income audit, using a formula exactly like the cans-of-peas illustration. The first step adds today's arrivals to the opening balance.

The City Hotel, Anywhere, U.S.A.		Page 1
03/16　Night Auditor's Report		

SALES			ROOM STATISTICS	
Rooms	$12,900.00		Total Rooms	320
Coffee Shop	1,524.80		House Use	−0−
Steak House	CLOSED		Out of Order	−0−
Cap'tn Bar	896.00		Complimentary	−0−
Telephone	990.76		Permanent	2
Laundry	100.51		Room Count	180
Total Sales	$16,412.07		Vacant	140
			House Count	210
Other Charges:				
Cash Advance	987.76			
Taxes Payable	540.00			
Transfers	693.15			
	$18,632.98			

ACCOUNTS RECEIVABLE		ROOM RATIOS	
Opening Balance	$44,651.07	% Occupancy	56.3
Charges	18,632.98	% Double Occupancy	16.7
Total	$63,284.05	Average Daily Rate	$71.67
Credits	950.00	RevPar	$40.35
Closing Balance	$62,334.05		

Exhibit 13–13　The night auditor's report to the manager is one of many reports prepared each night. It contains information about the hotel's accounts receivable and about room sales, the chief generator of accounts receivable. The left side of the exhibit reports on accounts receivable, the right side on room sales. The night auditor's report is an interim report. The daily report to the manager is prepared later and includes cash sales.

Today's opening balance is always yesterday's closing balance. This opening/closing relationship applies to every inventory count, be it cans of peas, accounts receivable, rooms occupied, or bottles of scotch. Consider the scotch. When the bar closes at 2 AM, there are six bottles of scotch. Twelve hours later, when the bar reopens, the same six bottles are there. The closing balance of day one and the opening balance of day two are always the same.

The reasoning applies to room statistics. The number of rooms occupied, the number of persons, and the dollar income is increased by today's arrivals and decreased by today's departures. The values determined by the income auditor using the computation that follows should agree with the results of the night audit.

Occasional changes involving neither arrivals nor departures must be either added in or subtracted out. These internal changes have several causes. Guests change rooms, hence a rate change. Guests also move to or from larger/smaller accommodations, hence a change in the number of rooms occupied. Sometimes members of the party leave while other members remain, hence a change in the number of guests. The simple mathematics is illustrated so:

	Room Count	House Count	Room Income
Opening balance	840	1,062	$174,200
+ Arrivals	316	391	80,100
= Total	1,156	1,453	$254,300
− Departures	88	122	16,400
= Total	1,068	1,331	$237,900
± Changes	+ 6	− 2	+ 1,730
= Closing balance	1,074	1,329	$239,630

Room Statistics.   Both the night auditor's report to the manager and the income auditor's daily report to the manager contain statistics. Statistics are merely

ROOM	No Guests	RATE	ROOM	No Guests	RATE	ROOM	No Guests	RATE	ROOM	No Guests	RATE	ROOM	No Guests	RATE	ROOM	No Guests	RATE
3101			3319			3615			3910			4206			4501		
3102			3320			3616			3912			4207			4502		
3103			S3322	4	80	3617			3914			4208			4503		
3104			3401			3618			3915			4210			4504		
3105			3402	2	66	3619			3916			4212			4505		
3106			3403	2	66	3620			3917			4214			4506		
3107			3404			S3622			3918			4215			4507		
3108			3405	2	68	3701			3919			4216			4508		
3110			3406			3702			3920			4217			4510		
3112			3407			3703			S3922			4218			4512		
3114			3408	1	58 −	3704			4001			4219			4514		
3115			3410			3705			4002			4220			4515		
3116			3412	3	72	3706			4003			S4222			4516		
3117			3414	1	59 50	3707			4004			4301			4517		
3118			3415	3	66 −	3708			4005			4302			4518		

ROOM	No Guests	RATE	ROOM	No Guests	RATE	ROOM	No Guests	RATE	ROOM	No Guests	RATE	ROOM	No Guests	RATE	ROOM	No Guests	RATE
3312			3606	2	66	3903			S4122			4418			4712		
3314			3607	2	66	3904			4201			4419			4714		
3315			3608	3	71	3905			4202			4420			4715		
3316			3610	1	66	3906			4203			S4422			4716		
3317			3612			3907			4204						4717		
3318			3614			3908			4205						4718		
TOTAL			TOTAL	57	3,731 00	TOTAL			TOTAL			TOTAL			TOTAL		

OCCUPANCY AND ROOM REVENUE REPORT   **Hotel Gary**   DAY *Monday*   DATE *9-18-*

EAST WING

Exhibit 13-14   A report on room occupancy is prepared nightly usually at the closeout hour. It is a snapshot of rooms occupied and vacant at that time on that date. This hand-prepared exhibit would be copied from the information in the room rack (Exhibit 13–9). Property management systems prepare the same report in a fraction of the time (see Exhibit 13–4, under section titled Before the Income Audit). Totals—of rooms occupied, number of guests and room income—should agree with the corresponding values of the audit. In a pencil-and-paper audit that would be columns 2, 3, and 6 of Exhibit 13–12. (*For ease in reading, several illustrations use small dollar values, which may not seem realistic.*)

special ways of grouping data in an orderly and usable manner. Statistics are the facts expressed in dollars, cents, or numbers. For example, instead of itemizing

Guest A	Room 597	$150
Guest B	Room 643	$130
Guest C	Room 842	$160

and so on, one might say there are 220 guests in 189 rooms paying a total of $27,198. A great deal of information has been grouped, classified, and presented to become a statistic.

Taking the next step, these room figures are expressed in ratios, which are more meaningful than the simple statistic. So the 189 rooms sold is expressed in relation to the number of rooms available for sale, 270. The result is a percentage of occupancy, a mathematical expression of how many rooms were sold in relation to how many could have been sold. Using those values, the percentage of occupancy is

$$\frac{\text{number of rooms sold (room count)}}{\text{number of rooms available for sale}} = \frac{189}{270} = 70\%$$

A frequent companion to the percentage of occupancy computation is the average daily rate (ADR). Both ratios appear in the night auditor's report to the manager. Sales per occupied room, as this figure is sometimes called, is the income from room sales divided by the number of rooms sold.

$$\frac{\text{room income}}{\text{number of rooms sold (room count)}} = \frac{\$27,198}{189} = \$143.90$$

A similar computation, RevPar, once called *sales per available room*, is derived by dividing room income by the number of rooms available for sale rather than by the actual number of rooms sold.

$$\frac{\text{room income}}{\text{number of rooms available for sale}} = \frac{\$27,198}{270} = \$100.73$$

The fourth most frequently cited ratio in the manager's daily report is the percentage of double occupancy. Double occupancy is the relationship of rooms occupied by more than one guest to the total number of rooms occupied. That is what the following ratio expresses:

$$\frac{\text{number of guests} - \text{number of rooms sold}}{\text{number of rooms sold}} = \frac{220 - 189}{189} = 16.4\%$$

Having finished the audit with the preparation of the night auditor's report to the manager, the night auditor lays aside pencils and erasers—or more likely, rubs stiff shoulders from working at the keyboard—and goes home to bed.

RECONCILING THE AUDIT

Whether computer prepared or a pencil-and-paper rendition, the night audit has several goals. Among them are validating accounts receivable, identifying departmental incomes, and preparing management reports. Property management systems make the job easy. Every service delivered to the guest, whether rooms, food or spa, is recorded simultaneously on the guest folio and the departmental income record. The two are already balanced and the data ready to be reported. Not so with pencil-and-paper audits, which rely on separate records: the signed guest voucher; the departmental control sheet, and the hand-posted folio.

Proving Room Charges

Room charges originate at the front desk so two of the records listed immediately above, vouchers and control sheets, are unnecessary for the rooms audit. Other departments test transcript totals against vouchers and control sheets. Room sales data (columns 6, 2 and 3 of Exhibit 13–12) are tested against the room rack.

Information that appears on the folio (name, number in the party, room assigned and rate charged) appears also on the room rack. The room count sheet (Exhibit 13–14) is a manual version of the PMS' room status report. (See the earlier discussions headed, Room Status Reports.) The hand-prepared audit tests the totals of the room count sheet against the transcript totals. Errors, if any, are uncovered and corrected.

The Housekeeper's Report.   Further verification of both the rack and the transcript come from the housekeeper's report. Housekeeping forwards the report to the desk at least twice daily. Although the illustrations that follow are presented in written form, the report is now filed electronically.

Room status is communicated by means of abbreviations that are widely understood across the industry (see Exhibit 13–15). Occupied rooms are reported with checkmarks ($\sqrt{}$), meaning OK. Sleep-outs, which are rooms with baggage but no overnight guests, are flagged with a B, for baggage. Occupied rooms with no baggage or just light baggage get an X mark (for nothing). Other codes mix handwritten and alphanumeric symbols.

The housekeeper's report (see Exhibit 13–16) is a composite report. It is a summary of reports coming from the floor housekeepers. Each sleeping floor is serviced by one or more floor housekeepers (see Exhibit 3–18), who report room status to the linen

Baggage: no occupant (sleep-out)	B
Check out: room on change	c/o
Cot	C
Do not disturb	DND
Double-locked room	DL
Early arrival	EA
No service wanted (Do not disturb)	NS
Occupied	$\sqrt{}$
Occupied, but dirty	OD
Occupied, with light baggage or no baggage	X
OK	ok
Out of order	O (also OOO)
Out of inventory	OOI
Permanent guest	P
Ready for sale	/
Refused service	RS
Stayover	s/o
Stayover, no service	SNS
Vacant	V (also no symbol at all)
Vacant and dirty (on change)	VD

Exhibit 13–15   Communication between the desk and housekeeping is critical if rooms are to be turned quickly and guests accommodated promptly. More and more that communication is electronic. Alphabetic and numeric symbols are used to facilitate housekeeping's report on the status of room readiness. (See also Exhibits 13–16 and 13–17.)

HOUSEKEEPER'S DAILY REPORT

Kayco Form No. 1209   DATE *10-6* _____ 19 __

ROOM NO.	OCCUPIED	VACANT	BAGGAGE	BED USED	ROOM NO.	OCCUPIED	VACANT	BAGGAGE	BED USED	ROOM NO.	OCCUPIED	VACANT	BAGGAGE	BED USED
2529	✓				3517		/			4211	s/o			
2530	✓				3518	✓				4212	s/o			
2531		c/o			3519	✓				4213		/		
2532		/			3520	✓				4214	ρ			
2533			B		3521	✓				4215				
2534		/			3522		c/o			4216		/		
2535		/												

Exhibit 13-16   The housekeeper's report summarizes the status of guest rooms as reported by floor housekeepers (see Exhibit 13–17). A reverse housekeeper's report, which flows from the desk to the linen room, is prepared as one of the PMS's many reports. It has replaced the morning report from the housekeeper and increased the importance of the housekeeper's afternoon report to the desk.

room. The linen-room staff merges the floor reports (see Exhibit 13–17) to complete the final report.

Discrepancies between the housekeeper's report and the desk are usually resolved by emailing and telephoning between the two locations. When differences still remain, someone is dispatched to look at the room. A bellperson might be sent, or a security officer. Or a more senior management type, the housekeeper, the assistant manager or the chief of security might "take a look." Credit managers are especially interested in light luggage reports and skippers. Several recent lawsuits have highlighted the need to investigate Do Not Disturb signs. Guests who leave DNS signs on the door must be checked before the day is out. An alert is warranted if the floor housekeeper notes a DNS on both the morning and afternoon reports. It is one fact if the guest forgot to remove the notice and something different if the guest is in distress, unable to remove the sign. Wise hoteliers telephone the room to verify the condition of the occupant. If no one answers, the room is entered, always by more than one person. Recording the circumstances in the front-desk log is an extra, prudent step.

The second report of the day is the chief means of uncovering sleepers, skippers, and whos. *Sleepers* are guests who have actually checked out but are still listed as occupants. *Skippers* are guests who have left without paying. *Whos* are unknown guests; someone is occupying a room but the desk doesn't know who it is.

Originally, the housekeeper's report was sent to the income auditor. Internal control is an issue when one person, the guest-service agent, sells the rooms, handles the payments, and keeps the records. Having another party check the status of the house versus the records of the desk established a degree of internal control. This is still important for small hotels. As front-office staffs grew larger, the housekeeper's report was no longer needed for internal control.

Property management systems have also altered the floor housekeepers approach to reporting occupied rooms. No longer do they bang on guest-room doors early in the morning. PMSs now prepare a *reverse housekeeper's report*, also called a *room occupancy*

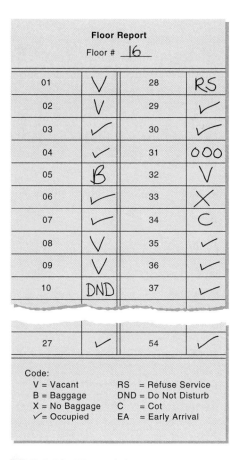

Exhibit 13-17   Exhibits 13–15, 13–16, and 13–17 are interrelated. Floor housekeepers report room status to the linen room. These reports are consolidated and furnished to the desk. This critical information keeps the desk up to date on room availability. Electronic check-outs and instant communication has improved the process immensely.

status report. It's one of the many night-audit reports listed previously. The linen room gets the report early the following morning. Now, the housekeeper knows the room count and the configuration of the floors before the day's work begins. Work schedules are refined before the crew arrives. Extra housekeepers are called in, or days off are scheduled for full-time staff. Assigning jobs earlier means the staff gets to work earlier.

> The balance of the chapter explains the pencil-and-paper audit. Understanding it helps in understanding the audit of the property management system. The concept is the same for both; obviously the procedures differ. Since pencil-and-paper audits are no longer used, readers may consider skipping ahead to the chapter summary.

Proving Charges Other Than Rooms

Let's review the steps of the pencil-and-paper audit. First, the night auditor posts all vouchers that arrive at the desk before the closeout hour. Then each folio is removed from the cashier's well (see Exhibit 10–3). Room rates and taxes are recorded on each folio and the folio is totaled. The total is carried forward to the column of the following day (see Exhibit 13–1). Next, the *vertical* column of each folio is copied onto a *horizontal* line of the transcript (see Exhibit 13–12).

Property management systems accumulate a running total of departmental charges. The value of each new sale is added electronically to the previous total. Pencil-and-paper systems wait for the manual night audit to do the same. Distributing the folio by transcript columns enables the auditor to obtain a total balance of sales by department (by column). Once totaled, the value can be compared to totals on the departmental control sheets (see Exhibit 10–7) that are maintained in each operating unit: food, beverage, and so on.

The Premise.   After all the folios, including the day's departures, are copied onto the transcript—and that may take several transcript sheets—the night audit is back to the basic premise: Do the totals of the columns, which are the sum of the postings to the individual folios, agree to the charges originating in the departments, as shown on the control sheets?

Although the form of the control sheet differs somewhat in the several departments (in some instances, only the cash register tape is available), the method of proving departmental charges is identical department to department.

Vouchers from the various departments are hand carried to the desk all during the day. After being posted, each voucher is marked to lessen the chance of duplicating the charge. Next, the checks (vouchers) are sorted by departments—a job made easier with different colors for each department—and filed into pigeonholes. There they remain for the night auditor, who totals them on an adding machine. The adding machine tape is then attached to the pile of vouchers.

Three different totals are available to the auditor for each department:

1. The total derived from the departmental control sheet. Each time a guest charges a departmental service to the folio, the departmental cashier makes an entry on the control sheet. At the end of the day, this sheet is totaled and forwarded to the night auditor.

2. The total on the adding machine tape of the individual vouchers, which have arrived at the desk one at a time. These are the communicative devices between the departmental cashier and the front-office billing clerk.

3. The total posted to the folio for that department. This total is the sum of the postings made to the folios. The auditor gets that value from the departmental column of the transcript.

If the system is in balance, the departmental control sheet (which records the event) has a total equal to the tape of the vouchers (which communicate the event) and to the sum of the folios (the ultimate record of the event). If the three totals agree, the auditors move to the next department. There, the three comparisons are made again.

The Search.   The audit begins in earnest when one of the values fails to reconcile. If two of the three totals agree, the search concentrates on the unequal total. There are several likely causes. Mathematical mistakes account for a number of the errors. The major ones—slides, transpositions, and additions—were explained earlier.

A control sheet total larger than the other two totals suggests a voucher (check) was lost en route from the department to the desk. It was never posted. Had the voucher been posted and then lost, the voucher total would be the smallest of the three.

Sometimes several columns of the transcript (food and beverage, for example) are smaller than the corresponding control sheets and vouchers, which are in agreement. Most likely a folio was stuck in the well and never appeared on the transcript. Such an omission impacts several departments. Simple oversights like this seem less simple in the early morning hours. Then, a check omitted from the departmental control sheet or a voucher filed before it was posted means long minutes of searching by the weary auditor.

Vouchers posted to the correct department but to the wrong guest account will not be evident to the auditor. All three totals will agree even though the wrong guest account is charged. This is not so with the reverse situation—when the charge is made to the proper folio but posted to the wrong department. Let's use a food-and-beverage example again. Assume a restaurant charge appears on the transcript in the beverage column. (The error might originate with the clerk's original folio posting, or the auditors might mistakenly copy from the folio to the wrong transcript column.) The food column total of the transcript would be smaller than the voucher and control sheet totals, which would be in agreement. The total of the beverage column is the clue to the error. That total will be larger than the voucher and control sheet totals by the same difference as the restaurant column was smaller.

One error special to the manual audit is particularly difficult to find. It occurs when the original voucher is misposted by the desk. The charge is recorded on the folio of a stayover guest but in a previous date's column. That's what would happen if the $6 bar charge of Exhibit 13–1 had been posted in the October 5 (10/5) column instead of in the 10/6 column. The figure never makes it to the transcript because it doesn't even appear as that day's business. Transcript totals that are smaller than voucher and control sheet totals highlight the problem. Finding it requires the auditor to sort vouchers by room-number sequence and compare each voucher to the particular transcript column, which is also by room-number sequence. Matching vouchers and transcript entries uncovers the mistake.

Finding and correcting errors is difficult because manual audits have numerous flubs. Mistakes are compounded, so simple column differences are often no clue at all.

It's easy to forget that reconciling the three balances is not the purpose of the audit. Reconciling balances is only a means to the end. As each error is uncovered, the record must be corrected. Either the folio is changed or departmental sales are restated, or both. Making the corrections ensures the guest of an accurate billing and determines the exact revenues of each department. As errors are uncovered, corrections are made and the audit moves to the next department.

Balancing the Transcript's Mathematics. Property management systems monitor the mathematics electronically. Pencil-and-paper audits require a manual mathematical check of additions and subtraction. Crossfooting the grand totals (adding horizontally) ensures the accuracy of all lines of the transcript. One further review of the whole process will explain why crossfooting the transcript totals proves the mathematical accuracy of each folio in the well.

Step 1: The night auditor posts room charges and taxes to the folios.

Step 2: The folios are totaled and the balances carried forward to the next day.

Step 3: Folios are copied onto the transcript. Within the figures are errors created by steps 1 and 2 and errors made during the day by the desk cashiers. Among the mathematical errors will be slides and transpositions, inaccurate figures, oversights, duplications, and mistakes in addition and subtraction. The audit is designed to uncover all these errors.

Step 4: The total of each transcript column is proved against other documents, as explained earlier, chiefly control sheets, vouchers, cash sheets, and the room count sheet. Corrections are made on the transcript and on the folio as errors are uncovered. This verification ensures the mathematical accuracy of all the departmental columns, which are vertical columns 6 through 19, except column 16 (see Exhibit 13–12).

Step 5: The opening balance columns, vertical columns 4 and 5, are now verified. Unlike columns 6 to 15, columns 4 and 5 are not income columns, so there are neither control sheets nor vouchers. The opening balance of each folio is the guest's cumulative debt, carried forward from yesterday. Therefore, the opening balances of today (columns 4 and 5, debit and credit) are compared to the closing balances of yesterday, yesterday's transcript columns 21 and 22.

The guest goes to bed the previous night owing columns 21 and 22 of yesterday's transcript and awakens the following morning owing the same exact amounts, now reflected in columns 4 and 5 of the new day. If today's opening balance does not agree with yesterday's closing balance—perhaps a folio has been left off today's transcript—a search begins for the discrepancy.

Step 6: Crossfoot (horizontally add) the totals of columns 6 to 15 to obtain a value. If the transcript is in balance, that value will equal the total of vertical column 16. This can be understood by doing the very same thing on any one horizontal line. Columns 6 to 15 on any horizontal line must equal column 16 of that line. Therefore, crossfooting the grand totals of columns 6 to 15 should equal the sum obtained by vertically adding column 16. (The total should equal the sum of its parts.)

If the sum of all the columns does not equal the total of column 16, there is an error on one or more of the horizontal lines, which is, of course, someone's folio. [That folio was added by the night auditor (step 2) and copied onto the transcript (step 3). Obviously, it was added or copied incorrectly.] Each horizontal line must be crossfooted until the mathematical error or errors that contributed to the total error is uncovered. Once uncovered, column 16 of that line will be changed, and since that line represents a folio—the line of figures was copied from the folio—the folio itself must also be corrected.

Step 7: Verify the three credits. Previous discussions have stressed the three methods of settling folios: cash, allowances, and transfers. Credit column 17 is the cash settlement and that transcript total is compared to the receipts reported on the cashiers' front-office cash sheets. (Similarly, disbursements on those sheets must agree to the cash disbursement column, column 13 of Exhibit 13–12.)

Column 18, allowances, is compared to the sum of the allowance vouchers granted at the desk that day. Column 19 is the most common credit, since it includes credit-card transfers. It is tested against column 14, transfer debits, because transfer credits and debits must always equal. Since most of column 19's transfers (transfers credit) are to the city ledger, balancing with column 14 (transfers debit) requires that the cumulative balance of the city ledger also be reported on the transcript. Exhibit 13–12 shows the equality, but the city ledger is abbreviated at the bottom of the exhibit.

Column 20 is missing on many transcripts. It might be used for advanced deposit credits if the hotel's clientele commonly used them, but that's very rare. More likely, it would be used to total credit columns 17, 18, and 19 as shown in Exhibit 13–12. As such, it would represent the sum of all credits as column 16 represents the sum of the day's debits (charges).

Step 8: Crossfoot and mathematically balance the entire transcript. First obtain the net opening balance by subtracting column 5, opening credit balance, from column 4, opening debit balance. To that difference add the total of column 16, which was tested by step 6. These total charges are next reduced by payments (credits), the sum of columns 17, 18, and 19 (or perhaps column 20; see step 7). The result is the net amount owed by accounts receivable.

Recall the pea analogy. Opening inventory (column 4 minus column 5) plus new purchases (column 16) minus peas used (columns 17, 18, 19) equals peas still on hand—or accounts receivable owed; that is, column 21 minus column 22. The transcript is a summary of accounts receivable, a summary of folios. The closing balance represents the total amount that all accounts receivable owe the hotel at the close of the day. It's possible for the hotel to owe one or more guests temporarily, so some lines (folios) will have credit balances, probably as a result of advanced deposits. For two different credit balance examples, see column 2 (10/6) of Exhibit 13–1 and the third horizontal line of Exhibit 13–12, column 22.

Step 9: Vertical addition is easier to visualize than horizontal crossfooting. It's just a more traditional way to do the mathematics. Then the proof, or the "formula" as it is sometimes called, looks like this (see Exhibit 13–12, line 2):

Opening balance, column 4 minus 5 (debit minus credit)	$63.60
+Charges and services used by guests, column 16 (debits)	39.60
−Payments made by guests, columns 17 to 19 (credits)	−0−
=Closing balance, column 21 minus 22 (debit minus credit)	$103.20

The closing balance is the cumulative balance of guests' debt to the hotel and is a debit balance.

The math can also be done by having column 16 represent the running total (see Exhibit 13–12, line 1). Then the formula would look different:

Opening balance, column 4 minus 5 (debit minus credit)	$19.00CR
+Charges and services used by guests, columns 6 to 15 (debits)	89.00DR
=Total, column 16 (cumulative debit balance before payments of the day)	70.00DR
−Payments made by guests, column 17 to 19 (credits)	−0−
=Closing balance, column 21 minus 22 (debit minus credit)	70.00

The result of the two approaches is the same. The difference is the handling of column 16. Some auditors use column 16 to reflect only the day's debits, as the top formula illustrates. Other auditors use column 16 to reflect the cumulative balance, including the balances of yesterday, the bottom illustration. Whichever is selected reflects the procedure used on the folios because the transcript is a copy of the folios.

SUMMARY

All businesses reconcile their accounts receivable, but only hotels do it nightly. They close the business day by means of the night audit. Guest folios (accounts receivable) are balanced and reconciled. Hotel guests come and go at all hours. Their folios must be current and accurate when called up. That's the primary job of the night audit. Since hotel sales are recorded mostly on folios—guests charge purchases to their rooms— reconciling the folios enables the night auditor also to reconcile the bulk of the day's income activity. That's the second aim of the night audit. With so much data gathered, the third purpose evolves almost automatically: Present the information in reports that help management do its job.

Uncovering clerical mistakes made by the desk throughout the day, getting accurate folios, was the original focus of the night audit. Its paper-and-pencil procedure (the transcript) dates to the 1920s. A new system appeared in the early 1970s, the property management system. As it matured, new capabilities such as point of sale (POS) terminals and call accounting (CA) systems were added. These electronic upgrades reduced the human errors substantially, almost to none. So at one and the same time, the tedious work of the night audit, such as posting room rates and taxes or transcribing transcript sheets, was reduced and the number of errors minimized.

The chapter retains these outdated procedures as a means of explaining what takes place within the heart of the computerized audit. PMS and hand-posted records have the same goals. With tedious hand-prepared audits, balancing the folio was the main thrust. With PMSs, the emphasis changes, but the almost automatic repair of folio errors is not visible. Readers can see a pencil-and-paper folio, voucher, and transcript that makes the records. They can see only the output, the results, of a PMS audit, a printout. Readers who follow the pencil-and-paper explanations of the chapter will better understand the modern audit.

The PMS has jumped ahead. No longer is it a tool of the audit only. Rather than a piece of equipment for the front desk, the hotel's computer is now the heart of its operation (see Exhibit 13–6). New capabilities have appeared, and many more are yet to come, as Chapter 14 explores.

RESOURCES AND CHALLENGES
Resources

WEB SITES

http://www.agilysis.com (Agilysis–Hospitality Solutions)—Alpharetta, GA. A large company with several divisions. Its hospitality segment is Lodging Management Systems with an IBM operating system. Heavy service in casino management.

http://www.hotelinfosys.com (HIS—Hospitality Information Systems)—Lake Forest, CA. HIS has two product lines, epitome (hotel) and core (food service). It functions on Windows, XP, Unix and iSeries. (Sometimes confused with HSI, primarily a supplier for the restaurant industry.)

http://www.hvsinternational.com (HVS International)—Mineola, NY. "A global consulting service focused on the hotel and other industries." The site offers a variety of reports, articles, statistics, and the well respected *Rushmore Letter*.

http://www.micros.com (MICROS-Fidelio International)—Beltsville, MD. By virtue of its ties to Micros, this subsidiary is a global supplier of integrated property-level information management systems (Micros Opera and Xpress) for the hospitality industry. Operates on a Windows configuration, but companies such as SBC Pure Consult have adapted it to Citrix.

Web Assignment

List three accessories (supporting programs) that you might add to your property management system. Identify the program and the supplier (go beyond this small list of three suppliers by searching the Web under property management systems) and note whether the items selected are innovations or old standbys.

INTERESTING TIDBITS

➤ In Dayton, Ohio, the Montgomery County Historical Society maintains a museum of NCR (National Cash Register) memorabilia, including both the NCR 2000 and the NCR 4200 posting machines, which were the workhorses of front-desk folios through the 1970s.

➤ Installing a PMS was a great uncertainty when the MGM Grand Hotel (now Bally's) opened in Las Vegas. So uncertain was management of the PMS's capability that a dozen NCR 4200 machines were purchased as backup. They were never used. Electronic locking systems were also untested and, therefore, rejected by the hotel. Soon after the opening, the old lock-and-key system was replaced.

➤ In 1998, Larry Chervenak, an earlier advocate of integration standards, was also a visionary. He foresaw the coming revolution in property management systems:

"For the past 25 years, the annual changes in the PMS market has been evolutionary. Now that market is on the brink of revolution. The key factor . . . is the rush toward PMS standardization by . . . hotel chains. It will impact every phase of the PMS market." *The Bottom-line*, June/July, 1998, p. 13.

Challenges

TRUE/FALSE

Questions that are partially false should be marked false (F).

____ 1. The night audit closes the hotel's day, which the American Hotel & Lodging Association has set at 1 AM, although exceptions are allowed upon petition.

____ 2. The closing balance of each day is the same as the opening balance of the following day; that's true whether the count is a running balances of cans of peas, bottles of scotch, or accounts receivable.

____ 3. Downtime reports are "dumped" 24 hours after they were printed; that's a waste!

____ 4. "Exception reports" are not usually prepared during the night audit; they are exceptions to the usual reporting because management has requested the special information.

____ 5. Not all charge sales are reported in the night audit; some accounts receivable have no folios.

PROBLEMS

1. Explain how the three backup reports discussed in the section "Downtime Reports" would be used in the event of a computer malfunction.

2. A guest checks in at 4:30 AM on Tuesday, January 8. Under hotel policy, the guest is to be charged for the room-night of Monday, January 7. The closeout hour of Monday, January 7, was 12:30 AM, January 8, and the room charge postings were handled automatically by the PMS at approximately 3 AM on that morning. The room rate is $72 and the tax is 5%; no other charges were incurred. Sketch a computer-prepared folio as it would appear when the guest departs on Wednesday, January 9, at 10 AM. Identify each posting by day and hour and briefly explain who made which posting.

3. **Given**

Rooms occupied	440
Rooms vacant	160
Total rooms sales	$32,330
House count	500

Required

The percentage of occupancy	_____
The percentage of double occupancy	_____
ADR	_____
RevPar	_____

4. Use Exhibits 13–3 and 13–12, and identify your answers by room numbers.

   a. Which guests, if any, arrived today?

   b. Which guests, if any, had advanced deposits?

   c. Which guests, if any, checked out today?

d. Which guests, if any, used credit cards at departure?

e. Which guests, if any, had amounts due from the hotel?

5. The discussion on reservation reports cites a central reservation report that includes fees. Explain who pays what fees and to whom. About how much might those fees be? (Refer to earlier chapters if necessary.)

6. Is this transcript in balance? If not, what error or errors might account for the discrepancy? What percentage of sales tax is being charged in this community?

Allowances	$ 100.00
Telephone	670.70
Transfers to	395.05
Rooms	9,072.00
Cash advance	444.25
Debit transfer	395.50
Beverage	1,920.00
Credit-card charges	14,482.07
Cash	10,071.22
Closing balance	3,670.41
Opening balance	48,341.50
Rooms tax	725.76
Food	3,000.10
Closing balance	43,007.33
Opening balance	185.00
Total charges	$64,384.81

AN INCIDENT IN HOTEL MANAGEMENT

When a Body Meets a Body

What a day! A traveling couple has stopped at this airport hotel for an overnight to break up 27 hours of travel from almost around the world. It is already late, almost 11:00 PM, when they finally get to their room.

What's that noise? A party in the room across the hall. After giving the partygoers an additional hour to finish up, the distraught guest calls the desk. No answer after some 10 rings. Every 10 minutes the caller rings the desk because the party has grown louder and louder. No answer. No answer. No answer.

Two hours after arriving, the man pulls on his trousers and goes down to the lobby. The lobby is pitch dark except for emergency lighting. "Wow, something has happened. Oh Gosh! There's a body on the sofa!"

The guest is startled even more than the guest-service agent/night auditor, who jumps up from the sofa and his deep sleep.

Questions: Was there a management failure here; if so, what?
What is the hotel's immediate response (or action) to the incident?
What further, long-run action should management take, if any?

ANSWERS TO TRUE/FALSE QUIZ

1. False. There is no set time for the hotel's day to close. Each hotel selects an hour that best fits its individual operation. Hotels with heavy lounge activities and dining/entertainment will most likely choose a later hour than that picked by a limited-service motor inn.

2. True. All perpetual inventories (running balances) are the same whether it's linens, cans of peas, bottles of scotch, paper supplies, or accounts receivable. The closing balance of one day is the opening balance of the next.

3. False. It isn't a waste. Downtime reports are prepared in the event the PMS goes down. If it doesn't crash, the data is outdated in 24 hours because a new day has come with new

data and new downtime reports. Be happy that downtime reports were not used!

4. False. Exception reports are a very important part of the night audit. "Exception" refers to data that seems unusual. Exception reports flag that information for management's quick examination. The question is false because it gives "exception" a totally different meaning than it has in audit reporting.

5. True. Not all charge sales are reported in the night audit. Nonregistered guests, who create accounts receivable with credit cards, have no folios. Also, registered guests may opt to use credit cards in lieu of folio signatures in restaurants and lounges.

C H A P T E R   1 4

Hotel Technology

Contributed by Cihan Cobanoglu, Ph.D., CHTP
Associate Professor of Hospitality Information Technology
University of Delaware

Outline

Innkeepers have never been technology leaders. Lodging is so segmented that no one company, or even one association, has had the resources for research and technical innovation. The hotel industry was at the forefront of the credit-card revolution (Chapter 11), but was unable to sustain its leadership; it lacked capital. The hotel industry was quick to adopt the computerized advantages of property management systems (Chapter 13), but relied on outside industries to make them work; it lacked technical know how.

Without a tradition of internal development, the industry has relied on others. That dependence does not diminish its enthusiasm for the new and the exciting. Hotel rooms undergo continuous upgrading and improvements. Hotels may follow in technological research, but they lead in adaptation. That is most apparent in lodging's ongoing effort to bring technology to the guest room.

TECHNOLOGY IN THE GUEST ROOM: HISTORICAL VIEW

Guests are pleasantly surprised to find cutting-edge technology in their hotel rooms, but they shouldn't be. Innkeepers have always marched ahead of their times. Hotels had bathtubs before the White House; elevators were first tested in hotels; "tubular connectors" (mail chutes) sped letters down from the upper floors; telephones first appeared in New York City's Netherland Hotel in 1894.[1] Hoteliers have always seized the moment, but they slipped behind temporarily when electronic technology crossed the nation's threshold.

A Look Back

Neither the general public nor the lodging industry experienced much change in inroom technology before 1970. Small refrigerators with ice-cube makers were one early innovation. In part, this was a means of reducing labor in the uniformed services division, which was responsible for delivering ice to guest rooms. Like other innovations (massage beds

---

[1]Lundberg, Donald. *Inside Innkeeping.* W. C. Brown Company, Publishers, Dubuque, Iowa, 1956. p. 91.

and early television sets) either an extra charge was made for the room or a coin was needed to activate the equipment.

New telephone systems—systems, not telephones—were also introduced early in the decade of the 1970s (see Exhibit 14–1). Previously, hotels often had but one trunk line (outgoing connection to the telephone company's lines). Long waits for connections, especially for long-distance calls, were not unusual.

Color television sets were well established in private homes before the industry saw the need. Then, like so many of the amenities discussed in Unit I, hoteliers began installing them in special guests rooms—soon throughout the property—to differentiate the hotel from its competitors. Amenity creep meant every hotel and every guest room was soon furnished with a TV, and then with color TV.

Although nothing like today's cell phones, the telephone was ubiquitous, and no hotel could afford to furnish a hotel room without one. HOBIC (Hotel Outward Bound Information Center) was a 1980 telephone innovation[2] (see Exhibit 14–1). It enabled front desks to track calls originating in guest rooms and charge them to folios. That was sweetened in 1981 when it became legal for hotels to add service charges, especially for interstate calls. Call accounting systems (CAS), the earliest of the new technologies, exploded during the 1980s. Telephone profits rose after AT&T's telephone monopoly was broken up in 1981. In less than a quarter century cell-phone technology relegated inroom instruments to being chiefly call receivers. But incoming calls generate no revenue. Hoteliers had to find new, offsetting income sources. One they called "resort services" or "hotel services" (see Chapter 9).

HOTEL GUESTROOM TECHNOLOGY BETWEEN 1970 AND 2000

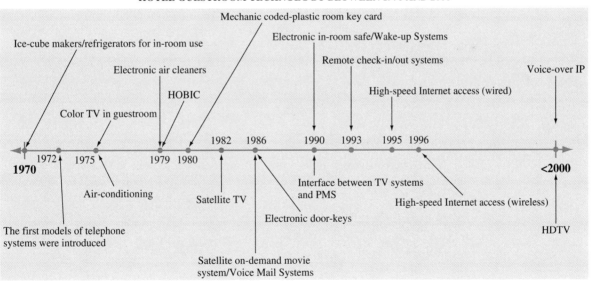

Exhibit 14–1   Thirty years of change, ranging from in-room refrigerators to Voice-over Internet Protocol, are tracked in this chronological chart of hotel technology.

---

[2]HOBIC is also called Hotel Billing Information Center, which is a more accurate description. It is a generic term defining the standard format of the telephone data coming to the desk for pencil-and-paper billing or to the property management system for electronic billing.

Electronic key systems came on the scene in 1986 and with them increased security and convenience. The 1990s decade brought new ideas. Television sets were interfaced with the hotel's PMS, enabling guests to view their folios. Guests began using the television for speedy check-out and by the mid-decade this had replaced the pencil-and-paper zip-out check-out (see Chapter 13).

The technology revolution accelerated as the new century began. High-speed Internet access (1995) was widely available. Gaining ground were Voice-over Internet Protocol (IP) phoning systems, high-definition TV, wireless Internet access, interactive entertainment systems, and more.

Costs and Benefits

Technology is part of today's culture; so is innkeeping. It is almost impossible, therefore, to imagine a hotel without some level of technology. If nothing else, even the smallest hotel is likely to have a property management system. Technology increases the efficiency of the staff and enhances the experience of the guest. Candidly, however, it may also detract from the guest's experience. Technology can be overdone. Try holding on through minutes of automated telephone directions before reaching, a live voice, if ever.

Once the industry sought technology to actually use it, benefits grew exponentially. Early efforts seemed to focus on buying technology just to buy technology. At first, hotels were notorious buyers of products that failed to work as promised, or worked, but provided no real benefit to the operation. Most of the companies that foisted products on the industry during the 1990s are no longer in business or no longer support the product that they once sold. Only three of the original 12 technology vendors that placed advertisements in the first issue of *Hospitality Upgrade* are still in business.[3] That's a function of the very rapid rate of innovation. Technology vendors matured as their products matured. More important to the economic health of hotelkeeping was the maturation and sophistication of the hotel buyer/user.

Comfortable with the technology, innkeepers are applying its potential to a range of uses. The Mandarin Oriental, for example, actually tracks its guests' favorite fruits. Computerized guest profiles make it possible to stock the welcoming fruit basket with the guest's preference based on previous selections. It's the kind of "wow" factor that makes for repeat business.

Without such "wow" factors, hotelkeeping could be commoditized. Chapter 2 outlined that danger. Airlines have suffered economically and many have gone through bankruptcy. Today's airline consumer looks at price above all else. Unable to distinguish one carrier from another, travelers view air travel as a commodity, not as an experience. Lodging must avoid this syndrome, and technology will help it do so.

Technology and the systems that it develops offer many tools. Among them, the ability to solve problems; the opportunity to improve profits through an effective utilization of resources; and positive returns from the use of information management. These advantages are highlighted in Exhibit 14–2.

Of course, technology carries costs as well, and Exhibit 14–2 itemizes these also. Security is on that list of negatives because it is at the forefront of business and governmental concerns. This places it high on the industry's watch list. One example is wireless Internet. It is a service that most hotel guests expect, especially those at business and convention hotels. But private conversations are subject to security breaches. Technology managers and operating executives must assess the risks and implement steps to

---

[3]*Hospitality Upgrade*, Spring, 2007.

The Pluses and Minuses of Hotel Technology	
Advantages	**Disadvantages**
• Accurate information	• Amenity creep
• Better operational controls	• Crashed systems
• Closer fiscal scrutiny	• Ergonomic issues
• Ease of use; minimal training	• Higher-priced employees
• Enhanced guest satisfaction and loyalty	• Initial investment
• Improved labor productivity	• Maintenance expenses
• Reduced operating costs	• Periodic upgrades
• Tighter fiscal controls	• Rapid obsolescence
• Speedier decision making	• Security losses

Exhibit 14–2   An alphabetized list of the advantages and offsetting disadvantages of hotel technology. The plus side wins, by far.

protect the hotel. Either a wireless security protocol such as Wi-Fi protected access (WPA) must be installed, or guests must be asked to sign a disclaimer at registration.

Ergonomics, the study of the relation between machines and humans,[4] is another worry linked with all technology. For lodging it involves the user/employee who may be exposed to eight hours of poorly designed office facilities, or even worse, radiation from computer monitors. Management must attend to both issues, the latter simply by using LCD (liquid crystal display) instead of CRT (cathode ray tube) monitors.

Cost plays a role in technology, as it does with every management decision. The relative price of technology has been in a downward spiral for many years, but new products come onto the market at high initial cost. The organization may need to invest today even though the cost will be lower in the future. Waiting may be too late. Systems must be updated and maintained if they are to contribute to the bottom line. The outlay to do so is evident; the gains much less clear. It poses the same questions as advertising outlays: Will my investment pay off? It's a management conundrum.

Locking Systems

Mechanical Locks.   Colonial innkeepers roomed several parties together. Indeed, strangers often slept in the same bed. Keys were not part of an early inn's inventory. Room security and personal space improved when mechanical keys were introduced (see Exhibit 14–3). Maintaining key inventories became a full-time job split between engineering, which made them, and the desk, which inventoried them (see Exhibit 14–4).

Iron, mechanical keys had several issues. Made of metal with hanging metal tags, they were very heavy. The weight encouraged guests to return them each time they left the building. Although few guests carried them away in pockets or purses, mechanical

---

[4]From the Web page of the International Ergonomics Associations: "Ergonomics (or human factors) is the scientific discipline concerned with the understanding of interactions among humans and other elements of a system, and the profession that applies theory, principles, data and methods to design in order to optimize human well-being and overall system performance."

Exhibit 14–3   Iron keys and mechanical locks were used by hotels well beyond the first half of the 20th Century. New technology made electronic locking systems possible and several highly publicized security lawsuits made hoteliers amenable to their use. *Courtesy of Getty Images, Inc.*

Exhibit 14–4   Compared to a manual key system, which requires tracking thousands of keys, electronic locking systems (ELSs) are easy to manage. ELSs rekey within minutes. Manual systems were so costly and timeconsuming that hotels rarely, if ever, rekeyed.

keys disappeared at an alarming rate. Way back in 1980 when a dollar had real value, Holiday Inn reported key replacement reached $1 million annually. The reason for the turnover was obvious. The tag contained the hotel's name and room number (see Exhibit 14–3). Locks were almost never changed so room thieves returned again and again to ply their trade with the same key.

The American Hotel Association, forerunner of the American Hotel & Lodging Association, convinced postal authorities to accept keys in the mail and return them to the individual hotel, which would pay postage due. That information was printed on the key tag. Some keys made it through; many fell into unauthorized hands.

Something needed to be done. Plastic tags was the first modification (see Exhibit 14–4). The first significant change came in the early 1980s when plastic keys (not plastic tags) with coded punched holes were introduced. They were not unique, meaning that the same key was used for subsequent guests, just as mechanical keys were. Guests liked them because plastic was lighter and easier to carry, especially to the beach or the pool. Hotels favored them since they carried no hotel identification. Room numbers were still required because the key was returned to the desk and recycled for the next occupant of that room.

Electronic Locking Systems (ELS).   Thus, the electronic lock became the third generation of locking systems. About 85% of all U.S. hotels now use one of the two versions of electronic locking systems: hard-wired or microprocessor–based.[5]

Hard-Wired Systems.   Hard-wired systems operate through a central master console that is interfaced to every key lock. This is an expensive installation, but a secure one. The guest-service agent programs a new key for each arrival and transmits that code to the room door through a hard-wired installation. By the time the guest reaches the assigned room, the key lock has the new code and accepts the guest's key. Key codes issued to previous guests are invalidated simultaneously.

Microprocessor–Based Systems.   Microprocessor–based systems are stand-alone installations. There are two types of these ELSs: one-way communication and two-way communications.

ONE-WAY COMMUNICATION SYSTEMS.   These use a microprocessor (a keycard console) with an electronic key encoder. The equipment is not very large; it sits on the counter at the desk. This device encodes new lock combinations on new guest keys as the guests complete their arrival process (see Chapter 8). When the key card is inserted into the lock (see Exhibit 14–5) on the guest-room door, the new combination automatically cancels the previous codes. The door lock contains a battery-powered microprocessor (see Exhibit 14–6) and card reader.

One-way communication systems offer several advantages over mechanical keys. Each is a unique key: Every guest (every party) gets a new key (see Exhibit 14–7). They are light weight, with a magnetic stripe which is not affected by water, sun, or sand.

Key cards are secure. They contain neither the hotel's identification nor the specific room number. They are easily replaced if lost, and the replacement immediately cancels the previous code. Cost is very low, about 10¢ a card. Besides, they are recyclable. Keys that are returned can be reprogrammed for another room and another guest. The system

---

[5]Ellis, Ray. "Lodging Has Seen Rapid Advances in Fire Safety and Security." *Hospitality Technology,* April 2004.

Solitaire 710-11

Exhibit 14–5   Entry to the guest-room door is controlled by a microprocessor (located at the front desk) that encodes a key (see Exhibit 14–7). The lock's microprocessor/card reader are powered by a long-life battery, illustrated by Exhibit 14–6. The lock reads the code and the guest gains entry. *Courtesy of Kaba Lodging Systems, ILCO, Montreal, Canada.*

also allows others to access individual rooms or groups of rooms. Thus, housekeepers, authorized bellpersons, and security agents can gain entry, but each entry leaves an audit trail, as shown in the final frame of Exhibit 14–8.

One-way communication systems have disadvantages, as their name implies. There is no security alert if the wrong key is inserted in the lock. It also takes a trek to the desk for a new key if the party changes rooms; not really a big issue. Their chief limitation is the "one-way" application, as the following section on two-way communications explains.

TWO-WAY COMMUNICATION SYSTEMS.   These systems are another step up. Consequently, they are more expensive to install and somewhat more complex to service. In the two-way installation, a central database communicates to the locks through either a hard-wired system or a wireless one. A major disadvantage of the one-way system is remedied with the two-way program. The guest key can open different doors throughout the hotel; not so with the one-way system. Guest-room keys can access the parking garage, the fitness room, the pool, the elevator, and the concierge floor (see Exhibit 14–8).

Exhibit 14–6   Electronic locking systems that are not hard wired depend on a long-life battery to be a practical installation. Hard-wired systems are more costly to install and are rarely used if the lock system is put in after the hotel's construction. *Courtesy of Kaba Lodging Systems, ILCO, Montreal, Canada.*

Exhibit 14–7   A cardkey with operating instructions for the three types of locks. The lock will not open unless the plastic card key is properly inserted. Each party gets a new, unmarked key, which is light weight and not affected by the elements. *Courtesy of Kaba Lodging Systems, ILCO, Montreal, Canada.*

Similarly, floor housekeepers who are assigned to different stations can gain access remotely to both areas of the hotel. Once a two-way system is in place, interfaces can be installed with the property management system (PMS) and the point-of sale (POS) system,

Key Cards.   Key cards are an essential element of every electronic locking system. But even here, there are variations. Magnetic stripe cards (see Exhibit 14–7) are the most common of the four types.

Magnetic Stripe Cards.   These cards contain three stripes or tracks. Hotels use the first track for their ELSs. The key card looks somewhat like a bank ATM card, but carries a whole set of separate codes. In addition to the lock access codes, key cards carry an expiration date. Some hotels use more than the single stripe/track. Casino/hotels make good use of the extra memory by encoding there the guest's slot-club number or frequent-guest number. While the guest racks up points for membership, the hotel/casino tracks the individual's activity. The information is used to rate the frequency and quality of the guest's play. Supermarket shoppers will recognize the idea from their food-chain cards.

Stripe cards can be encoded further to facilitate charges in dining rooms, lounges, and retail outlets. Personal information such as the guest's credit-card number is not on the key cards, although rumors abound that it is. It may happen one day, but executives from information technology companies and electronic locking system companies strongly refute this now.

Memory Cards.   As their name suggests, memory chips store data such as lock-access codes and other information. The smallest card stores about 2 kilobytes (Kbs) of data, enough to store 25 different key lock codes. Memory goes up from there: 8 Kbs

Guest Cards

Check-in:
Issue card to guest with relevant information.

Parking:
Access to parking facilities.

(Elevator) access:
Access to specified areas only.

Enter room:
Lock checks that keyboard has correct information (room #, unique hotel code, time window etc.).

Payment:
Use keyboard to pay for services at hotel (restaurant, souvenir store etc.).

Other areas:
Guests have access to conference room, gym, etc., with keycard.

Lost keycard:
Hotel issues new keycard.

Enter room w/new keycard:
New keycard replaces previous guest keycard in lock.

Check-out:
Hotel system reports what to bill (restaurant, etc.). Guest leaves and keycard is cancelled for access upon departure.

Staff operations

Issue keycard to employee:
Employee gets individual keycard.

Access:
Only access to specified areas.

Locklink/program lock:
Upload software and data to lock (room #, unique hotel code, set clock).

Housekeeping:
Not able to access room if privacy function is turned on by guest.

Low battery:
When low battery, employees will get 3 yellow flashes.

Lock link/read events:
Download lock events.

Exhibit 14–8   The advantages of two-way communication systems, whether hard wired or wireless, are highlighted here. Both guests and staff access various areas and services throughout the hotel. Security is increased and an audit trail provided. *Courtesy of VingCard Elsafe, an ASSA ABLOY company, Connecticut, U.S.A., and Stockholm, Sweden.*

can carry 125 different key lock codes; 64 Kbs as many as 1,350 key lock codes. Memory cards well serve staff members and managers who need access to multiple locks...and hotels have locks everywhere. A memory card costs between $2 and $4 each, in contrast to the 10¢ of the stripe card mentioned earlier.

Smart Cards.   Smart cards, chip cards, or integrated-circuit cards are any pocket-sized card with embedded, integrated circuits. They are capable of processing information. Smart cards store more information than memory cards. Because they also process data, smart cards can serve as an electronic purse or personal identification (ID). Their cost is upward of $10 each.

RFID Cards.   Radio frequency ID (identification) is the fourth class of cards and the last of the group. We examine them next.

TECHNOLOGY IN THE ROOM: THE NEW GENERATION

Biometric Locking Systems

Smart cards and memory cards separate manual and electronic innovation from the latest advances, biometric and radio frequency identification. The first generation of biometric ELSs was launched by Saflok in 2004. Saflok was among the earliest companies to work in biometrics. In 2006, IBM exhibited a biometric locking system that scanned the user's iris. *Guestroom 2010* was the name of that exhibition. It was sponsored by The Association of Hospitality Financial and Technology Professionals, which was looking ahead four years.

Arriving guests register their fingerprints or iris scans as part of Chapter 8's registration process. Desk clerks forward the information by wireless to the lock. The guest enters without delay when he or she reaches the room. Similar to the two-way system (see above), access can be made just as easily to other locks: the pool; the concierge floor; etc. Two issues have delayed general adoption throughout the industry, and elsewhere. The systems are expensive; all new technology is. More to the point, guests do not feel comfortable giving up sensitive information such as fingerprints and iris scans. Aversion grew greater after it was learned that even CIA and FBI files can be hacked. Replacing a key card is one thing; retrieving hacked iris IDs is something else entirely.

The science might be in place, but its acceptance awaits better security before guests will join in large numbers. Still, Boston-based Nine Zero Hotel uses an iris scanner to monitor access to its Cloud Nine suite.[6]

Radio Frequency Identification (RFID)

Identification using radio frequency is another innovation undergoing tests. It relies on storing and remotely retrieving data using devices called RFID tags or transponders. Similar to all other locking systems, the major parts of RFIDs are the lock and the tags, the keys.

RFID Locks.   RFID locks are battery operated, similar to the power used in microprocessor locks. This special lock (see Exhibit 14–9) looks to the RFID tag to grant access.

---

[6]Ellis, David. "Get ready for the hotel of the future." *CNNMoney*, February 15, 2006. http://www.money.cnn.com/2006/02/14/news/companies/hotels_future.

Exhibit 14–9   A Radio Frequency Identification (RFID) lock contains no open ports and no moving parts. Access is made by radio waves with the encrypted code carried on the tag, or key, or elsewhere, perhaps on a wristband. Physical contact with the door is eliminated: Look, ma, no hands! *Courtesy of Kaba Lodging Systems, SAFLOK, Troy, Michigan.*

The tag can be a standard plastic key card that other locking system use. Or it can be some other encoded device such as a wristband. The encrypted code, which is programmed into, say, a wristband, makes a unique communication credential. It carries the information that "instructs" the lock to permit or deny access to the door. Similar to other improved systems, each exchange is recorded and stored within the lock for audit as needed.

Exhibit 14–9 highlights one of the major innovations of the system: There is no moving part—no keyhole, no card-swipe slot. Opening the door takes no physical contact so there are several obvious advantages:

➤ No need to fumble for the lock opening in a dimly lit corridor
➤ Ease of access for the handicapped
➤ Less maintenance because dirt doesn't clog the aperture
➤ "Open Sesame," even with hands full of suitcases or packages

RFID systems, like previous systems cited, allows multiple access to garages, fitness rooms, and the like as well as to inroom equipment such as minibars or safes. Guests also use the system as an electronic wallet, putting "cash" in their own wristband or those of their children.

Energy Management and Climate Control Systems

After labor, energy is the industry's next largest operating expense,[7] as it is for the nation's airlines. According to the Environmental Protection Agency (EPA), the lodging industry spends nearly $5 billion annually on energy.[8] And costs are rising. Guest-room

---

[7]Whitford, Marty. "Energy-management Systems Save Hoteliers Money." *Hotel & Motel Monthly*, December, 1998.
[8]Terry, Lisa. "The Conservative Hotel." *Hospitality Technology*, March, 2003.

use consumes between 40% and 80% of the total cost, depending on the type and class of hotel. As a percentage, room consumption is smaller at hotels with large public areas.

Energy costs vary by the time of day. Utility rates peak just about the time that guests leave their rooms. Signage that prompts guests to turn off heating, lighting, and airconditioning when they leave the room has not been effective. Hotels began testing Energy Management Systems at the time of the first oil embargo, 1973. Now the industry has moved beyond the testing phase, using one of three approaches: centrally controlled systems; individually controlled systems; or network controlled systems.

Centrally controlled systems have not been well received and are, therefore, not in widespread use. Guests cannot adjust the room temperature. Control of the entire hotel rests with the engineering department. It sets a standard that old guests and young, northern guests and southern guests, national and foreigners must accept. They don't do so happily.

Individually controlled systems have been in place for a long time because they have been the guests' preference. Guests have the comfort of setting their own inroom temperatures and hotels the anguish of controlling costs.

Network-controlled systems strike a balance. Guests control comfort; hotelkeepers control energy costs. Guests control HVAC (heating, ventilation, and air-conditioning) while they are in the room. The hotel controls the temperature (and lighting) when guests leave the room. They do so with inroom sensors that operate within four levels of occupancy; sold; sold and occupied; sold but unoccupied; and unsold. Ceiling sensors electronically communicate the status of the room to the energy management system. Three types are in use.

Electronic Key Card Systems. A wall-mounted unit at the entrance to the room controls all electrical and HVAC devices. Nothing will operate until a magnetic stripe keycard, the room key, is inserted (see Exhibit 14–10). Obviously, when the guest leaves and takes the card, everything goes off. A one- or two-minute delay allows the guest ample time to exit. This, the simplest of the energy control systems, needs no inroom sensors. Installation costs are minimal and savings are real.

Inconvenience to the guests is part of the downside. Everything stops operating while guests are gone. They may return to very hot (or cold) rooms that take time to moderate, leaving them uncomfortable for a time.

Control is a serious weakness. The wall-mounted unit takes any card. Savvy guests get two cards or carry one from another hotel and leave the extra in the slot. Then everything runs without pause, defeating the very purpose of the system. For environmentally sensitive guests, it works perfectly.

Body-Motion Detection Systems. A motion detection system requires inroom sensors, and inhall sensors as well, since the installation should be extended beyond the guest rooms. When the ceiling sensor detects no motion, lights and HVAC equipment are shut down. These are sensitive instruments able to detect motion from adults, children, and pets. Cost is the chief disadvantage of the installation. Balance is its chief advantage—balance because energy-consuming equipment is not closed down completely, but is, rather, reduced to a preset level. Recovery and comfort are rapidly restored when the guest returns. The system recalls the last-entered temperature and operates until that is achieved.

Motion detection systems are not limited to guest rooms and corridors. They work well in public space such as banquet rooms. Here, too, nothing is absolute. Lights and temperatures are reduced, but a minimum of both assure safety for anyone passing through.

Exhibit 14-10   A wall-mounted receptacle controls utilities within the guest room. Guests insert their room keys to rev up power for HVAC and lighting. When exiting the room, they take their keys, shutting off energy service to the room. Except sometimes they don't: They leave a second key in the slot to retain the utilities. This device is used more often in the hot section of, say northern Australia, than in the U.S.A.

Like any equipment, the system doesn't work unless it is properly installed. Hidden angles and nooks in the room and bath may convey a nonoccupancy mode, which might shut down the system even when guests are present. Quiet sleepers may also be sensed as a vacancy. There are anecdotal cases, probably "urban myths," of such sleepers waking ill because the entire night passed without once triggering the HVAC.

Body-Heat Detection Systems.   Heat-detection systems are similar to motion installations, except they work from the body heat generated by guests and pets. Consequently, heat-detections systems are thought to be more reliable. Sensing no heat, the system reduces energy consumption to a preset level. Sensing occupancy, the system allows the guest to set the parameters.

Both types of detection systems interface with the hotel's property management system because the PMS holds information about occupancy. If the room is unsold, the system maintains HVAC at either the minimum level or none at all, as weather dictates. If the room has been sold, energy is regulated according to the room's immediate status: sold and occupied or sold but unoccupied.

"True" Detection Systems.   A new energy management system has been developed by *Smart Systems International*. Increased accuracy and reliability is achieved by combining body-heat detection and body-motion systems (see Exhibit 14–11). Thus, a truer detection system is achieved. An added feature, an adaptive learning system, controls the amount of time needed to return the temperature to the guests' set point

Exhibit 14-11   A "true" Detection System regulates inroom energy consumption by responding to both movement within the room and body temperature from persons and pets. Dual sensory systems increase reliability, but cost more. *Courtesy of Smart Systems International, Las Vegas, Nevada.*

once the room is reoccupied. Recovery time is typically set at 12 minutes when the system is installed, but hotels have the option to change the program at any time. Unlike fixed setback thermostats, drifting recovery time around outside weather conditions enhances guest comfort.

Digital thermostats are integral to all of the energy management systems (see Exhibit 14–12). They are standard equipment so guests recognize them and use them easily to control temperature while the room is occupied.

Networked Fire Alarm System

A 1946 fire in Atlanta was the nation's worst hotel conflagration until 1980, when an inferno at the MGM Grand in Las Vegas killed 85 and injured 700 persons.[9] Untouched areas that were protected by a sprinkler system contrasted sharply with sections that were not. Knowledge gained from the disaster spawned tighter fire regulations for hotels across the nation. Several technologies were developed both to help control the spread of a blaze and to communicate the double danger of smoke and fire.

The Hotel and Motel Fire Safety Act[10] was a delayed spinoff of the Las Vegas tragedy. Federal employees on official government business must stay in fire-safe accommodations. For the purpose of the act, every guestroom must have no less than an AC-powered smoke alarm. These are commonly called "hard wired." Installation must be in accordance with the National Fire Protection Association (NFPA) Standard 72. Battery-powered alarms do not meet that criterion. Batteries wear out and guests steal them. An AC-powered alarm with a battery backup is even more desirable, but is not mandated. Under the act, buildings of four stories or more must also have sprinklers. Inroom sprinkler systems represent a significant safety upgrade. The fire code in Las Vegas was changed so all hotels in that city now have inroom sprinkler systems.

---

[9]Stoller, Gary. "Better Fire Safety in Hotels Saves Lives." *USA Today*, November 20, 2005.
[10]The act is available at http://www.usfa.dhs.gov/applications/hotel/hm-faq.cfm.

Exhibit 14–12
Digital thermostats
support every
energy-saving sys-
tem. Many guests
have them in their
homes as well.
*Courtesy of Smart
Systems Interna-
tional, Las Vegas,
Nevada.*

Standalone alarms, similar to those used by homeowners, are not adequate for hotels with public space and hundreds of guest rooms. Large areas of hotel buildings are unattended for long periods. Lodging facilities need a networked fire-alarm system. An integrated fire-safety system saves lives, reduces fire damages, lowers insurance premiums and minimizes costly litigation. Components of such a system include a centralized computer or fire-command console that uses electronic and audiocontrol devices for fire alert, response, and protection.

A good fire system connects smoke detectors (see Exhibit 14–13) to a central management system by means of a wireless network. Sensing smoke, the detector notifies the closest receiving unit, which transmits the information to the central management system. Taken up a level, the fire system is also interfaced with a paging system. Security is paged and directed to the area or specific room to check the status. (False alarms do occur; see the case incident at the end of this chapter.) Well-managed hotels respond with trained fire teams composed of individuals from several departments. The manager on duty also responds and decides whether or not to call the public fire department.

Minibars

Minibars changed over time as technology improved the degree of automation. Some are still not automated; others are completely automated by means of microprocessors. In between are semiautomated models.

The convenience of minibars plays an important role in guest satisfaction, especially in full-service hotels. They must be important because guests willingly pay a handsome premium for the soft drinks, candy, liquor, snacks and personal items that minibars disburse.

Exhibit 14-13   Increased safety results when smoke detectors are interfaced to a central fire-control network. The federal Hotel and Motel Fire Safety Act requires these devices to be hard wired, not merely battery operated. *Courtesy of INNCOM international inc., Niantic, Connecticut.*

The minibar is a good profit center for the hotel. Mindful of guest expectations, some hotels provide (without charge) an empty refrigerator that occupants stock as they prefer.

Traditional (Nonautomated) Minibars.   Early versions of the minibar (see Exhibit 14–14)—and they are still popular—require a daily, manual count by a minibar employee. He or she must enter every occupied room, open the refrigerator, and count the contents. Each entry imposes on the guest and the guest's privacy. A voucher is prepared for anything consumed and given to the desk so charges can be made to the folio (see Chapter 10). Of course, each minibar then needs to be restocked.

Exhibit 14-14   Earlier versions–and many are still in use–of minibars required daily, manual counts to determine what charges needed to be posted to the guest's folio. Newer versions are tied electronically to the PMS so posting is automatic (see Exhibit 14–15). Restocking remains a manual job. (Counting and restocking are among the services supposedly covered by resort fees.) *Courtesy of Minibar North America, Inc., Bethesda, Maryland.*

To minimize labor costs some hotels tried eliminating the employee, relying on a honor system instead. It was penny wise and pound foolish. Labor was still needed to restock. Honor remains part of the procedure, nevertheless. The minibar inspector works during the day. Guests return to their rooms and use the minibars at night; they check out the following morning. Guest-service agents/cashiers routinely ask departing guests whether they used any minibar items in the past 24 hours. Some pay up; some do not.

Putting a "seal" on the minibar reduces labor costs. Guests must break the seal in order to retrieve an item. The staff member need only make a quick survey from the door. If the seal is intact, the associate moves on quickly to the next room. If broken, the count and restocking proceed as usual.

Semiautomated Systems.   Vendors came up with semiautomated minibars and completely automated ones in response to the several disadvantages of the initial equipment. One innovation built on the "seal" idea used on the nonautomated equipment. Whenever the bar door is opened, a door alert reports over telephone lines to the property management system. Staff members get a report that shows which rooms have used the minibar and, therefore, which have not. If there is no activity, the room is skipped. This reduces both labor costs and imposition on guests.

Automated (Microprocessor) Systems.   Automated minibars monitor and process sales transactions electronically. Each tray in the minibar is programmed to inventory a certain item (see Exhibit 14–15). A clock begins ticking whenever a product is removed from its designated space, giving the shopper 10 to 60 seconds for "inspection time." The cost of an item not returned within that window of time is charged automatically to the guest's folio.

Posting is accomplished through an interface between the automated minibar and the property management system. The PMS sends an unlocking signal to the inroom minibar as soon as the guest checks in. It is thus able to identify the item purchased, the time of the purchase, the amount of the purchase, and its tray location. A quick printout of minibar activity is possible if the guest disputes a charge at the desk.

		Total Purchases *Minibar*		
Minibar Bill for Room: 101		**TIME:** 12:54 **DATE:** SUNDAY 15 APRIL		
Date	*Time*	*Contents*	*Price (US $)*	*Location*
13 April	11:32:45	Imported Beer	3.50	Location 11
13 April	12:45:55	Tonic Water	1.50	Location 08
14 April	12:55:10	Gin	4.50	Location 07
14 April	12:55:12	Nuts	2.00	Location 13
15 April	09:02:12	Mineral Water	1.50	Location 15
15 April	09:03:01	Orange Juice	2.00	Location 17
15 April	14:32:34	Domestic Beer	3.00	Location 10
		Total Purchases	18.00 (inc tax)	

Guest checked in 11:25 13 April
* * * * * * * * * * * * * *THIS BILL FOR CHECKING PURPOSES ONLY* * * * * * * * * * * * *

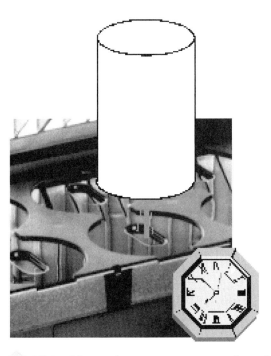

Exhibit 14-15   Each item in an automated minibar sits on a pressure-sensitive tray. Guests have time to examine the product and return it if unused. An electronic signal from the room to the folio by means of the property management system posts charges when the item is consumed. A record is maintained and quickly printed out if the guest protest the charges, see below. *Courtesy of Bartech System International, Millersville, Maryland.*

Relocking the minibar is part of the PMS's automatic check-out procedure. Just as is, say, putting the room on change. Also, the system tracks expiration dates on the products. Unfortunately, it does not restock automatically—at least not yet—so labor remains a significant cost. But the PMS helps even with labor. A daily report of total minibar consumption is one of many reports generated by the PMS during the night audit (see Chapter 13). Minibar employees use the report to requisition and draw refills for the following day.

REFILL REQUIREMENTS REPORT
Automated Minibar System
Date: 15 April

Refill requirements report for the following rooms/groups/zones: **ALL**

Item	Unit
Spa Still Water	22
Gordon's Gin	12
Canada Dry Tonic Water	14
Orange Juice	78
Vodka	45
Coca-Cola (Can)	76
Evian Water (50ml)	56
Seven-Up (Can)	14
Domestic Beer	45
Imported Beer	23

A complementary report, also from the previous night's audit, identifies which rooms get which replacements of the total inventory draw.

REFILL REQUIREMENTS REPORT
Automated Minibar System
Date: 15 April

Refill requirements report for the following rooms/groups/zones:
First Floor/Room By Room

	Quantity	*Item*	*Tray #*
Room: 103	1	Spa Still Water	6
	1	Gordon's Gin	9
	1	Canada Dry Tonic Water	3
Room: 109	1	Orange Juice	12
	2	Vodka	14
	1	Coca-Cola (Can)	4
Room: 115	1	Evian Water (50ml)	5
	2	Seven-Up (Can)	7
	1	Domestic Beer	8
	2	Imported Beer	17

Minibars began life as refrigerators. Guests still like to use them as such. They are perfect for storing half a sandwich, a baby's formula, or some medicine. Sometime space is so tight that an item must be removed to make room for the guest's personal needs. Newer models need to accommodate this secondary use because getting charged for an unused item is irritating, and trying to obtain an offsetting allowance is frustrating.

Inroom Safes

State laws require every hotel to maintain a safe or lose the protection of the limited-liability laws that each state has enacted (see Chapter 8). Large, common, iron safes behind the desk were the standard until small, personal, inroom safes were introduced (see Exhibit 14–1). Modern and secure, these inroom safes need only be large enough to hold a laptop computer and, perhaps, a camcorder or camera.

Initially, most hotels charge for inroom safes. Purchase contracts were often based on a split between the hotel and the safe provider. Hotels kept all the income after the purchase price was recovered. Most dropped the charge thereafter, offering the safe as another amenity. It was a messy arrangement otherwise. Tying the safe to the PMS was too costly a means of tracking use. So a "safe charge" was added to every folio during the night audit. Guests complained loudly about the charge, as they do still about "resort fees" (see Chapter 9).

Safes reduce theft. Electronic locking systems battle external theft; inroom safes reduce internal losses. Theft by employees (internal theft) is usually an impulsive act caused by temptation. Valuables in the safe remove the temptation. They also undercut the guest's effort at defrauding the hotel. Reduced insurance premiums are another savings. The safe is very heavy, almost impossible to carry, but is bolted down or magnetized nevertheless. Moreover, access to the protection is not evident.

Just as guest-room locks started with mechanical keys, so did inroom safes. Not nearly as heavy as the original door keys, guests signed for and obtained lock keys from the desk. Lost keys required a locksmith to open the safe and rekey the lock at the guest's expense. Today's electronic safes carry an override feature. Management can override the guest's code or the key card code if an emergency arises. It takes two inputs: an instrument that looks like a cell phone and maintains an override audit trail, and an override security code.

Electronic inroom safes upgraded asset security as electronic keys upgraded personal security. And, similar to the door lock, access to the safe progressed through several steps.

Magnetic Stripe Cards.   The keycard that opens the guest-room door can also serve as the safe key card (see Exhibit 14–16). These keys are either simple magnetic strip cards or the more advanced smart cards discussed earlier in the chapter.

Code-Based (Digital) Entry.   Exhibit 14–17 illustrates the code-based safe. Digital safes are superior to both the mechanical and key card safes because there is no secondary element (the key or the card) to be lost. Each new guest enters a personal code. Typically, guests use easily remembered numbers: birthdates, PIN numbers, home-security codes and the like.

Exhibit 14-16   Electronic inroom safes can be accessed in several ways. Here, a closet-located safe is opened by a keycard, either a simple magnetic card or one of the "smart" cards. *Courtesy of VingCard Elsafe, an ASSA ABLOY company, Connecticut, U.S.A. and Stockholm, Sweden.*

Exhibit 14-17   Digital code-based safes operate on a PIN number that each guest creates, usually one that the guest has used before. *Courtesy of VingCard Elsafe, an ASSA ABLOY company, Connecticut, U.S.A. and Stockholm, Sweden.*

Biometric Safes.   Biometric safes use the same technology as biometric door keys. Guests register either their fingerprint or their iris scan before using the safe. Biometrics are the most convenient of the systems because there is no key to lose or PIN code to forget. However, not all models accommodate multiple users at this time, so double occupancy poses an issue. The iris or fingerprint of one guest will not trigger the mechanism that was created with the biometrics of the room's companion. Exhibit 14–18 shows the biometric safe.

COMMUNICATION SYSTEMS

As members of the broad community, hotels respond to change, be it a social reordering or a technological innovation. Worldwide communication falls easily within both categories.

Exhibit 14-18   Biometric safes use the same technology as biometric door keys. Neither are yet in widespread use and will not likely be until users get over their reluctance to surrender very personal data. Biometric safes require no key and no PIN code. *Courtesy of Minibar North America, Inc., Bethesda, Maryland.*

A Brief History of Telephone Service

Between the early 1980s and the late 1990s, the telephone department was a big contributor to the hotel industry's bottom line. Departmental income exceeded 2.5% of total hotel revenues. Telephones were profitable because they were deregulated and automated. Telephone revenues fell victim to both social reordering and technological innovation. Departmental profits now contribute less than 1% of total industry revenue. Part of the decline must be attributable to changing habits and the introduction of the cellular phone. Part of the decline must be attributable to the excess charges that hotels levied on inroom telephone use, charges that drove customers away.

To encourage the growth of hotel telephones, the Federal Communications Commission (FCC)—which regulates *inter*state calls, not *intra*state calls (calls within a state)—issued a 1944 ruling. Telephone companies were directed to pay a 15% commission for all calls originating in hotels. Before direct-dial telephones, hotel operators connected guest callers to the telephone company's operators. When the call was completed, the company's operator would call the hotel operator and quote "time and charges." To those charges, the hotel added its 15% commission and hand-posted the total to the folio (see Chapter 10).

With the direct-dial telephone, which bypassed the telephone company's operator, charges were routed through a call accounting system (CAS). The CAS tracked the calls and the charges and reported them to the front-office cashier by means of a printer located at the front desk. Charges were posted manually to the folios. Progress continued: The CAS was interfaced with the PMS. Pencil-and-paper posting was used no longer.

It took almost 40 years (1981) before the FCC changed the rules again. This time, the required 15% commission was dropped, allowing each hotel to set its own surcharge. And charge they did. Revenue zoomed. At first guests went to telephone booths to avoid the excess surcharges; next came the cell phone. Both social change and innovation brought a rapid decline to inroom telephone use. That's why revenues began falling as the 20th century ended.

Internet Access

Internet access has paralleled the development of the cell phone. It, too, brings social reordering along with technological innovation. The rapid acceptance of both technologies created two different business models for the lodging industry. Some hotels offer Internet access without charge. They build the cost into the room rate. Some hotels charge for Internet access, usually at a daily rate. Charges for a 24-hour day range from as little as $6.99 to as much as $49.99. One explanation for the spread is the type of access.

Dial-Up Access.   The first generation of Internet access is dial-up. An inroom connection to the Internet provider is made by means of a computer modem and a data port in the telephone. Speed is poor, transmission is limited to 56 kilobits per second (Kbps). Still, many users, especially business travelers, prefer dial-up access because of the heightened security. They willingly trade away speed to get security.

High Speed with Wired Access.   Every high-tech advance that the text discusses has come in stages, both in technological developments and cost increments. That's also true of Internet access. Depending on the type of cable and bandwidth used by the hotel, the speed of the Internet connection varies between 1 Mbps and 100 Mbps (Megabits per second). The cost outlay for the hotel varies with each, but wired high speed is costly, whatever the system.

With wired access, sleeping rooms are furnished with an Ethernet cable. Guests attach their portable computers by means of a network interface card. To minimize the hotel's liability, guests are asked to sign a liability waiver before using the equipment. Most hotels require the waiver, whether the wired access is free or not.

High Speed with Wireless Access.   Lodging managers prefer wireless access to wired access for two reasons. Guests transact much of their business in public settings, such as lobbies and meeting rooms, where wired access is difficult to install and monitor. Moreover, a wireless installation is much less costly than a wired one. That brings the issue back to security.

Wireless means just that: The message goes into the air. The information can be captured by anyone and used for his or her personal gain. The user-guest knows that as well as the innkeeper, but security fears have not deterred the very rapid growth of wireless access.

The Institute of Electrical and Electronics Engineers (IEEE) has recommended standards for wireless and wired network communications. They are known as 802.11b, 802.11g, and 802.11a. Code 802.11b was one of the first standards for transmitting data up to 11 Mbps. The other two, newer standards, transmit at up to 54 Mbps.

It is repetitious to say, but every high-tech advance that the text discusses has come in stages: both technological developments and cost increments. A new jump in communication technology has already taken place, Voice-Over-Internet Protocol.

Future of Hotel Telephones

The decline in telephone revenues has been noticed: noticed big time! The search is on for new revenue sources. Guests might be enticed back to the hotel's facilities by means of a one-price, telecommunications bundle. As homeowners, guests are already getting bundled rates. Wyndham was among the first to launch the format, testing it within their frequent-guest program. Currently, all *Wyndham By Request*® members get free Internet access and free local and long-distance calls. The Westin at Chicago's O'Hare Airport charges $9.99 for 24-hour Internet access, but also offer a "Telecom Bundle." Its $16 per-day package includes high speed Internet access; long-distance calls within the U.S.; local calls; and operator assistance. Other properties are joining in the bundling, taking advantage of the rapid technical advances of VOIP.

Voice-Over-Internet Protocol (VOIP).   This upgrade is so new that the language hasn't yet solidified. One hears it called VoIP; VOIP; IP telephony; Internet telephony; Broadband telephony; Broadband Phone; and Voice over Broadband. Whatever the name, it routes voice conversation over the Internet or through any other IP-based network instead of the analog (twisted-pair-cable) phone lines. Improvements in VOIP have been rapid. Sound quality, which was poorer initially than analog transmission, has quickly reached analog levels.

Hotels need a broadband, high-speed Internet connection if they want to use VOIP. Most have the installation; certainly, members of a chain do. Hotels within a chain are usually connected by an IP network that supports the chain's data service. Telecommunication costs are drastically reduced if the individual hotel uses that same network for guests' long-distance calls. The property most likely pays a flat, monthly fee to the ISP (Internet service provider) for unlimited use of the network. This recreates the revenue center even as the per-call price charged to guests falls. Switching from traditional telephone lines to VoIP is not complicated.

The traditional, handset telephone can be reconfigured to the new technology by an analog adaptor, which converts analog signals to digital signals. The cost is minimal, about $50 per handset. That's much less costly than the $500 needed to replace handsets with VOIP digital phones. As the text mentioned earlier, technology costs continue to fall, so both figures will likely be less by the time the reader is using this information.

VOIP telephones don't look much different than their analog cousins (see Exhibit 14–19), but they are a world apart. They are also the future of hotel telephony. VoIP phones are a service and application delivery system all by themselves. The installation provides digital voice mail; alarm clocks; room service, spa, and golf interfaces; high-speed Internet access; an entry to *GameBoy*[11], a guest-room control console for lighting, television, DVD and temperature control; a digital hotel guide; and conference-call capability.

Wake-Up Systems

Most telephone installations include both voice mail and wake-up service, of which there are four types.

Manual Wake-Up Systems.   There is an extended history of manual wake-up systems because they have been in use long before any technological advances. Guests call the telephone operator requesting a wake-up call. The operator notes the room and time on a specially ruled time sheet and sets a special alarm clock that accommodates five-minutes differences. At the appropriate time, the alarm rings and the call is made to the room. Sometimes the call is early and sometimes it's late, depending upon the operator's call volume that morning.

Semiautomatic Systems.   These systems are one step up in automation. The guest still calls the operator, who manually enters the room and time into the system. It

Exhibit 14–19   Telephone equipment that accepts VoIP (Voice-over-Internet-Protocol) looks no different than the traditional instrument. Lower costs are driving its spreading use and holding out, perhaps, some chance of reinvigorating revenues from the hotel's telephone department. *Courtesy of Cisco Systems, Inc., San Jose, California.*

---

[11]*Game Boy* is a handheld, game console released as the first of its kind by Nintendo in 1989. Because it remains an all-time best seller, the name references the entire game genre.

is the system, not the operator, that makes the wake-up call. A prerecorded message might say, "This is your wake-up call; this is your wake-up call." Other options provide the date and day of the week and a brief weather report. The message is repeated every five minutes until the guest answers. After four or five tries, the system either shuts down or—the preferred—alerts security to make certain the guest is not in distress.

Fully Automated and Interactive TV Wake-Up Systems. With this system, guests bypass the hotel's telephone operator and make the connection by simply pushing a "wake-up" button. A digital voice walks the user through the several simple steps. For example, for 7:00 AM, the instruction says to punch in 0700. Then it asks for a confirmation. The telephone rings at the desired time and an automated message similar to that of the semiautomated system plays its tune and/or delivers its message. Sometimes it is a sales message: "Want to order room-service breakfast?"

Interactive systems employ an interface between the wake-up equipment and the television set. Guests set the wake-up call with the TV remote. Technologically advanced or not, every hotels furnishes inroom alarm clocks. Alarm clocks are one of the most important technology items in a business hotel.[12]

Voice Mail

Voice mail enables a caller to leave a message for an absent guest. Historically, a telephone operator took such a message, wrote it down, and left it the guest's mailbox (by room number) at the front desk; hence the term voice mailbox. Technology has removed the operator from the message procedure, as it has with wake-up calls. By so doing, the system improved the accuracy of the message, reduced labor costs for the hotel, and made delivery more timely. A blinking light on the telephone alerts the guest to the waiting message. No longer any need to trek to the desk.

Voice mail is more common in full-service properties than in transient lodging such as motor hotels. The advantages are numerous. Guests can leave messages as well as receive them. They can have messages forwarded to another room. The message can be personal and in the guest's native language, or defaulted to the standard English message built into the system. Access can be limited, requiring callers to use a special PIN number that the guest has created.

Pressing the call-message button activates the system when the guest returns. He or she is told that there are a given number of messages, some old, some new. Messages can be saved or deleted. The system is activated when a guest checks in. Some systems hold messages up to 24 hours after check-out, unless the room is assigned to a new guest in the interim.

OTHER TECHNOLOGIES

Inroom Entertainment Systems

Color television came to the hospitality industry in 1975 (see Exhibit 14–1). Within five years, almost every property offered it as an amenity. Today's generation of travelers expect rooms to have the same multimedia and entertainment choices that they use at

---

[12]Kistner, M., Cobanoglu, C., and Dickinson, C. "What Keeps the Hospitality Industry from Making the Right Technology Investments Even When They Are Staring Us in the Face." *International Hotel, Motel and Restaurant Show*, 2005. http://www.ahma.com/pdf/NewYorkHotelMotelShow-AHLA2005.pdf.

home. Inroom entertainment is a fast growing revenue center.[13] Visitors are willing to pay for movies, video-on-demand, inroom games and high-speed Internet access. Hoteliers have shifted their offerings from conventional cable to high-tech options such as high-definition, flat panel monitors and video-on-demand equipment. Guests want to watch what they want and when they want. So when interfaced with other systems, "entertainment" systems offer:

➤ Personalized welcoming messages on the TV screens of new arrivals

➤ Video-on-demand by means of pay-per-view (films and programs) that guests special order with options such as pause, rewind, and fast forward

➤ High-speed Internet, which usually includes free news and weather

➤ Wake-up calls interfaced to the television as explained previously

➤ Room service with pictures of the menu items displayed on the television screen

➤ Live feedback to management from surveys. Survey items that guests mark very low alert the manager on duty by means of a paging interface. Here's a unique opportunity for the hotel to "make it right" (see Chapter 7)

➤ Different language options, especially useful as international tourism booms

➤ Internet Protocol-based radio that captures broadcasts over the Internet from around the world. Thus, say, a Turkish guests can tune in Power FM, a popular radio channel from Turkey

➤ Folio viewing, billing, and settling as part of the departure process. Folios can follow guests to their homes or offices by land mail or Internet (see Chapter 10)

➤ Parental control of programming, blocking adult material from their children's sets

➤ Compatibility with MP3 players and portable DVD players that many guests now carry

... And that's just the start of what is still to come.

At the Desk

Technology's greatest impact has been at the desk. The property management system has quickened the speed of service; reduced labor cost; improved accuracy, and modernized the look and flow of the lobby. The PMS has been with us throughout the text, from the chapters on reservations and arrivals to those dealing with billing and auditing. Because, contradictory as it seems, the nonpersonal, self-service aspects of an electronically supported hotel strengthens the guest's perception of a caring management. Guests know that staff is available; that desk personnel will respond when needed. Knowing help can be summoned, guests appreciate the speed and anonymity of self-service. Travelers, especially business travelers, dislike waiting in line, whether they are arriving or departing. So the self-service kiosk that speeds the guest along simultaneously saves the hotel labor. One study estimated the labor savings to be between 15% and 20%! Another anomaly: Self-service kiosks may actually increase revenue. Unlike stumbling guest-service agents, kiosks easily prompt guests to buy up. Without awkwardness, kiosks plug the ancillary services of restaurants, lounges, spas, and nightclubs. Advertising revenue from lobby concessionaires and external merchants has proven to be another, unexpected plus.

---

[13]In-room entertainment system solutions. http://www.microsoft.com/industry/hospitality/solutions/inroomentertainment.mspx.

As Chapter 8 explained, self-check-in equipment accommodates arrivals with a swipe of their credit cards (see Exhibit 14–20). It accepts registrations, cuts keys, and prints instructions for finding the room. Property management systems continue handling guests' records during their stay, tracking everything through point of sale terminals (POSs), telephone call-accounting systems (CAs), in-room minibars and safes, electronic locks, and fire systems. And then back to the kiosk and its PMS interface for an electronic check-out.

Internet-based systems push the process forward. Check-ins via the hotel's Web site are accepted as early as seven days before arrival. Radisson Hotels led with this idea. "Express Yourself" features a three-step process. (1) Guests make reservations through any of the means discussed in Chapters 5 and 6. (2) Seven days before arrival the system sends emails inviting guests "to express" themselves by checking in. Personal preferences are accommodated: room location; no-smoking; king bed; etc. (3) The key is waiting when the guest arrives and offers identification. Other hotels offer Internet-based check-in by smart phones or personal digital-assistants such as Blackberry or Treo.

Similar hand-held devices are used by guest-service agents. Cross-trained staffers exit the desk. Then from the middle of the lobby, the rear of the line, by the curb, or in the parking lot or garage, guests are registered by wireless equipment that communicates with the PMS. It's service with a technological smile.

Stages in Hotel Technology

Control Panels.   Progress comes in steps. Gas light replaced candle light; electric light replaced gas light. Bedside switches augmented entry-door switches. Now, guest-room control panels (see the next generation, Exhibit 14–21) are showing

Exhibit 14–20   Guests, especially business guests, dislike the delays of standing in line. Strategically located equipment speeds guests along, whether they are arriving or departing. The photo shows the advantage. The guest in the foreground is handling his account while the guests in the background monopolize the guest-service agent. *Courtesy of Micros Systems, Inc., Columbia, Maryland.*

Room Control   Guest Services   Alarm Clock &   2-Line
                                               Digital Radio   Seakerphone

Exhibit 14–21   Bed-side panels, which control everything from window drapes to HVAC, are on the horizon, but not yet anywhere near a regular amenity. New technology has come in pieces and been installed in hotel rooms in pieces. An integrated control panels awaits an integrated installation. *Courtesy of INNCOM international inc., Niantic, Connecticut.*

up in a few avant-garde hotels. They go hand-in-glove with high-tech installations. Control panels are not yet widely used because technological installations have been piecemeal. It will take new construction to capture all the technology pieces from the start before control panels are common throughout the lodging industry. When that happens, a panel by the bedside will control temperature and ventilation (HVAC), lighting, window curtains, television, DVD player, radio, clock, digital *Gameboy*, and CD player. And who knows what else will be designed to upgrade service, speed, and earnings. One thing is certain: The industry would never have achieved any level of integration were it not for standardization.

Standardization: From HITIS and Beyond.   Lodging now employs many technologies, but getting to this stage has been a bumpy road. Early systems were unable to talk to one another. That incompatibility was an industrywide issue that slowed—almost halted—progress. Initially, the industry lacked knowledge of the subject. Appropriately, a decision was made to adopt an industrywide approach. The American Hotel & Lodging Association launched an initiative called Hospitality Industry Technology Integration Standards (HITIS).

The HITIS committee created a unified programming structure for the Property Management System and its related interfaces. Compatibility between, say, PMS equipment and POS terminals, or between the PMS and the CAS (call accounting system), didn't exist. One reason? Research costs forced each manufacturer to specialize in just one or two pieces of equipment. HITIS created standards and hoteliers were urged to specify them as part of their requests for bid (RFB) as early equipment was upgraded. And they did with good success.

OTA, OpenTravel Alliance, the next generation of cooperative effort, expanded the horizon from "Hospitality" to "Travel." Its goal states: " . . . our primary focus is the creation of electronic message structures to facilitate communication between the disparate systems in the global travel industry." The organization's Web site goes on to identify membership, including "Travel suppliers, defined as any company with primary control of inventory, including air carriers, car rental companies, hotel companies, railways, cruise lines, insurance companies, golf course owners, motorcycle, water or bicycle tour companies, etc."

Clearly, OTA's interest doesn't focus on lodging separately, but rather as one of its cross-industry sectors. Within the definition of a travel supplier, the hotel industry isn't as large as hoteliers imagine. As industry-buyers learned with HITIS, it takes cooperation among the immediate user-buyers to force uniformity from the manufacturer-sellers. A new association, HTNG, returned the momentum to the lodging industry.

Hotel Technology Next Generation (HTNG), a nonprofit organization, is more like HITIS than is OTA. All three organizations bring manufacturers, suppliers, consultants, and end-users together. HTNG's narrower universe concentrates on lodging, whereas lodging is but one segment within OTA. Within itself, lodging's focus is all inclusive, embracing the full scope of lodging technology: operations, telecommunications, inroom entertainment, customer information systems, and electronic installations.

Employing the initiatives of both of its predecessor organizations as well as its own, HTNG has begun certifying products, identifying them with a HTNG label and special logo. In so doing, it rejuvenates the work of HITIS. By using standardized interfaces rather than reinventing, as was done in the early effort, vendors save time and money. Knowing that larger companies will interface with them, smaller vendors are encouraged to participate. This broadens the scope of progress.

Whatever the organization one subscribes to, it works only if hoteliers buy from vendors that comply with universal standards. They have; so progress continues unabated.

SUMMARY

No longer is hotel technology viewed as an operating cost center. Today, it is a strategic item in the toolbox of the modern hotel executive. Technology impacts guests from the time of their intended stay through their arrival and departure, and into their next stay. It tracks, implements, and facilitates so many parts of the guest's stay and the hotel's operation that no summary list is practical.

For an industry as old as innkeeping, technology is but a kid. Still, it has awakened the old one and has shaken its traditions, including the sacred cow of "service." Few would argue that service has been diminished in any way by the use of property management systems, or inroom facilities, or better safety and security equipment. Technology is a great differentiator, separating the Mine Host profile of Chapter 3 from the modern hotel executive. We find it in almost a dozen applications in the guest room alone. Just as the single bed with a connecting bath has been replaced with supreme bedding and multiple shower heads, so has the operator-assisted telephone and the open window been replaced by VoIP phones and sophisticated HVAC systems.

The technological revolution has just entered the time line of the world's perspective. Relatively speaking, the lodging industry was late to the game. But the pace is accelerating Hoteliers need to be further ahead than merely getting ready.

RESOURCES AND CHALLENGES
Resources

WEB SITES

http://www.hitec.org Hospitality Financial Technology Professionals (HFTP)—Austin, TX. An association of hotel financial/technology companies and individuals that started as the National Association of Hotel Accountants (1952) and grew through several stages to the HFTP. The association premiered *Guestroom 2010* at its HITEC 2006.

http://www.htng.org Hotel Technology, Next Generation (HTNG)—Schaumburg, IL. Providing "leadership that will facilitate the creation of one (or more) industry solution set(s) for the lodging industry" is HTNG's mission statement.

http://www.opentravel.org OpenTravel Alliance (OTA)—Washington, D.C. An organization of and founded by companies in the travel industry, focusing "on the creation of electronic message structures to facilitate communication between the disparate systems in the global travel industry."

http://www.2getsmart.com Smart Systems International—Las Vegas, NV. A representative manufacturer and distributor of inroom energy control systems; one of many such technical companies to be found on the Web.

Web Assignment

Visit http://www.hitec.org and report on either the next or the previous HITEC meeting: What it means; where it was or is to be; the number of vendors; and two interesting aspects of the meeting's content.

INTERESTING TIDBITS

➤ The U.S.'s first coded lock system for hotels was installed in 1979 in the Westin Peachtree Plaza in Atlanta, Georgia.

➤ A elderly lady requested room 720 as she checked in. The guest-service agent explained that the room was taken. "Now don't lie to me, young lady." "No, I am sorry but that room is occupied. I can locate you close by." "It can't be taken! You see, I took the key when I was here last time. Aha!"

➤ The Lock Museum of Orange Country is located in Garden Grove, California. Among the exhibits are classic prison hardware such as leg irons and handcuffs, including those of the famous escape artist, Houdini. Closer to the hotel industry are old keys and locks, including the lock from Elvis Presley's dressing room at the MGM Grand in Las Vegas.

➤ Comcast Corporation unveiled a new technology in 2007 that created a data download speed of 150 Megabits per second (current maximum about 50 Mbps) and hinted that it would be available within "a couple of years."

➤ Robots were not discussed in this chapter, but Hotelier Grace Leo-Andrieu, whose hotel company is based in Paris, and is a consultant for *Travel + Leisure Magazine*, foresees their use as part of an inroom vacuuming and disinfecting system, as a back-and-foot massage amenity, or even as a food-and-beverage delivery system.

Challenges

TRUE/FALSE

Questions that are partially false should be marked false.

____ 1. By changing the name of their "Telephone Departments" to "The Department of Communications," hotels have been able to stop the revenue hemorrhaging that began about 1990, caused partly by hotels overcharging for inroom calls.

____ 2. Biometrics have been widely adopted by the lodging industry as the best means yet of increasing security of both guests' assets and persons.

____ 3. "True" detection systems are energy detection systems that sense body heat and body motion and thus achieve a truer reading of room occupancy than one or the other alone.

____ 4. Four nonprofit organization (alphabetically: HITIS, HTNG, OTA, PIN) have been launched during the past several years to establish standards for the manufacture and sale of hotel technology.

____ 5. The hotel PMS has been interfaced with the POS, the CAS, and HVAC to provide better service to guests and improved costs for the business.

PROBLEMS

1. The relationship of the telephone and hotel industries has changed significantly since the 1960s. List three major pieces of legislation, court rulings, findings by the FCC, or decisions by members of either industry that caused or contributed to the changes. How did each alter the way in which the hotel's telephone department operates?

2. Undoubtedly, some PMS vendors will comply with HITIS standards and others will not. What are the benefits and disadvantages to a hotel manager who purchases software from a vendor in compliance?

3. Most hotel operations charge a premium for the convenience of placing long-distance phone calls directly from the room. This premium may range from 10% to 25% above the cost of the call. Other properties charge as much as 10 or more times the cost of the call. Assuming that the hotel announces its surcharge with a notice, discuss the fairness of charging the guest such a premium. Is it ethical to charge a small premium (say, 10% to 25%)? Is it ethical to charge a large premium (say, 10 times the cost)? At what point does the hotel overstep the limits of "fairness"?

4. Using professional terminology correctly is important to understanding and being understood. Identify the following acronyms and briefly discuss what they represent:

   a. HOBIC
   b. WATS
   c. PMS
   d. FCC
   e. ELS
   f. OCC
   g. AT&T
   h. PBX
   i. RFID
   j. POS
   k. CAS
   l. AH&LA
   m. PPC
   n. VoIP

5. Be creative and imagine the hotel room of the future. Describe several guest-operated interfaces or devices that might be available in your fictitious hotel room of tomorrow.

AN INCIDENT IN HOTEL MANAGEMENT

The Bare Facts

Hotels USA, a small, West-coast chain, decided to go after the Asian market. It used a well-respected Asian marketing firm to create the "buzz." Among the hype: a fully electronic hotel. The effort had already showed positive results when a Javanese couple arrived one afternoon. Luckily—because they spoke no English—all their reservation papers were in order, including a four-day deposit. After much nodding and smiling, they were escorted to their no-smoking room as prescribed by the reservation.

At about midnight, the fire alarm went off in their room. Following fire-fighting procedures, four employees, all men, raced to the room with equipment and access keys. After a quick knock, they burst into the room! The amazed couple were standing naked in the middle of the room staring at the ceiling alarm. Screaming, the wife ran into the bathroom. The tallest man in the crew stood on a chair and "fixed" the fire alarm.

One hour later, the scenario played out once again, only this time the lady was clothed.

Questions: Was there a management failure here; if so, what?

What is the hotel's immediate response (or action) to the incident?

What further, long-run action should management take, if any?

ANSWERS TO TRUE/FALSE QUIZ

1. False. Changing the name is meaningless. Hotels need to change the structure in order to woo guests back, if that is even possible. Two strategies are being tested: (1) Bundle all telecommunications together to increase sales; and (2) Use ISPs (Internet service providers) to carry the calls as a means of lowering costs.

2. False. Guests are reluctant to surrender very personal attributes such as fingerprints and eye scans, and until that changes, biometric security systems will not gain position in hotels.

3. True. However, the more accurate sensing comes at a higher initial cost. How long it will take, to recover that incremental cost isn't clearly understood.

4. False. This is a "catch question." HITIS, HTNG, and OTA are organizations working to standardized equipment interfaces. PIN is a well known abbreviation for one's personal identification number. So it doesn't belong in the grouping.

5. True. And these three interfaces are just the start of a long list of current interconnects (minibars and key-lock systems, ELS, for example) and many more to come.

Glossary

Words in *italic* in each definition are themselves defined elsewhere in the Glossary. (Words not listed might be found in the Index.) cf. means "compare."

A card   A form once used with the *NCR front-office posting machines* to reconcile and report cash at the close of the first shift and alternate shifts thereafter; see also *B card*.

account balance   The difference between the *debit* (charge) and *credit* (payment) values of the *guest bill*.

account card   See *guest bill*.

account receivable   A company, organization, or individual, *registered* or not, who has an outstanding bill with the hotel.

accounts receivable ledger   The aggregate of individual *account receivable* records.

acknowledgment   Notice of a *confirmed reservation* by telephone, fax, email, letter, postcard, or preprinted form.

ADA   See *Americans with Disabilities Act*.

adds   Last-minute *reservations* added to the reservation list on the day of arrival.

ADR   See *average daily rate*.

adjoining rooms   Rooms that abut along the corridor but do not connect through private doors; cf. *connecting rooms*.

advance deposit   A deposit furnished by the guest on a room *reservation* that the hotel is holding.

advances   See *cash paid-outs*.

affiliated hotel   One of a chain, *franchise*, or *referral* system, the membership of which provides special advantages, particularly a national reservation system.

after departure (AD)   A *late charge*.

afternoon tea   A light snack comprising delicate sandwiches and small sweets served with tea, or even sherry; cf. *high tea*.

agency ledger   A division of the *city ledger* dealing with *travel agent* (agency) accounts.

agent   Representative of an individual or business; term that is a popular substitute for clerk, as in guest-service agent rather than room clerk.

AH&LA   See *American Hotel & Lodging Association*.

AIOD   Telephone equipment that provides Automatic Identification of Outward Dialing for billing purposes.

All-inclusive   *Plan* that includes all hotel services: room, food, beverages, entertainment for one price.

allowance   A reduction to the *folio*, as an adjustment either for unsatisfactory service or for a posting error. Also called a *rebate*.

amenities   Literally any extra product or service found in the hotel. A swimming pool, *concierge* desk, health spa, and so on, are all technically known as amenities. However, this term is used primarily for inroom guest products: as soap, shampoo, suntan lotion, mouthwash, and the like.

amenity creep   The proliferation of all guest products and services when hotels compete by offering more extensive *amenities*.

American Hotel & Lodging Association (AH&LA)   A federation of regional and state associations that are composed of individual hotel and motel properties throughout the Americas.

American plan (AP)   A method of quoting room *rates* where the charge includes room and three meals.

American Resort Development Association (ARDA)   A professional association of *timeshare* developers.

American Society of Association Executives (ASAE)   An organization of the professional executives who head the business and *SMERF* associations in the United States.

American Society of Travel Agents (ASTA)   A professional association of retail *travel agents* and wholesale tour operators.

Americans with Disabilities Act (ADA)   Established in 1990, the ADA prohibits discrimination against any guest or employee because of disability.

application service provider   Supports *central reservation systems* and *global reservation systems* with hardware and software.

arrival, departure, and change sheet   A pencil-and-paper form to record guest *check-ins*, *check-outs*, and *changes* under a hand audit system; sometimes three separate forms.

arrival time   The hour which the guest specifies as the time that he or she will arrive to claim the *reservation*.

ATM   Automatic teller machine provides self-service banking services. Often located in heavily trafficked public areas such as hotel lobbies or casino/hotels. User must have a *PIN*.

attrition   The failure of a convention *group* to fill its reserved *block* of rooms.

authorization code   (1) Response from a credit-card issuer that approves the credit-card transaction and provides a numbered code referral if problems arise; (2) a code for entry to a computer program.

available   The room is ready.

available basis only   (1) Convention *reservations* that have no claim against the *block* of convention rooms (see *blanket reservation*) because the request arrived after the *cutoff date*; (2) no reservations permitted because the rate being granted is too low to guarantee space, employee *reservations*, for example.

available rooms   The number of guest rooms the hotel has for sale—either the total in the hotel or the number unoccupied on a given day.

average daily rate (ADR)   The average daily *rate* paid by guests; computed by dividing room revenue by the number of rooms occupied. More recently called *sales per occupied room*.

back to back   (1) A sequence of consecutive *group* departures and arrivals usually arranged by tour operators so that rooms are never vacant; (2) a floor plan design that brings the piping of adjacent baths into a common shaft.

bank   Coins and small bills given to the cashier for making change.

bank cards   Credit cards issued by banks, usually for a smaller fee than that charged by *travel and entertainment cards*.

batch processing   A computer procedure that collects and codes data, entering it into memory in batches; cf. *online computer*.

B card   A form once used with *NCR's front-office posting machines* to reconcile and report cash at the close of the second shift and alternative shifts thereafter; see also *A card*.

bed and board   Another term for the *American plan*.

bed and breakfast (B&B)   Lodging and breakfast offered in a domestic setting by families in their own homes; less frequently, the *Continental plan*.

bed board   A board placed under the mattress to make a firmer sleeping surface.

bed night   See *guest day (night)*.

bed occupancy   A ratio relating the number of beds sold to the number of beds available for sale; *occupancy* measured in available beds rather than in *available rooms*.

bellcaptain   (1) The supervisor of the bellpersons and other uniformed service personnel; (2) a proprietary in-room vending machine.

bellcaptain's log   See *callbook*.

bellstand   The bellperson's desk located in the lobby close to and visible from the front desk.

Bermuda plan   A method of quoting room *rates*, where the charge includes a full breakfast as well as the room.

best available   A *reservation* requesting (or a confirmation promising) the best room available or the best room to open prior to arrival; cf. *available basis only.*

B folio   The second *folio* (the individual's folio) used with a *master account.*

blanket reservation   A *block* of rooms held for a particular *group*, with individual members requesting assignments from that *block.*

block   (1) A number of rooms reserved for one *group*; (2) a restriction placed in the *room rack* to limit the clerk's discretion in assigning the room.

book   To sell hotel space, either to a person or to a *group* needing a *block* of rooms.

bottom line   The final line of a profit-and-loss statement: either net profit or net loss.

box   Reservation term that allows no *reservations* from either side of the boxed dates to spill through; cf. *sell through.*

breakage   The gain that accrues to the hotel or tour operator when meals or other services included in a *package* are not used by the guest.

brunch   A meal served after breakfast but before lunch and taking the place of both.

bucket   See *cashier's well.*

budget motel   See *limited service.*

building cost rate formula   A rule-of-thumb formula stating that the average room rate should equal $1 for every $1,000 of construction cost; see also *rule-of-thumb rate.*

C-corporation   Used to distinguish standard corporations from nonstandard corporations, such as non-taxpaying *REITs.*

cabana   A room on the beach (or by the pool) separated from the main *house*; may even be furnished as a sleeping room.

café complet   Coffee snack at midmorning or midafternoon.

California length   An extra-long bed, about 80 to 85 inches instead of the usual 75 inches. Same as *Hollywood length.*

call accounting system (CAS)   Computerized program that prices and records telephone calls on the guest's electronic *folio* through a *property management system (PMS) interface.*

callbook   The bellperson's record of calls and activities.

call sheet   The form used by the telephone operator to record the room and hour of the *morning call*; replaced by automatic systems.

cancellation   A guest's request to the hotel to void a *reservation* previously made.

cancellation number   Coded number provided by the hotel or *central reservations office* to a guest who cancels a *reservation.*

case goods   Furniture that provides storage.

cash advance   See *cash paid-outs.*

cash disbursement   See *cash paid-outs.*

cashier's drop   A depository located in the front-desk area where others can witness cashiers depositing their *turn-ins.*

cashier's report   The cash *turn-in* form completed by a departmental cashier at the close of the *watch.*

cashier's well   The file that holds paper-and-pencil *folios*, often recessed in the countertop; also known as *tub*, *bucket*, or *pit.*

cash paid-outs   Monies disbursed for guests, either advances or loans, and charged to their accounts like other departmental services.

cash sheet   The *departmental control sheet* maintained by the front-office cashier.

casualty factor   The number of individual or *group reservations* (*cancellations* plus *no-shows*) that fail to appear.

central processing unit (CPU)   The *hardware/software* nucleus of the computer.

central reservations office (CRO)   A private or chain-operated site that accepts and processes *reservations* on behalf of its membership.

central reservations system (CRS)   The sophisticated *hardware* and *software* used by a *central reservations office* to accurately track and manage *reservations* requests for member properties.

change   Moving a party from one guest room to another; any change in room, *rate*, or number of occupants.

chargeback   Credit-card charges refused by the credit-card company.

check-in   All the procedures involved in receiving the guest and completing the *registration* sequence.

check-out   All the procedures involved in the departure of the guest and the settlement of the *account.*

check-out hour   That time by which guests must vacate rooms or be charged an additional day.

city ledger   An *accounts receivable ledger* of nonregistered guests.

city-ledger journal   The form used to record transactions that affect the *city ledger*.

class   The quality of hotel, with *average daily rate* the usual criterion.

closeout hour   Also called *close of the day*.

close of the day   An arbitrary hour that management designates to separate the records of one day from those of the next.

closet bed   See *Murphy bed*.

collar hotel   Identifies location of a hotel on the collar (outside rings) of a city.

colored transparency   A colored celluloid strip placed in the *room rack pocket* as a *flag* or indicator of room status, replaced by PMS.

commercial hotel   A *transient hotel* catering to a business clientele.

commercial rate   A reduced room *rate* given to businesspersons to promote *occupancy*.

commissionable   Indicates the hotel will pay *travel agents* the standard fee for business placed.

comp   Short for "complimentary" accommodations—and occasionally food and beverage—furnished without charge.

company-made (reservation)   A *reservation* guaranteed by the arriving guest's company.

concession   A hotel tenant (concessionaire) whose facilities and services are indistinguishable from those owned and operated by the hotel.

concierge   (1) A European position, increasingly found in U.S. hotels, responsible for handling guests' needs, particularly those relating to out-of-hotel services; (2) designation of the sleeping floor where these services are offered.

condominium   A multiunit dwelling wherein each owner maintains separate title to the unit while sharing ownership rights and responsibilities for the public space.

conference center   A *property* that caters to business meetings, corporate retreats and conferences. Generally considered smaller in size and more personable in nature than a convention hotel.

confirmed reservation   The hotel's *acknowledgment*, maybe in writing, to the guest's *reservation* request.

connecting rooms   *Adjoining rooms* with direct, private access, making use of the corridor unnecessary.

consortium   A new organization, formed by existing organizations (banks, developers, hotels) to carry out a particular enterprise.

continental breakfast   A small meal including some combination of: bread, rolls, sweet rolls, juice, or coffee. Often set up in bulk by the innkeeper or host; continental breakfasts are usually self-service.

Continental plan   A method of quoting room *rates* where the charge includes a *continental breakfast* as well as the room rate.

convention rate   See *run-of-the-house rate*.

convertible bed   See *sofa bed*.

corner (room)   An *outside room* on a corner of the building having two *exposures*.

corporate meeting package (CMP)   An *all-inclusive plan* quoted by *conference centers* and hotels for corporate meetings.

correction sheet   A form once used with *NCR front-office machines* to record posting errors for later reconciliation by the *night auditor*.

cot   See *rollaway bed*.

coupon   (1) A checklike form issued by *travel agents* to their clients and used by the clients to settle their hotel accounts; (2) a ticket issued by *tour groups* for the purchase of meals and other services to be charged against the *master account*. Also called a *voucher*.

credit   An accounting term that indicates a decrease in the *account receivable*; the opposite of *debit*.

cutoff date   The date on which unsold rooms from within a convention's *block* of reserved rooms are released for sale.

cutoff hour   That time at which the day's unclaimed *reservations* are released for sale to the general public.

daily rooms report   See *room count sheet*.

day rate   A reduced charge for occupancy of less than overnight; used when the *party* arrives and departs the same day. Also called *part day rate* or *use rate*.

D card   A form once used with *NCR front-office posting machine* as the machine equivalent of the *transcript*; the term is still used for the daily revenue report prepared now by the *property management system*.

dead room change   A physical change of rooms made by the hotel in the guest's absence so no tip is earned by the *last* bellperson.

debit   An accounting term that indicates an increase in the *account receivable*; the opposite of *credit*.

deluxe   A non-U.S. designation implying the best accommodations; unreliable unless part of an official rating system.

demi-pension (DP)   A non-U.S. method of quoting room *rates* similar to the *modified American plan (MAP)* but allowing the guest to select either luncheon or dinner along with breakfast and room; also called *half pension*.

density board (chart)   A noncomputerized *reservation* system where the number of rooms committed is controlled by type: *single, twin, queen*, etc.

departmental control sheet   A form maintained by each *operating department* for recording data from departmental *vouchers* before forwarding them to the front desk for *posting*. Replaced by *point-of-sale* terminals.

departure   *Check-out.*

deposit reservation   See *advance deposit.*

destination hotel   The objective of—and often the sole purpose for—the guest's trip; cf. *transient hotel.*

did not stay (DNS)   Means the guest left almost immediately after *registering.*

difference returnable   See *exchange.*

dine-around plan   A method of quoting *AP* or *MAP* room rates that allows guests to dine at any of several different but cooperating hotels.

display room   See *sample room.*

D.I.T.   Domestic independent tour or domestic inclusive tour; cf. *F.I.T.*

double   (1) A bed approximately 54 by 75 inches; (2) the *rate* charged for two persons occupying one room; (3) a room with a double bed.

double–double   See *twin–double.*

double occupancy   (1) Room occupancy by two persons; (2) a ratio relating the number of rooms double occupied to the number of rooms sold.

double-occupancy rate   A *rate* used for tours where the per-person charge is based on two to a room.

double-up   A designation of *double occupancy* by unrelated parties necessitating two *room rack* identifications and/or two *folios.*

downgrade   Move a *reservation* or registered guest to a lesser accommodation or *class* of service; cf. *upgrade.*

downtime   That time span during which the computer is inoperative because of malfunction or pre-emptive operations.

ducat   See *stock card.*

due back   See *exchange.*

due bank   See *exchange.*

due bill   See *trade advertising contract.*

dump   To *check out* early; with reference to *groups.*

duplex   A two-story *suite* with a connecting stairwell.

duvet   A bed comforter, much like a large pillow, filled with feather in a washable cover.

early arrival   A guest who arrives a day or two earlier than the *reservation* calls for.

EBITDA   See *house profit.*

economy class   See *tourist class.*

Ecotourism   Responsible travel to nature areas that conserves the environment and improves the well-being of local people.

efficiency   Accommodations that include kitchen facilities.

Elderhostel   Study programs for senior citizens that include travel and classes, often held on college campuses.

electronic data processing (EDP)   A data handling system that relies on electronic (computer) equipment.

ell   A wing of a building at right angles to the main structure.

emergency key (E-key)   One key that opens all guest rooms, including those locked from within, even those with the room key still in the lock; also called the great *grandmaster.*

English breakfast   A hearty breakfast of fruit, cereal, meat, eggs, toast, and beverage generally served in the United Kingdom and Ireland, but less often of late.

en pension   See *full pension.*

en suite   Forming a suite; adapted to ensuite to mean a room with a bath.

European plan (EP)   A method of quoting room *rates* where the charge includes room accommodations only.

exchange   The excess of cash *turn-in* over *net receipts*; the difference is returnable (due back) to the front-office cashier; also called *due back, due bank*, or *difference returnable.*

executive floor   See *concierge* (floor).

executive room   See *studio.*

exempt workers   Employees (supervisors) not covered by wage-and-hour laws.

exposure   The direction (north, south, east, or west) or view (ocean, mountain) that the guest room faces.

express check-out   Mechanical or electronic methods of *check-out* that expedite *departures* and eliminates the need to stop at the desk; also called *zip-out*.

extra meals   An *American plan* charge made for dining room service over and above that to which the guest is entitled.

family plan   A special room *rate* that allows children to occupy their parent's room at no additional charge.

family room   See *twin–double*.

fam trip   Familiarization trip taken by (offered to) *travel agents* at little or no cost to acquaint them with *properties* and destinations.

farm out   Assignment of guests to other *properties* when a *full house* precludes their accommodation.

fenced rates   One of several tools used by the reservations department to maximize room revenues under *yield management* systems, including nonrefundable, prepaid *reservations* and *reservations* not subject to change.

first class   A non-U.S. designation for medium-priced accommodations with corresponding facilities and services.

F.I.T.   Foreign independent tour, but has come to mean free independent tour, a traveler who is not *group* affiliated; by extension, frequent independent traveler, or full inclusive tour; cf. *D.I.T.*

flag   (1) A device for calling the room clerk's attention to a particular room in the *room rack*; (2) designating a hotel's membership in a chain or *franchise*.

flat rate   (1) See *run-of-the-house rate*; (2) same price for *single* or *double occupancy*.

float   The free use of outstanding funds during the period that checks and credit-card charges are in transition for payment.

floor key   See *master key*.

floor (release) limit   The maximum amount of charges permitted a credit-card user at a given *property* without clearance; the limit is established for the property, not for the user.

folio   See *guest bill*; also called an *account card*.

force majeure (forz mazhoer)   An unexpected and disruptive event that frees parties from contractual obligations; an act of God.

forecast   A future projection of estimated business volume.

forecast scheduling   Work schedules established on the basis of sales projections.

forfeited deposit   A *deposit reservation* kept by the hotel when a *no-show* fails to cancel the reservation; also called a lost deposit.

franchise   (1) An independently owned hotel or motel that appears to be part of a chain and pays a fee for that right and for the right to participate in the chain's advertising and reservation systems; (2) the chain's right (its franchise) to sell such permission; or the permission itself, or both.

franchisee   One who buys a *franchise*.

franchisor   One who sells a *franchise*.

free sale   Occurs when a *travel agent*, airline, or other agency commits hotel space without specific prior confirmation from the *property*. See also *sell and report*.

from bill number . . . to bill number   A cross-reference of *account* numbers when the bill of a guest who remains beyond one week is transferred to a new *folio*.

front   The next bellperson eligible for a *rooming* assignment or other errand apt to produce a *gratuity*; cf. *last*.

front office   A broad term that includes the physical front desk as well as the duties and functions involved in the sale and service of guest rooms.

front of the house   (1) The area of the hotel visible to guests in contrast to the back of the house, which is not in the public view; (2) all of the functions that are part of the *front office*.

full day   The measure of a chargeable day for accounting purposes; three meals for an *AP* hotel, overnight for an *EP*.

full house   Means 100% *occupancy*, all guest rooms sold; cf. *perfect fit*.

full pension   A European term for the *American plan*.

full service   Means a complete line of hotel services and departments are provided, in contrast to a *limited-service property*.

futon   A Japanese sleeping mat made of many layers of cotton-quilted batting that is rolled up when not in use.

garni   A non-U.S. designation for hotels without restaurant service except for *continental breakfast*.

general cashier   The chief cashier with whom deposits are made and from whom *banks* are drawn.

general manager (GM)   The hotel's chief executive.

ghost card   Nonexistent credit card or credit-card charges not supported by a signature.

global distribution system (GDS)   The *hardware, software,* and computer lines over which *travel agents,* airlines, on-line subscription networks, and others access *central reservations systems* and individual *property management systems.*

grande dame   French for an aristocratic lady; hence, an elegant, grand hotel.

grandmaster   One key that opens all guest rooms except those locked from within; see also *emergency key.*

gratuity   A tip given to an employee by a guest, sometimes willingly and sometimes automatically added to the charges; see also *plus, plus.*

graveyard   A work shift beginning about midnight.

greens fee   A charge for the use of the golf course.

group   A number of persons with whom the hotel deals (reservation, billing, etc.) as if they were one party.

guaranteed rate   The assurance of a fixed *rate* regardless of the hotel's *occupancy,* often given in consideration of a large number of *room-nights* per year pledged by a company.

guaranteed reservation   Payment for the room is promised even if the occupant fails to arrive.

guest account   See *guest bill.*

guest bill   An accounting statement used to record and display the charges and payments made by registered guests *(accounts receivable)* during their hotel stay. Also known as *folio* or *account card.*

guest check   The bill presented to patrons of the dining rooms and bars and, when signed, often used as the departmental *voucher.*

guest day (night)   The stay of one guest for one day (night); also called *room night* or *bed night.*

guest elevators   Lobby (front) elevators for guest use exclusively; employees are permitted only during guest service, as bellpersons *rooming (a guest);* cf. *service elevators.*

guest history   A record of the guest's visits, including rooms assigned, *rates* paid, special needs, credit rating, and personal information; used to provide better guest service and better marketing approaches.

guest ledger   All the *guest bills* owed by registered guests *(accounts receivable)* and maintained in the *front office,* in contrast to the group of *city-ledger* bills (nonregistered guests) maintained in the accounting or back office.

guest night   See *guest day.*

guest occupancy   See *bed occupancy.*

guest-service area   See *front office.*

half-board   See *modified American plan.*

half-pension   See *demi-pension.*

handicap(ped) room   A guest room furnished with special devices and built large enough to accommodate guests with physical handicaps.

hard copy   Computer term for material that has been printed rather than merely displayed.

hard goods   Guest-room furniture: beds, chairs, etc.; cf. *soft goods.*

hardware   The physical equipment (electronic and mechanical) of a computer installation and its peripheral components; cf. *software.*

HFTP   Hospitality Financial and Technology Professionals, an association specializing in hotel accounting, finance, and technology; formerly the IAHA, International Association of Hospitality Accountants.

hide-a-bed   See *sofa bed.*

high season   See *in-season rate.*

high tea   A fairly substantial late afternoon or early evening meal; cf. *afternoon tea.*

HITIS   An acronym for Hospitality Industry Technology Integration Standards, which are computer *interface* standards developed to facilitate the *interface* of computer systems from various vendors onto the hotel's *property management system.*

HOBIC   An acronym for Hotel Outward Bound Information Center, the telephone company's long-distance hotel network.

holdover   See *overstay.*

Hollywood bed   *Twin* beds joined by a common headboard.

Hollywood length   An extra-long bed of 80 to 85 inches instead of the usual 75 inches. Same as *California length.*

Hospitality Sales and Marketing Association International (HSMAI)   An international association of hotel sales and marketing managers.

hospitality suite (room)   A facility used for entertaining, usually at conventions, trade shows, and similar meetings.

hostel   An inexpensive but supervised facility with limited services catering to young travelers on foot or bicycle; cf. *Elderhostel*.

hotelier   Innkeeper or hotelkeeper.

hotel manager   Hotel executive responsible for the front of the house, including *front office*, housekeeping, and uniformed services; also called rooms manager, house manager, or guest-services manager.

hotel operating hours   Twenty-four hours per day; 7 days per week; 365 days per year.

hotel rep   See *rep(resentative)*.

hot list   A list of lost or stolen credit cards furnished to hotels and other retailers by credit-card companies.

house   A synonym for hotel, as in *house bank*, *house count*, *house laundry*; see also *property*.

house bank   See *bank*.

house call   Telephone call made to the outside of the hotel by a member of the staff doing company business; not subject to a *posting* charge, as guest calls are.

house count   The number of registered guests; cf. *room count*.

housekeeper's report   A report on the status of guest rooms, prepared by the *linen room* and used by the front desk to verify the accuracy of the *room rack*.

house laundry   A hotel-operated facility, usually on premises, in contrast to an *outside laundry* that contracts with the hotel to handle *house* and/or guest laundry.

house profit   Net profit before income taxes from all *operating departments* except *store rentals* and before provision for rent, interest, taxes, depreciation, and amortization; renamed as "earnings before interest, taxes, depreciation, and amortization (EBITDA)" by the 1977 edition and subsequent editions of the *Uniform System of Accounts* for hotels; see also *bottom line*.

house rooms   Guest rooms set aside for hotel use and excluded, therefore, from *available rooms*.

housing bureau   A citywide reservation office, usually run by the convention bureau, for assigning *reservation* requests to participating hotels during a citywide convention.

Hubbart room rate formula   A basis for determining room *rates* developed by Roy Hubbart and distributed by the *American Hotel & Lodging Association*.

HVAC   Acronym for heating, ventilation, and air-conditioning.

ideal average room rate   This formula assumes a hotel sells an equal number of rooms from both the least expensive upward and from the most expensive downward. The resulting average rate is a theoretical benchmark against which to compare actual operating results.

imprest petty cash   A technique for controlling petty cash disbursements by which a special, small cash fund is used for minor cash payments and periodically reimbursed.

incentive (group, guest, tour, or trip)   Persons who have won a hotel stay (usually with transportation included) as a reward for meeting and excelling sales quotas or other company-established standards.

inclusive terms   (1) Phrase that is sometimes used in Europe to designate the *American plan*; (2) indicates that a price *quote* includes tax and *gratuity*.

independent   A *property* with no chain or *franchise* affiliation, although one proprietor might own several such properties.

information rack   An alphabetic listing of registered guests with a room number cross-reference.

in-house   On the premises, such as an inhouse laundry; cf. *off premises*.

in-season rate   A *resort's* maximum rate, charged when the demand is heaviest, as it is during the middle of the summer or winter; cf. *off-season rate*, *low season*, *shoulder*.

inside call   A telephone call that enters the switchboard from inside the hotel; a telephone call that remains within the hotel; cf. *outside call*.

inside room   A guest room that faces an inner courtyard or light court enclosed by three or four sides of the building; cf. *outside room*.

inspector   Supervisory position in the housekeeping department responsible for releasing *on change* rooms to ready status.

interface   Computer term designating the ability of one computer to communicate with another; see *HITIS*.

International Association of Travel Agents (IATA)   A professional affiliation which both lobbies on behalf of the travel industry and identifies/verifies legitimate *travel agents* to other vendors.

Internet telephony   Telephone capability on Internet access; also called VoIP, Voice over Internet Protocol.

interstate call   A long-distance call that crosses state lines.

interval ownership   See *timeshare.*

intrastate call   A long-distance telephone call that originates and terminates within the same state.

in-WATS   See *wide area telephone service.*

IT number   The code assigned to an inclusive tour for identification and *booking.*

joiner   A guest who joins another guest or *party* already *registered.*

junior suite   One large room, sometimes with a half partition, furnished as both a *parlor* and a bedroom.

king   An extra-long, extra-wide *double* bed at least 78 by 82 inches.

kiosk   An information site (originally a booth) that may be staffed, but more likely provides access to the hotel's property management system for self-registration and self-check-out.

lanai   A Hawaiian term for "veranda"; a room with a porch or balcony, usually overlooking gardens or water.

last   The designation for the bellperson who most recently completed a *front*; cf. *front.*

last-room availability   A sophisticated reservations system that provides real-time access between the chain's *central reservations system* and the hotel's *in-house property management system.*

late arrival   A guest with a *reservation* who expects to arrive after the *cutoff hour* and so notifies the hotel.

late charge   A departmental charge that arrives at the *front office* for billing after the guest has *checked out.*

late check-out   A departing guest who remains beyond the *check-out hour* with permission of the desk and thus without charge.

least cost router (LCR)   Telephone equipment that routes the call over the least expensive lines available. Also called automatic route selector (ARS).

LEED   Leadership in Energy and Environmental Design is a benchmark created by the U.S. Green Building Council for buildings that meet energy and environmental standards.

light baggage   Insufficient luggage in quantity or quality on which to extend credit; the guest pays in advance.

limited service   A hotel or motel that provides little or no services other than the room; a *budget hotel (motel)*; cf. *full service.*

linen closet   A storage closet for linens and other housekeeping supplies usually located conveniently along the corridor for the use of the housekeeping staff.

linen room   The housekeeper's office and the center of operations for that department, including the storage of linens and uniforms.

lockout   (1) Denying the guest access to the room, usually because of an unpaid bill; (2) a key of that name.

log   A record of activities maintained by several *operating departments.*

lost and found   An area, usually under the housekeeper's jurisdiction, for the control and storage of lost-and-found items.

low season   See *off-season rate.*

maid's report   A status-of-rooms report prepared by individual room attendants and consolidated with other reports by the *linen room* into the *housekeeper's report.*

mail and key rack   An antiquated piece of *front-office* equipment where both guest mail and room keys were stored by room number.

maitre d'   The shortened form of maitre d'hôtel, the headwaiter.

market mix   The variety and percentage distribution of hotel guests—conventioneer, tourist, businessperson, and so on.

market niche   Identifiable, but often poorly served, subset of a market.

master account   One *folio* prepared for a *group* (convention, company, tour) on which all group charges are accumulated.

master key   One key controlling several *pass keys* and opening all the guests rooms on one floor; also called a *floor key.*

master franchise   A *franchisee's* right to resell pieces of the *franchise* to other *franchisees.*

menu   An array of function choices displayed to the computer user, who selects the appropriate function.

message lamp   A light on the telephone, used to notify an occupant that the telephone system has a message to relay.

meters   See *square meters.*

mezzanine financing   A high-interest, unsecured debt that may become equity in the hotel; often paid off when a regular mortgage is obtained.

minisuite   See *junior suite.*

minor departments   The less important *operating departments* (excluding room, food, and beverage) such as valet, laundry, and gift shop.

miscellaneous charge order (MCO)   Airline *voucher* authorizing the sale of services to the guest named on the form, with payment due from the airline. The manual form has been replaced by an automated MCO on ticket stock.

modified American plan (MAP)   A method of quoting room *rates* in which the charge includes breakfast and dinner as well as the room.

mom-and-pop   A small, family-owned business with limited capitalization in which the family, rather than paid employees, furnishes the bulk of the labor.

moment of truth   A popular term describing the interaction between a guest and a member of the staff, when all of the advertising and representations made by the hotel come down to the quality of the service delivered at that moment.

morning call   A *wake-up call* made by the telephone operator or automatically by the *property management system* at the guest's request.

move-in date   The date that a group, convention or trade show arrives to begin preparing for their meeting or exhibit; cf. *move-out date*.

move-out date   The date that a group, convention or trade show vacates the *property* after a meeting or exhibit; cf. *move-in date*.

Ms   An abbreviation used to indicate a female guest without consideration of marital status.

Murphy bed   A standard bed that folds or swings into a wall or cabinet in a closet-like fashion; trademarked.

NCR front-office posting machine   A mechanical device used to *post folios* and automatically accumulate *account receivable* and revenue balances; two popular models, the NCR (National Cash Register Company) 2000 and the NCR 42(00), neither of which are manufactured today, were replaced by electronic *property management systems*.

NCR paper   No carbon required; paper is specially treated to produce copies without carbon.

net rate   A room *rate quote* that indicates no additional commissions or fees are to be paid to *travel agents* or other third parties.

net receipts   The difference between cash taken in and *cash paid-outs*.

night audit   A daily reconciliation, which is completed during the *graveyard* shift, of both *accounts receivable* and incomes from the *operating departments*.

night auditor   The person or persons responsible for the *night audit*.

night auditor's report   An interim report of *accounts receivable*, room statistics, and incomes earned; prepared by the *night auditor* for the *general manager*.

nightbird   Euphemism for prostitute.

night clerk's report   Another name for the *room count sheet*.

no reservation (NR)   See *walk-in*.

no-show   A *reservation* that fails to arrive.

occupancy (percentage of occupancy, occupancy percentage)   A ratio relating the number of rooms sold *(room count)* to the number of *rooms available* for sale.

occupied   (1) A room that is sold or taken and is not available for sale; (2) someone is physically in the room at this time.

ocean front   A front room with an *exposure* facing directly on the ocean; cf. *ocean view*.

ocean view   Other than a front room, but with some view of the ocean; cf. *ocean front*.

off line   See *batch processing*.

off premises   Not on the *property*; cf. *in-house*.

off-season rate   A reduced room *rate* charged by *resort hotels* when demand is lowest; cf. *in-season rate*, *shoulder*.

off the shelf   Standardized, not customized, computer software.

off the street (OS)   See *walk-in*.

on change   The status of a room recently vacated but not yet available for new occupants.

one- (two-) pull dialing   One (two)-digit telephone dialing (or Touch-Tone) that connects the caller to hotel services such as room service and bellstand.

online (computer)   Computer facilities hooked directly to input and output devices for instantaneous communication; cf. *batch processing*.

opaque   A reservation Web site, not operated by the hotel, that identifies the actual hotel being booked only after the guest (who is shopping rates) commits a final payment.

open credit   Credit based only on a guest's signature.

operating departments   Those divisions of the hotel directly involved with the service of the guest, in contrast to support divisions such as personnel and accounting.

organic search results   By anticipating the user's key words and phrases, a Web site listing appears close to the top of the Internet display naturally, without artificially gaining placement through paid advertising. Also known as "pure results" or "natural search results."

out of inventory (OOI)   A significant problem has removed this room from availability. Although *out of order (OOO)* rooms are usually available in only a matter of hours, OOI rooms may be unavailable for days or weeks.

out of order (OOO)   The room is not available for sale because of some planned or unexpected temporary shutdown of facilities.

outside call   A telephone call that enters the switchboard from outside the hotel; a call that terminates outside the hotel; cf. *inside call.*

outside laundry (valet)   A nonhotel laundry or valet service contracted by the hotel in order to offer a full line of services; cf. *house laundry.*

outside room   A room on the perimeter of the building facing outward with an *exposure* more desirable than that of an *inside* room.

out-WATS   See *wide area telephone service.*

over or short   A discrepancy between the cash on hand and the amount that should be on hand.

overbooking   Committing more rooms to possible guest occupancy than are actually available.

override   (1) Extra commission above standard percentage to encourage or reward quantity bookings; (2) process by which the operator bypasses certain limits built into the computer program.

overstay   A guest who remains beyond the expiration of the anticipated stay.

package   A number of services (transportation, room, food, entertainment) normally purchased separately but put together and marketed at a reduced price made possible by volume and *breakage.*

paid in advance   A room charge that is collected prior to occupancy, which is the usual procedure when a guest has *light baggage*; with some motels, it is standard procedure for every guest.

paid-outs   See *cash paid-outs.*

paid search results   Advertisers position their Web sites at the top of the Web page by purchasing key words or phrases from search-engine companies.

parlor   The living room portion of a *suite.*

part day rate (guest)   See *day rate.*

party   *Front-office* term that references either the individual guest ("Who's the party in room 100?") or several members of the group ("When will your party arrive?").

pass key   (1) A sub *master key* capable of opening all the locks within a limited, single set of 12 to 18 rooms, but no other; (2) guest key for access to public space (spa, pool).

PBX   See *private branch exchange.*

penthouse   Accommodations, almost always *suites*, located on the top floor of the hotel, theoretically on the roof.

percentage of occupancy   See *occupancy.*

perfect fill   *Occupancy* of 100%, with every room actually occupied; cf. *full house* in which 100% *occupancy* might reflect guaranteed reservations that didn't actually show.

permanent guest   A resident of long-term duration whose stay may or may not be formalized with a lease.

personal digital assistant (PDA)   Hand-held computer, often with wireless capability.

petite suite   See *junior suite.*

petty cash   See *imprest petty cash.*

pickup   (1) The procedure once used with *NCR front-office posting machines* to accumulate the *folio* balance by entering the previous balance into the machine before posting the new charges; (2) the figure so entered.

PIN   Personal identification number. A secret combination of numbers and letters chosen by an individual as identification for accessing electronic equipment such as *ATMs.*

PIP   See *product improvement plan.*

pit   See *cashier's well.*

plan   The basis on which room *rate* charges are made; see *American plan* and *European plan.*

plus, plus   Shorthand for the addition of tax and tip to the check or price per cover.

pocket   A portion of a manual *room rack* made to accept the *room rack slips* and provide a permanent record of accommodations and *rates*; obsolete.

point-of-sale (POS) terminal   An electronic "cash register" providing *on-line* communications to the *property management system* from remote sales locations, in contrast to an input device at the *front office.*

porte–cochère   The covered entryway that provides shelter for those entering and leaving a hotel; French: coach gate [port-ko-shâr].

porterage   (1) Arrangements made to handle luggage; (2) the charge for luggage handling.

posting   The process of recording items in an accounting record, such as a *folio*.

power of the pen   Right to *comp* guest services.

preassign   *Reservations* are assigned to specific rooms that are *blocked* before the guests arrive; cf. *prereg(istration)*.

prereg(istration)   Registration is done by the hotel before the guest arrives, although the actual *(reg)istration card* is not completed. Used with groups and tours to reduce *front-office* congestion, since individual guests need not then approach the desk; cf. *preassign*.

private branch exchange (PBX)   A telephone switchboard.

product improvement plan (PIP)   Standards established by franchisors. A franchisees must meet PIP or risk losing its franchise.

projection   See *forecast scheduling*.

property   Another way to reference a hotel, includes physical facilities and personnel.

property management system (PMS)   A hotel's, that is a *property's*, basic computer installation designed for a variety of functions in both the back office and *front office*.

published rate   The full *rack rate* quoted or published for public information; the rate quoted without discounts.

quad   Accommodations for four persons; see also *twin–double*.

quality assurance   A managerial and operational approach that enlists employee support in delivering a consistently high level of service.

quality circle   A group of persons from different but related departments who meet on a regular basis for dialogue and problem resolutions as part of a *quality assurance* program.

quality management   See *total quality management* and *quality assurance*.

quality of the reservation   Differentiates *reservations* on how likely they are to be honored by the guest: *paid in advance reservation* vs. *guaranteed reservation* vs. 6 PM *cutoff hour*, etc.

queen   An extra-long, extra-wide *double* bed, about 80 to 85 inches long by 60 inches wide; see *California length*; see *king*.

queuing theory   The management of lines (queues of persons waiting their turn) in order to maximize the flow and minimize the inconvenience, but doing so with attention to operating costs. Also called *waiting-line theory*.

quote   To state the cost of an item, room *rates* in particular.

rack   See *room rack*.

rack rate   The full *rate*, without discounts, that one *quotes* as a room charge; so called because the *room rack* is the source of the information.

rate   The charge made by a hotel for its rooms.

rate cutting   A reduction in *rate* that attracts business away from competitors rather than creating new customers or new markets.

real estate investment trust (REIT)   A form of real estate ownership (public corporation) that became popular during the real estate recovery of the mid-1990s because of income tax advantages.

rebate   See *allowance*.

recap   A summary or recap(itulation) of several *transcript* sheets in order to obtain the day's grand totals.

referral   A *central reservation system* operated by *independent* properties in contrast to that operated by chains and *franchisors* for their *affiliated hotels*.

registered, not assigned (RNA)   The guest has *registered*, but is awaiting assignment to a specific room until space becomes available; see *on change*.

register (ing), registration   (1) Indication (completing and signing the *registration card*) by a new arrival of intent to become a guest; (2) register: the name for a book that served at one time as the registration record.

(reg)istration card   A form completed during *registration* to provide the hotel with information about the guest, including name and address, and to provide the guest with information about the hotel, including legal issues.

REIT   See *real estate investment trust*.

reminder clock   A special alarm clock that can be set at 5-minute intervals across a 24-hour day; once used by the *front office* for *wake-up calls*.

rep(resentative)   Short for *hotel representative*: An agent under contract, rather than an employee under salary, who represents the hotel in distant cities or for special activities, chiefly marketing activities, but sometimes gaming related.

reservation   A mutual agreement between the guest and the hotel, the former to take accommodations on a given date for a given period of time, and the latter to furnish the same.

reservation rack   A piece of *front-office* equipment, largely replaced by the *property management system*, providing an alphabetic list of anticipated arrivals with a summary of their needs, filed chronologically by anticipated date of arrival.

residential hotel   A hotel catering to long-stay guests who have made the *property* their home and residence; see also *permanent guest*.

resident manager   See *hotel manager*.

resort hotel   A hotel that caters to vacationing guests by providing recreational and entertainment facilities; usually a *destination hotel*.

RevPar   Short for revenue per available room, a ratio of room revenue to the number of *available rooms*.

road warrior   Slang for a frequent traveler battling the hardships and indignities of being on the road, that is, of traveling, for long periods of time.

rollaway bed   A portable utility bed approximately 30 by 72 inches; also called a *cot*.

rondoval   A *suite* in the round, special to honeymoon *resorts*.

room charge sheet   See *room count sheet*.

room count   The number of occupied rooms; cf. *house count*.

room count sheet   A permanent record of the *room rack* prepared nightly and used to verify the accuracy of room statistics; also called a *night clerk's report*.

rooming (a guest)   The entire procedure during which the desk greets, *registers*, and assigns new arrivals, and the bell staff accompanies them to their rooms (rooms them).

rooming slip   A form issued by the desk during the *rooming* procedure to the bellperson for guest identification, and left by the bellperson with the guest to verify name, *rate*, and room number.

room inspection report   A checklist of the condition of the guest room prepared by the *inspector* when the room attendant has finished cleaning.

room night   See *guest day (night)*.

room rack   A piece of *front-office* equipment, now replaced by the *property management system*, in which each guest room is represented by a metal *pocket* with colors and symbols to aid the room clerk in identifying the accommodations.

room rack slip (card)   A form prepared from the *registration card* identifying the occupant of each room and filed in the *pocket* of the *room rack* assigned to that guest; obsolete; cf. *room rack*.

rooms available   See *available rooms*.

room service   Food and beverage service provided in the privacy of the guest room.

rooms ledger   See *guest ledger*.

rule-of-thumb rate   A guideline for setting room rates with the hotel charging $1 in rate for each $1,000 per room construction costs; see also *building cost rate formula*.

run-of-the-house rate   A special *group* rate generally the midpoint of the *rack rate* with a single, flat price applying to any room, *suites* excepted, assigned on a *best available* basis.

ryokan   A traditional Japanese inn.

safe deposit boxes   Individual sections of the vault where guests store valuables and cashiers keep house *banks*.

sales per occupied room   See *average daily rate*.

sales rack   A piece of *front-office* equipment, now replaced by the *property management system*, used for the storage and control of *stock cards* (*ducats* or *sales tickets*).

sales ticket   See *stock card*.

salon   The European designation for *parlor*.

sample room   A guest room used to merchandise and display goods, usually in combination with sleeping accommodations.

Scottish breakfast   See *English breakfast*.

seamless connectivity   The next step beyond *last room availability. Travel agents*, airlines, on-line subscription networks, and others can access a *property's* room availability right down to the last room.

search engine optimization   Gaining maximum exposure on the Internet by an artful blending of *paid search results* and *organic search results* using the key words and phrases that most closely match the user's expected input. See also *organic search results* and *paid search results*.

season rate   See *in-season rate*.

segmentation   The proliferation of many hotel types as the lodging industry attempts to target its facilities to smaller and smaller market niches (segments).

sell and report   *Wholesalers*, tour operators, *reps*, airlines, and *central reservation systems free sell* rooms, periodically reporting the sale to the hotel; also called status control.

sell through   Denoting days for which no *reservation* arrivals are accepted; reservations for previous days will be accepted and allowed to stay through the date; cf. *box* date.

sell up   Convince the arriving guest to take a higher priced room than was planned or reserved.

service charge   A percentage (usually from 10 to 20%) added to the bill for distribution to service employees in lieu of direct tipping; see also *plus, plus*.

service elevators   Back elevators for use by employees (room service, housekeeping, maintenance, etc.) on hotel business and not readily visible to the guests; cf. *guest elevator*.

share   More than one person occupying the guest room.

shoulder   Marketing term designating the period between peaks and valleys; the time on either side of the *in-season rate* or the leveling off between two sales peaks.

Siberia   Jargon for a very undesirable room, one sold only after the *house* fills and then only after the guest has been alerted to its location or condition.

single   (1) A bed approximately 36 by 75 inches; (2) a room with accommodations for one; (3) occupancy by one person; (4) the *rate* charged for one person.

single supplement   An extra charge over the tour *package* price assessed for *single* occupancy when the total price was based on a *double-occupancy rate*.

sitting room   See *parlor*.

size   The capacity of the hotel as measured by the number of guest rooms.

skip   See *skipper*.

skipper   A guest who departs surreptitiously, leaving an unpaid bill.

sleeper   A departed guest whose record remains active, giving the appearance of an *occupied* room.

sleeper occupancy   See *bed occupancy*.

sleep-out   A room that is taken, *occupied*, and paid for but not slept in.

slide   The transcription error caused by a misplaced decimal, as when 36.20 is written 3.62.

smart card   A credit card or other card containing a microprocessor capable of interfacing with the *PMS* or other computer configurations.

SMERF   Marketing reference to Society, Military, Educational, Religious, and Fraternal organizations.

sofa bed   A sofa with fixed back and arms that unfolds into a standard *single* or *double* bed; also called a *hide-a-bed*.

soft goods   Linens; cf. *hard goods*.

software   The programs and routines that give instructions to the computer; cf. *hardware*.

special attention (SPATT)   A label assigned to important guests designated for special treatment; see *very important person*.

split rate   Division of the total room *rate* charge among the room's several occupants; see *share*.

split shift   A work pattern divided into two work segments with an unusually long period (more than a rest or mealtime) between.

spread rate   Assignment of *group* members or conventioneers using the standard *rate* distribution, although prices might be less than *rack rates*; cf. *run-of-the-house rate*.

square meters   Measurement used in the metric system: 0.093 square meters equal 1 square foot; 10.76 square feet equals 1 square meter.

star rating   An unreliable ranking (except for some well-known exceptions) of hotel facilities both in the United States and abroad.

star reservation   Indicates the arrival of a *very important person*, SPATT.

stay   See *stayover*.

stayover   (1) Any guest who remains overnight; (2) an anticipated check out who fails to depart; also called *holdover* or *overstay*.

stock card   Once used with a *sales rack* to represent the content of the *room rack pocket* when the room rack was distant and therefore inaccessible to the room clerk; also called a *ducat*.

store rentals   Income earned from shop leases; cf. *concession*.

studio   (1) A bed approximately 36 inches wide by 75 inches long without headboard or footboard that serves as a sofa during the day; (2) the room containing such a bed; cf. *sofa bed*.

suite   A series of *connecting rooms* with one or more bedrooms and a *parlor*; very large suites occasionally include additional rooms such as dining rooms; see *hospitality suite*.

summary transcript sheet   See *recap*.

supper   (1) A late-night meal; (2) the evening meal when midday service is designated as dinner.

swing   The work shift between the day *watch* and the *graveyard* shift; usually starts between 3 and 4 PM.

T&T   See *trash and towels*.

take down   Cancel *reservations* that are without an *advance deposit* after the *cutoff hour*; also called "dump"; cf: *dump*.

tally sheet   See *density board*.

TelAutograph   A historical piece of communication equipment that transcribes written messages.

timeshare   (1) A method of acquiring accommodations by which each occupant purchases the right to use the facility (room or apartment) for a specified period; an interval ownership; (2) term for users who share computer facilities.

time stamp   A clock mechanism that prints date and time when activated.

to-date   Designates a cumulative amount; the sum of all figures in the current period (usually monthly or annually) including the day or date in question.

total quality management (TQM)   A way to continuously improve performance at every level of operation, in every functional area of an organization, using all available human and capital resources. See also *quality assurance*.

tour group   See *package*.

tourist class   A non-U.S. designation for *limited-service* hotels whose accommodations frequently lack private baths; also called *economy class*.

trade advertising contract   An agreement by which hotel accommodations are swapped for advertising space or broadcast time; also called a *due bill*.

traffic sheet   A *departmental control sheet* used by the telephone department before *call accounting systems*.

transcript   A pencil-and-paper form once used by the *night auditor* to accumulate and separate the day's charges by departments and guests.

transcript ruler   The headings of a *transcript* sheet attached to a straightedge and used as a column guide at the bottom of the long *transcript* sheet.

transfer   (1) An accounting technique used to move a figure from one form to another, usually between *folios*; (2) the movement of guests and/or luggage from one point to another (e.g., from the airline terminal to the hotel); see *porterage*.

transfer folio   A special unnumbered *folio* used to carry non-computerized guest accounts beyond the first week's stay when the original folio was numbered and cross referenced to the *registration card*.

transfer from   The *debit* portion of a *transfer* between accounts or ledgers.

transfer journal   A *front-office* form once used to record *transfer* entries between different accounts or different ledgers.

transfer to   The *credit* portion of a *transfer* between accounts or ledgers.

transient guest   A short-term guest; see *transient hotel*.

transient hotel   A hotel catering to short-stay guests who sometimes stop en route to other destinations; cf. *destination hotel*.

transient ledger   See *guest ledger*.

transmittal form   The form provided by national credit-card companies for recording and remitting nonelectronic credit-card charges accumulated by the hotel.

transposition   A transcription error caused by reordering the sequence of digits, as when 389 is written as 398.

trash and towels   References basic service fee paid for each stay by occupants of *timeshares*.

travel agent (TA)   An entrepreneur who *books* space and facilities for clients in hotels and public carriers for which hotels usually pay a 10% commission.

travel and entertainment card (T&E)   A credit card issued by a proprietary company, or bank, for which the user pays an annual fee; cf. *bank card*.

Travel Industry Association of America (TIAA)   A nonprofit association of many travel-related agencies and private businesses working to develop travel and tourism in the United States.

tray service   The fee charged *American-plan* and *all-inclusive* guests for *room service*.

tub   See *cashier's well*.

turn away   (1) To refuse *walk-in* business because rooms are unavailable; (2) the guest so refused is a turn-away.

turn-downs   An evening service rendered by the housekeeping department, which replaces soiled bathroom linen and prepares the bed for use.

turn-in   The sum deposited with the *general cashier* by the departmental cashier at the close of each shift.

turnkey   A facility (computer, *franchise*, entire hotel) so complete that it is almost ready for use at the turn of a key.

twin   (1) A bed approximately 39 inches wide by 75 inches long to sleep a single occupant; (2) a room with two such beds, *twins*.

twin–double   (1) Two double beds; (2) a room with two such beds capable of accommodating 4 persons; see *quad*.

twins   Two *twin* beds.

type   The kind of market toward which the hotel is directed, traditionally: *commercial, residential,* and *resort*.

understay   A guest who leaves before the expiration of the anticipated stay.

Uniform System of Accounts for the Lodging Industry   A manual and dictionary of accounting terms, primarily incomes and expenses, to ensure industry-wide uniformity in terminology and use.

United States Travel and Tourism Administration (USTTA)   A division of the Department of Commerce responsible for promoting travel to the United States; successor to the U.S. Travel Service (USTS).

unoccupied   (1) An unsold room; (2) a room that is *occupied*, but is temporarily vacant, the guest is out.

u-owe-me   See *exchange*.

upgrade   Move a *reservation* or a currently registered guest to a better accommodation or class of service; cf. *downgrade*.

upsell   see *sell up*.

use rate   See *day rate*.

user-friendly   Computer design, application, or implementation that minimizes the user's fears, encouraging purchase and use of the equipment.

vacancy   The hotel is not fully *occupied*, so there are rooms available for sale.

very important person (VIP)   A reservation or guest who warrants *special attention (SPATT)* and handling.

VoIP   Voice over Internet Protocol. See *Internet telephony*.

voucher   (1) The form used by the *operating departments* to notify the front desk of charges incurred by a particular guest; (2) form furnished by a *travel agent* as a receipt for a client's advance *reservation* payment; see *coupon*.

waiting-line theory   See *queuing theory*.

wake-up call   See *morning call*.

walk (a guest)   To turn away guests holding confirmed *reservations* due to a lack of available rooms.

walk-in   A guest without a *reservation* who requests and receives accommodations.

walk-through   A thorough examination of the *property* by a hotel executive, *franchise* inspector, prospective buyer, etc.

watch   Another term for the work shift.

WATS   See *wide area telephone service*.

who   An unidentified guest in a room that appears vacant in the *room rack*.

wholesaler   An entrepreneur who conceives, finances, and services *group* and *package* tours that he or she promotes (often through *travel agents*) to the general public.

wide area telephone service (WATS)   Long-distance telephone lines provided at special rates to large users; separate charges are levied for incoming and outgoing WATS lines.

worldwide travel vouchers (WTVs)   Form of payments drawn against a well-known financial institution (usually a major credit-card company).

xenodogheionology   The study of the history, lore, and stories associated with inns, hotels, and motels (zeno-dog-hi-on-ology).

yield   The product of *occupancy* times *average daily rate*.

yield management   (1) Controlling room *rates* and restricting *occupancy* in order to maximize gross revenue *(yield)* from all sources; (2) a computerized program using artificial intelligence.

youth hostel   See *hostel*.

zero out   To balance the *guest bill* as the guest *checks out* and makes settlement.

zip-out   See *express check-out*.

Index

• • •